Scripture for the Eyes

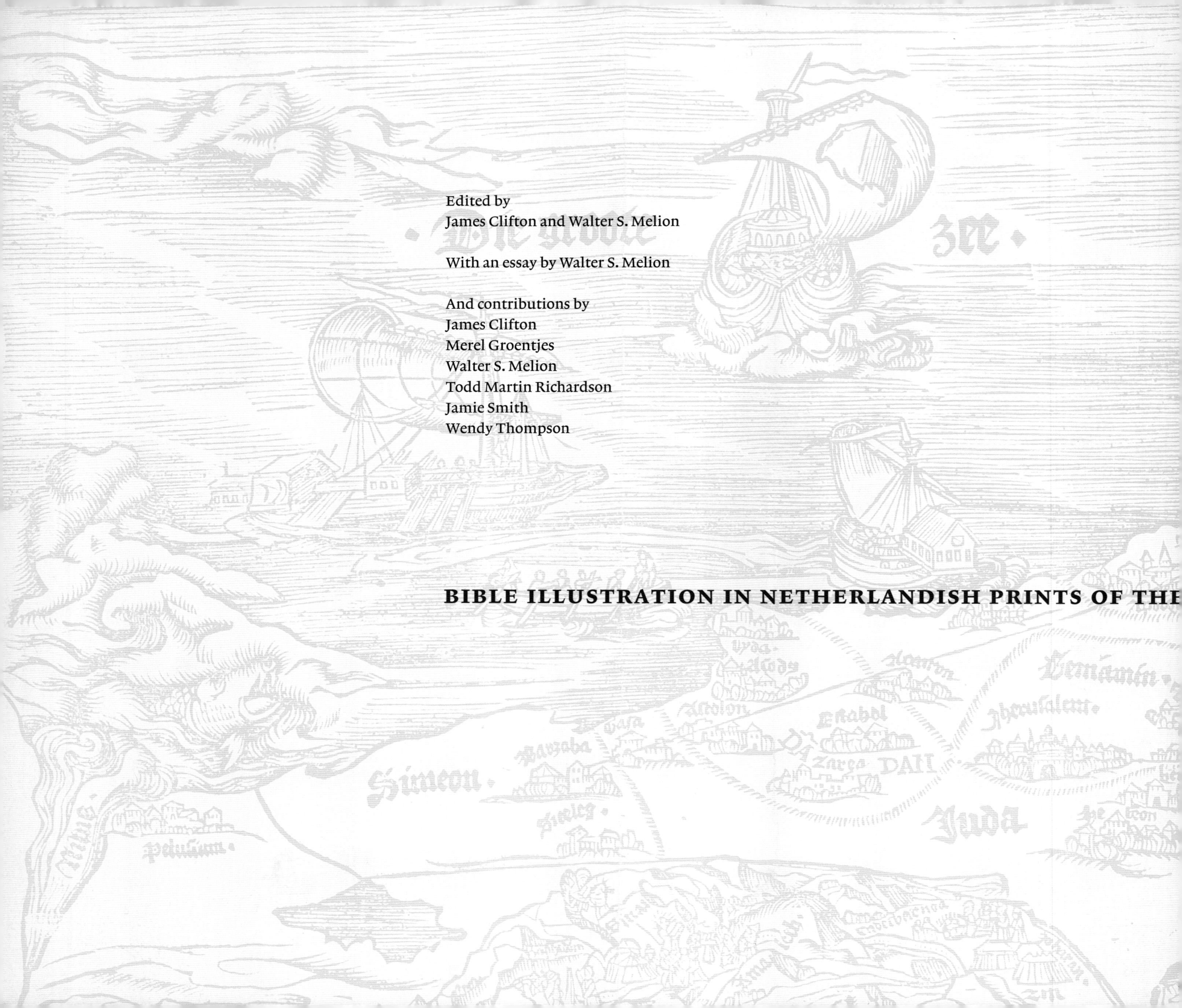

Edited by
James Clifton and Walter S. Melion

With an essay by Walter S. Melion

And contributions by
James Clifton
Merel Groentjes
Walter S. Melion
Todd Martin Richardson
Jamie Smith
Wendy Thompson

BIBLE ILLUSTRATION IN NETHERLANDISH PRINTS OF THE

SIXTEENTH CENTURY

Scripture for the Eyes

MUSEUM OF BIBLICAL ART
MOBIA

Museum of Biblical Art, New York
in association with D Giles Limited, London

This catalog accompanies the exhibition *Scripture for the Eyes: Bible Illustration in Netherlandish Prints of the Sixteenth-Century* on display at the Museum of Biblical Art June 5 – September 27, 2009; and at the Michael C. Carlos Museum, Emory University October 17, 2009 – January 24, 2010

© 2009 Museum of Biblical Art

First published jointly in 2009 by GILES
An imprint of D Giles Limited
2nd Floor, 162-164 Upper Richmond Road,
London SW15 2SL, UK
www.gilesltd.com
and
Museum of Biblical Art
1865 Broadway (at 61st Street),
New York City,
NY 10023, USA
Phone: 212-408-1500
Fax: 212-408-1292
info@mobia.org
www.mobia.org

Library of Congress Cataloging-in-Publication Data available

ISBN paperback: 978-0-9777839-3-9 (13 digit)
ISBN paperback: 0-9777839-3-6 (10 digit)
ISBN hardcover: 978-1-904832-66-9 (13 digit)
ISBN hardcover: 1-904832-66-0 (10 digit)

The exhibition was co-curated by Dr James Clifton, Director of the Sarah Campbell Blaffer Foundation and Curator in Renaissance and Baroque Painting, Museum of Fine Arts, Houston and Dr Walter S. Melion, Asa Griggs Candler Professor of Art History, Emory University.

Edited by James Clifton and Walter S. Melion

With an essay by Walter S. Melion

And contributions by
James Clifton
Merel Groentjes
Walter S. Melion
Todd Martin Richardson
Jamie Smith
Wendy Thompson

Catalog Design: Anikst Design, London
Produced by D Giles Limited, London
Printed and bound in Hong Kong

All measurements are in centimeters:
height precedes width.

Scripture for the Eyes is made possible, in part, by gifts from Roberta and Howard Ahmanson, Sandra and Robert Bowden, Darlene and Walter Hansen, Sarah and Reed Bowden, Magdalena and Graham Laws, and the O'Neil Family Fund.

Scripture for the Eyes is made possible, in part, by a generous contribution from American Bible Society, New York City and Case Systems, Midland, Michigan.

Front cover illustration: Jan Swart (ca. 1500-ca. 1560), *Jesus Preaching from the Ship* (detail), ca. 1525, woodcut, The New York Public Library.
Frontispiece: *Map of the Promised Land*, in *Den Bybel met groter neerticheyt gecorrigeert* (Antwerp: Hansken van Liesveldt, 1538), folio. By permission of the Trustees of The British Library. 3041.g.6.

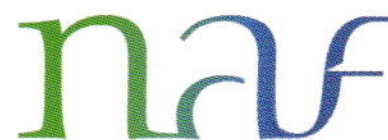

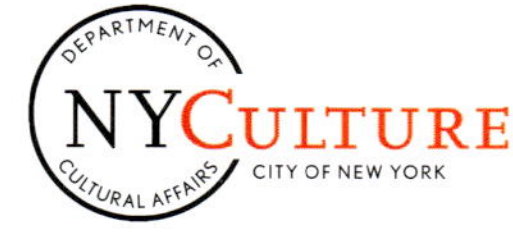

This project has received funding through a grant from the Netherland-America Foundation.

This program is supported, in part, by public funds from the New York City Department of Cultural Affairs.

Table of Contents

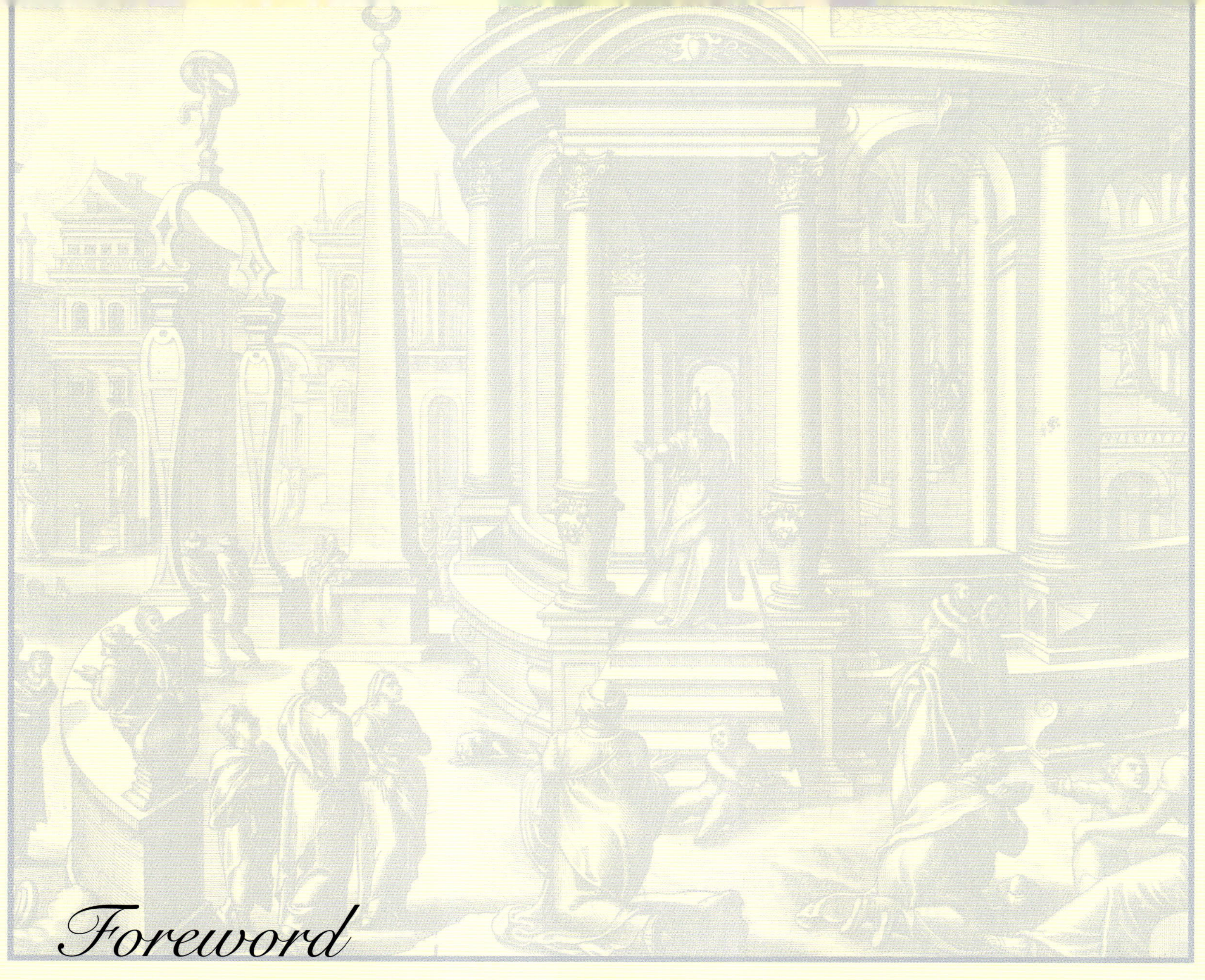

Foreword

*T*his exhibition originated in a conversation I had in the spring of 2004 with James Clifton. MOBIA was to open the following spring, and I was trying to find out what some of my colleagues were working on that would shed new light on art, the Bible, and their interconnection. I was fishing for ideas and hoping for collaborations, and Jim obliged. He told me that one of his enduring interests was the relationship between northern European religious prints and confessional conflicts in the sixteenth and early seventeenth centuries. Soon, he enrolled Walter Melion as co-curator and together they transformed the idea of this relationship, at a crucial historical point for both religion, marked by the Reformation, and artistic developments, transformed by the advent of the printing press, into the current exhibition, aptly entitled *Scripture for the Eyes*. As Walter points out in his introduction, the title says it all: the prints included in the exhibition represent a revolutionary new way to 'translate' scripture pictorially, for an audience with an unprecedented access to images. The access was facilitated by the development of new printing techniques and the flourishing publishing centers of the Low Countries; the need was reinforced by reformation thought advocating direct, personal experience of scripture.

This exhibition, woven together expertly by Jim's and Walter's deep knowledge and thoughtful analysis of this remarkable period in religious and artistic history, is a perfect match for MOBIA, a museum which connects those two threads of history and looks at one through the lens of the other. This type of analysis is particularly apt for the sixteenth century, which brought about remarkable changes in the way large numbers of people accessed, understood, and enjoyed biblical art. I am deeply grateful to Jim Clifton and Walter Melion for documenting the beginning of this fascinating process (which ultimately ushered in the modern era of art) with such knowledge, insight, and elegance. Their scholarship makes a very significant contribution to the field, and I trust will encourage further research.

The curators are the creators of the exhibition conceptually, but many other talented people are always involved in its actual making. At MOBIA, I thank my staff, who have courageously engaged with me on the journey of creating a new museum, and have worked tirelessly since we opened. I would also like to thank our partners at the Michael C. Carlos Museum in Atlanta, in particular the director, Bonnie Speed, for ensuring that the exhibition travels.

In the world of museums, great exhibition ideas sometimes remain just ideas due to lack of funding. I am most grateful to those people who helped us transform the idea for *Scripture for the Eyes*, not only into an exhibition that will be seen in New York and Atlanta, but also into this book, which will remain as a record of the show and a tool for future learning. This project would not have happened without the generosity of Roberta and Howard Ahmanson, Sandra and Robert Bowden, and Darlene and Walter Hansen. I would also like to thank Case Systems (Midland, MI); the Department of Cultural Affairs, New York City; the Netherland-America Foundation; Sarah and Reed Bowden; Magdalena and Graham Laws, and the O'Neil Family Fund. Last, but certainly not least, I should like to acknowledge and thank the American Bible Society for their generous support of MOBIA through the years, as well as of this particular exhibition.

The most rewarding part of a museum director's job remains working with talented, committed professionals, and being able to serve an interested and inquisitive public. Here at MOBIA, I am lucky to experience both. To all of you who have contributed to this exhibition and catalog, my deepest thanks.

Ena Giurescu Heller
Director

Acknowledgements

$\mathscr{L}$ike the prints discussed here, and like every exhibition and catalog, *Scripture for the Eyes* was a collaborative endeavor, the work of many hands and minds.

For scholarly advice and encouragement, we are much indebted to friends and colleagues: Karen L. Bowen, Wim François, Agnès Guiderdoni-Bruslé, August den Hollander, Leo Kenis, Petrine Knight, Mathijs Lamberigts, Peter Maes, Tanya Paul, and Elizabeth Wyckoff.

Our researches at print rooms and libraries were greatly facilitated by patient and helpful staff members, especially: Jonathan Bober, Senior Curator, Jack S. Blanton Museum of Art, University of Texas at Austin; Teresa M. Burk, Manuscripts and Rare Books Library, Emory University; Bernard Desprez, Researcher Jesuitica, Maurits Sabbebibliotheek, Katholieke Universiteit Leuven; Stephen Enniss, Eric Weinmann Librarian, Folger Shakespeare Library, Washington, D.C. (formerly Director, Manuscripts and Rare Books Library, Emory University); David M. Faulds, Rare Books Librarian, Manuscripts and Rare Books Library, Emory University; Margaret Glover, New York Public Library; M. Patrick Graham, Director, Pitts Theology Library, Emory University; Heidi Herr, Special Collections, The Milton S. Eisenhower Library, The Johns Hopkins University; Dirk Imhof, Curator of Rare Books and Archives, Plantin-Moretus Museum, Antwerp; Frank M. Jackson, Visual Resources Librarian, Art History Department, Emory University; Ingrid Kastel, Albertina Museum, Vienna; Luc Knapen, Bibliotheek Godgeleerdheid, Katholieke Universiteit Leuven; Liana Lupas, Curator, American Bible Society; Nadine Orenstein, Curator of Prints and Drawings, The Metropolitan Museum of Art, New York; Margaret Peddle, Pitts Theology Library, Emory University; Cynthia Requardt, William Kurrelmeyer Curator of Special Collections, The Milton S. Eisenhower Library, The Johns Hopkins University.

This exhibition is wholly dependent on the lending institutions, whose generosity extended to both their objects and the time of their staffs; we are exceedingly grateful to:

American Bible Society, New York; The Baltimore Museum of Art; Bibliothèque Royale de Belgique, Brussels; The British Museum, London; Georgia Museum of Art, University of Georgia; Manuscript, Archives, and Rare Book Library, Robert W. Woodruff Library, Emory University; The Metropolitan Museum of Art, New York; The National Gallery of Art, Washington D.C.; The New York Public Library; The Pitts Theological Library, Candler School of Theology, Emory University; Museum Plantin-Moretus/ Prentenkabinet, Antwerp; Rijksmuseum, Amsterdam; The Sheridan Libraries of The Johns Hopkins University, Special Collections.

We are especially grateful to our co-authors, Merel Groentjes, Todd Martin Richardson, Jamie Smith, and Wendy Thompson, for their contributions. Above all, we wish to thank Ena Heller, Director of the Museum of Biblical Art, for her invitation to curate this exhibition, and her staff for their effort to see it through to completion. On the curatorial side, Ellen Brueckner, Dean Ebben, Laura McManus, Paul Tabor, and intern Megan Welchel brought this complex exhibition together, negotiating multiple loans and creating a beautiful installation, as well as an array of programs that are at once scholarly, engaging, and accessible. On the publishing side, Ute Keyes and Michelle Oing, together with Sarah McLaughlin from our wonderful publishing partner Giles Ltd., have helped to print this catalog as both a research tool and a gorgeous art book. Debbie Bujosa, Lisa Dierbeck, and Megan Whitman have helped to publicize the exhibition and to raise the necessary funds.

Notes on the Book

Biblical quotations are taken from various translations without specification, or are translated by the author. All non-biblical quotations are translated by the author, unless otherwise noted, except those in the Preface that come from Nadal 2003 and are the work of Frederick A. Homann, S.J.

In the Vulgate (Latin) Bible and on most of the prints of the period, there are four books of Kings, but we conform throughout to the predominant modern usage in which 1 and 2 Kings of the Vulgate are 1 and 2 Samuel, and 3 and 4 Kings of the Vulgate are 1 and 2 Kings.

Most of the prints in this exhibition and book were cataloged by F. W. H. Hollstein, in a series of volumes that began to appear in 1947. In the past two decades, Hollstein's catalogs have been undergoing revision by various authors and publication in fully illustrated volumes that are described as either *Hollstein's Dutch & Flemish Etchings, Engravings and Woodcuts 1450–1700* or *The New Hollstein Dutch and Flemish Etchings, Engravings and Woodcuts 1450–1700*. Both Hollstein's original and the revised volumes have been of enormous importance to the study of early modern printmaking; without them this exhibition would have been scarcely feasible. In this book, Hollstein (or New Hollstein) numbers refer to volumes listed in the references section; page numbers are also given parenthetically in endnotes. Additional references to Hendrick Goltzius's prints are to Walter Strauss's catalog, also listed in the references. All other references are given in a short form linked to the bibliography.

The authors of the catalog entries are identified by their initials:

JC: James Clifton
WM: Walter S. Melion
MG: Merel Groentjes
TR: Todd Martin Richardson
JS: Jamie Smith
WT: Wendy Thompson

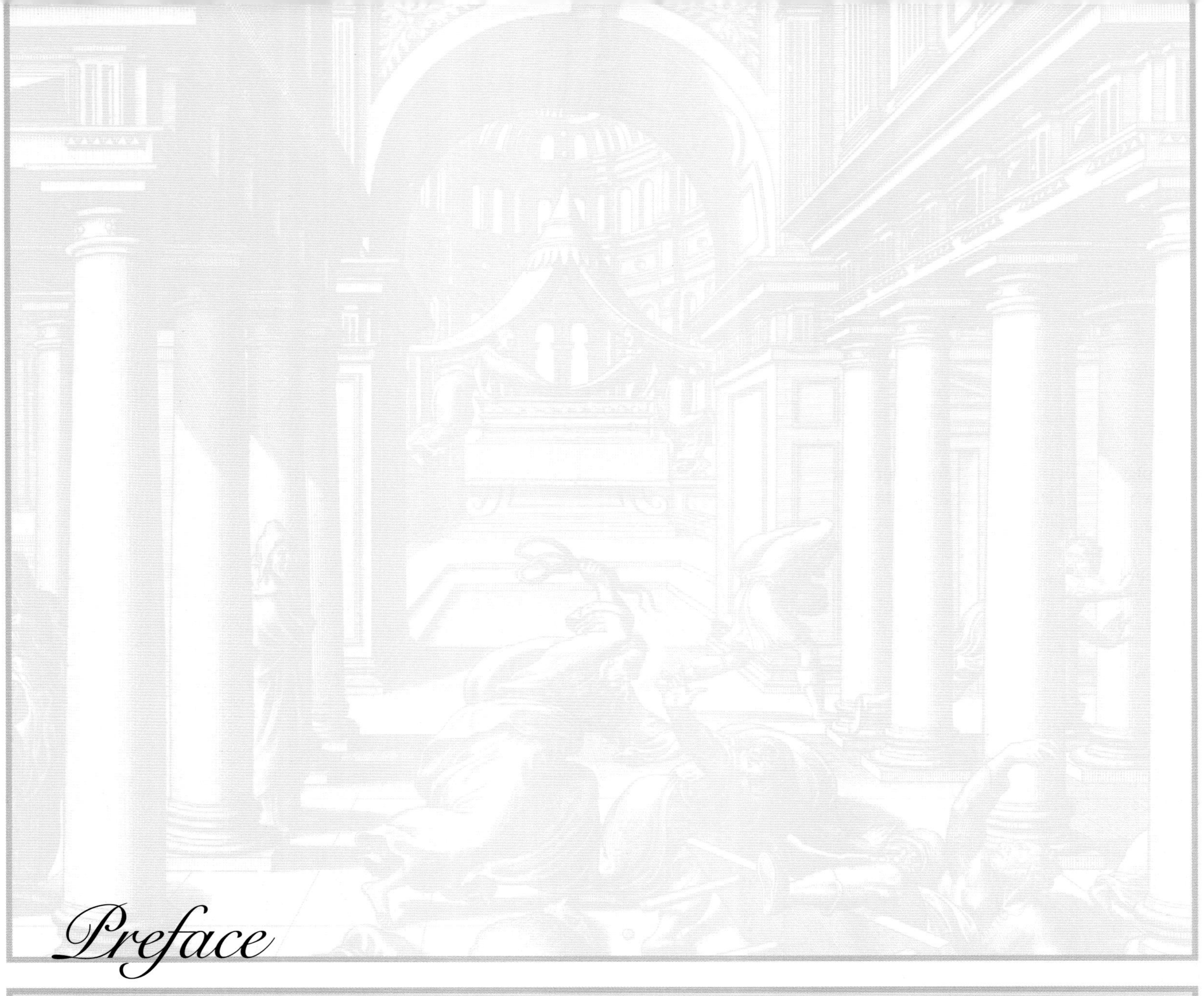

Preface

*A word to the wise. Expect no spiritual growth (which Christ
effects abundantly in souls open to Him in contemplation of His
sacred life) from a mere glance at the pictures or wonder at their
artistic beauty. Spend a whole day, even several days, with each
image. Read the Annotation and Meditation points slowly.
Meditate, contemplate, pray over the whole exercise.*
Diego Jiménez

Scripture played a central role in Christianity from its infancy, but
it was only with the introduction of moveable type in the fifteenth
century that it could reach a broad reading public, and only with
the Catholic reform and Protestant reformation movements of the
sixteenth century that that broad public was encouraged to develop
a culture of biblical study. The first Bible printed in the
Netherlands, the so-called Delft Bible of 1477, was not illustrated,
but woodblock prints were already used for scripture-based images
in the *Biblia Pauperum* (Bible of the Poor) and the *Speculum Humanae
Salvationis* (Mirror of Human Salvation), and very soon woodcut
illustrations, sometimes numbering in the hundreds, appeared in
Bibles. Early in the sixteenth century, printmakers began to
produce independent prints illustrating scripture, along with
illustrations of devotional books, and the trickle of such images at
the beginning of the century was a flood at its end, with thousands
of prints produced and marketed by scores of draftsmen, engravers,
and publishers. The work in the mid-seventeenth century of
Rembrandt, who is considered among the greatest visual
interpreters of the Bible, is unthinkable without the foundation of
more than a century of Netherlandish printmaking—much of it
innovative and brilliant in its own right—that preceded him.

The Protestant Reformation, with its emphasis on scripture
alone (*sola scriptura*) as the means to knowing, following, and
worshiping God, threatened the extra-scriptural apparatus that
the church had, over the centuries, erected as part of its faith,
including the use of images in liturgy and devotion. Martin Luther
was largely indifferent to ecclesiastical art, viewing it as *adiaphora*,
that is, inessential and harmless as long as improper attention was
not paid to it. But some reformers were much more hostile to
religious art, claiming its use to be idolatrous and calling for its
destruction. The Roman Catholic Church defended the use of
images at the Council of Trent in 1563, and the controversy over art
remained a point of contention among confessions.

The Reformation that roiled Germany from the late 1510s was,
for a few decades, more successfully suppressed in the Netherlands
by the Holy Roman Emperor, Charles V. But eventually the
Netherlands, too, were rent by discord, both religious and political,
especially under Charles's successor, Philip II of Spain, to whom the
Netherlands devolved on Charles's abdication in 1556. Eventually,
the political movement that sought independence from Spain,
achieved for much of the Netherlands through the Eighty Years'
War, was allied with the religious movements that sought
independence from the Catholic Church, and the politics of the
northern Netherlands, known as the United Provinces, came to be
dominated by Calvinist reformers, while the southern Netherlands,
retained by Spain, remained officially Catholic. But for the period
of most active printmaking covered by this book, from the mid-
sixteenth to the early seventeenth century, both politics and
religion in many communities in the Netherlands were in flux.
Antwerp, the most important center of both book production
(including Bibles) and printmaking, was under Calvinist control
from the late 1570s, until it was re-taken by the Spanish in 1585.
Protestants were then made to convert or to leave. The population
of the Netherlands had already been in movement for religious and
political reasons for decades, but in spite of attempts by governing
bodies, no community became confessionally uniform. Catholics
and Protestants (especially Lutherans and Calvinists) co-existed, if
sometimes unofficially and even secretly. In such an environment,
it is not surprising that publishers and printmakers (foremost
among them Christopher Plantin and Philips Galle) were reticent
about their own religious inclinations and marketed their works to
both Catholics and Protestants. Religious prints are largely devoid
of explicit confessional markers; they draw on scriptural sources
and focus on universally palatable moral and devotional themes
that might appeal to as broad an audience as possible.

In the later decades of the sixteenth century, it is a wonder that
much art was made at all. War and strife destroyed agriculture,
industry, and the arts, as many allegories of the period proclaim.

In his monumental book of artists' biographies published in 1604, Karel van Mander often referred to "art-hating Mars", whose devastations he had witnessed himself. Van Mander was particularly angered by acts of iconoclasm that had destroyed works of church art early in the Reformation in Germany, and in 1566 in the Netherlands. The hostility toward religious art betokened by iconoclasm led some artists to flee into exile, change their profession, or change the kind of art they made. The last dated paintings by one of the most important artists of the century, Maarten van Heemskerck, were executed in the year after the outbreak of iconoclasm, in which many of Van Heemskerck's works were destroyed by "the raging iconoclasts" (*de rasende beeldtstorminge*), as Van Mander calls them, and the artist may have given up painting to concentrate more of his energies on designing prints. Prints seem to have been the target of iconoclastic impulses much less than paintings and sculpture (although there are instances of the obscuring of representations of God the Father in later states of prints to make them inoffensive to Calvinists), probably in large part because they were intended for private rather than public consumption. They were small and usually not colored, and thus posed little threat of the idolatrous confusion of depiction and depicted, nor did they play a role in public liturgy. Those that were closely tied to scripture thereby appealed to a sacred text shared by all confessions, and could serve a common didactic need (although there were still voices raised against the use of imagery at all). With the removal of images from churches in the Netherlands, art, like the study of scripture with which it was allied, became more private and personal. The countless religious prints made in this period attest to the important role they played in the devotional life of many Netherlanders.

A now prevailing notion of the artist as a creative individual first emerged around 1500, at the beginning of what is often called the early modern period, achieving its full flowering in the romanticism of the early nineteenth century, then becoming naturalized and ossified in the twentieth century. The lives, work, and reputations of some early modern artists contributed in no small measure to this myth. The prevalence of the assumptions on which it is based are evident in the *auteur* theory of cinema, which argues that the director is the supremely responsible artistic agent of film, a medium which in all but its most extreme examples is *de facto* a collaboration, dependent on the creative efforts of many people, many of the contributions of whom lie outside the purview or control of the director. Film-making provides perhaps the best contemporary analogue for the production of many of the sixteenth- and early seventeenth-century prints in this exhibition. To be sure, there were some painter-engravers, such as Lucas van Leyden, who accomplished most aspects of the printmaking process themselves, but especially from the mid-sixteenth century on, as printmaking became more frequently a profession in itself rather than a sideline for painters, there was an increasing division of responsibility.

The production of a print required the conception of the idea, the drawing of the composition, the cutting of the woodblock or metal plate, the pulling of impressions on paper, and the publication of the final product, as well as, occasionally, inscription writing, calligraphy, and hand-coloring. An individual might fulfill more than one of these roles, even all of them. The publisher of the print, who was ultimately responsible (even legally) for its form, content, and dissemination, might exercise great control over all aspects of the production or might simply publish prints that had been produced by others, even decades earlier. Thus, the personal source of the intellectual content, or even its visual form, is often not clear, and it is difficult to assert that a print is *by* a single person. Such ambiguity does not detract from the profundity of works such as the compositions conceived by Dirck Volckertsz. Coornhert, drawn by Van Heemskerck, and then engraved by Coornhert (see cat. 34); or Benito Arias Montano's emblem- book *David*, produced in close collaboration with the publisher Philips Galle (see cat. 22). The *Evangelicae Historiae Imagines* and the *Adnotationes et Meditationes in Evangelia*, large companion volumes of illustrations of, and meditations on, Gospel texts for the liturgical year, derive meaning not just from the author, the Jesuit Jerónimo Nadal (Hieronymus Natalis), but also from Ignatius of Loyola, the founder of the order, who suggested the project to Nadal, as well as several draftsmen, engravers, publishers, consultants (one of whom complained that there were too many people involved), and the Jesuit who saw the work to completion after Nadal's death,

Diego Jiménez. The result, decades in the making, is among the most beautifully illustrated and richly meditative books of the early modern period (see cat. 9, 28), and yet it stands at the furthest remove from the modern idea of a work of art as the product of a unique, solitary, creative "genius."

In terms of technical and artistic quality, scripture illustrations in the sixteenth century ranged from small, simple woodcuts to elaborate, sophisticated, and painstakingly cut engravings. At one end of the spectrum, the subject matter and religious function of the prints seem to have been of paramount importance, and most buyers, regardless of social or educational class, might well be as content with a crude, pirated copy as with a fine original. To be sure, there is no doubt that collectors and connoisseurs valued the aesthetic qualities of prints of contemporary artists or earlier masters, even in some instances to the point of disinterest in the iconography or devotional function of the works. But high artistic quality does not necessarily exclude or even overshadow doctrinal meaning and devotional function. Skilled artifice might manifest personal devotion, as in the case most saliently of prints by Hendrick Goltzius, or it might play a significant role in the viewer's religious reception of the works. The *Evangelicae Historiae Imagines* demonstrates that style was not something extraneous to the didactic and devotional purposes of religious images, but was a vehicle for them. In the dedication of the *Adnotationes et Meditationes in Evangelia* to Pope Clement VIII, Jiménez noted that the very best artists were recruited so that the images would not be confusing and thus frustrate the purpose of the book; the "subtle style," along with the text, would "invite the reader to open the book and meditate on its pages with loving attention"; and the book would "give a new and vibrant picture of the Gospel." Philips Galle described the subject of the exquisite *David*, in the dedication to Philip II, as "eminently suited to be exhibited for the use and pleasure of pious students of the Catholic religion, and to be expressed and embellished by the diligence and industry of the art of engraving, furnished and exercised by me chiefly for the cultivation of piety." Likewise, Georgius Cassander commented in his prefatory verse to the Latin edition of Willem van Branteghem's and Lieven de Witte's illustrated *Life of Christ* (*Iesu Christi vita*, 1537) that the useful and the pleasing are mixed in De Witte's woodcuts (see the Introduction, 16–17,25).

Although many of the prints produced in the Netherlands in the sixteenth century are specific to the time and place, early modern printmaking was an international phenomenon, in both production and consumption. Already at the beginning of the century the graphic work of the German artist Albrecht Dürer was known, collected, and imitated, from the Netherlands to Italy, as was the work of the Netherlander Hendrick Goltzius at the end of the century. Members of the Flemish Sadeler family operated in Antwerp, Munich, Prague, and Venice. Inscriptions on Netherlandish prints often appeared in more than one language, especially Dutch, French, German, and the most pan-European of languages, Latin. This latter language spoke especially to educated humanists, including scholars, theologians, artists, and publishers, who spread across Europe but maintained close ties with each other through correspondence and travel.

The sixteenth-century Netherlandish school of printmaking is among the most prolific and brilliant in the history of European art, and much of the work was produced in engagement with a stimulating, if also challenging, religious environment. Yet, as specific to its time and place as the work might be, it played an important role in the development of European art, and its treatment of scriptural themes, especially in the handling of the complex interplay between image and sacred text, resonates even now, as neither imagery nor scripture has lost its force. The full apprehension of such scriptural images, as Diego Jiménez's admonition to the reader of the *Adnotationes et Meditationes in Evangelia*, quoted at the beginning of this preface, suggests, may not come easily, but it continues to repay the effort.

James Clifton

Scripture for the Eyes

Bible Illustration in the Sixteenth-Century Low Countries

Walter S. Melion

*T*he title *Scripture for the Eyes* encapsulates the argument of this exhibition, which focuses on biblical prints produced in the Low Countries (present-day Belgium and The Netherlands) between 1500 and 1600: namely, that pictorial images of persons and events from the Old and New Testaments, as well as other kinds of picture based on scripture, such as moral allegories deriving from the parables of the prophets and Christ, offered a clarifying lens through which the word of God was received, pondered, and interpreted by sixteenth-century readers and viewers. Cities such as Amsterdam in the northern province of Holland, and especially Antwerp in the southern province of Flanders, were great publishing centers. Indeed, as Paul Arblaster has recently shown, Antwerp's printing district, formed by the junction of two streets, the Kammenstraat and the Lombardenvest, was the main international source of vernacular Bible editions between 1523 and 1545, not only in Dutch, but also in French, English, Danish, Italian, and Spanish.[1] By the second quarter of the sixteenth century, the neighborhood defined by these streets, along with the Steenhouwersvest, had also become home to the *figuerdruckers* (printmakers), *vormsnyderen* (plate and block cutters), and *printeren* (printers and print publishers), who benefitted from close proximity to the Onze-Lieve-Vrouwepand, the city's chief art market from 1460 to 1560, as Jan van der Stock has demonstrated in his magisterial study of printmaking in early modern Antwerp.[2] And, as Bart A. Rosier makes clear in his comprehensive history of printed Bible illustration in the Low Countries between 1479 and 1599, publishers in Antwerp and Amsterdam, followed a bit later by the important university town Leuven (Louvain), became from the mid-1520s the leading suppliers of Bibles embellished with woodcuts.[3]

In 1526, the printer-publisher Jacob van Liesveldt issued the first complete Bible in Dutch: *Dat oude ende dat nieuwe testament* (*The Old and New Testament*), based largely on Luther's translation of the Old Testament (from Genesis to the Song of Songs) and completely on his translation of the New Testament.[4] Published in Antwerp, this Bible contains fifty illustrations, mainly to the historical books of the Old Testament, deriving primarily from the woodcuts in various Luther editions published in Wittenberg, such as *Das alte testament deutsch* and *Das ander teyl des alten testaments*, illustrated

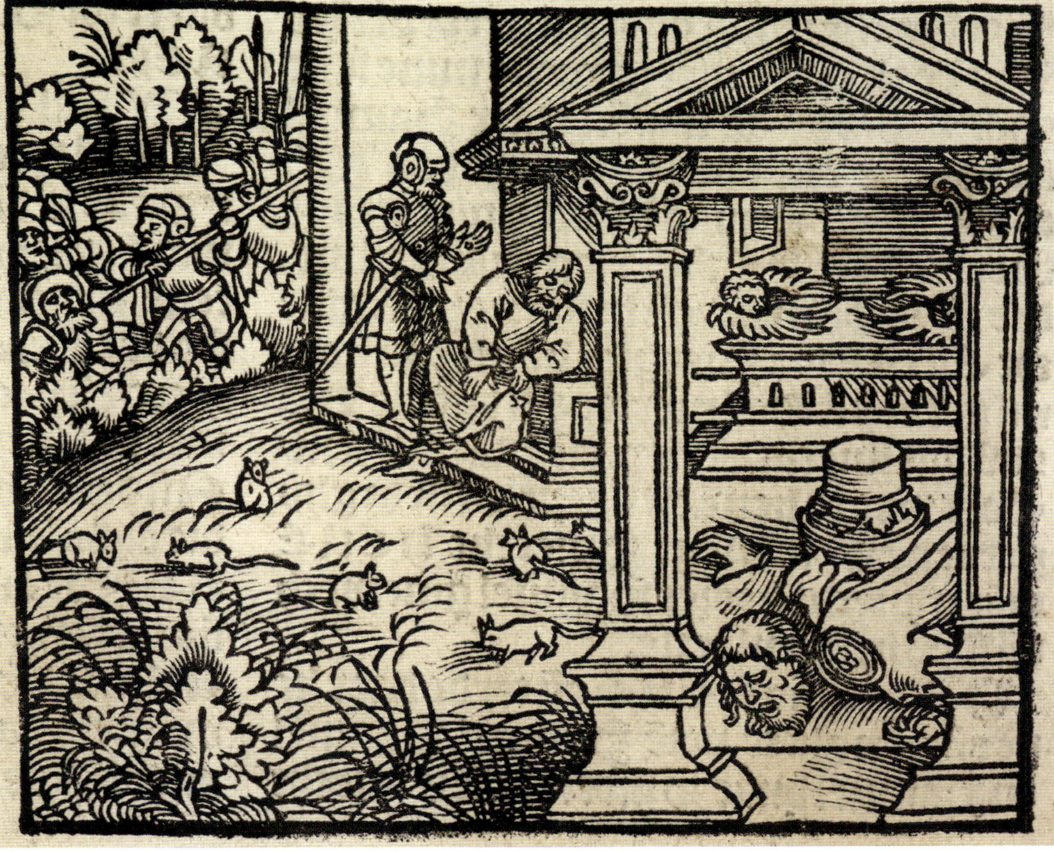

Fig. 1

respectively by Hans Lufft and Lucas Cranach the Elder (fig. 1).[5] Other Dutch Bibles soon followed, such as Willem Vorsterman's *De Bibel* of 1528, subtitled *Tgeheele Oude ende Nieuwe Testament met grooter naersticheyt naden Latijnschen text gecorrigeert* (*The Whole Old and New Testament Revised after the Latin Text*); likewise published in Antwerp, this Bible is based on two Lutheran editions that Vorsterman's scholarly advisers adapted to harmonize with the Latin Vulgate, the canonical Latin text attributed to Saint Jerome and authorized by the Roman Catholic Church (fig. 2).[6] Jan Swart of Gouda designed (and perhaps cut) the woodcuts illustrating the Old Testament, while Lucas van Leyden, amongst other masters, designed and cut the woodcuts illustrating the New.[7]

Fig. 1

The Ark Held Captive in the Temple of Dagon; Eli Learns that the Ark Has Been Captured and his Two Sons Slain; Battle between the Philistines and Israelites, woodcut, in *Dat oude ende dat nieuwe testament* (Antwerp: Jacob van Liesveldt, 1526), folio (D7v). By permission of the Trustees of the British Library. C.110.g.4.

Whereas Swart's designs are startlingly original, those in the
Van Liesveldt Bible, like the prints illustrating the Old Testament
in most Dutch Bibles predating Christopher Plantin's *Biblia Regia*
(*Royal Bible*, also known as the *Polyglot Bible*) of 1568–73, derive
from four German sources: the Cranach workshop's prints for
Luther's Old Testament of 1524 and 1525, Erhard Schön's biblical
prints in Jacob Sacon's *Biblia cum concordantiis veteris et novi
testamenti* (*Bible with Concordances of the Old and New Testament*) of
1519, Hans Sebald Beham's *Biblische historien* (*Bible Histories*) of 1533,
and Hans Holbein's *Historiarum veteris instrumenti icones* (*Historical
Images of the Old Testament*) of 1538.[8] Amongst the sources for prints
illustrating the New Testament, the most important were Lieven
de Witte's innovative woodcuts in Willem van Branteghem's *Dat
leven ons Heeren Jesu Christi* (*The Life of Our Lord Jesus Christ*), a so-
called Gospel harmony that, as its title indicates, reconciles the
four Gospels into a continuous narrative sequence (fig. 3).[9] De
Witte's prints, like the harmonic sequence they illustrate, are the
first consistently to embed the foreground action within detailed
landscapes containing corollary scenes preceding and/or
following the main scene; they are also the first to combine
images of Christ preaching with subsidiary scenes portraying His
parables (figs. 9–11). Examples of several of these publications—
the Van Liesveldt and Vorsterman Bibles, and the Plantin *Royal
Bible*, which inaugurated the switch from woodcut to engraving as
the preferred method of Bible illustration—are featured in the
exhibition, of course, but I mention them here principally to
suggest the close ties between book and print publishing, that
characterize the production of scriptural prints in the Low
Countries between 1500 and 1550.

We might sum up the situation as follows: the translation of
biblical text into biblical images went hand in hand with the
translation of the Bible into the vernacular and, in the case of the
Biblia Regia, from biblical languages such as Hebrew, Syriac, and
Chaldee, into Latin.[10] In Antwerp (the city where the pertinent
archives have been most closely studied) this correlation between
rendering the Bible in text and in image arose within a social
situation in which print and book publishing were implicitly
associated as "free arts"—that is, trades that could be practised
without the requirement of guild membership and its attendant

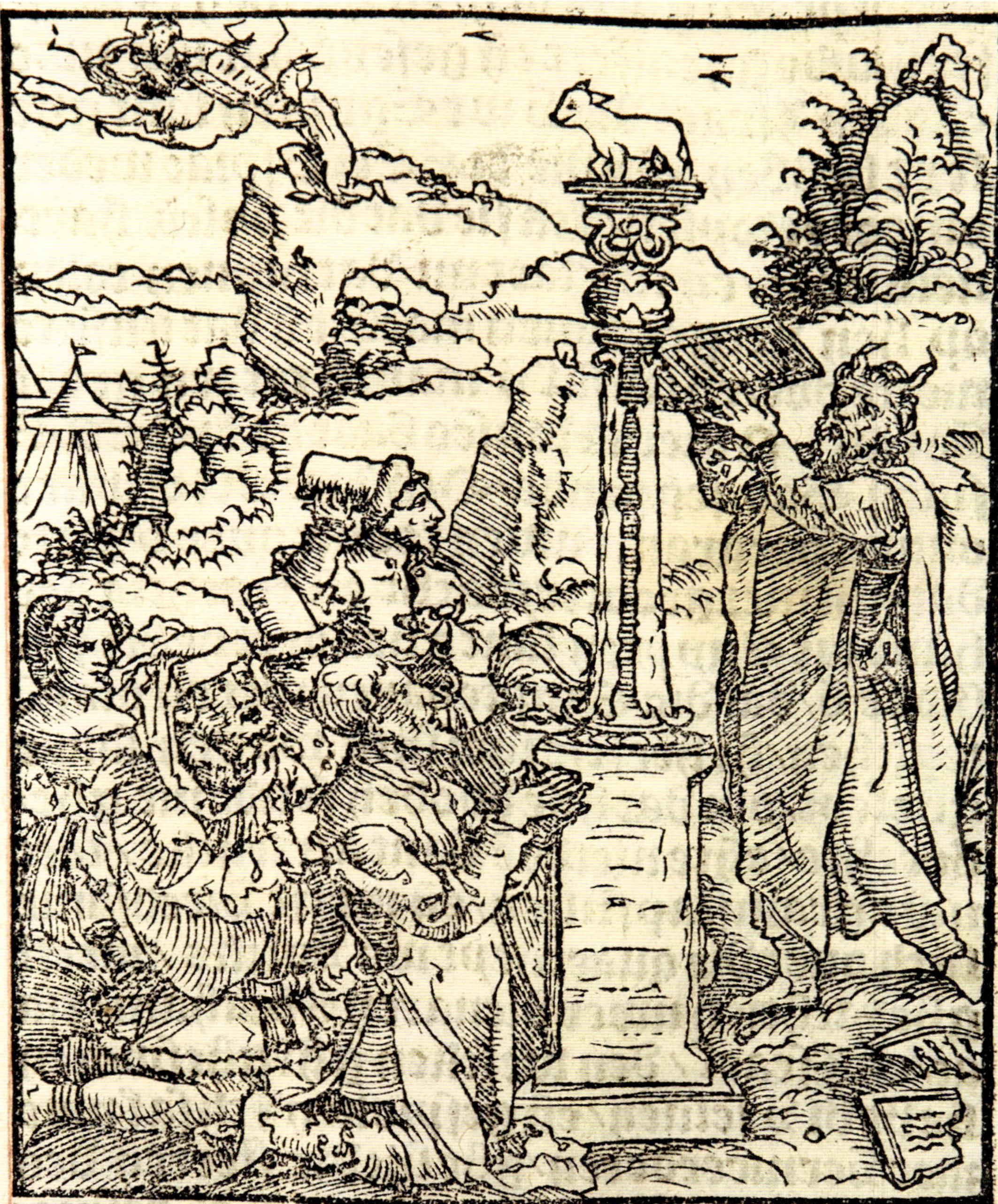

Fig. 2

regulations.[11] Unlike textile printers, who worked with brushes and paint, printers of letterpress and of pictorial images were not required to join the Guild of St. Luke, since they utilized paper and ink, scribal materials traditionally free of guild rules. This situation obtained until 1558, when the Antwerp city council, bowing to pressure from the central government in Brussels, compelled printers of books and pictures, as well as book dealers and bookbinders, to enroll in the guild, which was empowered to oversee their publications and ensure their moral character and religious conformity.[12] An earlier statute of 1546 had already forced the printers to apply for a work permit attesting their probity and orthodoxy.[13] What is interesting here is the degree to which printers of books *and* pictures appear to have been linked, or at least affiliated.

Artists like Jan Swart and Lucas van Leyden also designed and published independent prints and print series portraying biblical scenes, both in woodcut and engraving. Book publishers generally commissioned woodcuts for inclusion in Bibles; carved from blocks, they could be combined with movable type and, having been set by the compositor, inked and printed on a block-press. Engraving involves a very different technique: whereas the woodcutter uses knives and gouges to carve out the woodblock, the engraver uses burins to incise lines into the surface of the copperplate. Burins are cutting tools consisting of a lozenge-shaped tine with a needle-sharp tip that is pushed into the metal to score linear grooves; the copperplate is inked, then carefully wiped so that ink remains only in the grooves, and finally printed in a roller- rather than block-press. The skilled engraver manipulates a wide spectrum of hatches and cross-hatches to secure tonal and textural effects commensurate with finished drawings in various media and, in exceptional cases, with painting. Before the mid-sixteenth century engravings were rarely used as book illustrations, and few incorporated inscriptions either quoting or paraphrasing scripture, although brief references to specific passages sometimes occur. The relation between the illustrative woodcut and the scriptural places to which it attaches can differ markedly from that between the independent woodcut or engraving and the scriptural places it encapsulates. Let us now look at a few examples.

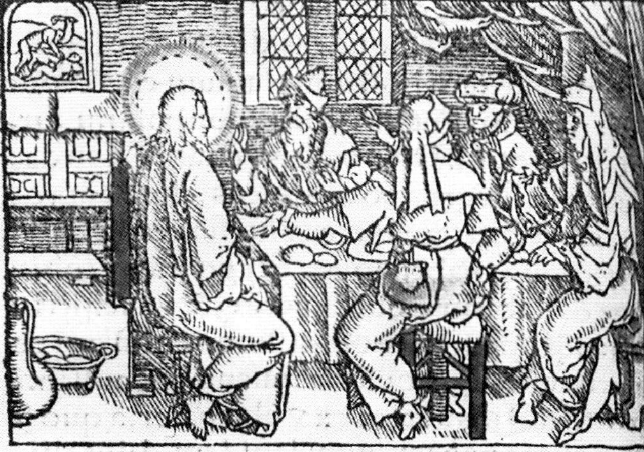

Præposteræ ceremonię

LVC. XI.

ROgauit IESVM quidam pharisæus vt pranderet apud se. IESVS autem ingressus accubuit. Pharisæus autē qui vidisset admiratus est, quod non prius lauisset ante prandium. Et ait dominus ad illum: Nunc vos pharisæi exteriora poculi, catinicq mundatis, & quod intus est vestri, plenum est rapina & malicia: stulti, nonne qui fecit quod foris est, etiam id quod intus est fecit. Veruntamen quod superest, date eleemosinam, & ecce omnia munda sunt vobis. Sed væ vobis pharisæis, quia decimatis menthā & rutam, & quoduis olus, & præteritis iudicium & charitatem Dei, Imo hæc oportuit facere, & illa nō omittere. Væ vobis pharisæis, quia diligitis primas cathedras in synagogis, & salutationes in foro,

Fig. 3

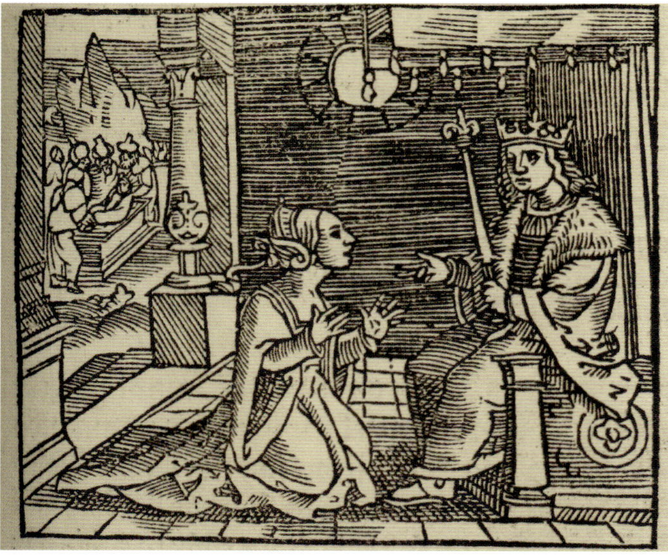

Fig. 4

In Marten de Keyser's *La saincte Bible* of 1530 and the 1532 edition of Vorsterman's *De Bibel*, both published in Antwerp, the image prefacing 1 Kings 1 portrays a beautiful woman kneeling before an enthroned young king; a burial scene takes place in the left background (fig. 4).[14] The placement of this print identifies its subject, which would otherwise be difficult if not impossible to ascertain. 1 Kings 1 tells the story of the beautiful Shunamite maiden Abishag who was chosen to sleep beside the aged and infirm King David, in order that she might keep him warm.[15] A marginal gloss in the Vorsterman Bible explains that Abishag is a "figurative image of Mary the mother of God" (*figuere van die moeder Gods Maria*), drawing an implied parallel between Mary's perpetual virginity and Abishag's chastity: as Mary bore Jesus yet remained a virgin, so Abishag slept with David and yet preserved her maidenhood. The background scene must therefore depict King David's burial. However, as Bart Rosier has argued, the king's youth would seem to indicate that he is Solomon who, having just acceded to the throne, listens to his supplicant mother Bathsheba's plea that Adoniah, Solomon's older half-brother, be allowed to marry David's former handmaid Abishag (1 Kings 2:19 – 23).[16] Although Solomon responded by publicly honoring his mother, he ultimately denied

her request, instead avowing his divinely sanctioned right to rule by commanding that Adoniah, who had declared himself David's presumptive heir, be immediately executed. Rosier quite reasonably suggests on the basis of Vorsterman's marginal note, that both he and De Keyser were overlaying a new reading upon the established, prefigurative image of Solomon and Bathsheba. In traditional typology, which pairs Old Testament types with the New Testament anti-types they were seen to adumbrate, Bathsheba's audience with Solomon was read as a prefiguration of the coronation of the Virgin as Queen of Heaven by Christ the King. Manuscripts and blockbooks of the *Biblia pauperum* (*Poor-Man's Bible*) had disseminated this typological pair (in fact triangulated it with another Old Testament type, Esther before Ahasuerus).[17] By connecting this image to 1 Kings 1, De Keyser and Vorsterman invite the reader-viewer to construe it anew, indeed to misread it as the meeting of David and Abishag that looks forward to the mystery of the Incarnation (the making flesh of God in Christ through the instrument of the Virgin's womb).

It may be worth asking, however, whether the image works concurrently in other ways, reading the text as well as being read by it. The print may perhaps be interpreted as a kind of frontispiece to the opening chapters of 1 Kings: it clearly illustrates 1 Kings 2:10, the burial of King David in Jerusalem, and this reference to chapter 2 invites the reader-viewer further to read it in light of 1 Kings 2:19– 23; seen thus, it would relate to chapter 1 by way of the topic of the royal audience, Abishag, whose presence in the scene would then be strongly implied rather than explicitly portrayed. After all, an image of Solomon and Bathsheba perfectly distills the meaning of chapters 1 and 2 of 1 Kings, since both chapters concern the royal succession and the important role played by Bathsheba in securing it; the divinely mandated legitimacy of her son Solomon is asserted definitively by his power over his half-brother's life. The term *figuere* might just as well apply to Bathsheba pictured in the image as to Abishag denominated in the adjoining text, for both women prefigure Mary the mother of God, though in different ways. One answer to the question, why is the print placed here rather than within chapter 2, would be that it thereby serves to emphasize that Solomon rules in David's place, commanding as much power over his mother as did David over his handmaid. The placement of

Fig. 4
David and Abishag, woodcut, in
La saincte Bible en Françoys
(Antwerp: Martin Lempereur
[Marten de Keyser], 1530), folio
(Q6r); and in *Den Bibel. Tgeheele
Oude ende Nieuwe Testament*
(Antwerp: Willem Vorsterman,
1532), folio (s6v). American
Bible Society.

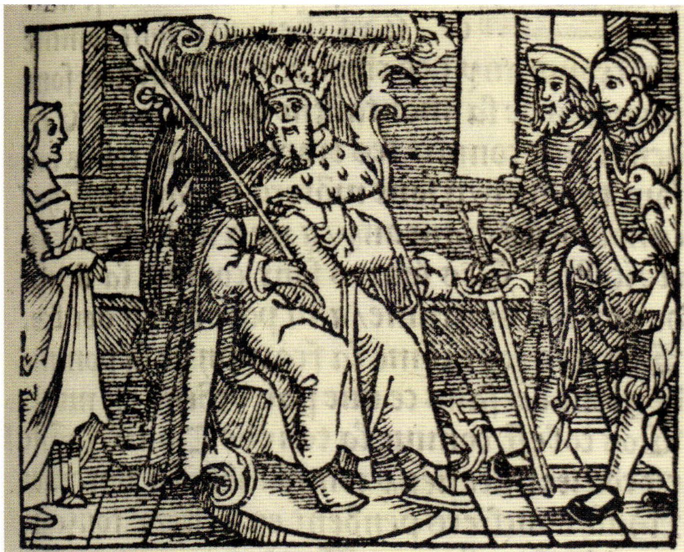

Fig. 5

Bathsheba before Solomon, in other words, underscores the thematic unity of the opening chapters of 1 Kings. The print fulfills this function even if it is read as multi-valent–that is, as representing David and Abishag, and then, in a revised reading, Solomon and Bathsheba. And nor does such a dual reading preclude the application of the standard typologies. On the contrary, it may be fair to state that the image draws upon such an enriched array of possible meanings precisely because it operates in tandem with the scriptural text(s), and moreover, that the image invites a reading of chapters 1 and 2 as a coherent entity focusing on the relation between David and Solomon and on the theme of divinely sanctioned rule. This theme is itself prefigurative, for as God chose Solomon to succeed David, so too, in a lineage from David, did God choose to bring forth Christ.

Images of Solomon were especially susceptible to readings anchored in multiple scriptural places, perhaps because he is so prevalent in the historical books 1 Kings and 1 and 2 Chronicles, and also the presumed author of Proverbs, Ecclesiastes, the Song of Songs, and the Wisdom of Solomon. Rosier provides three examples of Solomon's ability to function as a signpost pointing to various biblical books, whence pertinent passages are gathered and collated. He describes these prints as variants of the author portrait. If the placement of these images as chapter heads makes their subjects discernible, it also, conversely, encourages us to consider how diverse text passages qualify each other by attaching to a single pictorial locus. In the De Keyser Bible of 1530, as well as the Vorsterman Bibles of 1532 and later, the Song of Songs opens with a picture of Solomon enthroned between attendant figures; he addresses the woman at his right, while two courtiers standing at his left, one armed, the other holding a falcon, watch this exchange closely (fig. 5).[18] In this context, the woman is best identified as the bride of the Canticle, whom the poet lovingly extols, and who in turn beholds her beloved approach in the likeness of King Solomon seated upon his silver and golden palanquin and wearing the royal crown (Song of Songs 3:6–11). The print functions equally well as a frontispiece to the next biblical book, the Wisdom of Solomon, that opens with an invocation of justice: "Love righteousness, you rulers of the earth." Seen from this vantage point, the seated Solomon exemplifies the ruler who loves righteousness, and the personification of the beloved bride doubles as the personification of justice, whom Solomon instructs godly men to seek and to love. She also embodies wisdom, for in the Wisdom of Solomon 8:2–3, Solomon calls mighty wisdom his noble and beautiful bride, whom he desired to marry even from his youth. By the same token, the courtiers stand for the powerful men whom Solomon admonishes throughout the Wisdom of Solomon to imitate him in loving justice and wisdom. The complementarity of these passages becomes apparent in and through their association with one and the same image that plays the part of a switchboard, inviting us to consider how the love of the bride and bridegroom is like the ruler's love of justice and wisdom.

In the De Keyser Bibles of 1530 and 1534, the Vorsterman Bibles of 1532 and later, and various other Dutch Bibles, 2 Chronicles 1 opens with an image of King Solomon kneeling before an altar on which the menorah burns brightly (fig. 6).[19] The scene loosely illustrates 2 Chronicles 1:3-5, Solomon's burnt offering at the bronze altar made by Bezalel, on the high place at the tent of meeting in Gibeon, but it also conflates the Wisdom of Solomon 8:21–9:1–18, Solomon's prayer for the divine gift of wisdom: "Send her forth from the holy heavens, and from the throne of thy glory send her, that she may be

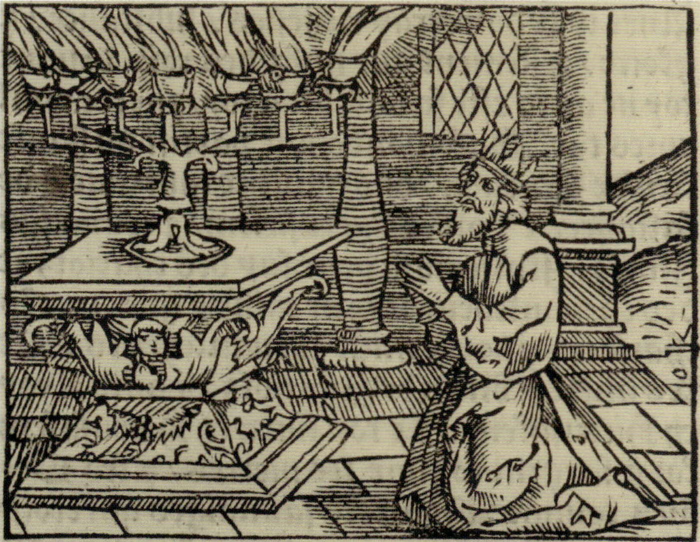

Fig. 6

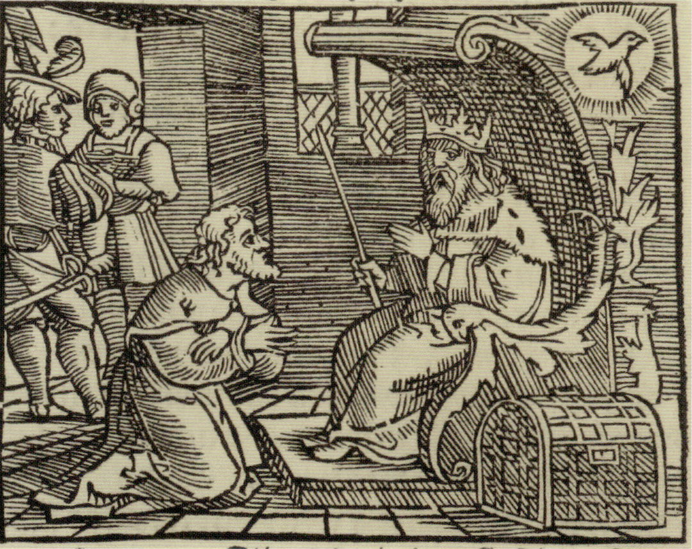

Fig. 7

with me and toil, and that I may learn what is pleasing to thee." 2 Chronicles 1:7–13 recounts how God appeared to Solomon in the night after his burnt offering, promising to grant whatever he might wish and rewarding him with wisdom, riches, possessions, and honor, when he prudently chose wisdom above all things. The print of *Solomon Praying for Wisdom* instead reconciles 2 Chronicles 1 and the Wisdom of Solomon 8, construing Solomon's ritual sacrifice as an extended prayer of supplication for wisdom, the precise words of which are revealed in the Wisdom of Solomon 9. The nature of divine wisdom and the intensity of Solomon's love of it, set forth in the Wisdom of Solomon, are seen to inform the events that inaugurate his reign, recorded in 2 Chronicles 1.

The image of a supplicant kneeling before an enthroned king, above whose throne the Holy Spirit hovers in the form of a radiant dove, appears at the start of Ecclesiastes, the Wisdom of Jesus Sirach, and Psalm 39 in the De Keyser Bible of 1530 and the Vorsterman Bible of 1532 (fig. 7).[20] Ecclesiastes provides one frame of reference: the seated king speaking to the supplicant would be Solomon the Preacher and King over Israel, "who applied [his] mind to seek and to search out by wisdom all that is done under heaven," and having learned true wisdom, now instructs his people

(Ecclesiastes 1:12–14). The treasure chest beside the throne alludes to the silver and gold "gathered for myself...and the treasure of kings and provinces," that here signify all those other possessions after which mankind strives, and which the Preacher appraises as mere folly, "a striving after wind" (Ecclesiastes 1:17 and 2:8). The Wisdom of Jesus Sirach frames the image in a different if complementary fashion: the king over whom the Holy Spirit presides would stand for the Lord from whom "all wisdom comes" and "is...for ever," and "who is wise, greatly to be feared, sitting upon his throne" (Wisdom of Jesus Sirach 1:1). By the same token, the supplicant would both embody and exemplify the fear of the Lord that "is the beginning of wisdom" (Wisdom of Jesus Sirach 1:14). Psalm 39 offers a third frame of reference: the supplicant before his lord denotes the Psalmist beseeching God to deliver him from all transgressions, grant knowledge of life's transience, and confer the gladness of peace (Psalm 39:4–6, 8, 12–13). The treasure chest now alludes to those transient things that "man heaps up, and knows not who will gather" (Psalm 39:6). The triple repetition of the *Suppliant before a King* calls attention to the themes linking Ecclesiastes, the Wisdom of Jesus Sirach, and Psalm 39— most importantly, the necessity of heavenly wisdom in the

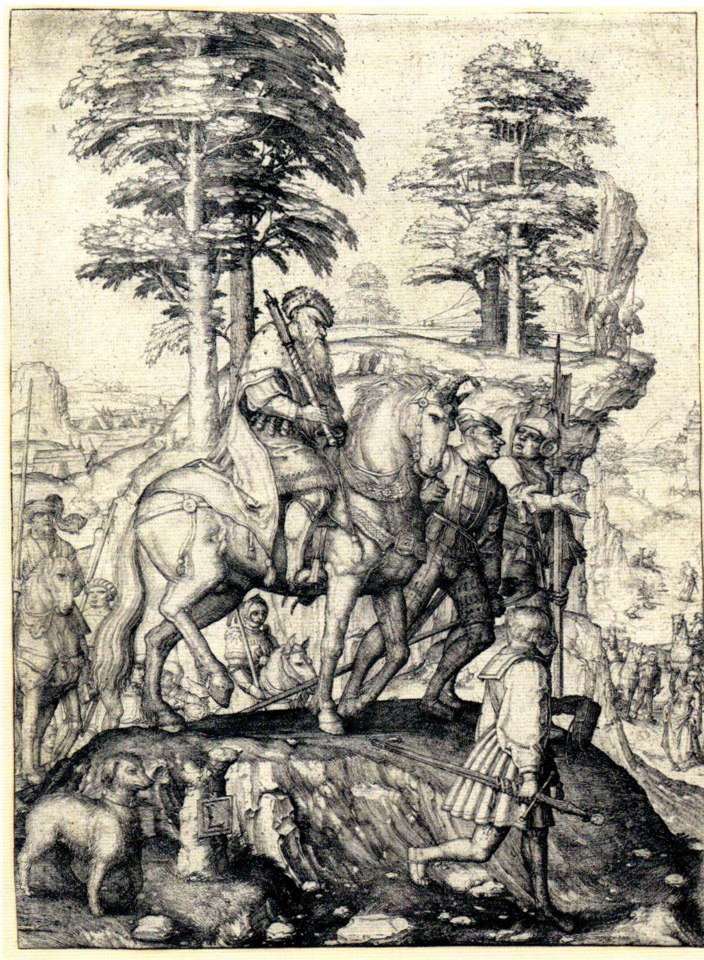

Fig. 8

presence of which all terrestrial things, including life itself, are counted as naught—as well as to the divinely inspired wisdom of their respective authors, Solomon, Jesus Sirach, and David. The dove of the Holy Spirit, as Rosier suggests, may further signify the Holy Spirit of discipline, invoked in the Wisdom of Solomon 1:1–6, that dwells in uprightness and sincerity of heart but flees deceitful souls, foolish thoughts, and the shame of unrighteousness.[21] Here its presence affirms the righteousness of the ruler dispensing wisdom from his throne, whose justice is

known to God: "God is witness of his inmost feelings, and a true observer of his heart, and a hearer of his tongue; because the Spirit of the Lord has filled the world, and that which holds all things together knows what is said" (Psalm 39:6–7).

As these examples from illustrated Bibles make clear, a single print may allude to interrelated scriptural passages from multiple sources, or alternatively, it may be repeated to suggest linkages amongst scriptural books. What of independent prints? Before the mid-sixteenth century when inscriptions became commonplace, the subjects of such prints were chiefly known by reference to pictorial templates, such as the *Biblia pauperum* or *Speculum humanae salvationis* (*Mirror of Human Salvation*), the former consisting of New Testament antitypes (one per page) flanked by two Old Testament types and four prophets, the latter of New Testament antitypes (one per opening) followed or preceded by three Old Testament types. Lucas van Leyden's celebrated engraving of *David and Abigail*, issued ca.1508, derives from a famous typological analogy going back to these sources: the supplicant Abigail pleading before David for the life of her household prefigures the merciful Virgin pleading before Christ for the salvation of the Church; and as Abigail clearly foresaw that the Lord would make David victorious, so Mary fervently believed in the triumph of Christ (fig. 8).[22] However, Lucas alters the standard formula: instead of foregrounding the encounter between the two protagonists, he depicts an earlier moment from the story, positioning David at the summit of a steep hill, the diminutive figure of Abigail at its base. She holds a peace offering, perhaps a branch of olive, and looks up, having caught sight of David; behind her is one of the camels laden with gifts of food that she has brought in hope of appeasing his righteous indignation against her husband Nabal. Although the foot-soldier armed with a halberd begins to gesture in Abigail's direction, David has not yet seen her; he sits atop a caparisoned steed, towering over his men, his commander's baton raised, his face sternly expressive of the desire to be avenged. The foreshortened view of David's face, like the precipitous vista from the cliff-top, underscores the strangeness of our vantage point and betokens our unusual point of entry into this otherwise familiar story. Although Lucas includes just enough detail to make his subject matter discernible, his alterations firmly detach it from the typological reading that had heretofore been

Fig. 8
Lucas van Leyden, *David and Abigail*, ca. 1508, engraving, 270 x 192 mm. By permission of the Trustees of The British Museum.

conventional. If Abigail has yet to intercede, she can no longer be interpreted as a symbol of the Virgin's intercession. Instead, Lucas induces us to read 1 Samuel 25 carefully, to examine whence and why she has come, whither and to what end David and his army are marching, and to dwell on the passions at play, his anger and her anxiety. The extreme divergence in scale that separates them serves to characterize him, in the words of 1 Samuel 25, as the lord magnified by the Lord's favor, and conversely, to emphasize her intention of humbling herself as his lowly handmaid (1 Samuel 25:24, 28–30). These devices function as prompts to close reading: they encourage us to consult the Bible in search of the historical event and its meaning, rather than substituting the typological consensus for the scriptural source.

Jan Swart, the chief illustrator of the Old Testament scenes in the Vorsterman Bibles of 1528 and 1532, produced an independent woodcut of the rarely illustrated scene of *Jesus Preaching from the Ship* (Matthew 13:1–9, Mark 4:1–20, Luke 8:1–14) around 1526 (see cat. 32).[23] Swart explores the compositional device developed by Lucas in his engraving of *David and Abigail*: rather than foregrounding Jesus, he distances and even marginalizes him; the ship aboard which Jesus preaches to the crowd gathered on the shore has been positioned near the print's right-hand border. The four richly dressed figures standing on the rocky mound at center tower above everyone else, dominating the image. Instead of seeing and hearing Christ, they converse amongst themselves, although the declamatory gesture of the man wearing a stove-pipe hat, along with the extended thumb of the pointing figure beside him, indicate that Christ is the topic of discussion. The turbaned figure at right grasps the pommel of his sword, indicating his hostile intent. Since the bearded man facing forward wears a levitical mitre, he may be identified as a priest, while his companions are likely scribes and Pharisees. (In the left middle-ground, another Pharisee, dressed in the long robes denounced by Jesus in Matthew 23:5, hurries to join the shore-side congregation.) Barely visible in the distant field at center left is a peasant sowing seed; flocks of birds have gathered before and behind him, and others swoop down in his direction. Even more diminutive than Christ, the husbandman bodies forth the subject of his sermon: the parable of the sower.

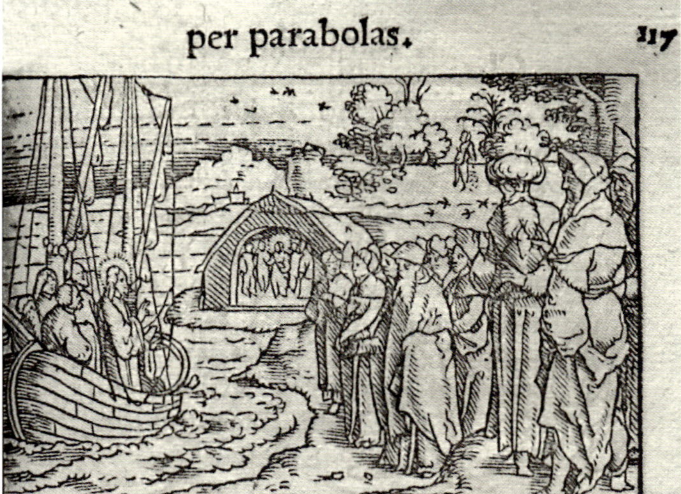

per parabolas.   117

Qui habet aures ad audiendum, audiat. Interrogabant aūt eum discipuli eius, dicentes: quæ esset ista parabola. At ille dixit: Vobis datū est nosse mysteria regni Dei, ceteris aūt per parabolas, vt videāt non videāt, & audientes nō intelligant. Est aūt hæc parabola: Semen est sermo Dei. Qui aūt iuxta viā, hi sunt qui audiunt deinde venit diabolus, & tollit sermonem de corde eorū ne credentes seruentur. Nam qui su per petram, ij sunt, qui quum audierint, cū gaudio suscipiunt sermonem, & hi radices non habent, qui ad tempus credunt, & in tēpore tentationis recedunt. Quod aūt in spinas cecidit, hi sunt q audierūt, & a solicitudinibus & diuitijs ac voluptatibus vitæ euntes suffocātur, nec reserūt fructum. Quod aūt in bonā terrā, hi sunt qui in corde honesto ac bono audiētes sermonem retinent, & fructum afferūt per patientiā.
H.3.

Fig. 9

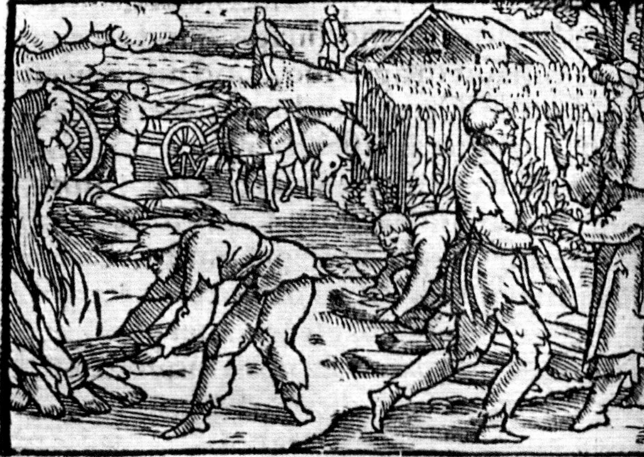

Parabola

MAT. XIII.

ASsimilatum est regnū cœlorū homini se-
minanti bonū semen in agro suo, sed dor-
mientibus hominibus venit illius inimicus, & seminauit zizania inter triticum, abijtq́;
Quum aūt germinasset herba, & fructum fecis-
set, tunc apparuerūt & zizania. Accedentes autem serui patrisfamilias, dixerunt illi: Domine,
nonne bonum semen seminabas in tuo agro?
Vnde igitur habet zizania? Ille vero dixit illis: Inimicus homo hoc fecit. Serui aūt dixerūt
illi. Vis igitur abeamus & colligamus ea? At ille dixit, Non, ne dum colligitis zizania, eradi-
cetis simul cū illis & triticū, sinite pariter cresce-
re vtraq; vsq; ad messem, & in tempore messi
dicam messoribus. Colligite primū zizania,
& colligate in fasciculos ad comburendum ea,
Triticum vero congregate in horreum meū.

Fig. 10

Swart makes it possible to identify Jesus: he is haloed, framed by masts and spars, and stands as the object of the crowd's attention, the goal toward whom the figures at left process. He also marks the junction of numerous diagonals. Nonetheless, he is difficult to make out, and nor is the subject of the print readily apparent until one has found him (and perhaps not even then). Like Lucas, Swart compels us to refer to scripture, and again like Lucas, he matches the pictorial format to the meaning of the source texts. This is something that the illustrations to be found in the Bibles we have been examining rarely attempt, and it would be fair to assume that their small size precluded such thematic manipulations of scale and composition. (Both Swart's woodcut and Lucas's engraving are nearly folio-size prints, whereas the woodcuts in the Liesveldt, Vorsterman, De Keyser, and other Bibles generally take up no more than an eighth or at most a quarter of a folio.) Swart makes Jesus difficult to spot, because the subject of his sermon is the difficulty of seeing and hearing the truth he embodies. He is preaching, as the synoptic Gospels testify, about the nature of the word he promulgates and the ways in which it is received; that is to say, what he is actually doing, the very act of speaking, is also what he is speaking about. The crux of his sermon is the parable of the sower that stands for, as well as exemplifies, his use of parables to communicate religious truths: "All this Jesus said to the crowds in parables; indeed he said nothing to them without a parable. This was to fulfill what was spoken by the prophet: 'I will open my mouth in parables, I will utter what has been hidden since the foundation of the world'" (Matthew 13:34–35 and Psalm 78:2).

The speech that Jesus delivers from the ship concerns a sower who scatters seeds onto a path where birds come and devour them, onto rocky ground where they quickly sprout and are soon scorched, onto thorns that grow up and choke them, and onto good soil where they mature into a thirty-, sixty-, or hundredfold of grain. The background vignette of the sower corresponds exactly to this imagery: he stands amidst companies of birds, with boulders at his left and dense undergrowth at his right. The meaning of the parable is revealed by Christ to the disciples (watching and listening to him intently from shipboard in the print), who, immediately after his sermon, ask him why he speaks in parables. He answers that he does so to fulfill the prophecy of Isaiah: "You

Fig. 10
Lieven de Witte, *The Parable of the Wheat and the Tares,* woodcut, in Willem van Branteghem, *Iesu Christi vita, iuxta quatuor Evangelistarum narrationes* (Antwerp: Mattheus Cromme, 1537), octavo (p. 141); and in *Dat leven ons Heeren Christi Jesu figuerlijck uuten text der vier Evangelisten* (Antwerp: Mattheus Cromme, 1537), octavo (p. 141); and in *Dat nieuwe Testament ons Heeren Jesu Christi* (Antwerp: Mattheus Cromme, 1538), octavo (K5v). Katholieke Universiteit Leuven, Maurits Sabbebibliotheek.

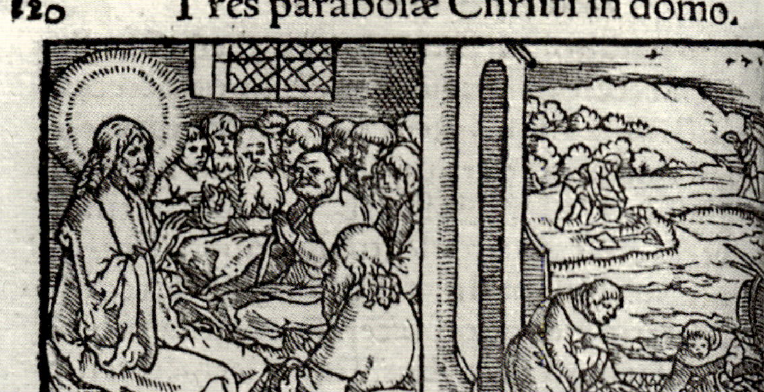

Simile est regnū cœlorū thesauro absconso
in agro, quē repertū homo abscondidit, & præ
gaudio quod habet sup eo abit, & oīa quæ
cunqʒ habet vēdit, ac mercatur agrū illū. Rur
sum simile est regnū cœlorū homini negociato
ri querenti pulchras margaritas: q cū inuenerit
vnā preciosam margaritā, abiēs vendidit oīa
quæ possidebat, & mercatus est illā. Rursum, si
mile est regnū cœlorū verriculo iacto in mare,
& ex omni gñe cōtrahēti: qd cū impletū fuisset
subduxerūt in litt⁹, & sedētes collegerūt q bona
sunt in vasa, q vero mala foras abiecerūt. Sic fu
turū est in consummatiõe seculi, Venīēt angeli,
&segregabūt malos de medio iustorū, &mittē
eos in caminū ignis, illic erit ploratus & stridor
dentiū: dicit eis Iesus, Intellexistis hęc oīa? Dicūt
ei. Etiā dñe. At ille dixit ei: Propterea oīs scri
ba doctus ad regnū cœlorū similis ē hoī patrisfa
milias, q de ꝑmit ē thesauro suo noua et vetera.

Fig. 11

shall indeed hear but never understand, and you shall indeed see but never perceive. For this people's heart has grown dull, and their ears are heavy of hearing, and their eyes they have closed, lest they should perceive with their eyes, and hear with their ears, and understand with their heart, and turn for me to heal them." He then divulges what he expects the disciples to ascertain in the parable, unfolding it to elucidate the prophecy: the seeds are the Gospel, the "word of the kingdom"; the path is the ignorant heart whence the devil, to wit the birds, snatches away the word before it can take root; the rocky ground is the heart that joyfully receives the word but whose enthusiasm instantly withers when faced by tribulation or persecution; the thorns are the earthly cares and pleasures that entangle the heart, choking the word before it can bear fruit; and finally, the good soil is the heart that hears and understands the word, allowing it to take root, mature, and produce plentifully (Matthew 13:18–23). Only the privileged few who have been given "to know the secrets of the kingdom of heaven" will discover the parable's true meaning; having digested the teachings of the Old Testament, they are equipped to apprehend what Christ now teaches, which will germinate and flourish within them, even as it withers and dies in those who are blind and deaf to him: "For to him who has will more be given, and he will have abundance; but from him who has not, even what he has will be taken away" (Matthew 13:11–12). Parables on this account have a double function, as comparison of the parallel versions of this episode in Matthew 13, Mark 4, and Luke 8 makes apparent. According to Matthew 13:13, parables assist the undiscerning to know what they otherwise would only half-see and half-hear: "This is why I speak to them in parables, because seeing they do not see, and hearing they do not hear, nor do they understand." But Mark 4:11–12 and Luke 8:10 construe parables differently, as a means of separating those with from those without the capacity of perception: "To you has been given the secret of the kingdom of God, but for those outside everything is in parables; so that they may indeed see but not perceive, and may indeed hear but not understand; lest they should turn again, and be forgiven." (Mark 4:33–34 adds that Jesus, though he spoke publicly in parables, explained them privately to his disciples.) Jesus concludes by compounding the parable of the sower with additional parables—of

Fig. 11

Lieven de Witte, *Christ Preaches the Parable of the Kingdom of Heaven from the House*, woodcut, in Willem van Branteghem, *Iesu Christi vita, iuxta quatuor Evangelistarum narrationes* (Antwerp: Mattheus Cromme, 1537), octavo (p. 144); and in *Dat leven ons Heeren Christi Jesu figuerlijck uuten text der vier Evangelisten* (Antwerp: Mattheus Cromme, 1537), octavo (p. 144); and in *Dat nieuwe Testament ons Heeren Jesu Christi* (Antwerp: Mattheus Cromme, 1538), octavo (L3r). Katholieke Universiteit Leuven, Maurits Sabbebibliotheek.

the wheat and the tares, of the grain of mustard seed, of the leaven and three measures of meal — that describe the kingdom of heaven awaiting whosoever comes to know and embrace the truths he purveys (Matthew 13:24–34, Mark 4:26–32).

In the woodcut, the priest, scribes, and Pharisees gathered on the hillock, who neither look at nor listen to Christ, embody the men of evil hearts, from whom "the evil one comes and snatches what is sown." They stand between us and the congregation on the shore, blocking access to Christ; in this sense, they represent the path where the seeds of faith are quickly devoured. The dead and living trees at the left draw attention to the difference between the faithful and the faithless, the plant that withers and dies and the "greatest of shrubs [that] becomes a tree, so that the birds of the air come and make nests in its branches" (Matthew 13:31). The hostile intent of the turbaned man grasping his sword while dismissively thumbing Christ, recalls a related passage in Matthew 21, suggesting that these men are representatives of the "chief priests and the Pharisees [who] heard his parables [and] perceived that he was speaking about them," and then plotted to arrest him (Matthew 21:45–46). The soldier staring at the crowd, seated just behind this man, enforces this interpretation. The pharisee, peasant, and elegantly dressed woman at left, who hurry to join the congregation, perhaps represent the hearts that rush to embrace the word, only to fall away when difficulties arise. Amongst the throng ostensibly here to attend to Christ, the many heads looking away or toward each other belong to those whose many cares distract them from the word, causing the seeds he sows to be choked by thorns. They are the souls prophesied by Isaiah and censured by Christ, whose hearts fail to understand and who neglect to "turn for [him] to heal them" (Matthew 13:15). By contrast, the women listening attentively in the front rank, like the disciples on the ship, are they whose eyes and ears, being blessed truly to see and hear, turn wholly toward Christ (Matthew 13:16). They may be the women described in Luke 8:2–3, who followed him as he preached, having been healed of evil spirits and infirmities: Mary Magdalene, Joanna, and Susanna. Our ability to read the image in terms of Matthew 13, Mark 4, Luke 8, and of complementary passages such as Matthew 21:45–46, and effectively to apply the parable as did Christ to his congregation,

discriminating between the kinds and degrees of adherence they display, gives us the opportunity to measure our understanding of his words, and to determine whether we possess fertile hearts in which the "secrets of the kingdom of heaven" are apprehended. It may be accurate to describe the print as a spiritual *machina* (apparatus) that permits us to test the nature and potency of our scriptural understanding. And this returns us to the question of compositional mode with which our discussion commenced. The difficulty of finding and dwelling on the figure of Christ in the print stands for, or better enacts the difficulty of parsing the parables he delivers, descrying their significant images and accurately interpreting them. To see this print and to know it are to experience vividly what it was like to see and know Christ at first hand through the parabolic medium that was his chosen vehicle for disseminating the Gospels.

The exploitation of the conditions of viewing as an heuristic pictorial device that challenges us better to grasp the meaning of scripture—to experience what it meant to encounter Christ through the application of sense, heart, and mind—appealed to both Catholic and Lutheran viewers of printed images throughout the sixteenth century. This is one of many respects in which it is often difficult, or well-nigh impossible, rigidly to demarcate confessional positions where biblical prints are concerned.[24] As indicated above, such compositional exploration is characteristic of independent prints and print series. In Willem van Branteghem's *Iesu Christi vita, iuxta quatuor Evangelistarum narrationes* (*Life of Jesus Christ According to the Gospel Accounts of the Four Evangelists*) of 1537, the superb woodcuts by Lieven de Witte include a series of three prints, respectively illustrating Christ preaching the parable of the sower from the ship and complementary parables from the house (Matthew 13:3-9, 18–23, Mark 4:2–9, 13–20, Luke 8:5–15), the parable of the wheat and the tares (Matthew 13:24–25), and Christ preaching the parables of the kingdom of heaven from the house (Matthew 13:44–48) (figs. 9–11).[25] Two of these prints, *Christ Preaching from the Ship* and the *Parable of the Wheat and the Tares*, reappear in Mattheus Cromme's *Dat nieuwe Testament ons Heeren Jesu Christi* (*New Testament of our Lord Jesus Christ*) of 1538, where the former serves to evoke the parables told at the feast of Levi (Luke 5:29–39) as well as illustrating Luke 8, and the latter illustrates

Matthew 13 (figs 9–10).[26] In the Vorsterman Bible of 1528, we find a print of the *Parable of the Sower* at the start of Matthew 13;[27] in the 1532 edition, it illustrates both Matthew 13 and Luke 8.[28] When these prints incorporate the figure of Christ, he is clearly visible as the source of the parables, the content of which appears in the background or in a subsidiary scene adjacent to that of Christ preaching; alternatively, the parable takes up the whole scene, and the figure of Christ is absent. Nowhere are we presented with the problem of finding him, as a surrogate for the experience of spiritual discernment that parables elicit and dramatize. Additionally, there is another respect in which independent prints differ from embedded images. Before the appearance of inscriptions at mid-century, reader-viewers of prints like Jan Swart's *Christ Preaching from the Ship* could spread their nets widely, accommodating readings from numerous scriptural passages in their efforts to decode the image. As the pictures in illustrated Bibles are not merely read by the texts they illustrate, so independent prints redound upon those texts they portray, calling forth important themes worth pondering, such as the form and function of the parables used by Christ to teach doctrine by means of lively verbal images—the farmer sowing, the servant reaping, or the woman leavening. Understood in this way, *Christ Teaching from the Ship* may be seen as an image about the legibility, relevance, and instrumentality of Christian image-making.

Thus far, I have focused on prints produced in the first half of the sixteenth century. Although illustrated Bibles like those of Van Liesveldt, Vorsterman, De Keyser, and others, continued to be published—Hans de Laet's Dutch translation of the Latin Vulgate, authorized by the Catholic theological faculty of the University of Leuven, being an interesting case in point—the situation changed somewhat at mid-century with the establishment in Antwerp of the print-publishing houses of Hieronymus Cock, Philips Galle, Gerard de Jode, Hans and Mynken Liefrinck, Pieter Baltens, and others.[29] Many if not most of these publishers specialized in the production of engraved prints and print series, taking responsibility for the coordination of the designers, engravers, and copperplate-printers, often supplying such materials as paper and copperplate, and finally marketing the printed images. It became standard practice in signed prints to use the term *invenit* (invented) for the designer, *fecit* (executed) for the engraver, and *excudebat* (issued) for the publisher. Legal documents indicate that the latter was held primarily responsible for the content of the prints he purveyed.

Book publishers in Antwerp, amongst whom the most accomplished and successful was the typographer Christopher Plantin, tended to collaborate with such print publishers in the production of illustrated volumes. As Karen L. Bowen and Dirk Imhof have recently demonstrated in their monograph on Plantin and the development of engraved book illustration in the sixteenth century, he was chiefly responsible for the shift toward engraving in luxury publishing after the mid-1560s.[30] Plantin relied mainly on the printing house of Mynken Liefrinck, a successful seller, printer, and colorer of maps and images. She supplied the folio-size title-page and five frontispieces to Plantin's magnificent *Biblia sacra Hebraice, Chaldaice, Graece, & Latine* (*Sacred Bible in Hebrew, Chaldee, Greek, and Latin*), also known as the *Biblia regia* or *Biblia polyglotta* (*Royal Bible* or *Polyglot Bible*), published between 1568 and 1573, under the editorial supervision of the prominent Spanish theologian Benito Arias Montano (fig. 12).[31] Along with the liturgical *Horae beatissimae Virginis Mariae* (*Hours of the Most Holy Virgin Mary*) of 1570, the emblematic *Humanae salutis monumenta* (*Monuments of Human Salvation*) of 1571, and the *Biblia sacra* of 1583, the *Biblia polyglotta* marked a threshold, after which engraving became a medium of choice for ambitious illustrated Bibles and other scriptural texts, such as catechisms, liturgies, emblem books, and meditative treatises, addressed to elite audiences, both lay and clerical.[32] Like earlier Bibles featuring elaborate title-pages that play upon the relation between the Old and New Testaments, the *Polyglot Bible* opens with a figured title that alludes allegorically to the joint authority of both covenants.[33] Various editions of the Van Liesveldt Bible, for instance, open with an aedicular title-page printed in woodcut and letterpress: Moses sits in a scalloped niche at the summit of the folio, pointing at the tablets of the law; as the composer of the Pentateuch, the first five books of the Bible, he is given pride of place amongst the divinely inspired authors of the Old and New Testaments (fig. 13).[34] Moses establishes the historical and thematic axis on either side of which stand pairs of prophets and evangelists. His primacy also illustrates the argument of Van Liesveldt's preface, that the Old Testament should be valued no less than the New, since it contains the salvific promises to be fulfilled in and through Christ. His pointing gesture also directs our gaze beyond the tablets of the law toward the figures of Mark and John who hold writing tablets inscribed with representative texts from the New Testament. The complementary relation between the Old Law and the New is made clear by the attitudes of the prophets and evangelists who display their texts to each other and look intently into each other's eyes. At right, Moses's successor Joshua holds a citation from Joshua 1:8, God's command to meditate day and night on the book of the law, rather than merely reciting it. Below him, David, his attribute the harp at his side, holds a citation from Psalm 18 [19]:8, proclaiming that the Lord's precepts are pure, and that they enlighten the eyes of the spirit. Both texts emphasize that the Mosaic law consists first and foremost not of strictures to be observed, but more importantly of the divinely transmitted word, enshrined in the holy book (*boec*) and holy law (*gebot*) that must serve both as meditative source (*mer peyst daerom dach ende nacht*—"but rather meditate upon it day and night") and source of enlightenment (*ende si velichten die oogen*— "and they illuminate the eyes"). At left, Marc holds a citation from chapter 16:15 of his Gospel, Christ's command to go into all of the world and preach the Gospel to all creation. Below him, John holds a citation from chapter 1:10 of his second epistle, warning that anyone bringing a doctrine other than that of Christ must be neither received nor greeted. Relayed by Joshua, God's command to meditate upon the divine word transposes into that of Christ, relayed by Mark, universally to broadcast it. David's promise that the divine word shall clarify spiritual sight becomes John's admonition to welcome and enshrine only the word of Christ within the heart. Beneath the privilege ostensibly authorizing this edition (*cum gratia et privilegio*—"by grace and privilege"), Jacob van Liesveldt's printer's mark, emblazoned on an escutcheon held by two putti, mediates between the prophets and evangelists, as if to imply that he has hearkened to their words precisely, embracing both testaments by publishing this Bible.

What makes Plantin's *Polyglot Bible* distinctive is the coherent development of the testamentary theme in a series of introductory

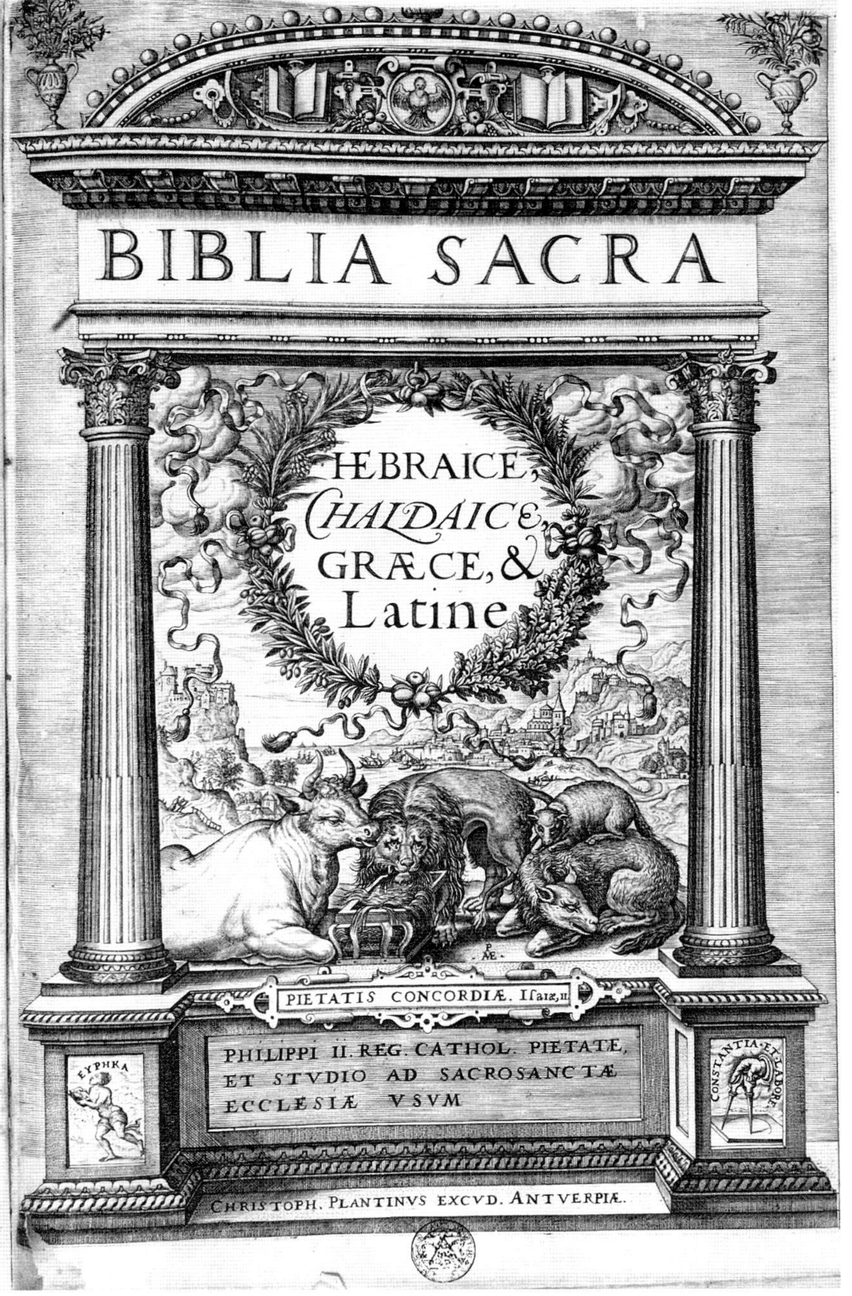

Fig. 12

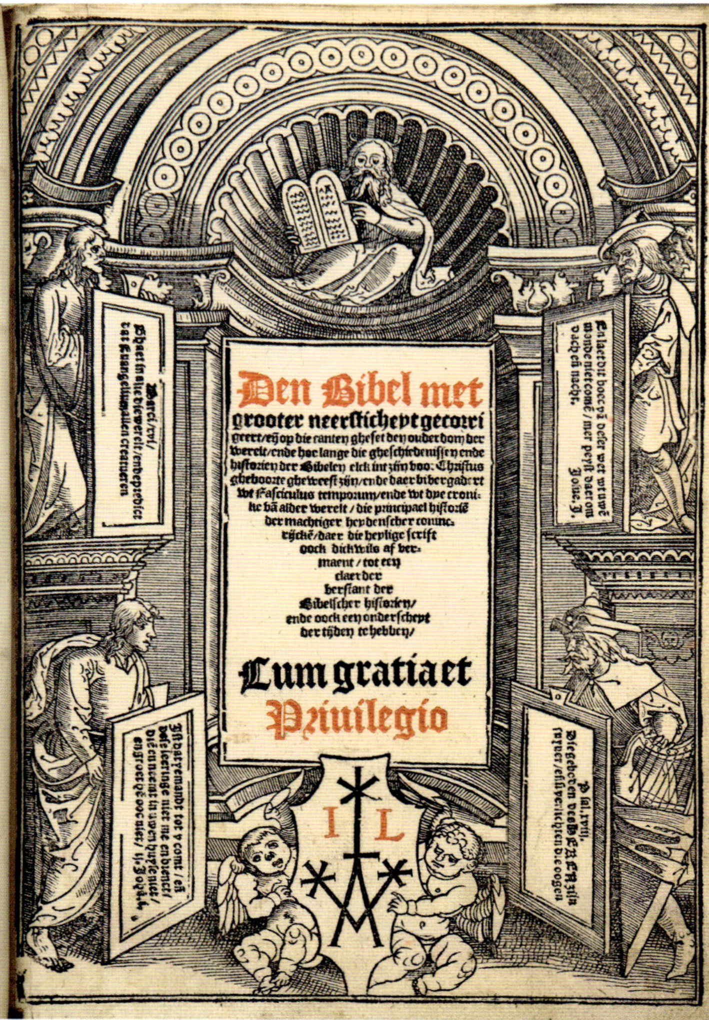

Fig. 13

images —the title-page and succeeding five frontispieces attaching to volumes 1, 2, 4, and 5 of the eight-volume work—illustrating scriptural texts having to do with the historical journey of the revealed word as the divinely sanctioned instrument of human salvation (see cats. 2–5).[35] That these engravings are integral is made apparent by the explanatory text focusing on the title-page and frontispieces, *Tabularum in Regiis Bibliis depictarum brevis explicatio* ("Brief Expository Discourse on the Plates Depicted in the Royal Bible"), composed by Plantin as one of the forewords in volume 1. Arias Montano, the probable iconographer of these images, further expounds the scheme uniting the title-page and frontispieces in the general preface opening volume 1, *De divinae scripturae dignitate, linguarum usu & Catholici Regis consilio, praefatio* ("On the Dignity of Divine Scripture, the Use of Languages, and the Good-Judgment of the Catholic King [Philip II]"). Since these illustrative engravings are some of the most sophisticated and elaborate biblical prints dating from the second half of the sixteenth century in the Low Countries, I want to dwell on their hermeneutic function by way of concluding these general remarks on Dutch and Flemish Bible illustration. I shall then proceed to discuss the organization of the exhibition "Scripture for the Eyes" under five thematic categories, encapsulated by the descriptive rubrics "Sacred History and Geography," "Visual Exegesis," "Worship," "Morality," and "Politics and Polemics."

Let us begin by briefly summarizing the argument of the title-page and frontispieces with reference to Plantin's concise exposition. Engraved by Pieter van der Heyden after an anonymous master (perhaps Crispijn van den Broeck, also known as Paludanus), the title-page portrays a pedimented gateway over which an effigy of the Holy Spirit presides, flanked by open codices of the Old and New Testaments (fig. 12).[36] Ornamental fruits and flowers emblematize the spiritual pleasures of close reading. From the entablature inscribed *Biblia Sacra* hangs an immense wreath plaited from branches of four species—palm, willow, olive, and oak —that respectively represent, as Plantin states, the four peoples — Jewish, Chaldean, Greek, and Roman—in whose languages Holy Writ was first transmitted. As the enwreathed terms *Hebraice*, *Chaldaice*, *Graece*, and *Latine* (each written in a distinctive script) make clear, these are the languages on which the *Biblia polyglotta* is

Fig. 13

Fig. 13
Title-Page of *Den Bibel met grooter neersticheyt gecorrigeert* (Antwerp: Jacob van Liesveldt, 1538), folio. American Bible Society.

based.[37] A short epigraph paraphrasing the argument of Isaiah 11, the prophecy of the advent of the Prince of Peace, identifies the peaceable scene beneath the wreath as an image of the *pietatis concordiae* (harmonies of piety, that is, the many kinds of peace issuing from fear of the Lord).[38] Isaiah envisions the coming of Christ as the restoration of paradisiacal harmony: "The wolf shall dwell with the lamb, and the leopard shall lie down with the kid, and the calf and the lion and the fatling together, and a little child shall lead them. The cow and the bear shall feed; their young shall lie down together; and the lion shall eat straw with the ox" (Isaiah 11:6–8). The crib at which the lion and ox feed refers to the nativity of Christ, who was placed in a manger. As Sylvaine Hänsel has noted in her monograph on Arias Montano as an iconographer, the imagery of the title-page, specifically the lamb lying upon the back of a wolf, also derives from Isaiah 65:25, the prophecy of the glorious restoration of Sion to the descendants of the servants of God: "The wolf and the lamb shall feed together, the lion shall eat straw like the ox."[39] The lamb symbolizes Christ the Lamb of God that pacifies vulpine sin. This prophetic edifice that allegorizes the triumph of Christ, bringer of peace, as foreseen by Isaiah, rises from a podium incised with a short text ascribing the *Polyglot Bible* to Philip II, whose pious zeal caused it to be compiled for the use of the Church. On the column bases appear the *imprese* (symbolic devices) of Arias Montano—Archimedes impelled by his love of discovery, exclaiming *Eureka!* and gazing at heaven, his source of divine inspiration— and of Plantin—hand manipulating the compass, one tine fixed, the other circling, within the motto *Constantia et labore* (by means of constancy and labor).[40]

There immediately follows the frontispiece engraved by Pieter van der Heyden after Crispijn van den Broeck, dedicated to Philip II as the chief agent of the *Biblia polyglotta* project (see cat. 2a).[41] The entire scene is suffused by the brilliant light of the rising sun, whose light makes even the cast shadows semi-transparent. The personification of *Pietas Regia* (Royal Piety) stands upon a podium, one hand resting on the royal arms, the other holding the *Biblia polyglotta* before the altar of the Holy Trinity (inscribed *Deo P. F. SS. Patrum Nostrorum S.*—"Sacred to the Father, Son, and Holy Spirit of Our Forefathers"). An angel crowns her with an olive wreath, symbol of Philip's triumphant pursuit of the arts and sciences, and

hands her a palm frond, symbol of military triumph. The palm tree hung with trophies of war and the olive tree hung with implements of the manual and liberal arts develop the theme of the king's double triumph, as also do the emblems of the hand grasping a sword (on the podium inscribed *aut gladio*—"either by the sword") and of the hand grasping a scepter topped by a pair of eyes (on the podium inscribed *aut verbo*—"or by the word"). Plantin informs us that the sword-hand signifies the king's obligation to enforce the laws of his kingdom against all violators of public peace and virtue, while the sceptered hand (identified by Plantin as a caduceus) signifies the constant assiduity and vigilance with which the king improves the republic's laws and adorns it with good morals.[42] Every other element in this allegory of royal piety avows that Philip is the living image of Josiah, King of Judah, who re-established the book of the law and caused the scriptures to be transcribed and disseminated. The dedicatory inscription on the front and side of the pedestal beneath Royal Piety praises Philip for having purified religion and renewed religious devotion, and further, for having revived the memory of King Josiah. At the base of the palm and olive trees are plaques paraphrasing 2 Kings 22–23: they extol Philip for having purged his kingdom of heretics and schismatics by force of arms, just as Josiah eliminated the haruspices of the false god Baal, and for having supported the Church and promoted its liturgy, just as Josiah repaired the house and worship of the Lord. The large plaque above Royal Piety quotes 2 Kings 23:3: "And the king stood by the pillar and made a covenant before the Lord, to walk after the Lord and to keep his commandments and…to perform the words of this covenant that were written in this book." Whereas Josiah keeps the book of the law, Philip, as Josiah Redivivus, upholds the whole of the Bible by sponsoring the *Biblia polyglotta*.[43] Plantin concludes his account by affirming that this allegory, like the pedestal inscribed entirely in the antique style (*antiqua inscriptionum phrasi*—"in the ancient epigraphical style or diction"), derives wholly from scripture (*ex sacrae Scripturae locis*—"from sacred scriptural places").[44] Its pictorial style or diction, in other words, is fully scriptural. In fact, this is true of all the frontispieces.

The second frontispiece to volume 1, perhaps engraved by Pieter van der Heyden (after an unknown artist), refers specifically to its contents—Genesis to Deuteronomy in Greek, Hebrew, Latin, and

Aramaic (Chaldee) (see cat. 2b).[45] The tablets of the law, displayed by angels in the pediment of an elaborate gateway, preside over a landscape containing six episodes of divine revelation from Genesis and Exodus: (upper right) God promises Noah, who kneels beside the thank-offering made after the flood, that he shall never again destroy the sinful world and every living creature in it (Genesis 8:20–22); (upper left) God promises Abram asleep by the carcasses of the sacrificial animals he has offered, that his descendants, having been freed after four hundred years of exile and bondage, shall take possession of all the land "from the river of Egypt to the great river…Euphrates" (Genesis 15:9–21); alternatively, this scene may depict Jacob's sacrificial offering at Beersheba, where God appeared and instructed him to go into Egypt, whence eventually, accompanied by the Lord, his people would come forth a great nation (Genesis 46:1–4); (center) Jacob wrestles with the angel at the ford of Jabbok, refusing to let him go until he receives his blessing, being christened Israel, and sees the face of God (Genesis 32:22–30); (center left) God promises Jacob dreaming at Haran of the stairway to heaven, that he shall possess the land upon which he lies, that his numerous progeny shall spread abroad and be blessed by all the families of the earth, and that whithersoever he goes, he shall return to this land accompanied always by the Lord (Genesis 28:10–16); (lower left) the angel of the Lord appears to Moses in a flame of fire out of the midst of a bush on Mount Horeb, whence God then commands him to approach unshod, promises to deliver his people from their bondage in Egypt unto a land flowing with milk and honey, and instructs him, as a sign of his God-given authority, to cast his rod upon the ground, where the people will see it turn into a serpent (Exodus 3–4:1–5); (lower right) the glory of God settles upon Moses on Mount Sinai, where he receives the tablets of the law written by the finger of God and is instructed to build the tabernacle and honor the sabbath (Exodus 24:12–31:18). The designer of the print, undoubtedly advised by Arias Montano, has introduced angelic messengers into all these scenes, even though an angel is mentioned only in Exodus 3:2. (I shall presently address this anomaly in my discussion of the title-page and frontispieces together.) Plantin explains that the frontispiece verifies the divine authority of the Pentateuch that conserves God's promises of human salvation, teaching the will of the Lord and the obligations he places upon humankind.[46] This authoritative doctrine, taught by means of the word, now openly and perspicuously, now figuratively and enigmatically, requires to be believed, revered, and observed because it issues not from any human source but truly from God. Paul confirms as much in Hebrews 1, stating that the authority and fidelity of these books is most assured, having been tried and tested by the ministry of angels acting in God's name, neither only once nor in only one way, but in many places and manners, as attested by the greatness of many divinely chosen eyewitnesses (Hebrews 1:1, 7, 14, and 2:1–3).[47] In making these claims, Plantin amplifies the short quotation from Hebrews 1:1 inscribed on the plaque hanging from the pediment: "In many and various ways God spoke of old to our fathers." His reference to the figured and enigmatic word takes up the gist of the pithy motto, incised on the podium below, that distills the argument of 1 Corinthians 10: *Arcani consilii apparatio* ("Framework of hidden purpose"). Paul refers to Exodus 13–14, 16–17, averring that the cloud that sheltered the Israelites, the sea through which they passed, the dewy manna they ate and drank, and the rock that watered them, were a kind of baptism into Moses prefiguring the supernatural Rock of Christ in whom the faithful may now be baptized. These things that guided the chosen people, like the punishments that chastened them, have been written down "for our instruction," in order that we may discern in the experience of Israel and its altar sacrifices the blessing of Christ made manifest through our sacramental participation in his body and blood (1 Corinthians 10:9–11, 15–18). And so, Plantin continues, citing God's repetition in Genesis 9:8–17 of his promise to Noah never again to annihilate the world, the salvific promises enshrined in his covenants under the old dispensation were reiterated, in order that humankind, trusting in divine intention, might be encouraged to expect the salvation of Christ.[48] This is the sense in which the salvation promised to Moses at the burning bush, and earlier variously to Noah, Abraham, and Jacob, figuratively contains the Christian doctrine of human salvation (*in qua humanae salutis ratio ut in figura continebatur*).[49] The texts on the podia supporting the flanking columns—*Vere domus Dei ista* ("Truly this is the Lord's house") and *Et haec parta caeli* ("And this is the gateway of heaven")—

underscore this message concerning the parallel salvations to be discerned in the Old and New Testaments. The passage from Psalm 119 [118]:130 on the strapwork plaque bearing the entire edifice—*Declaratio sermonum tuorum illuminat* ("The unfolding of thy words gives light")—serves to strengthen the hermeneutic impulse that the allegory calls forth, urging us to read the covenants of Israel as testimonies of the coming of Christ. We may presume that the olive branch held by the left-hand angel on the pediment signifies the spiritual fruit to be obtained from such interpretative effort, while the cup held by the right-hand angel signifies the eucharistic "cup of blessing" latent in the divine promises recorded in the Pentateuch as an earnest of Christ (1 Corinthians 10:16).

Engraved by Jan Wierix after an unknown artist (perhaps Crispijn van den Broeck), the frontispiece to volume 2 (Joshua to 2 Chronicles in Greek, Hebrew, Latin, and Aramaic) portrays the Israelites led by Joshua crossing the river Jordan (Joshua 4:14–24) (see cat. 3).[50] He oversees his people from the river bank at right, his military baton raised in a gesture of command. The priests carrying the ark of the covenant stand in mid-stream, their presence having stopped the river's waters. Representatives of the twelve tribes gather stones to be erected as a memorial of the miraculous passage and a testament that the "hand of the Lord is mighty" (the monument is already visible just beyond the ark) (Joshua 3:24). Amongst the Israelites, the armed tribes of Reuben and Gad, along with the half-tribe of Manasseh, predominate. The plaque above quotes Hebrews 2:2, changing it from a conditional statement to a declaration: "The message delivered by angels has been made firm."[51] (The original reads: "For if the message delivered by angels was sure, and every transgression or disobedience received a just retribution, how shall we excape if we neglect so great a salvation?") This epigraph places the crossing of the river Jordan in a lineage from the God-given promises arrayed in the frontispiece to volume 1, which are here seen to be reaffirmed, indeed fulfilled, by this miracle that re-enacts the crossing of the Red Sea under Moses. Plantin develops this theme, observing that the Old Testament not only contains the book of the law but also memorializes the terrestrial promises (*promissa terrena*) undertaken by God with his chosen people, by means of which he represents or shadows forth the promise of the heavenly kingdom to come.[52]

Through the fulfillment of those earlier covenants exemplified here by the entry of the Jews into the promised land, God confirms them in their hope of eternal salvation, if only they persist in believing and obeying him; for relayed by angelic ministers, the word of God was shown to be ineluctable, when the Israelites, having finally entered Canaan, dwelt there for generations, claiming it as an inheritance and possessing the fruits of their labors.[53]

The penultimate frontispiece, engraved by Jan Wierix after an anonymous master, encapsulates the meaning of the prophetic books gathered in volume 4 (Isaiah to Maccabees in Greek, Hebrew, Latin, and Aramaic) (see cat. 4).[54] Vineyards planted around a cruciform plaza fill the steeply receding vista, at the center of which rise a circular watchtower and a large winepress. Husbandmen wearing ancient and contemporary, lay and clerical dress tend the vines within the double-walled garden, its entrance portico inscribed *Domus Israel* (House of Israel), a reference to Isaiah 5:7, but also to Ecclesiasticus 24:8, 17, God's promise that divine wisdom shall "make [her] dwelling in Jacob, and in Israel receive [her] inheritance," and "like a vine" cause "loveliness to bud" and "blossoms [to become] glorious and abundant fruit." Two further plaques identify Isaiah as the chief source of this vinicultural imagery. At left, *Delectatio plantationum Domini* ("Pleasure of the Lord's planting") derives again from Isaiah 5:7: "For the vineyard of the Lord of hosts is the house of Israel, and the men of Judah are his pleasant planting." (Implicit here is also an allusion to Isaiah 27:2–3, God's promise to tend and water his people like a solicitous vine-dresser: "A pleasant vineyard, sing of it! I, the Lord, am its keeper: every moment I water it. Lest any one harm it, I guard it night and day.") At right, *Quid enim debui facere vineae meae quod non feci?* ("For what ought I to do for my vineyard, that I have not [already] done?") derives from Isaiah 5:4: "What more was there to do for my vineyard, that I have not done in it?" Isaiah 5, a love song addressed by the prophet to God, attentive custodian of the spiritual vineyard, likewise describes the watchtower and winepress that he builds within it (Isaiah 5:2). The imagery compounded in this frontispiece is not only prophetic but also Christian; it illustrates the parables of the kingdom of God told in Matthew 20 and 21 and Luke 20, as well as the famous simile likening Christ to the true vine whose branches (his followers), pruned by God the vine-dresser, either bear abundant fruit or, failing that, are discarded. Jesus bases these parables on Isaiah 5:1–7, so that viewing the image through this parabolic lens is to see the New Testament reading the Old, or rather, to learn how Christ himself authorizes such a reading. Matthew 20:1–16 concerns the generosity of God: like the householder who hires laborers to cultivate his vineyard, setting the day's wage and paying it to all irrespective of whether they work two, five, eight, or eleven hours, God rewards all the faithful, making the last first, and the first last. Matthew 21:28–41 incorporates two parables: the first describes the man with two sons, the first of whom initially refuses to labor in his father's vineyard, then repents and goes to do it, the second of whom agrees to labor but never goes; the first son stands for believers in Christ who repent of their sins, the second for the chief priests and elders whose self-righteousness precludes belief. The second parable, also told in Luke 20:9–16, compares God to the householder who plants a vineyard, encircles it with a hedge and sets a winepress within it, builds a watchtower, and then lets it out to tenants before leaving for another country. He later sends a series of servants and finally his son to collect the fruit of the harvest, but all are rebuffed, beaten, or killed by the laborers seeking to expropriate the vineyard. Just as the householder ultimately puts these false men to death, so God punishes sin and tenants the spiritual vineyard with new laborers "who will give him the fruits in their seasons."

These parables invite us to draw a parallel between the House of Israel and the Church of Christ that have cultivated in tandem the garden where Christ the true vine was eventually planted, grew, and bore fruit.[55] As Christ the Messiah is the harvest to be gathered by Israel, according to the prophecies of Isaiah, so he is the sacramental vintage to be pressed by the Church, as his parables indicate and the Eucharistic winepress at upper right signifies. Christ is also the true heir to the vineyard, whom the false tenants kill, and whose sacrificial death calls forth new laborers to displace the old. Plantin underscores this reading of the image, stating that it argues (*haec tabula argumento*) for the great attention, solicitude, and vigilance expended by God on the cultivation, ornamentation, and augmentation of his Church, just as previously he taught the people of Israel to know the divine will and cultivate true religion through the prophets and their divinely mandated actions, embassies, and prophecies.[56]

The print accommodates these prophetic and parabolic images, harmonizing and amplifying them. The householder stands on the main path leading from the entry gate to the tower, his exhortatory gesture signaling the authority he exercises over the laborers. The tall tree growing to the tower's right probably refers to Luke 13:6–9, the parable of divine forbearance that tells of the man who planted a fig tree in his vineyard; three years later, having ordered it to be cut down when there was still no fruit, he yet relented when his vine-dresser encouraged him to cultivate the tree for one more year. The many wild beasts—wolves, lions, bears, boars, a serpent, and a dragon—laying siege to the garden evoke the ravening beasts that beset the Psalmist and prophesy the Passion of Christ in Psalm 22 [21] (the Good Friday Psalm). They also recall Isaiah 1:8, that portrays Israel, the daughter of Sion, as a vineyard besieged by her enemies; so too, Isaiah 27:1–3 avows that the Lord, keeper of the vineyard, must guard it night and day, even after slaying Leviathan the "twisting serpent and…the dragon," while Isaiah 5:5 cautions that God himself shall threaten the vineyard, breaking down its wall and trampling its vines, if it yields only wild grapes, that is, fails properly to be cultivated into the Lord's fruitful garden.

The final frontispiece, engraved by Jan Wierix after an anonymous master (perhaps Crispijn van den Broeck), illustrates the baptism of Christ (Matthew 3:13–16, Mark 1:9–11, Luke 3:21–22, John 1:29–34) (see cat. 5).[57] Although the scene includes elements taken from all four Gospels, it corresponds most closely to details from Matthew and John. Having just been baptized by John the Baptist, Jesus climbs out of the river Jordan, and the heavens open; the Spirit of God descends like a dove, alighting on Jesus, and a voice from heaven declares that, "This is my beloved Son, with whom I am well pleased" (Matthew 3:16–17). Seeing the heavenly Spirit descend upon Jesus, John recognizes him as the Son of God who "baptizes with the Holy Spirit," of whom he has borne witness (John 1:33–34). The print therefore shows the precise moment when the last of the prophets recognizes the Messiah promised and foretold throughout the Old Testament. He carries the shell with which he baptizes in his right hand, stares at the dove hovering over Christ, and raises his left in a combined gesture of astonishment and attestation. On both shores, the people coming to be baptized respond to his awe-inspiring testimony. That God the Father is not

portrayed, or rather, appears as the radiant source of the dove's
ethereal light, agrees with the synoptic Gospels that distinguish
between the Holy Spirit, seen by Christ (Matthew 3:16, Mark 1:10)
and John (John 2:33), and the voice of the Father, heard by all (as
implied in Matthew 3:17, Mark, 1:11, and Luke 3:22). The quotation
excerpted from Hebrews 1:1–2—*Novissime diebus his locutus est nobis
Deus in filio, quem constituit heredem universorum*—characterizes the
baptism of Christ as the promulgation of the Son, whose ministry
of the word, promised by God to the patriarchs and prophets, is
now made manifest through the mystery of Incarnation: "In many
and various ways God spoke of old to our fathers by the prophets;
but in these last days he has spoken to us by a Son, whom he
appointed as the heir of all things." The rays of light connecting
Christ, the dove, and the heavenly source alludes to Hebrews 1:3:
"He reflects the glory of God and bears the very stamp of his nature,
upholding the universe by his word of power." As Plantin puts it,
this plate demonstrates that divine authority has established the
truth of the New Testament no less than of the Old. (*Novi Testamenti
fidem non secus atque Veteris divina auctoritate constare, tabula hae
indicat.*) The presence of John the Baptist, who by many miracles
and manifest signs bore witness to the light of Christ, the minister
and interpreter of the New Testament, makes evident that God
wished to confirm this Testament by a "greater and more explicit
apparatus of deeds and words" (*maiori & illustriori rerum &
testimoniorum apparatu confirmari hoc Testamentum voluit Deus*).[58]

The frontispieces bring the viewer ever closer to the advent of
Christ: promised by angelic ministers seen at small scale beyond a
framing archway in the frontispiece to volume 1, prefigured by the
crossing of the Jordan in the riverbed of which we stand with the
Israelites in the frontispiece to volume 2, signified by the prophetic
and parabolic imagery of the vineyard that fills our field of vision
urging us to enter the *Domus Israel* in the frontispiece to volume 4,
and finally revealed on the bank of the Jordan beside whose
cleansing waters we await his approach with the other neophytes
(see cats. 2–5). The scale of the figure of Christ exceeds that of any
other in this graduated sequence. Arias Montano's general preface,
as indicated above, explains how this sequence coheres. He begins
with a series of philosophical and theological postulates. "Nothing
is more appropriate and necessary to the human spirit," he

explains, "or more proper to the due ordering of life than sure
knowledge of oneself, firm insight into the reasons for one's
existence, and precise judgment of those things that lend [us]
dignity and distinction and lead to the utmost felicity."[59] If we now
run through all the orders of things from the first elements to the
celestial firmament, we who possess cognition and sense will find
that nothing fails to reveal the reason, order, and counsel of the
governing mind that we call God. Having made this discovery, we
will ascertain our God-given affinity with the Creator. Just as man
is endowed with whatever excellent virtues other creatures possess,
so through his power of mind and reason he transcends them, for
he approaches to God "as if bearing in himself a certain likeness to
or kinship with that which is highest in the universe."[60] "And since
it is agreed that there resides in human nature a singular and
peculiar virtue of knowing and desiring the proper end [of life] and
those means by which it may be attained, as well as of judging and
rejecting those means inappropriate to this end, so it is most seemly
to institute rules of life and conduct in keeping with the exercise of
this great virtue, so that complying with this rare dignity we may
arrive at the wished-for result by a noble and excellent route."[61]
Arias Montano now reaches the first crux of his argument: "It
therefore follows that man must not only journey diligently
[through life] but also know whence his journey begins, its route,
method, and destination, as well as in what the glory of a well-
executed journey consists, and having explored these things, he
must keep them [always] in mind."[62] But if our vocation is twofold
—to journey and to know the nature of one's journey—how are we
to discern the parameters of our passage through life, first
mapping out this notional itinerary and then implementing it?

The chief obstacles to be overcome are, firstly, the devil, who
endeavors always to confound the self-knowledge inherent in
mankind, and secondly, the cognitive defects of the human mind
that relies upon ratiocination in order to search out and discover
truth. Although this investigative impulse arises naturally from
the power of true invention and apprehension, that the mind
exercises ably and eagerly (*mens veri inveniendi & cognoscendi avida &
capax natura sua*), nevertheless, thought often goes astray,
proceeding from poorly formulated first principles, or reckoning in
an obscure or disorderly fashion. As a consequence, in their efforts

to find universal precepts and institutes that might properly facilitate the journey through life, philosophers have instead established mutually exclusive sects that confound any sure sense of our true origin and certain end. Truth has rarely if ever appeared simple and unvarnished (*veritatem…vel rarissimè nudam & simplicem apparuisse*), having been transmitted "in the semblance of false, inane, and ambiguous fables, or so entwined by difficult questions, arguments, and artifices that however much we avow truth to be altogether desirable, it can hardly benefit us imparted in this way."[63] Only God could free us from such entanglements and perplexities, and so, "having resolved to advance, amplify, and bless the human race, created and brought forth voluntarily from himself for the sake of the greatest good and honor, he executed at their appointed times the plans that he had most wisely initiated: amongst which, this one — since true knowledge of both human and divine matters was veiled in a tempest, and human minds impeded by the deepest obscurity and the greatest confusion of errors, fictions, and idolatry, God shone the most sweet and brilliant light of his word upon the world, confirming that same light in his own voice clearly audible to the human race, and through miracles, portents, and signs, the wide-ranging dissemination of the Holy Spirit, and most grave punishments [meted out] against traducers and insolent opponents [of his word]."[64]

The sacred word, issuing from and authorized by divine Wisdom, is identical with "that selfsame Truth briefly compassed within the [scriptural] books"; available to all who consult them, these beneficial sources preserve the knowledge of divine and human affairs, as well as containing mysteries penetrable to holier and more experienced men (that is, theologians and formally trained exegetes).[65] The light of the word (*haec lux*) "incites and enkindles souls strenuously and zealously to embark upon the difficult journey of virtue; it informs and illuminates judgment in the examination of all systematic doctrines, disciplines, and arts, and in the distinguishing of truth from falsehood, honor from dishonor. The sacred word lays the true and certain foundation of everything that the human mind may justly fashion and determines the sum total of all the rules that it is right and expedient for humankind raise up."[66] Most importantly, the holy word "reveals [God] as the divine author of everything good, who expels all that is evil, his son being high priest and conciliator," and it "sets forth the whole plan and labor of human salvation fit to be conferred by Christ and obtained by the human race."[67] Scripture does this in two ways, for by the action of the Spirit the word consists of two parts that jointly aim to advance human salvation, but differ with respect to times, ministers, usages, and efficacy (*pro temporum verò ac ministrorum rationibus, & efficientia, atque usu distinctae*). Arias Montano paraphrases Psalm 119 [118] that expounds the commandments and exalts the promise of salvation implicit in them: he avers that the Old Testament contains the written law (Pentateuch), along with the prophecies that foretell and comment on the New, proclaiming Christ its future minister; the New Testament discloses the law of grace exemplified in the Gospels and the books drawn from them (Acts and the Epistles).[68] In another paraphrase, this time of 2 Corinthian 3:3, he applies the metaphor of light to both books: whereas the Old Testament is "the lamp lighting the roads of life trod by men," the New Testament is "the light shining upon minds internally," through which "the promised gifts of the Holy Spirit are more freely bestowed, by whose efficacy the mysteries of both testaments are known and confirmed," so that the truth "formerly inscribed in stone" is now "written upon [faithful] hearts."[69] Students of the word prosper in all they undertake; they are like the branch planted beside streams of water, that bears fruit in season, its leaves never withering (Psalm 1:3). For they realize the unity of the word, seeing that "the message declared by angels was valid" (Hebrews 2:2).[70] Moreover, they perceive how calamitous it is to neglect the word, as did the kings of Israel after the reign of Josiah, who strayed from his example, failing to observe God's commandment in Deuteronomy 17:18, that the word be copied in a book and read daily, so that the law and its statutes may be maintained.[71] Arias Montano ascribes the religious divisions now tearing the Christian world apart to the false interpretations of scripture engineered by the devil and disseminated by his agents: "The authority and dignity of divine letters having been revealed and commended to human wisdom, prudence, and good sense, the devil then sprinkled the deadly venom of perverse and depraved interpretation, by the power of which he corrupted many ingenious and judicious minds, destroyed innumerable souls, and miserably disordered the Christian republic."[72] He proposes to remedy this sad state of affairs with the *Biblia polyglotta*, its parallel texts issuing from close study of the four biblical languages, its scholarship inspired by the Holy Spirit, sanctioned by the Church, and endorsed by Philip II: "that the [devil], author of all evils, and his ministers be given no opportunity of adding anything…to the [present] danger, God inspired Philip II…to consider how the sacred books, ancient languages, and best translations might diligently be gathered and composed, seeing that…the study of piety and of pure religion is acknowledged to be the principal, noblest, and firmest foundation for the establishment of the state."[73]

The title-page allegorizes the condition of Christian unity that Arias Montano hopes to restore through the philological and exegetical apparatus of the Royal Bible (fig. 12). This unity originates in the divine harmony of the scriptural texts that are his quadrilingual sources. The image declares the book's ambitious hope of restoring the peace embodied by Christ the Prince of Peace, prophesied in Isaiah 11, and seen proleptically to be fulfilled in Isaiah 65. The frontispiece personifying Royal Piety acknowledges Philip as the agent of this restorative project, on the model of King Josiah who perfectly complies with the Deuteronomic injunction to transcribe, publish, and preserve the word, the book of the written law and of the law of grace (see cat. 2). The sequence of frontispieces that follow constitutes stages in the journey of the revealed word, whose beginning in the Pentateuch, progress through the historical books, operation through the prophets, and destination in Christ we behold at the start of volumes 1, 2, 4, and 5. These images are interwoven through the inscription and illustration of mutually applicable biblical passages. On the Pentateuch frontispiece, for instance, the excerpt from Psalm 119 [118] draws attention to the salvific promises latent in the Lord's commandments and testimonies that we are called upon to unfold, as the general preface indicates (see cat. 2b). The interpolation of mediating angels into all the scenes of patriarchs conversing with God follows from Hebrews 1, quoted above, which compares the angelic messengers of the old covenant to the inimitable messenger Christ, whom the angels worship. The reference to Hebrews also implicitly compares the

message conveyed by Christ to that delivered by the prophets: "In many and various ways God spoke of old to our fathers by the prophets; but in these last days he has spoken to us by a Son, whom he appointed the heir of all things, through whom also he created the world…When he had made purification for sins, he sat down at the right hand of the Majesty on high, having become as much superior to angels as the name he has obtained is more excellent than theirs. For to what angel did God ever say, 'Thou art my Son, today I have begotten thee'?.. And again, when he brings the first-born into the world, he says, 'Let all God's angels worship him.' Of the angels he says, 'Who makes his angels winds, and his servants flames of fire.' But of the Son he says, 'Thy throne, O God, is for ever and ever'" (Hebrews 1:1–5, 6–7).

Seen in this light, the frontispiece prefigures the Pauline doctrine of unmediated access to the word through Christ the Word made flesh. The end of the journey, actual and metaphorical, upon which God's chosen people, and we as readers of the Bible, have embarked is already clearly

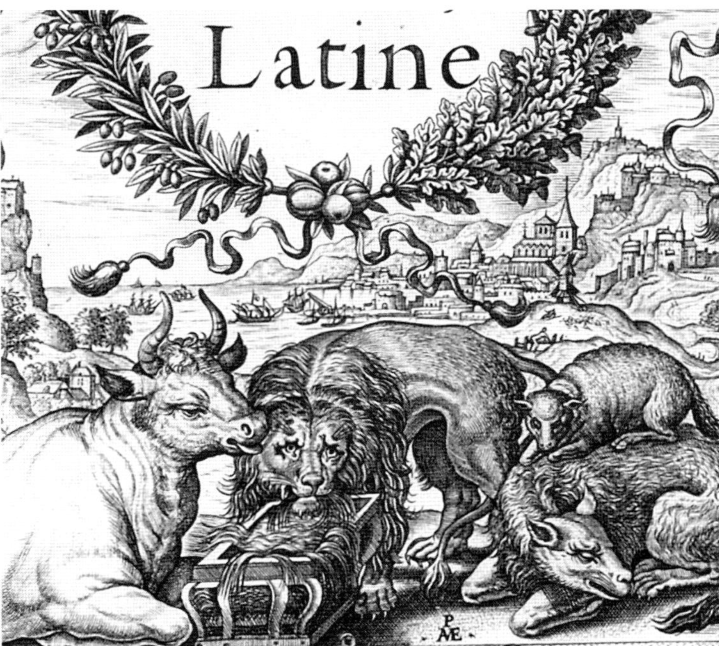

Fig. 12 (detail)

acknowledged at its start. Or perhaps it would be truer to say, in the words of another epigraph from this frontispiece, that we discern this journey's start and finish by viewing it through the interpretative apparatus—*arcani consilii apparatio*—that makes known the nature and scope of the divine plan of salvation.

The frontispiece to volume 2 accentuates the theme of journeying in conformation to the divine will: Joshua 4:21–24 construes the collection of the twelve stones, set up to commemorate the crossing of the river Jordan, as an affirmation of God's power to fulfill the promise prefigured by the crossing of the Red Sea (see cat. 3). Hebrews 2:2, quoted above, in turn construes this crossing over as the figurative adumbration of Christian salvation, which is seen to fulfill the angelic promises assembled in the previous frontispiece. As the Israelites entered the promised land, so Christ has secured the "great salvation" that must be recognized and embraced: "For if the message declared by angels was valid and every transgression or disobedience received a just retribution, how shall we escape if we neglect such a great salvation? It was declared at first by the Lord, and it was attested to us by those who heard him, while God also bore witness by signs and wonders and various miracles and by gifts of the Holy Spirit distributed according to his own will" (Hebrews 2:2–4). As the general preface cites Hebrews 2:2 to emphasize the unity of the word, so here the linking of Joshua 4 and Hebrews 2 insists upon the seamless fabric of God-given promises.

The frontispiece to volume 4, as we have seen, functions jointly as prophecy and parable, showing how the journey of the revealed word imbricates the Old Testament and the New (see cat. 4). The frontispiece seems to suggest that cultivation of the spiritual vineyard entails reading scripture as if one were crossing over from one resonant meaning (the House of Israel) to another (the Church of Christ). The notion that Isaiah, amongst the prophets, especially requires such an integral reading goes back to Jerome, who states in his *Prologus in Esaiam prophetam* ("Prologue to the Prophet Isaiah"), that this singularly eloquent prophet deserves to be described more as an evangelist (*quòd non tam Propheta dicendus sit quàm Evangelista*), or put differently, that he partakes equally of both testaments. This prologue introduces the Book of Isaiah in the *Biblia polyglotta*: "So clearly

does he follow up the universal mysteries of Christ and his Church, that you would think he composes a history of the past, rather than prophesying the future."[74] Jerome later expands upon this observation, noting that Isaiah, though he prophesied in Jerusalem and Judah before the Babylonian captivity, seems sometimes to speak of the present, sometimes to speak of the return from Babylon, but mostly concerns himself with the vocation of the Jews, their divine calling as God's chosen people, and with the advent of Christ.[75]

The final frontispiece functions as a capstone to the series, amplifying and completing the prior images and texts (see cat. 5). The fiery light of divine inspiration in the Pentateuch frontispiece becomes the far brighter light of the Holy Spirit, whose "promised gifts," to quote the general preface, "are more freely bestowed" under the dispensation of Christ. The small figures of angels and patriarchs, separated from the viewer by a layered archway, become the large figures of John the Baptist and Jesus, the former facing the viewer, the latter advancing toward him. The crossing of the river Jordan in the frontispiece to volume 2 becomes the climbing forth of Christ from that same river at the moment his divinity and thereby the promised coming of the Messiah are revealed. The memorial stones gathered by the Israelites become the single stone upon which Christ treads, an allusion to Psalm 118 [117]:22–23, that identifies him as the cornerstone of faith: "The stone which the builders rejected has become the head of the corner. This is the Lord's doing; it is marvelous in our eyes." In Luke 20:17, Jesus subsumes this prophetic image into the parable of the vineyard, construing the cornerstone as himself. The passage from Hebrews 1:1 quoted in the Pentateuch frontispiece is completed by the passage from Hebrews 1:2: the "many and various ways God spoke of old to the Fathers" transform into the embodied word "spoken to us by the Son, whom [God] appointed the heir of all things." Likewise, the prophecy and parable of the vineyard in the frontispiece to volume 4 are elucidated by the image of the cornerstone deriving from the complementary parable told by Christ in Matthew 21:42–43 and Luke 20:17–18: after converting Isaiah's prophecy into the parable of God's spiritual vineyard, he immediately follows by describing himself as the cornerstone prophesied in Psalm 118 [117]: "The very stone which the builders rejected has become the head of the corner." Spurned by the chief priests and elders, he is the foundation-stone of the new edifice of faith, just as he is the rightful heir of the divine householder whose tenanted vineyard we cultivate. As our passage through the frontispiece sequence allows us to enact a virtual journey leading from the mediated transmission of the divine word—by angels, by such spokesmen as Joshua, and by such prophets as Isaiah—to its unmediated incarnation in Christ, so our reading and viewing of this interconnected sequence enable us to assess "whence this journey begins, its route, method, and destination," and thus to comply with the twofold vocation outlined and enjoined in the preface—to journey and to know the nature of one's journey.

Scriptural images summarizing the contents of the Polyglot Bible's various parts have proved crucial to this process. They have functioned as prompts to close reading, illustrating and expounding selected texts that conversely illuminate and explain the images they inscribe. The unity of the images issues from and insists upon the unity of the texts from Genesis, Exodus, Joshua, Psalms, Isaiah, Matthew, Mark, Luke, John, Corinthians, and Hebrews, that are made to read each other, or better, woven into a tightly-knit fabric of interpretation. Arias Montano was well aware of the interpretative power of this text-image apparatus, as the reader's preface following the general preface makes clear. Entitled *Eiusdem Benedicti Ariae Montani alia ad lectorem praefatio, in qua de totius usu, dignitate, & apparatu ex ordine disseritur* ("Another Preface by the Selfsame Benito Arias Montano, in which the Use, Dignity, and Framework of the Whole Work Are Treated in Sequence"), this introductory text first defends the authority of the sources consulted, the utility of the translations provided, and the beauty of the typeface imprinted (especially in Syriac), before praising the book's illustrations as compact hermeneutic instruments par excellence, that amply uncover the meanings densely encoded into scripture: "In order that nothing pertaining to the splendor of this royal project be judged wanting, individual plates skillfully engraved in copper have duly been inserted in places, by means of which selected passages and the divine mysteries lying hidden within them are examined, and though these plates are small, their argument is lengthy and truly divine, as any studious person may observe."[76]

Sacred History and Geography

Let us turn now to the five subdivisions of this exhibition and their topical headings. I shall dwell at greater length on the initial three—sacred history and geography, visual exegesis, and worship—than on the final two—morality and politics-polemics, since the former touch upon issues that may be less familiar to the general reader. The first rubric—sacred history and geography—refers to the study of biblical events, places, and chronology, at the intersection of antiquarian and religious scholarship. Just as philologists attempted to situate words in context, the better to evaluate their usage, so certain theologians believed that scriptural truths could better be understood if their material character and circumstances—the times and settings in which they had transpired, the persons, offices, and institutions that had performed them, the ceremonial and liturgical rites that had accompanied them—were systematically set out and evaluated. Arias Montano makes this case in the reader's preface cited above, in the subsection on the *Apparatus sacer* ("Sacred Apparatus"), the three-volume appendix containing dictionaries, grammars, and assorted philological and antiquarian tractates, that attaches to the *Biblia polyglotta*. Volume 8, entitled *Exemplar, sive de sacris fabricis liber* ("Exemplar, or Book on Sacred Edifices"), contains seventeen tractates illustrated by sixteen engravings, the majority folio-size, including an historical-topographical map of the city of Jerusalem, reconstructions of the levitical vestments and ritual implements associated with the tabernacle and the temple, and elaborate plans, elevations, and perspectival views of Noah's ark and the Temple of Solomon (figs. 14–18).[77] More than simply utilitarian or ornamental, these illustrated appendices function as interpretative guides, the pictorial images especially requiring close attention:

"Since it is clear to all that the calculation of places and times and the exact knowledge of weights and measures greatly enhance the clarity and pleasure to be gained from the exposition of things and the investigation and establishment of their truth, so for this reason in two books we have followed up all the rules of geography and topography, selected from scriptural

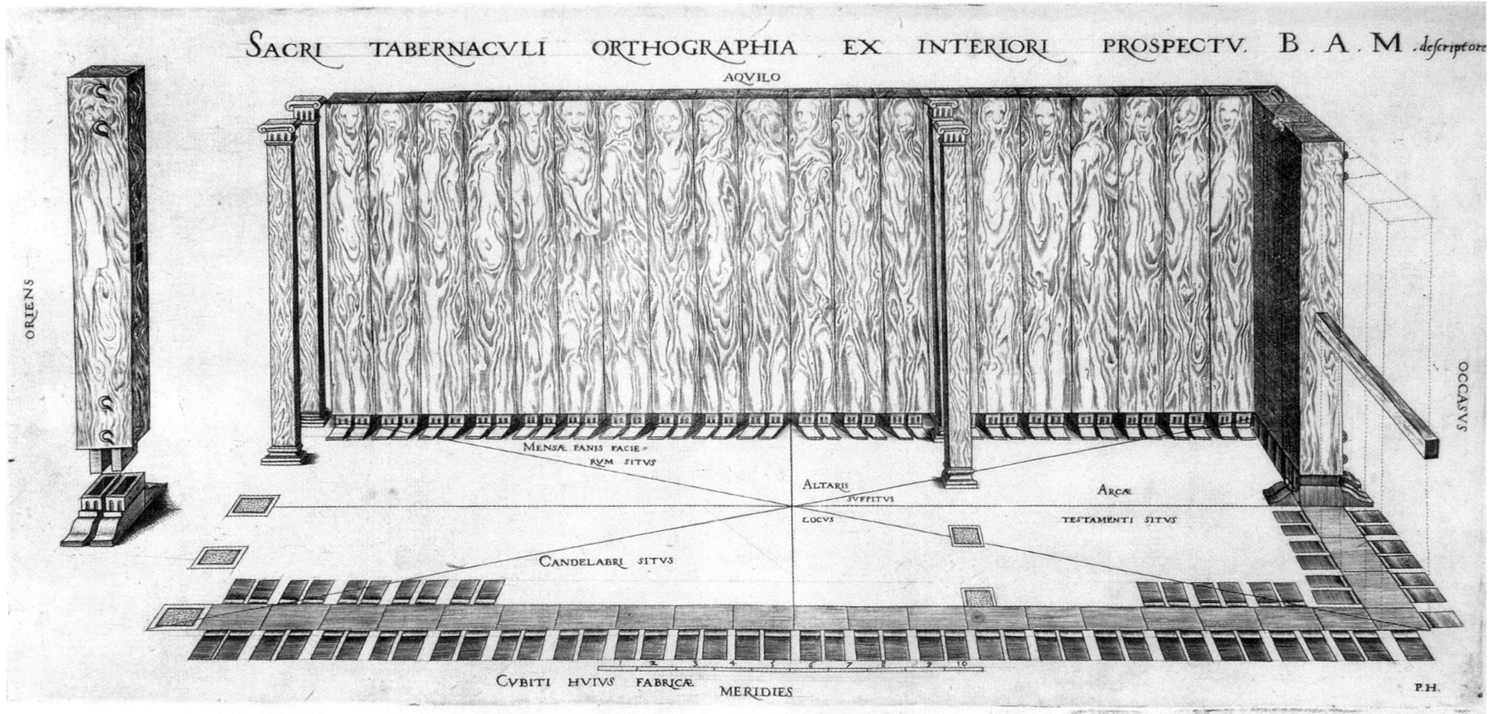

Fig. 14

Fig. 14
Pieter Huys after an anonymous artist, *Interior Elevation of the Tabernacle,* engraving, in volume 8 of Benito Arias Montano, ed., *Biblia Sacra Hebraice, Chaldaice, Graece, & Latine,* 8 vols. (Antwerp: Christopher Plantin, 1568–73), large folio. Plantin-Moretus Museum, Antwerp. Photo: Peter Maes.

descriptions and annotations, and sufficient for the expounding of sacred texts. Next we have delivered a brief and sure account of the long sequence of times and ages flowing from the creation of the world to Christ. In closing, we present an appraisal of weights, diligently researched and fitly adorned with precepts and with altogether pleasing and worthy examples of sacred architecture. Nothing could be more necessary or desirable than these tractates for the explication of the arcane and secret meanings contained by the divine prophecies. But no-one who has not first observed and become thoroughly acquainted with the skillful and clearly divine structure of the images (*artificiosa, ac divina plane imaginum structura*), which as noted above you shall here see engraved and inserted pertinently, may duly acquire the true knowledge concealed and as it were lying hidden in the selfsame images of those historical matters (*earum historiarum…sub ipsis imaginibus absconditam, & quodammodo, ut ita dicam, latentem*)."[78]

The reference to the divine order apparent in these images originates in the conviction, spelled out in the tractate *Beseleel, sive de Tabernaculo* ("Beseleel, or On the Tabernacle"), that the exemplars revealed to Noah, Moses, and other chosen instruments of the divine will, after which they caused such monuments as the ark and the tabernacle to be constructed, were entirely spiritual, fashioned from invisible matter wholly by divine artifice (*spirituale illud quidem, & invisibili materia, divino plane artificio constructum*). God promulgated these *exemplaria,* better and more lucid than any manmade templates, to be imitated by human artifice (*sed nulla descriptio aut melior aut clarior; quam exemplaris ipsius proposita forma; quam artificio imitari contingat*). Arias Montano adds that he hopes likewise to supply a spiritual description based in the supreme artifice displayed by God; however, constrained like Noah and Moses by his humanity and the terrestrial materials available, he accepts that he must rest content to expound the visible form of these monuments, expressing nothing but a rough image of their divine perfection (*sed illam visibilem formam, quam illius exemplaris velut rudem imaginem in terris exprimere licuit*).[79]

The plan, elevation, cross-section, and side views of the tabernacle, along with the perspective view of the sacred precinct surrounded by the tents of Moses, Aaron, and the twelve tribes (the latter engraved by Jan Wierix after a design by Pieter van der Borcht), demonstrate how detailed and informative the descriptive images were expected to be (figs. 14–16).[80] Arias Montano adheres punctiliously to the descriptions in Exodus 26, 27, 36, 38, and 40, prefacing his account with an inventory of the precious materials offered by the Israelites to bear witness to their willing spirit of oblation and their desire diligently to do the will of God (Exodus 25:1–7): in addition to gold, silver, and bronze, *hyacinthum* (a wool woven from threads colored by oriental hyacinths), *purpura* (the reddish purple of pomegranate seeds), *coccus bis tinctus* (the double-dyed red commonly known as *cremesinum*), *byssus* (very fine, strong, and lustrous Egyptian linen), *pili caprarum* (the water-resistant fleece of she-goats), *pelles arietum rubricatae* (rubricated ram-skins), *pelles janthinae* (badger-skins tinted violet-blue), and *ligna sitim* (various genera of cedar wood harvested in the wilderness of Moab, not far from the settlement of Pharan).[81] This list, along with the illustrative images, gives a clearer sense of the tabernacle's appearance and of the texture, weight, and weave of the triple-tiered coverings draped over it, than the scriptural text alone can provide. The same holds true for the Temple of Solomon, the account of which, both textual and pictorial, scrupulously follows 1 Kings 6 and 2 Chronicles 3:1–13 (figs. 17–18).[82] Arias Montano strives for the utmost clarity, especially in his enumeration of the building's measurements, since the temple where the Israelites kept common cause with divine doctrine and sacred precepts, signifies simply and perpetually the pattern of the one, holy, and Catholic Church to be constructed by God from all humankind (*unius Ecclesiae exemplar habuisse debuit*).[83] And so, the temple's plan and elevation are made perspicuous: the main building followed the dimensions of the tabernacle, being 60 cubits long by 20 wide, excluding the portico, its proportions based on the standard practice of sculptors squaring any block to a size three times as tall as wide. The galleries encircling the temple on the northern, southern, and western sides were three stories high, the first extending five cubits from the temple wall, the second six, the third seven; for each story the transverse beam supporting the

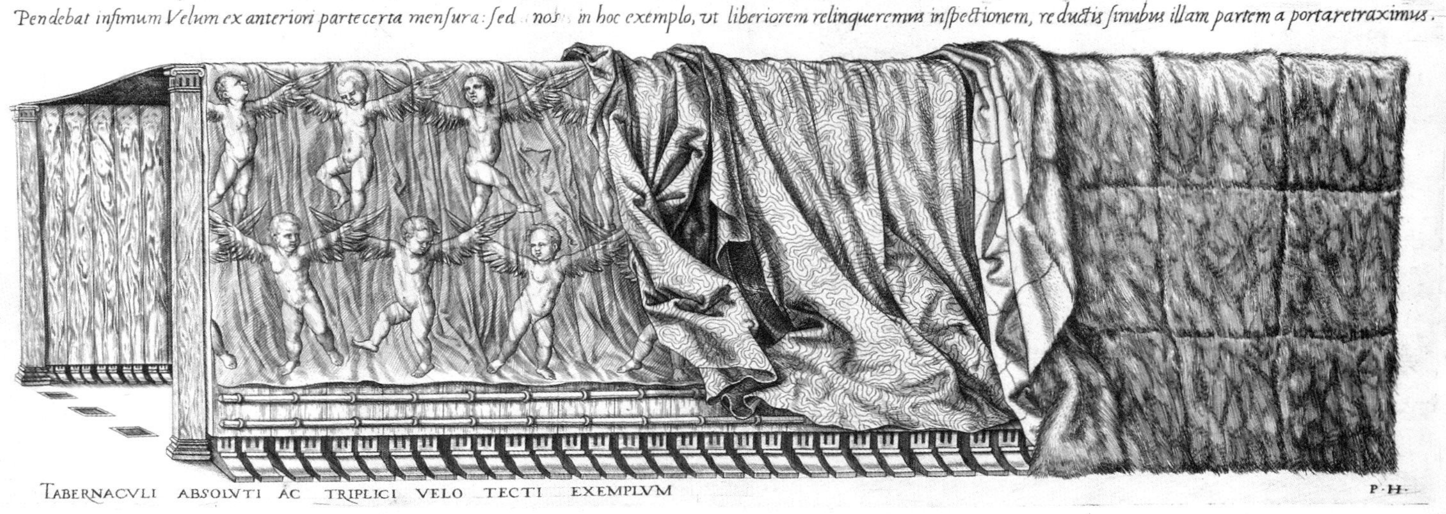

Fig. 15

Fig. 15
Pieter Huys after an anonymous artist, *The Ark Covered by the Three Veils*, engraving, in volume 8 of Benito Arias Montano, ed., *Biblia Sacra Hebraice, Chaldaice, Graece, & Latine*, 8 vols. (Antwerp: Christopher Plantin, 1568–73), large folio. Plantin-Moretus Museum, Antwerp. Photo: Peter Maes.

floor above rested on the temple wall, which decreased in thickness by one cubit for every five cubits of height, in order to accommodate the beam.[84] In conjunction with the illustrations, such instructions make the structural fabric and wall articulation extremely clear and cogent.

Published separately as an addendum to the *Biblia Polyglotta*, the *Bird's-Eye View of the Temple of Solomon* supplements the series of illustrations elucidating the Solomonic Temple; it provides a prespectival view of the temple precinct complementary to the earlier bird's-eye view of the Mosaic tabernacle amidst the encamped tribes (fig. 19).[85] Franciscus Raphelengius included it in the *Antiquitatum Iudaicarum libri IX.* (*Nine Books of Jewish Antiquities*), an independent edition of the antiquarian tractates from Arias Montano's *Apparatus*.[86] The image was also sometimes interpolated into copies of the *Biblia Polyglotta* bound after 1576. In the *Apparatus* and the *Antiquitatum Iudaicarum libri IX.*, the illustrative sequence leading from Noah's ark to the ark of the covenant and the tabernacle, thence to the Temple of Solomon on the Temple Mount, draws attention to the action of divine providence. As Arias Montano explains in the subsection entitled *Ariel, sive, de templi fabrica et structura* (*Ariel, or, On the Fabric and Structure of the Temple*), God first chose to inhabit the exilic tabernacle, that was moved from one solitary place to another, until he selected the Ephraimite city of Shiloh as the ark's fixed abode; which having rejected, God then chose Jerusalem, exalting David and the tribe of Judah, whom he commanded along with all Israel to build him a house (1 Paralipomenon 21:16–30, 22:1–19).[87] Arias Montano defines the temple as the crucible where religious identity is fashioned: "Therefore the temple ought to be [a place] of habitation for the one God, where whosoever desires eagerly to be numbered among God's people should keep common cause with religious affairs and doctrines."[88] Its significance has been ever simple—to adumbrate the one, holy, Catholic Church to be established by God from all the families of men on earth.[89] Although the Temple of Solomon was thus unique, other ancient temples likewise served religiously to unify the peoples who worshipped within them: this is why the ancients forbade individuals to build private or votive temples, lest their personal attachments foment discord and fracture the religious

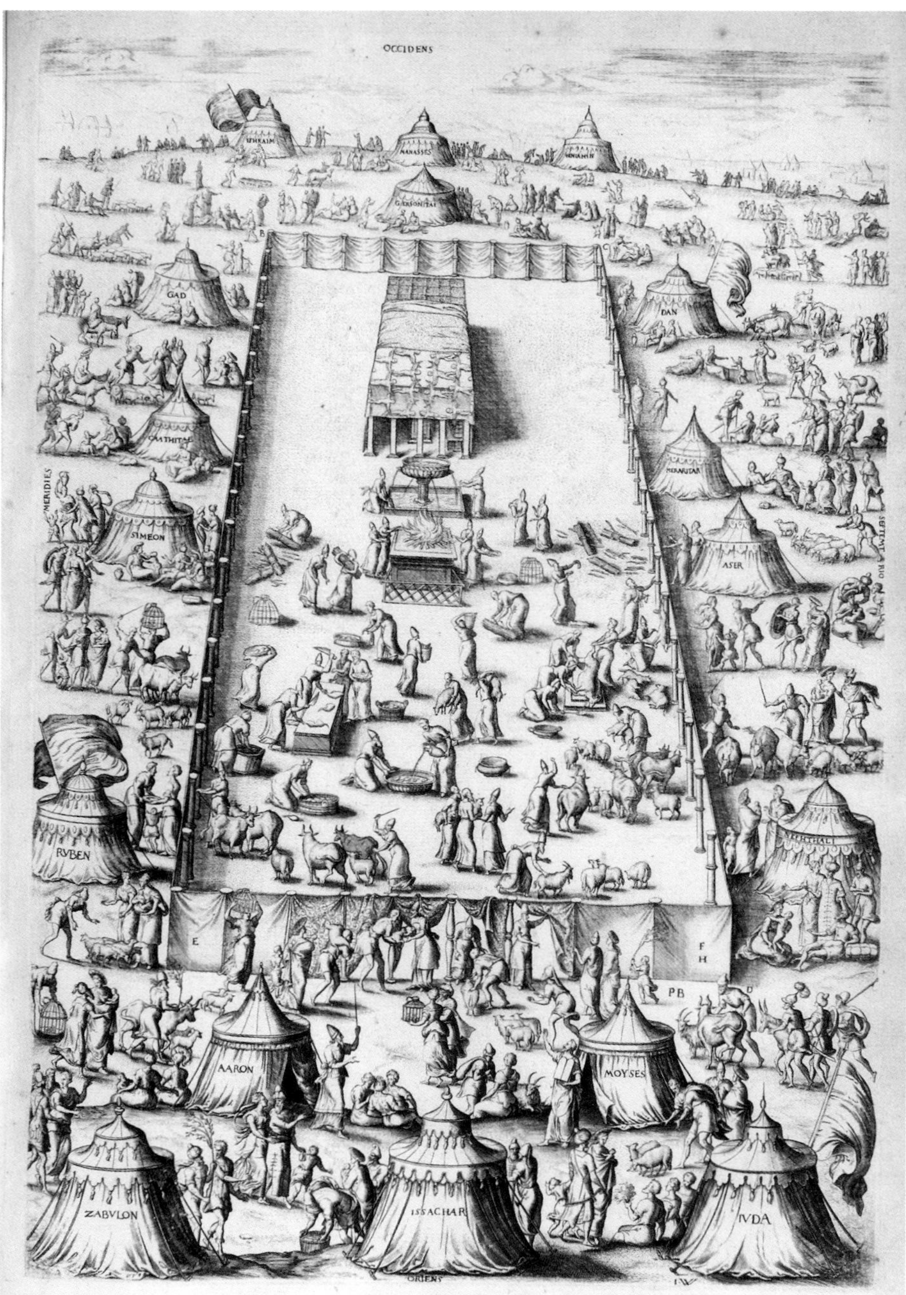

Fig. 16

community.[90] The perspective view of the temple, its atria, portals, and passageways receding toward a single vanishing point, its prominent central axis clearly delineated, its courtyards thronging with priests and congregants converging from the north, south, and east, exemplifies the building's sacred function as a source of *religionis communio* (religious community, but also, communion). The resemblance between the perspective construction here, in the *Bird's-Eye View of the Tabernacle*, and in the *The Laborers in the Vineyard* frontispiece, implies that they form part of a spiritual lineage: the tabernacle, the temple, and the Church were all consecrated successively as the sanctuary of God (the vineyard also stands for the soul, which being a microcosm of these institutional vessels, likewise partakes of their privilege of housing God).[91]

The neo-Aristotelian preface to the *Exemplar* justifies the reliance on pictorial images as a means of knowing scriptural truth. Since divine inspiration and natural instinct fuel the universal desire for knowledge, all men are inclined to preserve and nurture those bodily senses by means of which they may come to know the most things.[92] On the model of Solomon, whom God granted largeness of mind (1 Kings 4:29), that is, knowledge of all good arts (*omnium bonarum artium cognitionem*), judicious men have developed the faculty of curiosity (*curiositas*) that impels ingenious wits to seek out the causes and investigate the reasons of all things, either through first-hand experience or through the reading and writing of texts.[93] From these textual monuments (*literarum monumentis*) have arisen several literary species: finely judged disputations (*disputationes*), narratives of worthy exploits (*rerum gestarum narrationes*), descriptions of the customs and predilections of peoples and nations (*descriptiones morum, ac studiorum uniuscuiusque gentis, nationumque singularum*), and histories of illustrious men and their memorable words and deeds (*historiae quibus illustrium virorum memorabilia recensentur dicta, & praeclara praedicantur facinora*).[94] This last category not only operates textually but also visually, through the works of painters, sculptors, and other artificers, visible to everyone (*verùm etiam à pictoribus, sculptoribus, variisque artificum operibus ante oculos uniuscuiusque sunt posita*). Arias Montano itemizes the many kinds of *historiae* susceptible to textual and pictorial representation, expanding their scope to encompass manufactured things:

"Not only feats of arms, public actions and transactions, concord and community, disagreement and discord, and other such things wont often to occur; but also the public and private works of individuals, have been subjects written about…and rendered for the sake of public utility, solemnity, and display. Of which genre are: foundations, sanctuaries, edifices of any kind, temples, city-gates, triumphal arches, porticos, atria, boulevards, bulwarks, walled towns, city walls, suburban villas, vineyards, gardens, country villas, ramparts, gymnasia, palaestra, stadia, theaters, amphitheaters, bridges, fountains, pyramids, obelisks, triumphal cars, coaches, two-wheeled war chariots, thrones, tripods, tables, benches, and other innumerable works that, springing from human ingenuity or industry, are perfected and adorned by human artifice. To which are added: ornaments, varieties of dress, and diverse forms of uniform, by means of which peoples and families are distinguished, and also companies and commissions discharged publicly and privately."[95]

Because all these things pertain to some useful end, the ancients deemed them worthy to be recorded in texts and expressed in pictures and other kinds of image, that they might become known to absent persons and to posterity.[96] In addition, amongst all the "exercises of ingenuity" (*omnes optimas ingenij exercitationes*) invented by the ancients and adopted by the moderns, *historiae* have this further advantage: they can conserve the narrative sequence of whatever actions are recorded.[97] As these remarks reveal, the category *historia* applies both to frontispieces such as the *Crossing of the River Jordan* and to descriptive images such as the various views of the *Tabernacle* and *Temple of Solomon*. Moreover, given the kinds of object included under the term *historia*, it would seem to subsume or at least incorporate the term *descriptio*.

Many things, Arias Montano continues, even though little or no trace of them survives, simply by dint of having once existed, are deemed worthy of being restored to sight (*vindicata in conspectum*).[98] Consumed by age, threatened by oblivion, they are yet renewed by descriptions and histories that preserve them for future generations. This ought to hold true even more for those monuments brought forth by the will of God, which we must make every effort to conserve and cultivate diligently, for to retain such things is to partake of his divine nature (*divini…ingenij*).[99] After all, God wished the mysteries of divine wisdom to be inferred not only from the arguments of scripture, but also from its ornaments—namely, monuments such as the ark, tabernacle, and temple—since every word of scripture (the specifications of these edifices included) proceeds from the Holy Spirit for our benefit.[100] We may therefore suppose that students of scripture ought to expend the greatest effort in deciphering its every part, given that the Fathers published the sacred books to exercise pious souls in reading and investigating them. (Arias Montano adds the disclaimer that this is surely true, even though what the Church proposes as canonical and necessary to believe and to perform is sufficient for securing salvation.) So inexhaustible are the figures and mysteries contained in both testaments (*figuras & mysteria quae in sacris leguntur libris*), that the things described therein, however much they have been expounded, remain susceptible to further exposition.[101] (By *figuras*, Arias Montano signifies the visual symbols that encode divine truths; by *mysteria*, he denominates these truths conveyed by means of symbolic instruments.) This is where pictorial images come into play, the use of which as interpretative devices the Fathers have themselves endorsed: "The [students of scripture] have observed that the Fathers were wont to be led to know the light and the truth also through images and diagrams (*etiam imaginibus illis, ac delineamentis*)."[102] Arias Montano deploys just such a biblical figure to support this assertion, citing Matthew 13:52: "And he said to them, 'Therefore every scribe who has been trained for the kingdom of heaven is like a householder who brings out of his treasure what is new and what is old.'" The scriptural scholar, in other words, is like the householder who uncovers hidden treasures, searching them out in the Old Testament and the New, or alternatively, bringing forth from these sources both established and newly discovered truths. Chief amongst the implements allowing him to plumb the treasure trove of scriptural figures and mysteries are the historical and descriptive images that facilitate the discovery of truths issuing from the kingdom of heaven.

The pictorial images Arias Montano especially promotes are topographical and architectural.[103] Like the biblical figures to be found throughout both testaments, religious buildings by their very nature, by the art with which they are fashioned, and by the significance of that which they house, belong to the "apparatus of wisdom" comprised by the sacred books (*in sacris continetur libris sapientiae apparatum pertinet*).[104] Indeed, in their significance they surpass all other buildings (although they were built according to the same rules and orders appertaining to Greek and Roman architecture). For this reason, ignorance of architecture, like lack of training in ancient languages, has led many to misunderstand the Bible. And so, Arias Montano precisely because he is well-versed in ancient languages and the rules of ancient architecture, was led to devise this scholarly apparatus—the *Apparatus sacer*—in which the status of the buildings discussed, like that of other divine works, may be measured from their high art, the mystery they contain, and the force and sense of the scriptural words used to describe them.[105] He concludes by commending to the reader-viewer the elegant structure of the images and the brief yet comprehensive explanations, with which the buildings of Noah, Moses, and Solomon have been exhibited and the mysteries they enclose designated. His labors in this regard are fully consonant with the many and great labors that went into these edifices fabricated at God's command.[106]

Topographical and geographical maps were another kind of historical image, that allowed the reader-viewer to chart and thereby to participate in the sacred journeys of biblical personages, their *itineraria* (itineraries) and *peregrinationes* (pilgrimages). In the *Biblia, dat is, de gantsche Heylighe Schrift, grondelick ende trouwelick verduytschet* (*Bible, that is, All of Holy Writ Thoroughly and Faithfully Translated into Dutch*), published in 1589 by Jan Paedts Jacobszoon and Jan Bouwenszoon of Leiden, three maps respectively portray the *Holy Land*, the *Exodus*, and the *Peregrinations of the Apostle Paul* (figs. 20–21).[107] This Bible belongs to a family of reformed Bibles known as the *Deux-Aes*, thirty-eight editions of which appeared in the northern Netherlands between 1538 and 1600.[108] Appended to the *Peregrinations of the Apostle Paul* is a short text avowing the utility of topographical maps (*caerten van lantbeschrijvinghen*): they are a reliable and pleasurable source of information that clarifies our understanding of biblical history, as the "cartographical portrait of

Fig. 17
Pieter Huys after an anonymous artist, *Plan and Interior Elevation of the Solomonic Temple*, engraving, in volume 8 of Benito Arias Montano, ed., *Biblia Sacra Hebraice, Chaldaice, Graece, & Latine*, 8 vols. (Antwerp: Christopher Plantin, 1568–73), large folio. Plantin-Moretus Museum, Antwerp. Photo: Peter Maes.

Fig. 18
Pieter Huys after an anonymous artist, *Exterior Elevation of the Solomonic Temple*, engraving, in volume 8 of Benito Arias Montano, ed., *Biblia Sacra Hebraice, Chaldaice, Graece, & Latine*, 8 vols. (Antwerp: Christopher Plantin, 1568–73), large folio. Plantin-Moretus Museum, Antwerp. Photo: Peter Maes.

A Porticus vel aVLAM
B Sanction
C Sanctium sanctorum
D Murus inferior nudus
E Coronis trimembris
F Ornamentum muri ex ligno auro obducto.
G Fenestræ
H Prioris contignationis locus
I Locus vacuus et obscurus inter contignationem et tectum.
L Muri crassitudo et reductus.
M N O Tres contignationes cellarum.
P Coronidis trimembris specimen
Q Portici sciographia
R Ornamenti interioris specimen.
SACRÆ ÆDIS SCIOGRAPHIÆ PARS.
A B C
SACRÆ ÆDIS ICNOGRAPHIA EX BENEDICTI ARIÆ MONTANI DESCRIPTIONE.

Fig. 17

P.H.
TEMPLI CVM PORTICV ET CELLIS ABSOLVTA ORTHOGRAPHIA ex descriptione Bened. Ariæ Montani.
Conuenit orthographia cum Icnographia mensioris ad Vnguem. Membra omnia respondent Architecturæ Israelitarum

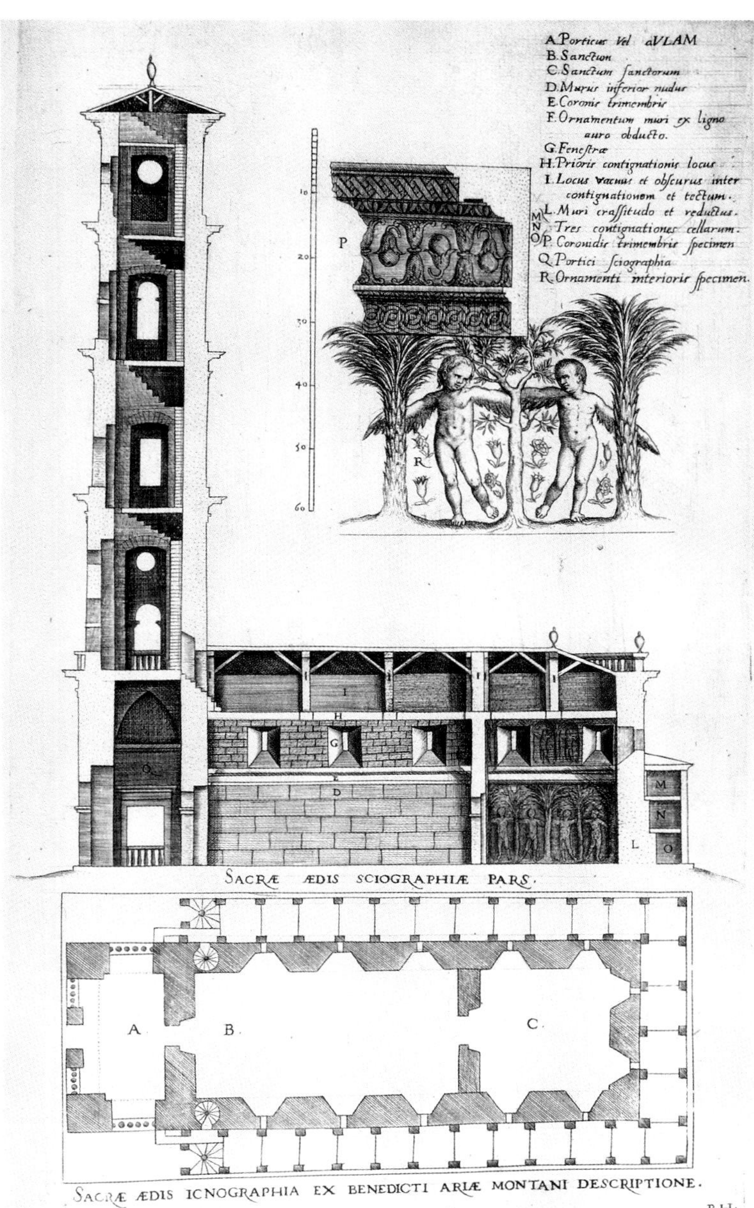

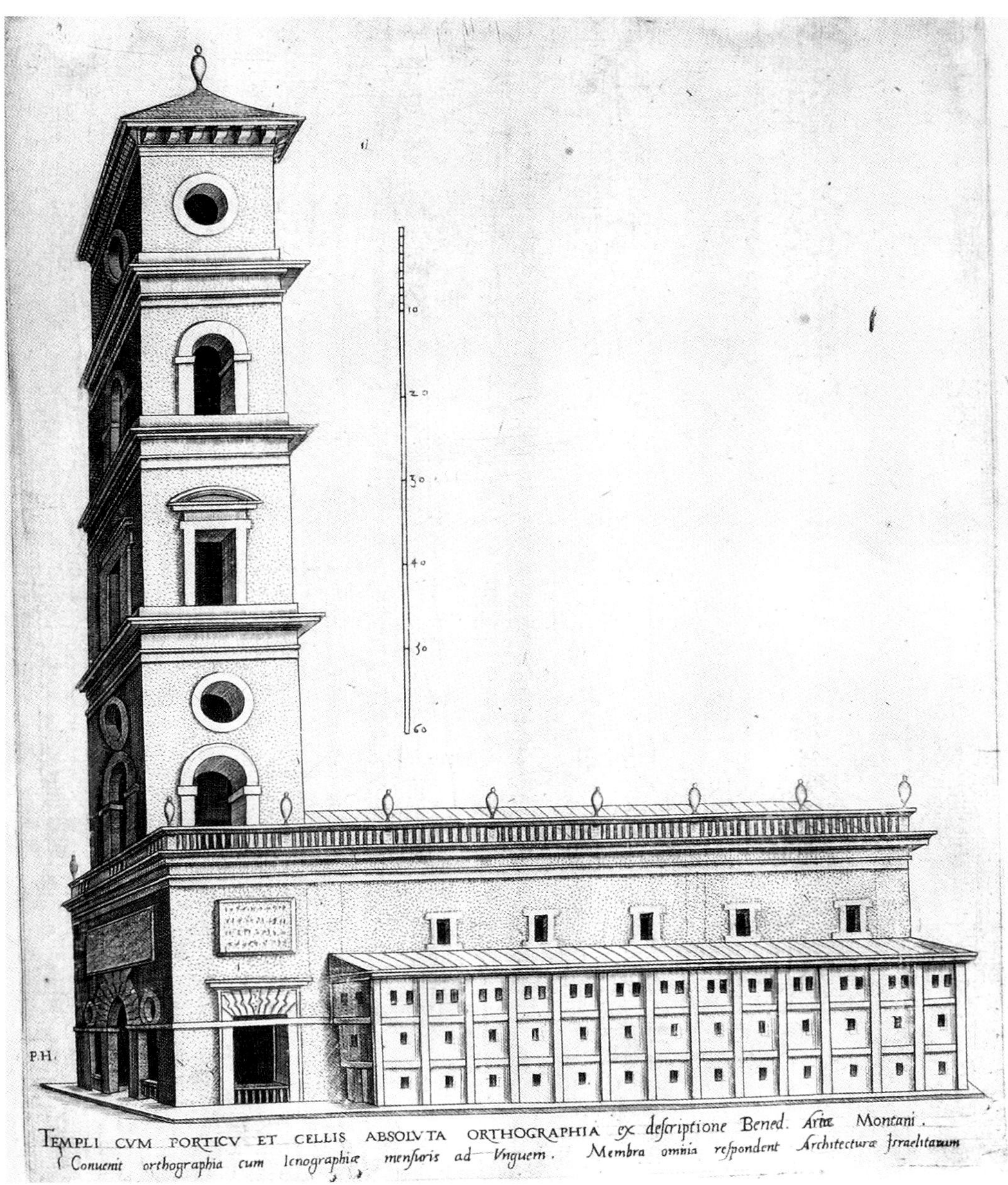

Fig. 18

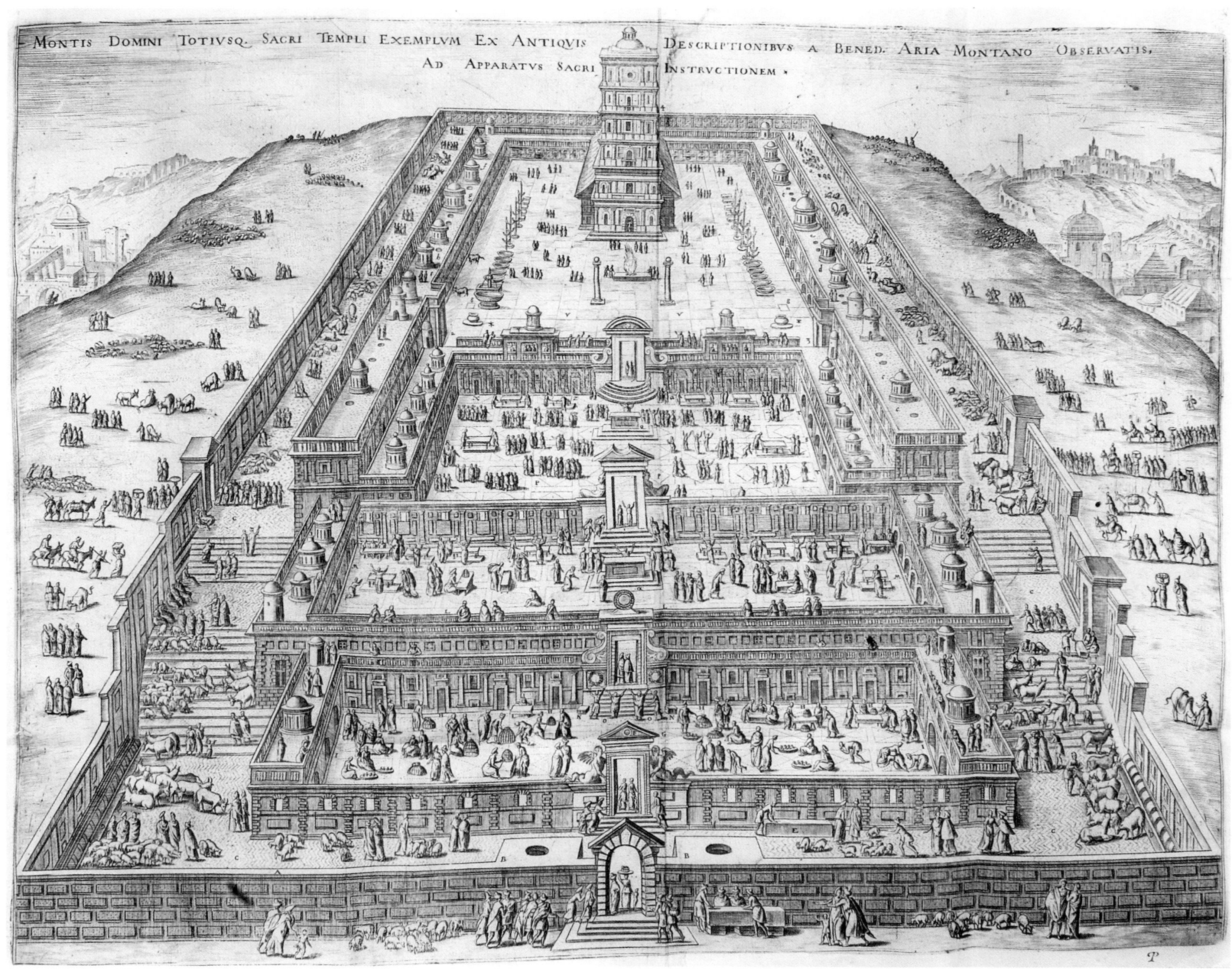
MONTIS DOMINI TOTIVSQ. SACRI TEMPLI EXEMPLVM EX ANTIQVIS DESCRIPTIONIBVS A BENED. ARIA MONTANO OBSERVATIS,
AD APPARATVS SACRI INSTRVCTIONEM.

Fig. 19

the lands, provinces, and cities traversed by Paul during… his apostleship" testifies.[109] This map, like that of the *Exodus*, is primarily historical not geographical; it incorporates fewer towns and cities than contemporary maps, such as that of the *Holy Land*, because it focuses exclusively on those places mentioned in the New Testament, of which none has been omitted.[110]

Entitled *Chart Showing the Passage and Migration of the Children of Israel, when They Wandered for Forty Years out of Egypt into the Arabian Wilderness, thence into Canaan*, the map of Exodus delineates the route taken by Moses and the Israelites, their forty-one encampments clearly numbered, as enumerated in Numbers 33 (fig. 20).[111] These numbers are keyed to an explanatory text printed on the reverse of the map, that associates the places with definite events and etymologizes the place-names. Playing upon the dual meaning of the Latin term *locus* and Dutch *plaets* (place, as a locality, a site in space, and as a citation, a passage in a text), the text also refers each of the cartographical places to relevant scriptural places. To read the map, then, is to read scripture; the exilic sites are prompts, that refer the reader to specific passages, and storehouses of the citations consulted and committed to memory. Additionally, as the explanatory text puts it, the map and its apparatus, by precisely situating the biblical events, improve the reader's comprehension of the histories still to be recounted (*tot breeder verclaringhe van dien, ende om tot beter verstant der Bibelscher Historien te comen*).

The third encampment, for example, is Etham, which corresponds to Exodus 13:21; located beside the great desert, it is the place where the Lord first appeared to his people, by day as a column of cloud, by night as a column of fire.[112] The fourth, Hahiroth, corresponds to Exodus 14:10; in this deep valley close to the Red Sea, Pharaoh cornered the Israelites, who escaped only when God, responding to the fervent prayers of Moses and the people, shielded them within a cloud-bank.[113] The eighth encampment, Sin, between Elim and Mount Sinai, the wilderness where the Israelites wandered in a circle, is the place where, according to Exodus 16:8, they murmured against God a second time.[114] The eleventh, Raphidim, signifies "great health and salvation" (*der stercken heyl ofte ghesontheyt*), but Moses renamed it Massa (*versoeckinghe*—"temptation") and Meriba (*twist*—"strife")

because here the people tempted him, finding fault with the Lord.[115] The explanatory text refers us to a series of linked passages, that amplify the themes of temptation and strife associated with Raphidim-Massa-Meriba. It directs the reader to Psalm 95:8: "Harden not your hearts, as at Meriba, as on the day at Massa in the wilderness."[116] This verse is annotated Hebrews 3:7: "So he designates another day, saying through David what he said long ago to the people: 'Today is the day that you shall hear his voice, and so do not harden your hearts.'"[117] This refers in turn to Psalm 95:7: "For he is our God, and we are the people of his pasture, and the sheep of his hand."[118] This passage then points to Psalm 23:2 (and also to Psalm 29:13, 100:3 and Ezekiel 34:31): "He makes me lie down in green pastures. He leads me beside still waters."[119] This chain of references converts Raphidim into a place of scriptural prophecy and commemoration, through which passages from the Old and New Testaments transit, read each other, and amplify the meanings implicit in the place-names Massa and Meriba. The events evoked by the sequence of forty-one encampments constitute a virtual summa of the vicissitudes of Moses, as recounted in Numbers; the content of this book, as distilled in one of the Bible's prefaces, "Argument of All the Books of the Old Testament," serves perfectly as a description of the map: "In this book one may see with what exemplary patience and merciful devotion Moses constantly endured the ignominious abuse of foreigners and his own people; and yet he was himself flawed."[120] This last observation alludes to Mount Abarim, the last exilic site, whence Moses, having disobeyed God by failing publicly to sanctify the water-miracle in the wilderness of Sin, beheld the promised land but was forbidden to enter it (Deuteronomy 34:1). If the *Chart* offers an exemplary digest of Moses's virtues, it also serves as a negative exemplum of the chosen people's failings. The map situates, and the explanatory text recounts, the many incidents of defiance and disobedience toward God and Moses during the journey to Canaan, that the "Argument" encapsulates as "the recalcitrance of the people," their frequent "agitation, confusion, and insurrection," and the punishments that ensued. The three vignettes at lower right of the *Twelve Tribes Encamped around the Tabernacle*, the *Chapel of the Nativity at Bethlehem*, and the *Church of the Holy Sepulcher*, invite us to draw a parallel between the journey of the

Fig. 19
Hieronymus Wierix (?) after Pieter van der Borcht (?), *Bird's-Eye View of the Temple of Solomon*, ca. 1575, engraving, in Benito Arias Montano, *Antiquitatum Iudaicarum libri IX., in quis, praeter Iudeae, Hierosolymorum, & Templi Salomonis accuratam delineationem, praecipui sacri ac profani gentis ritus describuntur… adiectis formis aeneis* (Leiden: Franciscus Raphelengius, 1593), quarto. Plantin-Moretus Museum, Antwerp. Photo: Peter Maes.

De Caerte vant theylich landt
twelckmen noemt (landt van
belosten daer de Heylighe schrift
Oude en nieuwe Testament zoo
veel van vermelt

MARIS MEDITER
RANEI
PARS
MARE MEDITERRANEVM
PHOENITIVM
MARE AEGYPTIVM
MARE MAGNVM
Libanus
COELE.
SYRIAE
PARS.
Damascus
ITVRALA
AMMONI-
TARVM
regio vel PHI
LADELPHIA.
Hippus mons
ARABIAE DESER
TAE PARS
Dispositio sepul-
turae Dominicae
Forma Capelle
in Bethlehem
Die reyse der kinder
van Israel wt Egip-
ten int landt van be
losten met haren le-
gers daer sy ghe-
reyst hebben
AEGYPTVS
Delta
P
paruu
MARE
RVM
ARABIA
TRACADEA
DESERTVM
SIN DE
MARIS
RVBRI PARS
SERTVA PHATANITA
Sicimite vel
Cinei Arabes

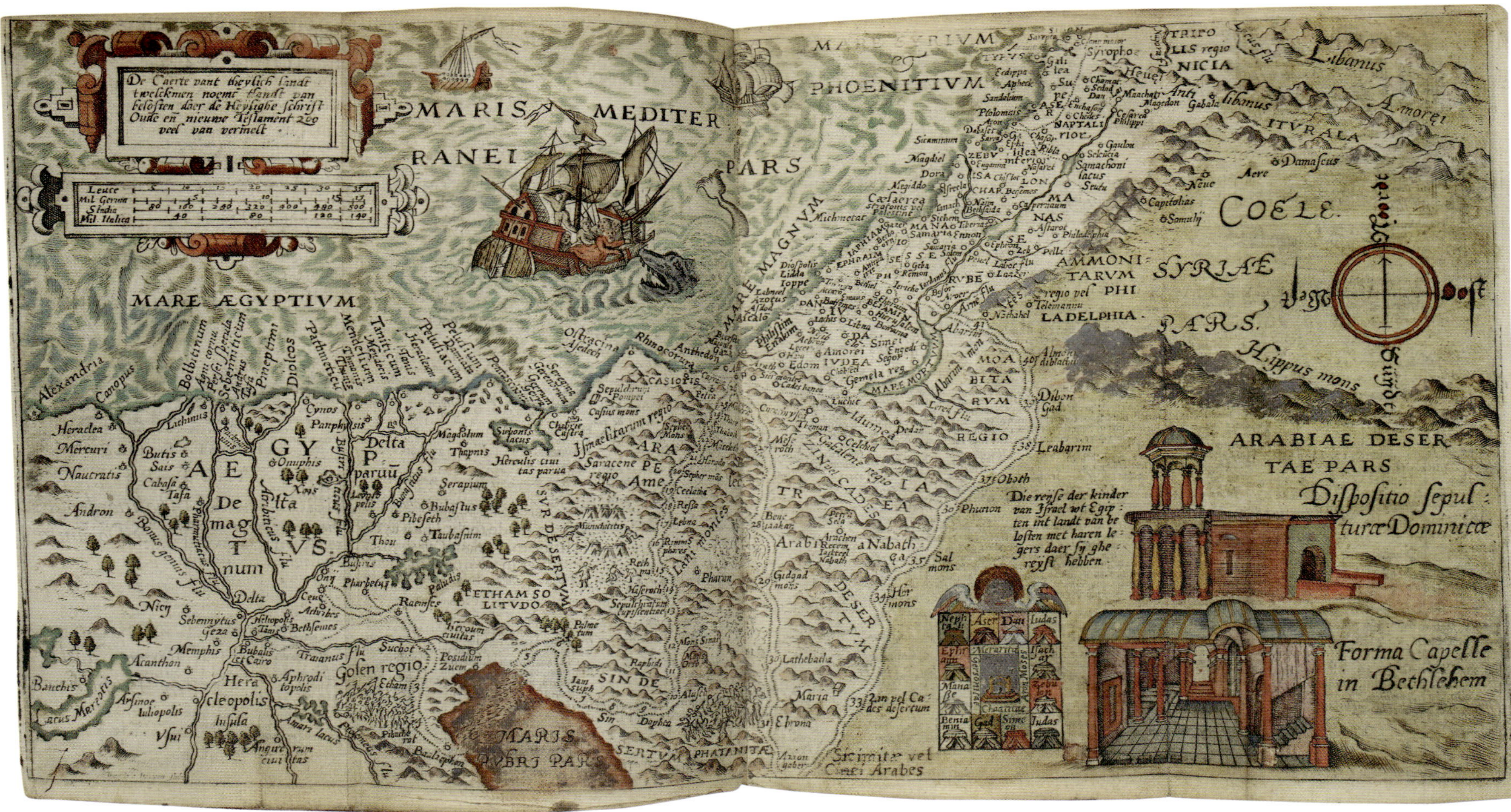

Fig. 20

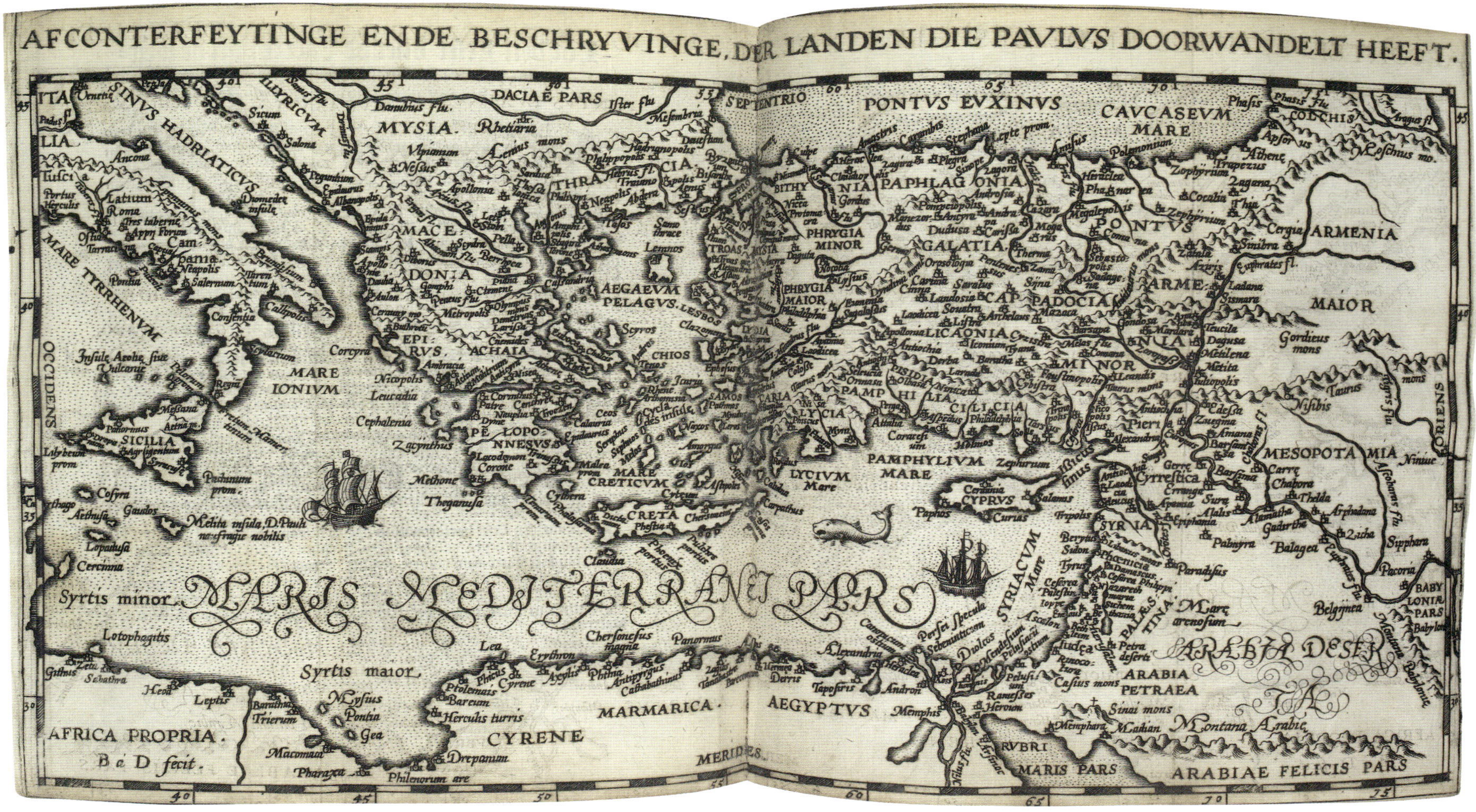

Fig. 21

Fig. 21
Baptista van Doetecum, *Map of
the Mediterranean Illustrating the
Peregrinations of the Apostle Paul*,
engraving, in *Biblia, dat is, de
gantsche Heylighe Schrift* (Leiden:
Jan Paedts Jacobszoon and Jan
Bouwenszoon, 1589), octavo. By
permission of the Trustees of the
British Library. 3040.b.14

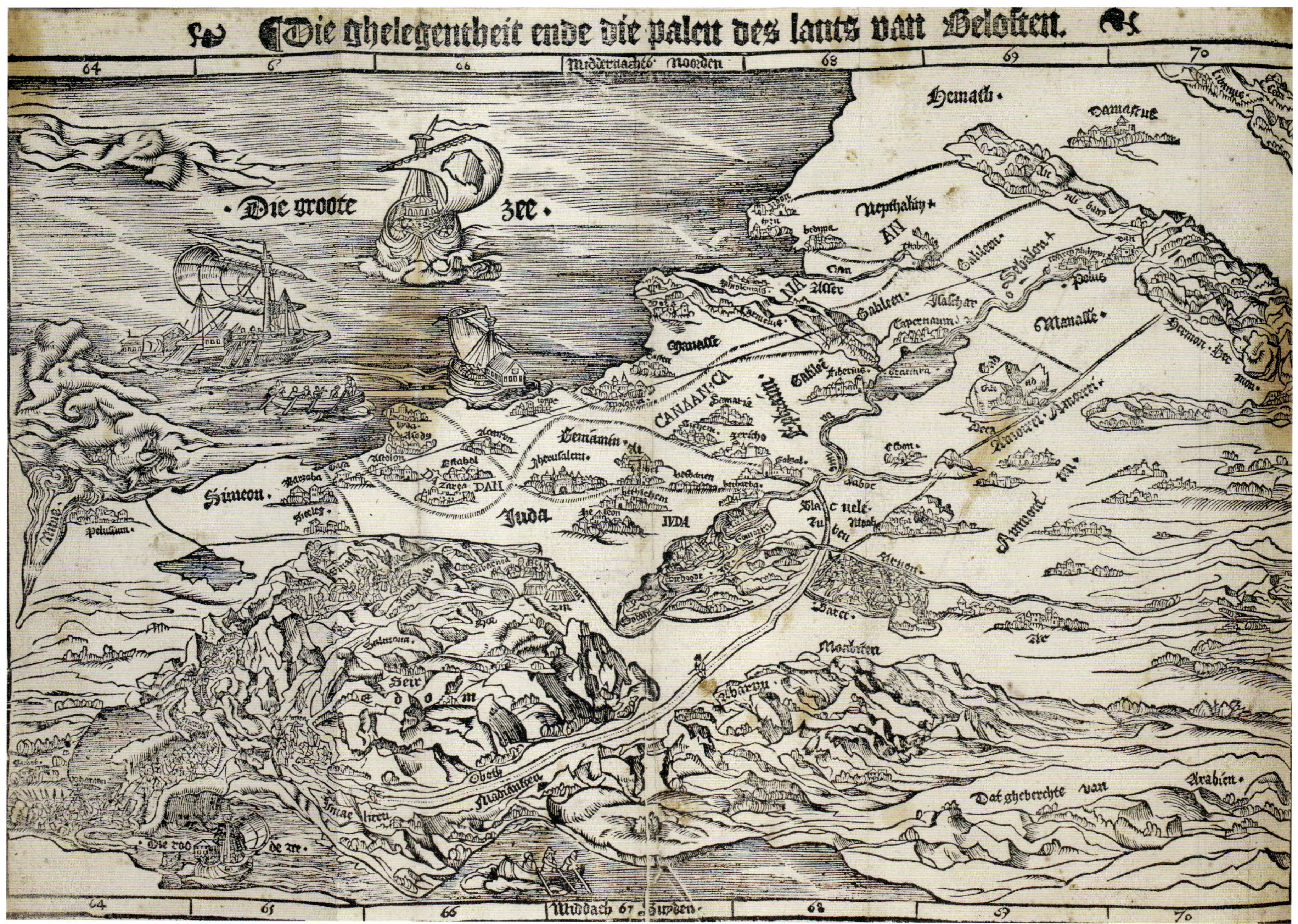
Die ghelegentheit ende die palen des lants van Beloften.
Middernacht Noorden
Die groote Zee
Hemath
Damascus
Nepthalim
AN
NA Aser
Galilea
Sebulon
Naphtar
Capernaum
Manasse
Hermon Berch
Manasse
Canaan
Benjamin
Jherusalem
Juda
IVDA
Simeon
Pelusium
Seir
Edom
Obot
Moabiten
Abarim
Arabien
Dat gheberchte van
Middach Zuyden

Israelites toward the promised land and the life journey of Christ from birth to death, that fulfills the promise of eternal salvation, made first to the chosen people and then to all humankind.

The complementary map of Paul's apostolic voyages, entitled *Chart of the Holy Apostle Paul's Pilgrimage*, expands to encompass the entire Mediterranean basin, showing that the promised salvation of Christ, the scope of which is universal not local, has superseded the more limited scope of the promised land of Canaan (fig. 21).[121] The epigraph inscribed above identifies the map as a "descriptive portrait of the lands traversed by Paul." The explanatory text printed after the map lists the places he visited along with the deeds he performed in them; each entry is flanked by three calendars counting the year from the birth of Christ, from the conversion of Paul, and from the imperial accession (starting with the Emperor Tiberius). Source texts in Acts and the Epistles are noted, along with the times and places when the latter were written. We learn, for example, that in the year 56 (after Christ), 22 (after the conversion), 14 (of Claudius), Paul wrote the Second Epistle to the Thessalonians en route from Athens to Jerusalem. In the year 61, 27, 5 (of Nero), he wrote the First Epistle to Timothy in Ephesus, en route from Ephesus to Macedonia, and the Second Epistle to the Corinthians, at Philippis, charging Titus and Luke to deliver it.[122] Other benchmarks are likewise noted: for instance, in the year 42, 8, 4 (of Tiberius), he, Barnabas, and the other disciples were first called Christians.[123] The brief references to the Epistles, like the short summaries of the Epistles in the introductory "Argument," connect them to Paul's sermons. These summaries supply the content of the Epistles, whose geneses are recorded in the map and its accompanying text, and it seems likely that the summaries and map text were consulted in tandem. To take one example, together they inform the reader that the Epistle to the Romans, written in the year 56, 22, 14 (of Claudius), concerns the doctrine of grace and faith, teaches that justification begets penitence, and confirms the calling of the gentiles, as well as the rejection and re-adoption of the Jews.[124] Viewed in this light, Paul's pilgrimage in Christ's name, from conversion to martyrdom, marks stages in the consolidation of Christian doctrine.

The maps of the *Exodus* and the *Peregrinations of the Apostle Paul* are inserted into Numbers 33 and Acts 28 respectively. In various editions of the Van Liesveldt Bible, the map *Position and Borders of the Promised Land* is inserted into Numbers 22–24, where it illustrates Balaam's three-fold prophecy of the triumph of Israel and oracle of the advent of Christ (fig. 22): "I see him, but not now; I behold him, but not nigh: a star shall come forth out of Jacob, and a scepter shall rise out of Israel" (Numbers 24:17).[125] In the edition of 1538, the woodcut map follows the small print of *Balaam and the Angel*, generally inserted into Numbers 22, that illustrates the prophet's indignant ass miraculously reproving its master (fig. 23).[126] Unlike the beast, Balaam has failed to descry the angel blocking his path, but he now sees him, his eyes having been divinely opened. Called by Balak, King of Moab, to curse the invading Israelites, he promises the Lord that he shall speak only the word that God bids him to speak. As *Balaam and the Angel* depicts the moment when he is granted the power of spiritual sight, so the map represents his expanding spiritual vision of Israel's future glory (fig. 22). The highlands of Moab lie east of Edom, south of the Ammorite kingdom, and north of the Arabian mountains. Balak meets

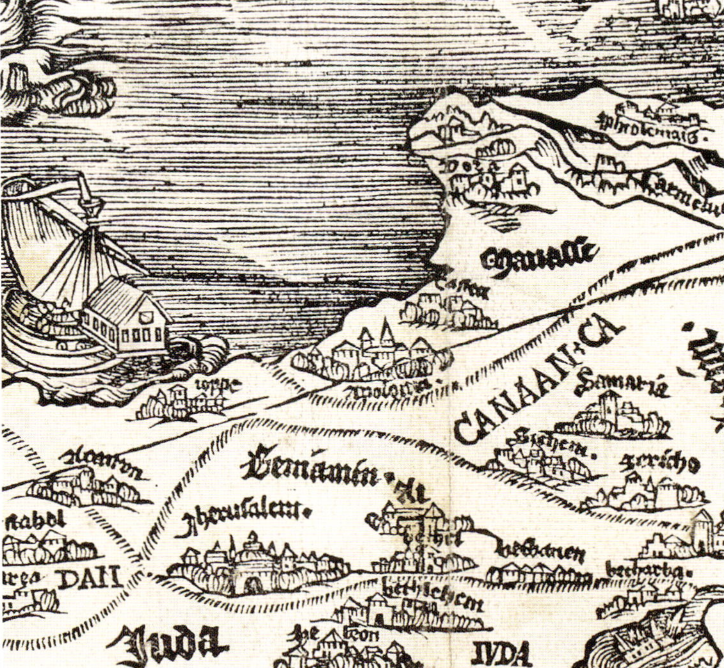

Fig. 22 (detail)

Balaam at the river Arnon, the boundary between Moab and the Ammorites, and takes him to a high place whence he sees the full extent of the encamped Israelites (*aen dat eynde des volcx*).[127] The result is the first prophecy of Israel, focusing on its fecundity, righteousness, and singular destiny: "For from the mountains I see him, from the hills I behold him; lo, a people dwelling alone, and not reckoning itself among the nations! Who can count the dust of Jacob, or number the fourth part of Israel? Let me die the death of the righteous, and let my end be like his!"[128] The exasperated Balak, hoping to make Balaam curse a part if not all of Israel, then brings him to a place on Mount Pisgah whence less of the Israelite camp is visible (*daer ghi dat eynde van Israel siet, ende doch niet al en siet*).[129] There ensues the second prophecy, exalting Israel led from Egypt by the power of the Lord: "God brings them out of Egypt;… now it shall be said of Jacob and Israel, 'What has God wrought!'"[130] This oracle expands to encompass the map's southwestern quadrant: Egypt, the highlands of Edom and Midian, and the route tracing the Exodus, as well as the vignettes portraying Moses's and the Israelites' crossing of the Red Sea, Moses promulgating the tablets of the law, and Moses raising the brazen serpent. In desperation, Balak leads Balaam to the summit of Mount Peor (just west of the wilderness of Zin), asking him to refrain from blessing Israel, if he cannot curse it. Balaam lifts up his eyes, and seeing all the encamped tribes of Israel, issues his final prophecy, his vision dilating to reveal the full extent of this people's future ascendancy: "The [oracle of the] man whose eyes are opened…who sees the vision of the Almighty, falling down, but having his eyes uncovered: How fair are your tents, O Jacob, your encampments, O Israel! Like valleys that stretch afar, like gardens beside a river."[131] There follows the oracle of the advent and triumph of Christ, prefigured in the triumph of the chosen people: "I see him, but not now; I behold him, but not nigh: a star shall come forth out of Jacob, and a scepter shall rise out of Israel; it shall crush the forehead of Moab, and break down all the sons of Sheth. Edom shall be dispossessed, Seir also, his enemies, shall be dispossessed, while Israel does valiantly."[132] In the topographical map, this visionary prophecy corresponds to the panoramic vista opening out to include Canaan and the twelve tribal territories, their names clearly designated. The battle vignette bounded by the tributaries Arnon

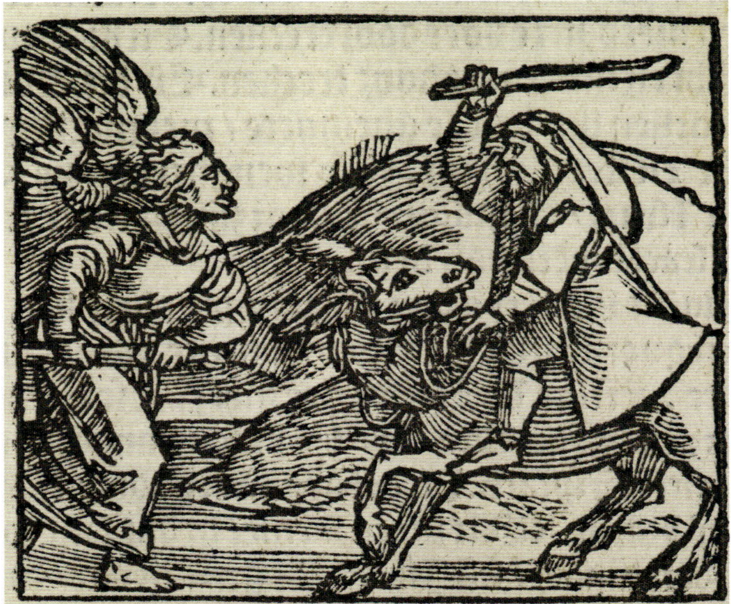

Fig. 23

and Saret stands for the military victory prophesied by Balaam.

Visual Exegesis

Exegesis is the systematic interpretation of scripture, the word of God, with reference to the authoritative sources—the Latin translation of the Bible known as the Vulgate of Saint Jerome, the sermons and exegetical treatises of the Greek and Latin Fathers, commentaries such as the *Glossa ordinaria*, theological summae by churchmen such as the scholastic exegete Thomas Aquinas, and readings promulgated by conciliar and papal decree. In the sixteenth century, scholars trained in humanist philology scrutinized the scriptural source texts, placing pressure upon, if not quite questioning, the singular authority of the Latin Vulgate; and as we have seen, new translations of the Bible began to proliferate, as instruments of religious reform–Catholic, Lutheran, and Calvinist. In many vernacular Bibles, as well as in newly edited versions of the Vulgate, printed images were used as hermeneutic instruments. In the Van Liesveldt, Vorsterman Bibles, and De Keyser Bibles, as discussed above, illustrative prints mark complementary biblical passages, suggesting how they may be read mutually to comment upon each other and themselves. Independent prints such as Swart's *Jesus Preaching from the Ship* function as pictorial prompts, urging us to consider the nature and meaning of parables, how and why Christ uses them as interpretive devices. Here again, we are asked to consider the relation between the New Testament and the Old, the manner in which the one reads the other, and more generally, the ways that scripture can be seen to read itself.

In the Van Liesveldt and Vorsterman Bibles, especially the early editions of 1526 and 1528 respectively, in which there are fewer New Testament images, it becomes apparent that much time, energy, and expense have been lavished on the copious illustration of the Old Testament (fig. 24). The Vorsterman Bible of 1528 contains ninety-four illustrations of the Old Testament (seventy-seven by Jan Swart), in addition to ninety-one of the New Testament (of which Swart also designed the Apocalypse series). Bart Rosier counts forty-one Old Testament illustrations in the Van Liesveldt Bible of 1526, and 84 in the edition of 1532 (counting repeats);[133] in the 1538 edition, the Old Testament illustrations number 122, copied or adapted from Symon Cock's *Historien ende prophecien* (*Histories and Prophecies*) of 1535, whereas the New Testament illustrations, printed from the blocks used to illustrate Willem van Branteghem's *Dat leven ons Heeren* (*The Life of Our Lord*) of 1537, number 162 (again counting repeats).[134] This remains a substantial number of Old Testament prints; given the fact that the images are often quite detailed, it would seem fair to assume that they play some sort of interpretative rather than merely ornamental role. The reader's prefaces to these various editions justify this assumption, indicating that the Old Testament has been richly illustrated to draw the reader's attention, ensuring that he shall stop, read, and ponder, rather than simply scanning or skipping this important part of the Bible.

Van Liesveldt's preface opens by disavowing those readers whose simpleness and lack of learning cause them to ignore or contemn the Old Testament; they falsely assume that it was meant only for the Jews, that its warrant has been made null and void, or that it consists merely of historical exploits without any deeper meaning.[135] On the contrary, the Old Testament enshrouds the New: it is the swaddling in which the infant Jesus lies wrapped (or alternatively, the winding sheet in which the sacrificial Christ lies

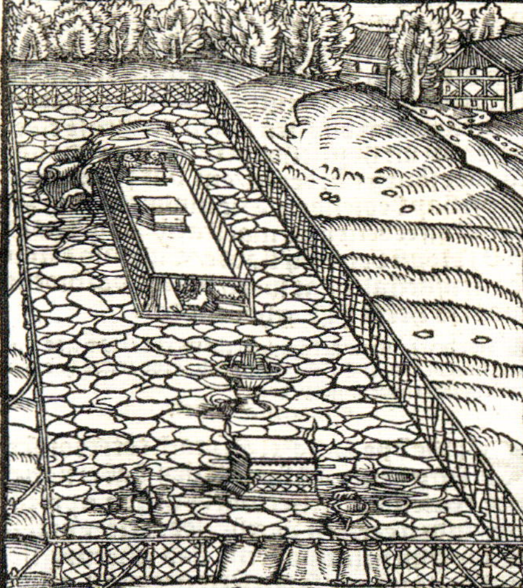

Fig. 24

buried), that can be unfolded to reveal how surely he is promised, how fully he is made manifest throughout the Old Testament (*dat oude Testament is ons als die wendeldoecken daer Christus in ghewonden leyt, ende daer wy hem oock in vinden sullen*).[136] The New Testament itself confirms the truth of this assertion, as many passages testify. In John 5:39, 46–47, for instance, Christ insists that the Old Testament must be searched for evidence of himself, and referring to Numbers 21:9 and Deuteronomy 18:15, declares that Moses bears him witness.[137] In 2 Timothy 3:8, 14–17, Paul states that all of scripture must be perused for what it teaches about salvation through faith in Christ Jesus.[138] In Romans 1:1–2, he counsels that the Gospel is promised through the prophets, and in 1 Corinthians 15:3–4 (in conjunction with Romans 1:3 and 2 Timothy 2:8), he avers that born of David's blood, Christ died and was raised for the remission of sins (alluding to Psalm 16 [15]:10, Isaiah 53, Daniel 9:26, Zechariah 13:7, and Hosea 6:2).[139] Likewise, the Epistles of Peter (1 Peter 1:10–12 and 2 Peter 1:19) reiterate this truth (alluding to Daniel 8:15, 9:24–26, 12:4, 9, 13 and Isaiah 52:13–53:12).[140] And in Acts 7:37, Stephen, whom Van Liesveldt calls the first Christian martyr of the Old Testament, invokes Moses's prophecy of Christ, while in Acts 17:11, Luke observes that the Jews of Beroea (near Thessalonica) assiduously searched the scriptures—that is, the Old Testament—for validation of what Paul was preaching.[141] Just as the Jews looked for confirmation of Paul's sermons in the Old Testament, before the New had been written down, so the latter, once it had been transcribed, continued to be ratified by the former.[142] It follows that Christians should value the Old Testament no less than the New, for the New does not disavow but rather fulfills the Old, attesting that the many divine promises made by the grace of God have now been graciously kept. Indeed, if the Old Testament teaches the law, the New Testament brings the law to fruition; together they inculcate fear and love of the Lord, inspiring trust in God, whose joint sanctuary they constitute.[143]

The *Prologhe* ("Prologue") to the Vorsterman Bible, composed by the book's editors, defends the Old Testament even more emphatically. This Bible as a whole belongs to whosoever keeps and perfects the word of God, rather than simply reading or hearing it. Woven into a single scriptural fabric, it resembles the goatskin veil covering the tabernacle (*daer offeren wy gheyten vellen*), and has been brought forth as a kind temple offering (*maer een offer inden schat des tempels*).[144] Like Van Liesveldt, the editors emphasize that the Old Testament neither merely chronicles past events nor demands to be consulted only for its spiritual sense, but rather requires to be read as the vessel of the living spirit of God, that vivifies as surely as the letter of the law kills. In other words, the Old Testament is more than the book of the law; rather, it is the living complement of the New.[145] The New Testament demonstrates that this is so by extensively quoting the Old. Luke 4:21 (based on Isaiah 61:1–2) is cited: "Today this scripture has been fulfilled in your hearing." And also 1 Corinthians 15:3–4 (based on Isaiah 53:5–12 and Psalm 16:8–9): "that Christ died for our sins, in accordance with the scriptures, that he was buried, that he was raised on the third day in accordance with the scriptures." And finally, Romans 1:1–4, that ascribes the Gospel also to the prophets: "for the gospel of God which he promised beforehand through his prophets."[146] If the Old Testament instructs us patiently to hope for eternal life by trusting in scripture, the New Testament must be seen to fulfill the promises made figuratively by the prophets, as Christ himself indicates in John 15:25, citing Psalms 35:19 and 69:4 to prophesy his Passion: "It is to fulfill the word that is written in their law, 'They hated me without cause.'"[147] The editors employ metaphors and tropes that stress the complementarity of the two testaments: all of scripture is the Red Sea, through which the Israelites, led by Moses, obediently came to Christ; scripture is also the crib where the shepherds found the infant Christ wrapped in swaddling, when Herod's priests and wise men failed to do so.[148] The two testaments constitute a chiasmus: as in the New Testament, laws and precepts supplement the teachings of grace, so in the Old, the promises of grace supplement the laws and precepts, for the patriarchs and prophets were preserved by their faith in Jesus Christ.[149] Moreover, in their summary of Deuteronomy, the editors quote Matthew 15:9 (based on Isaiah 29:13), in which Christ distinguishes his doctrine from the vain teachings of men, to explain the Mosaic distinction between true religion and idolatry. It is to clarify this distinction, the editors claim, that they have edited both the Gospel and the Law. In doing so, they have discerned that there are three kinds of laws operative in the Old Testament and the New: those that curb evildoing; those that establish the liturgy; and most importantly,

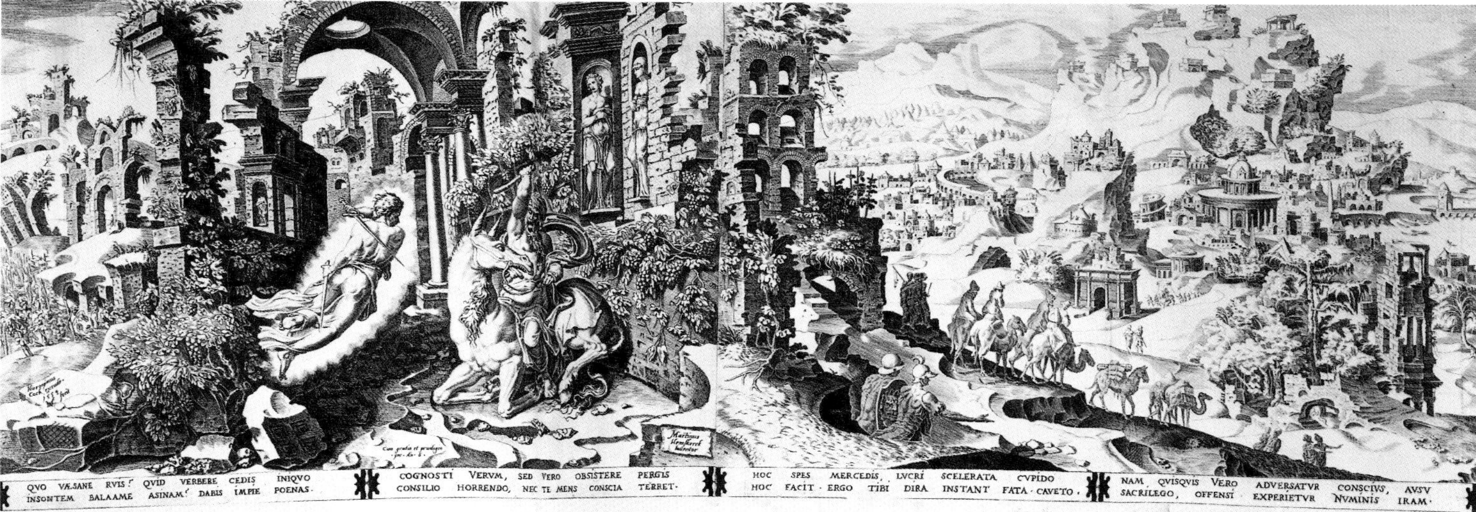

Fig. 25

those that promote love of God and one's neighbor.[150] If then, under the old dispensation, knowledge of sin and fear of the Lord ensured that the law was kept, the law of love was also exercised, so that the distinction between the two covenants is one of degree not kind. So too, knowledge of sin begets longing for the salvation of Christ under both dispensations.[151] Such comments help to account for the proliferation of Old Testament illustrations in the Bibles we have been briefly examining.[152] By their sheer numbers, these images call on the reader-viewer to delve into the Old Testament, as did Christ, Paul, and the evangelists, who recognized it as an indispensable source of the New.

Learned artists familiar with the Bible, such as the draftsman Maarten van Heemskerck and his collaborator the engraver Dirck Volckertszoon Coornhert, occasionally portrayed traditional subjects in novel ways that call attention to exegetical conundra. Etched and engraved by Coornhert after a design by Van Heemskerck, *Balaam and the Angel* juxtaposes two accounts of the prophet, based respectively in the Old Testament and the New (fig. 25).[153] In effect, the print poses an heuristic problem, combining contradictory readings of Balaam, that prompt us to question our understanding of his dual significance as a harbinger of the Incarnation and a negative exemplum of simony. *Balaam and the Angel* inventively illustrates Numbers 22:22–30, embedding the scene within a panoramic vista extending over two oblong plates. In format and argument, the print diverges from the typological mode of presentation codified for this subject in the *Biblia pauperum* (*Poor-Man's Bible*) and *Speculum humanae salvationis* (*Mirror of Human Salvation*), where the prophet's encounter with the angel prefigures the Annunciation.[154] This association derives from the exegetical tradition that reads Numbers 24:17 as an oracle of the Incarnation: "I see him, but not now; I behold him but not nigh: a star shall come forth out of Jacob, and a sceptre shall rise out of Israel."[155] Although Van Heemskerck uses the landscape to allude to this prophecy, as we shall see, he mainly characterizes Balaam as the flawed prophet invoked in 2 Peter 2:15, Jude 1:11, and Revelation 2:14. Balaam is shown as a prophet blind to the presence of the messenger angel, and hostage to vengeful rage. Having been summoned by Balak the Moabite king, and received God's permission to travel with the king's representatives, his way is thrice blocked by an angel sent to communicate the divine will.[156] Fearful of the angel, the prophet's she-ass turns away and is savagely beaten for her pains. When Balaam raises his hand against her for the third time, she miraculously chastises him for his unjust and merciless rage.[157] Van Heemskerck describes the sites of the second and third detours—the narrow path between vineyards and the walled boundary against which the she-ass retreated—and he portrays Balaam just before the Lord opens his eyes and causes him to see the minatory angel with drawn sword. In response, Balaam acknowledges his sin of failing to recognize the angelic presence of God. The Latin inscription underscores the prophet's failings, accusing him of impiety, injustice, cupidity, and iniquitous rage: "Whither do you hasten, madman? Balaam, why with unjust rod do you strike the innocent she-ass? You shall but punish impiously. Knowing the truth, you yet proceed to oppose it, your counsel being dreadful, and nor does a knowing conscience deter you. The hope of reward, the wicked longing for riches makes you do this. And therefore the fearful Fates pursue you. Beware! For whoever knowingly opposes truth with sacrilegious intent shall incur the wrath of an offended God."[158]

This text construes Balaam as the flawed prophet negatively exemplified in Revelation 2:14, Jude 1:11, and especially 2 Peter 2:15.[159] The latter passage provides the basis for the image and the inscription: "Forsaking the right way they have gone astray; they have followed the way of Balaam, the son of Beor, who loved gain from wrongdoing, but was rebuked for his own transgression; a dumb ass spoke with human voice and restrained the prophet's madness." Balaam stands for the false prophets and teachers whom Peter decries for distorting the "knowledge of our Lord Jesus Christ."[160] Having failed to discern the angel, unaware of his sinful ignorance, he stands for "whoever...is blind and shortsighted and has forgotten that he was cleansed from his old sins."[161] Enraged and vengeful, he epitomizes the "corruption that is in the world because of passion."[162] He embodies the opposite of the true follower of Christ, whose virtues concatenate—self-knowledge linking to self-control, self-control to steadfastness, steadfastness to godliness, godliness to brotherly affection, and brotherly affection to love.[163] The pagan ruins filling the landscape refer to the "ancient world" that God "did not spare" and the "cities...he condemned...to extinction" as examples of the wages of sin.[164]

The panoramic vista that so amply expands the viewer's field of vision adumbrates Balaam's prophetic vision of the future greatness of Israel and the glorious coming of the Messiah. In Numbers 22–24, as noted earlier, Balak takes Balaam to three high places, whence he commands him to curse the Israelites encamped on the plains of Jericho: the bare height of Bamoth-baal, then the summit of Mount Pisgah, and finally the summit of Mount Peor. From these vantage points, he first sees the "nearest of the people" (that is, the encamped Israelites), and then the whole of "Israel encamping tribe by tribe."[165] As his field of vision opens out to embrace all of Israel, so his oracular blessings amplify, to enumerate Israel's future victories over Moab, Edom, Seir, and Amalek, which foreshadow the triumph of Christ.[166] The panoramic vista can be seen to allude to this visionary panorama of cities destroyed and nations come to destruction, that Balaam shall yet see once his eyes have been spiritually opened: "The oracle of Balaam the son of Beor, the oracle of the man whose eye is opened, the oracle of him who hears the words of God, who sees the vision of the Almighty, falling down, but having his eyes uncovered."[167] In sum, the print juxtaposes two accounts of the prophet—the one based on Numbers 22–24, the other on 2 Peter 2, Jude 1, and Revelation 2—that together constitute a meditative crux upon which we are invited to reflect. The two readings of Balaam issue from two exegetical traditions: in the one case he epitomizes spiritual blindness, in the other spiritual discernment. The print urges us to consider how the former condition transforms into the latter, when the eye once closed becomes the eye now opened.[168]

Other prints invite an exegetical response by illustrating unfamiliar or unprecedented scenes. Designed by Otto van Veen, engraved by Hieronymus Wierix, and published by Jan Baptiste Vriendt, all based in Antwerp, the *Entombment* of ca. 1600 depicts a new pictorial subject that combines elements of an entombment and a pietà (representation of the Virgin cradling the dead Christ) (fig. 26).[169] It might justly be entitled *Showing of the Corpus Christi*, since the male figure at right firmly raises the lifeless but radiant body of Christ, removing him from Mary's lap in order better to display him to the viewer. This figure is the aristocratic prophet Isaiah, identifiable by his ermine-lined mantle, his deictic gesture of pointing, and the inscription below, that quotes from Isaiah 11:10: "Him the Gentiles shall beseech, and his sepulchre shall be glorious." This excerpt forms part of the great prophecy about the spiritual kingdom of Christ and the universal peace he confers (already familiar from our discussion of the *Biblia Polyglotta*):

"And there shall come forth a rod out of the root of Jesse, and a flower shall rise up out of his root. And the spirit of the Lord

shall rest upon him: the spirit of wisdom, and of understanding,
the spirit of counsel, and of fortitude, the spirit of knowledge,
and of godliness. And he shall be filled with the spirit of the fear
of the Lord. He shall not judge according to the sight of the eyes,
nor reprove according to the hearing of the ears….The wolf shall
dwell with the lamb, and the leopard shall lie down with the kid;
the calf and the lion, and the sheep shall abide together, and a
little child shall lead them….In that day, the root of Jesse, who
standeth for an ensign of the people, him the Gentiles shall
beseech, and his sepulchre shall be glorious….And he shall set
up a standard unto the nations, and shall assemble the fugitives
of Israel" (Isaiah 11:1–3, 6, 10, 12).

Laid upon the winding sheet, or better, impressed upon it, the *corpus
sacrum* is portrayed as if it were indeed the ensign raised for all to see
and be converted. (The sheet further refers to the corporal, the linen
cloth upon which the priest lays the consecrated host, the
sacramental body of Christ, during the Mass.[170]) The prophet, even as
he exhibits Christ for our benefit, jointly consoles Mary, looking into
her eyes and pointing toward her son, whose radiance portends his
oracle of the glorious Resurrection to come ("and his sepulchre shall
be glorious").[171] He reminds her that, distraught as she is at her
separation from Jesus, she must, like Christ himself, learn to judge
what she sees not corporeally, "according to the sight of the eyes," but
spiritually according to the "spirit of wisdom, and of understanding,
the spirit of counsel, and of fortitude, the spirit of knowledge, and of
godliness…[and] of the fear of the Lord." In other words, she is urged,
as are we, to utilize spiritual sight, harnessing it to meditate on the
relation between the Passion and the Resurrection. Visual exegesis is
the means to this end: by interpolating Isaiah into a scene that calls
for interpretation precisely because he is anomalously present, but
also because it is neither a pietà nor entombment simply, Van Veen
encourages us to read the mystery of Christ's sacrificial death in
terms of Isaiah 11, and conversely, to read Isaiah 11 in terms of this
Christian mystery. The second inscription, probably composed by
Van Veen, who was a learned poet, painter, and emblematist,
amplifies the meaning of the verse quoted above. The paradoxically
deathly yet glorious sepulchre, that stands for all the other paradoxes
reconciled by Christ—the wolf and the lamb, the leopard and the

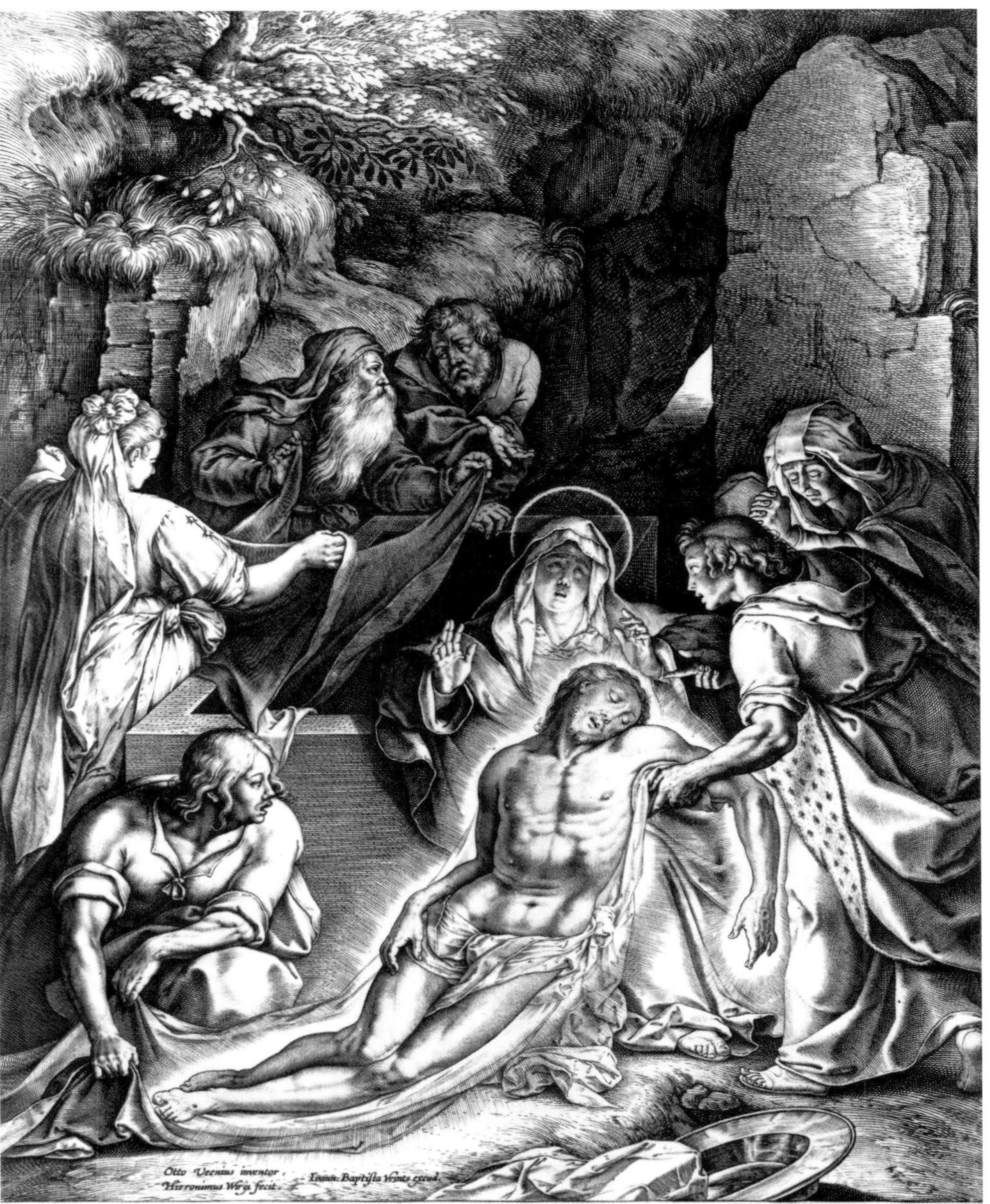

IPSVM GENTES DEPRECABVNTVR, ET ERIT SEPVLCHRVM EIVS GLORIOSVM. ESA. II.

Per varios casus, per tot tormenta, labores,   Conditur hic Christi venerandum corpus Iesu:
   Quæ tulit, affixus victima facta cruci;   Mors vilis, tumulo gloria magna fuit.

Fig. 26

kid, the lion and the calf—becomes on this account a metaphor for the complementary relation between the mysteries of the Passion and Resurrection, the former so ignominious, the latter so triumphant. Van Veen teases out this relation: "Having borne various misfortunes, innumerable labors and torments, affixed as a sacrifice upon the cross, the body of Jesus is here fashioned as an object of veneration: base death became in the tumulus great glory."

Along with the other figures gathered at the tomb—John grasping the shroud, Nicodemus, Joseph of Arimathea, and the Magdalene lining the tomb with a second shroud—another figure is visible at right (beside her, a second woman is barely discernible). Dressed like a sybil or prophetess, this elderly woman smiles at what she sees, presumably recognizing the promise of salvation that the sacrificial Christ bodies forth. Whereas she can be seen to understand the meaning of Isaiah's oracle, Joseph and Nicodemus seem earnestly to discuss what it is that the prophet expounds. Her face brightly lit by the glow emanating from Christ, she must be the elderly prophetess Anna, who identified him as the Messiah, proclaiming his salvation to "all that looked for the redemption of Israel" (Luke 2:36–38). She was present at the Temple when Simeon, inspired by the Holy Spirit, extolled the infant Christ as "a light to the revelation of the Gentiles, and the glory of thy people Israel." Here she bears witness to Simeon's luminous imagery of salvation, that he affirmed to have seen by the grace of God: "Now thou dost dismiss thy servant, O Lord, according to thy word in peace; because my eyes have seen thy salvation, which thou has prepared before the face of all peoples" (Luke 2:29–31). The light of Christ also alludes to the imagery of Isaiah 2, which calls upon the faithful to "walk in the light of the Lord," and to be mindful of the "glory of his majesty," which shall be everywhere visible when he comes once again in glory to judge humankind, destroying its idols (that is, overweening pride in human works and affection for physical things). This prophecy attaches to the later prophecy of the sepulchre made glorious; it refers to the risen Christ, who having conquered death, shall return to save or damn the human race. Also implicit is an allusion to the Canticle of Anna (namesake of the temple votaress who recognized Christ) in 1 Kings 2:1–10; this song of praise doubles as a prophecy of the Messiah who "prevails

by his own strength," exalting the low and humbling the high, just as he is himself humiliated in glory, glorious in humiliation. Anna's words construe the Christ of God as an expression of his infinite power to raise by lowering, and as such, they are an oracle of the sacrificial Christ as agent of redemption:

"My heart hath rejoiced in the Lord, and my horn is exalted in my God: my mouth is enlarged over my enemies, because I have joyed in thy salvation. There is none holy as the Lord is: for there is no other beside thee, and there is none strong like our God…. The Lord killeth and maketh alive, he bringeth down to hell and bringeth back again. The Lord maketh the poor and maketh the rich, he humbleth and he exalteth….For the poles of the earth are the Lord's, and upon them he hath set the world. He will keep the feet of his saints, and the wicked shall be silent in darkness, because no man shall prevail by his own strength…. The Lord shall judge the ends of the earth, and he shall give empire to his king, and shall exalt the horn of his Christ."

Van Veen's invention is the virtual *locus* through which these scriptural texts transit, intersect, and resonate: the image and its inscriptions animate them by prompting us to read the prophecies mutually and in tandem, anchoring all of them in the visibly manifest *corpus Christi*. That Van Veen utilizes the term *conditur* (is formed, fashioned) suggests that the body of Christ is a work of divine artifice, but at the same time it refers to the pictorial image that represents this mysterious body, proffering it as an exegetical instrument. The fact that the scene he delineates is not actually described in the Gospels drives home his point about the power of the image to mobilize exegesis.

Pictorial images generally functioned as exegetical implements within an intricate text-image apparatus. A most interesting case of such an apparatus is the *Imagines et figurae bibliorum* (*Images and Figures of the Bible*) of ca. 1592, published by Franciscus Raphelengius (son-in-law of Christopher Plantin) in Leiden, which consists of 60 oblong folio plates of the Old Testament and 38 of the New (figs. 27–33).[172] Trilingual commentaries in Latin, French, and Dutch accompany the Old Testament scenes, explaining the process of interpretation they are meant to engender. The pseudonymous author of these commentaries was Jacobus Villanus (Hendrik Jansen van Barrefelt, also known as Hiël), the second leader of the Family of Love, the spiritualist community founded in The Netherlands by Hendrik Niclaes, whom Van Barrefelt, a breakaway disciple, succeeded as the sect's prophet. The publisher Raphelengius likewise adopted a pseudonym, issuing the book under the moniker Renatus Christianus. (The use of pseudonyms suggests that both author and publisher feared that the book's content might be deemed heterodox.) Christopher Plantin had initiated the project as early as 1582, overseeing the production of the etched plates from Leiden, where he resided between 1583 and 1585, but he seems to have abandoned it after returning to Antwerp in 1585, leaving the plates in the possession of Raphelengius. It is unknown who commissioned Van Barrefelt's text, which comments only on the Old Testament scenes and may have been written at a relatively late stage, but the book's overall argument suggests that he guided the coherent selection of biblical passages to be illustrated. The designer and etcher was Pieter van der Borcht, who had earlier worked on the *Biblia polyglotta*.

Amongst the explanatory materials printed at the end of the Old Testament sequence (often published independently of the New Testament sequence), the *Interpretationes sive explicationes imaginum aliquot historiae biblicae* ("Interpretations and Expositions of Several Images of Biblical History") summarizes the hermeneutic applied consistently throughout the *Imagines et figurae Bibliorum*: "These images taken from history properly figured (*ab Historia proprie figurativa*) have been adapted and distilled into testimonies of the essential truth that any Christian (divine grace assisting and renunciation of oneself leading the way) can and ought to discern and ascertain in his heart and soul, for the salutary renewal of life and the peace of God, in the unity of the Holy Spirit, through his son Jesus Christ, our eternal Lord and Savior, who was, is, and will be forever and ever in the Trinity."[173] The epigraph from 1 Corinthians 15:47 implies that every image will be read in a binary way—externally and internally, humanly and divinely, temporally and eternally—that transforms the reader-viewer accordingly: "The first man, being terrestrial, is from the earth; the second, being celestial, is from heaven."[174] Three biblical passages, cited at the close of the

reader's preface that immediately follows, correlate these dual modes of reading-viewing with other dualities—the distinction between the Old Law and the New, between shadowy prophecy and the radiant light of truth that fortifies it, and between the provincial ministry of the prophets and the essential ministry of Christ. Hebrews 10:1 discriminates between the promise of the "law having a shadow of the good things to come (*umbram habet lex futurorum bonorum*)," and its realization in the Gospel, the "very image of those [good] things (*ipsam imaginem rerum*)."[175] Deuteronomy 30:11–15 situates in the heart this true image that supersedes its adumbration: "For this commandment which I command you this day is not too hard for you, neither is it far off. It is not in heaven, that you should say, 'Who will go up for us to heaven, and bring it to us?' Neither is it beyond the sea, that you should say, 'Who will go over the sea for us, and bring it to us, that we may hear it and do it?' But the word is very near you; it is in your mouth and in your heart, so that you can do it. See, I have set before you this day life and good, death and evil."[176] 2 Peter 1:19 assures us that prophecy is fulfilled within ourselves, as an internal process revealing the true image described by Paul: "And we have the prophetic word made more sure. You will do well to pay attention to this as to a lamp shining in a dark place, until the day dawns and the morning star rises in your hearts."[177]

The reader's preface elaborates upon these conceits in what is effectively an exegesis of Revelation 14:12, 16:4–7 and especially Romans 7:6: "But now we are discharged from the law, dead to that which held us captive, so that we serve not under the old written code but in the new life of the Spirit." These exegeses are used to argue that the very process of reading an image is itself exegetical, and in turn, this process proves constitutive of a dynamic of self-reformation that converts the beholder into a true image of Christ.[178] Van Barrefelt begins by stating his intention of transforming terrestrial into spiritual sight: he hopes to uncover the soul's eyes, so that the reader, his heart having been opened by the grace of Christ, may descry the essential works of God, which he at first administers figuratively to the figurative man (*mira et essentialia Dei opera, quae initio per figurale ministerium homini figurali ostendit*).[179] This figurative ministry ultimately prevents humankind from beholding the splendor of the divine essence or

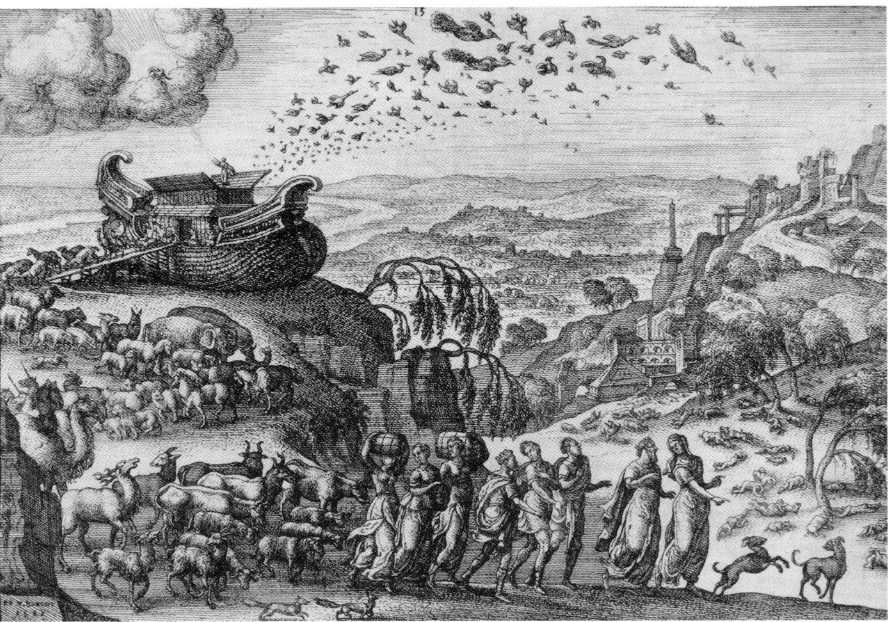

Fig. 27

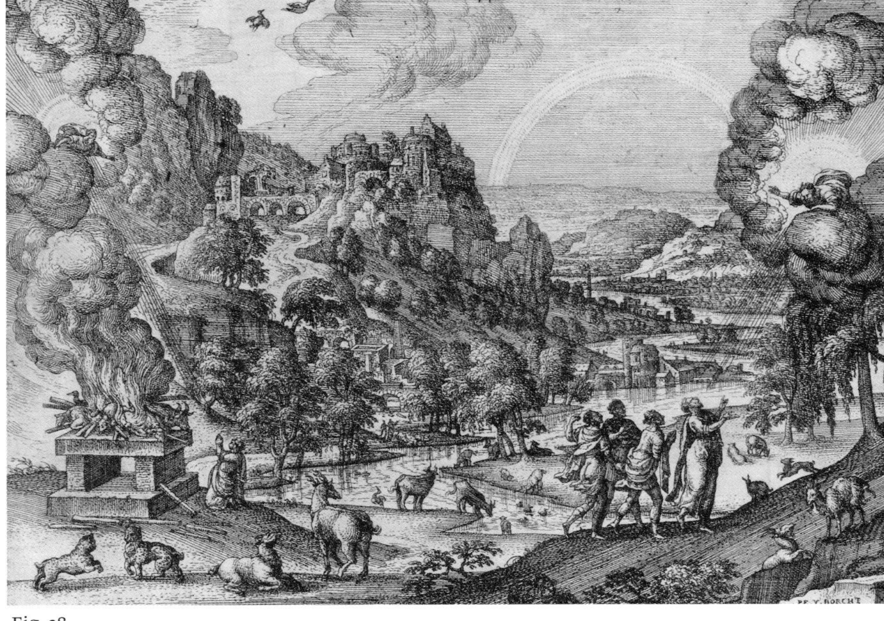

Fig. 28

attaining it spiritually; the figurative must therefore be translated by divine grace into the essential, through the agency of Christ.[180] By "figurative" Van Barrefelt seems to mean "purely descriptive"; the figurative man entirely relies on the "imaginative intellect" (*imaginarij intellectus sui viribus*), dwelling on its superficial images to the neglect of divine interpretation (*divinam interpretationem*); he attempts to arrive at the knowledge of God by essentially terrestrial means, relying upon his senses, especially the sense of sight, because he believes himself to be righteous.[181] Van Barrefelt aims to oppose this perversion of the senses by embedding figurative resources within an exegetical framework: he starts with scriptural images because God himself operates figuratively, that is, by means of visible forms and pictures; he then comments briefly upon the legitimate scriptural sense of these images, reading them with recourse to the biblical passages whose true meaning these images and figures intimate. This meaning, to be discerned exegetically, is anchored always in the spirit and essence of Christ (*secundum Spiritum & Essentiam Christi*).[182] So for Van Barrefelt, the pictorial images that initially illustrate the figurative sense of things (*iuxta ministerium tabulis formisque exprimendi*) are the very images and figures that finally indicate the legitimate sense of scripture (*legitimum sensum, sive basim & fundamentum Scripturae…ad quam figurae & imagines nos ducunt*). The reader, guided by Van Barrefelt, far from reading these images as mere histories (*historias nudas*) must acutely focus his interior

intellect on those things that the images teach and recollect; at the same time, he must engage in spiritual exercises, searching his heart for the consolatory presence of God and the traces of his divine essence.[183] Van Barrefelt reminds the reader that the Bible was written so that men might learn to distinguish good from bad within themselves; the scriptural texts and the images illustrating them are not so much historical narratives as spiritual instruments for the renewal of life (*nihil praeter historicam narrationem è Scriptura homines haurirent, ignari renovationis vitae*).[184] In sum, there are two ministries that God in his holy wisdom has permitted us to exercise and himself exercises in us, the figurative and the essential, and for this reason, images and figures ought to be considered in these two ways; with the proviso that any figurative ministry, justly exercised, must at last be attuned to the sacred essence of God.[185] This process is continuous, leading from the figurative to the essential, from historical events to their spiritual significance, as John 3:6, 1 John 3:14, and 1 Corinthians 15:40–47 imply: "There are also celestial bodies, and bodies terrestrial…it is sown a natural body; it is raised a spiritual body. If there is a natural body, there is also a spiritual body…Howbeit that is not first which is spiritual but that which is natural; then that which is spiritual. The first man is of the earth, earthy: the second man is of heaven."[186] In this context, these citations signify the process of visual exegesis that Van Barrefelt endorses; their exegesis, in other words, comes to stand for the exegetical process

Fig. 27
Pieter van der Borcht, *Noah, his Family, and the Animals Leaving the Ark*, 1582, etching, no. 13 in Hendrik Jansen van Barrefelt [Hiël], *Imagines et figurae bibliorum; Images et figures de la Bible; Beelden ende figuren wt den Bybel* (Leiden: Franciscus Raphelengius, 1592), oblong quarto. Plantin-Moretus Museum, Antwerp. Photo: Peter Maes.

Fig. 28
Pieter van der Borcht, *Noah's Sacrifice after the Flood and his Covenant with God*, ca. 1582–85, etching, no. 14 in Hendrik Jansen van Barrefelt [Hiël], *Imagines et figurae bibliorum; Images et figures de la Bible; Beelden ende figuren wt den Bybel* (Leiden: Franciscus Raphelengius, 1592), oblong quarto. Plantin-Moretus Museum, Antwerp. Photo: Peter Maes.

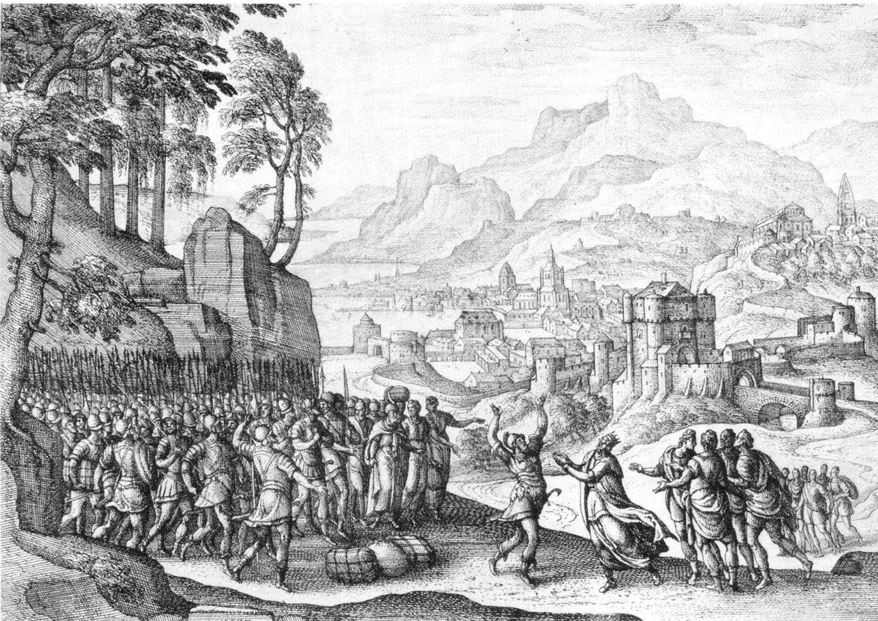

Fig. 29

leading from figurative to essential viewing.

We can better understand how this exegetical system operates by looking at a group of seven *imagines* illustrating biblical episodes when God himself communicated through images. Van der Borcht consistently sets these events within panoramic vistas that emphasize that they take place within the wide world, accessible figuratively to the senses, but also that their significance extends essentially to embrace all of creation. Image 13 portrays *Noah, his Family, and the Animals Leaving the Ark* (Genesis 8:18–19) (fig. 27).[187] Van Barrefelt begins by describing it simply: "In this image and figure you see how God, having called back the punitive flood, caused the ark to settle on Mount Ararat."[188] He explains that God thereby exemplifies his benevolence and divine grace, calling us to acknowledge these divine virtues and turn toward him. As a figurative example, the image demonstrates that instruction and doctrine under the Law bring forth malediction and the fear of damnation for our sins.[189] As an essential example, it represents Noah's ark as the image of the sacred ark that God causes to descend upon Mount Sion, bringing new instruction and doctrine into our hearts, that announce our salvation and humble us with the news that the curse of sin has been lifted.[190] Implicit in the distinction between the exemplifying force of the figurative and the essential image is the further distinction between two kinds of instruction and doctrine, that of the Old and New Testaments, of the Law and the Gospel.

Image 14 depicts *Noah's Sacrifice after the Flood and his Covenant with God* (Genesis 8:20–22, 9:8–17) (fig. 28).[191] Noah kneels beside the sacrificial altar at left, illuminated by God who answers his prayer; he stands with his sons at right, again illuminated by God who expounds the rainbow arcing over the distant horizon. Van Barrefelt describes the image as follows: "In the image and figure you may see how God placed the rainbow in heaven, after Noah had made the sacrificial thank-offering."[192] This figurative sign conveyed God's intention never again to destroy the world in flood. As the exemplary significance of the figurative sign was readily discernible, so our spirit may discern the meaning of the ardent, essential sign.[193] It signifies the fiery charity, along with the water of purity, to be found in all godly souls. On the contrary, for worldly souls, these same elements evoke the fire of horror that accompanies the water of damnation.[194] That the theme of fiery charity can beget the opposed theme of fiery horror demonstrates how the divine sign may be read as an essential image of salvation or damnation, of God's power to save or to damn, depending on who views it—the pure or sinful soul. So the figurative sign comes essentially to stand for the duality of divine signs, whose meanings are contingent on the condition of the viewer's soul. If the state of our souls determines how we read those signs, the converse is also true: how we read them allows us to read our soul's true state.

Image 22 illustrates *Abraham and the King of Sodom* (Genesis 14:21–24) (fig. 29).[195] Abraham stands before the 318 armed men of his house, with whom he recovered Lot and his family, as well

Fig. 29
Pieter van der Borcht, *Abraham and the King of Sodom*, ca. 1582–85, etching, no. 22 in Hendrik Jansen van Barrefelt [Hiël], *Imagines et figurae bibliorum; Images et figures de la Bible; Beelden ende figuren wt den Bybel* (Leiden: Franciscus Raphelengius, 1592), oblong quarto. Plantin-Moretus Museum, Antwerp. Photo: Peter Maes.

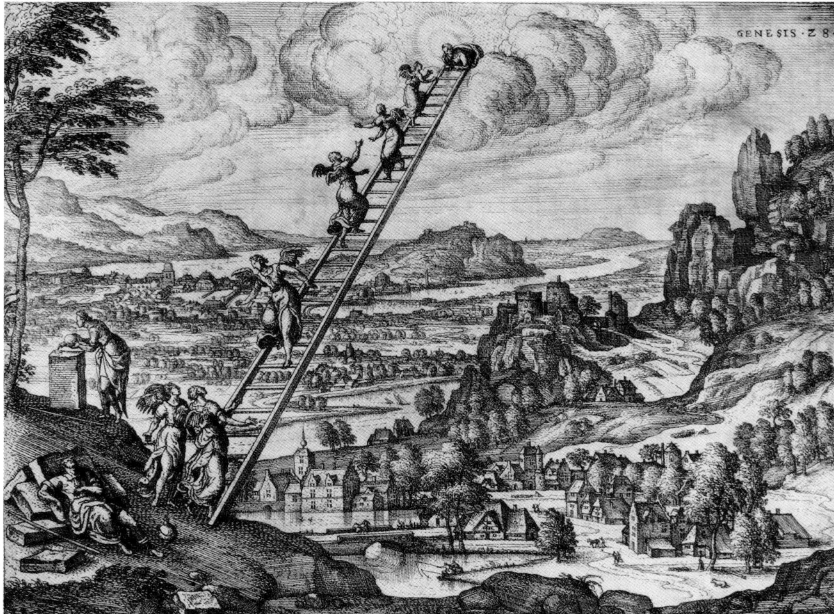

Fig. 30

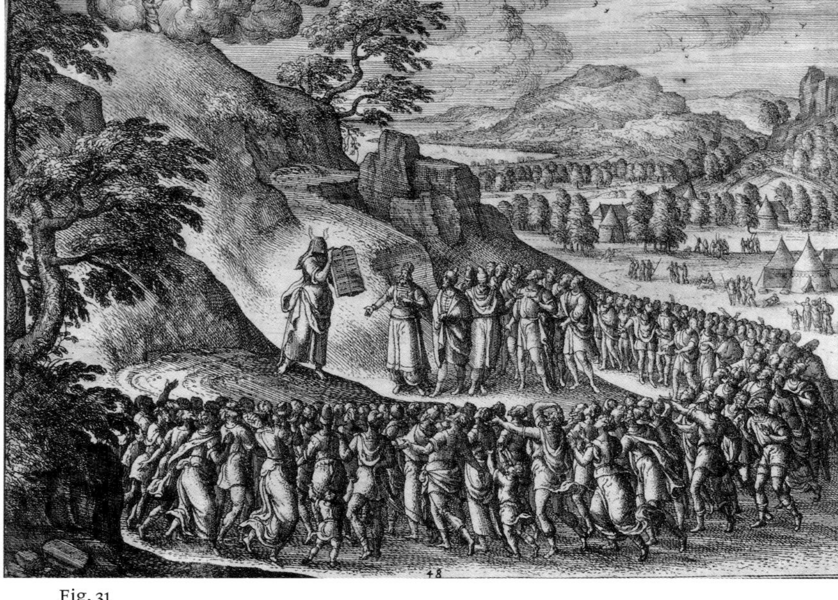

Fig. 31

as the people and property of Bera, King of Sodom, that were taken captive by Chedorlaomer, King of Elam and his royal allies. When the King of Sodom offers him all the captured goods, asking only for the return of his people, Abraham declines, raises his arms heavenward, and repeats the oath he had earlier sworn before God, promising to accept nothing but the gifts given him by the Lord. Van Barrefelt first quotes Abraham's response to the King of Sodom and then observes that God here supplies an example showing how he fills us with images and perfects them internally: "[This image] exemplifies essentially and truthfully that the perfect essence of God makes his images and figures prominent in us and brings them to essential perfection. Against the King of Sodom, Abraham the father of faith raises his hands to God, [which stands for] the salutary, obedient faith that gives him power and strength to resist the essence of rebellious, corruptible, and terrestrial arrogance, as he truly testifies: 'My divine nature covets neither your terrestrial property nor intelligent genius, lest such property claim to have enriched my salutary faith. Let your property forsooth be yours, and give back only what the young men have eaten. May you, the terrestrial essence of rebellion, bear your damnable burden, but let the principle of tender and youthful faith that flees property as do I, share in [my] virile old age.' Or again: 'Keep your mundane essence, and suffer the divine nature to live in its salutary essence.'"[196] Van Barrefelt opposes two essential principles — the

temporal desire to possess earthly goods and the spiritual desire to preserve an ever-fresh faith—that are embodied in two exemplary figures. Abraham, having declined the king's gift, construes himself by his words as the essential image of divine obedience and fidelity, and conversely, construes the King of Sodom as the antithetical image of worldly disobedience and rebelliousness. He is thus seen and heard to embody the power of the exegete, who takes a figurative image and recasts it as an essential one, with a view to strengthening the faith.

Image 38 represents *Jacob's Dream and his Anointing of the Stone at Bethel* (Genesis 28:10–22) (fig. 30).[197] He sleeps at the base of the visionary ladder, along which angels ascend and descend between heaven and earth, God and Jacob. He appears again on the hillock at left where he sanctifies his pillow-stone, vowing to serve the Lord so long as God shows himself to be with him. Having given a descriptive account of the vision of Jacob, Van Barrefelt classifies it as a *documentum*—instructive example—whose figurative function and essential meaning he then expounds.[198] Figuratively speaking, the rock of Jacob reifies the incorruptible essence of God eternal, upon which Jacob—also named Israel, victor, by divine mandate—rested, and which he later erected as the habitation and throne of God, the tangible form of his essential divinity. As such, the pillow-stone instructs us likewise to trust in God, finding our rest in him.[199] These are figurative meanings in two senses: the Bible makes them explicit, and they were apparent to

Jacob himself. Van Barrefelt now parses the essential image; he identifies the rock of Jacob as the living rock commemorated by Peter (1 Peter 2:4–8, an exegetical adaptation of Isaiah 28:16), who calls Christ the cornerstone and fellow Christians the building blocks of the spiritual edifice of the Church: "a living stone, rejected indeed of men, but with God elect, precious, ye also, as living stones, are built up a spiritual house….Because it is contained in scripture, 'Behold, I lay in Sion a chief cornerstone, elect, precious.'"[200] The heavenly stairway stands for this edifice, built up from affection and charity, links in the chain (or better, rungs in the ladder) connecting humankind to the essence of God; the angels climbing up and down this pathway signify the grace of inspiration that mediates between the human and divine spheres.[201] Understood in this way, the essential image can be seen to illustrate Peter's epistolary exegesis of Isaiah, amplifying its central metaphor of Christ the cornerstone.

Image 48 portrays *Moses Showing the Tablets of the Law to the Israelites* (Exodus 34:29–33) (fig. 31).[202] Moses appears twice: he receives the tablets from God atop Mount Sinai, and then, his radiant face veiled, reveals them to Aaron and the people. The people's poses and gestures, like the distance they keep, express their initial fear at the sight of Moses's shining face. As usual, Van Barrefelt opens by describing the figurative image: "In the image and figure may be seen Moses, the servant of God, speaking with [the Lord] on the mountaintop, and descending with the tablets of the ten commandments; and having drawn nigh to the Israelites, he set forth the law of justice that kills sin's unjust desires."[203] The figurative function of this exemplary image is made clear: it compels us to consider that the law was given for the slaying of those sensual passions and desires that arise from the sinful flesh. Like the Israelites, we are thereby urged to repent and emend the terrestrial life of sin.[204] But as Van Barrefelt now demonstrates, the function of this image, like that of all images and figures, is more expansive than this, for its scope is both figurative and essential. He calls this fuller function the *ministerium imaginum* (ministry of images). As the Israelites embraced servitude under the law of Moses, so we continue to observe the commandments, endeavoring to kill the sins we harbor; but having effected the death of sin, we must look past the figurative image of the law,

discerning the essential image of Christ, whose law vivifies the spirit even as it kills the flesh.[205] The ministry of Moses, the prophets, and Christ himself points finally to this new law that renews the salutary life and leads ultimately to salvation. Van Barrefelt equates servitude to the Mosaic law (*hoc legale servitium*) with the viewer's servitude to the figurative image (*imaginarium servitium*); if one fails to see through the law of Moses to the law of Christ, moving from the figurative to the essential image, then one's engagement with the ministry of images will prove entirely futile and fruitless. And so, we are encouraged to view the image of Moses promulgating the ten commandments, first as the figurative image of ourselves receiving the carnal ministry of the law that kills the sins of the flesh (*secundum carnem ministerium*), and then as the essential image of ourselves receiving the spiritual ministry of the law that restores the soul in Christ (*legem Christi, quae vivificat in Spiritu*).

Image 54 depicts *King Josiah Being Shown the Book of the Law* (2 Kings 22:8–11) (fig. 32).[206] The king's secretary Shaphan reads from the book, while the high priest Hilkiah, standing just behind the lectern, addresses the king. Josiah rends his garments, having learned that he and his people have failed to keep the law. After describing the scene, Van Barrefelt reinterprets its every detail, construing King Josiah as the Essence of God (*Deus essentialis*), the book of the law as essential justice (*essentialem iustitiam*), the temple of Jerusalem as the temple of the heart (*in templo cordis*), Josiah's desire to restore the law as our desire to be reborn from the essential Godhead (*cupiemus nasci ex essentiali Deitate*), and external observance of the letter of the law as the heart's internal observance of the generative law of God (*in penetrali pectoris huius…liber legis divinae generationis iterum inveniatur*).[207] Like and yet unlike King Josiah, we must strive to apprehend the essence of God, in order that he may preside over our souls, revealing in our innermost hearts the essence of divine justice, that our terrestrial hearts, fixated on the book of the law, have lost. Roused by this epiphany (*eaque ostensione*), we shall yearn to be reborn from the essential Godhead, our desire hastening our rebirth.[208] With this end in view, all humankind should endeavor daily to find and read within the temple of the heart the divinely generative book of the law.[209] Van Barrefelt's

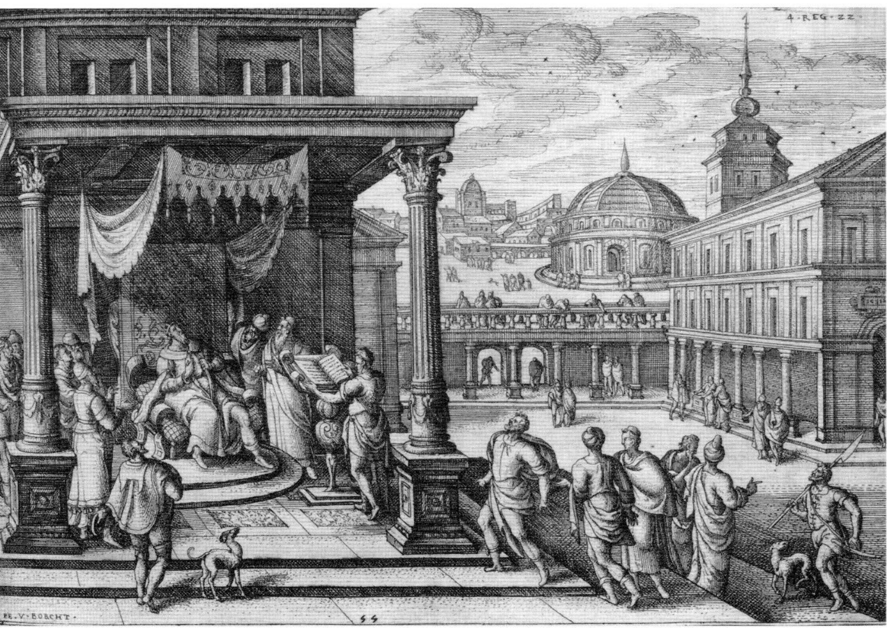

Fig. 32

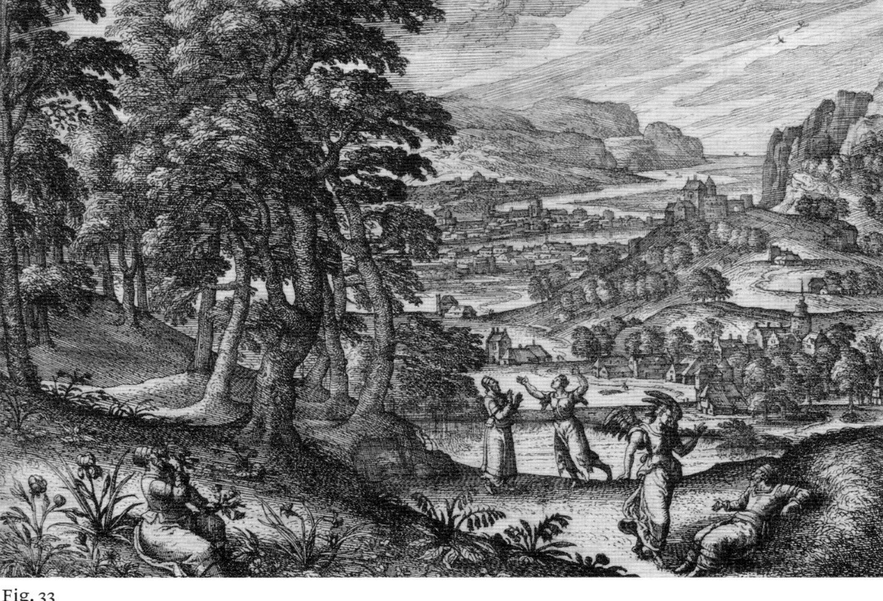

Fig. 33

reflexive commentary insists that the king's act of reading be re-read as the essential image of this very act of re-reading, that discovers everywhere in scripture, even 2 Kings 22, the renewing spirit of God.

Finally, image 55 represents the rarely illustrated scene of *The Prophet Ezra Eating the Flowers of the Field, Seeing the Vision of the Mourning Woman, and Learning from the Angel Uriel the Vision's Meaning* (4 Esdras 9:24–47, 10:1–24, 29–59) (fig. 33).[210] As instructed by the angel of the Lord, Ezra repairs to the flowery meadow (at left), beholds the mother who has lost a son (at center), and learns that the woman personifies Sion, her son Jerusalem (at right); both have fallen but shall be restored in the fulness of time. The angel further states that this vision of the edifice God purposes to build could be revealed only in a solitary place, pristine and devoid of human habitation. According to Van Barrefelt, the figurative image shows the prophet going into the uninhabited place where God wishes to speak with him.[211] The essential image exemplifies a psychological truth: we shall all be parted from our imaginary desires, when, at the end of time, all thought and sense are transformed in Christ, whose essence contains no variableness of perception or cognition.[212] In that time and place, the Lord will converse with the soul, making it sure of the divine will, as Matthew 6:6 testifies: "But when you pray, go into your room and shut the door."[213] So this image from Esdras admonishes us to depart from human things and instead advance toward the essence of God, in whom our hearts, made party to divine

mysteries, are renewed in the spiritual life. This injunction concerns the necessity of contemplative prayer; it is predicated on an exegetical translation of 4 Esdras 9–10 into Matthew 6:6, that foresees in the figurative image of the prophet Ezra eating flowers, the essential image of the human heart united mystically with the divine presence. In this act of reading as viewing, exegesis is the pivotal instrument that transforms the image from descriptive *figura* into meaningful *essentia*.

Worship

The rubric "worship" refers to the full spectrum of religious devotion, public and private, encompassing liturgical as well as meditative prayer. Whereas liturgical images generally illustrate the sacraments, such as the Eucharist and the ritual of the mass that embeds it, meditative images often provide visual templates, such as episodes from the Passion of Christ, to be imprinted internally, as part of the penitential process of self-reformation, known as the *imitatio Christi* (imitation of Christ), that aims to conform the soul to the image of its Savior. The *Passio Domini nostri Iesu Christi, sive scopus meditationis Christianae* (*Passion of Our Lord Jesus Christ, or the Goal of Christian Meditation*) of 1523, can serve to exemplify the form and function of the scriptural prints illustrating meditative treatises (figs. 34–35). Commissioned by the pious merchant and literary enthusiast Pompeius Occo, the *Passio* consists of sixty-four woodcuts designed by Jacob Corneliszoon van

Fig. 32
Pieter van der Borcht, *King Josiah Being Shown the Book of the Law*, ca. 1582–85, etching, no. 55 in Hendrik Jansen van Barrefelt [Hiël], *Imagines et figurae bibliorum; Images et figures de la Bible; Beelden ende figuren wt den Bybel* (Leiden: Franciscus Raphelengius, 1592), oblong quarto. Plantin-Moretus Museum, Antwerp. Photo: Peter Maes.

Fig. 33
Pieter van der Borcht, *The Prophet Ezra Eating the Flowers of the Field, Seeing the Vision of the Mourning Woman, and Learning from the Angel Uriel the Vision's Meaning*, ca. 1582–85, etching, no. 56 in Hendrik Jansen van Barrefelt [Hiël], *Imagines et figurae bibliorum; Images et figures de la Bible; Beelden ende figuren wt den Bybel* (Leiden: Franciscus Raphelengius, 1592), oblong quarto. Plantin-Moretus Museum, Antwerp. Photo: Peter Maes.

Oostsanen, mainly portraying scenes from the life of Christ, printed opposite texts by various Christian poets, both ancient and modern, including Prudentius, Proba Falconia, Jacobus Montanus Spirensis, and Alardus Amstelredamus, the book's chief editor.[214] The publisher Doen Pieterszoon of Amsterdam entrusted Alardus with the task of selecting poems for the prints, and in turn, the scholar-priest Alardus collaborated with Theodoricus Syrenius, a fellow Christian humanist.[215] Addressed to Syrenius, Alardus's preface outlines what we may call his meditative poetics. He opens with a commercial simile: it might seem inequitable to lend Theodoricus the Christian poems Alardus has amassed without charging him interest; but knowing that the clergyman is too poor to repay the debt, he rests content by transferring some of his editorial obligations to Theodoricus, whom he asks to edit these poems annotated by Alardus, suitably matching the selected texts to the available images.[216] Should Theodoricus wish to find better poems, let them be apposite, pious, and profound, in order that they who thirst after salutary poesy may come to desire these Christian sirens more than the Homeric ones.[217] (Alardus puns on the virtual homophones Syrenus and *Sirenes*.) If, like Odysseus and his men, they find themselves drawn to the sirenic rocks, let it be love of Christian learning, not sweetness of the poet's voice, or his song's novelty and variety that seduces them. Or rather, they should wish to hear with holy ears these Muses' songs, even as they stand transfixed by the dulcet tones, their desirous hearts wounded, so that crossing over to the Father's shores (namely, at their deaths), they may be joyful and more knowing (of God and themselves).[218]

Alardus now affirms the Christian nature of these poems, assembled from multiple sources and attached to images, as if they were a "patchwork duly stitched together" from the interwoven "threads of which the reader may fashion a most beautiful garment."[219] By this he means that the reader-viewer should fit to himself the fabric of Christ's life, broadcast in words and images, and conversely, should conform his body and soul to Christ. Whosoever reads these poems shall declare with Saint Paul, that he now knows nothing but the presence of Jesus Christ and his crucifixion, meditation on which has accomplished even the most difficult tasks.[220] For nothing is so hard to attain, that our spirit may not accomplish it by meditating on our desire to be with Christ Jesus

(*quod non efficiat si hoc sibi sentiat animus noster, quod fuit in Christo Iesu ut magnopere velit*).[221] Our tribulations having united us with him, we shall discover how quickly our bodies are restored from such exertions; and our souls shall bring forth great deeds, having harvested the fruits of this poetic orchard densely planted with mature trees.[222] Amongst the episodes from Christ's infancy, ministry, Passion, and Resurrection, the poetic texts and images of his Passion will prove especially efficacious; having been gathered up, they will impress themselves on our tender hearts, like a bundle of most bitter myrrh, whose pungency attracts, allures, and inflames the spirit of smell, making it all the more sensitive. Absorbed in this way, the life of Christ will fill the "bifold valley of the heart," "abiding there," making it "pliant and [spiritually] fruitful (*molle intra pectus bifidam quod ducit in ubera vallem, coniectus commoretur*)."[223] Alardus is alluding to the meditative tradition that compares the life of Christ to a fragrant garden planted in the soul, whose scents compel us to breathe in the intense sweetness of Jesus, especially manifest in the Passion.[224] He closes by comparing himself and his co-editor Syrenus to bees flying amongst aromatic fields of thyme in mountaintop valleys and pastures, whence they furnish honey from the springtime flowers; or again, they are like indefatigable ants bearing seeds gleaned during their long and frequent marches.[225] Food is a metaphor for the nourishing and delicious sustenance to be garnered from this meditative source. And so, these poems excerpted from various sources and harmonized in their proper places into a complete life of Christ, have been united (and joined to the images) like elms linked by tender vines, like the lotus and its watery element, like the myrtle and the riverbank, like the spider's finely woven web, like the silkworm's thread.[226] So too, Alardus implies, these pregnant moments from the life of Christ must be entwined seamlessly with our souls, so that we become inextricably bound to Christ. Adamus Verdunius Hagensis asseverates in a closing addendum, that these poets, most perfect in every genre, strongly defend the faith against all impiety, that of pagans and heretics especially, enriching it by means of excellent literary monuments. After all, Saint Paul himself did not disdain to adduce poetry as a scriptural witness (Acts 18:28), nor feared to enlist the poet Epimenides as a prophet (Acts 17:28 and Titus 1:12).[227] (The reference is to the *Cretica* of Epimenides, that proclaims the eternity of

Godhead, cited by Paul without attribution.)

The two images of the *Last Supper* and their poems demonstrate how this poetics works in practice (figs. 34–35). The first scene shows Jesus officiating at the Passover meal; holding the prescribed staves, the apostles stand around the dining table, the paschal lamb clearly visible at the center (fig. 34). The two foreground figures flanking the table raise pieces of unleavened bread to their mouths. Alardus's long poem, entitled *Ritus edendi paschalis agni* ("Rite of Eating the Paschal Lamb") retails in great detail the paschal ritual and the events it commemorates.[228] He opens by focusing on the time of the year and the day when the Passover was first celebrated —the tenth day of the first month of the year, at first dusk, "when birds fleet of wing return to their nests."[229] Closely following Exodus 12:1–27, 43–49, he then describes how this day of rest must be kept, the paschal lamb chosen, the paschal meal eaten (with unleavened bread, with wild lettuce and woodland herbs, with loins girt, hands clasping long staves, and feet shod [the one detail Jacob Corneliszoon fails to include]), who may attend (not Jews only, but also sojourners, hired servants, and resident foreigners, so long as they are circumcised), how many (as many households as are sufficient to consume the lamb and its inwards), and what the newly established rite represents (the unfermented flour carried during the Exodus, the daubing of doorposts with the blood of the lamb, and the passing over of the angel sent by God to slay every firstborn man and animal, from the son of the great Pharaoh in his fortress to that of the bondswoman destitute and imprisoned).[230] The second scene complements the first (fig. 35): based on Matthew 26, Mark 14, Luke 22, and John 13, it shows Christ making a combined gesture of blessing and instruction; he and the apostles sit, rather than stand, and ritual implements such as the staves are absent, though the presence of the paschal lamb indicates that this is a continuation of the previous scene. John lies upon the breast of Jesus, as detailed in John 13:23; clutching the money-bag, Judas sits in the foreground, farthest from Jesus. Although Christ's raised right hand expresses benediction, thereby evoking the prayerful institution of the Eucharist in the synoptic Gospels, it also signifies that he is teaching, and as such, illustrates the long disquisition in John 14–16. The poem combines verses from the fourth books of Iuvencus the Presbyter's *Evangelical History* and Sedulius's *Miracles of*

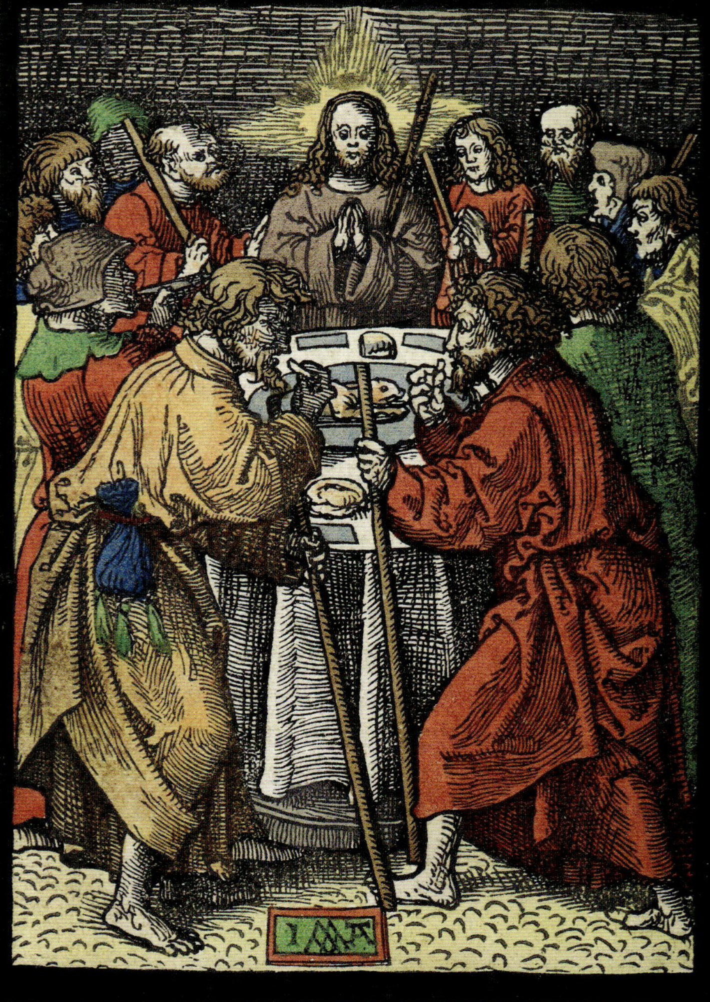

Fig. 34

God. Like the previous poem, it begins by fixing the time of day (early evening when the twelve apostles were reclining at table), which is now only specified, not prescribed.[231] The poets then launch into a paraphrase from the four Gospels, describing how Christ prophesied his impending death and imminent betrayal and avowing that the human race will suffer but a while for its sins, whereas the miserable Judas will be punished forever.[232] However, unlike the *Ritus edendi*, this poem focuses not on the specific punishments sent by God, but on the sinner's experience of sin and on the mercy of Christ. Judas is characterized as "greatly weighed down by his knowing heart," and Jesus, when asked by Judas whether the suspicion touches him, refrains from all accusation, merely answering, "I perceive that you say so" (Matthew 26:25).[233] Shifting gear at mid-verse, the poem turns from the themes of human sin and divine mercy, and instead distills what Jesus taught about the Eucharist: "He taught the disciples that he was conveying his sacred body. 'Receive this,' he says, 'in memory of me.' After this, the Lord took a chalice full of wine, blessed it with words of thanks, and administered it, teaching that he was distributing his blood. And he says, 'This blood shall remit the sins of the people; drink this my blood.' These are the covenants of peace."[234] The closing line is a compressed paraphrase of John 14:27: "Peace I leave with you; my peace I give to you; not as the world gives do I give to you. Let not your hearts be troubled, neither let them be afraid." The reference to the "covenants of peace" (*foedera pacis*) explicitly distinguishes the subject of this poem from that of the *Ritus edendi*, which stipulates the newly prescribed rite of Passover, the elaborate rules of which must be scrupulously observed under the covenant of the law (*ecce novo vetus hoc celebrabitis ordine pascha*). The rituals recalling and assuaging the wrath of God become the ritual reconciling men and God. The complementary images, similarly composed yet different in detail, depict in sequence how the Passover celebration becomes the Christian Mass. Together with the poems, they urge us to meditate on the fundamental distinction between the Jewish and Christian sacraments, the first a shield against divine vengeance, the second a conduit of divine grace.

The greatest meditative treatise of the sixteenth century is arguably Benito Arias Montano's *Humanae salutis monumenta*

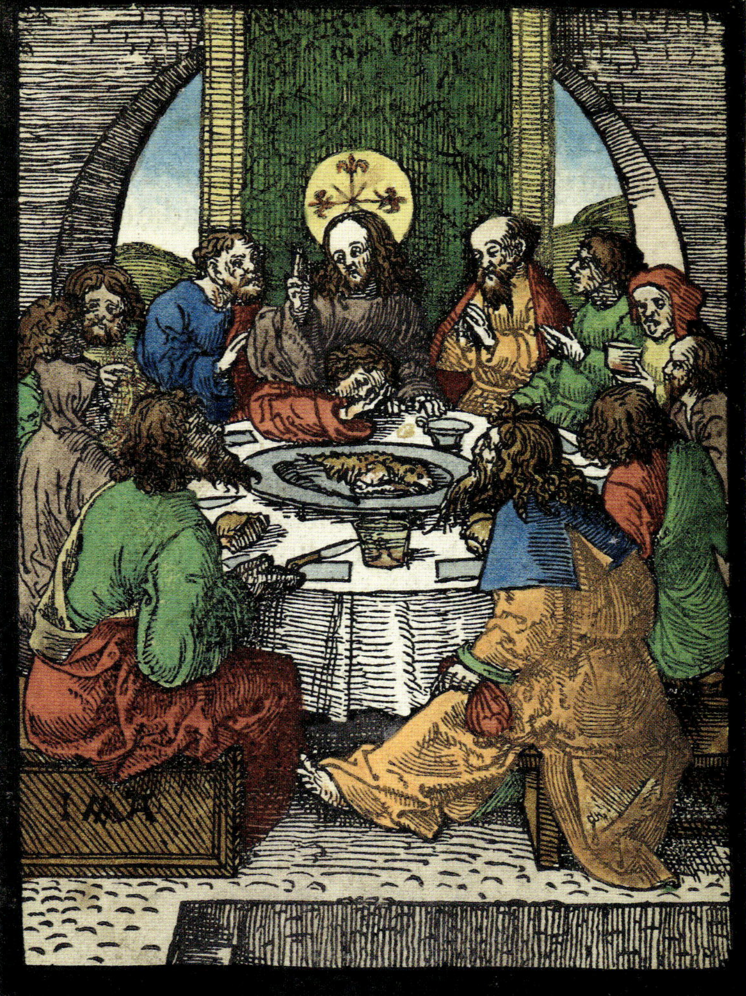

Fig. 35

(*Monuments of Human Salvation*), the first scriptural emblem book published in the Low Countries (and one of the first ever), the first to combine engraved illustration with letterpress, and the first to integrate the overall content of a picture Bible (the history of human salvation) with the text-image format of an emblem (consisting of an *imago, lemma,* and *subscriptio,* that is, a mutually referential picture, caption, and commentary) (figs. 36–43).[235] Published by Christopher Plantin in 1571, the book is composed of seventy-one engravings chronicling key episodes from salvation history: the sequence begins with portraits of Moses and Christ, the founders of the Old Law and the New (*Bust of Christ* and *Moses with the Ten Commandments*), continues with scenes from Pentateuch, Joshua, 2 Samuel, the prophets, the Gospels, and Acts (starting with the *Fall of Adam and Eve,* that necessitates the redemption of sin), and concludes with two paradigms of salvation conceived as the perfection of spiritual seeing (*Ananias Healing the Blindness of Saul* and the *Last Judgment,* at which God shall finally be seen face to face, *facie ad faciem*). The pictorial *monumenta* are enframed by three texts: above, a short motto in Roman capitals (*inscriptio*), followed by a distich in italics, that comments on the relation between the image and the motto; below, a dedication in small Roman capitals (*dedicatio*), that consecrates the image to some theme. Printed on the folios recto, the engravings open onto Horatian odes in various meters that further explicate their significance. Since the format of this book was so novel, and its ingenious argument so complex, Plantin composed an appendix that briefly expounds the odes, along with selected mottos, inscriptions, and dedications.

Many of Arias Montano's odes are explicitly reflexive in that they comment on the relation between corporeal and spiritual vision and construe the viewing of sacred images as a meditative instrument par excellence, that allows the votary better to discern the state of his soul, spurring him to reflect on his relation to Christ Redeemer. Written in response to the pictures, as the constant use of the titular phrase *in tabulam* ("on the image of") indicates, the language of the poems is intensely visual. The *Monumenta* thus makes us constantly aware of how and why we behold its poetic and pictorial images as we search through biblical history, striving to uncover the key mysteries of human salvation. The cogency, ingenuity, and subtlety of Arias Montano's argument are especially evident in a subset of scriptural emblems about the form, function, and meaning of the divinely sanctioned images to be found throughout the Bible. To begin, take the *monumenta* portraying Moses and Isaiah, both of whom are characterized as prophets (figs. 36–37). *Moses with the Ten Commandments* portrays him displaying the tablets of the law; his face aglow, he descends Mount Sinai, returning to the Israelite encampment visible below (fig. 36).[236] The motto identifies his showing of the tablets as the "beginning of true wisdom,"[237] while the distich hails Moses as a leader of men and benign exegete of God, who was also the first historian (namely, the author of the Pentateuch).[238] The dedication is to Moses the faithful minister of the Lord.[239] The *Ode Sapphica II* ("Sapphic Ode II") describes his relation to the law in visual terms: he is the "brightly shining scion of the house of Levi," the "proper witness to the renewed promise of salvation," whose command over "true portents" constrained the Egyptian sorcerers to cease "dissimulating counterfeit images."[240] Having returned to his people, he was "soon recognized as the messenger of the heavenly Father" and the "minister and guide to his afflicted race."[241] By his fearless example, "he showed how dangers might be overcome"; by his exposition of the "laws fearful to kings and peoples, yet pleasing to the divine will" he shines "with stunning nobility."[242] In his commentary, Plantin underscores the theme of vision; he points out first of all that the motto—*Verae sapientiae rudimenta*—alludes to 1 Corinthians 1:24, which refers to Christ as the Wisdom of God, but also to Galatians 3:24, which applies the same title to the Old Law.[243] On this basis, Moses, minister of the law, is called the "preceptor of Christ," who leads humankind toward the Wisdom of God. This is why the ode states that Moses, having "risen by the will of God" and "ornamented at every age by evidence of greatness," was "at length made manifest as liberator" and "constituted as supreme legislator."[244] The closing phrase— *obstupendo clarus honore*—distills and collates Numbers 12:8, Exodus 34:29, and 2 Corinthians 3:7, passages that refer to Moses's privilege of beholding God and to the splendor of his face made luminous by the presence of divinity.[245] His vision of God and his transformed visage prefigure the dispensation of the Spirit and its greater brightness, that is beheld under the new dispensation of Christ, according to 2 Corinthians 3:7–8: "Now if the dispensation

Fig. 36
Abraham de Bruyn after Pieter van der Borcht, *Moses with the Ten Commandments,* ca. 1570–71, engraving, no. 2 in Benito Arias Montano, *Humanae salutis monumenta B. Ariae Montani studio constructa et decantata* (Antwerp: Christopher Plantin, 1571), octavo. [Ornamental frame engraved by Pieter Huys.] Katholieke Universiteit Leuven, Maurits Sabbebibliotheek.

Fig. 37
Jan Wierix after Pieter van der Borcht, *The Prophet Isaiah,* ca. 1570–71, engraving, no. 26 in Benito Arias Montano, *Humanae salutis monumenta B. Ariae Montani studio constructa et decantata* (Antwerp: Christopher Plantin, 1571), octavo. [Ornamental frame engraved by Pieter Huys.] Katholieke Universiteit Leuven, Maurits Sabbebibliotheek.

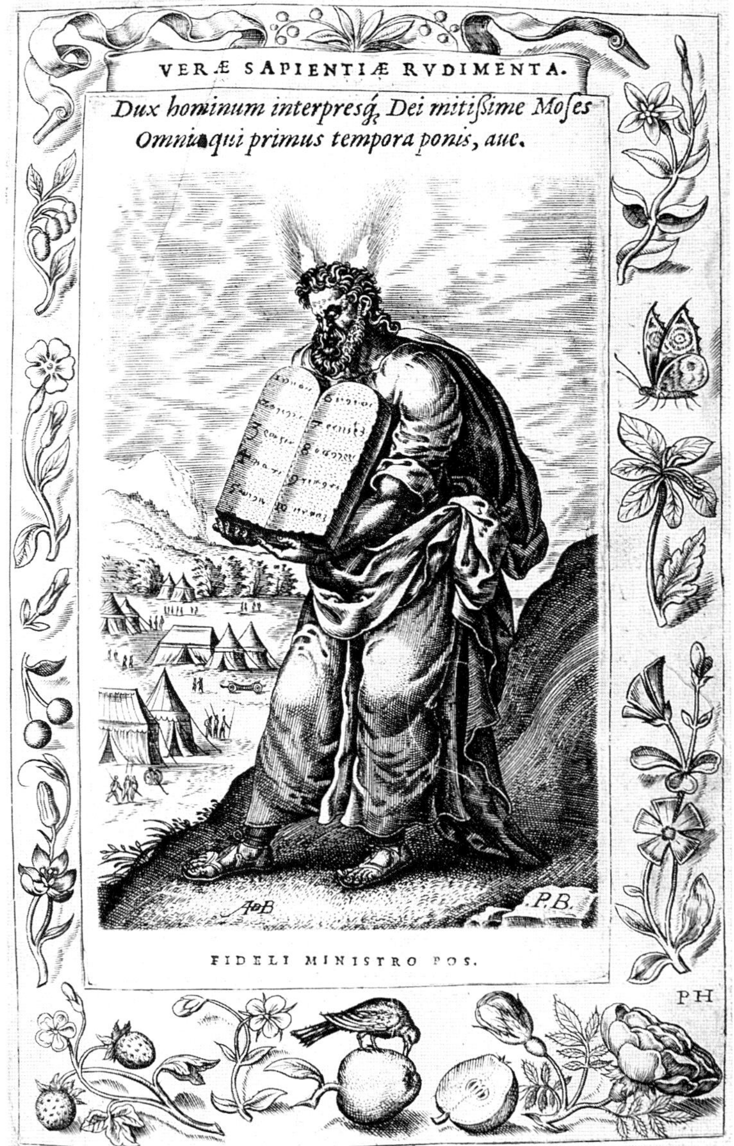

VERÆ SAPIENTIÆ RVDIMENTA.
Dux hominum interpresq́, Dei mitißime Moses
Omniaqui primus tempora ponis, auc.
FIDELI MINISTRO POS.
PH

Fig. 36

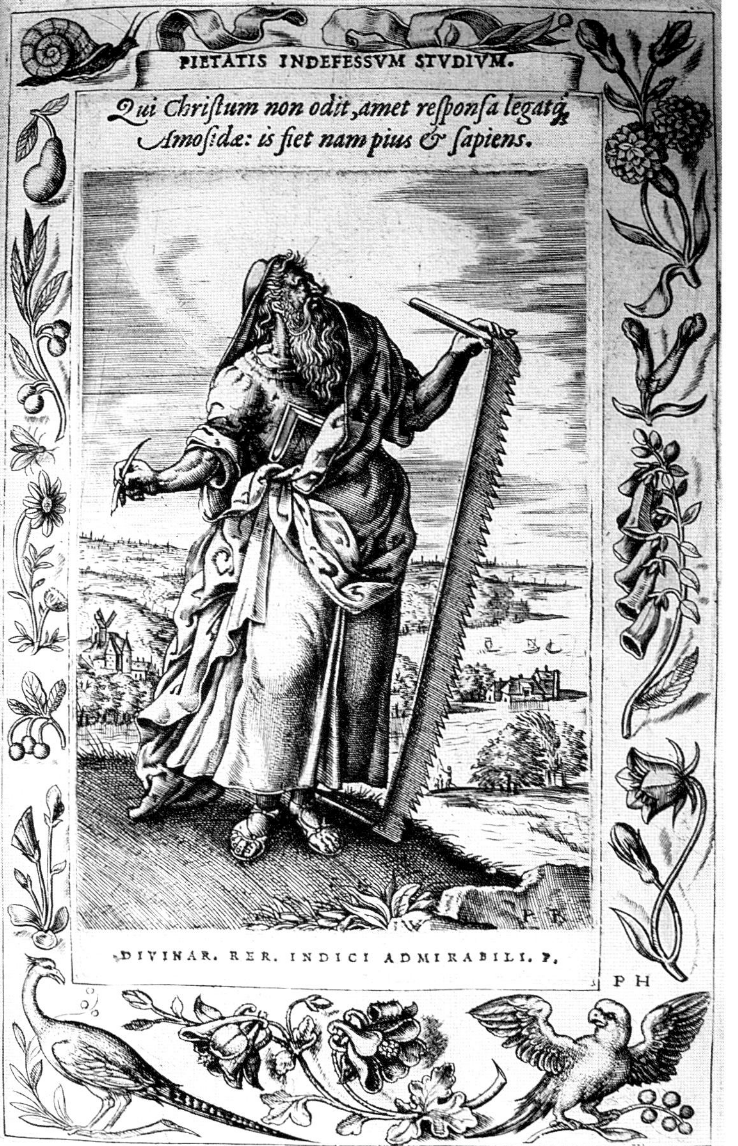

PIETATIS INDEFESSVM STVDIVM.
Qui Christum non odit, amet responsa legatq́,
Amosidæ: is fiet nam pius & sapiens.
DIVINAR. RER. INDICI ADMIRABILI. P.
PH

Fig. 37

of death, carved in letters of stone (namely, the Mosaic law), came with such splendor that the Israelites could not look at Moses's face because of its brightness, fading as this was, will not the dispensation of the Spirit be attended with greater splendor?" Paul's assertion derives from the passages in Numbers and Exodus, that extol Moses's unmediated access to the word and vision of God. Numbers 12:8 declares solemnly that Moses saw the image of God: "with him will I speak mouth to mouth, even manifestly, and not in dark speeches; and the form of the Lord shall he behold." Exodus 34:29 asseverates that "when Moses came down from Mount Sinai, with the two tables of the testimony in his hand…[he] wist not that the skin of his face shone by reason of his speaking with God."

The *Prophet Isaiah* portrays him pen in hand, holding the saw with which he was martyred, his book of prophecy tucked into his mantle (fig. 37).[246] He gazes up toward the radiant source of divine inspiration. The motto commemorates his "indefatigably zealous devotion," the distich, his prophecies that make Christian readers both pious and wise, and the dedication, his power of disclosing divine things.[247] Based on the so-called "autobiography" in Isaiah 6–8, supplemented by 2 Kings 18–20, the *Ode dicolos tetrastropohos XXVI* ("Ode in Dicolos Tetrastrophos XXVI") likens the prophet to a beholder of divinely fashioned images, which his prophecies then eloquently disclose: "Knowing the limits of times past, as well as his own future, he saw all things depicted in the house of heaven, as if he were a spectator. Has any prophet been so keen to discern whatsoe'er the great world holds, even from its earliest days— morals, histories, imperial cities, and all the generations of men?"[248] If he teaches souls their divine obligations, refreshes wearied minds, and lifts the mortifying bonds of enforced labor, he does so by means of ingenious and eloquent prophecies unequaled in beauty, force, and richness of sense.[249] These are visual oracles: "By your report, the king sees lifetimes surely revealed, indeed prolonged, when the sun, like an eyewitness, [is seen to] traverse the day already traversed in prophecy."[250] Plantin interprets the motto as an avowal of Isaiah's commitment to his prophetic vocation, as chronicled in 2 Kings 18–20.[251] The dedication affirms that this vocation entailed the full disclosure of Christ, the Gospel, and God's secret plan for human salvation, the crystal-clear

signification of which the ode lavishly praises.[252] Together, *Monumenta II* and *XXVI* mark two important thresholds in salvation history, when human eyes were opened spiritually, first by the unveiling of the law by the visibly radiant Moses, and then by the revelation of Christ by the inimitably perspicuous Isaiah. Let us now examine several *monumenta* that narrate key episodes in the history of humankind's visual awareness of God.

Jacob's Dream illustrates the patriarch reclining upon the pillow-stone, the architectonic stairway to heaven visible beside him (fig. 38). He appears again in the background, anointing the altar built of the stones upon which he dreamt of the Lord. The motto praises the "humane divinity" of God; the distich observes that God would not have deigned to honor men by speaking to them, were he not capable of perfecting the human race; and the dedication acknowledges the "benevolence of God."[253] Entitled *In somnium Iacob* ("On the Dream of Jacob"), the *Ode dicolos distrophos VIII* ("Ode in Dicolos Distrophos VIII") asserts that the divine covenants entrusted to the Fathers, believed for generations, yet "read all the while in the form of a rough image," are now perceived by Jacob with greater clarity, "having been divulged" while his tired limbs slept, but his mind remained ever alert.[254] Jacob saw heaven standing open, its ample threshold sparkling, palpably manifest. Having there observed God whose "[holy] face governs the fiery sun, snowy winters, the furious, violent sea," he learned that the sure way leading to the innermost sanctuary of eternal heaven lies open to all; and "seeing the angels pass to and fro between heaven and earth," he realized that "commerce with God was being offered to the human race," and so he professed and adored the bountiful Lord.[255] The ode finishes with an implied disclaimer about the nature of visionary experience: since the brief compass of a poem could never enclose this "divine opus" that meanders from the highest stars, through the upper air, to the heavy earth, the poet aims merely to evoke the patriarch's expanded field of vision, that transcends the rough image of God's promised salvation upon which humankind had hitherto relied.[256] Plantin interprets the motto *Humana divinitas* as a reference to the mystery of the Church, envisioned by Jacob as the place where God shall dwell amongst men and deify them. Implicit in this motto is the heavenly vision of God promised in 1 John 3:2: "Beloved, we are God's children now; it

Fig. 38
Pieter Huys after Pieter van der Borcht, *Jacob's Dream*, ca. 1570–71, engraving, no. 8 in Benito Arias Montano, *Humanae salutis monumenta B. Ariae Montani studio constructa et decantata* (Antwerp: Christopher Plantin, 1571), octavo. [Ornamental frame engraved by Pieter Huys.] Katholieke Universiteit Leuven, Maurits Sabbebibliotheek.

does not yet appear what we shall be, but we know that when he appears we shall be like him, for we shall see him as he is."[257] The inscription *Dei philanthropiae* signifies God's philanthropic love; expressed in the vision of Jacob and the Church it prefigures, this love dignifies the human race, elevating it in a manner that "requires to be represented" in proof of 1 John 4:10: "In this is love, not that we loved God but that he loves us."[258] The ode emphasizes that the visionary "image shown to Jacob" may be regarded as a "summa" of all the prior promises made by God; it "represents them in a special way," signifying his intention of reigning from within the human soul, as if it were his sanctuary.[259] The angelic vision also illustrates the friendship intimately binding celestial and human spirits.[260] In closing, Plantin construes the poem itself as a literary counterpart of Jacob's dream; he claims that it not only conveys but actually exemplifies — that is, allows us to experience — the truth bodied forth by the vision of the stairway connecting Jacob to heaven and to the very throne of God.[261] In other words, it projects us into the patriarch's visionary experience of his relationship with his Creator.

Moses and the Burning Bush represents the patriarch keeping Jethro's flock on Mount Horeb, where he encounters the burning bush, obeys the Lord's command to put off his shoes from hallowed ground, and learns to cast his rod as proof of his divinely sanctioned authority (fig. 39).[262] The motto designates the miraculous portent as a "specimen of divine power."[263] The distich declares that the light of grace remains constant, nourishing pious men, even amidst the world's tempests.[264] The dedication admonishes us to be mindful of divine mercy.[265] Entitled *In tabulam Mosis, rubi incendium mirati* ("On the Image of Moses Marveling at the Burning Bush"), the *Ode tricolos tetrastrophos XII* ("Ode in Tricolos Tetrastrophos XII") dwells on the nature and meaning of the portentous image that seized Moses's attention. Refined beyond measure, familiar with all the high arts of Egypt, knowledgeable of every creature on land and in the sea, capable even of numbering the starry firmament, Moses yet dared not apprehend, even less to handle, this unwonted genus of thing beyond the scope of human knowledge and invention.[266] The poet urges us to follow Moses in conceding that this sight (*speciem*) transcends our power either to grasp what we see, or even to question it; if we wish at least to admire what we cannot know, we

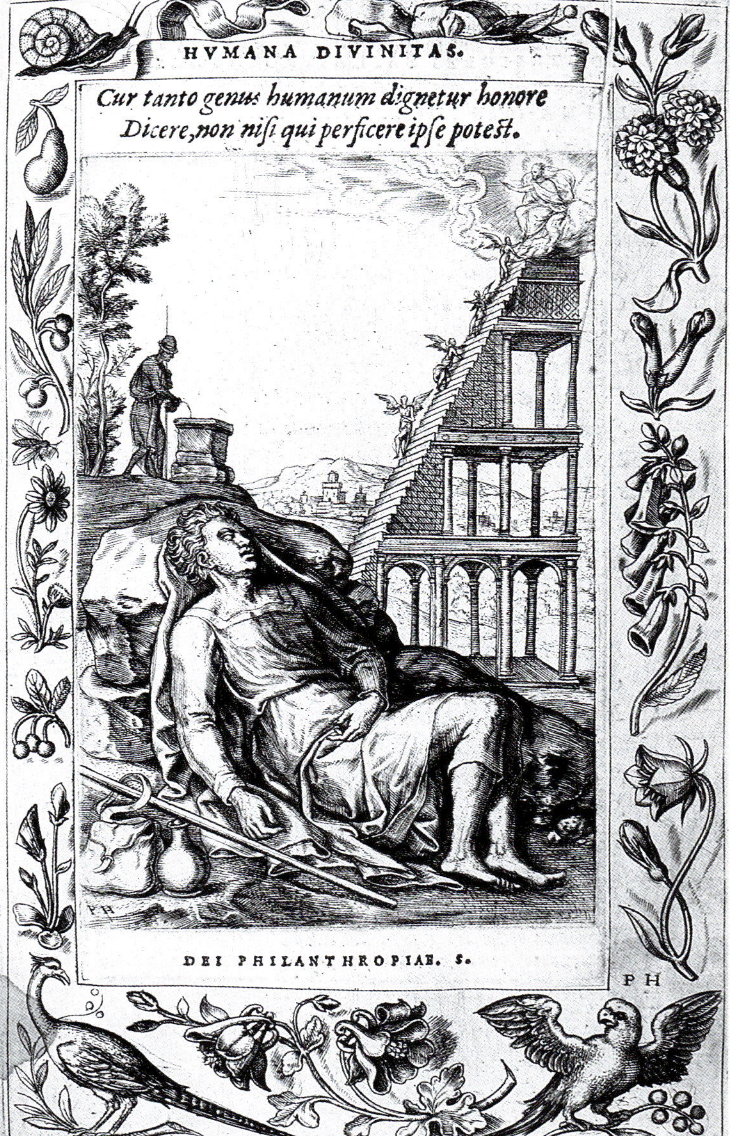

Fig. 38

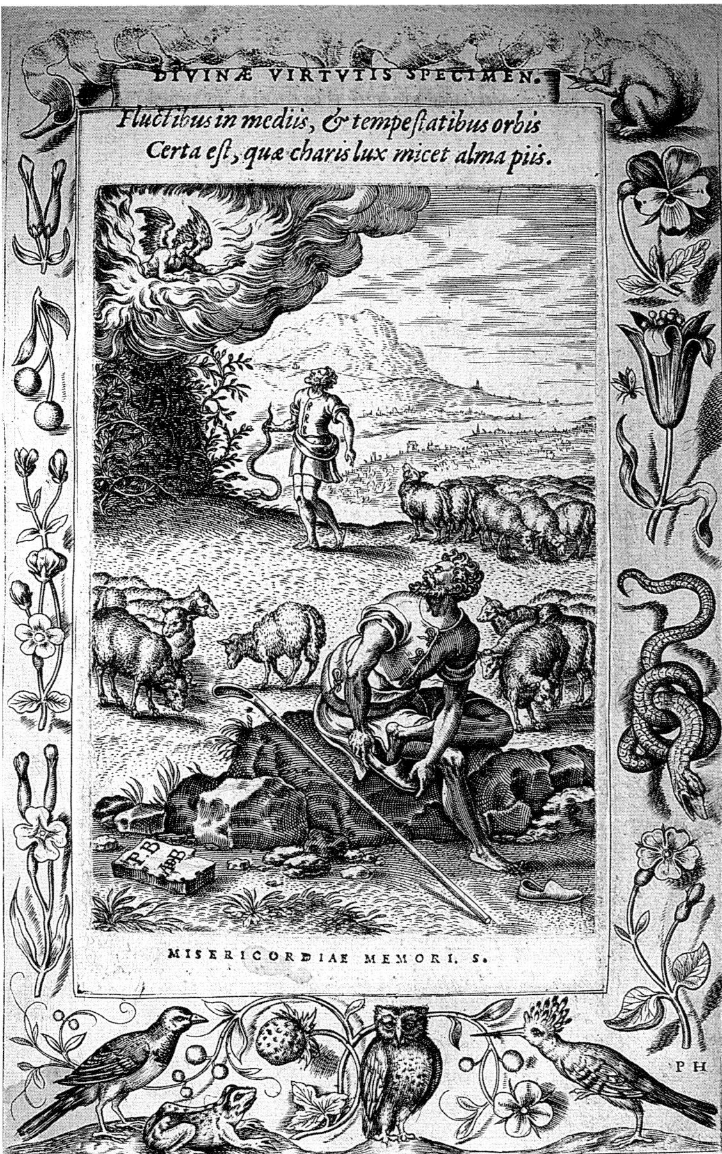

Fig. 39

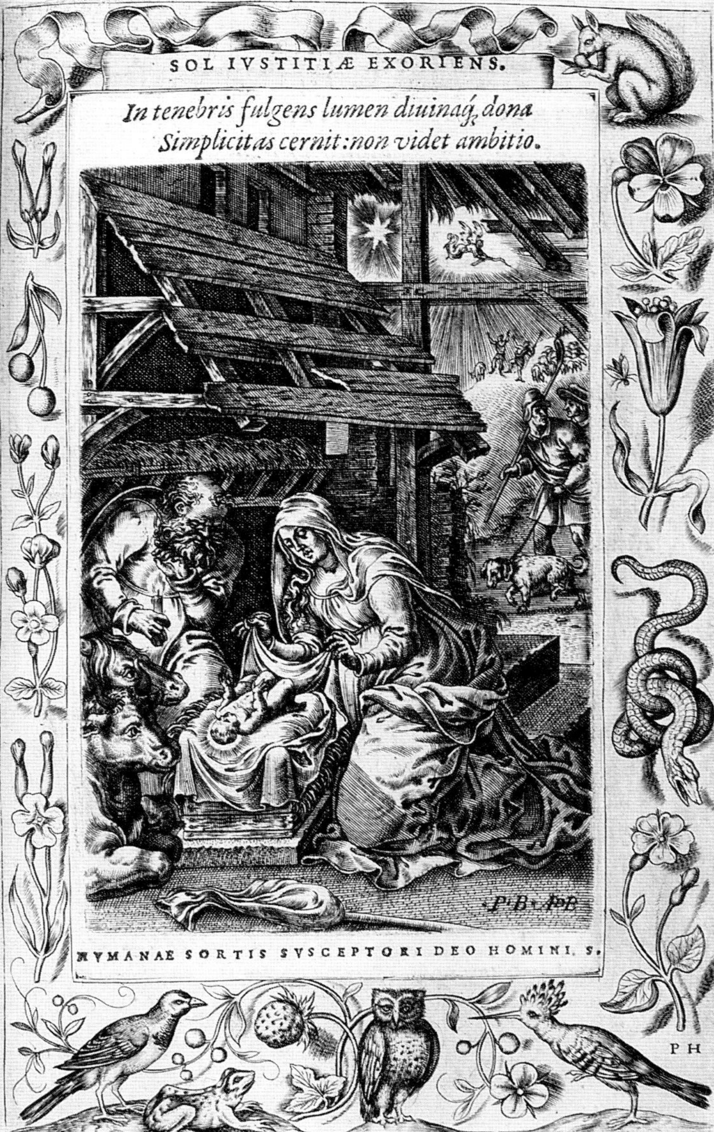

Fig. 40

Fig. 39
Abraham de Bruyn after Pieter van der Borcht, *Moses and the Burning Bush*, ca. 1570–71, engraving, no. 12 in Benito Arias Montano, *Humanae salutis monumenta B. Ariae Montani studio constructa et decantata* (Antwerp: Christopher Plantin, 1571), octavo. [Ornamental frame engraved by Pieter Huys.] Katholieke Universiteit Leuven, Maurits Sabbebibliotheek.

Fig. 40
Pieter Huys after Pieter van der Borcht, *Nativity*, ca. 1570–71, engraving, no. 33 in Benito Arias Montano, *Humanae salutis monumenta B. Ariae Montani studio constructa et decantata* (Antwerp: Christopher Plantin, 1571), octavo. [Ornamental frame engraved by Pieter Huys.] Katholieke Universiteit Leuven, Maurits Sabbebibliotheek.

must "cast off earthly cares and a prideful spirit," for this species of image is divine not human.[267] How then, the poet seems to ask, does one approach a divine image of this sort? The answer is to read it as a symptom of divine artifice: Moses and we are enjoined to approach this singular *speciem* as simple disciples eager to learn with what potency the "efficacious fire [of God] transforms the world's forms," newly reshaping their outward appearance. This is the fire that formerly dispersed "darkness, chaos, and nothingness, instilled harmony amongst the world's constituent parts, [demarcated] their limits, and [conferred their] manifold beauty."[268] Finally, more than simply exemplary, this fire is also figurative, for it functions as the image of divine love, fashioned by divine design "in the visible likeness of a flame," that "furnishes earthborn humanity with [divine] life and restorative light."[269] By turns, the ode makes us aware that "this unwonted genus of thing" is an exemplary and meaningful "sight." Read in this way, the pictorial *monumentum* can be seen to portray him contemplating his visual encounter with the miraculous flame that exemplifies the power of divine artifice and signifies the power of divine love. Plantin amplifies this poetic account of the image through which God communicated with Moses. The motto *Divinae virtutis specimen* indicates that the non-consuming fire is a *typus* (representative image, that is, an image that stands for a class of phenomena) and *specimen* (specimen, that is, exemplifying image) of divine virtue, that "animates pious and humble men by the heat of its efficient power," rendering them "holy and remote from vulgar and profane conduct."[270] Such fire has the capacity to convert whatever it touches: what was formerly inflamed (*calefactus*, that is, troubled, as if by human passion) is changed into something sacred. And yet it is seen variously by different viewers, as is evident from the fact that the proud and contumacious Egyptians experienced the fire of divine virtue differently from the Israelites.[271] This is why, Plantin explains in his comments on the ode, such images of the mysteries of salvation must be divinely expounded by teachers expert in religious doctrine. Otherwise their true significance will prove elusive, for human wisdom is contingent, and the divine plan to redeem the world is beyond the ken of men.[272] (He remarks that the presence of the fiery angel instructing Moses implies the necessity of such teachers.) These assertions amount to a justification of the *Humanae*

salutis monumenta and its emblematic apparatus.

The *Israelites Crossing the River Jordan* portrays representatives of the twelve tribes gathering memorial stones to mark their entry into Canaan, the land promised by God; bearing the ark, the Levites stand amidst the riverbed, the commemorative monument already visible just beyond them (see cat. 7a).[273] The motto, "fruit of constancy," like the dedication to "steadfast God," emphasizes that the Israelites have closely followed the word of God, who now rewards their fidelity.[274] The distich likewise reiterates this theme, which the *Ode sapphica XVII* ("Sapphic Ode XVII"), entitled *In tabulam Israëlitarum Iordanem transeuntium* ("On the Image of the Israelites Crossing the River Jordan"), adapts into an appreciation of the constant faith shown by the Israelites in their single-minded application of spiritual sight.[275] Inspired by the word of God, they have pursued the path divinely "exposed to view," keeping their eyes ever fixed on high heaven.[276] They are implicitly presented as beneficiaries of the lessons learned by Moses in his encounter with the divinely imparted *speciem*, set forth in *Monumentum XII*. Like him, they attend to what God has given them to see, a point Plantin underscores in his summary of the ode's argument that those who hasten to perform the tasks set by God may justly conceive a great hope of finding their loving faith rewarded.[277]

The nature and scope of the vision of God, conferred on those who faithfully strive to see him, alter in the *monumenta* focusing on the life of Christ (figs. 40–42). The votary's field of vision expands and brightens, as his corporeal and spiritual eyes behold episodes from the infancy, ministry, Passion, and Resurrection of Christ. The *Nativity* depicts Mary and Joseph staring intently at the newly born child, whose radiance illumines the penumbral stable (fig. 40).[278] The annunciation to the shepherds occurs in the distance, and two shepherds approach the shed, while overhead, the star of Bethlehem burns brightly. The framing texts relate what was seen at the Nativity: the "rising sun of justice," "the fulgent light and divine gifts that [virtuous] simplicity descries amidst the shadows, but [blind] ambition fails to see," "God the mortal recipient of human destiny."[279] Entitled "On the Image of the Nativity of Jesus," the poem takes the form of a lament, subtitled *Naturae humanae naenia XXXVIII* ("Lament of Human Nature XXXVIII"). Voiced by nature personified, it recounts what she witnessed with fearful consternation and joyful astonishment at the birth of Christ: the splendid babe coming forth from the virgin womb, a tender child human by choice rather than by nature, or again, born of nature and sustained by her gifts, yet surpassing her in every way.[280] The mixed emotion of the lament arises both from nature's joy at seeing herself augmented by the child's divinity, to which she is irrevocably joined, and from her sorrow at seeing him diminished by grief, toil, and death, the burdens she perforce confers on the human race.[281] Plantin emphasizes that the Nativity was marked by unwonted sights. With reference to the motto *Sol iustitiae exoriens*, he observes that the light shone into the night to signify the rising sun of salvation, soon to penetrate the world's darkness; this is the "wonderful spectacle" that the shepherds desired to behold.[282] In turn, their act of beholding is construed as a *signum* (visible sign) of the child's vocation of bringing light into the world. As the dedication *Humanae sortis susceptori Deo homini* asserts, the infant Christ, having assumed human form, bears the "image of a servant" (*formam servi*).[283] For its part, the "Lament" speaks in the voice of human nature admiring the *formam* of the newborn Christ and the *signum* of his birth.[284]

The *Adoration of the Magi* delineates the many transits of gaze binding Mary, Joseph, and the kings to each other and to Christ (fig. 41).[285] Mary stares at Jesus, who gazes at the eldest magus, whose eyes are humbly lowered; as Jesus blesses the kneeling king, he is watched by the second magus, while the youngest king and Joseph look at one another. The motto dubs Christ the "light of peoples," and the distich states that it is true wisdom to know and cherish God, whom the dedication identifies as Christ, "immortal deity and true man, king and liberator."[286] The pictorial image makes explicit the connection between knowing, cherishing, and beholding Christ, a nexus explored in the *Ode tricolos tetrastrophos XL* ("Ode in Tricolos Tetrastrophos XL"), entitled *In tabulam adorationis Magorum* ("On the Image of the Adoration of the Magi"). The ode compares the Epiphany to a panoramic vista: as the first light of day becomes visible from the summit of Mount Pisgah (whence Balaam espied the Israelites, and Moses the promised land), while dawn's purple rays remain hidden from valleys wreathed in mist, so kings hailing from Persia and Parthia first saw rising the fair splendor of Christ,

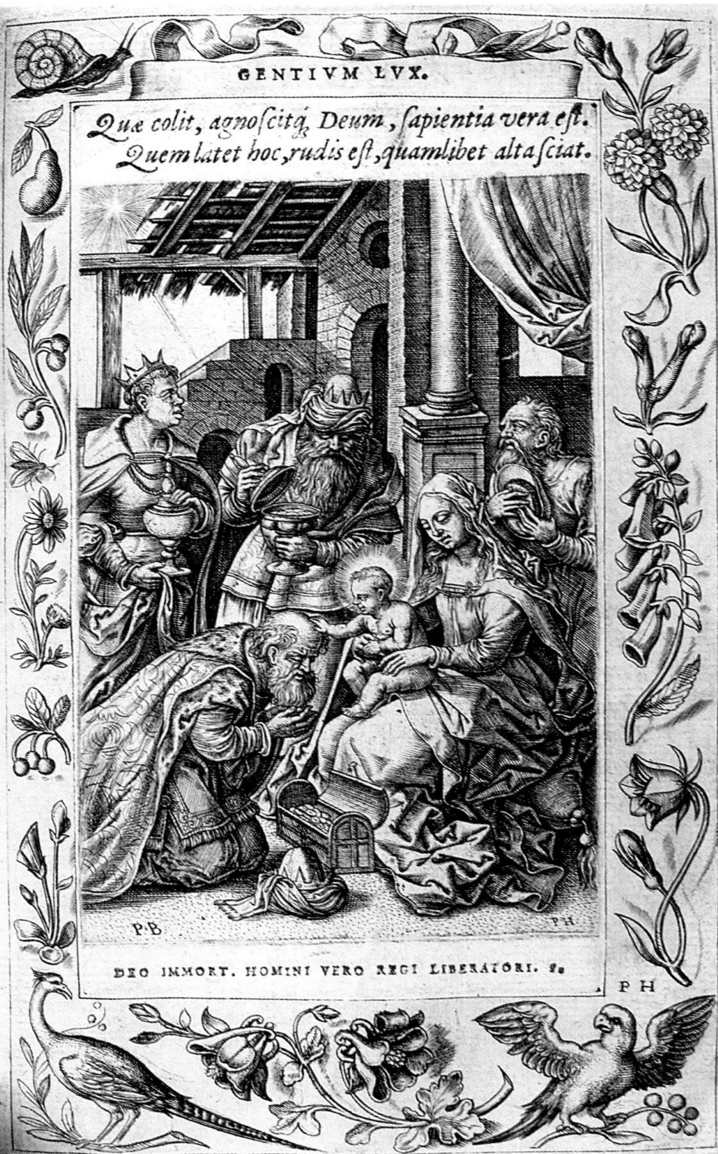

Fig. 41
Jan Wierix after Pieter van der Borcht, *Adoration of the Magi*, ca. 1570–71, engraving, no. 40 in Benito Arias Montano, *Humanae salutis monumenta B. Ariae Montani studio constructa et decantata* (Antwerp: Christopher Plantin, 1571), octavo. [Ornamental frame engraved by Pieter Huys.] Katholieke Universiteit Leuven, Maurits Sabbebibliotheek.

Fig. 41

whereas the mad tyrant (Herod) and his inconstant people, indeed all of Jerusalem, as if blind, failed to discern the advent of the Savior.[287] The bright golden light of a newly visible star first revealed his presence, its novelty representing the world's renewal.[288] And having anon found and admired Christ the king, the magi perceived that the holy face of God, greater than that of any mortal child, was being revealed to their bodily and spiritual eyes (*oculis animoque*).[289] Image and text work together to engage us in the magi's experience of Christ, whom as gentiles they first came to know through the observation of nature (the fiery star), and then through the direct revelation of his incarnate divinity and its salvific significance, a point Plantin makes lucidly in his comments on the ode.[290] In his reading of the motto—*Gentium lux* —he cites the *Nunc dimittis* (Luke 2:29–25), Simeon's prayer acknowledging Christ as "a light for revelation to the Gentiles, and for glory to thy people Israel." From his birth, Plantin notes, he shone brightly, a light demanding to be seen and known (*cognoscendus*).[291]

Two final *monumenta* explore how Christ instructs by means of images, amplifying the image of himself promulgated at the Nativity and broadcast at the Epiphany (figs. 42–43). The *Marriage Feast at Cana* portrays the moment when he converts water into wine; his gesture doubles Mary's, showing that he does her bidding (fig. 42).[292] The motto emphasizes that the miracle signifies the "renewal of nature" in Christ, while the dedication celebrates him as the "benign guardian," whose kind offices saved the faltering marriage feast.[293] The distich declares that compared to this event, everything in the world seems paltry.[294] The *Ode sapphica XLVI* ("Sapphic Ode XLVI"), entitled *In tabellam signi à Christo in Cana editi* ("On the Image of the Sign Brought Forth by Christ at Cana"), interprets the miracle as an earnest of Jesus's desire to marry our souls to himself; it is the dowry he settles upon us, the wondrous sight that transforms Cana in Galilee from a mere place into a living witness of his divinity.[295] The personified Cana stands for us: she finds herself transformed (*renovata*), no less than the water become wine; its changed state astonishes her, eliciting the desire to be conjoined to Jesus, the heavenly spouse, whose divine power she acknowledges. For she sees "fixed forms alter," and is herself altered by this spectacle (*munera*), as should we also be by seeing as

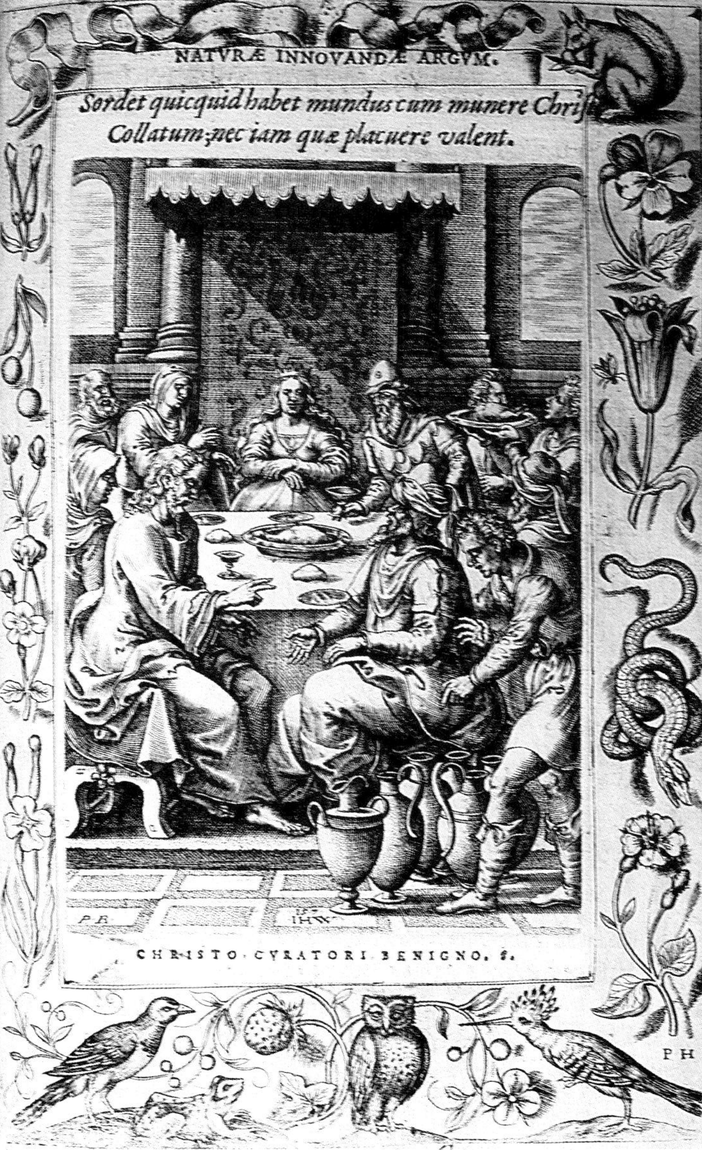

Fig. 42

Fig. 42
Jan Wierix after Pieter van der Borcht, *The Marriage Feast at Cana*, ca. 1570–71, engraving, no 46 in Benito Arias Montano, *Humanae salutis monumenta B. Ariae Montani studio constructa et decantata* (Antwerp: Christopher Plantin, 1571), octavo. [Ornamental frame engraved by Pieter Huys.] Katholieke Universiteit Leuven, Maurits Sabbebibliotheek.

does she.[296] We shall therefore emulate her in bearing witness to the divine spouse who fulfills the promise implicit in the "venerable wine of Noah" (the reference is to Genesis 9:20–23, the drunkenness of Noah, as a prefiguration of Christ's redemptive death): having drawn "flowing waters from a vitreous fountain" and turned them into (eucharistic) wine, Christ demonstratively offers the gift of salvation as a marriage-portion.[297] Plantin reiterates this complex meaning in his comments on the ode's reading of the miracle at Cana as the "first [visible] sign of the power of Christ."[298]

The *Triumphal Entry of Christ into Jerusalem* depicts him showing himself to the people as their lawful king and savior, as the motto "the setting forth of salvation,"and dedication "to the true king made manifest" affirm (fig. 43).[299] The distich warns that he must be welcomed, for otherwise, having shown himself gracious, he shall become a severe judge.[300] Entitled *In tabulam Christi regis Ierosolymae declarati* ("On the Image of Christ the King Evinced to Jerusalem"), the *Ode sapphica LI* ("Sapphic Ode LI") expounds the image of Christ revealed to the city (and to us), advising how it should be received. The conditions under which he was seen were conducive to the utmost clarity of vision. The sun had never shone more beautifully than on that day when Jerusalem beheld the "cherishable face of [her] great king," formerly veiled by prophetic song but now fully exposed to view by Christ himself.[301] The poem contrasts the candor of Christ the king, who restores the sinful world, allowing himself to be discerned by "sure signs," and the deceitfulness of the devil, who wounds the world with sin, perpetrating unspeakable acts of deception.[302] So too, the genuine honors bestowed on Christ are distinguished from the feigned praises and counterfeit honors heaped upon proud rulers, whom the flattering, ambitious, and changeable hearts of their fearful people inflate so falsely. Likewise, such blandishments are opposed to the triumphal acknowledgment of Christ as his people's high king and supreme priest.[303] In conclusion, the ode calls upon these people, amongst whom we are projected, to recognize the ritual entry as the veridical image of Christ's Messianic identity.[304] *Monumentum LI* refashions the image they first staged as instruments of the divine will, converting it into a meditative image under the sanction of Christ. Plantin makes this

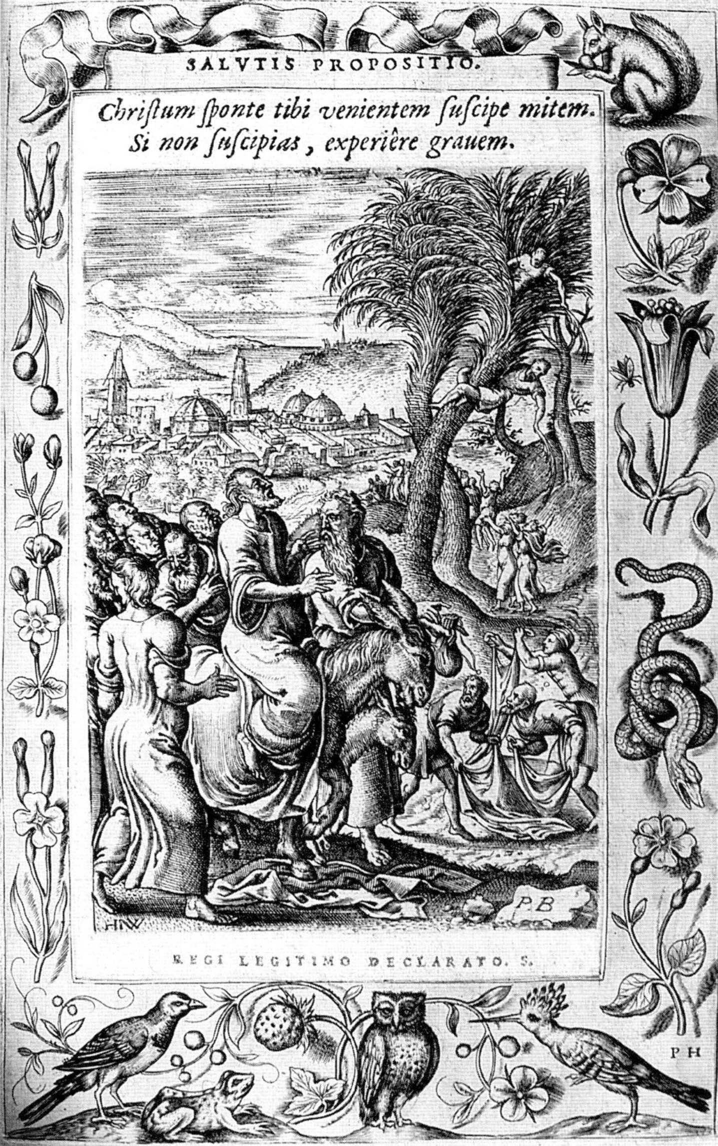

Fig. 43

case in his brief comment on the motto *Salutis propositio* (which he rephrases as *Salutis oblatio*—"offering of salvation"). Here the Son of God, having been sent into the world, "gives himself to be seen and known" as the expression of God's love for the human race.[305] His account of the dedication—*Regi legitimo declarato*—reinforces this claim: "Whom God had revealed and proclaimed by the prophets, he [now] caused to be beheld by sure signs."[306] He adds that the ode focuses on the paradoxical image presented by Jesus: showing no traces of mundane pride, yet perforce recognizable as "Christ the king, lord of future time, and priest of salvation," he enters Jerusalem in accordance with the signs foretold by the prophets. The people applaud him not from fickle affection, hope for advancement, or fear of reprisal, but because they superimpose on the prophetic images of the Messiah, their memories of the miracles they have seen Jesus perform and the doctrine they have heard him teach.[307] These mnemonic and oracular images inform the paradoxical image of Christ humbly triumphant, that anchors the meditative imagery of *Monumentum LI*. In urging us to consider the image of Christ, the monument epitomizes the theme that runs through the entire sequence we have been examining—the place of divinely mandated images within the history of human salvation recounted in the Bible.

Morality, and Politics and Polemics

The two final categories are complementary, which is why I discuss them together; they raise important issues, as the catalog entries will show, but are sufficiently transparent to warrant shorter treatment here. "Morality" refers to the ethics of private and public behavior, as measured against the example set by Christ and his chief imitators, the apostles and disciples, and for Roman Catholic viewers, the Virgin Mary, John the Baptist, and the saints. (Lutheran and Reformed viewers tended to privilege the sole example of Christ, just as *sola fides*, faith in him alone, was acknowledged to be the sole criterion of salvation.) The key term is *exemplum* (example), a rhetorical figure of speech that entails foregrounding a protagonist whose moral (or immoral) character is expressed in this person's consequential actions. *Periphrasis* is an allied rhetorical figure that describes the action's circumstances. If moralizing prints operate by means of example and periphrasis,

political and polemical prints can be said to do so as well, but with this difference (one of degree rather than kind): they focus on rulers, heads of state and prelates of the Church, whose secular or ecclesiastical policies are approved, or in the case of polemical prints, harshly judged. Such prints are always *epideictic*, another rhetorical term, that refers to the oratory of praise or blame.[308] In the sixteenth century, when various positions were staked out under the banner of religious reform (as much Catholic as Protestant), political prints were often also dogmatic, or at least religious, in argument, as is clear from the *Pietas Regia* frontispiece of the *Biblia Regia* (see cat. 2). As we saw earlier, this allegory draws parallels between Philip II and King Josiah: both were great military leaders, and both were zealous supporters of religious orthodoxy. Josiah's restoration and promulgation of the book of the law is compared to Philip's patronage of the Polyglot Bible as an instrument of Roman Catholic renewal. In his exposition of the frontispiece, Plantin avers that Philip is seen to surpass all other princes, past or present, in several respects: first of all, his cultivation of the true religion, but also his administration of justice, and equally his promotion of the liberal arts, as well as of literature, painting, sculpture, and such utilitarian arts as agriculture and navigation.[309] In this way, Philip exemplifies the ideal Christian ruler, whom Arias Montano characterizes in the general preface as a propagator of the word of God, surpassing the Kings of Israel in his piety and observance of divine law: "In order that the devil and his ministers be given no further opportunity of gravely endangering [the Christian commonwealth], God inspired Philip II, the Catholic King of Spain, that most powerful prince wholly devoted to Christian piety…to ruminate how the scriptural texts, languages, and translations, having been collated, might diligently be compiled, seeing as…the study of piety and true religion are the best, greatest, and firmest foundation of the stable state."[310] A most interesting counter-example is the Exodus map from the Dutch Reformed *Biblia* of 1589, which as we have seen illustrates the itinerary recounted in Numbers 33 (fig. 20). The rationale of Numbers is summarized as follows in the prefatory *Argumenten aller boecken des Ouden Testaments* ("Arguments of All the Books of the Old Testament"): "In this book are many things pertinent to politics and civic government, as well as to religion, and especially this: that just as priests should not repudiate the civic government, so magistrates should not repudiate what pertains to religion."[311] Distilled by the map, the Exodus enshrines this political moral that adapts the principle of *cuius regio, eius religio* (whose region, his religion), enshrined at the Peace of Augsburg in 1555. The moral adjusts this tenet, calling for the mutual recognition of secular and sacred spheres of authority.

Engraved by Jan Wierix after designs by Gerard van Groeningen, the *Story of the Maccabees* consists of eight scenes chronicling the exploits of Judas Maccabeus (figs. 44–51).[312] It was first published ca. 1574 by Gerard de Jode in Antwerp. Judas is portrayed as the exemplary ruler, who battles to defend the true faith against Greek religion and culture. Although the series exalts his orthodoxy, it refrains from explicitly equating Judas's religious zeal to that of a Roman Catholic, Lutheran, or Reformed zealot. For example, the key passages from 2 Maccabees serving as proof texts for the Roman Catholic doctrines of the resurrection of the body (7:9, 11; 14:46), of judgment, reward, and punishment after death (6:26), of purgatory and the efficacy of prayers for the dead (12:42–45), and of the intercession of the saints (15:12–16) are left unillustrated.[313] (Conversely, the fact that these passages are not invoked should not automatically be read as endorsing *in absentia* an implicitly Protestant position.) Instead, the series offers general exempla that evade a strict confessional reading, or alternatively, accommodate mutually exclusive readings.

Scene 1 illustrates *Antiochus Epiphanes Sacking the Temple of Jerusalem* (1 Maccabees 1:20–24); his soldiers slaughter the Jews and despoil their liturgical paraphernalia (fig. 44).[314] Two carry off the seven-branched candelabrum, while golden vessels and a fragment from one of Solomon's pillars of bronze are heaped beside Antiochus's steed. Shocking as this carnage and impiety appear, the inscription closely follows 1 and 2 Maccabees in ascribing them to God himself, who punishes his apostate people for having abandoned his cult and his law. Scene 2 illustrates *Mattathias Killing an Apostate Jew and the King's Officer at Modein* (1 Maccabees 2:23–26): Mattathias the father of Judas gives vent to righteous anger at the king's altar, where he kills a hellenizing Jew (shown wreathed and wearing a Roman cuirass) (fig. 45).[315] In the presence of his fellow Jews, he has already slain the king's officer

who was forcing them to worship before the royal idol. (The likeness of Mattathias's raised sword to that of the idol is fiercely ironic.) In the distance, observant Jews gather their belongings and desert the city in the company of Mattathias. The inscription paraphrases the first half of 1 Maccabees 2, identifying Mattathias as a "priest and zealous follower of the divine law who slew the king's prefect and the Jew about to offer sacrifice to pagan gods, and then fled, taking with him his sons and those God-fearing Jews that remained true [to their faith]." Scene 3 illustrates *Antiochus's Soldiers Killing the Jews Who Would not Fight on the Sabbath* (1 Maccabees 2:33–38); having sought refuge in the wilderness, they are slain in the hiding places where they chose to die blamelessly rather than profaning the Sabbath (fig. 46).[316] The inscription paraphrases the second half of 1 Maccabees 2: "Lest they violate the Sabbath, the Jacobites refrain from battle and from arms, reckoning it better to die innocently than to transgress the precepts of God." Scene 4 illustrates *Judas Maccabeus Cleansing the Temple on Mount Sion* (1 Maccabees 4:42–51); his men demolish the altar of burnt offering defiled by a pagan idol, while artisans dress whole stones for rebuilding the sanctuary (fig. 47).[317] The inscription paraphrases the third quarter of 1 Maccabees 4, declaring that Judas and his army set about the task of purifying and restoring the temple after they had defeated the army of Antiochus. Scene 5 illustrates the *Consecration of the Altar of Burnt Offerings on the Anniversary of its Profanation* (1 Maccabees 4:52–58); the high priest kneels before the distant altar, upon which burns a praise-offering of deliverance, while in the foreground the congregation falls to its knees and prays, or devoutly consults the book of the law (fig. 48).[318] This corresponds to 1 Maccabees 4:53: "they rose and offered sacrifice, as the law directs." The inscription paraphrases the fourth quarter of 1 Maccabees 4, emphasizing that the people blessed God who had prospered them, on the day and at the time when the sanctuary had formerly been desecrated. Implicit here as elsewhere in 1 and 2 Maccabees is the theme of divine mercy that succeeds divine indignation. Scene 6 illustrates *Judas Maccabeus Displaying to the People of Jerusalem the Head and Right Hand of Nicanor* (1 Maccabees 7:47–49); having defeated Nicanor, who was sent by Demetrius Seleucus to destroy Israel, Judas flaunts the head and hand with which he arrogantly

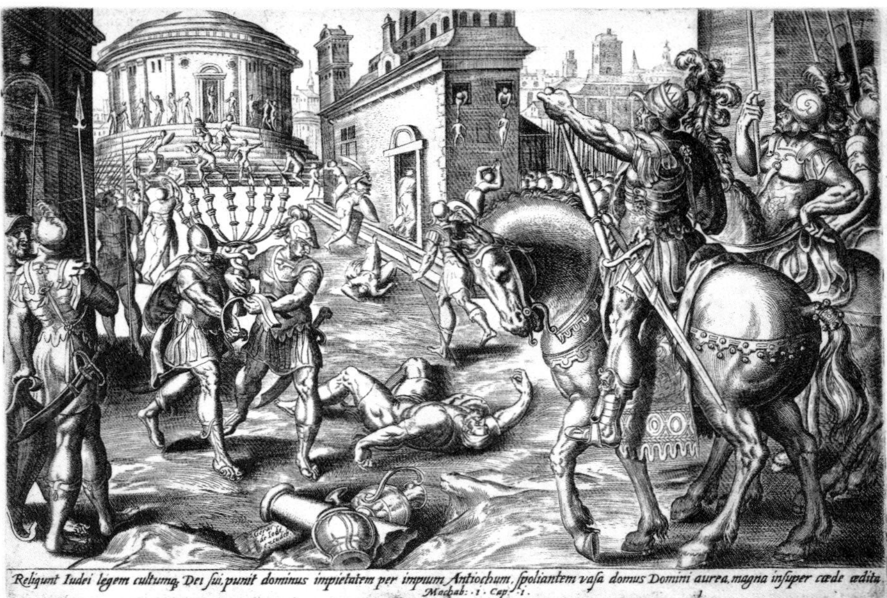

Fig. 44

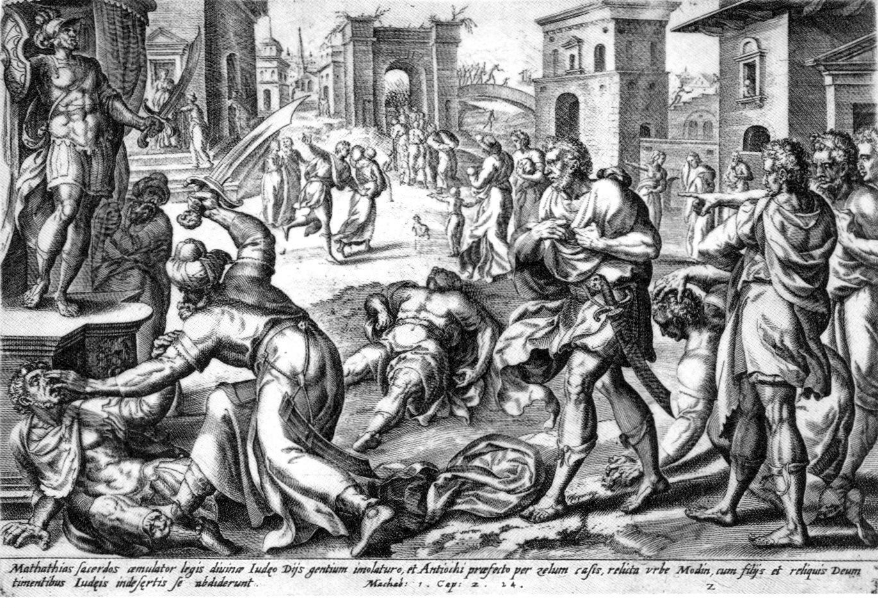

Fig. 45

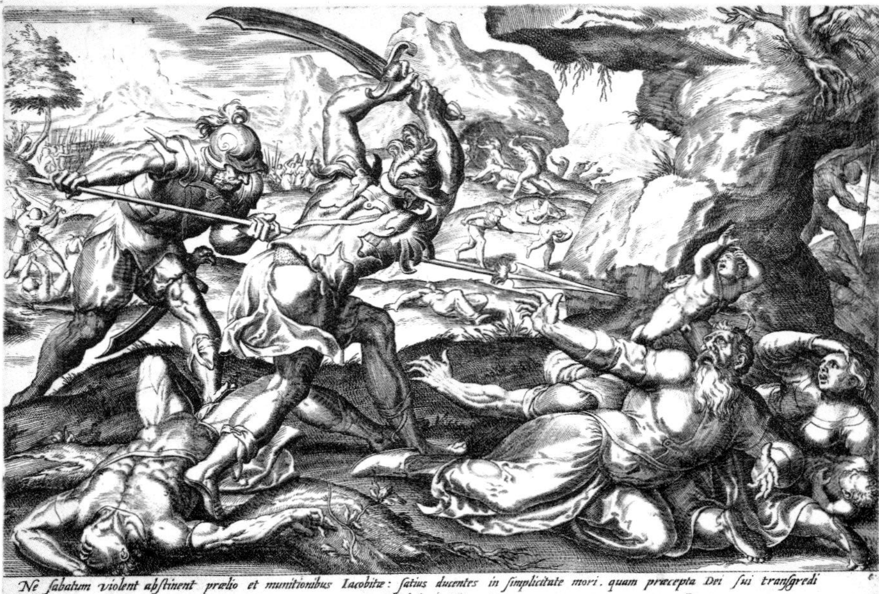

Fig. 46

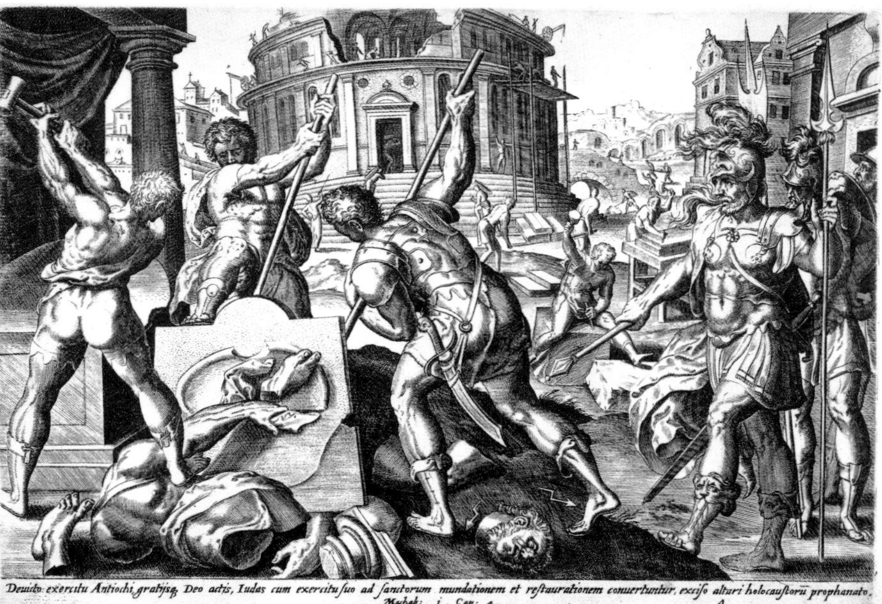

Fig. 47

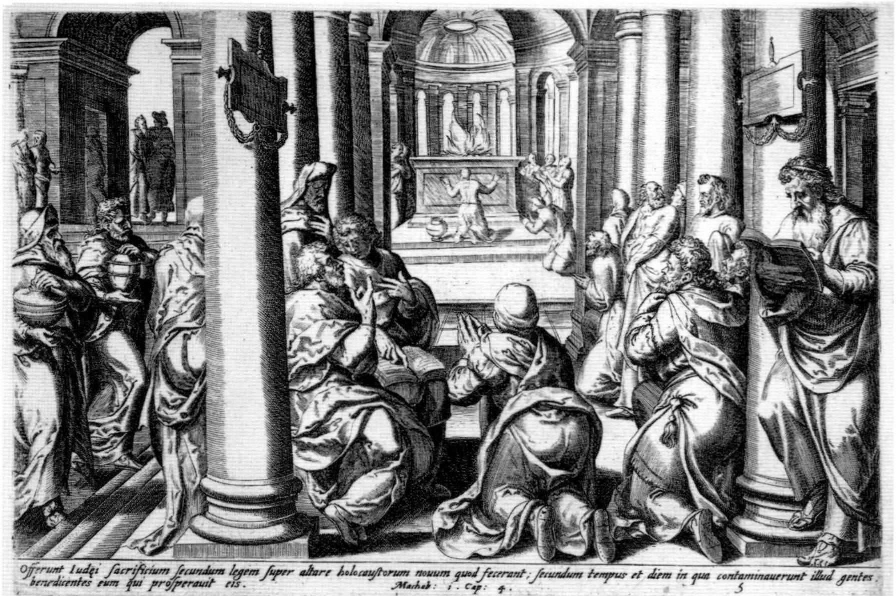

Fig. 48

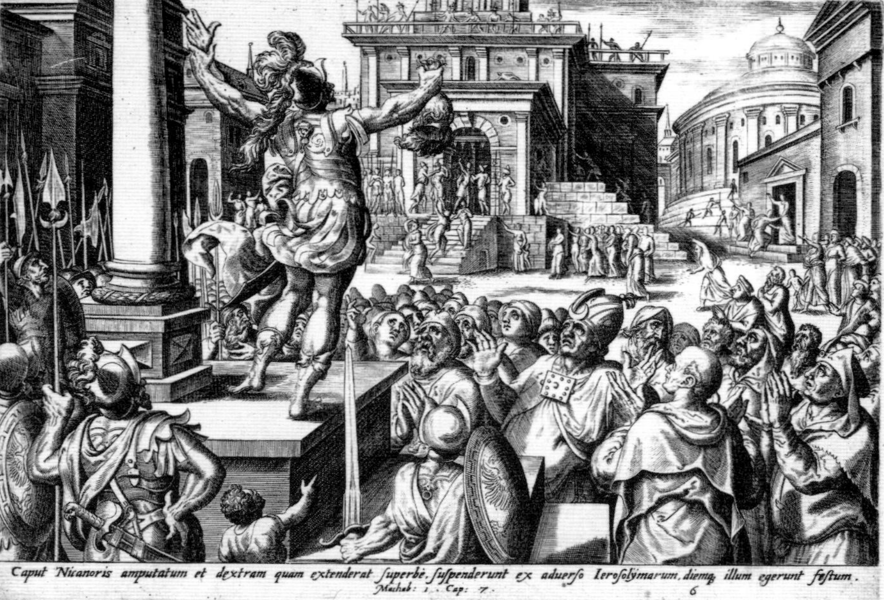

Fig. 49

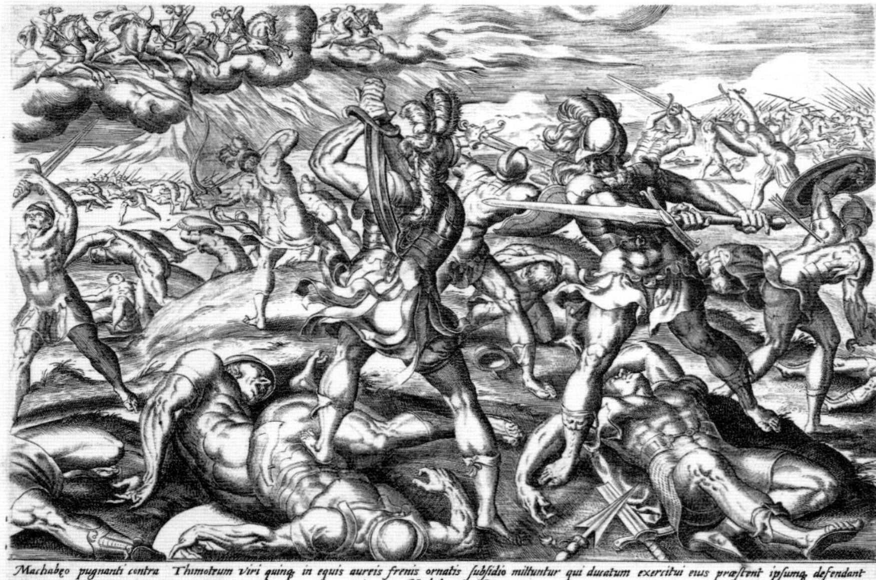

Fig. 50

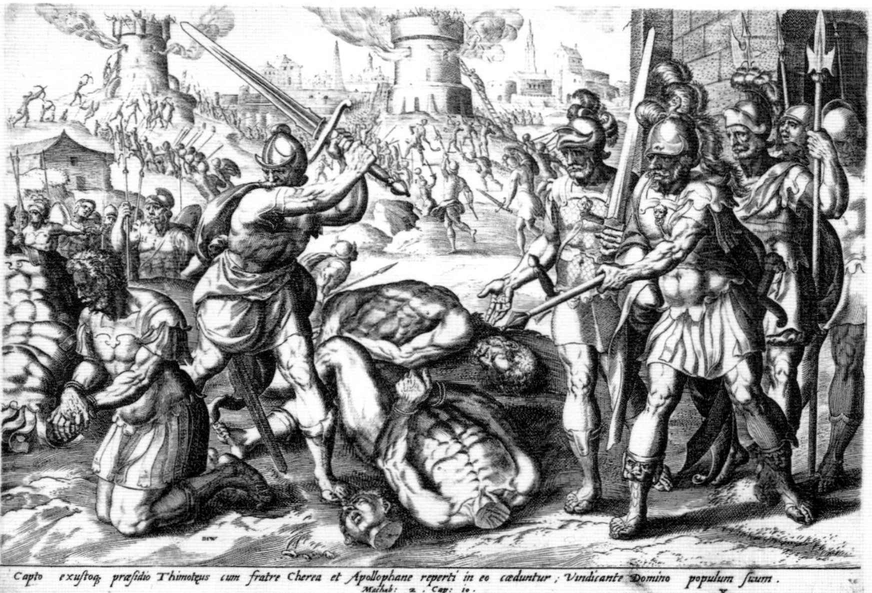

Fig. 51

mocked, derided, and defiled the priests and elders, and threatened to burn down the house of the Lord (fig. 49).[319] The event takes place on a plaza outside one of the city's main gates; amongst the attentive audience stand soldiers, elders, and the high priest (wearing a mitre). That several onlookers fold their hands in prayer or extend them in the *orans* gesture (also indicative of astonishment) suggests that they construe the ostentation as evidence of divine deliverance. God is seen to have answered the priests' prayer of supplication, quoted in 1 Maccabees 7:37–38: "Thou didst choose this house to be called by thy name, and to be for thy people a house of prayer and supplication. Take vengeance on this man and on his army, and let them fall by the sword; remember their blasphemies, and let them live no longer." The inscription paraphrases the closing section of 1 Maccabees 7, adding that this feast day was henceforth celebrated annually.

The two final scenes are taken from 2 Maccabees (figs. 50–51). Scene 7 illustrates the *Five Heavenly Warriors Joining Forces with Judas Maccabeus against the Army of Timotheus* (2 Maccabees 10:29–31); Judas and Timotheus duel amidst the melée, while the "five resplendent men on horses with golden bridles" emerge from fiery clouds above (fig. 50).[320] The inscription paraphrases from the close of 1 Maccabees 2:10, stating that the heavenly horsemen were sent to provide military guidance and support and to defend Judas. The strong implication is that God has answered Judas's prayer of supplication in 2 Maccabees 10:26, in which he asks the Lord "to be gracious to them and to be an enemy to their enemies and an adversary to their adversaries, as the law declares." Scene 8 illustrates *Judas Maccabeus Storming the Stronghold of Gazara and Executing Timotheus, his Brother Chaereas, and Apollophanes* (2 Maccabees 10:32–38); behind the execution scene, Judas's soldiers attack and burn the fortified towers where Timotheus's supporters blasphemed against God (fig. 51).[321] The inscription paraphrases the close of 2 Maccabees 10, stressing that God has vindicated his people, giving them victory over Timotheus. As a whole, the series praises the leadership of Judas: the scion of a pre-eminent family, he follows the laudable example of his father Mattathias, rising to the defense of his defenseless people; having marshaled them into an army, he retakes Jerusalem and reinstates the temple, the liturgy, and the law. He shows the people that he acts an instrument of divine justice,

ascribing his victories to God, who is seen to sanction his military actions. His first thought is always of God: when he displays Nicanor's head and hand, he reaffirms the power of divine mercy; when he commands the execution of Timotheus, he does so to signify that his people have been divinely justified. Finally, like his father, he fights against idolatry, striving to preserve and recover the true religion, cleansing it of pagan novelties, and punishing blasphemers and apostates. In every respect, the pious and valorous Judas, though not himself princely, could function as a mirror of princes, both Catholic and Protestant. This last point is worth emphasizing: for example, whereas a Lutheran or Reformed viewer might interpret the purification of the sanctuary as a coded critique of popish idolatry, a Roman Catholic viewer might interpret the restoration of the temple as an implied critique of Lutheran and Reformed attempts to amend the liturgy. So too, although Mount Sion can be seen in general terms to represent the edifice of faith, the question of which faith is left open.

In closing, let us look at a famous meditative text that doubles in places as a moral treatise. Composed by the Jesuit Jerónimo Nadal, the *Adnotationes et meditationes in Evangelia* (*Annotations and Meditations on the [Liturgical] Gospels*) consists of 153 chapters, each based on an *imago* (pictorial image) portraying one or more scenes from the life of Christ (cat. 59, figs. 52–53).[322] The sequence constitutes a Gospel harmony focusing on the infancy, ministry, Passion, and Resurrection of Christ. Sponsored by the Jesuit order, the book was issued in 1595/96 by the publisher Martinus Nutius of Antwerp. Jan, Hieronymus, and Antoon Wierix headed the team of engravers that produced the sequence of 153 folio-size prints after designs by Bernardino Passeri and Maarten de Vos. (Entitled *Evangelicae historiae imagines*, this sequence has its own frontispiece.) The book served as a complement to Ignatius's *Spiritual Exercises*, instructing scholastics enrolled at the order's colleges in the *imitatio Christi* (imitation of Christ), the basis of the Jesuit vocation. I want briefly to examine *imagines* 90, 91, and 92, that illustrate the parable of the Pharisee and the publican and the parable of the vineyard. These images illustrate chapters 135, 90, and 91 respectively. Like all the chapters in the *Adnotationes et meditationes*, these consist of descriptive annotations attaching to lettered places within the image, and of meditative spiritual exercises reflecting upon the image's meaning.

Engraved by Antoon Wierix, *imago* 90 illustrates the *Parable of the Pharisee and the Publican* read on the tenth Sunday after Pentecost (Luke 18:9–14) (see cat. 9).[323] Told by Christ en route from Samaria to Jerusalem, the parable concerns a self-righteous Pharisee and a penitent publican, both of whom go to the temple to pray, the former exalting, the latter humbling himself before God. Christ affirms that God shall show mercy to the sinner, just as surely as he shall chasten the proud Pharisee. The extraordinary bird's-eye view of the temple and its three courtyards (labeled C) positions Christ at the first interior gateway (A); the small distant figure of the Pharisee (D) advances toward him, whereas the large foreground figure of the publican attends him from a distance (E). Caption B identifies the crowd around Christ as composed partly of proudly contemptuous men, partly of men listening attentively to his sermon. That the Pharisee and the publican approach Christ, author of the parable they inhabit, rather than the temple proper, and that both are in scale to him, and he to them (though from near and from far), implies two things: first, that he is speaking about them, but also to them, so that virtually no distinction seems to obtain between his auditors and the parable's protagonists, or by implication, between us and them; second, that he is as much a protagonist as they, that the parable, in other words, is as much about him as them. This is part of the moral point of almost every parable, of course, for most are exemplifying allegories about Christ and our relation to him, although image 90 and its corollary annotations and meditation drive this point home with extraordinary force and ingenuity, as we shall see. Annotation A likewise applies the parable to Christ, placing its genesis just after his triumphal entry into Jerusalem (cf. Matthew 21:8–10 and Mark 11:8–10): just as the humble publican was exalted, so Jesus was glorified when he entered Jerusalem, and having been justly exalted, so like the Pharisee (though unjustly yet voluntarily) he was humiliated in the Passion.[324] If this is true of Christ, it should surely be true of us, annotation E argues; like the publican, with compunction of heart, we must beg simply and humbly for our sins to be pardoned. We shall do this more readily if we match each of the publican's words, spoken in supplication—*Deus propitius esto mihi*

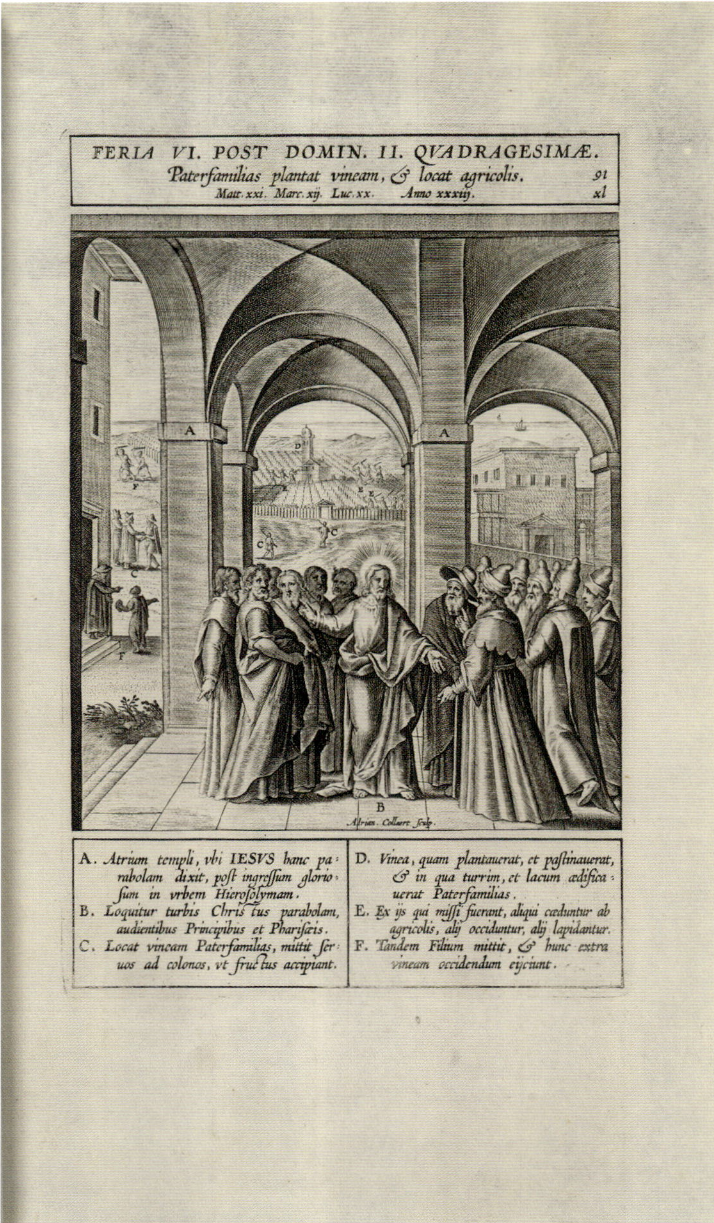

A. Atrium templi, vbi IESVS hanc parabolam dixit, post ingressum gloriosum in vrbem Hierosolymam.
B. Loquitur turbis Christus parabolam, audientibus Principibus et Pharisæis.
C. Locat vineam Paterfamilias, mittit seruos ad colonos, vt fructus accipiant.
D. Vinea, quam plantauerat, et pastinauerat, & in qua turrim, et lacum ædificauerat Paterfamilias.
E. Ex ijs qui missi fuerant, aliqui cæduntur ab agricolis, alij occiduntur, alij lapidantur.
F. Tandem Filium mittit, & hunc extra vineam occidendum eijciunt.

Fig. 52

peccatori ("Be merciful, God, to me, a sinner.")—to one of the five wounds Christ received on the Cross; that is, if we identify these words so closely with Christ, that they become images of his wounded body.[325] Seen in this light, the parable spoken by Christ becomes a parable about him.

The meditation reflects further upon the moral lesson to be drawn from the parable, which is compared to the message of Psalm 138 [137]:6 (as well as of James 1:9, 26): "For though the Lord be high, yet hath he respect unto the lowly: But the haughty he knoweth from afar."[326] We are counseled to stand with the publican, crying out from the depths of our sinful souls, from where we shall hear Christ addressing us: "For if anyone approaches, raised up by arrogance and negligence, I shall not hear him; but anyone profoundly abject of heart, I shall hear all the more, for the farther he withdraws, the closer he approaches."[327] The meditation amplifies this paradoxical imagery of nearness in farness, inviting us to associate the image of Christ with the crouching figure of the publican at the front left of *imago* 90. As we recite the publican's five words, sharing his penitential frame of mind, we must visualize the five principal wounds of Christ, as if seeing them newly inflicted, our devotion thereby growing through faith and hope in the propitiation of sin he effects. More than this, we must consider how like the publican was Christ incarnate who assumed our very humanity, sharing in our labor and our pain, even unto death; and conversely, how we grew closer to God through the merciful agency of Christ.[328] So, viewing the penitent publican's distance from Christ (and nearness to us) is tantamount to acknowledging his proximity to lost and profligate sinners (like ourselves), whose penitential awareness of their profligacy and abjection brings them closer to the glory and mercy of Christ. In this metaphorical register, consciousness of sin as distance from God becomes the penitential instrument that brings us close to him, so that the condition of farness effectively propels us into its opposite, the condition of nearness to God.

Imagines 91 and 92 illustrate the parable of the householder who plants a vineyard, which is read on the sixth weekday after the second Sunday in Lent (this is the same parable illustrated in the frontispiece to volume 4 of the *Biblia Regia*) (figs. 52–53). *Imago* 91

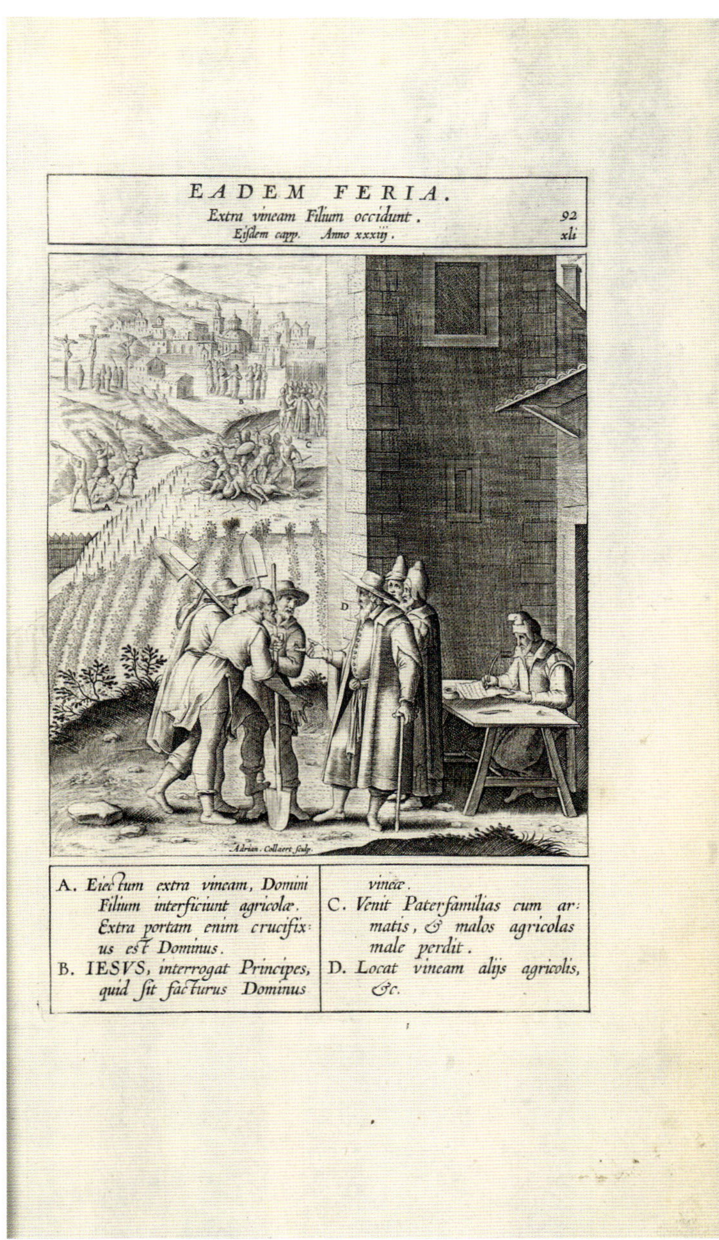

Fig. 53

Fig. 53
Adriaen Collaert after Bernardino Passeri, *The Householder Leases the Vineyard to New Tenants*, ca. 1593, engraving, *imago* 92 in *Evangelicae historiae imagines*, in *Adnotationes et meditationes in Evangelia quae in sacrosancto Missae Sacrificio toto anno leguntur* (Antwerp: Jan Moretus, 1607), large folio. John Work Garrett Library, The Johns Hopkins University.

portrays Jesus (B) lecturing the apostles (at his right) and the chief priests and elders (at his left) (fig. 52).[329] He stands within the atrium of the temple (A), the imagery of the parable unfolding behind him: the vineyard planted, trenched, and furnished with a winepress and a watchtower (D); the servants sent by the householder to collect the vineyard's fruits (C); these same servants beaten, stoned, and slain by the tenants (E); and finally, the householder's son driven from the vineyard and slain (F). The annotations explain the parable's readily discernible moral—namely, that we are under an obligation to God, who awaits payment for the life he has granted us.[330] The householder stands for God, the tenants for us, the vineyard for our bodies and souls, the tenancy for the effort, labor, and industry with which we should tend the vineyard of God, the servants for the prophets sent to collect what is owing to God, the slain son for Christ sent to gather fruits of the vine.[331] The meditation develops the theme of divine obligation. Having cleared the soil of the soul, God plants Christ, the true vine, the living Word that has the power to save; from which vine the spiritual life is propagated like a new branch, whence in turn virtuous offshoots—gifts of the Holy Spirit—spring up.[332] The wine of the vineyard is the merit each of us accrues in this life (*meritum scilicet aliquod vitae tuae*), for which God holds us accountable.[333] The term *meritum* denotes "good works," in the sense of virtuous deeds exemplifying moral character and conduct. The image of the son slain compels us to represent to ourselves how we tread down Christ when we sin, rejecting the blood of his promise, reacting with contumely to the spirit of grace.[334] On the contrary, engaging in good works on the model of Christ (the *imitatio Christi*) can best be visualized as a kind of ingrafting of oneself, the branch, to the true vine, Christ, through whom we become green, bringing forth leaves and grapes in abundance.[335] For Nadal, morality issues from the meditative life, fundamental to which is the heartfelt image of Christ engendered by the soul's visual faculty; this image derives from the engraved *imago,* beheld closely and internalized by means of the annotations, and then manipulated in the meditation. Meditative manipulation involves the rhetorical amplification of the pictorial image, which is re-figured by means of verbal images that clarify and complicate its implicit meaning. This process,

that negotiates from external to internal sight, is remarkably like the process of parable formation, that clothes Christ and his gospel in verbal images requiring to be internalized and interpreted. With regard to the *Adnotationes et meditationes*, we might put this reflexively: by meditating on parables, we ascertain that meditation is a wellspring of the moral life.

Imago 92 makes apparent that Christ, the source of the parable, dwells at its heart, as the parabolic subject (fig. 53).[336] *Imagines* 91 and 92 are inverted pendants: whereas in the former Christ stands front and center, the imagery of the parable unfolding behind him, in the latter, the householder assumes center stage, while Christ shifts to the background, where he questions the elders about the parable. *Imago* 91 reads front to back; *imago* 92 back to front: ejected by the villainous tenants, the lord's son is murdered, just as the Lord was crucified outside Jerusalem (A); Jesus asks the elders what the lord of the vineyard shall do (B); the householder comes with armed men to lay waste to the false husbandmen (C); he transfers tenancy of the vineyard to other laborers (D). The transposition of Christ (*imago* 91) and the householder (*imago* 92) suggests that the parable's author is also its key protagonist, the divine proprietor who apportions the vineyard and evaluates its husbandmen (Christ as divine judge). By the same token, the transposition of Christ teaching to the background, where he is surrounded by scenes pertaining to his sacrificial death and the punishment of sin, indicates another conclusion to be drawn—namely, that the Father offers his Son to redeem the fruits of the vineyard, that is, to call us to account, rewarding and punishing according to our just deserts. The annotations analogize *imagines* 91 and 92, as well as pointing out internal analogies. Annotation A, for instance, correlates the murder of the son and the crucifixion of the Son of God.[337] Annotation D specifies that both images may be read in two ways: spiritually, Christ is seen to teach (*imago* 91) and the householder to enact (*imago* 92) the dismissal of the faithless Synagogue and election of the faithful Church; morally, they jointly warn us to embrace spiritual gifts, husbanding them wisely, lest by our moral perversity we incur the harsh justice of Christ, and having been shattered, are brought to naught.[338] Both truths, the spiritual and the moral, are conveyed through affective images having the power to touch our hearts in the manner of the parables.

Conclusion

Let us look at one final example of scriptural illustration that implicitly claims the warrant of Christ himself. In the Van Liesveldt Bible of 1538, the opening onto Luke 4 and 5 contains two images: at left, Christ reads from the Book of Isaiah, or rather is handed the book to read (alternatively, he may be closing the book, having just recited Isaiah 61:1–2, as described in Luke 4:16–21) (fig. 54); at right, he forgives the sins of a bedridden paralytic, whose friends, "finding no way to bring him in…went up on the roof and let him down with his bed" (Luke 5:18–26) (fig. 55).[339] Both scenes reveal how Christ mobilizes the eyes as instruments of faith. In the temple, he speaks in the voice of the prophet, paraphrasing the opening verses of Isaiah 61, which he supplements with a promise to restore the spiritual sight of those blindly awaiting the fulfillment of this prophecy: "The Spirit of the Lord is upon me, because he has anointed me to preach good news to the poor. He has sent me to proclaim release to the captives and recovering of sight to the blind, to set at liberty those who are oppressed, to proclaim the acceptable year of the Lord." Jesus then closes the book, as if symbolically foreclosing the Old Testament, and announces, "Today this scripture has been fulfilled in your hearing" (Luke 4:21). He makes this assertion while "the eyes of all in the synagogue were fixed on him" (Luke 4:20), adding that few of them will accept the living testimony he proffers, just as "no prophet is acceptable in his own country."[340] Luke 4:16–21 constitutes, therefore, the visual manifestation of Jesus as the Christ, howsoever few if any beholders prove willing to affirm him as the Messiah. Moreover, he can be seen to present himself as the visual exegesis of Isaiah 61: his presence bodies forth visually the truth that the era of grace, formerly adumbrated by the prophet, has now at last commenced. The print by Lieven de Witte portrays this exegetical presence, showing Christ seated in the temple, surrounded by Levites and Pharisees who see and yet do not see him, lacking spiritual discernment (fig. 54). The image aims paradoxically to represent their failure of sight, exposing to view what was theirs to behold, had their eyes been truly opened. The complementary print depicts another example of visual proof (fig. 55). Christ heals the paralytic in front of the scribes and Pharisees, in order to demonstrate that he is the Son of man, who "has authority on earth to forgive sins" (Luke 5:24). This time, the miracle they are given to see converts them: "And amazement seized them all, and they glorified God and were filled with awe, saying, 'We have seen strange things today'" (Luke 5:26). In the subsidiary scene at the right, they marvel at the paralytic walking home with his mattress on his back. Both prints illustrate how Christ calls upon his auditors to know him by exercising their faculty of vision (figs. 54–55). That he thus endorses the power of sight to shore up belief, constitutes an implicit endorsement of the images describing his evangelical ministry, as divine exegete and thaumaturge. Their scriptural form and function, in other words, derives from Christ himself, who relied upon the eyes as agents of religious persuasion.

At the start of this introductory essay, the claim was made that scriptural prints offered a clarifying lens through which sixteenth-century reader-viewers in the Low Countries received, pondered, and interpreted the word of God. Various kinds of relation between biblical images and texts were then examined, first a selection of illustrative woodcuts taken mainly from Dutch Bibles published in Antwerp before 1550, second some single-leaf prints requiring prior knowledge of the Bible, and third a series of frontispieces from the *Biblia Regia,* that put forward a deeply learned and integrated reading of the Old and New Testaments. Finally, biblical prints were classed under rubrics identifying five principal visual functions and treatments of the Bible: "Sacred History and Geography" (philological, antiquarian, or cartographical); "Visual Exegesis" (hermeneutical); "Worship" (liturgical or meditative); "Morality" (ethical); and "Politics and Polemics" (epideictic and periphrastic). All these functions call forth an inventive reader-viewer capable of construing the Bible as an historical, doctrinal, devotional, ethical, or political source. The catalog that follows will, I hope, reveal the range of these approaches to this most crucial of sixteenth-century books, that came increasingly to be read through printed images.

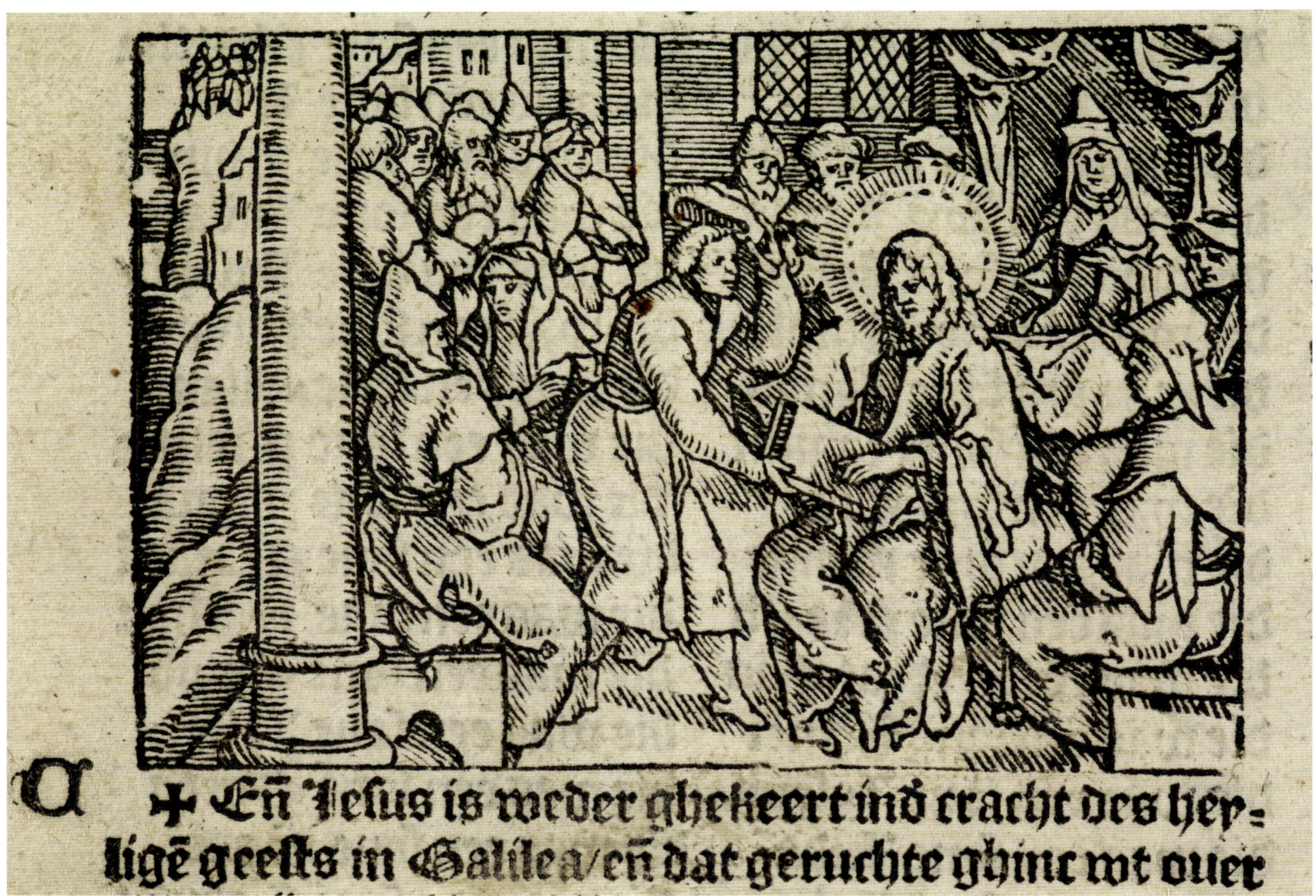

Fig. 54

Fig. 54
Lieven de Witte, *Christ Reads the Book of Isaiah in the Temple*, woodcut, in *Den Bybel met groter neersticheyt gecorrigeert* (Antwerp: Hansken van Liesveldt, 1538), folio (2LL6v). By permission of the Trustees of the British Library. 3041.g.6.

Fig. 55
Lieven de Witte, *Christ Heals the Paralytic*, woodcut, in *Den Bybel met groter neersticheyt gecorrigeert* (Antwerp: Hansken van Liesveldt, 1538), folio (2LL7r). By permission of the Trustees of the British Library. 3041.g.6.

ż.a
ŝ.a

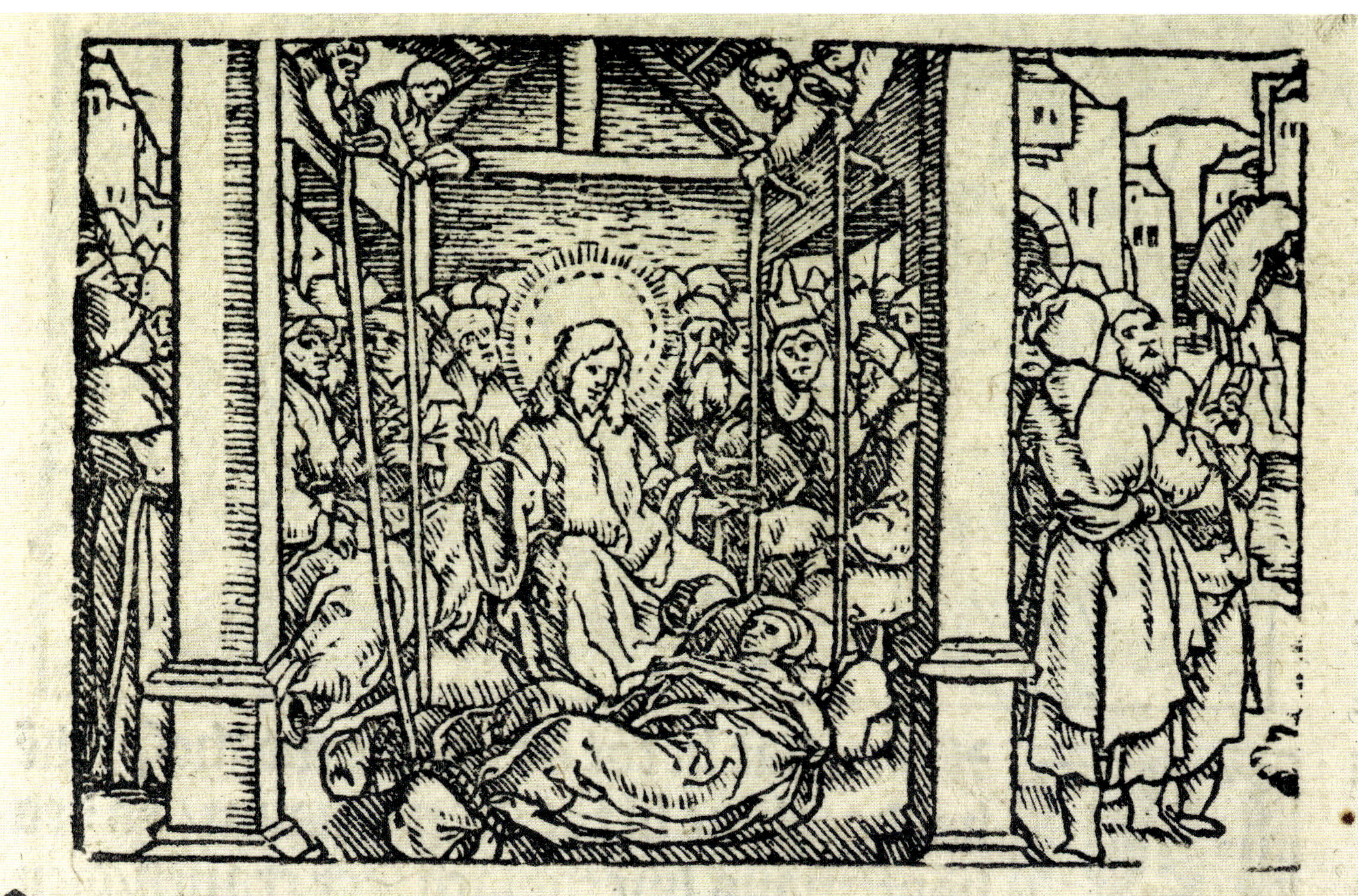

✠ Eñ het gheschiede op eenen dach/ dat hi leerde/
eñ daer satē pharizeen eñ Scriftgeleerdē/ die gecomē

Fig. 55

Notes

1. Arblaster 2004, 9–11.

2. Van der Stock 1998, 59–69.

3. Rosier 1997, 1:12–50.

4. On the various editions of the Van Liesveldt Bible, including the 1538 edition published under the name of Jacob's son Hansken, see ibid., 14–15, 23–24, 27–28, 31–32.

5. On Lutheran sources of Old Testament illustrations in the Van Liesveldt Bible, see ibid., 14–15.

6. On the various editions of the Vorsterman Bible, see ibid., 16–23.

7. On Jan Swart's illustrations of the Old Testament for the Vorsterman Bible, see ibid., 16–17; on the New Testament illustrations by various artists, including Lucas van Leyden, 17–18.

8. On these German sources of Old Testament illustrations, see ibid., 3–4. On Plantin's *Biblia Regia*, see ibid., 44–45, 80–83.

9. On *Dat leven ons Heeren Christi Jesu* (Antwerp, 1537), the Dutch edition of Van Branteghem's *Iesu Christi vita,* printed by Mattheus Cromme for Adriaen Kempe van Bouckhout, see Veldman 1986a, 263–64; and Veldman and Van Schaik 1989. On Van Branteghem's illustrator De Witte, see ibid., 13–16, and Rosier 1997, 1:28–29. Figure 3, *Christ Confutes the Accusation of Ritual Negligence*, illustrates Luke 11:37–52; Christ warns the Pharisees that they shall be held accountable for the blood they and their ancestors have spilled, "from the blood of Abel unto the blood of Zacharias, who was slain between the altar and the temple." The house altarpiece at left depicts the substance of this admonition, revealing the legacy of sin that extends from the killing of Abel to the present.

10. On official attitudes to vernacular Bible translation before and after the promulgation in 1546 of an index of forbidden books, see Den Hollander 2003; François 2004; and François 2006. The promulgation of a "proto-index" in 1529 resulted in attempts to conform Bible editions to the Vulgate, as later editions of the Vorsterman Bible indicate. That the *magistri lovanienses* (theological faculty of Leuven University) later banned the 1534, 1544, and 1545 editions of this Bible, resulted from their disapproval of paratextual elements such as the prologue and glosses, on which see Den Hollander 2003, 18–19.

11. On printing as an unregulated "free art," see Van der Stock 1998, 27–57, esp. 27–31, 36–37, 56–57, on its identification as a scribal art.

12. On the statute of 1558 and its political ramifications, see ibid., 39–43.

13. On the statute of 1546, see ibid., 45.

14. De Keyser 1530, fol. Q6r; on the De Keyser Bible of 1530, see Rosier 1997, 1:19–20, 178–83. Vorsterman 1532, fol. s6v; on the Vorsterman Bible of 1532, see Rosier 1997, 1:22–23, 189–96.

15. On the print of *Abishag before David*, see ibid., 1:97–100.

16. Ibid., 1:97–98.

17. On the *Biblia pauperum* as a source of Swart's woodcuts for the Vorsterman Bible of 1528, see ibid., 1:86; on the *Biblia pauperum* as a source of biblical typology, see Auerbach 1953; Henry 1983; Henry 1984; and Henry 1987, 3–18.

18. De Keyser 1530, fol. n1v; on this print, see Rosier 1997, 1:111. Vorsterman 1532, fol. G2v; on the Vorsterman Bibles of 1532 and later, see Rosier 1997, 1:189–96, 200, 254–55.

19. De Keyser 1530, fol. X3r; Vorsterman 1532, fol. 2zlv. On this print, see Rosier 1997, 1:95–96; on the De Keyser Bible of 1534, 1:201–204.

20. De Keyser 1530, fols. g8r, m3v, o7r; Vorsterman 1532, fols. B1r, F5v, H3v. On this print, see Rosier 1997, 1:111–12.

21. Rosier 1997, 1:112.

22. On Lucas's *David and Abigail*, see New Hollstein (Van Leyden) 24 (pp. 52–53), with full bibliography on this print. On Lucas's distinctive approach to narration and its heuristic implications, see Parshall 1978.

23. On Swart's *Jesus Preaching from the Ship*, see Hollstein (Swart) 5 (p. 110).

24. On the adaptability of most Bible illustrations to both Catholic and Protestant readings, see Rosier 1997, 1:116–22. On attitudes toward religious formalism and resistance to sectarian politics in later sixteenth-century Antwerp, see Harris 2004; for a case study of confessional fluidity in a later print by Hieronymus Wierix, see Melion 2009, 243–60.

25. Van Branteghem 1537, 139, 141, 144.

26. Cromme 1538, fols. C2r, K5v, L3r.

27. Vorsterman 1528, fol. 2B7r.

28. Vorsterman 1532, fols. 2B5v, 2E6v.

29. On De Laet's Bibles of 1556, 1560, and 1565, see Rosier 1997, 1:39–40. On Cock, Galle, De Jode, the Liefrinck's, Baltens, and other print publishers in Antwerp, see Van der Stock 1998, 143–72.

30. Bowen and Imhof 2008, especially 31–176.

31. On Liefrinck, see ibid., 54–57, 345–346.

32. On these benchmarks in the history of engraved illustration, see ibid., 84–121.

33. Arias Montano 1568–73; on this title-page, see Hänsel 1991, 26–31; and Rosier 1997, 1:80–81, 322.

34. Van Liesveldt 1526; on this title-page, see Rosier 1997, 1:73–74. The 1526 title-page block, reused in 1534, instead serves to introduce the New Testament in Van Liesveldt 1538, which opens with a new title-page, copied from Luther's German Bible of 1533–34; on the 1538 title-page, see Rosier 1997, 1:214.

35. On the sequence of title-page and frontispieces, see Hänsel 1991, 26–35; Rosier 1997, 1:80–83, 322–25; and Bowen and Imhof 2008, 91–92. On the significance of the illustrations *qua* engravings, see ibid., 84–106; on the likelihood that Arias Montano himself chose the medium of engraving, 99. On Arias Montano's contributions to the project, not only as editor and iconographer, but also as draftsman, see Hänsel 1991, 27–28.

36. On the title-page, see Hollstein (Wierix Book Illustrations) 1 (1:4), with full bibliography. On Van der Heyden and Van den Broeck as artists who worked with Plantin, see Bowen and Imhof 2008, 326–29, 338–39. The title-page contains several inscriptions: besides the title, the epigraph—*Pietatis concordiae. Isaiae,*

11.—and the dedication —*Philippi II. Reg. Cathol. Pietate, et studio ad sacrocanctae Ecclesiae usum.*

37. Cf. Plantin 1568, unfoliated: "Huic tabulae addita est corona quatuor arborum ramis connexa, quae usum quatuor linguarum sacrarum ad unam Christianae Religionis disciplinam significat. Constat enim Israeliticam regionem generosarum palmarum copia insignem fuisse, Babylonicam salicibus abundasse, Graecos olivae imagine fuisse significatos, apud quos Athenae celeberrimum gymnasium Palladi consecratum fuit, Palladi autem oliva dedicabatur. Latinorum verò symbolum quercus fuit, Saturno prisco sacra."

38. Cf. ibid.: "Prima tabula continet significationem concordiae omnium Imperiorum in Christianae Religionis cultum & studium. Assyriorum enim & persarum, nec non Graecorum & Latinorum nationes certis animantium imaginibus indicantur: quas omnes in Christi Regni obedientiam conspiraturas Isaias Praedicebat. Habitabit lupus cum agno, & pardus cum hoedo accubabit: vitulus, & leo, & ovis simul morabuntur, & puer parvulus minabit eos. Vitulus & ursus pascentur, simul requiescent catuli eorum, & leo quasi bos comedet paleas. Isai. 11."

39. Hänsel 1991, 29.

40. Cf. Plantin 1568: "Sub columnarum basibus duo symbola sunt, ex altera parte Archimedis nudi cum libro procurrentis imago, ab Aria Montano iamdiu delecta, certa quadam suorum studiorum significatione. Ex altera verò

parte Plantini Typographi symbolum est circinus, altero pede fixo, altero laborante."

41. On this allegorical frontispiece, see Hänsel 1991, 31–33; and Rosier 1997, 1:323. The frontispiece incorporates several inscriptions. On the plaque above: "Stetitque rex super gradum, et foedus percussit coram Domino, ut ambularent post Dominum; et custodirent praecepta eius, et sucitarent verba foederis huius, quae scripta erant in libro illo. 4. Reg. 23." On the base below: "Philippo II. Hispaniar. Regi Catholico, quod religionem expiandam, pietatemq. instaurandam curaverit pos."; and "Iosiae, monumentum renovat." On the smaller plaques beneath the two trees: "Ob deletos aruspices Baal. 4. Reg. 22."; and "Ob templi sartatecta curata. 4. Reg. 22."

42. Plantin 1568: "Ex altera autem parte, qua bellorum trophaea sunt, manus est in lapide titulari constituta, gladium tenens, quae alterum Regis munus significat, hoc est, Iustitiae plenam & severam administrationem in eos qui publicam honestatem & pacem vel vi, vel iniuria inferenda, vel fraude facienda violant. Ex altero verò caduceus sive Regium sceptrum est, oculis adhibitis vigilantibus: hoc altera manu tenetur, quae in lapide etiam titulari constituta est. Haec verò imago Regiam sedulitatem, vigilantiam, diligentiam & constantiam significat in emendanda legibus, ac moribus adornanda republica. Illius partis inscriptio est, AUT GLADIO: huius verò, AUT VERBO. Nam vel hoc,

vel illo modo (ut magis expedite pro rerum, personarum ac temporum ratione videatur) perpetuò Regem in gubernanda repub. attentum esse oportet."

43. Cf. ibid.: "Huius autem Catholicae Religionis fovendae, colendae, & propagandae causa hoc sacrorum Bibliorum omnibus antiquis atque sacris linguis constans opus, diligentissimè atque integerrimè impressum, instaurandum curaverit; ad Iosiae Regis pientissimi exemplum, qui inventum in templo divinae legis exemplar in multa exempla descriptum populo exhibuerit; lege lata, ut ille solus Deus coleretur, eoque modo quem liber ille praescriberet."

44. Ibid.: "Hanc autem totam rationem ex sacrae Scripturae locis petitam antiqua inscriptionum phrasi basis ipsa exponit."

45. On the second frontispiece, see Hänsel 1991, 33; and Rosier 1997, 81–83. The design has recently been attributed to Pieter van der Borcht; see New Hollstein (Van der Borcht Book Illustrations) 423 (2:3). On Van der Borcht, see Bowen and Imhof 2008, 322–26. The frontispiece contains three epigraphs: above, "Multifariam multisq. modis olim Deus ad patres locutus est. Hebr. 1."; below, "Arcani consilii apparatio. 1. Corinth. 10." and "Declaratio sermonum tuorum illuminat. Psal. 118."

46. Plantin 1568: "Tertia tabula veteris Testamenti, hoc est quinque librorum Mosis, auctoritatem indicat, cuius ratio breviter exponetur. Testamentum Vetus divinarum humanarumque rerum notitiam imprimis continet, & divinorum

etiam de humana salute promissorum, Deique voluntatis, humanorumque officiorum doctrinam, tum aperto & perspicuo, tum figurato & aenigmatico sermone hominibus exhibet."

47. Ibid.: "Hoc autem ita se habere, Divus Paulus in primo epistolae ad Hebraeos capite confirmat, asserens Angelorum ministerio Dei nomine olim non semel nec uno modo, sed multifariam multisque modis illorum librorum & rerum, quae in illis continentur, auctoritatem & fidem spectatissimam certissimamque fuisse, idque nobis constare multis & maximis testibus à Deo delectis."

48. Ibid.: "Nam post salutem orbi ab aquis restituam Deus per angelus Noe alloquutus, in fide & spe salutis expectandae confirmavit, & promissi ac propositi sui repetitione & expositione animavit, sicut scriptum est, Statuam pactum meum vobiscum. Gen. 9."

49. Ibid.: "Praeterea Mosen apud ardentem atque illaesum rubum Angelus Dei nomine, de parata iam proximeque futura filiorum Israel salute alloquutus est, in qua humanae salutis ratio ut in figura continebatur."

50. On the third frontispiece, see Hänsel 1991, 33–34; Rosier 1997, 323; and Hollstein (Wierix Book Illustrations) 1.1 (1:4). On Jan Wierix as an artist who worked with Plantin, see Bowen and Imhof 2008, 353–56. The plaque above is inscribed with the epigraph: "Qui per angelos dictus est sermo factus est firmus. Heb. 2."

51. This passage from Hebrews anchors

the exegetical tradition that reads Joshua, who leads his people into the land of promise, as a figure of Jesus; further, his law is regarded as the second law of Moses, that more fully adumbrates the dispensation of Christ. On Joshua as a type of Christ, see Danielou 1960, 229–75.

52.   Plantin 1568: "Prima tabula continebat legis à Deo latae certissimam fidem, omni populo publicè factam, ut ex postrema illius imagine observavimus. Sed quia Vetus Testamentum non solùm leges à Deo sancitas, verùm etiam promissa terrena continebat, quibus velut umbra aut imagine quadam caelestis regni promissa significabantur; oportuit illa praestari & expleri, atque illorum exemplo edito confirmari etiam spem caelestium promissorum, quae tandem credentibus atque obedientibus obtinenda erant."

53.   Ibid.: "Ideoque in secundo tomo, qui Iosue, libros Iudicum ac Regum continet, appingitur ingressus filiorum Israel in regionem promissam: quem, ubi tempus à Deo praescriptum accessit, nullae vires, aut opes, nulla potentia, nulla consilia humana impedire potuerunt: immò & flumina ipsa contra naturae cursum reducta, admirabili concessione iuverunt. Atque ita qui per Angelos dictus est sermo, factus est firmus. Id enim constitit populo Israelitico in regionem deducto promissam, ibidemque diutissimè commorante, atque populorum labores, ut Psaltes ait, possidente."

54.   On the fourth frontispiece, see Hänsel 1991, 34; Rosier 1997, 1:323; and Hollstein (Wierix Book Illustrations) 1.2

(1:4). The entry portal is inscribed with the epigraphs "Delectatio plantationum Domini" and "Quid enim debui facere vineae meae quod non feci?"

55.   Within the exegetical tradition founded by Justin Martyr, Clement, and Eusebius, the parallel drawn between the House of Israel and the Church of Christ is seen to arise from within the Book of Isaiah itself, chapters 1–39 of which signify the era of promise, that is fulfilled by the era of grace prophesied in chapters 40–66; on the Book of Isaiah as a unified witness to the time of Jesus, that also prefigures the distinction between the two eras, see Seitz 1989, 103–116.

56.   Plantin 1568: "Quartus tomus Prophetarum scripta continet, qui variis legationum, vaticiniorum & actionum generibus Israelitarum populum divinae voluntatis cognoscendae, ac purae religionis colendae rationes docuerunt, atque in huiusmodi administrando munere multa eademque gravissima multi ex illis pertulerunt. Quamobrem vineae Domini exercituum imagine hic tomus ornatur, cuius descriptionem ex Isaiae vaticinio, atque ex Evangelica lectione petere licebit. Est autem haec tabula argumento maximae solicitudinis, curae, ac diligentiae, quam Deus in Ecclesia sua excolenda, ornanda, amplificandaque ponit."

57.   On the fifth frontispiece, see Hänsel 1991, 35; Rosier 1997, 323; and Hollstein (Wierix Book Illustrations) 1.3 (1:5). Inscribed below is the epigraph, "Novissime diebus his locutus est nobis. Deus in filio quem constituit haeredem

universorum. Heb. 1."

58.   Plantin 1568: "Novi Testamenti fidem non secus atque Veteris divina auctoritate constare, tabula haec indicat: eamque tanto digniorem esse, quanto Angelis Dei ipse Dei filius, huius Testamenti minister & interpres, praestat: quantoque maiori & illustriori rerum testimoniorum apparatu confirmari hoc Testamentum voluit Deus. Antè enim quàm Evangelium à Christo enuntiaretur, Iohannes Baptista, multis miraculis ac manifestis signis ab ipso infantis à matre concipiendi tempore ad baptismi exerciti usque dies, illustris extitit. Hic venit in testimonium, ut testimonium perhiberet de lumine."

59.   "Benedicti Ariae Montani Hispalensis in sacrorum Bibliorum quadrilinguium regiam editionem, de divinae scripturae dignitate, linguarum usu & Catholici Regis consilio, praefatio," in Arias Montano 1568–73, vol. 1, unfoliated [*4r]: "Inter omnes cogitationum, consiliorum, actionum, curarum, studiorúmque rationes, quibus humanus animus in hac mortali vita teneri atque exerceri potest, nullum genus est quod vel naturae ipsius magis proprium & consentaneum, vel utile ac necessarium magis, vel ad vitam instituendam commodius aptiúsque sit, quàm certa & clara sui ipsius cognitio, nec non vera ac perspicua originis propriae, & caussae, quamobrem editus natúsque fuerit, notitia, ac demum omnium eorum, quae vel ad ipsius dignitatem & amplitudinem facere, vel ad extremam felicitatem conducere ac pertinere

possunt, exacta, optiméque subducta ratio."

60.   Ibid., unfoliated [*4v-*5r]: "Una autem hominis natura caeterarum perfectionibus omnium, dignitate, pulchritudine, virtute, habilitate, & aptitudine adeò antecellit, ut nihil egregii in caeteris inveniatur, cuius ille virtutem & vivam imaginem magna ex parte in se agnoscendam non ostendat: neque inferiores tantùm species rerum exprimat, sed mentis vi & rationis, (cuius est praecipuè particeps) ipsum optimum atque maximum Deum, cognatione ferè quadam, aut certè illustrissima & praestantissima similitudine attingat, quandamque in se universi veluti summam vel reipsa habeat, vel specie referat."

61.   Ibid., unfoliated [*5r]: "Quoniam verò in hominis natura singularem ac praecipuam quandam virtutem, qua caetera omnia animantium genera carent, eámque ultra agendi facultatem ad consequendum proprium finem vim quandam esse constat, qua finis ipse, atque eae res, quae ad eum maximè faciunt, cognosci & optari; eae etiam quae non aptae, aut incommodae iudicantur, dignosci, vitari, ac reiici possunt; cúmque huiusmodi in ipso virtus ut praestantissima, purissima, atque efficacissima, ita praecipuè propria sit: consentaneum maximè fuerit, omnes vitae actionúmque rationes, huius tantae virtutis, ubi facultas arbitriúmque per aetatem accesserit, usu exercitationéque instituere, atque hoc modo, tam admirabili dignitati respondere, sibíque

constare, ac nobili & probato cursu ad optatum exitum pervenire."

62.   Ibid., unfoliated [*5r–*5v]: "Itaque homini non solùm iter suum diligenter facere, sed unde initium, quae viae ratio, quis modus, & quis tandem sit finis, quaenam bene confecti itineris gloria constet, imprimis cognoscere, exploratúmque habere maximè convenit."

63.   Ibid., unfoliated [*(1)r]: "tamen varia & fallaci, inani & ambigua fabularum specie involutam, vel tantis quaestionum, argumentationum & artificiorum difficultatibus implicitam, ut non magis ferè prodesse ita traditam, quàm omnino desideratam affirmare possimus."

64.   Ibid., unfoliated [*(1)v]: "Verum enimverò benignissimus & clementissimus Deus, qui hominum genus maximi boni atque honoris caussa à se ultro creatum atque editum, eiusdem misericordiae & propositi constantia provehere, amplificare & beare destinarat, magna ad eam rem atque abdita consilia sapientissimè à se inita, quoad rem totam perfecit, suis temporibus est executus: ex quibus unum illud fuit, ut, qua tempestate vera divinarum humanarúmque rerum cognitio, maxima errorum, fabularum & idololatriae confusione, & obscurissima caligine detentis hominum mentibus, tegebatur, clarissima & suavissima verbi sui lux, fidelissimorum ministrorum operae ac diligentiae credita, tandem mundo illucesceret, eadémque propria voce hominibus clarissimè audita, miraculis, portentis, signis, & Spiritussancti varia

distributione, ac demum gravissimis in obtrectatores & contumaces animadversionibus comprobata confirmaretur."

65.   Ibid.: "Hoc enim sacrum verbum à divinae sapientiae consilio & auctoritate profectum, veritas ipsa est, quae brevibus librorum voluminibus, inexhaustos divinarum & humanarum rerum cognitionis thesauros continet, in quibus, quae hominibus & cognitu dignissima & utilissima facillimáque sunt, & quaedam maximi etiam momenti, quae provectioribus & sanctioribus aperiri solent, mysteria continentur."

66.   Ibid., unfoliated [*(2)r]: "haec animos ad difficile virtutis iter strenuè ac studiosè capessendum incitat atque accendit: haec ad doctrinarum, disciplinarum, atque artium omnium rationes examinandas, veráque à falsis, & honesta à turpibus discernenda, iudicium illustrat & informat. Hoc etiam verbum fundamentum iacit veritatis, & certitudinis earum omnium rerum quas humana mens confingere rectè potest. Hoc demum rationum omnium, quas hominibus subductas esse oporteat & expediat, integram summam praefinit."

67.   Ibid.: "Praeterea malorum omnium expulsorem, & bonorum auctorem Deum Christo filio eius pontifice & conciliatore ostendit, ac totum humanae salutis, tum ab ipso afferendae, tum hominibus ipsis obtinendae consilium negotiúmque exponit."

68.   Ibid., unfoliated [*(2)v]: "Altera lucerna est, quae mortalium pedibus adhibita, semitas vitae illustrat, & ad

clariorem expectandam lucem excitat."

69.   Ibid.: "Altera lumen est etiam ad mentes interius illustrandas aptissimum & commodissimum, quo lumine clarius ea omnia, quae maximè hominibus nosse expedit, ipsis innotescunt, in quos expeditiora Spiritus sancti dona promissa conferuntur, cuius efficientia utriusque testamenti mysteria cognosci, ac re ipsa comprobari possunt, propter egregiam quandam virtutem, quam in seipsis ex divino beneficio experiri fideles novi testamenti cultores possunt, qui quidem id in cordibus conscriptum agnoscunt, quod antea lapidibus incisum legebant."

70.   Ibid., unfoliated [*(3)r]: "Qui per Angelos dictus est sermo firmus factus est." Implicit in Arias Montano's use of Hebrews 2:2 is the argument of Hebrews 2:3; just as the word of God justified the message declared by angels, so the salvation of Christ justifies both testaments, knitting them together indissolubly: "It was declared at first by the Lord, and it was attested to us by those who heard him, while God also bore witness by signs and wonders and various miracles and by gifts of the Holy Spirit distributed according to his own will."

71.   Ibid., unfoliated [*(3)r-v]: "Atque huius sacrae disciplinae utilissimum & maximè necessarium, aptissimumque studium iis penes quos rerum summa est, Regibus, Principibus Magistratibúsque summopere commendatur; eiusdémque observantia & cultus in publicis & privatis obeundis rectéque gerendis negotiis proponitur, sicut de Israelitis regibus,

quos pietatis studio atque etiam divinae disciplinae auscultatione à Christianis superari oportet, scriptum est: 'Postquam autem sederit Rex in solio regni sui, describet sibi Deuteronomium Legis huius in volumine, accipiens exemplar à sacerdotibus Leviticae tribus, & habebit secum, legetqúe illud omnibus diebus vitae suae.'" Arias Montano finishes this thought two pages later; see ibid., unfoliated [*(4)v]: "Etenim simulac hostis ille divinum verbum in eum neglectionis locum, apud homines deducere potuit, quàm certam ipsis miseriam, quantas calamitates importarit, Iosiae regis aetatem mox consecuta tempora apertè satis declaravêre."

72.   Ibid., unfoliated [**1r]: "Inprimis enim divinarum literarum auctoritatem & dignitatem commendatam, atque humanae sapientiae, prudentiae, & iudicio omni (ut par erat) praelatam: postea perversarum interpretationum & depravationum exitiali veneno inspersit; cuius vi plurimorum hominum ingenia & iudicia corrupit, innumerabilésque perdidit animas, ac denique Christianam miserè perturbavit Rempublicam."

73.   Ibid., unfoliated [**3v]: "ne res tanti ponderis ac momenti ab illo malorum omnium auctore, illiúsque ministris, in id…discrimen, adduceretur; eámque mentem Philippo II…iniecit, ut inter quamplurima consilia, quae pietatis, & divini cultus, publicae utilitatis sacrosanctae Ecclesiae, ac denique totius Reipublicae Christianae gratia, ab ipso prudentissimè inita, fortissimè suscepta, felicissimèque sunt peracta,

de sacris etiam libris, antiquis linguis, & earum optimis interpretationibus, qua fieri potest diligentia, inter se collatis, excudendis, is etiam deliberaret; utpote, cui inter plurimas ad communem salutem, & tranquillitatem multarum gentium, & nationum à se gubernandarum divinitus datas, & fidelissimè susceptas curas, unum pietatis ac religionis purae studium, praecipuum, & maximum, atque ad omnem publicam rem stabiliendam firmissimum fundamentum esse constat."

74. "B. Hieronymi presb. prologus in Esaiam prophetam," in Arias Montano 1568–73, 4:3: "Ita enim universa Christi Ecclesiaeque mysteria ad liquidum prosecutus est; ut non putes eum de futuro vaticinari, sed de praeteritis historiam texere."

75. Ibid.: "Prophetavit autem Esaias in Hierusalem & in Iudaea, necdum decem tribubus in captivitatem ductis: ac de utroque regno nunc commixtim, nunc separatim texit oraculum. Et cùm interdum ad praesentem respiciat historiam, & post Babyloniae captivitatem reditum populi significet in Iudaeam; tamen omnis eius cura de vocatione gentium, & de adventu Christi est."

76. "Eiusdem Benedicti Ariae Montani alia ad lectorem praefatio. In qua de totius operis usu, dignitate, & apparatu ex ordine disseritur," in Arias Montano 1568–73, vol. 1, unfoliated [**6v]: "Ne verò quidquam, quod ad regij planè operis splendorem pertinere videbatur, praetermissum existimes: singulae

tabulae, aere artificiosè celatae, suis locis insertae sunt. Quibus tabulis singulorum textuum, ac divinorum mysteriorum, quae sub eis latent, explicatio, licet exiguo loco contenta, longo tamen ac divino prorsus argumento tractatur; ut studiosus quisque animadvertere poterit."

77. On the *Exemplar* and its illustrations, see Hänsel 1991, 35–53; Rosier 1997, 324; and Bowen and Imhof 2008, 91–99.

78. Arias Montano 1568–73, vol. 1, unfoliated [***1r] ("Eiusdem Benedicti Ariae Montani alia ad lectorem praefatio"): "Sed quia cuius patet, tum ad res explicandas, tum etiam ad certam rerum veritatem indagandam, ac tandem etiam constituendam, ex locorum, temporúmque ratione, & ponderum, ac mensurarum exacta cognitione plurimum lucis, & delectationis accedere: omnia Geographiae, & Topographiae praecepta, quae quidem ad sacrarum lectionum explicationem satis esse possunt, ab ipsis sacris descriptionibus, & annotationibus excerpta, duobus libris prosecuti sumus. Temporis deinde, ac aetatis illius, quae iam inde à condito orbe ad Christum usque longa serie effluxerat, exquisitae, certam quandam, ac brevem rationem tradimus. Sub finem, ponderum aestimationem diligenter examinatam, ac sacrae architecturae praeceptionibus, atque exemplis iucundis omnino, & dignis quae ab omnibus perdiscantur, concinnè exornatam exhibemus. Quibus nihil ad arcanos & occultos divinorum oraculorum sensus explicandos, aut

aptius, aut magis accommodatum requiri, aut desiderari potest. Nulla enim ratione unquam fiet, ut veram cognitionem earum historiarum, quas hîc egregiè caelatas, aptéque, & appositè, ut supra admonuimus, suo loco collocatas, conspicies, sub ipsis imaginibus absconditam, & quodammodo (ut ita dicam) latentem, quis rectè assequatur, nisi prius artificiosa, ac divina planè imaginum structura ei cognita, ac perspecta sit."

79. "Ben. Ariae Montani Hispalensis Beseleel, sive de Tabernaculo," in Arias Montano 1568–73, 8:6: "Materiae comportationem formae descriptio consequitur quàm rectissimè: sed nulla descriptio aut melior aut clarior, quàm exemplaris ipsius proposita forma; quam artificio imitari contingat. Fuit autem exemplar admirandum Moysi in monte à Deo ostensum, spirituale illud quidem, & invisibili materia, divino planè artificio constructum, Deoque habitatori gratissimum, & praeter omnes terrenas fabricas oportunissimum: cuius aliquam etiam spiritualem descriptionem nos indicaturos speramus, artifice summo demonstrante ipso Deo. Sed illam visibilem formam, quam illius exemplaris velut rudem imaginem in terris exprimere licuit, nunc explicare contenti sumus. Ostensum est igitur verum ipsum exemplar Prophetae admiranti & discenti, S. S. E. Iuxta omnem similitudinem tabernaculi, quod ostendam tibi, & omnium vasorum, & cultuum eius si facietis illud." On this passage, see Hänsel 1991, 44.

80. On the prints illustrating the tabernacle and its place within the Israelite encampment, see ibid., 41–47; the choice of archaeological subjects goes back to Nicholas of Lyra's *Postilla*, as Hänsel shows. On the *Postilla*, the first illustrated edition of which was published by Anton Koberber at Nuremberg, see Rosier 1997, 1:69–70. On Wierix's print of Moses, Aaron, and the twelve tribes camped around the sanctuary, see New Hollstein (Van der Borcht Book Illustrations) 424 (2:3); and Hollstein (Wierix Book Illustrations) 1.4 (1:5).

81. "Beseleel, sive de Tabernaculo," in Arias Montano 1568–73, 8:5.

82. On the prints illustrating the temple, see Hänsel 1991, 47–53; and Rosier 1997, 1:324. On Arias Montano's reconstruction as a precursor to the *In Ezechielem explanationes* of Juan Bautista Villalpando and Jerónimo Prado, see Lazure 2000, 167.

83. "Ariel, sive, de templi fabrica et structura," in Arias Montano 1568–73, 8:9–10: "His accedit templi significatio; quae cùm simplex perpetuò fuerit, unius Ecclesiae exemplar habuisse debuit, quam postea unam, sanctam, catholicam ex omnibus terrae familiis sibi constructurus erat Deus."

84. Ibid., 11–12.

85. The print is inscribed *Montis Domini totiusque sacri Templi exemplum ex antiquis descriptionibus a Bened. Aria Montano observatis, ad Apparatus sacri instructionem* (*Exemplar of the Lord's Mount and of All the Holy Temple, as Observed by Benito Arias*

Montano on the Basis of Ancient Descriptions... for Insertion into the Sacred Apparatus). The term *Apparatus* refers to volume 8 of the Polyglot Bible, which incorporates the *Exemplar, sive, de sacris fabricis liber* (*Exemplar, or Book on Sacred Edifices*), as we have seen. On the *Antiquitatum Iudaicarum libri IX.*, and this print in particular, see Hänsel 1991, 50–52; and Bowen and Imhof 2008, 103, 334, 379.

86. The book's subtitle distills its antiquarian function: *in quîs, praeter Iudeae, Hierosolymorum, & Templi Salomonis accuratam delineationem, praecipui sacri ac profani gentis ritus describuntur...adiectis formis aeneis* (*in which, besides the Accurate Portrayal of Judea, Jerusalem, and the Temple of Solomon, Are [also] Described the Principal Rites of the Clergy and Laity...by means of the Attached Copperplate Engravings*).

87. According to 1 Kings 2:12–36, God refuses further to dwell at Shiloh because of the sacrileges committed by the high priest Heli's sons. Through the prophet Gad, he then orders David to build the altar of burnt offerings on the site of Araunah the Jebusite's threshing floor (2 Kings 24:18–25; 1 Paralipomenon 21:18). When David finds that his prayers offered at this altar are answered, he decides here to build the temple, ultimately leaving completion of this sacred task to Solomon (1 Paralipomenon 22:1, 17–19). Arias Montano identifies this site as Mount Moriah, where the sacrifice of Isaac took place; see "Ariel, sive, de templi fabrica et structura," in Arias Montano 1593, 208.

88. Ibid., 206: "Templum igitur hominibus ad unius Dei cultum unum esse tunc oportuit, in quo eandem sacrorum & doctrinae rationem omnes tenerent, quicunque in Dei populi numero conscribi studerent."

89. Ibid.: "His accedit templi significatio; quae cùm simplex perpetuò fuerit, unius Ecclesiae exemplar habuisse debuit, quam postea unam, sanctam, catholicam ex omnibus terrae familliis sibi constructurus erat Deus." The phrase *exemplar habuisse debuit* (ought to have held the pattern) clearly designates the prefiguration of a type, hence my use of the term "to adumbrate."

90. Ibid.: "Antiquis fas non fuit, templum privato consilio aut voto aedificare, ne ea re religionis communio discinderetur, dum singuli suis, ac suorum inventis studentes simultatem excitarent ac foverent. Erat praetereà magnum periculum, ne pro vero cultu alienus iniretur, orbe terrarum vanorum deorum vanissimis cultibus distracto.

91. The *Bird's-Eye View of the Temple* corresponds closely to the antiquarian description in *Ariel*: although the temple sharply recedes toward the vanishing point, its measurements are clearly discernible: the main block is about half as high as it is long, and three times longer than it is wide, while the tower-vestibule is double the building's length. Beyond the temple courtyard are three trapezoidal atria, somewhat wider in the east than the west (as Arias Montano puts it, "in form like a lion, wider at the breast than the rear"). Solomon considered these spaces so important that he forestalled to ornament, denominate, or consecrate the temple until they were completed. (Ibid.: "Neque anteà templum aut ornavit, aut nominavit, aut initiavit quàm omnes hae partes essent absolutae: videlicet sancta, aedes, & atrium quod interius dictum est.") Demarcated by exterior walls of stone and interior walls of wood, these atria, especially the innermost of the three, are lined with *exedrae* (auxiliary halls) reserved for various functions, such as ritual washing, the collection of alms, and the slaughter of animals. Arias Montano observes that these exedrae were crucial components of the temple; in order properly to function, the temple cult required its ministers, and so too, the atrium required its exedrae. (Ibid.: "ita ut atrium illud sine eiusmodi exedris intelligi non possit: ut neque ministerium sine ministris.") The numerous arcades presumably also lead into the *coenacula* (dining chambers) and *cubicula* (sitting or storage rooms), used by the Levites as dwelling places and treasuries. The atrium closest to the temple courtyard, its eastern portal built by Joatham, was primarily reserved for priestly usage. The people as a whole, including the king, were wont to gather three times a year for religious ceremonies in the middle atrium, known as the *atrium Israel*. Women congregated in the outermost atrium, known as the *atrium foeminarum*, where there were female and male zones. As the kings of Israel presided over the *atrium Israel*, ensuring that the divine rites were maintained, so they invoked God on the people's behalf in the *atrium foeminarum* (also known as the *atrium novum*). Arias Montano gives as an example 2 Paralipomenon 20:5–12, Josaphat's prayer to the Lord for protection against the Moabites and Ammonites. (Ibid.: "Cumque stetisset Iosaphat in medio coetu Iudae & Ierusalem in domo Domini ante atrium novum.") Finally, enclosing the temple precinct and the three atria is a perimeter wall within which runs an open corridor lined with benches.

92. "Benedicti Ariae Montani Hispalensis in volumen quod exemplar, sive de sacris fabricis inscribitur, ad divinorum librorum studiosos lectores praefatio," in Arias Montano 1568–73, 8:2: "Omnes enim homines ab ineunte aetate, divino quodam afflatu, naturaeque instinctu, sciendi desiderio tenentur, & suapte natura eos corporis sensus conservant, ac fovent, quibus ad plurimarum se rerum cognitionem pervenire posse credunt."

93. Ibid.: "Siquidem ei cordis latitudinem à Deo datam esse legimus: quam quidem omnium bonarum artium cognitionem plerique interpretantur. Ex hoc autem doctorum hominum iudicio quaedam est nata curiositas, quae multorum solicitavit ingenia: eaque non modò in praesentium, verùm etiam in praeteritarum, futurarumque rerum cognitione exercuit, atque ad omnium rerum causas, rationesque investigandas impulit."

94. Ibid.

95. Ibid.: "Neque verò res gestae, atque ea quae in communi hominum usu, commerciisque versantur, itemque

concordia, & societas, dissidia & discordiae, & caetera huiuscemodi quae saepiùs evenire solent; sed etiam tum publica, tum privata uniuscuiusque opera, scribendi argumenta plerisque fuerunt, sive illa communis utilitatis, sive etiam pompae, & ostentationis gratia confecta fuerint. De quo genere sunt: moles, aedes, aedificia, templa, portae, arcus, porticus, atria, plateae, moenia, urbes, muri, turres, suburbana, vineae, horti, villae, aedificationes, gymnasia, palaestrae, circi, theatra, amphitheatra, pontes, fontes, pyramides, obelisci, currus, carpenta, esseda, sedes, tripodes, mensae, scamna, atque alia penè innumerabilia, quae vel ab humano sunt profecta ingenio, vel industria, & artificio perpolita sunt & exornata. Quibus accedunt & illa: gestamina, vestimentorum diversitates, diversae ac variae insignium formae, quibus & Gentes & familiae dignosci possent, collegia publicorum & privatorum functiones munerum."

96. Ibid., 2–3: "Quae quidem omnia, quoniam ad aliquem usum spectare possunt, ab antiquis digna sunt habita, quorum formae, rationesque omnes vel literis consignarentur, vel picturis & imaginibus exprimerentur: ut hac illae ratione, aut absentibus innotescerent, aut per manus veluti traditae ad posteros pervenirent."

97. Ibid., 3: "Porrò in historiis saepiùs fit mentio earum rerum quas iam enumeravimus, eaeque vix possunt intelligi, nisi in ordinem redactae alicuius opera explicentur."

98. Ibid.: "Pleraque verò ex iis quorum aut exiguus, aut omnino nullus est usus, vel ob id solum quòd aliquando extiterunt, digna sunt habita, quae è tenebris vindicata in conspectum darentur hominum: vel priusquam vetustate consumpta oblivione delerentur sempiterna, tum descriptionibus, tum etiam historiis renovarentur, & posteritati conservanda traderentur."

99. Ibid.: "Quocirca, ea quae non sine singulari Dei voluntate sunt edita, & quorum adhuc summae auctoritatis remanent monumenta aspectu pulcherrima, scitu dignissima, atque adeò hominibus ipsis utilissima; dubium non est, quin ab hominibus & diligenter conservari, & continuo studio excoli debeant."

100. Ibid.: "Qua verò ratione Deus, verae scientiae, sapientiaeque mysteria, non aliundè quàm ex sacris verbi sui libris peti iussit, eadem quoque ea omnia, quae non tam argumenta, quàm suae sunt ornamenta sapientiae, ex iisdem hauriri voluit."

101. Ibid.: "Etsi enim multa in unoquoque earum rerum genere sunt explicata: plura tamen adhuc latere ac desiderari putarunt. Existimarunt itaque, operae se pretium facturos si hoc laboris non solùm in iis quae in novo, verùm etiam in veteri Testamento describuntur, susciperent, & ad eas se figuras & mysteria quae in sacris leguntur libris explicanda conferrent."

102. Ibid.: "Animadverterunt etiam imaginibus illis, ac delineamentis veteres illos ut plurimùm esse usos, atque illis ipsis ad lucis & veritatis cognitionem perduci solitos fuisse."

103. On Arias Montano's use of maps to foster antiquarian scholarship, see Shalev 2003; on his use of maps as meditative instruments, see Melion 1999, 68.

104. Arias Montano 1568–73, 8:3: "Omnem enim scribam (inquit is) doctum in regno caelorum similem esse decet homini patrifamiliâs, qui profert de thesauro suo nova & vetera. At verò inter ea omnia rerum genera quae ad eius quae in sacris continetur libris sapientiae apparatum pertinent, sacrarum structura fabricarum non minus sua ipsius natura, & arte, quàm ea quam in se continet, significatione est admirabilis."

105. Ibid.: "Et quidem nonnulla scitu maximè digna, vel ob sacrae linguae, vel etiam Architecturae ignorationem, aut praetermissa, aut certè eo quo debuerunt modo, neque intellecta, neque tradita esse comperimus. Eum enim qui utraque non sit praeditus facultate, multorum tum verborum, tum rerum significationem ad rerum illarum cognitionem necessariam ignorare necesse est. In illis enim divinis operibus hic est constitutus ordo, ut ea, scilicet, primùm ex eo quod in se habent mysterio, mox ab arte (quae in iis est praestantissima) ac postremò ex verborum, quibus describuntur, vi & usu cognoscantur."

106. Ibid.: "Vobis itaque pij ac studiosi in Christo fratres, tum arcae illius à Noë aedificata, tum tabernaculi à Mose erecti, atque etiam eorum aedificiorum, quae à Salomone sunt instituta, rationes omnes qua potuimus, & sedulitate & brevitate expositas, elegantique imaginum structura repraesentatas exhibemus. Hic quoque nonnullas eorum mysteriorum, quae iis in rebus continentur, & quorum causa tot, tantaeque operum moles olim à Deo sunt institutae, veras explicuimus significationes: ex quibus quidem arcana illa tum admirabilia, tum cognitu dignissima intelligi poterunt & cognosci."

107. On this Bible and its maps, etched and engraved by Baptista van Doetecum, see New Hollstein (Van Doetecum) 861–63 (4:43–44), with full bibliography. The map of the *Holy Land* is inscribed: *Dit is die Beschrijvinghe des landts van beloften twelck-men noemt dat Heijlighe landt.* ("This is the Promised Land, Commonly Called the Holy Land.") The map of the *Exodus* is inscribed: *De Caerte van theijlich landt twelckmen noemt tlandt van beloften daer de Heijlighe Schrift Oude ende nieuwe Testament zoo veel van vermelt.* ("Map of the Holy Land, Called the Promised Land, of which the Old and New Testaments Recount so Much.") The map of the *Peregrinations of the Apostle Paul* is inscribed: *Afconterfeytinge ende beschryvinge, der landen die Paulus doorwandelt heeft.* ("Portrayal and Description of the Lands through which Paul Wandered.") Peter Verhaghen of Dordrecht and Cornelis Janszoon of Delft jointly published the first illustrated edition of the *Deux-Aes* Bible in 1581, on which see Rosier 1997, 1:45. On the *Map of the Holy Land Illustrating the Exodus*, see Delano-Smith and Ingram 1991, 34.

108. On illustrated editions of the Deux-

Aes Bible, which was first issued in 1562, see Rosier 1997, 1:45–47. As Rosier notes, the term *Deux-Aes* derives from a marginal note to Nehemiah 3, which refers to the numbers two and one on a die: "The poor must bear the cross; the rich give [them] nothing. *Deux aes* [two-one] has nothing; *six cinque* [six-five] gives nothing; *quater dry* [four-three] offer help freely." Whereas "two-one" and "six-five" stand for the poor and the rich, "four-three" stands for the middle class. Nehemiah 3:5 deprecates the Tekonites, whose nobility "did not put their necks to the work of their Lord," during the campaign to rebuild the Jerusalem wall.

109. Jacobszoon and Bouwenszoon 1589, [inserted between fols. 482v and 483r]: "Alle Gheleerden, oock mede de ervarentheyt selve ghetuyghen overvloedich hoe seer dat de Caerten van lantbeschrijvinghen niet alleen profijtich, maer oock nootwendich, ende daerenboven geneuchlick zijn, den ghenen die in trecht verstant der Bibelscher Historien begheeren toe te nemen." The map of Paul's evangelical journey therefore serves to facilitate comprehension of the Bible: "Onder welcken drien [caerten] dese de laetste inhoudt de afcontrefeytinghe aller landen, Provincien, ende Steden, die de heylighe Apostel Paulus, gheduyrende den tijt zijns beroeps ende Apostelampts, doorgereyst is."

110. Ibid.: "Ende alsoo wy gaerne bekennen dat in dese beschrijvinghe niet soo veel namen van Steden en sullen ghevonden werden, als wel in eenighe andere oude Caerten dit selfde stuck oock tracteerende: So moghen wy ons oock daerenteghen wel beroemen, ende mitsdesen beloven, dat dese teghenwoordige veel beter dienen sal tot verclaringhe des Nieuwen Testaments, dan wel de andere souden doen."

111. "Dat xxxiij Capittel Numeri, Tellinghe Reyse Israëls. Dat vierde boeck Mose. Caerte aenwijsende den wech ofte tochte der kinderen Israel, doe sy veertich jaren lanc uyt Aegypten lancx henen de woestijne van Arabien trocken, tot in tlant Canaan," in ibid. [map inserted between fols. 65v and 66r; explanatory key printed on reverse of map]: "Dese Caerte teeckent af ende vertoont ons de 42. legeringen ofte rust-plaetsen ghelijck de selfde beschreven zijn Nume. 33. mitsgaders der selfden Graden van hare lengde ende breede: oock hoe wijt dat d'eene legheringhe van d'ander ghehouden zy gheweest, tselfde by den by ghevouchden ghetalen lichtelick can af meten. Ende tot breeder verclaringhe van dien, ende om tot beter verstant der Bibelscher Historien te comen, dient oock tgheen dat in de uytlegginghe der namen achter-volcht wort in voor-ghenomener ordeninghe nae tcapittel Numeri 33." On this map, etched and engraved by Baptista van Doetecum, see New Hollstein (Van Doetecum) 861 (4:43); and Delano-Smith and Ingram 1991, 34. The cartouche above left reads: "De Caerte vant theylich landt twelckmen noemt tlandt van beloften daer de Heylighe schrift Oude ende nieuwe Testament zoo veel van vermelt."

112. "Caerte aenwijsende den wech ofte tochte der kinderen Israel," in Jacobszoon and Bouwenszoon 1589: "*Etham*, stercte ofte volcomenheyt. Daer henen siet David, Psalm. *74.37*. De derde wooninge ofte rustplaetse was in *Etham* aen het eynde vande groote woestijne. Aldaer verscheen hen ten eersten de Heere, dat hijse den rechten wech leydede des daechs in eener wolcken-calumne, ende des nachts in een vyer-calomne, dat hy hen luchtede dach ende nacht. Exo. 13.21."

113. Ibid.: "*Hahiroth*. Hare vierde legeringe heet *Hahiroth*, een groot diep dal, niet verre vande Roode ofte *Schelfzee* tegen *Baalaephon* ende legerden tegen oster *Migdol*. Hier syn sy van Pharao ende zynen heyre achterhaelt ende benauwet ghewoorden, alsoo dat sy seer vreesden, doch dewijle sy totten Heere riepen, ende Moses in den ghebede vyerich was, zijnse door de wolcke, die den Aegyptenaren duyster, maer den Israeliten claer lichtende was, seecker ende overhindert tot aen de *Roode-zee* ghebracht. Exod. 14.10. etc."

114. Ibid.: "*Sin*, dat is, een doornbossche, ofte oock haet ende nijt. Van Elim wederkeerende na tZuyden, maeckten sy hare sevenste legeringe wederom aen de *Roode-zee* inder woestijne *Sin*. Deze zee wort genoemt *Iam-suph*, van wegen des riets ofte der biesen ende schelffen die daer omtrent overvloedich wiessen: ofte oock van wegen des rooden gronts, want het Hebreeusch woort *Suph*, beteeckent root, ofte biesen, riet ofte liesen, etc. De Griecksche Oversetters noemen dese zee *Mare Erythraeum*. Plinius noemt het de *Arabische* ofte *Persische* custen tot aen dese zee, wijst de beschrijvinghe in der Caerten duydelick aen. Nume. 33.10. Plin. li. 6. c.24."

115. Ibid.: "*Raphidim*, dat is, der stercken heyl ofte ghesontheyt. *Massa*, heet versoeckinge. *Merica*, heet twist. Siet Psalm 95.8. etc."

116. Ibid., fol. 219r-v: "Heden so ghy zijne stemme hoort, so verstockt uwe herte niet/ als tot *Meriba* geschiede, als tot Massa in der woestijne."

117. Ibid., fol. 511r-v: "So bescheyt hy wederom eenen dach: Heden, seggende door David, na so veel tijts, gelijck geseyt is: Heden, ist dat ghylieden zijn stemme hoort, so en verhart uwe herten niet."

118. Ibid., fols. 219r: "Want hy is onse God, ende wy het volck zijner weyden, ende schapen zijner handen."

119. Ibid., fol. 204v: "Hy weydet my op een groene landouwe, ende voert my ten verschen water."

120. "De Argumentum aller boecken des Ouden Testaments: vervatende den sin ende meyninghe der ghener diese geschreven hebben, nae de orden des tijts: Numerus. Cap. 36," in Jacobszoon and Bouwenszoon 1589, unfoliated [*ij verso]: "Desgelijcx machmen in dit boeck sien, met wat wonderlicker lijtsaemheyt, ende goedertieren vromicheyt, Moses gestadichlick dat ongenadich overlast verdragen heeft, also wel van zijnen eygenen volcke als van de vreemde: ende is nochtans niet sonder feyl."

121. "Handelinghen der Apostelen. Schipvaert Pauli. Paulus te Roome. Dat xxviij Capittel. Tot den Leser over de

Caerte van de Pelegrimagie des heyligen Apostels Pauli: Dewelcke behoort ghestelt te worden fol. 483," in ibid., [map inserted between fols. 482v and 483r; explanatory key printed on fol. 483r-v]. Describing Paul's travels after his conversion, the latter text is entitled: "Ordentlicke vertellinghe der Jaren, na de bekeeringhe S. Paul. Bewijsende den tijt zijnder pelgrimagien, ende der Sendtbrieven tot den Ghemeynten gheschreven." On this map, see New Hollstein (Van Doetecum) 863 (4:44); and Delano-Smith and Ingram 1991, 105–106. The map is inscribed above: "Afconterfeytinge ende beschryvinge der landen die Paulus doorwandelt heeft."

122.   "Ordentlicke vertellinghe der Jaren, na de bekeeringhe S. Paul," in Jacobszoon and Bouwenszoon 1589, fol. 483r: "De beroerte die te Ephesen was, ghestilt zijnde, reyst hy nae Troas, ende van daer na Macedonien. [Op dese reyse: Namelick, van Ephesen nae Macedonien, schrijft hy den eersten brief tot Timotheum, dien hy tot Ephesen gelaten hadde.]   Ende te Philippis zijnde, schrijft hy den tweeden brief totten Corinthen: dien hy met Tito ende Luca derwaerts sent. 2. Corinth. 2. ende 13. Actu. 20."

123.   Ibid.: "Daer na wort hy van Barnaba na Antiochien geleyt: Alwaer de Discipulen eerstmael Christenen genoemt worden. Actuum 11."

124.   Ibid.: "Hy blijft te Corinthen xviij maenden. Actu. 18. Ende van daer schrijft hy totten Romeynen."

125.   On this map, which first appeared in the Liesveldt Bible of 1526 and the Vorsterman Bible of 1528, see Delano-Smith and Ingram 1991, XXII–XXIV, 25–26; copied from the map of Exodus in Christopher Froschauer's German Old Testament of 1525, this map ultimately derives from Lucas Cranach's woodcut wall map issued sometime between 1508 and 1518. Delano-Smith and Ingram argue that the map exemplifies Luther's conviction, based on Hebrews 11:23–29, that the Exodus demonstrates faith in the fidelity of God, rather than prefiguring the sacrament of Baptism or the Resurrection of Christ.

126.   On *Balaam and the Angel*, copied after the print in Symon Cock's *Historien ende prohecien* of 1535, see Rosier 1997, 1:216.

127.   Van Liesveldt 1526, "Dat boeck Numerus. Dat. xxiij. Capittel," unfoliated [Gij recto] A: "Ende des morgens nam Balak Bileam met hem, ende si gingen wech op die hoochte van Baal, dat hi van daer sien conde tot aen dat eynde des volcx."

128.   Ibid., B: "Want van die hooge steenrotse sie ic hen wel, ende vanden huevelen merck ic hen. Siet dat volc sal alleen woonen, ende onder die heidenen niet gerekent worden. Wie can gerekenen dat stof Jacobs, ende dat getal des vieren deels van Israel. Mijn siele moet sterven die doot der oprechtiger, ende mijn eynden moeten worden gelijc deser lieden eynden."

129.   Ibid., C: "Balak antwoorde, coemt doch met mi aen een ander plaetse, daer ghi dat eynde van Israel siet, ende doch niet al en siet, ende vermaledijtse aldaer."

130.   Ibid., D: "God heeftse wt Egipten geleyt…Tsijnder tijt salmen tot Jacob seggen, ende tot Israel wat God doet."

131.   "Dat boeck Numerus. Dat. xxiiij. Capittel," in ibid., unfoliated [Gij recto-verso] A-B: "Die man wiens oogen geopent sijn seyt…die des almachtigen gesicht was, die daer neder viel, ende sijn oogen werden geopent. O Jacob hoe schoon sijn uwe tenten, ende uwe woningen. O Israel, si sijn ghelijc breede groene dalen, ghelijc die hoven aent water."

132.   Ibid., unfoliated [Gij verso] D: "Ic sal hem sien, mer nu niet. Ic sal hem aenschouwen, mer niet van na bi. Een sterre sal daer comen wt Jacob, ende een Septer sal daer wt Israel op comen, ende hi sal verslaen die overste der Moabiten, ende verwinnen alle die kinderen Seth. Edom sal sijn erve sijn. Ende Seir sal sijnder vianden erve sijn. Israel sal stercke wercken doen."

133.   Rosier 1997, 1:157–59, 196–200.

134.   Ibid., 1:213–22.

135.   Van Liesveldt 1526, unfoliated [first folio recto after the title-page]: "Aenghesien dat die ongheleertheyt ende simpelheyt van veel menschen, den text der heyligher schriftueren des ouden Testaments, zeer cleyn achten, ende als nyet daer af en houden, meynende dat alsulcken schrifture allen den Joden gegheven si, ende dattet allen nyet dan voor slechte gheschiedenissen ende historien te verstaen en is."

136.   Ibid.: "Nyet teghenstaende dat ons Christus gheheelick daer door bewesen ende belooft wort. Ende dat oude Testament is ons als die wendeldoecken daer Christus in ghewonden leyt, ende daer wy hem oock in vinden sullen."

137.   Ibid.: "alsoo ons Christus oock selve betuycht, Johannis int. v. segghende, Ondersoect dye schrifuere, want die selve gheeft ghetuyghenisse van mi."

138.   Ibid.: "ende Paulus ghebiet Thimotheum, dat hy niet en soude laten, maer daghelics die schirftuere ondersoecken ende lesen."

139.   Ibid.: "Oock totten Romeynen int eerste, Dat evangelium is van Godt inder schriftueren belooft. Ende in die eerste totten Chorintheren int. xv. seyt Paulus, dat Christus nae inhout der schriftueren is van Davids bloede ghecomen, ghestorven, ende opgeresen vander doot."

140.   Ibid.: "Desghelijcs so wijset ons oock Petrus in sine epistolen totter schriftueren."

141.   Ibid.: "Aenghesien dattet dat nieuwe testament so crachtelijck bevesticht, ende die Apostelen hebben haer predicatie daer mede moeten beschermen, also ooc sinte Steven die eerste martelaer des ouden Testaments, Christum bewees, door dat oude Testament, ghelijct blijct int werck der Apostelen, int sevende capittel, ende int. xvij. des selven schrijft die Evangelist Lucas, dat die van Thessalonica daghelics ondersochten die schriftuere, oft si also inhielt als Paulus predicte, ende dat is kenlijck, ende seker dat het die schriftuere des ouden Testaments was, want dat nieuwe noch niet beschreven en was."

142.   Ibid.: "ende dat nieuwe moeste ooc door dat Oude bevestighet worden."

143.   Ibid.: "daer om sullen alle Christen menschen dat oude Testament van gheender minder weerden houden, dan dat nyeuwe. Ende dat nieuwe Testament en is anders niet dan een vervullinge des ouden Testaments, ende een clare vercondinge, ende predicatie, hoe dat dye hooghe belosten, des alderhoochsten, onser salichmakinghen, ons nu ghegheven zijn, ende dat door Christum, dye welcke ons vander ghenaden, ende goedertierenheyt des vaders, in menigherley sproken des ouden Testaments belooft was. Daerom salmen die heylighe schriftuere, beyde des Ouden ende des nieuwen Testaments, houden… Ende dit is oock die principael ende nootlijcke sake, waer om dat dit boeck te lesen, ende met ootmoediger herten te ondersoecken is, op dat wy Godt leeren vreesen, lief hebben, ende betrouwen."

144.   "Die Prologhe. Die Correctuers deser translatien wenschen, allen den ghenen die desen onsen arbeyt sien ende lesen sullen, warachtige kennisse des vaders, door Jesum Christum den sone, ende die gratie des heylighen gheests, ende die heylighe schrift, alsoo te lesen, datmen daer door verbetert mach worden, ende alle sonden te laten," in Vorsterman 1528, unfoliated [*.ij. recto]: "maer een offer inden schat des tempels, daer dander ghout ende silver, dandere costelijcke steenen offeren, daer offeren wy gheyten vellen."

145.   Ibid., unfoliated [*.iij. recto]: "ende bidden den Heere dat hi ons sinen gheest gheve, om die seghelen op te Breken. Op dat dan die ghene die die heylige schrift sullen lesen, niet dwalen en souden, in die lettere die doot slaet, maer dat si leven mueghen, door den gheest die levende maect. Soo vermanen wi den menschen nader gratien, die ons Godt ghegeven heeft dat si dat Oude testament, niet soo cleyne en achten, als die somighe doen, diet achten alleen den Joetschen volcke ghegheven, ende nu voort wt te sine, ende dattet niet dan van voorleden geschiedenissen en schrive, meenende ghenoech aenden nieuwen testamente te hebben, ende datment alleen ghestelijcke sinnen int Oude testament sal soecken, want deser opinie, is teghen dat Nieuwe testament, dwelc vol is int alligeren der schriften des ouden testaments." The passage argues equally against a strictly historical or purely anagogical reading of the Old Testament, instead urging the reader to consult it as a pendant to the New.

146.   Ibid., unfoliated [*.iij. verso]: "Ende dies gelijcs Luce. iiij. seyde die Heere, dat die schriftuere Isaie in hem vervult was. Ende. S. Pauwels ghebiet Timotheum naerstich te wesen int lesen der heyligher schrift. Ende totten Romeynen int eerste Capittel, seyt hi, dattet Evangelium belovet is van Godt inder schrift. Ende na dinhout der schriftueren, is Christus van Davids bloet gecomen, ghestorven, ende vander doot verresen. i. Corin. xv. Ende hier af is alle dat Nieuwe testament vol."

147.   Ibid.: "Hierom is te weten dat, dat Oude testament gheheel somtijts, een boeck der wet ghenoemt wort, als onse Heere inden Evangelie seyt. Om dat vervult soude worden, dat woort dat gheschreven staet in haer wet, Si hebben mi ghehaet sonder sake, Johannis. xv."

148.   Ibid.: "Dit is die roode zee, daer die ghehoorsame kinderen van Israel int leytschap Moysi, tot Christum comen. Ende die hoovaerdige Egiptenaers met Pharao haeren leytsman, in verdroncken. Dit is die cribbe daer die herders vonden Jesum in doexkens ghewonden, den welcken Herodes ende dier Joden bisschoppen ende leeraers niet en vonden. Al schijnt die letter naect, die schat is al te costelijc, te weten, die eewighe waerheyt, wijsheyt, ende wech, die daer in verborghen is."

149.   Ibid.: "Maer ghelijc int Nieuwe testament, neffens die leeringhen der gratien, wetten ende gheboden zijn, om tvlees den gheeste onderdanich te maken, ende den gheest te regeren naer die Evangelische gratie, aengesien, dat in dit tegenwoordich leven, dye gheest gheen volcomen heerschappie, over dat lichaem en heeft. So zijn int Oude testament biden wetten ende gheboden, beloften der gratien, daer die heylighe vaders ende Propheten mede onder die wet staende, door dat gheloove ende betrouwen inden toecomende salichmaker Christum Jesum, behouden zijn, ghelijck wi. Ende ghelijck des Nieuwen testaments hooft leeringe is, gratie ende vrede door verghevinge der sonden in Christo. Also is des Ouden testaments leeringe, Die wet te leeren, die sonden te thoonen, duecht te eyschen. Ende daer en boven, onder tijtlicke geloften, worden beteekent, geestelijcke ende eewighe goeden, die ons door Christum comen ende die glorie der duechdelijcken. Ende onder die tijtelijcke dreyghementen, worden ons beteekent, die pine der hellen, ende tverlies der glorien ende dat afscheyden van Godt almachtich."

150.   Ibid., unfoliated [*.iiij. recto]: "Int Boeck Deutronomium, na dat tvolck gheplaecht was, om haer ongehoorsamheyts wille, ende wt vreesen met straffinghen, wat bekeert was… so verhaelt Moyses die geheele wet, met alle die gheschiedenissen die hen gemoet waren, sonder tghene, dat den priesterlijcken staet aenghinc. Alsoo verclaert hi die wet Goods, met die liefde Goods, ende totten naesten, ende metten geloove tot God, want dat willen alle die geboden Gods….Want dit leven sonder Gods dienst niet ghezijn en can, soo ghaf Godt hen soo vele geboden, daer toe om Gode te dienen, dat si niet van noode en hadden, anderen te versieren oft te doen, maer alleen wast ghenoech, dat si den woorden Gods ghehoorsaem waren, want hadmen hen laten versieren, wat si ghewilt hadden, si waren gheneycht tot afgoderien, si souden lichtelijck ghevallen hebben. Ende als die Heere leert Matthei int vijfthienste capittel haer schriftgeleerden, om haer eyghen ghiericheyt, versierden insettinghen, teghens Gods gheboden. Hierom hebben wi oock so naerstich gheweest, om dit Oude ende Nieuwe testament te corrigeren, om dat die menscen na Goods geboden souden mueghen leven, ende laten al dat teghen die Evangelische leeringhe is….Noch isser te weten, datter driederhande wetten zijn, die sommighe

om quaet te keeren, ende dese zijn om der quader wille ingheset, ghelijcker vele inden ouden testamente zijn…Ende die ander wetten ende geboden, zijn tot ceremonien des dienst Gods. Maer boven alle, ghaen die gheboden der liefden, dye wt een oprechte gheloove spruytende is."

151. Ibid., unfoliated [*.iiij. recto-verso]: "Daerom als die liefde Godts ende des naesten dat eyscht, sien wi, dat Godt inder nootsakelijcheyt daer in gedispenseert heeft, ende dat somtijts die heyligen wt dingeven des heyligen gheests duyterste der wet niet volbracht en hebben, als David theylige broot adt, ende desgelijc meer.…So is dan Godts wet van noode te weten, want daer in beschrijft Moyses, hoemen God vreesen, betrouwen, gelooven, ende beminnen sal, ende dat die menschen haer sonden kennen ende na Godts gratie haken souden, ende dat wi gheen betrouwen in ons noch inden mensche stellen, maer onse eyghen cranckheyt bekennen ende Christum met zijn gratie om hulpe soecken, ende alsdan sal die mensche sinen naesten gunstich worden ende goet doen, gelijc Godt hem door Christum gedaen heeft, ende so leert hi die te voren van sonden beghonste te wachten ende die wetten Godts wt vreesen volbracht, nu wt liefden die volbrengende, ende heeft Godt lief, ende sinen naesten, in die welcke twee woorden die Propheten ende die wet, vervult worden, also die heere Christus, inden Evangelie Mat. xxij. spreect. Ende die Propheten en hebben dit selve niet ongeroet gelaten, vanden salichmaker den Propheet diemen hooren

sal. Dit is dan dat finael van Moyses boecken, die welcke die Apostolen oock gebruyct hebben, om die predicatie des Evangelijs mede te stercken, ende die cracht der wet te thoonen." The editors add that the knowledge of sin, instilled by the Pentateuch and the prophetic books, begets and intensifies the longing for Christ: "Die andere Propheten ende geschiedenissen, van Josue, den Rechteren, der Coningen, ende dier ghelijck, en zijn anders niet tot gheenen eynde geschreven, dan Moyses boecken, want si doen tselve dat Moyses doet ende keeren die valsche Propeten dat si tvolc niet en souden verleyden ende afkeeren vander rechter kennisse der wet, ende ten rechten verstande om die sonde te weten ende henselven te kennen, ende zijn eyghen crancheyt ende te spiegelen aen die punitie der sonden, ende alsoo die gratie Christi te begheren."

152. Having insisted that Christ may be discerned in the Old Testament, as he is seen in the New, the editors conclude with what amounts to an implicit defense of biblical images, urging the reader to seek salvation through Christ, keeping his cause ever in view ("om namaels ten eewigen leven te comen, bi Jesum Christum, wiens sake wi voor ooghen hebben").

153. The print contains signatures identifying Coornhert as the person who executed the print (*DVC fecit*), Van Heemskerck as the inventor of the image (*Martinus Hemskerck Inventor*), and Hieronymus Cock as the publisher who commissioned it (*Hieronijmus

Cock excude.*). The terms *fecit* (executed), *invenit* or *inventor* (invented or inventor), and *excudebat* (published) became standard for reproductive prints, that is, prints produced by teams of specialist draughtsmen, printmakers, and publishers, at mid-century. Coornhert and Van Heemskerck, both based in Haarlem, collaborated closely between 1548 and 1559; the print publisher Cock, founder of the Antwerp firm *Aux Quattre Vents*, began working with them in 1553. This was one of several large prints he commissioned in the early 1550s to establish his reputation as a publisher of note. Other large-format prints issued by Cock include Giorgio Ghisi's *Saint Paul Preaching in the Areopagus* (*School of Athens*) of 1550 and *Disputà* of 1552, both after Raphael, and *Last Supper* of 1551 after Lambert Lombard, on which see Boorsch and Lewis 1985, 61–70. Having secured an imperial privilege (*Cum gratia et privilegio. per. An. 6.*), Cock started marketing this important print in 1554. The privilege, which protected the print from illicit copying for a period of six years, indicates that *Balaam and the Angel* was a valuable asset in which Cock had invested time, energy, and capital; on the significance of the privilege, see Ilja Veldman in Rijksmuseum 1986, 263. On Van Heemskerck and the publishers and reproductive engravers whom he supplied with drawings, see Veldman 1986b, 13–16.

154. The *Biblia pauperum* attaches two Old Testament types, as well as two pairs of prophets, to each New Testament

antitype; the *Speculum humanae salvationis* increases the figurative types to three, on which, with specific reference to *Balaam and the Angel*, see ibid.

155. The sceptre belongs to Christ the King, whose nativity the star of Bethlehem announces.

156. The soldiers and caravan descending the hillside are Balak's messengers sent to transport Balaam to Moab.

157. So furious is Balaam, that he threatens to kill the she-ass: "And Balaam said to the ass, 'Because you have made sport of me. I wish I had a sword in my hand, for then I would kill you'" (Numbers 22:29).

158. "Quo vaesane ruis? Quid verbere cedis iniquo/ Insontem Balaame asinam? Dabis impie poenas.// Cognosti verum, sed vero obsistere pergis/ Consilio horrendo, nec te mens conscia terret.// Hoc spes mercedis, lucri scelerata cupido/ Hoc facit. Ergo tibi dira instant fata. Caveto.// Nam quisquis vero adversatur conscius, ausu/ Sacrilego, offensi experietur numinis iram."

159. In Revelation 2:14, John reprimands the church of Pergamum for preserving the "teaching of Balaam, who taught Balak to put a stumbling block before the sons of Israel, that they might eat food sacrificed to idols and practice immorality." The three idols standing in niches of the ruined temple behind Balaam (two at right, one at distant left) perhaps allude to the prophet's association with idolatry. Jude 1:11 adduces Balaam as a venal practitioner of

divination for hire.

160.   2 Peter 1:8.

161.   2 Peter 1:9.

162.   2 Peter 1:4.

163.   2 Peter 1:5–7.

164.   2 Peter 2:5–6. Among the ruins are a Roman triumphal arch and the Septizonium, as Veldman observes; see Ilja Veldman in Rijksmuseum 1986, 263.

165.   Numbers 22:41, 24:2.

166.   Numbers 24:17–24.

167.   Numbers 24:3–4. In this respect, Van Heemskerck's landscape functions something like the inserted map in the Van Liesveldt Bible of 1538.

168.   The radiant angel unseen by Balaam enhances the viewer's sense that he is virtually blind.

169.   On this print, see Hollstein (Wierix) 384 (2:184). On Van Veen, see Haberditzl 1908, 220; Van de Put 1920; Norris 1940; De Maeyer 1955a, 62–82; De Maeyer 1955b; Müller-Hofstede 1957; Müller-Hofstede 1959; Hughes 1980; Vlieghe 1981; Foucart 1985; Walch 1985; Vogl 1987; Grieten 1995; Vlieghe 1998, 18–19, 283; Bertini 1998; Foucart 1998; Van Mander 1994–99, 6:52–68; Patigny 2003; and Melion 2009, 331–65.

170.   The large basin at the threshold of the image holds the saving blood of Christ.

171.   Van Veen interpolates Isaiah on the model of the printed *Biblia pauperum*, in which prophets comment upon the typological relation between Old Testament prototypes and their New Testament antitypes. However, there the prophets function as framing elements,

whereas Van Veen brings Isaiah into the Passion scene, showing how integral is the relation between the two testaments.

172.   On this book, see Hamilton 1981; Visser 1988; Engammare 1994; Dekoninck 1999; Dekoninck 2004; Mielke 2005, vii–xiv, esp. vii–viii; and Bowen and Imhof 2008, 213–15. The various editions are listed in New Hollstein (Van der Borcht Book Illustrations) 235–334 (1:3–5). On the complicated publication history of the *Imagines et figurae bibliorum*, initiated by Christopher Plantin in the early 1580s, but finally issued clandestinely by Franciscus Raphelengius ca. 1592–93, see especially the article by Visser; and on the spiritualist beliefs espoused implicitly throughout the book, see the articles by Dekoninck.

173.   "Interpretationes sive Explicationes imaginum aliquot historiae biblicae," in Van Barrefelt 1592, unfoliated [first folio recto after *imago* 60]: "Quae reductae & accommodatae ab Historia propriè figurativa ad testimonia veritatis essentialis: quam Christianus quilibet (adiuvante divina gratia, & praeeunte renuntiatione sui) potest & debet in anima ac pectore percipere atque agnoscere: ad vitae salutarem renovationem, & pacem cum Deo, per filium eius aeternum Dominum & Salvatorem nostrum Jesum Christum, in unitate sancti Spiritus, qui in Trinitate unus Deus fuit, est, & erit in saecula."

174.   Ibid.: "Primus homo de terra terrenus: secundus homo de caelo caelestis, etc." The afterword explains that the process of viewing, facilitated

by the commentaries, progresses from external to internal vision: the terrestrial significance of the historical events is first described, after which the essential truths they contain are then discerned. As we shall see, Van Barrefelt conceives of this process as continuous and exegetical, leading always from the figurative, temporal, and perceptible image of contingent things, to the essential, eternal, and spiritual image of Christ. That the illustrations embed the biblical episodes within panoramic landscapes, constitutes a challenge to the viewer, who must first find them and then focus in on their Christian meaning. Although the mode of visual interpretation may at first seem familiarly typological, in practice the transition from figurative to essential reading seems quite abrupt, the spiritual image difficult to apprehend, so that Van Barrefelt's masterful guidance proves ineluctable. It may therefore be argued that the book implicitly stages his authority as religious leader.

175.   Ibid., unfoliated [third folio recto after *imago* 60]: "Umbram habet lex futurorum bonorum, non ipsam imaginem rerum."

176.   Ibid.: "Hoc praeceptum quod praecipio tibi hodie, non est occultum à te, neque remotum est. Non in caelo est, ut dicas, Quis ascendet pro nobis in caelum, ut tollat illud nobis, & recitet nobis illud, ut impleamus illud? Neque trans mare est, ut dicas, Quis transfretabit pro nobis mare, ut afferat illud nobis, ut impleamus illud? Sed propinquum est tibi verbum valdè in ore tuo & in corde

tuo, ut facias illud. Vide, proposui tibi hodie vitam & bonum, mortem item & malum."

177.   Ibid.: "Habemus firmissimum Sermonem propheticum: cui rectè facitis quod attendatis, velut lucernae splendenti in obscuro loco, usque dum dies elucescat, & lucifer exoriatur in cordibus vestris."

178.   On Barrefelt's ambivalent attitude toward pictorial images, which he embeds within an emblematic apparatus that both privileges and transcends the figurative *imago*, see Dekoninck 1999, 107–111, 120–25. On the Familist beliefs implicit throughout the *Imagines et figurae*, and especially on Barrefelt's faith in illuminative *renovatio* and its source in the Holy Spirit, see Dekoninck 2004, 54–55.

179.   Van Barrefelt 1592, unfoliated [first folio verso after *imago* 60]: "Tibi, amice Lector, oculos pectoris ante omnia precamur per Christum Jesum: qui idem ianuam tui cordis reseret, ut sentire et agnoscere in teipso possis mira et essentialia Dei opera, quae initio per figurale ministerium homini figurali ostendit."

180.   Ibid.: "In quo tamen ministerio, divinae & caelestis Essentiae splendorem plenè adspicere et adipisci in spiritu humanitas non potest, donec per divinam gratiam in essentiale ministerium Christi transferatur & veluti transplantetur."

181.   Ibid.: "Quoniamque eadem humanitas nixa imaginarij intellectus sui viribus, divinam interpretationem negligit, & censet ad notitiam Dei

pervenire se in terrestri Essentia posse, eique in iustitia propria plenè satisfacere: ideo varij & diversi ministeriorum figuralium inter homines suborti ritus (quod nos, benignissimo Deo favente, per simplex ministerium Jesu Christi in nobis vidimus & invenimus) per quos carnei isti sensus, perverso iudicio, à Dei pace & à se dissidentes abeunt, & in sectas sparguntur.”

182. Ibid.: “causam habuimus (ut obviam iremus depravationi huic sensuum) Dei operationem de qua Scriptura testatur, partim iuxta figurale ministerium tabulis formisque exprimendi, partim adiungendi breviter legitimum sensum, sive basim & fundamentum Scripturae secundum Spiritum & Essentiam Christi, ad quam figurae & imagines nos ducunt.”

183. Ibid.: “Sperantes fore, ut Deus Lectori per suum Spiritum cor aperiat & illustret; uti cernat sentiatque, quid Deus per figurale ministerium requirat ab homine, & quis eius instituti finis. Quo facto non dubiè à perverso illo iudicio desistet, quod sibi è figurale essentia sumpserat: idque in se potius vertet, ut Dei pacificus Spiritus in eo regnet & domicilium sibi collocet ad renovationem vitae in Christo. Quam ut adipiscatur, monemus seriò Lectorem, ut interioris intellectus omnem aciem intendat in admonitionem doctrinamque harum figurarum, nec ita eas transeat tamquam historias nudas. Nimirum ut operationem Dei in cordibus sentiat; et solatium potius divinae Essentiae intus percipiat quàm ministerij figuralis.

Atque ita utetur iis hoc ipso fine, quo eas dedimus: nempe ad suam salutem, Dei gloriam, & ad vitae renovationem in Christo.”

184. Ibid.: “tamen hoc scriptum ideo, ut quisque in se bonum & malum discat novisse; et istud spernere, illud apprehende. Quod nisi esset, nihil praeter historicam narrationem è Scriptura homines haurirent, ignari renovationis vitae.”

185. Ibid., unfoliated [second folio recto after *imago* 60]: “Felix ille qui scripturam ita in se legit, ad suam salutem: quod cuique animadvertendum, ut in tempore figurale suum minsterium & iustitiam Deo in sancta Essentia sua tradat et offerat, ac permittat illum extruere sibi suum regnum per Christum…Nam omnium rerum, quas Deus homini subministrat, & quas ipse homo sibi attribuit, aut adsumit; Deus sibi iudicium servat, qui manet in sancta sua Essentia solus iudex super caelum & terram. Idque tam in figurali quàm essentiali ministerio. Sunt enim duo Ministeria, quae Deus sancta sua Sapientia exerceri permisit, & ipse in homine exercet.”

186. Ibid.: “Ideoque Lector intelligat & attendat, dupliciter considerari has figuras debere. Primò figurativè, deinde essentialiter: è quibus quod figurativum est cessat, alterum manet in vitam aeternam. Quare magis vertendus animus ad id quod essentiale est, quàm figurativum, magisque in pectus defigendum. Quia hoc docet duntaxat et gubernat primum hominem, qui è terra est; illud alium hominem qui è caelo;

sicut Paulus testatur in I. ad Corinth. cap. 15. & Joh. 3. & variis Scriptura locis. Existimamus igitur figuras has cum sua interpretatione usui esse posse Lectori timenti Deum, ut in anima & pectore sentiat sensum intimum Scripturarum.”

187. On *imago* 13, see New Hollstein (Van der Borcht Book Illustrations) 248 (1:9).

188. Van Barrefelt 1592, unfoliated [folio verso of *imago* 12]: “In hac imagine & figura vides, Deum remittentem vindictam Aquae, deponere Arcam Noë in monte Ararat.”

189. Ibid.: “Quod nobis in exemplum, ut agnoscamus & fateamur benignitatem & divinam gratiam, quam exhibet vindicta completa; ut corde puro & libero convertamur ad eum: & quemadmodum Arcam suam in figura descendere iussit in montem Ararat: (idest, in legalem instructionem doctrinamque, quae maledictionem adducit & metum damnationis super peccatis) ita placeat ei iubere descendere sanctam suam Arcam essentialem in montem Syon.”

190. Ibid.: “Hoc est, ut demittat instructionem doctrinamque sanctae Essentiae suae in cor nostrum, idipsum deiiciat & humiliet, ut annuncietur ibi salus in qua desinit & finit maledictio damnationis.”

191. On *imago* 14, see New Hollstein (Van der Borcht Book Illustrations) 249 (1:9).

192. Van Barrefelt 1592, unfoliated [folio verso of *imago* 13]: “In imagine & figura licet hîc cernere, Postquam Noë cum gratiarum actione holocaustum obtulisset, Deum posuisse Arcum in caelo.”

193. Ibid.: “Signum non ultra mundum periturum aqua. Quod nobis pro exemplo est, ut moniti signo figurativi arcus caelestis, animum applicemus ad ardens essentiale signum Dei.”

194. Ibid.: “Quod est ignea charitas, cum aqua puritatis in omnibus animis divinis. Quae charitas item notat omnibus profanis animis & remotis à Deo, Ignem horroris cum amara aqua condemnationis. Ita ut quisque pro sua parte visurus sit hoc signum divinum, ad potentiam Dei recipiendam, sive ad salutem, sive ad damnationem.”

195. On *imago* 22, see New Hollstein (Van der Borcht Book Illustrations) 257 (1:11–12).

196. Van Barrefelt 1592, unfoliated [folio verso after *imago* 21]: “Quod evenit nobis in exemplum, ut essentialiter & reipsa sentiamus, Deum per Essentiam suam perfectam imagines & figuras suas in nobis implere & essentialiter perficere. Ita ut Abrahamus (pater fidei) manus ad Deum tollat contra regem Sodomorum: Id est obedientia salutaris fidei, robur & vires ei dat contra contumaciam rebellis corruptae Essentiae terrestris, & reipsa testatur: Natura mea divina nihil concupiscit è terrestri tua Proprietate vel Sapientia ingenij, ne in tua Proprietate glorieris, quòd me (salutarem fidem) ditaveris, sed tua (proprietas nempe) tibi sunto, & mihi da quod iuvenes comederunt. Id est, Tu rebellis terrestris Essentia fer damnabile tuum onus, sed permitte ut tenerum & iuvenile principium fidei, quod mecum abiit à Proprietate, partem habeat cum virili

senio. Hoc est: Serva terrestrem tuam Essentiam, & sine divinam naturam vivere in Essentia sua salutari."

197.   On *imago* 38, see New Hollstein (Van der Borcht Book Illustrations) 273 (1:16).

198.   Van Barrefelt 1592, unfoliated [folio verso after *imago* 37]: "Quod scriptum nobis ad documentum, ut ipsi in eodem lapide Jacobi quiescamus, qui est incorrupta & incorrumpenda aeterna Essentia Dei."

199.   Ibid.: "In quem lapidem Jacobus (qui idem Israël dicitur, quia victor) inclinat in natura Dei: & erigit eum (Essentiam divinam) in domicilium & sedem Dei."

200.   Ibid.: "estque vivus ille lapis, quem Petrus Apostolus commemorat."

201.   Ibid.: "In eo enim loco scalae eriguntur è terra ad caelum, per quas angeli ascendunt, & descendunt. Quae sunt Affectio & Charitas erectae in Humanitate usque ad caelestem Essentiam, cùm Jacobus desiderium peccandi in ea contrivit. Per quam Affectionem seu Charitatem in sanctam Essentiam Dei angeli administri ascendunt & descendunt. Qui sunt inspiratio inter divinitatem ac Humanitatem."

202.   On *imago* 48, see New Hollstein (Van der Borcht Book Illustrations) 283 (1:19).

203.   Van Barrefelt 1592, unfoliated [folio verso after *imago* 47]: "Videre licet in imagine & figura, Moysen Dei servum cum Domino in monte locutum, & cum duabus tabulis decem Mandatorum descendere; atque cominus ad Israëlem

accedere, ut legem ei iustitiae proponat, quae iniustas cupidines peccatorum occidit."

204.   Ibid.: "Quod nobis pro exemplo accidit, ut legem iustitiae ex Essentia divina in cordibus nostris consideremus ad occisionem voluptatum & cupidinum, quae exoriuntur in nobis è carne: idque ad poenitentiam & emendationem terrestris peccatricis vitae."

205.   Ibid.: "Et cùm hoc legale servitium sub Moyse accompleverimus in morte peccatorum, accipimus demum, ut S. Paulus ait, legem Christi, quae vivificat in Spiritu. Quae est renovatio salutaris vitae, ad quam lex & Prophetae, & Christus secundum carnem ministerium suum extendunt. Quod si innovata ea vita in Christo, propter imaginarium servitium, non subsequitur, ministerium imaginum vanum est (id est infructiferum) in nobis."

206.   On *imago* 54, see New Hollstein (Van der Borcht Book Illustrations) 290 (1:21).

207.   Van Barrefelt 1592, unfoliated [folio verso after *imago* 53]: "Quod nobis pro exemplo, ut nos quoque expectemus nunc & sollicitè observemus Regem Josiam (qui est Deus essentialis) ut regnum animae nostrae obtineat, nobisque librum legis (essentialem iustitiam) in penetrali pectoris huius ostendat: quem librum in terrestri pectore amisimus."

208.   Ibid.: "Eaque ostensione mirificè incitabimur & cupiemus nasci ex essentiali Deitate.   Quae cupiditas sive desiderium ad partum incitat: et

quamdiu illa in Deum non est, non potest humanitas instrui à divinitate."

209.   Ibid.: "Ideo omnis Humanitas meritò anhelare debet, ut liber legis divinae generationis iterum inveniatur, ut quotidie legi possit in templo cordis."

210.   On *imago* 55, see New Hollstein (Van der Borcht Book Illustrations) 291 (1:21).

211.   Van Barrefelt 1592, unfoliated [folio verso after *imago* 54]: "Hic videre licet in imagine & figura, Prophetam in agrum ire, ubi flores virent, sed homines non habitant: atque illic Deus cum eo sermonem vult instituere."

212.   Ibid.: "Hoc nobis in exemplum, ut in extremo hoc fine temporum, cum omnibus sensibus & cogitationibus, ab imaginariis desideriis affectibusque avellamur; et transeamus ad simplicem Essentiam Christi, ubi varij sensus & cogitationes non habent locum."

213.   Ibid.: "Illic Spiritus Domini cum Anima sermonem instituet, & certam eam reddet suae voluntatis. Ita etiam Dominus testatur: *Cùm orare voles, abi in cubiculum tuum & occlude ianuam*. Quod nobis documentum et monitum est, ut à Proprietate nostra eamus in Essentiam Dei: ubi arcana sua Dominus aperiet & inseret pectori Humanitatis ad vitam novam in spiritu."

214.   The pictorial sequence begins with the *Fall of Man* and the *Expulsion from Paradise*, the events that necessitate the coming of Christ, and closes with *Pentecost*, the shoring up of the Church as the divinely sanctioned instrument of salvation, and the *Last Judgment*. There follow two addenda—the *Virgin of Sorrows*

and the *Virgin and Child*—that focus on Mary as chief witness to the life and especially Passion of Christ.

215.   On the *Passio Domini nostri Iesu Christi*, see De Graaf 1958, 25–26; and Kölker 1963, 55–60. The publisher Dodo Pietersz may originally have ordered the woodcuts to illustrate an earlier Passion book, commissioned by the canon Hans Reff in 1520, on which see ibid., 57–60.

216.   "Alardus. Amstelredamus. F. Theodorico Syrenio. S. D. P." in Amstelredamus 1523, unfoliated: "Non aequum esse censeo suavissime Syreni, ut quicquid est mihi Christianorum Poetarum, non sine qualicumque studiorum meorum iactura, tot tantisque mensibus haud cunctanter tibi, sine ullo foenore commodem. Nam tametsi referendi facultas tibi ut omnium rerum plus satis indigo quippe religioso desit, promptam tamen adesse voluntatem nihil ambigo, qua merito, nisi plane impudentiusculus forem flagitator, utcumque contentus esse & possem & deberem.…Proinde te etiam atque etiam rogo, ut omnibus omnium librorum horum marginalibus oris gnaviter explicatis, obiter annotata a nobis carmina fideliter describas primum, deinde suis quaeque imagunculis adijcias." Alardus desires to transfer his editorial obligations to Theodoricus, because the latter has the spare time to edit these poems (*plus satis otij suppetat tibi*) and wields the elements of poetry elegantly (*perquam aeleganter elementa depingas*). The term *depingas* (represent by painting) suggests that Theodoricus

skillfully paints with words.

217. Ibid.: "haec sicubi meliora forsitan occurrant (occurent autem complurima modo exactius evolvas) quam subindicavimus, ea fac diligenter excerpas. Sed apposita, sed pia, sed recondita digeras oportet omnia."

218. Ibid.: "Cogita mi Syreni plus quoddam tibi nunc praestandum, quam quod Homerus ille de Syrenum cantibus finxit. Fingit autem ille eas non vocum suavitate, aut novitate quadam, & varietate cantandi revocare eos solitas qui praetervehebantur, sed quia multa se scire profitebantur, ut homines ad earum saxa discendi cupidate adhaerescerent. Tibi vero nunc adnitendum atque adeo adnitendum, ut quisquis vere salutarem sitiat poesim, vereque Christianos audire Syrenes discupiat."

219. Ibid.: "Vale, ac vide necubi dormites in hisce centunculis probe consarcinandis, stamina tibi atque subtegmina, & licia concinnavi tu deinde pulcherrimam vestem ipse facito, iterum Vale."

220. Drawn from masters famed for their literary style and Christian piety, the verses are construed as agents of Pauline conversion, that cause their reader to become like Saint Paul, recognizing nothing but Jesus Christ, envisaging him crucified for our sins. Together with the images, the poems are intended to act like a lens focussing one's corporeal and spiritual eyes upon Christ—hence the book's subtitle *scopus meditationis* (target of meditation).

221. Ibid.: "Imo curabis ut quisquis

haec carmina lectitarit, ilico cum .D. Paulo iam non se dicat quicquam scire, vel apud quemvis, nisi Iesum Christum & hunc crucifixum. Scio difficillimum esse ad quod hortor, sed aliquam graviora vehemens crucifixi meditatio praestitit. Nec alia ratio par tanto negocio. Equidem nihil est tam arduum in rebus humanis, quod non efficiat si hoc sibi sentiat animus noster, quod fuit in Christo Iesu ut magnopere velit."

222. Ibid.: "Novi enim tuum illud corpusculum, invictum est, infatigabile est, ut non aliunde magis reparare vires, quam de laboribus ipsis videatur. Demetenda erit igitur haec sylvula maturissimis, denissimisque arbustis undique confertissima, unde semper redit labor actus in orbem."

223. Ibid.: "Ut vel hinc nobis congestus aliquis amarissimae fasciculus mirrhae, molle intra pectus bifidam quod ducit in ubera vallem, coniectus commoretur, atque subinde pectori appraessetur, qui vel algentissimum olfacientis animum vehementer alliciat, demulceat, & inflammet."

224. On this sensory imagery of the soul's garden and its meditative functions, see Falkenburg 1994.

225. "Alardus. Amstelredamus. Lectori," in Amstelredamus 1523, unfoliated: "Ut redit, itque frequens longum formica per agmen/ Granifero solitum dum vehit ore cibum/ Aut ut apes saltusque suos, & olentia nactae/ Pascua, per flores & Thyma summa volant/ Sic ruit ad ad sacros vates Syrenius, atque/ Floribus e vernis dulcia mella parat." As the subtitle

indicates, this subsection is addressed to the reader, rather than specifically to Theodorico Syreno.

226. Ibid.: "Aliud eiusdem ad eundem/ Nec melius teneris iunguntur vitibus ulmi,/ Nec plus lotos aquas, litora myrtus amat./ Nec vaga tam tenui discursat aranea tela,/ Tam leve nec bombix pendulus urget opus/ Singula quam varijs excerpta poemata libris,/ Conveniunt, proprijs quaeque relata locis."

227. "Adamus Verdunius Hagensis Ad pium lectorem," in Amstelredamus 1523, unfoliated: "Habes hic optime lector adventum, vitam, obitum, Resurrectionem quae Servatoris nostri Iesu Christi versibus doctis, iuxta ac pijs, ex diversis & religiosissimis quibusque Christianae religionis poetis. Quos & plurimos fuisse constat, & omni literarum genere excultissimos, ut qui non raro fidem nostram a gentilium, & haereticorum impietate vindicarint, eamque eximijs literarum monumentis egregie locupletarint.... Facessant igitur, inquam, & desinat carpere, raptare, imo lacerare divinam ipsam poeticen, quasi quae nil nisi moribus officiat, quaeque nihil in medium afferat, unde pietatem liceat discere. Quum eam ipse .D. Paulus non dedignatus sit in testimonium adducere, & poetam Epimenidem, prophetam appellare non sit veritus, cumque videant tot, tam pios, tamque insignes sanctae ecclesiae proceres huic operam navasse, huic qui praecipua fidei nostrae misteria concredidisse."

228. The "Rite of Eating the Paschal

Lamb" derives from the principal poem in Alardus's short tractate, *Ritus edendi paschalis agni* (Amsterdam, 1523), likewise published by Doen Pieterszoon, on which see De Graaf 1958, 26–30; and Kölker 1963, 60–64.

229. "Ritus edendi paschalis agni per .Alar .Amstel.," in Amstelredamus 1523, unfoliated: "Annus exactis ubi transit mensibus orbis. Ex. 12./ Primum sume diem mensis cognomine Nisan,/ Dum cava dimidiae sinuantur cornua lunae/ Subque diem decimum praesto sit victima semper/ Inde die quarto caligine noctis aborta./ Quando agitat levibus pro prima crepuscula pennis/ E pastu volucres ad nota cubilia vesper."

230. Ibid.: "Immundo grave olens coitu, peregreque reversus/ Differet in mensem purgata mente sequundum/ Servabunt patrios pereginus, & advena cultus/ Qui solenne statis peragit non pascha diebus/ Hunc inopina premet mors, hunc et acerba sequentur/ Nil operis nisi quod spectat peragant ad escam./.../ Quod si forte nequit, dum quaeritur agnus haberi/ De grege tunc sumant hoedum quemcumque licebit./ Sanguine cuius utrumque linent postemque, domumque,/ In quibus hoc comedent epulum promiscua turba,/ Fascibus hissopi tinctis in sanguine, passim/ Postibus asperso laquearia sanguine manent.. Illitus eniteat supero de limine sanguis./ Hic erit inditio, multosque relinquet inultos./.../ Prodigiosa scatet quo nunc Aegyptus ad unum,/ A primogenito Pharaonis in arce sedentis/ Afflictamque gravi gentem

terrore prementis/ Ad primogenitum captivae, et matris egenae/ Una nocte, sed ignota, nimiumque tremenda,/ Vindice transadiget gladio, impureque necabit/ Omnis et Aegyptus quae sit divina potestas/ Sentiet, et sero sapiet rex ipse superbus,/ Ac poenas tandem ille dabit, dabit impius acres./.../ Agresti cum lactuca, et sylvestribus herbis,/ Non fermentato cum pane subinde recocto,/ Multam sub noctem coeuntibus undique turbis./ Festinanter edant, ne Aegyptius opprimat hostis/ Transitus est domini, dictum cognomine Phase/ Et caput, ossa, pedes, femur, intestina vorantor."

231.   "Iuven. presby. libro .4. evange. histo.," in ibid.: "Vespere tum primo bis sex recubantibus una/ Discipulis, tali divinat voce magister."

232.   Ibid.: "Sed soboles hominum quondam praescripta subibit/ Supplicia ad tempus, miserabilis ille per aevum,/ Qui iustum tradet, quanto foelicior esset,/ Si nunquam terris tetigisset limina vitae./ At iudas graviter tum conscia pectora pressus."

233.   Ibid.: "Nunquid ait Iudam talis suspitio tangit?/ Respondit dominus, te talia dicere cerno."

234.   Ibid.: "Haec ubi dicta dedit, palmis sibi frangere panem:/ Divisumque dehinc tradit: sanctumque precatus,/ Discipulos docuit sanctum se tradere corpus./ Hoc ait accipite vobis nostri monumentum./ Hinc calicem sumit dominus, vinoque repletum/ Gratis sanctificat verbis: potumque ministrat./ Edocuitque suum se divisisse cruorem./ Atque ait, hic sanguis populi delicta remittet./ Hunc

potate meum. Aeternae haec foedera pacis."

235.   On this scriptural emblem book, see Ríos 1928; Mauquoy-Hendrickx 1978–83, 3:438–65, nos. 2172–2225; Navarro López 1990–91; Navarro López 1991; Hänsel 1991, 68–89; Hänsel 1993; Navarro López 1996; Alcina Rovira 1997; Alcina Rovira 1998; Sanchez Salor 1998, 159, no. 20; Sese Sanz 1998; Melion 1999, 65–67; Bowen 2003; Melion 2005a, 90–98; New Hollstein (Van der Borcht Book Illustrations) 899–946 (3:52–62); Hollstein (Wierix Book Illustrations) 3 (1:23–36); Bowen and Imhof 2008, 107–121; and Melion 2009, 39–104.

236.   On *imago* 2, see New Hollstein (Van der Borcht Book Illustrations) 899 (3:52). On the engraver Abraham de Bruyn, see Bowen and Imhof 2008, 329–31.

237.   Arias Montano 1571, unfoliated [*imago* 2]: "Verae sapientiae rudimenta."

238.   Ibid.: "Dux hominum interpresque Dei mitissime Moses,/ Omnia qui primus tempora ponis, ave."

239.   Ibid.: "Fideli ministro pos."

240.   "In tabulam Mosis Prophetae. Ode Sapphica II.," in ibid., unfoliated [*ode* 2]: "Clara Levitum soboles, Deo nec/ Non viris charum caput, ac puellis,/ Quem pater Nilus puerum innocenti/ Sustulit alveo:// Si quid angusto celebrare versu/ Possumus magnum, tibi nostra mixtis/ Vox ferat, Moses, fidibus dicati/ Carminis hymnum.//.../ Praepotens herbis magicoque cantu/ Thana mentitas simulare formas,/ Mox tibi veris agitata monstris/ Victaque cessit."

241.   Ibid.: "Redditus tandem populo

tuorum/ Nuncius magni superûm parentis,/ Rector afflicti & generis minister/ Nosceris idem."

242.   Ibid.: "Impiger ductor populi timentis,/ Pectora ut verbis recreas disertis;/ Ipse, quae nunquam metuis, pericla/ Vincere monstras.// Numinis purae placitura menti/ Iura, quae gentes metuántque reges,/ Certus interpres capis, obstupendo/ Clarus honore."

243.   Christopher Plantin, "Tabula II. argumentum," in ibid., 3: *Verae sapientiae rudimenta*.] Christum Dei sapientiam Paulus appellat, 1. Cor. 1. 24. Idem etiam Gal. 3. 24 legem antiquam, cuius minister Moses fuit, paedagogum hominibus ad Christum fuisse dicit."

244.   Christopher Plantin, "Ode II.," in ibid.: "Mosis laudes canit, quem ab ipso usque ortu Dei consilio delectum, variis per omnem aetatem amplitudinis testimoniis ornatum, tandem libertatis ducem declaratum, & legislatorem summa auctoritate constitutum fuisse ait."

245.   Ibid.: "*Obstupen. clarus honore*.] Gloriam & auctoritatem ex Dei colloquio Mosi additam indicat, Exod. 34. 29. 2. Cor. 3. 7."

246.   On *imago* 26, see New Hollstein (Van der Borcht Book Illustrations) 919 (3:57); Hollstein (Wierix Book Illustrations) 3.6 (1:24, 32).

247.   Arias Montano 1571, unfoliated [*imago* 26]: "Pietatis indefessum studium." "Qui Christum non odit, amet responsa legátque/ Amosidae: is fiet nam pius & sapiens."   "Divinar. rer. indici admirabili p."

248.   "In tabulam Isaiae Prophetae. Ode dicolos tetrastrophos. XXVI..," in ibid., unfoliated [*ode* 26]: "Prudens praeteriti temporis, ac tui/ Venturique modos, & seriem canis,/ Spectator veluti videris omnia/ Depicta in superûm domo.// Quis vatum propior cernere ab ultima,/ Quicquid magnus habet mundus, origine,/ Mores, historias, imperia urbium,/ Cuncta & saecula gentium?"

249.   Ibid.: "Quae vis eloquij, quae ingenij queat/ Exaequare modos, & decus ac tui/ Dicendo rapidum fluminis impetum,/ Sensu & multiplices notas?"

250.   Ibid.: "Vitae certa tuo tempora nuntio/ Rex prolata videt, ductaque longius,/ Cùm Sol pollicitis additur arbiter/ Decursum relegens diem."

251.   Christopher Plantin, "Argument. Tab. XXVI. de Isaia," in ibid., 14: *Pietatis indefessum studium*.] Huius rei exemplum in Isaia statuitur egregium, qui creditum sibi propheticum munus summa fide, magna pietatis & publicae salutis cura, usque ad mortem diligentissimè gessit. Ille suorum temporum scripsit historiam, hoc est, partem librorum Regum."

252.   Christopher Plantin, "Argumentum dedicationis," in ibid.: *Divinarum rerum indici admirabili*.] Nam nullus antiquorum prophetarum de divinis rebus, de humanae salutis ratione arcana, de Christo, de omni denique Evangelio plenius & significantius scripsit quàm Isaias."

253.   Arias Montano 1571, unfoliated [*imago* 8]: "Humana divinitas." "Cur tanto genus humanum dignetur honore/ Dicere, non nisi qui perficere ipse potest."

"Dei philanthropiae s."

254. "In somnium Iacob. Ode dicolos distrophos. VIII.," in ibid., unfoliated [*ode* 8]: "Quae patribus firmata olim sunt foedera primis,/ Novique coepta ab orbis ante termino,/ Et quae prima hominum, quaeque altera credidit aetas,/ Rudi sed usque pervoluta imagine:/ Haec eadem iam clara magis, monstratáque cernit/ Suo Iacobus expedita tempore./ Qui dum humilis, fugiensque minas fratrisque furores,/ Deum vocaret, inque vota posceret;/ Et placido iam membra daret recreanda sopori,/ Labore pressa, mente sed vigil magis."

255. Ibid.: "En certus docilisque, poli manifesta videbat/ Patentis ampla permicare limina;/ Innixamque solo scalam, quae vertice summo/ Poli tonantis alta templa vinceret;/ Multifidoque gradu terris deduceret imis/ Ad usque tecta fulgidi orbis aurea./ Illic supremam sedem, pater ipse benignè/ Fovens, tenebat efficace numine;/ Quo vultu solisque ignes, hyemesque nivales,/ Et impotentis impetum maris regit./ Hâc iter ad superos didicit, certamque patere/ Viam perennis usque ad intima aetheris./ Iamque oblata hominum generi commercia divûm/ Videns, fatetur atque adorat excitus./ Cernit enim aligeros, non agmina rara, ministros/ Identidem altos ferre per gradus pedem:/ Inde hominum terras invisere, rursus & isthinc/ Tonantis alta commeare limina."

256. Ibid.: "Tunc pavet agnoscitque domum portamque supernam./ Opus sed astra quod pererrat ultima,/ Quodque premens terras, praetervolat aethera,

in arctum/ Vocare carmen & referre sit nefas."

257. Christopher Plantin, "Tabul. VIII. Argum.," in ibid., 5: "*Humana divinitas*.] Videns Iacob mysterium ecclesiae, in qua habitaturus erat Deus trinus & unus, Verè, inquit, terribilis est locus iste, & non est nisi domus Dei, & porta caeli. Cùm autem Deus in hominibus inhabitat, homines ipsos deificat. Videte, inquit Iohannes, qualem charitatem dedit nobis pater, ut filij Dei nominemur & simus, 1. Iohan. 3. 1."

258. Christopher Plantin, "Inscriptio," in ibid., 5–6: "*Dei philanthropiae*.] Tantam dignitatem deificationis nostrae divino erga homines amori acceptam referendam esse indicat. In hoc est charitas, inquit Iohannes, non quasi nos dilexerimus Deum, sed quoniam ipse prior dilexit nos, 1. Iohan. 4. 10."

259. Christopher Plantin, "Argum. Odae VIII.," in ibid., 6: "Omnium promissorum, quae olim patribus facta fuerant, de serpentis capite conterendo, de benedictione familiarum terrae in semine Abrahae, summam quandam iam speciali quodam modo relatam, in illa ostensa Iacobo imagine indicatam fuisse ait."

260. Ibid.: "Quandoquidem omnia illud continebant arcanum, Deum, diaboli deleta tyrannide, in hominibus, ut in propria sibíque sanctificata domo, regnaturum, magnámque futuram esse spirituum caelestium, & hominum amicitiam, & familiaritatem."

261. Ibid.: "Est hoc magnae significationis mysterium, de quo poëta

aliâs plenius soluta oratione disseret. Adeo autem excellentis argumenti est, ut caelum usque ad ipsum Dei thronum penetret; quamobrem eleganti figura in ipso amplificationis incremento Ode ipsa finem sibi praescripsit."

262. On *imago* 12, see New Hollstein (Van der Borcht Book Illustrations) 908 (3:54).

263. Arias Montano 1571, unfoliated [*imago* 12]: "Divinae virtutis specimen."

264. Ibid.: "Fluctibus in mediis, & tempestatibus orbis/ Certa est, quae charis lux micet alma piis."

265. Ibid.: "Misericordiae memori. s.," in ibid., unfoliated [*ode* 12]: "Quamvis tu Phariis cultior artibus,/ Caelo dinumeres astra nitentia;/ Et res noveris unus,/ Quas tellus fovet ac mare;// Humanam fugiunt haec sapientiam,/ Et nostro positos ingenio modos,/ Queis atiingere mundi/ Vix conclusa licet polis."

266. "In tabulam Mosis, rubi incendium mirati. Ode tricolos tetrastrophos. XII."

267. Ibid.: "Quod si tantus amor discere, quam novam/ Mirator speciem conspicis;/ infimas/ Curas exue terrae,/ Et fastus animi graves."

268. Ibid.: "Hic iam veridica voce docebere,/ Quàm magnis valeat viribus efficax/ Ignis vertere mundi/ Formas in speciem novam.// Namque ille & tenebras, & chaos, & nihil/ Quondam discutiens intulit optimi/ Mundi consona membra,/ Finesque, & varium decus."

269. Ibid.: "Idem gratus amor perpetuò bonus,/ Flammae quem specie non temere vides,/ Vitam reddere & almam/ Lucem terrigenis parat."

270. Christopher Plantin, "Tabul. XII.

Argum.," in ibid., 8: "*Divinae virtutis specimen*.] Ignis ille quem Moses vidit, cuius vi rubus ardens non urebatur, divinae virtutis specimen quoddam & velut typum fuisse ait. Fovet enim divina virtus pios, modestos atque se advenientem excipientes, eosdémque calore efficientiae suae animat, sanctósque reddit, & à vulgari & prophana consuetudine remotos, ut illo igne totus locus olim calefactus sanctus dictus est."

271. Ibid.: "Idem verò ignis superbos & contumaces, atque sceleratos vi sua exurens consumit: alteram vim Israelitae ex Aegypto educti, alteram Aegyptij illorum hostes experti sunt."

272. Christopher Plantin, "Odae XII. Argum.," in ibid.: "Inducto colloquio cum Mose velut Angeli alloquentis indicat, divinae misericordiae mysteria maximè quae ad salutem hominum pertinent, maiora esse quàm ut humana sapientia absque Dei ipsius doctrina assequi possit. Illa enim cum ex singulari & arcano Dei consilio proficiscantur, Deum doctorem sui postulant, qui tamen facilis & benignus contingat iis, qui fide, charitate, modestia, & caeteris oportunis virtutibus probatos se discipulos praebeant."

273. On *imago* 17, see New Hollstein (Van der Borcht Book Illustrations) 909 (3:54) [mistakenly identified as the *Crossing of the Red Sea*]; and Hollstein (Wierix Book Illustrations) 3.4 (1:24, 32) [mistakenly identified as the *Crossing of the Red Sea*]. On the engraver Pieter Huys, see Bowen and Imhof 2008, 342–45.

274.   Arias Montano 1571, unfoliated [*imago* 17]: "Constantiae fructus." "Fideli Deo s."

275.   Ibid.: "Felix qui monitisque Dei verbisque benigni/ Audiit, ille sacrae compos erit patriae."

276.   "In tabulam Israëlitarum Iordanem transeuntium. Ode sapphica XVII.," in ibid., unfoliated [*ode* 17]: "Sed fides constans animíque magni,/ Quae semel certo radiata verbo,/ Tramitem ostensum subit, atque caeli/ Prospicit alti// Templa, lux unde & favor, ac potentis/ Vis tenax verbi, penetrare praesens/ Turbidi fluctus maris, ac secundo/ Grati a ductu."

277.   Christopher Plantin, "Odae XVI. [sic] Argum.," in ibid., 10: "Docet, non timidis, otiosis, pigris & incredulis, atque laborum detrectatoribus divinorum promissorum eventum usúmque contingere, sed iis qui fide & charitate innixi proposito sibi studium fortiter percurrunt, summa spe reportandi praemij concepta, ex divinis sermonibus efficacissimis ad animos fideli addendos, quibus omnis difficultas frangatur & superetur."

278.   On *imago* 38, see Hollstein (Wierix Book Illustrations) 3.15 (1:25, 33).

279.   Arias Montano 1571, unfoliated [*imago* 38]: "Sol iustitiae exoriens." "In tenebris fulgens lumen divinaque dona/ Simplicitas cernit: non videt ambitio." "Humanae sortis susceptori Deo hominis."

280.   "In tabellam natalis Iesu. Naturae humanae naenia. XXXVIII.," in ibid., unfoliated [*ode* 38]: "Virgineo splendens infans ut prodiit alvo,/ Atque illaesa dedit templa pudicitiae:/ Quae iam uteri intacti

stupuit Natura tumorem,/ Nunc pavet insolitum laeta puerperium./.../Nulla mihi in te iura puer, quòd puer & tener es./ Ergo me superas, sine me qui nasceris infans./ Quòd si me superas, es puer ergo Deus."

281.   Ibid.: "O puer & certè Deus, ô mihi iungeris, ut te/ Partibus excipiam, muneribusque meis./ O Deus, & verè puer, ô tibi iungor, ut aucta/ Amplius ipsa tuo numine perficiar./ Accipies ex me curam puer; atque labores,/ Mortis onus (tibi sic quòd placet) accipies./ A te ego, sed pacem Deus, acceptamque salutem,/ Et posse aeternae rumpere vincla necis."

282.   Christopher Plantin, "Argum. Tab. XXXVIII.," in ibid., 18: "*Sol iustitiae exoriens.*] Christus orbem in tenebris iacentem illustraturus, virtutis suae signum ipso ortu suo dedit, luce per noctem illustrante, & Angelis canentibus, pastoribusque simplicibus admirandum spectaculum vocatis."

283.   Christopher Plantin, "Dedicatio," in ibid.: "*Humanae sortis susceptori Deo homini.*] Qui factus est homo ex semine David, formam servi accipiens, per omne infirmitatis humanae genus (peccato excepto) tentatus."

284.   Christopher Plantin, "Naeniae Argument.," in ibid.: "Natura humana mirata novum genus infantis, agnoscit Deum in mundum venisse hominem, qui, infirmitatibus ipsius susceptis, renovationem admirandam efficiat."

285.   On *imago* 40, see Hollstein (Wierix Book Illustrations) 3.17 (1:25, 33).

286.   Arias Montano 1571, unfoliated [*imago* 40]: "Gentium lux." "Quae colit,

agnoscitque Deum, sapientia vera est./ Quem latet hoc, rudis est, quamlibet alta sciat." "Deo immort. homini vero regi liberatori. s."

287.   "In tabulam adorationis Magorum. Ode tricolos tetrastrophos. XL.," in ibid., unfoliated [*ode* 40]: "Ut Pisghae in altis aetherei iugis,/ Candentis aut de culmine Libani/ Surgentis aurorae salubris/ Conspicitur prior usque fulgor;// At quisquis errat vallibus infimis,/ Caliginosis nubibus obsitus,/ Hic nocte in atra nescit amens/ Purpurei radios diei;// Sic dum Tyrannum cum populo levi/ Exercet amentem ambitio impia,/ Praesentis adventum salutis/ Non Solyme malè caeca sentit.// Sed qui remotos Persidos incolit/ Parthosque tractus, hic alienior/ Splendoris exortum sereni/ Prospicit, & veniens adorat." The poetic conceit likening the Epiphany to the viewing of an awe-inspiring vista derives ultimately from 2 Peter 16, in which the apostle affirms the connection between faith and vision; "the power and coming of our Lord Jesus Christ," he declares, was beheld incontrovertibly when the "eyewitnesses of his majesty" saw him transfigured on Mount Thabor.

288.   Ibid.: "Ostensus astri laetior aurei/ Fulgor, non antè stellifero in polo/ Conspectus ignis, innovandi/ Auspicium referebat orbis."

289.   Ibid.: "Quem mox repertum laetior & Magus/ Miratus, ultra quàm soleat puer/ Mortalis, ostendisse sanctum/ Vultum oculis animóque cernit."

290.   Christopher Plantin, "Odae XL. Argum.," in ibid., 18: "Solem exortum

antea videri ab iis, qui in montibus versantur, quàm ab iis qui in nebulosis vallibus errant: ita Christi numen & nomen prius cognitum est Gentibus, qui Deum ex naturae observatione verè et simpliciter quaerebant, quàm à Iudaeis, malitia, ambitione, & cupiditate excaecatis, & à propria veraque doctrina ob propriam culpam alienatis."

291.   Christopher Plantin, "Argum. Tab. XL.," in ibid.: "*Gentium lux.*] Christus lumen fuit ad revelationem Gentium, Luc. 2. Qui statim ut natus est, magis affulsit congnoscendus."

292.   On *imago* 46, see New Hollstein (Van der Borcht Book Illustrations) 928 (3:58–59); and Hollstein (Wierix Book Illustrations) 3.22 (1:27, 34).

293.   Arias Montano 1571, unfoliated [*imago* 46]: "Naturae innovandae argum." "Christo curatori benigno s."

294.   Ibid.: "Sordet quicquid habet mundus cum munere Christi/ Collatum; nec iam quae placuere valent."

295.   "In tabellam signi à Christo in Cana editi. Ode sapphica. XLVI.," in ibid., unfoliated [*ode* 46]: "Sic & arcanis sociare taedis/ Gentis humanae genus expetitum,/ Et sibi magnis emere adiugandum/ Dotibus ardet:// Possit ut nostrae recreata gentis/ Iuncta divino soboles marito,/ Splendidi sedes habitare caeli/ Regnaque divûm."

296.   Ibid.: "Prima miratrix Galilaea Canas/ Obstupet testis renovata rerum/ Munera, & magnum probat esse Iesu in/ Pectore numen."

297.   Ibid.: "Dum videt certas variare formas,/ Iurat & prisci latices Noachi,/

Fonte quas nuper vitreo fluenteis/ Hauserat undas."

298.   Christopher Plantin, "Odae XLVI. Argum.," in ibid., 20: "Docet hoc carmen Christum praesentia sua nuptias legitimas à Patre suo institutas ornasse, & significasse etiam amorem suum erga Ecclesiam, quam sibi spirituali & arcano matrimonio copulare instituerat; deinde huius rei confirmationem & virtutis Christi signum primum celebrat, aquam in vinum conversam."

299.   On *imago* 51, see New Hollstein (Van der Borcht Book Illustrations) 932 (3:59); and Hollstein (Wierix Book Illustrations) 3.26 (1:28, 43). Arias Montano 1571, unfoliated [*imago* 51]: "Salutis propositio." "Regi legitimo declarato s."

300.   Ibid.: "Christum sponte tibi venientem suscipe mitem./ Si non suscipias, experiêre gravem."

301.   "In tabulam Christi regis Ierosolymae declarati. Ode sapphica LI.," in ibid., unfoliated [*ode* 51]: "Pulchrior nunquam, licet usque fastos/ Iebusum à priscis repetas colonis,/ Sol prius luxit Solymûm beatae aut/ Gratior urbi;// Quàm peroptatis ubi tempus annis/ Obtulit magni faciem colendam/ Regis, arcano cecinere qualem/ Carmine vates."

302.   Ibid.: "Hunc ut exceptum populi valerent/ Cernere, & certis celebrare signis,/ Vexit insuetus iuga ferre lentae/ Pullus asellae// Principem, non ut quibus intumenti/ Folle ventosum vitiosa pectus/ Urget, infestis populo, cupidoque/ / Ambitióque."

303.   Ibid.: "His potestatum specie superba/ Arrogat laudes metus,

atque honores,/ Multa mentitos malè blandientis/ Munera linguae.// Huic sed aeternos meruere plausus/ Dona doctrinae memorata divae,/ Atque morosis medicina praesens/ Addita morbis."

304.   Ibid.: "Vidimus castos pueros canoro, ac/ Virgines Regem coluisse versu,/ Et salutarem meminisse, & alto/ Aethere missum.// Quin & insonteis oleae virentis/ Pacis auctori pia turba frondes/ Spargit, & vestes properatque, avetque/ Sternere eunti.// Nam probat sanctum potiusque dignum/ Evehi iunctis humeris colentum, / Quem Deus terris iubet esse regem,/ Pontificemque."

305.   Christopher Plantin, "Argument. Tabul. LI.," in ibid., 21: *Salutis oblatio.*] Ultro nos Deus dilexit; ultro filium suum in mundum misit, ut dissolveret opera diaboli: ultro filius ipse spectandum agnoscendúmque se praebuit."

306.   Christopher Plantin, "Dedicatio," in ibid.: *Regi legitimo declarato.*] Quem Deus certis signis spectandum per prophetas indicari ac praedici curaverat."

307.   Christopher Plantin, "Odae LI. Argum.," in ibid.: "Canit laetissimam illam diem Ierosolymis illuxisse, qua rex Christus pater futuri seculi, & salutis pontifex urbem ingressus est, agnoscendus signis per prophetas praedictis, humilis & mansuetus, non fastu illo mundano regum & principum damnoso & gravi. Quibus vulgus vel spe, vel metu, vel levitate magis aliquando quàm iudicio blanditur & adulatur. Sed Christo turba plaudebat propter memoriam miraculorum & doctrinae."

308.   On Pieter Baltens, active in Antwerp between 1540 and 1584, as a publisher of epideictic political prints, see Van der Stock 1998, 158–72.

309.   Plantin 1568: "Haec tabula à Benedicto Aria posita est, ad Philippi Regis pietatem significandam, & studium erga Catholicam Religionem ostendendum. Huius enim Regis cura & felicitas maxima multis exemplis in utraque administrandi Regni ratione probatur. Si verò pacis commoda observemus, affirmare etiam possumus, nullum multis ab hinc annis Principem extitisse, qui in Religione colenda, Iustitia administranda, literarum promovendis studiis, & eruditis viris ornandis, denique literis, pictura, sculptura, caeterisque liberalibus aut honestis artibus aut vitae commodissimis, quales sunt agricultura & navigatio, illustrandis & amplificandis, huic anteponi possit."

310.   "Benedicti Ariae Montani…in sacrorum Bibliorum quadrilinguium regiam editionem…praefatio," in Arias Montano 1568–73, vol. 1, unfoliated [**3v]: "ne res tanti ponderis ac momenti ab illo malorum omnium auctore, illiúsque ministris, in id…discrimen, adduceretur; eámque mentem Philippo II. Catholico Hispaniarum Regi, & Principi potentissimo, & Christianae pietatis studiosissimo, iniecit, ut…de sacris libris, antiquis linguis, & earum optimis interpretationibus, qua fieri potest diligentia,, inter se collatis, excudendis, is etiam deliberaret; utpote…unum pietatis ac religionis purae studium, praecipuum,

& maximum, atque ad omnem publicam rem stabiliendam firmissimum fundamentum esse constat."

311.   "De Argumentum aller boecken des Ouden Testaments…Numerus. Cap. 36," in Jacobszoon and Bouwenszoon 1589, unfoliated [*ij verso]: "In dit boeck zijn veel dinghen, die dienen tot het Politische ende burgherlicke Regiment, ende tot de Religie: ende voornemelick dit, dat daer bewesen wort, dat de Priesters de saken der burgerlicker regeeringhe niet en verwerpen: ende die het burgerlick Regiment bedienen, en verwerpen niet dat de Religie aengaet."

312.   On this series, see New Hollstein (Van Groeningen) 51–58 (1:83–85); and Hollstein (Wierix) 62–69 (1:68–70). The *Story of the Maccabees* recalls such series as the *History of King Josiah*, engraved by Philips Galle after Maarten van Heemskerck, or the *History of Athaliah*, engraved by Harmen Muller after Maarten van Heemskerck, which portray events from the historical books of the Old Testament, that had rarely been illustrated (especially 1–2 Samuel, 1–2 Kings, and 1–2 Chronicles). These series, often focusing on the theme of royal piety, and regularly featuring scenes of religious renewal and the destruction of idols, began to proliferate in Antwerp and Haarlem after 1550, as Eleanor Saunders has shown; see Saunders 1978–79.

313.   The use of 2 Maccabees to defend these key doctrines of the Tridentine Church goes back to the homilies of Gregory Nazianzus, and John Chrysostom, on which see Ziadé 2007;

on 2 Maccabees 12:42–45 as a proof text for the doctrine of purgatory, in support of the Mass for the Dead, see Göttler 2005, 139–42. As Göttler notes, in the Tridentine Missal this passage forms part of the Epistle read during the commemorative Mass on the anniversary of someone's death.

314. On print 1 from the *Story of the Maccabees*, see New Hollstein (Van Groeningen) 51 (1:83); and Hollstein (Wierix) 62 (1:68–69). The inscription reads: "Reliquunt Iudei legem cultumque Dei sui, punit dominus impietatem per impium Antiochum, spoliantem vasa domus Domini aurea, magna insuper caede aeditu. Machab: 1. Cap: 1."

315. On print 2 from the *Story of the Maccabees*, see New Hollstein (Van Groeningen) 52 (1:83); and Hollstein (Wierix) 63 (1:69). The inscription reads: "Mathathius sacerdos aemulator legis divinae Iudaeo Dijs gentium imolaturo, et Antiochi praefecto per zelum casis, relicta urbe Modin, cum filijs et reliquis Deum timentibus Iudaeis indesertis se abdiderunt. Machab: 1. Cap: 2."

316. On print 3 from the *Story of the Maccabees*, see New Hollstein (Van Groeningen) 53 (1:84); and Hollstein (Wierix) 64 (1:69). The inscription reads: "Ne sabatum violent abstinent praelio et munitionibus Iacobitae: satius ducentes in simplicitate mori, quam praecepta Dei sui transgredi. Machab: 1. Cap: 2."

317. On print 4 from the *Story of the Maccabees*, see New Hollstein (Van Groeningen) 54 (1:84); and Hollstein (Wierix) 65 (1:69). The inscription

reads: "Devicto exercitu Antiochi, gratijsque Deo actis, Iudas cum exercitu suo ad sanctorum mundationem et restaurationem convertuntur, exciso altari holocaustorum prophanato. Machab: 1. Cap: 4."

318. On print 5 from the *Story of the Maccabees*, see New Hollstein (Van Groeningen) 55 (1:84); and Hollstein (Wierix) 66 (1:70). The inscription reads: "Offerunt Iudaei sacrificium secundem legem super altare holocaustorum novum quod fecerant; secundum tempus et diem in qua contaminaverunt illud gentes, benedicentes eum qui prosperavit eis. Machab: 1 Cap: 4."

319. On print 6 from the *Story of the Maccabees*, see New Hollstein (Van Groeningen) 56 (1:85); and Hollstein (Wierix) 67 (1:70). The inscription reads: "Caput Nicanoris amputatum et dextram quam extenderat superbè, suspenderunt ex adverso Ierosolÿmarum, diemque illum egerunt festum. Machab: 1. Cap: 7."

320. On print 7 from the *Story of the Maccabees*, see New Hollstein (Van Groeningen) 57 (1:85); and Hollstein (Wierix) 68 (1:70). The inscription reads: "Machabaeo pugnanti contra Thimoteum viri quinque in equis aureis frenis ornatis subsidio mittuntur qui ducatum exercitui eius praestent ipsumque defendant. Machab: 2. Cap: 10."

321. On print 8 from the *Story of the Maccabees*, see New Hollstein (Van Groeningen) 58 (1:85); and Hollstein (Wierix) 69 (1:70). The inscription reads: "Capto exustoque praesidio Thimotaeus cum fratre Cherea et Apollophane reperti

in eo caeduntur; Vindicante Domino populum suum. Machab. 2. Cap. 10."

322. Nadal 1607. On the 1594, 1595, and 1607 editions of the *Adnotationes et meditationes*, see Daly and Dimler 2005, 164–69, nos. J.1053–J.1055. On the *Adnotationes et meditationes*, see Rooses 1888; Nicolau 1949, 63, 114–20, 121–32, 166–70, 194, 205, 455, 464; Rodríguez de Ceballos 1974; Buser 1976; Mauquoy-Hendrickx 1976, 28–34; Freedberg 1978, 436–40; Fumaroli 1980a, 259–60, esp. n. 67; Wadell 1985, 9–17, 46–48; Freedberg 1989, 181–82, 185, 472–73; Moffitt 1990; Fabre 1992, 163–239, 263–95; Rheinbay 1995, 35–106; Spengler 1996; Von zur Mühlen 1997; Gabriele Wimböck in Baumstark 1997, 497–98, cat. no. 164; Melion 1998; Bailey 2003, 10–11; Dekoninck 2004; Melion 2003; Smith 2002, 40–46; Dekoninck 2005,157–370 passim, especially 234–37, 287–89, 303–05; Melion 2005b; Stroomberg 2007; Melion 2007a; and Lazure 2007.

323. On *imago* 90, see Hollstein (Wierix Book Illustrations) 56.76 (2:41). The captions read: "A. Christus in templo, in porticu Salomonis docens."; "B. Magnifici quidam homines, qui alios aspernabantur prae se, et alia multitudo audiens."; "C. Templum cum atrijs."; "D. Pharisaeus proxime stans ad ianuam atrij Sacerdotum arrogantissimè, & stultissimè orat."; "E. Publicanus longe stans tundit pectus, et oculos non audens tollere in coelum, humillimè orat; Deus propitius, etc. redit domum iustificatus, contra quam Pharisaeus."

324. Nadal 1607, 525: "Christus cum

Apostolis in porticu Salomonis, ubi hanc parabolam dixit, postquam receptus fuerat gloriosè in civitatem."

325. Ibid.: "Haec Publicani oratio caelos penetravit, & ei peccatorum veniam conciliavit. Sunt haec quinque verba efficacissima, praesertim si ea ad quinque Christi vulnera referamus, similiter animo contriti ut Publicanus."

326. Ibid., 525–26: "Ex hoc Evangelio nunc te [ego Jesus] erudiam. Cave igitur, orationem Pharisaei, ne imiteris: illam Publicani amplectere; atque adeò contrà, quàm facit Pharisaeus, tu ora...tu modestia animi, atque humilitate cordis, ex te nihil boni in te agnosce; quae à Deo beneficia accepisti, ea te tua improbitate corrumpere semper, nec percipere quemadmodum à Deo proficiscantur, ut ex infinito illo fonte omnis misericordiae & gratiae fluant, illius esse dona." The references *Psal. 138.*, *Iac. 1.*, and *1.Cor. 12.*, appear in the margin.

327. Ibid., 526: "non enim audio ego, si quis ad me accedit, sua incogitantia atque arrogantia erectus; sed qui ex profunda cordis sui humilitate; quantò longiùs recedit, tantò accedit propiùs, & magis à me exauditur."

328. Ibid.: "Corripe verò peccata tua, contunde & contere cor tuum, decute omnem peccandi affectum; & facto principio novo fidei in me, & spei, & devotionis contra peccata tua, Publicani quinque verba dicas ad quinque mea praecipua vulnera, quae pro te in cruce accepi; illa eò referens, quasi nunc videas illa vulnera infligi, unde vim recipiant.... Propitius es tu Domine; scio enim quòd

te proposuit Pater tuus propitiatorem pro omnium peccatis: utere tua propitiatione in me; non potuisti enim propiùs ad nos venire vel fieri, qui non solùm nostram humanitatem, labores, poenas assumpsisti, sed mortem etiam nostram. Ita fuisti verum propitiatorium in quo Deus ad nos veniret propè, misertus nostri, ac delens peccata nostra per te."

329.   On *imago* 91, see New Hollstein (Collaert) 1719 (7:29).   The captions read: "A. Atrium templi, ubi Jesus hanc parabolam dixit, post ingressum gloriosum in urbem Hierosolyman."; "B. Loquitur turbis Christus parabolam, audientibus Principibus et Pharisaeis."; "C. Locat vineam Paterfamilias, mittit servos ad colonos, ut fructus accipiant."; "D. Vinea, quam plantaverat, et pastinaverat, & in qua turrim, et lacum aedificaverat Paterfamilias."; "E. Ex ijs qui missi fuerant, aliqui caeduntur ab agricolis, alij occiduntur, alij lapidantur."; "F. Tandem Filium mittit, & hunc extra vineam occidendum eijciunt."

330.   Nadal 1607, 130: "[Annotation B] Iesus cum discipulis circumstante plebe, astantibus Principibus Sacerdotum & Pharisaeis, loquitur ad plebem, obliquè taxans omnes, praecipuè tamen Principes; & non obscurè significans quo pacto accepti fuerunt Dei Prophetae & sapientes ab eorum maioribus, ac vehementer illorum animos in necem ipsius concitatos flagellans." Cf. annotation C: "Postremò inflammatus desiderio fructus ex vinea percipiendi, mittit unigenitum filium sibi charissimum, cum certo periculo

mortis, ut vel ea ratione fructus vineae sibi proveniret."

331.   Ibid.: "[Annotation D] Non solùm plantasse vineam intelligendus est Paterfamilias, sed pastinasse ac coluisse. In vinea item turrim aedificaverat ad custodiam, torcular praeterea, sive machinam ad vinum ex uvis exprimendum atque excipiendum, vineam sepe undique munierat, denique Agricolis locaverat. Itaque nihil potuit facere vineae suae quod non fecerit, nihil conductoribus Agricolis commodare quod non commodaverit. Peregrè verò proficiscitur, ut intelligant Agricolae studio suo, industria, labore colendam vineam, atque Patrifamilias proventum summa cum probitate ac fide repraesentandum."

332.   Ibid., 131: "Hanc paravit ad custodiam, & adversariorum propulsationem: vitem verò *Christum* ad tuum palmitem emittendum, conservandum, promovendum; ad folia, & flores, & uvas producendas, ex quibus ultimum fructum colligere posses. Et dedit torcular, suae crucis divinum mysterium, & meritum suae passionis & mortis; per quod exprimere possis vinum meriti tui, & vitam aeternam; quod ex tuo palmite tandem exacturus est Deus."

333.   Ibid.: "At verò ubi primùm ad liberum usum rationis venisti, redige in memoriam, & vide quoties qui in te plantavit vineam Deus officij tui te admonuit, ut vinum illi dares tuae vineae, meritum scilicet aliquod vitae tuae."

334.   Ibid.: "Itaque vacuam illam gratiam

reddidisti, & quod ferè fecisti, iniurius illi gratiae fuisti, primùm quidem illum malè accipiendo, & affligendo indignis modis, aliquando etiam planè exstinxisti." Cf. ibid., 131–32: "Tu tamen, quoties his praetermissis, vel etiam neglectis, Filium Dei, quod in te est, interfecisti ac conculcasti, & contra Dei voluntatem peccasti?"

335.   Ibid., 132: "Cave miserrime, redi ad vitem, exstirpa vitem Daemonis, inseret te rursum Christus viti salutari & caelesti…. Haec Christus per torcular suum, per lacum sanguinis sui contulit ad iustificationem tuàm, dein ad meritum vitae aeternae."

336.   On *imago* 92, see New Hollstein (Collaert) 1720 (7:29). The captions read: "A. Eiectum extra vineam, Domini Filium interficiunt agricolae. Extra portam enim crucifixus est Dominus."; "B. Iesus, interrogat Principes, quid sit facturus Dominus vineae."; "C. Venit Paterfamilias cum armatis, & malos agricolas male perdit."; "D. Locat vineam alijs agricolis, etc."

337.   Nadal 1607, 134: "Crudeliter interficiunt coloni Filium Patrisfamilias è vinea exturbatum: extra portam enim Christus Dominus crucifixus est."

338.   Ibid.: "Utramque imaginem potes ad spiritum referre; nam apertè exauctoratio Synagogae describitur, & Ecclesiae electio. Tamen gravissimè admonemur singuli, ut divinas visitationes vel inspirationes non negligamus, vel reijciamus; ne, amissis donis, incidamus in Christi iustitiam per vitae nostrae perversitatem,

& conquassentur vires nostrae & confringantur."

339.   Van Liesveldt 1538, fol. 2LL6v (*Christ Reading from the Book of Isaiah*) and fol. 2LL7r (*Christ Heals the Paralytic*). On this edition of the Van Liesveldt Bible, which incorporates the New Testament prints originally designed by Lieven de Witte for Willem van Branteghem's *Iesu Christi vita* (Antwerp, 1537), see Rosier 1997, 1:213–22.

340.   As examples, he cites the case of Elijah, who was sent alone to the widow of Zarephath, and of Elisha, who cleansed only Naman (Luke 4:24–27).

Sacred History and Geography

So the men started on their way; and Joshua charged those who went to write the description of the land, saying, "Go throughout the land and write a description of it, and come back to me; and I will cast lots for you here before the Lord in Shiloh." So the men went and traversed the land and set down in a book a description of it by towns in seven divisions; then they came back to Joshua in the camp at Shiloh, and Joshua cast lots for them in Shiloh before the Lord; and there Joshua apportioned the land to the Israelites, to each a portion.

Joshua 18:8–10

The Ark of the Covenant with the Mercy Seat and
two Cherubim Made of Gold
The Table Made of Acacia Wood
The Lampstand Made of Pure Gold
The Altar of Burnt Offering
The Laver Made of Bronze
Woodcuts, each ca. 10.8 × 8.9 cm
In *De Bibel. Tgeheele Oude ende Nieuwe Testament met*
grooter naersticheyt naden Latijnschen text gecorrigeert.
…Met schoonen figueren ghedruct ende naerstelijc weder
oversien (Antwerp: Willem Vorsterman, 1528)
American Bible Society, New York

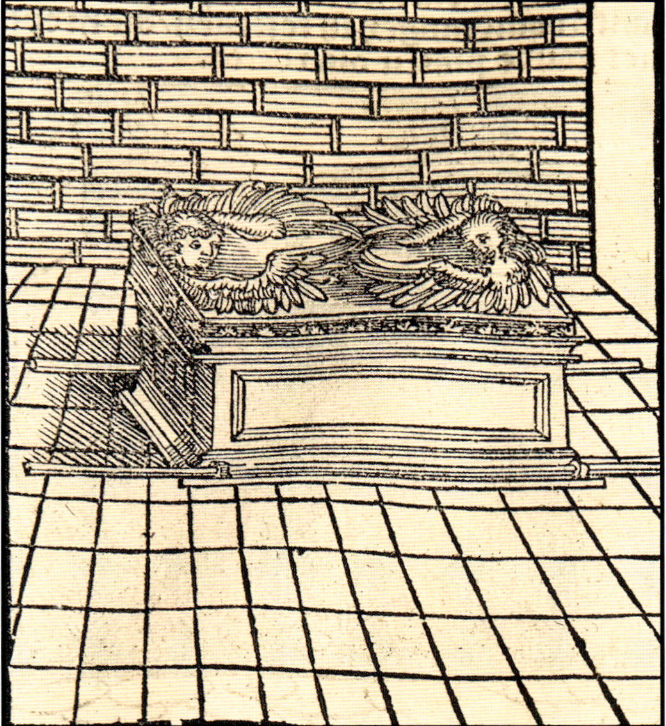

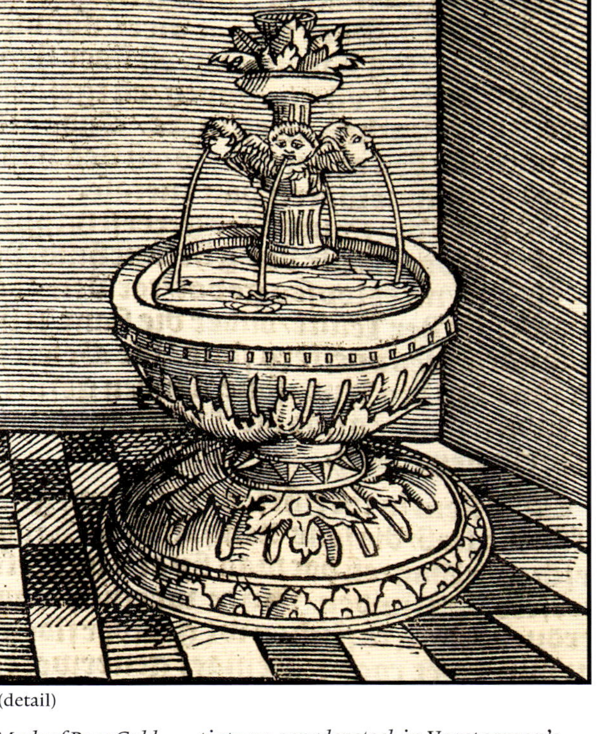

1 (detail)

1 (detail)

Beginning in Exodus 25, the Lord gives Moses lengthy instructions for the fashioning of a sanctuary, also called a tabernacle, and its furnishings, including the ark of the covenant. Much of the text is repeated, even verbatim, beginning in Exodus 36 in the description of the objects, which were made by "Bezalel and Oholiab and every skillful one to whom the Lord has given skill and understanding to know how to do any work in the construction of the sanctuary" (Exodus 36:1). The sanctuary and its furnishings had long been illustrated in medieval manuscripts of the Bible and related texts. Particularly important were illustrations to the extensive biblical commentary by Nicholas of Lyra (ca. 1270–1349), called the *Postilla super totam Bibliam*,[1] both in manuscripts and, from 1481, printed books.

Willem Vorsterman's Bible of 1528 was the second complete Bible published in Dutch translation—based on the Latin Vulgate and Martin Luther's translation into German—and it is particularly notable for its extensive series of woodcuts by the Groningen artist Jan Swart.[2] Most Netherlandish Bible illustrations of the first half of the sixteenth century depended on prior German examples, but Swart was exceptional in creating new compositions, which, in turn, served as models for subsequent illustrations. Several of the non-narrative illustrations of the sanctuary and its furnishings, however, including the five on the facing pages of Exodus 37 and 38 in Vorsterman's Bible (f3ᵛ–f4ʳ), do depend on earlier images, in this instance on the woodcuts in editions of Luther's Old Testament in German published in Wittenberg in 1523.[3]

Vorsterman's woodcuts offer large, detailed depictions of *The Ark of the Covenant with the Mercy Seat and Two Cherubim Made of Gold* (Exodus 37:1–9; also described in Exodus 25:10–22); *The Table Made of Acacia Wood* (Exodus 37:10–16; also 25:23–30); *The Lampstand Made of Pure Gold* (Exodus 37:17–24; also 25:31–40); *The Altar of Burnt Offering* (Exodus 18:1–7; also 27:1–8); and *The Laver Made of Bronze* (Exodus 38:8; also 30:17–21). It is unusual in Vorsterman's Bible that so many illustrations are placed close together in a single opening, but separating the major objects described in the text rather than combining them in compositions as in Jacob van Liesveldt's Bible of 1526, which Vorsterman knew, allows for greater attention to each. The emphasis on these objects attests to an archaeological impulse, enacted in a close, literal reading of scripture. Yet even with extensive textual descriptions, artists had to negotiate ambiguities. The description of the cherubim positioned at the ends of the mercy seat (the cover of the ark, also called the propitiatory; *genadenstoel*, in Vorsterman's translation), for example, says that they "spread out their wings above, overshadowing the mercy seat with their wings. They faced one another; the faces of the cherubim were turned toward the mercy seat" (Exodus 37:9). Vorsterman's woodcut represents them as bodiless cherubs, of a type long known in Netherlandish art, albeit with much greater wing-spans to accomplish their task here of "overshadowing" the mercy seat, as the RSV calls it (the Vulgate's *tegentes* and Vorsterman's *ouerendecten* suggest, less evocatively, simply covering), whereas they could also be envisioned as full-scale, standing angels.[4]   JC

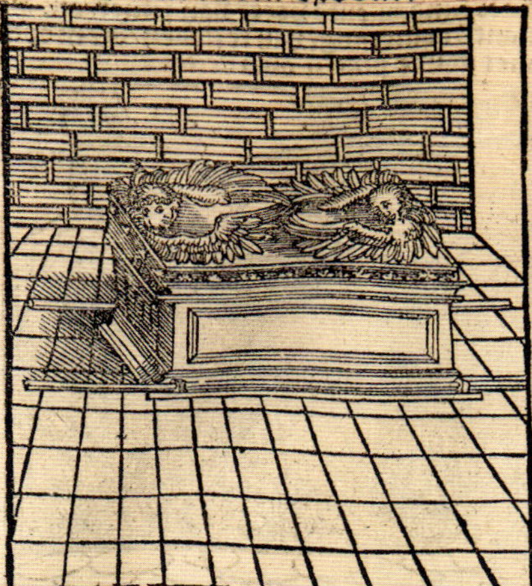

G Vanden alder fijnsten goude/ twee cubitus en een halue lanck/ en ander half cubitus breet/ en hi maecte twee Cherubim van ge= slagen goude/ aen die twee eynde des genade stoels/ een Cherubim aen deen eynde/ dan= dere aen dat ander eynde. En die Cherubim breyden wt haer vlogelen van boue ouer/ en decten also de genadestoelen sage malcanderen

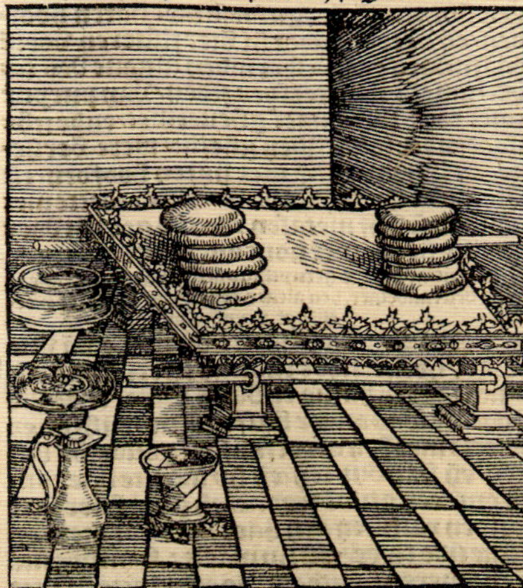

¶ En de genade stoel. En hi maecte de tafele van Vueren houte/ twee cubitus lanc een breet en ander half cubitus hooge/ en verguldese

met finen goude/ en hi maecte daer ouer al om een gulden lijste/ en op die lijste een gulde croon vier vinger breet/ en bouen die selue noch een ander gulden croone/ En hi goot daer toe vier gulde ringe/ en dede se aen die vier hoecke aen de voete tege die croone/ en hi stack die hantboome daer inne/ datmen die tafele soude moge drage/ En hy maecte die hantboome van vueren houte/ en dese met goude/ datme die tafelen daer mede soude drage/ En hy maecte ooc haren tot verscepden gebruyc der tafelen/ azijn hat= tey/ flesschen troesens wieroocvaten/ van supueren goude daermen dochtighe offer= hande mede soude offeren.

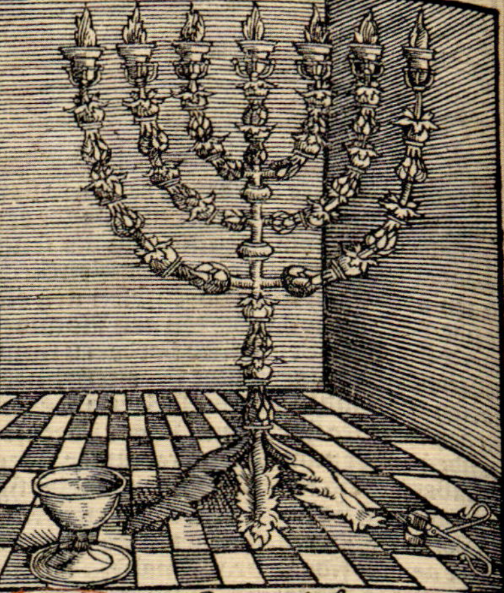

¶ En hi maecte den candelaer geslage van de alder fijnste goude/ van wies boom scach= te nappe/ronde clootkes/ en oock lilien wt quame ses ae beyde side die scachte wt der eender side/en die wt der andere side nappe in maniere va noteya en elcke scacht eyron de clootkes/ en daer mede lilie en drie nappe gelijc note aende andere scacht en ronde clootkens en daer mede lilie het werc deses schachte was gelijc die daer ginge wt den strupt des candelaers onder die twee schachten aen die plaetsen tsamewerde ses schachte voortcome de wt eenen boom/ En die clootkens en die schachte gingen wt he/ en ware alle gader geslagen werc wt den alderfijnsten goude.

lampen en hi maecte .vij. lichters) met hare keers snutters en blusuaten vanden alder fijnste goude/ Den candelaer en alle zijn ghereescap woech een talent gouts.

Hy maecte oock den outaer des rueck= wercx van vueren houte/int viercant heb bende die breede eens cubitus/ ende in die hoochte twee/wt sinen hoecken spruytede hoomen/ en hi ouerdecten met den alder supuersten goude met den rooster/ en die weegen en die hoomen/ en hi heeft hem in den omganck een croone gemaect/ en twee gulden ringhen onder die croone/ aen elc= ke side/op datmen daer hantboomen in ste= ken soude/ dat den outaer daer mede soude moghen ghedraghen worden/ Maer die hantboomen maecte hy van vueren hout= e/ en ouerdectese met gouden platen/ En hy maecte die heylighe salfolie/ ende ruec werck vanden alder fijnste specerien/ na die conste des apotekers.

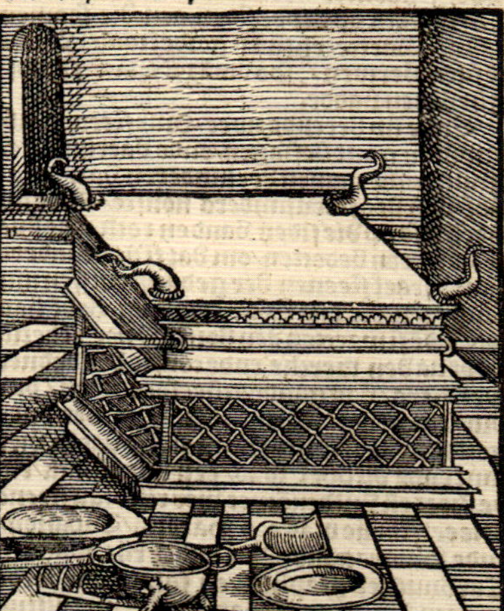

¶ Hoe den brantoffer altaer ghemaect wert/ dat meta= len vat en den voorhof/ en tghetal van dat rvole offerde

¶ Dat. xxxviij. Capittel.

O Nde hi maecte des brantoffers outaer van vueren houte/ vijf cubitus lanck en breet int viercant/en drie cubitus hooge wiens hoomen daer wt quamen vanden vier hoecken/ en ouerdecten met metalen platen/En hi maecte alderley ghereescap van metale tot des outaers gebruyc/ sie= potten/scuppen/becken/crauwels/vper= pannen/ Ende hy maecte aende outaer

eenen rooster/gheliick een nette/ van me= tale/ en onder die int middese des outaers een vloerken/en hi goot vier ringhen aen die vier hoecken des metalen roosters tot vueren houte/en ouertrocse met metalen platen/ en hi dede in die ringhen die aen die siden des outaers wtstake/ Maer die outaer en was niet dicht/ maer van gehou= wen barderen bi een gheuoecht binnen hol.

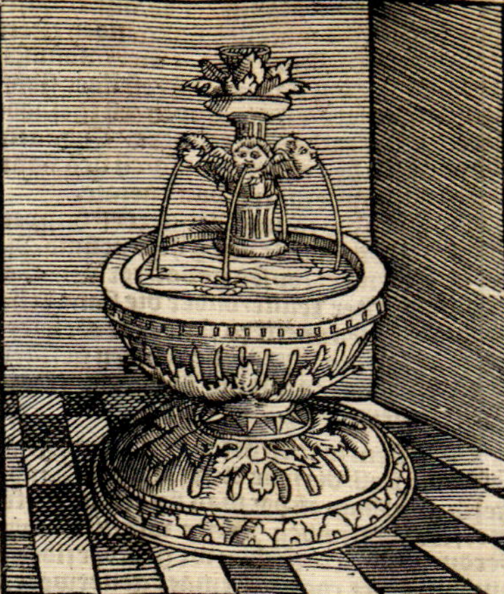

¶ En hy maecte dat wateruat met sinen voete van metale/ van die spiegelen der vrouwen) die voor die dueren des taberna= kels te waken pleghen.

¶ Ende hi maecte den voorhoue teghen die zuyder side een voorhanghende cleedt hondert cubitus lanck van ghetweernder witter siden/met haere twintich casomne en twintich voete va metale/maer de hoof= den en tghesneden werck van siluere/des selfs gheliicken tegent noorden/ hondert cubitus met twintich casomnen/en twin= tich voeten van metale/maer haer hoofden en dat ghesnede werck van siluere/Maer in die side die westwaert siet/ware cleedere van vijftich cubitus met thien cosomne en thien voete van metale/maer haer hoofden en verheue werc van siluere/Maer tegen de oosten bereyde hi cleedere van vijftich cubi= tus. Vijfthien op elcke side der poorte aen den voorhof met drie casomnen/en die voe= ten/dat alle die ghespannen cleederen des voorhofs ware van witter ghetweernder

f iiij.

2a

Pieter van der Heyden (ca. 1530–ca. 1576)
After Crispijn van den Broeck (?) (1524–89/91)
Royal Piety (Pietas Regia)
ca. 1568
Engraving, 37.6 × 24.6 cm
In volume 1 of Benito Arias Montano, ed., *Biblia Sacra Hebraice, Chaldaice, Graece, & Latine, Philippi II. Reg. cathol. pietate, et studio ad sacrocanctae ecclesiae usum* (*Sacred Bible in Hebrew, Chaldee, Greek, and Latin, [Provided] by the Piety and Devotion of the Catholic King Philip II for the Use of the Most Holy Church*), 8 vols.
(Antwerp: Christopher Plantin, 1568–73)
Pitts Theology Library, Emory University

2b

Pieter van der Heyden (ca. 1530–ca. 1576)
After Pieter van der Borcht (?) (ca. 1535–1608)
The Pentateuchal Covenants of God to the Patriarchs
ca. 1568
Engraving, 37.2 × 26.5 cm
In volume 1 of *Biblia Sacra Hebraice, Chaldaice, Graece, & Latine, Philippi II. Reg. cathol. pietate, et studio ad sacrocanctae ecclesiae usum* (*Sacred Bible in Hebrew, Chaldee, Greek, and Latin, [Provided] by the Piety and Devotion of the Catholic King Philip II for the Use of the Most Holy Church*), ed. Benito Arias Montano, 8 vols.
(Antwerp: Christopher Plantin, 1568–73)
New Hollstein (Van der Borcht Book Illustrations) 423
Pitts Theology Library, Emory University

*H*aving decided to sponsor Christopher Plantin's project of publishing a polyglot Bible, that would supersede the 1517 Alcalá *Polyglota* of Cardinal Jiménez de Cisneros, Philip II sent the theologian Benito Arias Montano to Antwerp, designating him the supervisory editor.[5] The *Biblia Sacra*, also known as the *Biblia Polyglotta*, appeared in stages between 1568 and 1573. Volume 1 contains Genesis to Deuteronomy; volume 2, Joshua to 2 Chronicles; volume 3, Ezra to the Wisdom of Jesus Sirach; volume 4, Isaiah to Maccabees. All four volumes supply the text in Greek, Hebrew, Latin, and Aramaic. Volume 5 contains the New Testament in Greek, Latin, Syrian, and Aramaic. Volumes 6–8, known as the *Apparatus*, consist of scholarly appendices in Old Testament Hebrew, New Testament Greek, and Latin. The Polyglot Bible is richly illustrated: in addition to the allegorical title-page, *The Unity of the Biblical Languages*, there are five frontispieces: two in volume 1—*Pietas Regia (Royal Piety)* and *The Pentateuchal Covenants of God to the Patriarchs*; one in volume 2—*The Israelites Crossing the River Jordan*; one in volume 4—*The Laborers in the Vineyard of the Lord*; and one in volume 5—*The Baptism of Christ*. Illustrations also accompany the named treatises in volume 8: *Phaleg*, *Chanaan*, and *Chaleb* respectively include maps of the ancient world with its God-given toponyms in Hebrew, of the land of Canaan before its conquest by Joshua, and of the land of Israel after its settlement and distribution among the twelve tribes; *Nehemiah* includes an historical map of Jerusalem and its major monuments; *Thubal-Cain* includes the image of a shekel; and *Exemplar, sive, de sacris fabricis liber* (*Exemplar, or the Book on Sacred Edifices*) includes a total of 11 images —the *Ark of Noah*, the *Plan of the Tabernacle*, the *Plan and Elevation of the Tabernacle*, the *Exterior Side-View of the Tabernacle*, the *Tabernacle Veils*, the *Ark of the Covenant*, the *Camp of the Israelites*, the

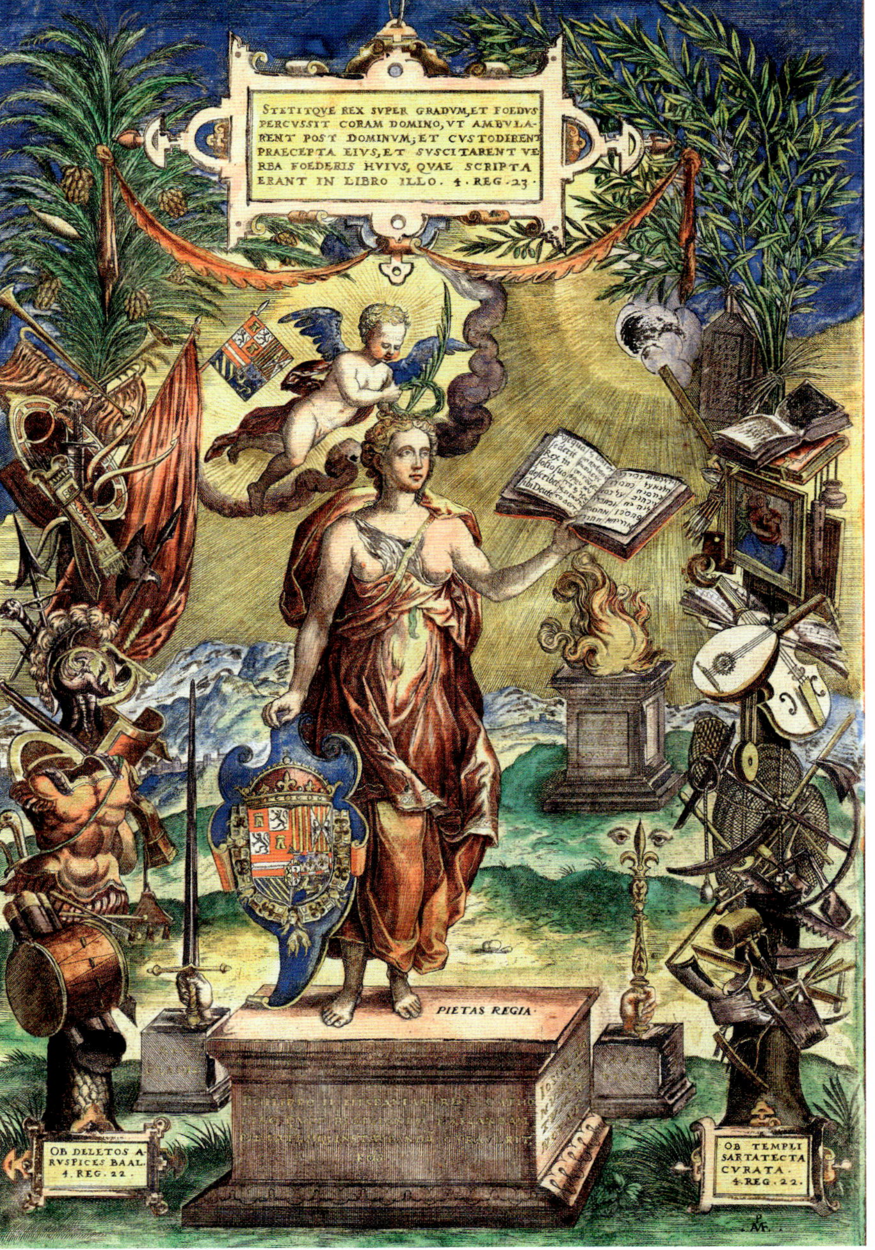

2a

Plan of Solomon's Temple, the *Plan and Section of the Temple, with Samples of Decoration from the Holy of Holies*, the *Exterior View of the Temple*, and *Aaron in the High Priest's Vestments*. Arias Montano oversaw the design of all the illustrations and may even have executed preliminary drawings for the use of specialist draughtsmen such as Pieter van der Borcht and Crispijn van den Broeck.[6]

The dedicatory frontispiece of the *Biblia Regia* features an allegorical personification of royal piety, that embodies King Philip II's fervent devotion to the Catholic faith, exemplified by his sponsorship of the publisher Christopher Plantin's new polyglot bible project.[7] Standing upon a podium inscribed *Pietas Regia* (*Royal Piety*), the king's coat of arms beside her, she holds forth a votive copy of the bible, offering it at the altar of the Holy Trinity, which appears at the right. She is flanked by emblematic devices signifying Philip's triumphant pursuit of the arts of war (the palm tree hung with trophies, and the emblem of a sword-hand rising from a base inscribed *aut gladio*—"either by the sword") and of peace (the olive tree hung with tools of the manual and liberal arts, and the emblem of a handheld sceptre topped by a pair of eyes, rising from a base inscribed *aut verbo*—"or by the word"). The source of all these regal achievements, the allegory affirms, is the king's exceptional piety. The large plaque above Royal Piety quotes 2 Kings 23:3, comparing Philip to Josiah, King of Judah, who restored the book of the law and re-promulgated the scriptural books.

The second frontispiece of the *Biblia Sacra* attests the divine authority of Pentateuch, the five Mosaic books of the Old Testament (Genesis, Exodus, Leviticus, Numbers, and Deuteronomy).[9] Visible through the archway, angels transmit the word of God to the patriarchs: (upper right) God promises Noah that he shall never again destroy the sinful world (Genesis 8:20–22); (upper left) God promises Abram that his descendants shall take possession of all the land "from the river of Egypt to the great river…Euphrates (Genesis 15:9–21)"; (center) Jacob wrestles with the angel at the ford of Jabbok and sees the face of God (Genesis 32:22–30); (center left) God promises Jacob that he shall possess the land upon which he lies, and that his numerous progeny shall populate it (Genesis 28:10–16); (lower left) God promises to deliver his people from their bondage in Egypt unto a land flowing with milk and honey (Exodus 3–4:5); (lower right) God conveys to Moses the tablets of the law, instructing him to build the tabernacle and honor the sabbath (Exodus 24:12–31:18).   WM

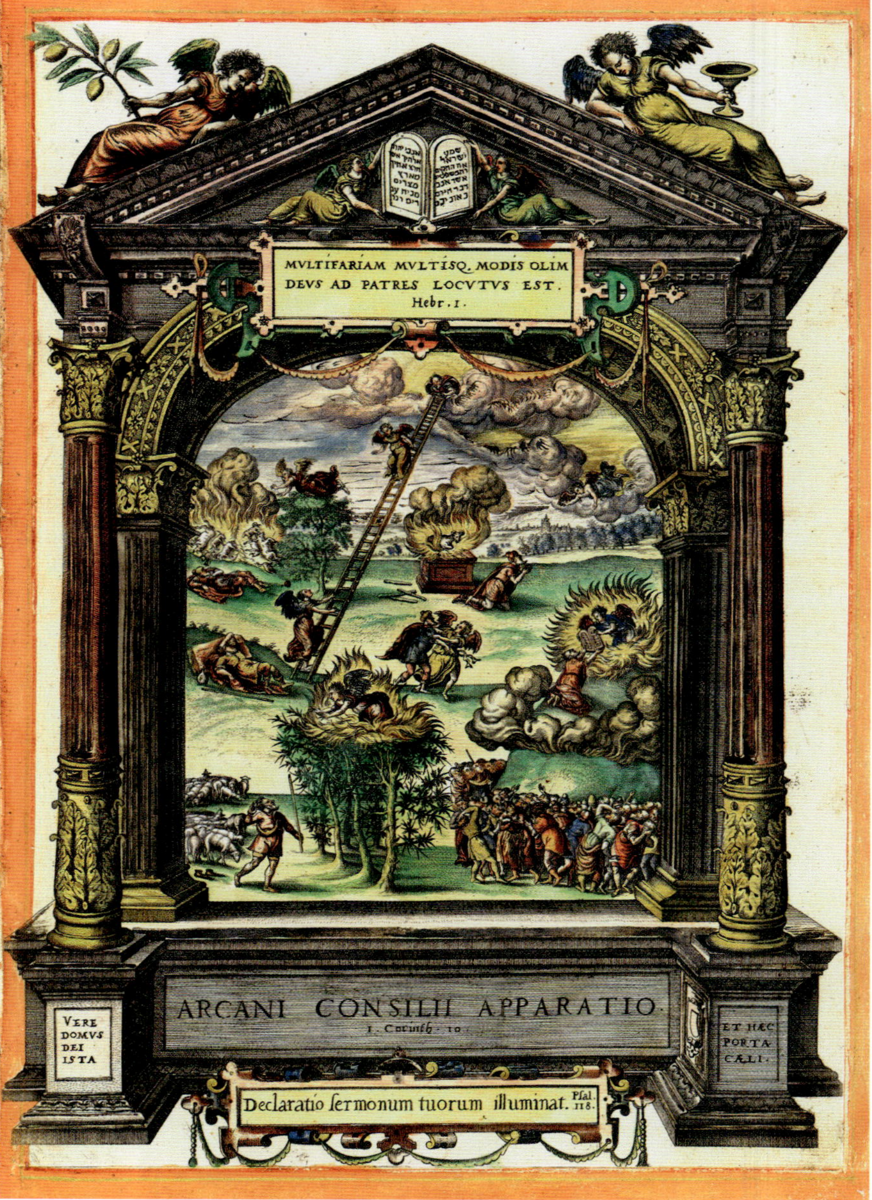

2b

Jan Wierix (1549–ca. 1618/20)
After Crispijn van den Broeck (1524–89/91)
The Israelites Crossing the River Jordan
ca. 1568
Engraving, 37 × 24.3 cm
In volume 2 of *Biblia Sacra Hebraice, Chaldaice, Graece, & Latine, Philippi II. Reg. cathol. pietate, et studio ad sacrocanctae ecclesiae usum* (*Sacred Bible in Hebrew, Chaldee, Greek, and Latin, [Provided] by the Piety and Devotion of the Catholic King Philip II for the Use of the Most Holy Church*), ed. Benito Arias Montano, 8 vols. (Antwerp: Christopher Plantin, 1568–73)
Hollstein (Wierix Book Illustrations) 1.1
Pitts Theology Library, Emory University

*T*he third frontispiece of the *Biblia Sacra* conflates several events retailed in Joshua 4:1–14: Joshua stands with Caleb on a headland in the middle distance, his commander's baton raised to indicate that he has instigated the crossing; the Levites bear the ark of the covenant in the midst of the dry riverbed that the tribes traverse; their representatives gather the twelve stones, one for each tribe, to be erected as a memorial "that the waters of the Jordan were cut off before the ark of the covenant of the Lord, when it passed over the Jordan (Joshua 4:7)."[10] The monument is already visible just beyond the ark. The "waters coming down from above [that] stood and rose up in a heap far off" take the form of a stream, levitating sinuously toward the distant right (Joshua 4:16).[11] The excerpt from Hebrews 2:2, inscribed on the plaque above, interprets the crossing as the fulfillment of the angelic promises depicted in the previous frontispiece, *Pentateuchal Covenants of God to the Patriarchs* (cat. 2): "The word spoken by angels has been made firm."   WM

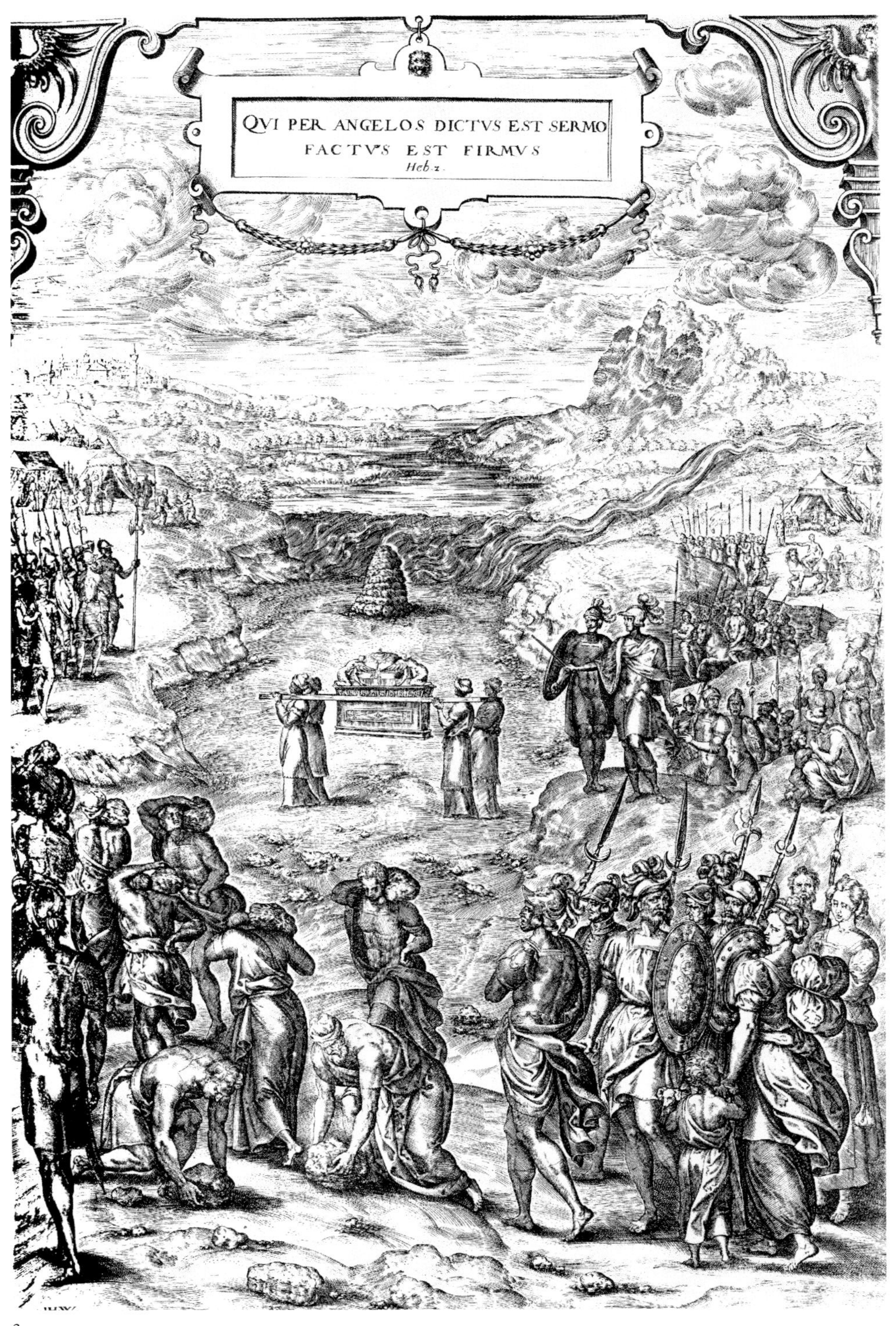

3

4

Jan Wierix (1549–ca. 1618/20)
After Pieter van der Borcht (?) (ca. 1535–1608)
The Laborers in the Vineyard of the Lord
ca. 1568
Engraving, 36.7 × 24 cm
In volume 4 of *Biblia Sacra Hebraice, Chaldaice, Graece, & Latine, Philippi II. Reg. cathol. pietate, et studio ad sacrocanctae ecclesiae usum* (*Sacred Bible in Hebrew, Chaldee, Greek, and Latin, [Provided] by the Piety and Devotion of the Catholic King Philip II for the Use of the Most Holy Church*), ed. Benito Arias Montano, 8 vols. (Antwerp: Christopher Plantin, 1568–73)
Hollstein (Wierix Book Illustrations) 1.2
Pitts Theology Library, Emory University

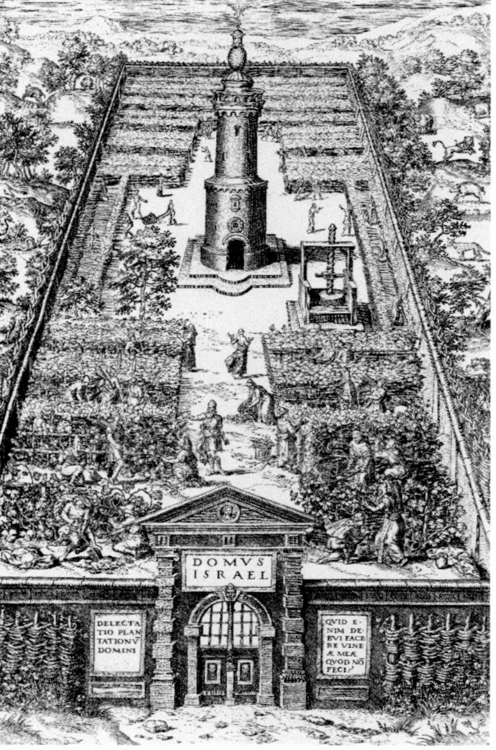

4

*T*he fourth frontispiece of the *Biblia Sacra* portrays a walled vineyard where husbandmen busily set about the tasks of digging, pruning, and harvesting.[12] Labeled *Domus Israel* (House of Israel), a reference to Isaiah 5:7, the vineyard also illustrates a further excerpt from Isaiah 5:7 (*Delectatio plantationum Domini*—"Pleasure of the Lord's planting"), and an excerpt from Isaiah 5:4 (*Quid enim debui facere vineae meae quod non feci?*—"For what ought I to do for my vineyard, that I have not [already] done?"). However, the garden imagery is not only prophetic but also parabolic, for it derives from Christ's parables of the kingdom of God in Matthew 20 and 21, which in turn are based on Isaiah 5:7. In Matthew 20:1–16, Jesus compares God to a householder who hires laborers to cultivate his vineyard; in Matthew 21:28–41, he describes God as the proprietor of a vineyard, who plants it, encircles it with a hedge, sets a winepress within it, builds a watchtower, and finally lets it out to tenants, whom he then leaves to do their work. At harvest time, he sends messengers to collect the vineyard's yield, but all are maltreated, even his son, whom the tenants slay. The owner therefore enlists armed men to punish the perfidious tenants, replacing them with laborers whose efforts bear better and truer fruit (see cat. 17b). Like Matthew 20, this parable signifies God's expectation that we should cultivate the vineyard of the soul in order to bring forth good works. The frontispiece operates as an exegetical hinge linking the Old and New Testaments: Isaiah affirms that God shall care for his spiritual vineyard Israel, and Christ, the living embodiment of that divine solicitude, appropriates the prophet's imagery to affirm the loving justice of God, who generously supplies the vineyard with everything it needs to prosper, but expects in exchange to receive its harvest, that is, to reap the soul's spiritual fruits. That the image has a double purchase is further indicated by the figures in the garden, who are dressed both in ancient and in modern dress.   WM

5

Jan Wierix (1549–ca. 1618)

After Crispijn van den Broeck (1524–89/91)

The Baptism of Christ

ca. 1568

Engraving, 38.5 × 24.5 cm

In volume 5 of *Biblia Sacra Hebraice, Chaldaice, Graece, & Latine, Philippi II. Reg. cathol. pietate, et studio ad sacrocanctae ecclesiae usum* (*Sacred Bible in Hebrew, Chaldee, Greek, and Latin, [Provided] by the Piety and Devotion of the Catholic King Philip II for the Use of the Most Holy Church*), ed. Benito Arias Montano, 8 vols. (Antwerp: Christopher Plantin, 1568–73)

Hollstein (Wierix Book Illustrations) 1.3

Pitts Theology Library, Emory University

*T*he fifth frontispiece of the *Biblia Sacra* illustrates the baptism of Christ, as the fulfillment of the prophecies of Isaiah portrayed in the *Title-Page* and the *Laborers in the Vineyard of the Lord*.[13] Glorified as the Son of God, he is the Prince of Peace envisioned in Isaiah 11; revealed as the Lamb of God, he comes forth to plant the spiritual vineyard described in Isaiah 5. Sanctioned by the Father, he is the son sent to collect the harvest of souls, as foretold by Christ himself in his parabolic adaptation of Isaiah 5 in Matthew 21 and Luke 20. As the Messiah "who takes away the sin of the world," he keeps the salvific promises made to the patriarchs in the *Pentateuchal Covenants*.[14] He emerges from the river Jordan, "exalted in the sight of all Israel," as was Joshua after the miraculous events represented in *The Israelites Crossing the River Jordan*.[15] As the Israelites gather stones to commemorate the power of the Lord, so Christ steps upon a square stone that identifies him as the cornerstone of faith, the stepping stone to salvation, which to reject is perilous: "What then is this that is written: 'The very stone which the builders rejected has become the head of the corner'? Every one who falls on that stone will be broken to pieces; but when it falls on any one it will crush him." The passage from Hebrews 1:2, inscribed below, completes the passage from Hebrews 1:1, inscribed on the *Pentateuchal Covenants*. Together they declare that God is no longer distant; formerly delivered by his chosen messengers, the word of God has been renewed in Christ the Son, who now speaks directly to us: "In many and various ways God spoke of old to our fathers by the prophets; but in these last days he has spoken to us by a Son, whom he appointed the heir of all things." Therefore, the final frontispiece summarizes and completes its predecessors, just as the New Testament distills and perfects the Old.   WM

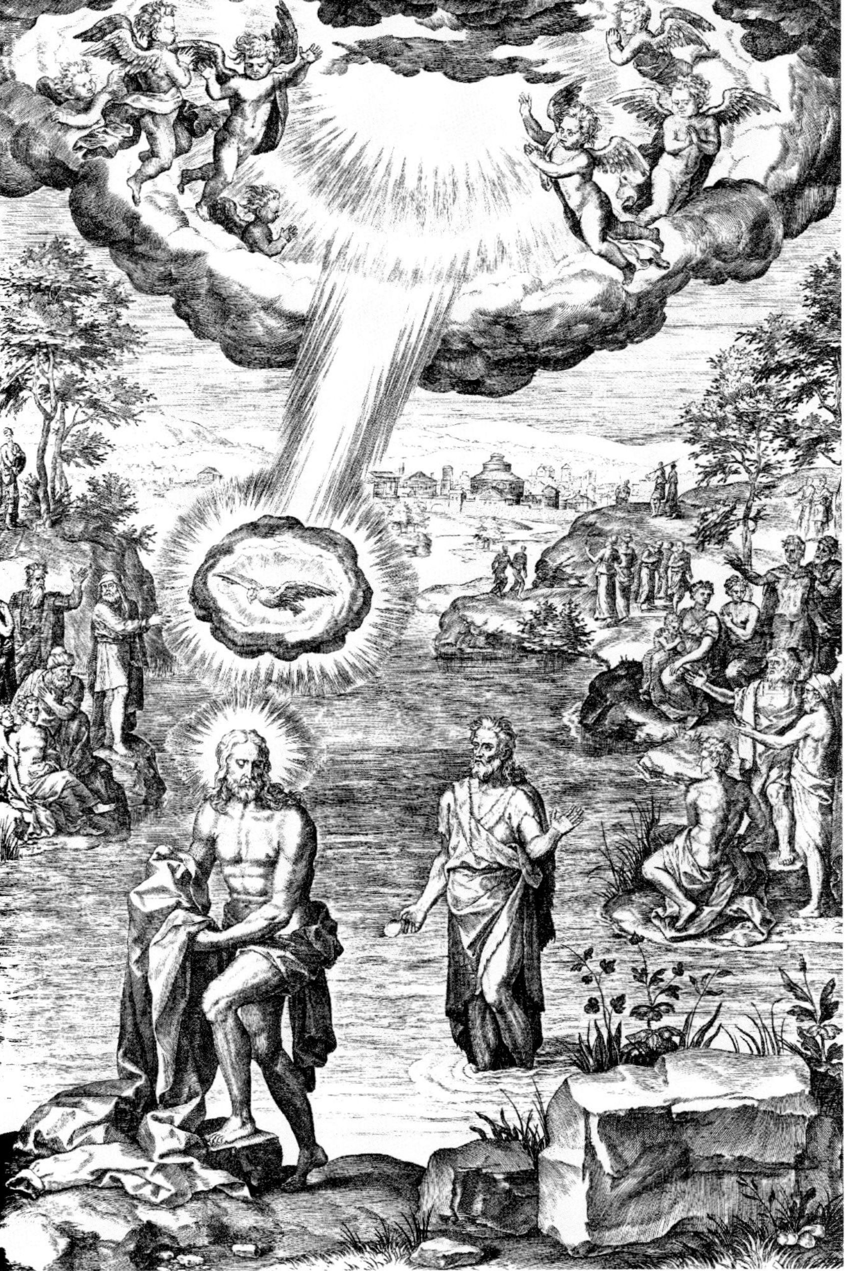

5

6

Pieter Huys (?) (ca. 1520–before 1586)
After Peter Laickstein (active 1550s)
True Image of Ancient Jerusalem, Principally for the Explication of Sacred Scripture and Other Histories of that City, Collated from [Various] Authors with the Traces of Ruins and the Site Itself (*Antiquae Ierusalem vera iconographia ad sacrae lectionis praecipue et aliarum de illa urbe historiar. explicationem. Ex collatione auctorum cum ruinarum vestigijs ac situ ipso.*)
ca. 1568
Engraving, 27.7 × 23cm
In volume 8 of *Biblia Sacra Hebraice, Chaldaice, Graece, & Latine, Philippi II. Reg. cathol. pietate, et studio ad sacrocanctae ecclesiae usum* (*Sacred Bible in Hebrew, Chaldee, Greek, and Latin, [Provided] by the Piety and Devotion of the Catholic King Philip II for the Use of the Most Holy Church*), ed. Benito Arias Montano, 8 vols. (Antwerp: Christopher Plantin, 1568–73)
Pitts Theology Library, Emory University

*T*he *Biblia Sacra* contains three antiquarian maps, respectively portraying the ancient world with Hebrew place-names, the land of Canaan before the Israelite conquest, and the land of Israel settled by the twelve tribes, in addition to the *True Image of Ancient Jerusalem*, a topographical map of the holy city showing its fortified boundaries and chief monuments from David's conquest of the Jebusites (the site's original inhabitants) to the Crucifixion of Christ. For Benito Arias Montano, the editor of the *Biblia Sacra*, as Zur Shalev has shown, the maps fulfilled several functions: they established the antiquarian basis for a literal-historical reading of Scripture, provided evidence of the operation of divine providence, invited reflection on the physical and spiritual journeys of biblical personages, and inspired meditation on the soul's pilgrimage through this life, as it searches for God.[16] In the preface to *Nehemias, sive, de antiquae Ierusalem situ, volumen: a Benedicto Aria Montano Hispalensi descriptum* (*Nehemiah, or, Tractate on the Site of Ancient Jerusalem*), Arias Montano recalls that his beloved former teacher Iago Vasquez Matamoro had taught him the value of cartography, having himself described the Holy Land and its antiquities in words (*tum literis*) and in maps (*tum etiam tabulis*).[17] As the verbal accounts were precisely recorded (*omnia exactè notavit*), so the visual accounts were drawn precisely by Matamoro himself (*tum etiam tabulis à se depictis*). Matamoro had given the young Arias Montano the essential means of understanding the biblical places: "He often showed me—a boy hanging upon his verbal report of all that region's localities—how each was formerly and is today; so that as an adolescent, I could promptly compare those [reports] to the pictorial images of places that he described and portrayed, among which was a great and most elegant exemplar of the whole city of Jerusalem and its environs, which I was given. But I shall refrain here from recounting how much the image of those sacred places, imprinted upon my mind by that man, contributed to my knowledge of the many things contained in both the Old and New Testaments."[18] He has now represented the site of ancient Jerusalem (*antiquum Ierosolymorum demonstratum situm*), on the basis of his combined reading of Scripture and of topographical works.   WM

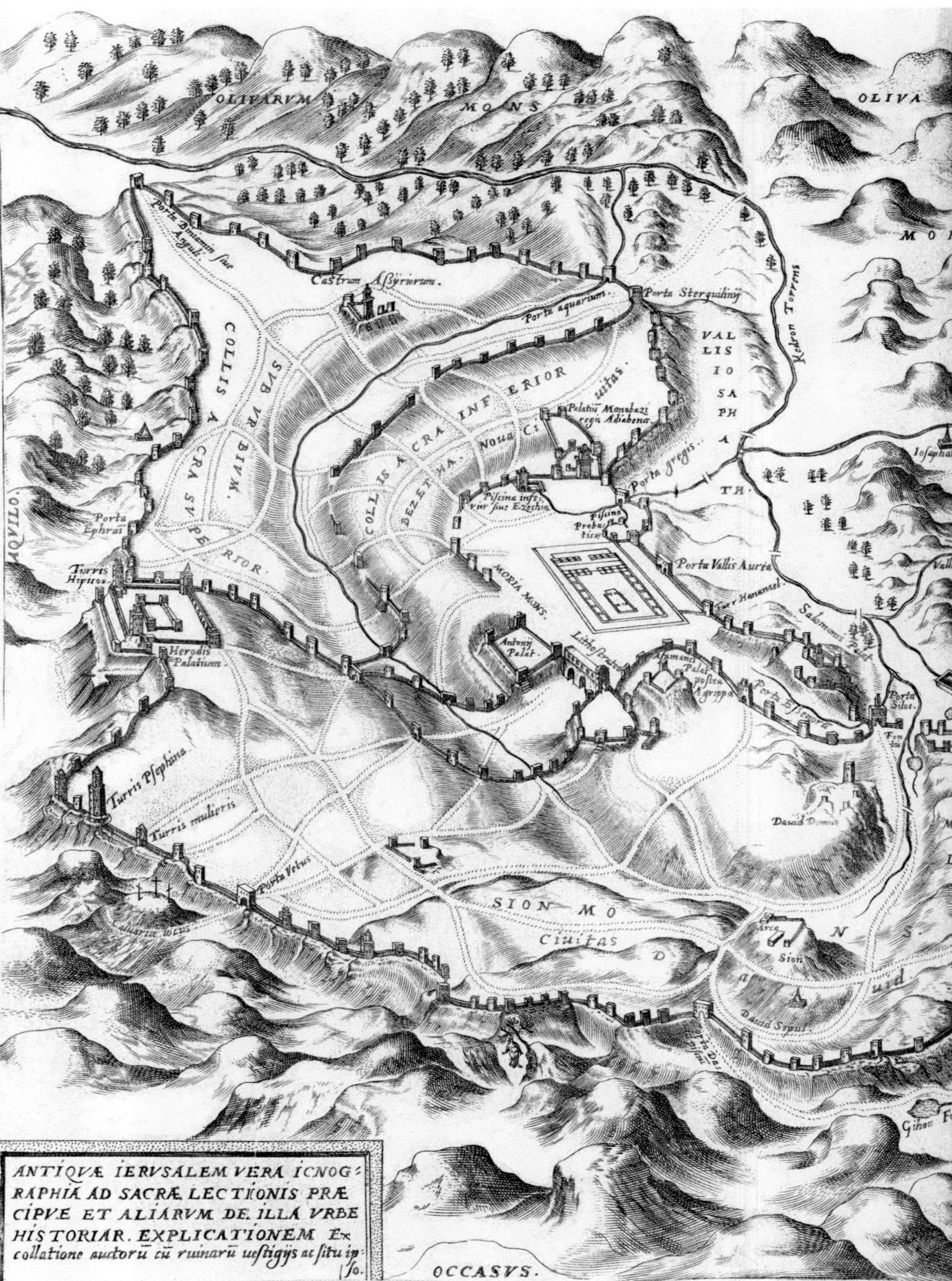

7a

Pieter Huys (ca. 1520–before 1586)

After Pieter van der Borcht (ca. 1535–1608)

The Israelites Crossing the River Jordan

ca. 1570

Engraving, 11.3 × 7.4 cm

Monumentum 17 in Benito Arias Montano, *Humanae salutis monumenta B. Ariae Montani studio constructa et decantata* (*Monuments of Human Salvation Assembled and Versified through the Effort of B. Arias Montano*) (Antwerp: Christopher Plantin, 1571)

John Work Garrett Library, Johns Hopkins University

7b

Abraham de Bruyn (1538/40–87)

After Pieter van der Borcht (ca. 1535–1608)

Joshua Distributes Land to the Seven Tribes

ca. 1570

Engraving, 11.5 × 7.4 cm

Monumentum 19 in Benito Arias Montano, *Humanae salutis monumenta B. Ariae Montani studio constructa et decantata* (*Monuments of Human Salvation Assembled and Versified through the Effort of B. Arias Montano*) (Antwerp: Christopher Plantin, 1571)

New Hollstein (Van der Borcht Book Illustrations) 912

Robert W. Woodruff Library, Emory University

*C*omposed by the Spanish theologian Benito Arias Montano, who was also a poet, philologist, and antiquarian, the *Humanae salutis monumenta* (*Monuments of Human Salvation*) consists of 71 engravings illustrating key episodes in the history of human salvation, beginning with portraits of Moses and Christ, the founders of the Old Law and the New (*Bust of Christ* and *Moses with the Ten Commandments*), and concluding with the *Last Judgment*.[19] The pictorial *monumenta* are enframed by three texts: above, a short motto in Roman capitals (*inscriptio*), followed by a distich in italics, that comments on the relation between the image and the motto; and below, a dedication in small Roman capitals (*dedicatio*), that consecrates the image to a theme. Printed on the folios recto, the engravings open onto Horatian odes, printed on the preceding folios verso, that expound the redemptive significance of the pictorial images. The *Monumenta* is one of the earliest scriptural emblem books; it belongs to the serious, yet agreeable genre of the *oblectamentum* (that which gives pleasure), a literary and artistic species that marshals the resources of pictorial and typographical artifice to instruct, amuse, and spiritually renew its reader-viewer.[20]

Since the book's format was so novel, and its ingenious argument so complex, the publisher Christopher Plantin composed two explanatory prefaces, as well as an appendix that briefly analyses the odes, along with selected mottos, inscriptions, and dedications. He explains that Arias Montano has fashioned two kinds of literary *genera*: the *genus architectonicum* is formed of a pictorial image surrounded by corollary texts; the *genus poëticum* is formed of poetic texts that explore themes beyond the scope of the pictures and "architectonic" texts.[21] Both kinds deal in images, either visual or verbal, and together the architectonic and the poetic imagery allow Arias Montano to visualize the redemptive operations of divine providence in human history.

The *Israelites Crossing the River Jordan* (*monumentum* 17) illustrates Joshua 3:7–14 and 4:1–10. The Levites stand amidst the

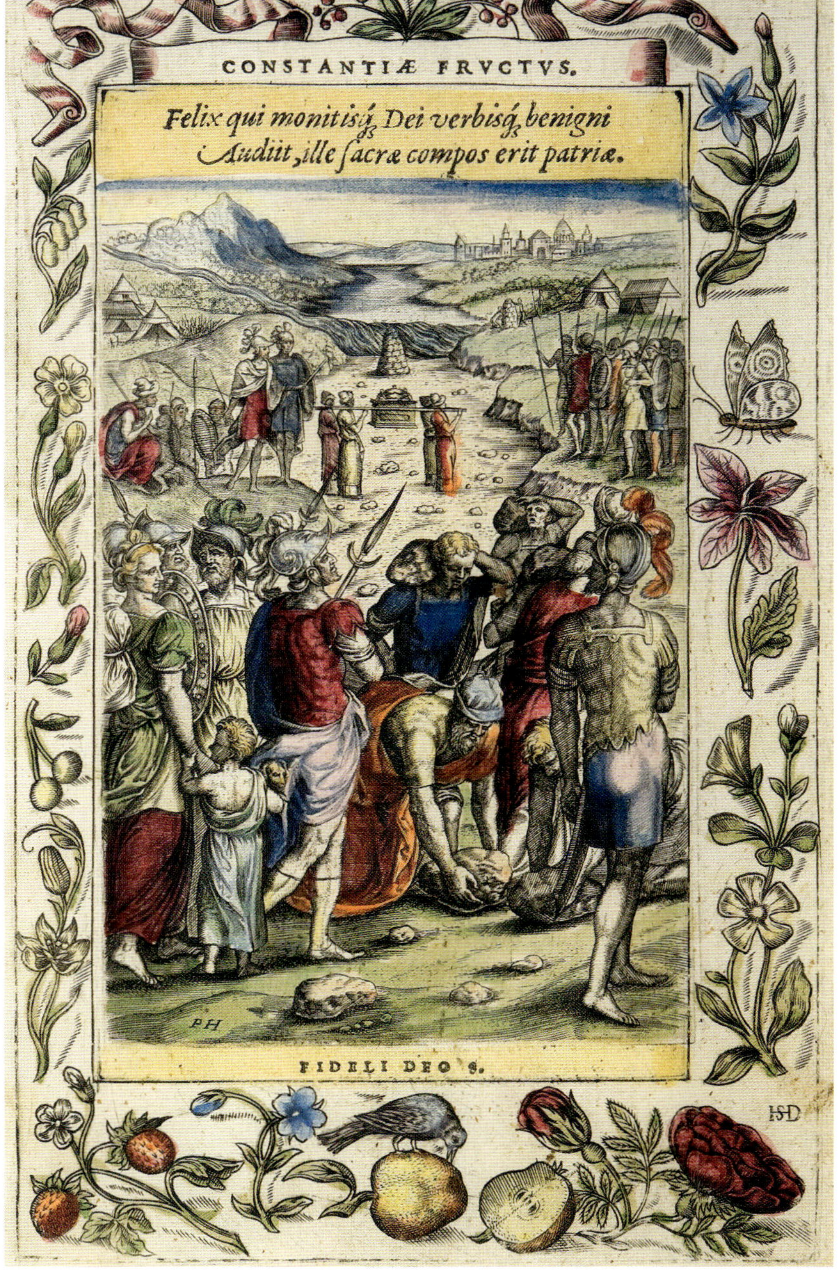

7a

dry riverbed, the ark upon their shoulders, while representatives of the twelve tribes gather memorial stones to mark their entry into the promised land. Joshua and Caleb, the only members of their generation to have reached Canaan, survey the scene from a headland in the middle distance. As discussed in the "Introduction," this print forms part of a sequence of *monumenta* focusing on the redemptive value of sacred images and the relation between corporeal and spiritual vision.[22] The motto describes the crossing as the "fruit of constancy" (*constantiae fructus*), a reference to Joshua and Caleb's firm conviction that God would guide his people in all their "going through the great wilderness."[23] The dedication to "steadfast God" emphasizes that the Israelites have closely followed the word of God, who now rewards their fidelity.[24] The distich likewise makes this point, recalling that only those who have heeded his benign admonitions will possess a fatherland.[25] The *Ode sapphica XVII* ("Sapphic Ode XVII"), entitled *In tabulam Israëlitarum Iordanem transeuntium* ("On the Image of the Israelites Crossing the River Jordan"), adapts the theme of constancy, praising the faith shown by the Israelites in their single-minded application of spiritual sight. Inspired by the word of God, they have pursued the path divinely "exposed to view," keeping their eyes ever fixed on high heaven.[26] In the same way the faithful must persevere in the journey mandated by God (*quamque contento repetenda cursu munera dia*) if they are to obtain the kingdom of peace (*quietis regna beatae*).[27]

Joshua Distributes Land to the Seven Tribes (*monumentum* 19) illustrates Joshua 18:2–10.[28] Representatives of the seven tribes still without land are sent to survey the promised land, "writing a description of it with a view to their inheritances" (Joshua 18:4). Van der Borcht envisions this as an exercise in sacred cartography, with Joshua apportioning the land according to the chart drawn up by the scouts. The motto refers to the scene as the "result of perseverance" (*perseverantiae exitus*); while the distich inquires, "Who but the man who believed and strove should declare that so much could be so quickly subdued?"[29] The dedication bears witness to the power and truth of God (*Deo veraci potentis.*). The ode sings the praises of the divine judge, whose counsel no mortal powers can withstand: his astonished followers are made lords of kingdoms that they conquer even before they can surview them.[30] In his annotation to the motto, Plantin cites two scriptural passages that bear on the Christian meaning implicit in image.[31] In Matthew 10:22 Christ sends forth his twelve disciples to journey through Palestine spreading the Gospel; he compares them to soldiers who put the land to the sword, thus implying that he is like Joshua who despatched the Israelites to conquer Canaan. In 2 Timothy 2:5 Paul admonishes his disciple to endure in Christian mission like a good soldier on campaign. Whereas *monumentum* 19 stresses that the Israelites, having seen how easily they conquered Canaan, discerned the power of God, *monumentum* 17 stresses that they kept God always in view, fixing their

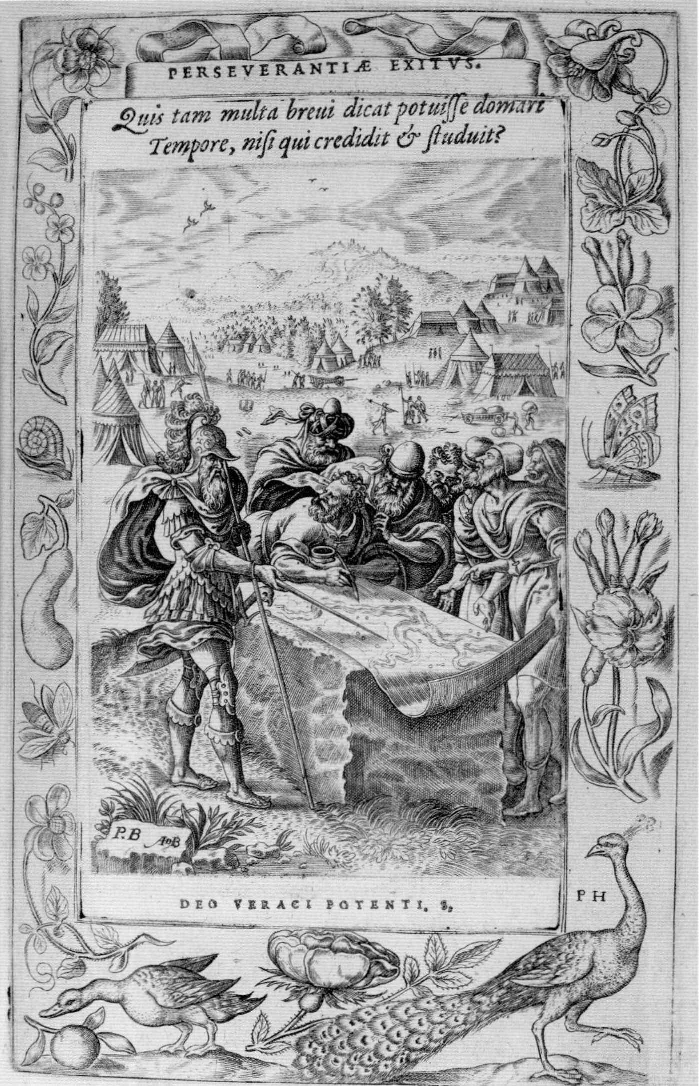

7b

eyes on the heavenly promise of spiritual salvation. Or put differently, in one instance corporeal sight confirmed their trust in the Lord; in the other spiritual sight sustained their faith in God.　WM

8a

Lucas van Doetecum (active 1554–72)
(and Johannes van Doetecum [d. 1605]?)
After Gerard van Groeningen (active 1561–ca. 1576)
Zacharias Emerges Mute from the Temple
Pl. 1 from *Memorabilivm novi testamenti, in templo
gestorvm icones tredecim elegantissimi ac ornatissimi*
ca. 1572
Etching and engraving, 20.4 × 28.9 cm
New Hollstein (Van Doetecum) 617;
New Hollstein (Van Groeningen) 79
The British Museum, London, 1928,1212.18

8b

Lucas van Doetecum (active 1554–72)
(and Johannes van Doetecum [d. 1605]?)
After Gerard van Groeningen (active 1561–ca. 1576)
The Jews Throwing Stones at Christ
Plate 10 from *Memorabilivm novi testamenti, in templo
gestorvm icones tredecim elegantissimi ac ornatissimi*
ca. 1572
Etching and engraving, 20.3 × 28.9 cm
New Hollstein (Van Doetecum) 626;
New Hollstein (Van Groeningen) 88
The British Museum, London, 1928,1212.28

8c

Lucas van Doetecum (active 1554–72)
(and Johannes van Doetecum [d. 1605]?)
After Gerard van Groeningen (active 1561–ca. 1576)
Christ Driving the Money Changers from the Temple
Plate 12 from *Memorabilivm novi testamenti, in templo
gestorvm icones tredecim elegantissimi ac ornatissimi*
ca. 1572
Etching and engraving, 20.2 × 28.7 cm
New Hollstein (Van Doetecum) 628;
New Hollstein (Van Groeningen) 90
The British Museum, London, 1928,1212.30

Active in Antwerp during the second half of the sixteenth century, Gerard van Groningen designed, sometime before 1572, a series of thirteen images depicting events involving the life of Christ and the Jewish Temple.

The first image is a representation of Zacharias, a high priest, stepping out of the Temple unable to speak. The story comes from Luke 1, which tells of the coming birth of John the Baptist. While burning incense in the temple, Zacharias was visited by an angel of the Lord, who informed him that his prayers had been heard and that his wife, Elizabeth, would give birth to a son, whom he was to name John. After Zacharias responded in doubt, noting his and his wife's elderly age, the angel answered, "I am Gabriel and I have been sent to speak to you and to tell you this good news. And now you will be silent and not able to speak until the day this happens, because you did not believe my words" (Luke 1:22).

Standing at the top of a flight of stairs leading to the temple, Zacharias gestures toward the waiting crowd to indicate his inability to communicate.[32] The architectural style of the temple and buildings in the background is an eclectic assembly and resembles designs by Sebastiano Serlio, whose *Book of Architecture* became a popular reference for Northern artists after it was published in 1553.[33] In the far right background, the angel brings God's message to Zacharias at the altar.

The fifth installment of the series is a depiction of the Jews throwing stones at Christ, an event conveyed at the end of John 8. The Gospel chapter begins with the story of the Pharisees confronting Jesus with a woman caught in adultery. When they asked him whether or not she should be stoned to death, Jesus responded by saying, "Let he who is without sin, cast the first stone" (John 8:7). After the woman was freed unharmed, Jesus proclaimed that he had come directly from God and, as a result, should be deemed above their forefather Abraham, a particularly offensive assertion to the Jews. The crowd responded in dismay and "At this, they picked up stones to stone him, but Jesus hid himself, slipping away from the temple grounds" (John 8:59).

Singled out by the halo of light around his head, Christ is shown in mid-stride in the center-right foreground and surrounded by multiple figures with stones in their hands. The temple architecture is generally classical in style, with Corinthian columns and detailed decorative tracery on the walls and ceiling. The event takes place in an outer court—given the preceding story of the adulteress, probably the court of women. In the distant background, curtains are parted to reveal the altar with a temple vessel in the middle and two stacks of shewbread on either side. To the left of the table stands a brazen laver (wash basin), which according to 1 Kings 7:25, stood upon twelve oxen and functioned as a place for the priests to purify themselves prior to entering the temple Holy Place (see cat. 19).[34]

The central, one-point perspective visually juxtaposes the figure of Christ in the foreground and the altar in the background, which is situated at the vanishing point. To understand the theological connection, it is necessary to remember that the chapter begins with the Pharisees asking Jesus if the woman caught in adultery should be stoned. While the woman was released unpunished and forgiven by Christ, "he who is without sin" now receives her just penalty. The stoning of Christ in the foreground, then, serves as the typological fulfillment of the priestly sacrifices and ritual cleansing of sins represented by the altar and laver in the background.

The seventh image in the series depicts Christ driving the moneychangers from Herod's Temple in Jerusalem. The moneychangers served pilgrims visiting the temple by exchanging various foreign currencies for Jewish and Tyrian money, the only coinage that could be used for temple ceremonies, such as for the purchase of animals to sacrifice for sins.

Similar to the previous image, Christ is located in the central foreground of an architectural setting that is generally classical in style. He lunges forward with his right arm raised and a whip in his hand. The man before him collapses to the ground, pleading for mercy, while another figure falls behind a table that Christ has overturned. Coins litter the floor. On the right, men escape Christ's wrath while, on the left, the temple leaders, who were so concerned by the crowd's awe of Jesus, conspire to kill him. On the floor in front of Jesus lies a dead, bound lamb.[35] In the distant background, curtains are parted to reveal the "Holy of Holies," or Ark of the Covenant, which contains the tablets of the Ten Commandments. As described in Exodus

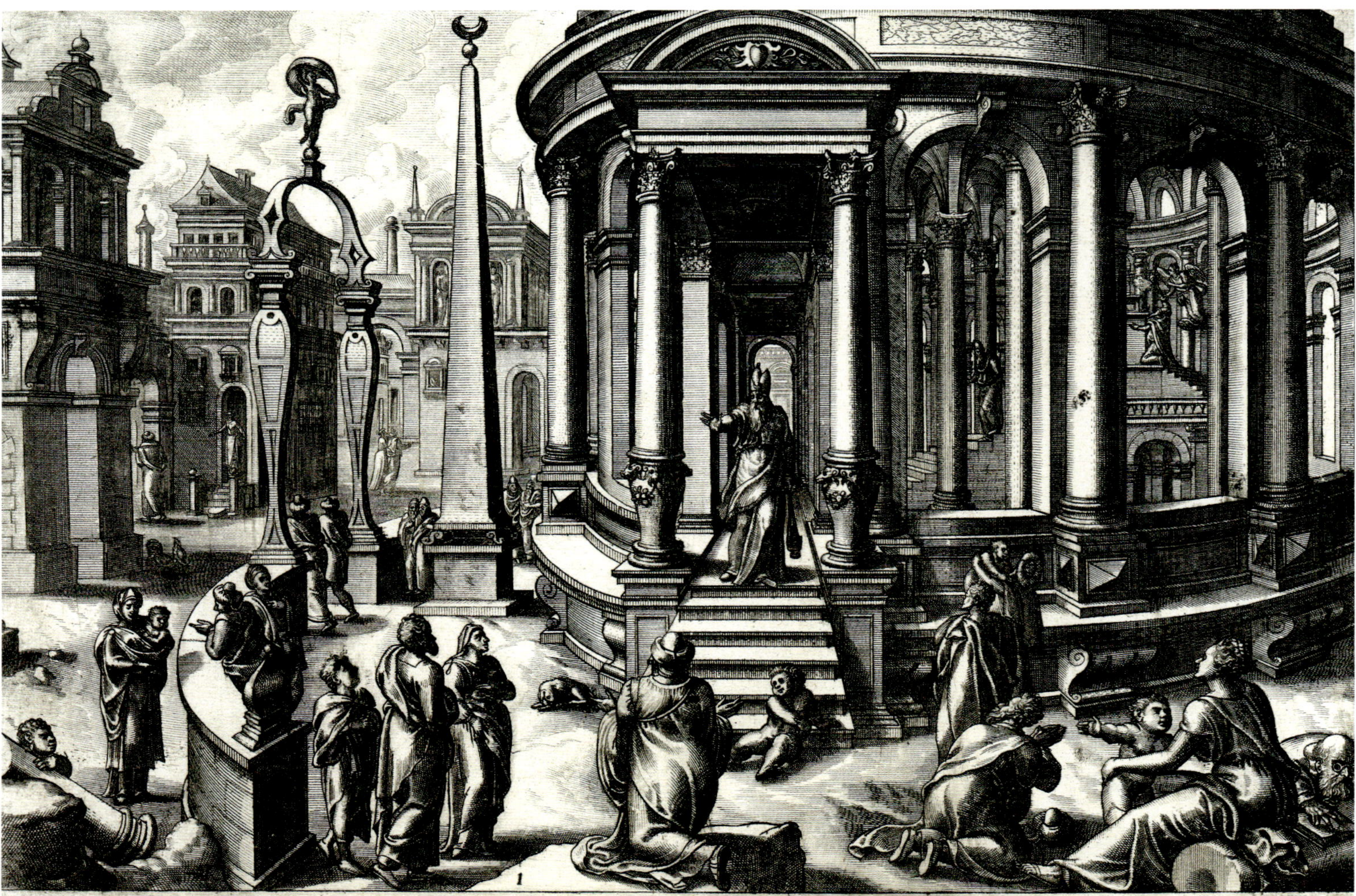

8a

25:22, cherubim are situated on either side of the ark with their wings stretched out to cover the Mercy Seat, the place where the high priest would sprinkle blood once a year for the forgiveness of the people's sins (see cat. 1).

The central, one-point perspective design of the image once again theologically connects the action in the foreground with the Ark of the Covenant in the background. In the foreground, Christ has overturned the money changers' table. In its place lies the bound lamb, a symbol that foreshadows the crucifixion and death of Christ on the cross. Whereas pilgrims exchanged their foreign currency for the local coinage of the temple in order to purchase temporary forgiveness through animal sacrifice, Christ drives out the money changers and replaces them with a new currency for salvation. In the foreground the sacrificial lamb, the New Covenant, fulfills once and for all the Law of Moses contained in the Ark of the Covenant in the background, rendering burnt sacrifices to God unnecessary. Such an image, that scorns profits made from religious ritual and so clearly situates Christ as the sole means of salvation, would have found a particularly receptive audience in the reform-minded Netherlands of the sixteenth century.   TR

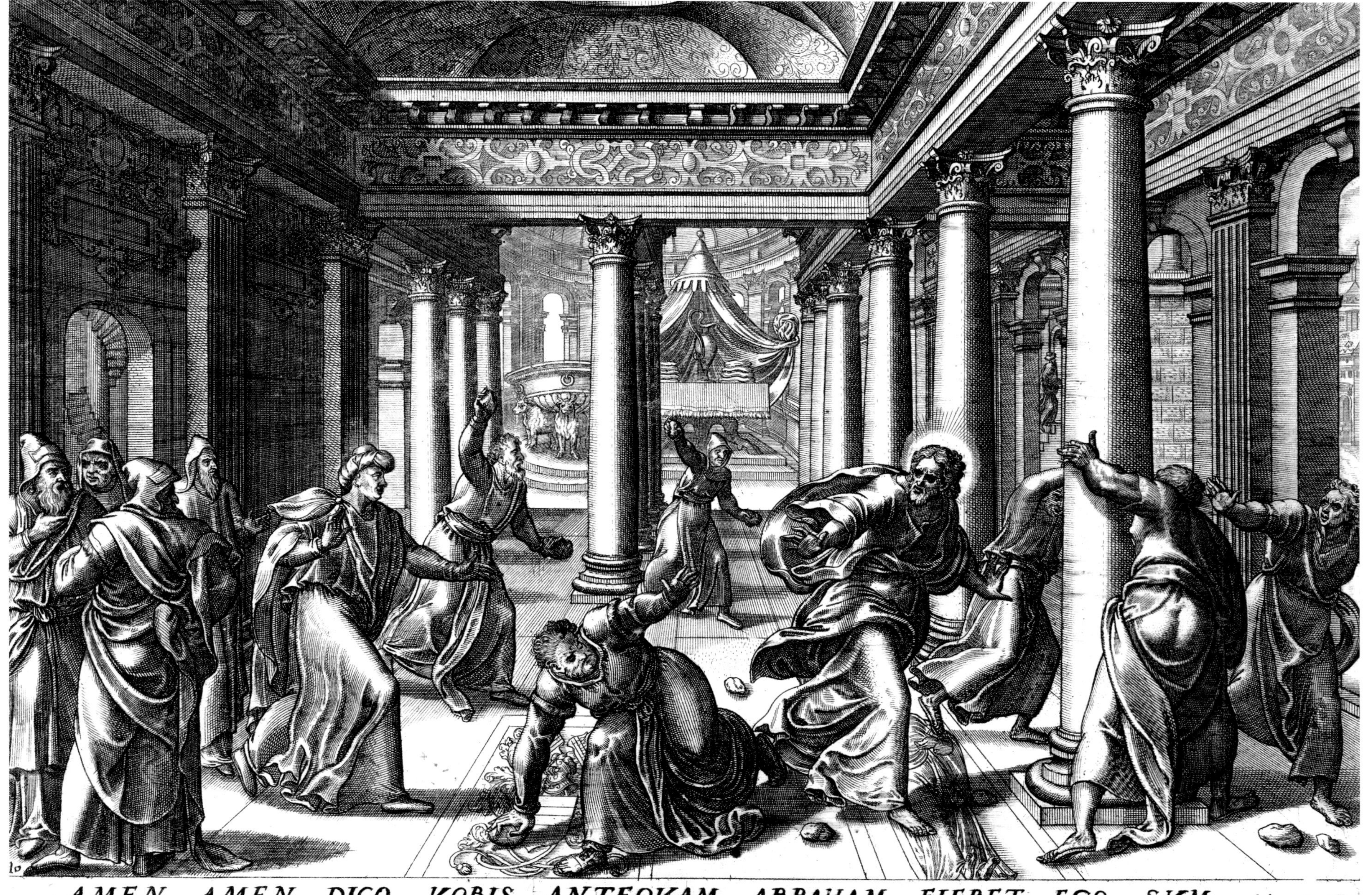
AMEN AMEN DICO VOBIS ANTEQVAM ABRAHAM FIERET EGO SVM . Iohan. 8 .

8b

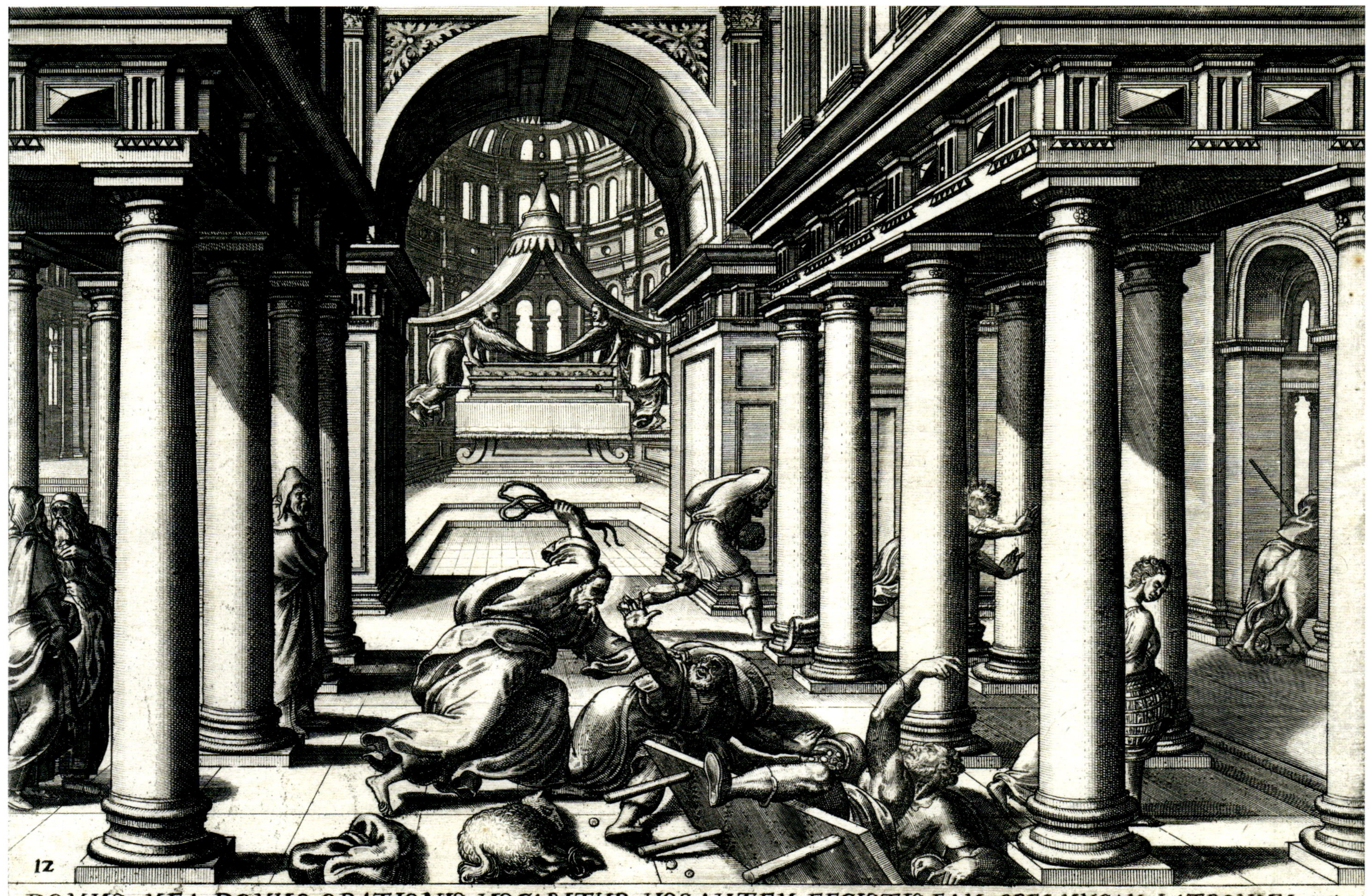

DOMVS MEA DOMVS ORATIONIS VOCABITVR. VOS AVTEM FECISTIS EAM SPELVNCAM LATRONVM. Math. 21

8c

Antoon Wierix (1555/59–1604)
After Bernardino Passeri (ca. 1540–96)
Parable of the Pharisee and the Publican
(*De Pharisaeo & Publicano*)
ca. 1593
Engraving, 23.2 × 14.7 cm
Imago 90 in Jerónimo Nadal, *Adnotationes et meditationes in Evangelia quae in sacrosancto Missae sacrificio toto anno leguntur. Cum Evangeliorum concordantia historiae integritati sufficienti. Accessit & index historiam ipsam Evangelicam in ordinem temporis vitae Christi distribuens* (*Annotations and Meditations on the Gospels Read in the Most Holy Sacrifice of the Mass during the Whole Year, with an Integral Concordance of Gospel History, and in Addition, an Index Arranging Gospel History in the Chronological Order of the Life of Christ*), 2nd ed. (Antwerp: Martinus Nutius, 1595)
Hollstein (Wierix Book Illustrations) 56.76
John Work Garrett Library, Johns Hopkins University

*C*omposed between 1568 and 1576 by the Jesuit Jerónimo Nadal, and first published in 1595, the *Adnotationes et meditationes in Evangelia* (*Annotations and Meditations on the Gospels*) consists of 153 folio engravings illustrating the chief events of Christ's life. Mainly engraved by the Wierix brothers of Antwerp (Jan, Hieronymus, and Antoon), who worked after *modelli* by Bernardino Passeri and Maarten de Vos; these images attach to extensive annotations and meditations composed by Nadal.[36] The texts are closely related to the images by means of *notae* (keys): the chief elements of each print are lettered, and these alphabetic markers match the lettered captions engraved below; the captions are repeated in letterpress at the start of every chapter. Lettered pericopes then identify the Gospel passages illustrated by the print, and finally, there follow the lettered annotations, likewise correlated to the lettered pictures. Most chapters conclude with a meditation on Christological themes ordered (though not lettered) according to the scheme of the captions and annotations. The order in which the images are read therefore determines the order of the annotations and meditations constituting the bulk of Nadal's text. The *imagines* (images) are bound into the book in one of three ways: galleried at the start or close of the volume, in which case they follow the sequence of Christ's life (as indicated by the Arabic numeral incised at upper right), or interpolated into the chapters they illustrate, in which case they follow the sequence of the liturgical calendar (as indicated by the Roman numerals incised just below the Arabic).[37]

Whereas the annotations follow the rhetorical principle of *definitio per descriptionem* (definition by description), that is, descriptively amplify the images by elaborating upon the circumstances of place and time, persons and things, the meditations figuratively interpret the religious meanings implicit in the evangelical scenes, discerning their doctrinal, ecclesiological, and spiritual significance.[38] The *Parable of the Pharisee and the Publican* illustrates the moral lesson taught by Christ in Luke 18:10–14. Standing before the Portico of Solomon (A), he teaches in the temple courtyard (C), spurned by some, attended by others (B). He tells the story of the presumptuous Pharisee (D), who, exalting himself before God, shall

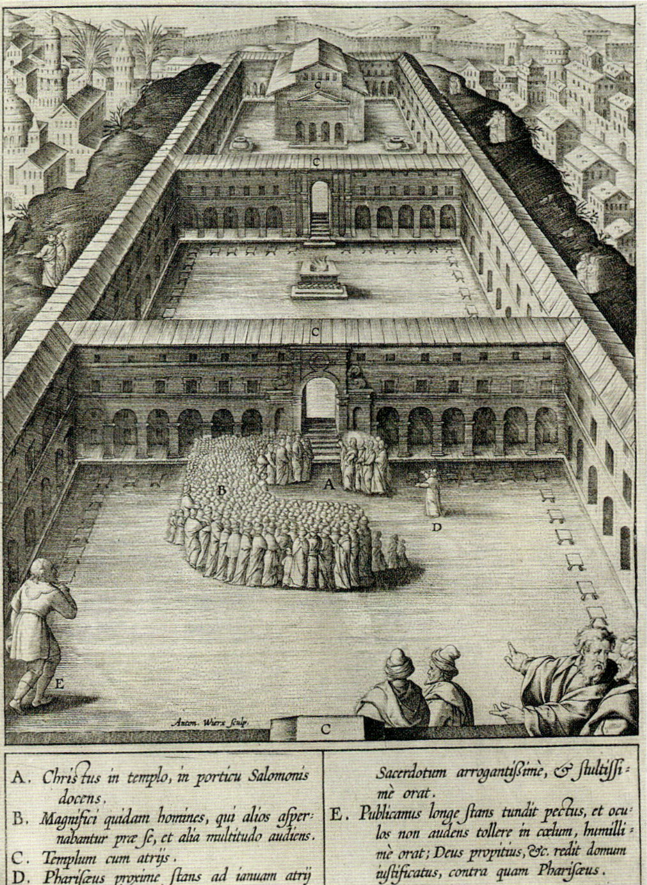

A. *Christus in templo, in porticu Salomonis docens.*
B. *Magnifici quidam homines, qui alios asper-nabantur prae se, et alia multitudo audiens.*
C. *Templum cum atrijs.*
D. *Pharisaeus proxime stans ad ianuam atrij*
Sacerdotum arrogantissimè, & stultissi-mè orat.
E. *Publicanus longe stans tundit pectus, et ocu-los non audens tollere in coelum, humilli-mè orat; Deus propitius, &c. redit domum iustificatus, contra quam Pharisaeus.*

9

ultimately be abased, and of the humble Publican (E), who, abasing himself before God, shall ultimately be exalted.[39] The annotations observe that the parable applies to Christ himself, who had just entered Jerusalem in triumph, but who would soon be humiliated upon the cross; so too, mortified in the Passion, he would yet be glorified as the redeemer. The meditation applies this paradoxical imagery to the mystery of the Incarnation, in which divinity is humbled, and humble humanity made divine. It also urges the reader-viewer to approach God with a penitent heart, as did the publican. Considerations such as these respond to the print's extraordinary perspectival construction, which depicts the publican as larger than the diminutive figure of the Pharisee, and for that matter, of Christ. That the parable's author is virtually indistinguishable from the parable's protagonists implies that the story Christ tells concerns himself. That the publican looms so large suggests his spiritual dignity; that Christ appears so small confirms his supernal humility. WM

From morning until evening he explained the matter to them, testifying to the
kingdom of God and trying to convince them about Jesus both from the law of Moses
and from the prophets. Some were convinced by what he had said, while others refused
to believe.

Acts 28:23–24

Allaert Claesz (active ca. 1520–26)
Baptism of the Eunuch
1524
Engraving, 26 × 19.5 cm
Hollstein (Claesz) 77
The British Museum, London, 1858,0417.1014

*I*n *Baptism of the Eunuch* Allaert Claesz illustrated an episode in Philip's ministry that began when an angel urged the Apostle to go from Jerusalem to Gaza. There he found the treasurer to Queen Candace of Ethiopia, a learned eunuch, in a chariot reading the book of Isaiah. When Philip asked if he understood the scripture, the eunuch solicited help in comprehending it. Philip explained that Isaiah prophesied Christ's works. After the eunuch declared his belief that Jesus was the Son of God, Philip granted his request for baptism.

Claesz integrated narrative elements of figures, water, a chariot, and Jerusalem into a detailed landscape. In a style reminiscent of Early Netherlandish painting, the engraver carefully articulated various textures, tonalities and surfaces. He distinguished Philip's physiognomy from that of the Ethiopian treasurer and his attendant with differences in skin tone, musculature and facial structure. Yet the figures are unified by complementary poses within a harmonious composition. Philip and the eunuch inhabit separate halves of the picture, the intervening space occupied only by Philip's cross-staff and outstretched hand. Christ's emblem and the baptismal gesture mediate between the Apostle and the foreign convert. The arrangement reinforces the biblical message that Christ's works elucidated scripture and

engendered the belief upon which the eunuch's baptism was predicated.

Claesz's pictorial theme of unity through understanding agrees with Flemish theologian Jan van Ruusbroec's conception of Christ as the intermediary between man and God, who reconciles all that is foreign and discordant.[40] The Dutch devotional petition, "Father…Let me never become a stranger,"[41] demonstrates the concept's popular currency. Vernacular religious education was coeval with the impetus toward familiarity with God. A Brother of the Common Life, Gerard Zerbolt van Zutphen (1367–98), cited the eunuch's baptism in his argument for holy scripture to be written in Dutch, instead of exclusively in Latin. He referred to Jerome's observation that, though the eunuch came "from the ends of the world," Philip "showed him Jesus, who was concealed beneath the letter."[42] Gerard reasoned that common language illuminates Bible lessons as Philip's preaching of Jesus illuminated Isaiah's obscure meanings.[43] Claesz's graphic style parallels the vernacular elucidation advocated by Gerard. In this engraving, he explicitly described the exotic forms of a domed temple, a chariot and Ethiopian figures to compose a fluent and comprehensive pictorial exegesis of the scriptural event.[44]   JS

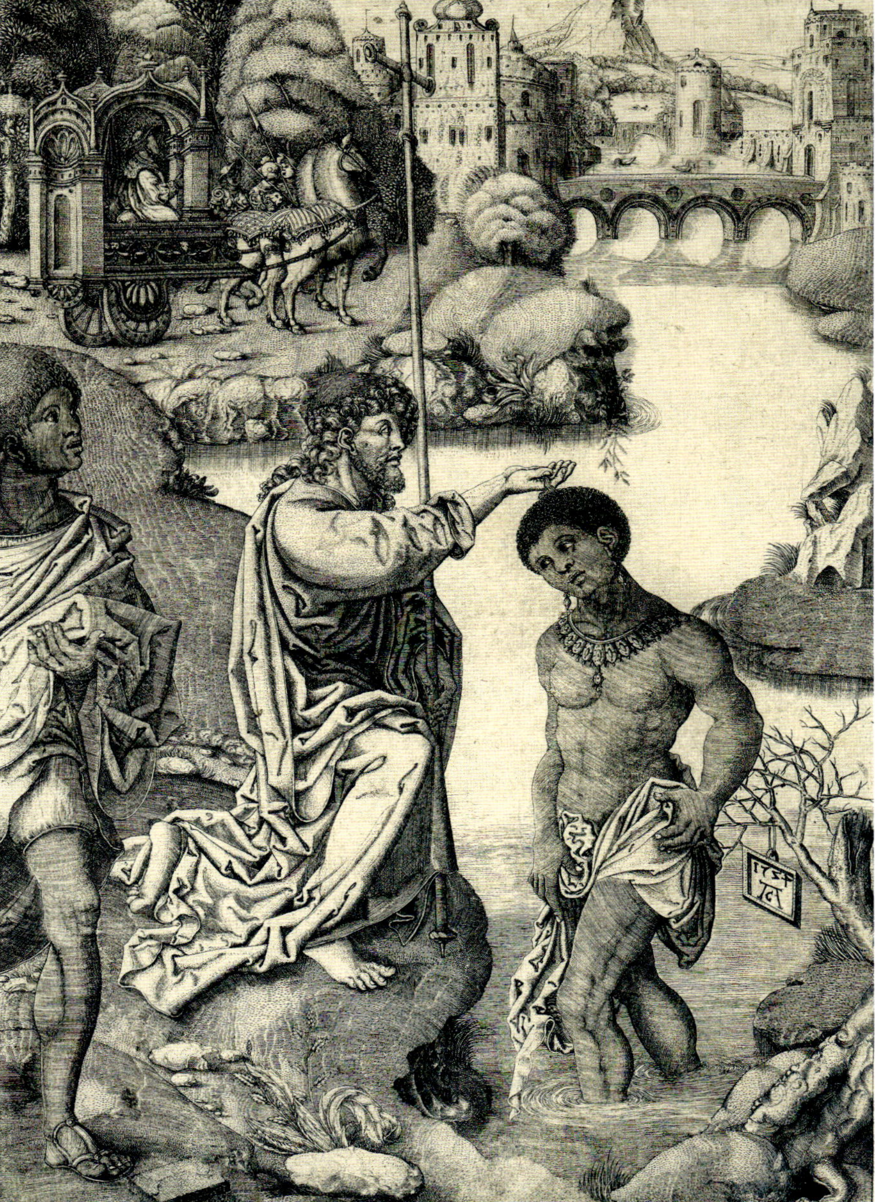

10

11

Jacob Cornelisz van Oostsanen (ca. 1475–1533)
After Lucas van Leyden (ca. 1494–1533)
*Moses Receiving the Tablets of the Law, The Agony in the
Garden, and Esther before Ahasuerus*
ca. 1530
Woodcut, ca. 18 × 26.5 cm
New Hollstein (Van Leyden), 287–310
Rijksmuseum, Amsterdam, RP-P-BI-6315B

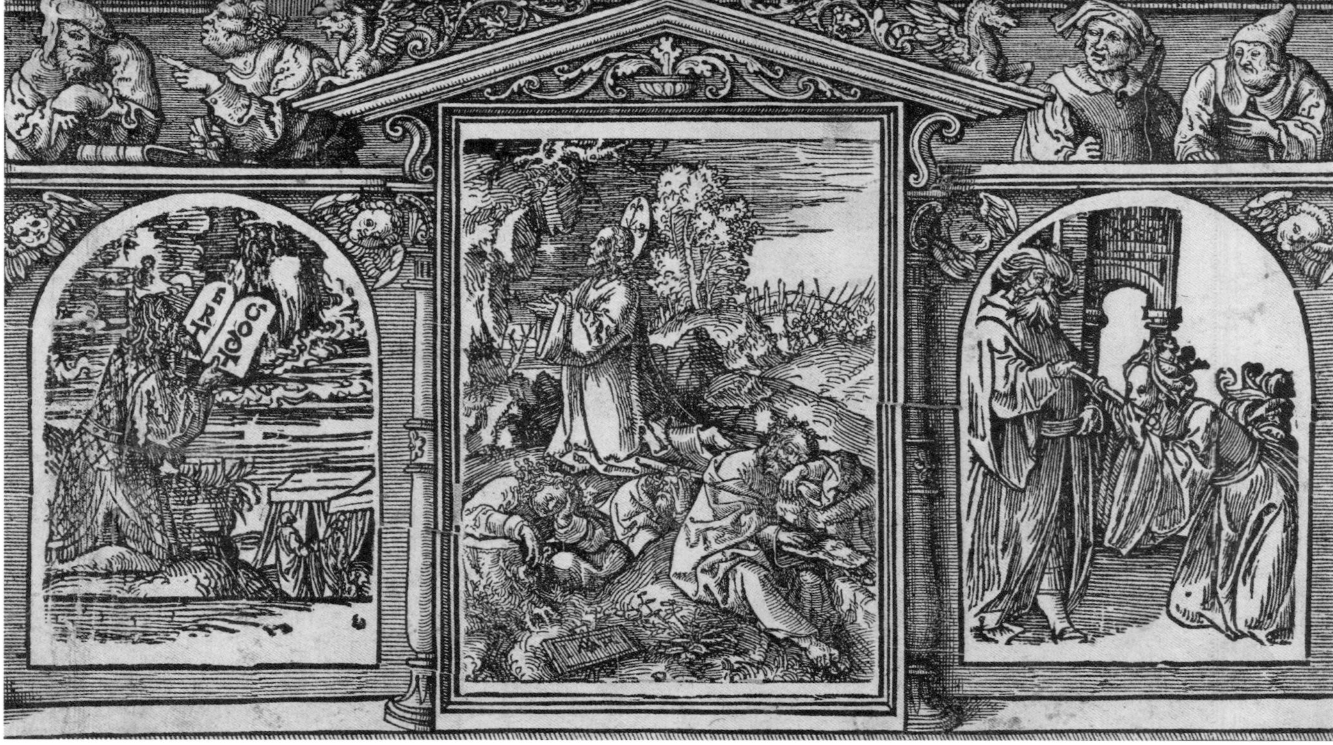

11

Amsterdam publisher Doen Pietersz.
compiled a *Biblia Pauperum* from
woodblocks by Jacob Cornelisz. van
Oostsanen and designs by Lucas van
Leyden.[45] Pietersz. typologically grouped
Old and New Testament events in the
tradition of the *Biblia Pauperum* and
Speculum Humanae Salvationis, illustrated
books popular in the Netherlands during
the fifteenth century.

Pietersz. presented an uncommon
arrangement of the Agony in the Garden
between Moses and Esther.[46] At left,
Moses, receiving the Old Covenant, prefigures Christ's establishment of the New
Covenant at his Passion.[47] At center, Christ
prays, as the inscription states: "Father, if
thou wilt, remove this chalice from me:
but yet not my will, but thine be
done"(Luke 22:42).[48] The chalice embodies the bitter cup of Christ's Passion and
signals that the covenant of the Eucharist
will supercede the Old Law.

At right, Esther intercedes with her
Persian husband, King Ahasuerus. The
selfless act that saved Esther's people am-
plifies the sacrifice that authorized
Christ's as judge and intercessor before
God the Father.[49] Previously, Esther was
grouped with Maria Mediatrix[50] or Mary's
Coronation and Solomon enthroned with
Bathsheba.[51] These precedents cast Esther
as a type for Mary's roles, as intercessor to
Christ, and his metaphorical Bride, the
Church.[52] Three scenes engraved above
reinforce Esther's identification with
Mary. Michal helping David escape
(1 Samuel 19:12), at left, and Rebecca dis-
patching Jacob (1 Samuel 19:12), at right,
prefigure Mary's protective function in
the Flight into Egypt (Matthew 2:14), center. Pietersz.'s ordering of biblical scenes
explicates salvation offered to worshipers
by the church.   JS

12

Hieronymus Wierix (1553–1619)
Christ in the Wine Press
ca. 1605
Engraving, 14 × 9.2 cm
Hollstein (Wierix) *737*
The Metropolitan Museum of Art, New York

*S*ince the early twelfth century, artists have drawn on a passage in Isaiah for one of the most remarkable images in Western Art.[53] "I have trodden the winepress alone, and from the peoples no one was with me; I trod them in my anger and trampled them in my wrath; their juice spattered on my garments, and stained all my robes" (Isaiah 63: 3). As early as Tertullian (d. ca. 225), the passage was interpreted with reference to Christ's Passion. Gregory the Great (d. 604) has Christ as both treader and trodden: "He has trodden the winepress alone in which he was himself pressed, for with his own strength he patiently overcame suffering."[54] But it was not until the late fourteenth century that a more literal representation of an unblemished—even triumphant—Christ treading in the winepress was replaced by a bleeding, thorn-crowned Christ squeezed within the press.[55] The metaphor of the winepress and representations of it paralleled and informed the late medieval emphasis on the torments of Christ's Passion, in which a veritable river of blood issued from Christ's body, gushing even from his mouth and his fingernails.[56] The press was specifically equated with the cross of Christ—"Torcular est sancta crux," in the words of the twelfth-century *Hortus deliciarum* by Herrade of Landsberg[57]— and from the early fifteenth century the beam of the winepress is represented as the cross, emphatically making the connection between the image and the Passion.[58] The subject appeared in virtually every possible medium, in both private and public contexts, and varied widely in composition and iconography. It was very popular in the fifteenth century and again toward the end of the sixteenth century, with its Counter-Reformatory emphasis on the eucharist,[59] although it was also used in Protestant contexts.[60]

In Hieronymus Wierix's engraving,[61] blood spouts from Christ's five wounds into a vat filled with grapes on which he stands. Christ's blood runs from a tap into chalices held by angels kneeling in the foreground, making explicit the eucharistic meaning of the subject.[62] The appeal to Catholic viewers is enhanced by the presence of Saint Peter at the left and especially the Virgin Mary—her heart pierced by a sword—at the right.

In Wierix's composition, the press consists simply of the cross levered onto Christ from a large screw operated by God the Father, offering in sacrifice his son, a motif that had appeared early in the iconographic development of Christ in the Winepress. The dove of the Holy Spirit, sitting atop the cross, completes the Trinity.   JC

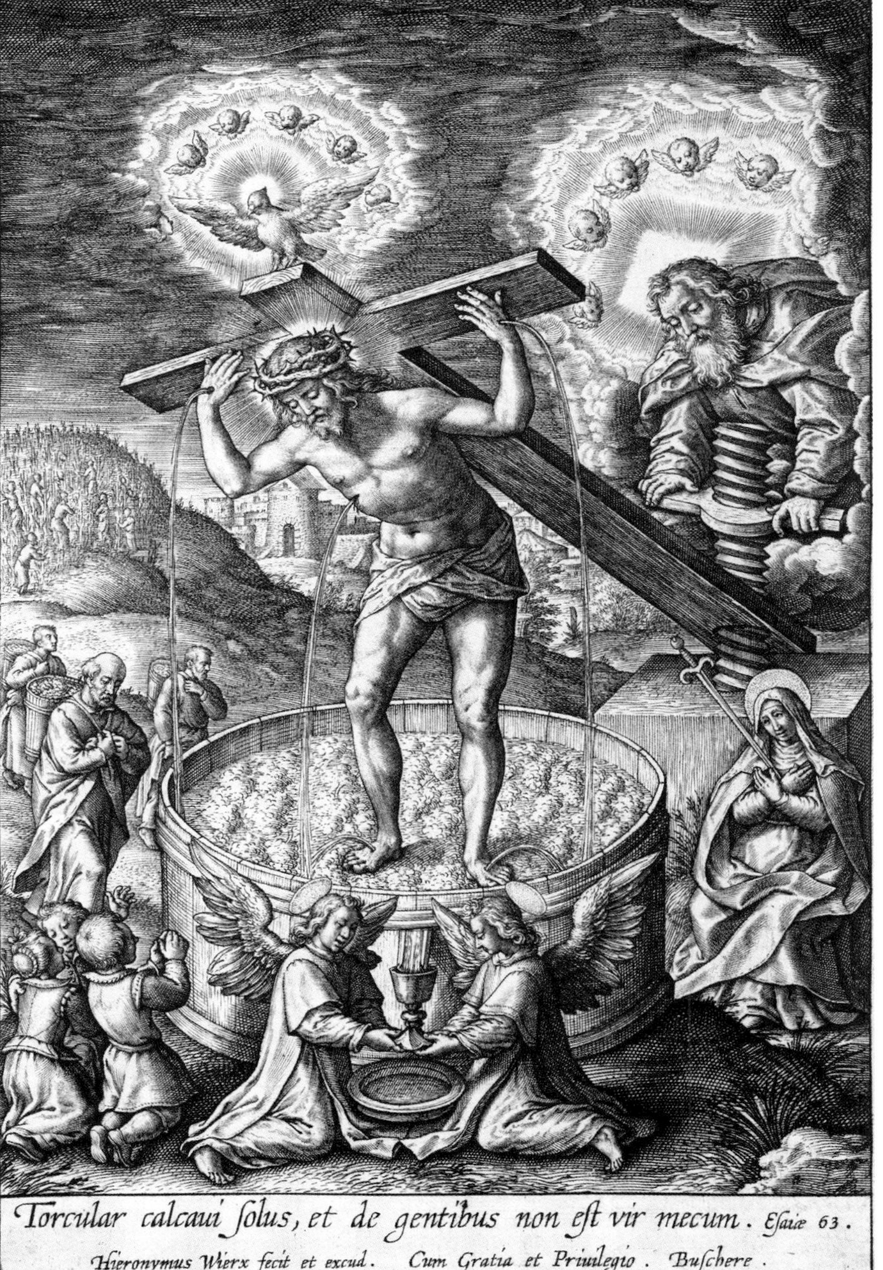

12

Adriaen Collaert (ca. 1560–1618)

After Joannes Stradanus (1523–1605)

Man of Sorrows

ca. 1585–1600

Engraving, 18.7 × 25.5 cm

New Hollstein (Collaert) 505

The Metropolitan Museum of Art, New York

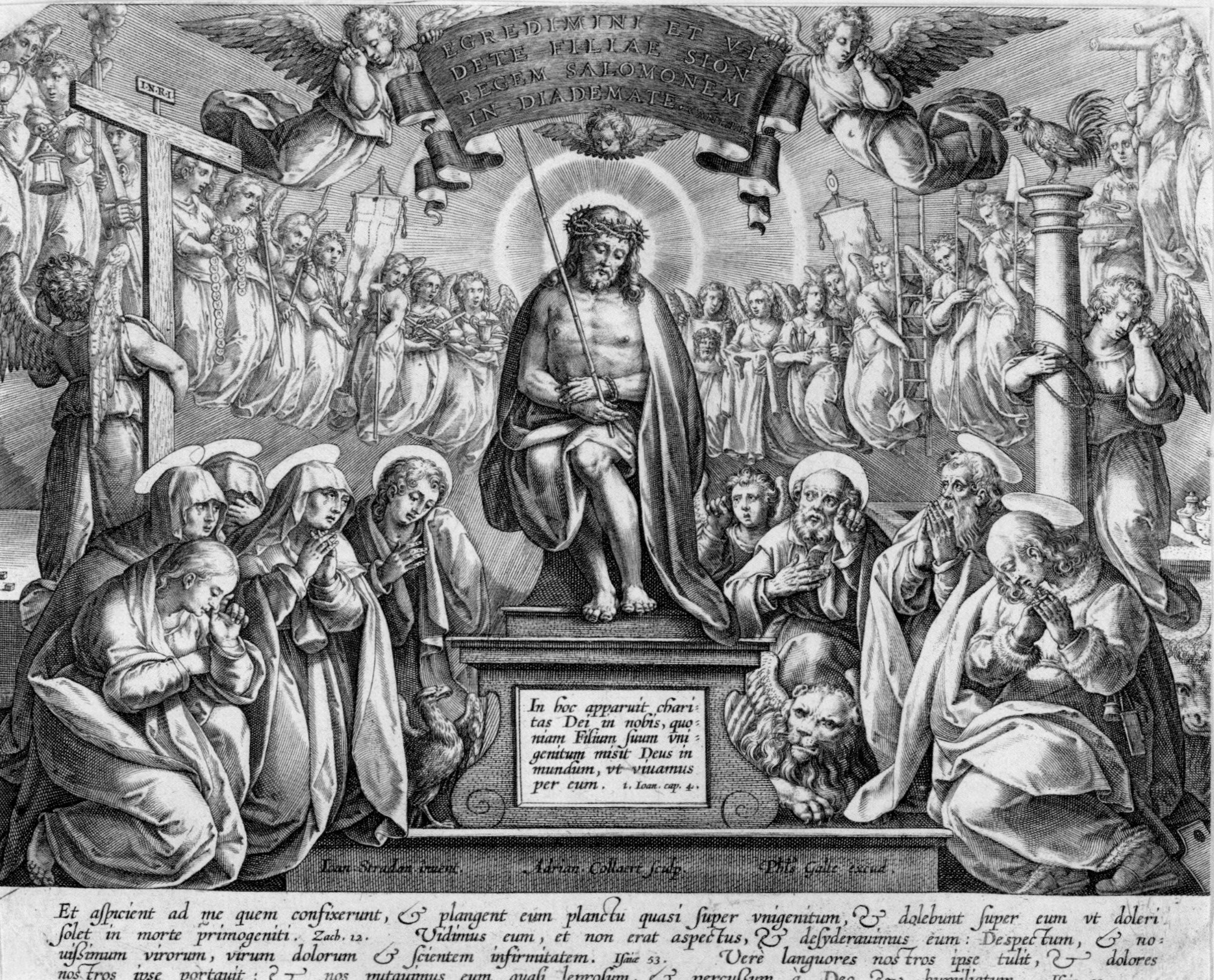

13

The *Man of Sorrows*, designed by Joannes Stradanus, engraved by Adriaen Collaert, and published by Philips Galle in Antwerp, exemplifies the use of biblical subjects for an iconic rather than narrative composition, entailing a devotional rather than illustrative function of the print.[63] The static, symmetrical composition leads the viewer's eye to the suffering Christ at the exact center. This Christ is taken from a Mocking or Ecce Homo, his head crowned with thorns, his bound hands holding a reed sceptre, a robe thrown across his shoulders. But he is situated in a literally nondescript space, without narrative action, aside from the adoration and commiseration of the three Marys and four Evangelists gathered around him. The *arma Christi*, or Instruments of the Passion, held by angels—the thirty pieces of silver for which Judas betrayed him; the column to which he was tied while beaten; the cock that crowed after Peter denied him three times; the hammer and nails with which he was hung on the cross; the cross itself; and so on—induce meditation on particular moments in Christ's Passion without directly depicting them, by provoking the viewer to reconstruct mentally the narrative in which they played a part.[64]

The texts do not explicitly tell the Passion story; neither does the image. Several of the texts, all direct biblical quotations, refer to or incite the act of looking at Christ (or, rather, Old Testament prefigurations of him). On the banderole held by angels at the top of the print, a passage from the Song of Solomon (3:11) exhorts the viewer: "Come out and look, O daughters of Zion, at King Solomon, in his crown." The passage from Zechariah (12:10) prophesies "when they look on the one whom they have pierced, they shall mourn for him, as one mourns for an only child, and weep bitterly over him, as one weeps over a firstborn." One of the two passages in the subscription from Isaiah 53 (one of the Old Testament chapters most commonly adduced to refer to the suffering Christ) acknowledges the discomfort of this looking: "We have seen him, and there was nothing in his appearance that we should desire him. He was despised and rejected by others; a man of suffering" (53:2–3), a passage read during Holy Week.[65] In the passage from 1 John (4:9) quoted in the inscription just below Christ, he is posited as the visible manifestation of God's love: "God's love was revealed [or appeared, or was made visible] among us in this way: God sent his only Son into the world so that we might live through him." Thus, the viewer is called upon by both text and image to confront, through looking and meditating, the paradox of God's love manifest in the suffering of his son. JC

14a–h

Philips Galle (1537–1612)

After Maarten van Heemskerck (1498–1574)

Vicissitudes of the Jewish People (*Clades Judaeae Gentis*)

1569

A series of twenty-two engravings, each ca. 14 × 20 cm, from which:

a. *Frontispiece*

b. *Noah's Sacrifice*

c. *The Mocking of Noah*

d. *The Chaldeans Carrying Away the Pillars of the Temple of Jerusalem*

e. *The Chaldeans Carrying Away the Temple Treasures*

f. *The Adoration of the Shepherds*

g. *The Adoration of the Magi*

h. *The Destruction of Jerusalem by Titus*

New Hollstein (Van Heemskerck) 237, 238, 239, 254, 255, 256, 257, 258; New Hollstein (Galle) 103, 104, 104, 120, 121, 122, 123, 124.

Museum Plantin-Moretus/Prentenkabinet, Antwerp–UNESCO World Heritage, Inv. No. OP 7641, Cat. No. II/G.137 (a); Inv. No. OP 7642, Cat. No. II/G.138 (b); Inv. No. OP 7643, Cat. No. II/G.139 (c); Inv. No. OP 7658, Cat. No. II/G.154 (d); Inv. No. OP 7659, Cat. No. II/G.155 (e); Inv. No. OP 7660, Cat. No. II/G.157 (f); Inv. No. OP 7661, Cat. No. II/G.159 (g); Inv. No. OP 7662, Cat. No. II/G.160 (h)

Five years before his death in 1574, Maarten van Heemskerck designed the extensive print series known as the *Clades Judaeae Gentis* (*Vicissitudes of the Jewish People*): twenty-two prints depict key events from Jewish history, some well-known, others rarely if ever illustrated.[66] Van Heemskerck had previously illustrated several of these scenes, but here he has drastically reduced the figures in favor of elaborate landscapes filled with ruins.

The series opens with an unexpected frontispiece prominently featuring a self-portrait of the artist, surrounded by ruins and fallen monuments and several dedicatory texts. This is followed by eighteen scenes in pairs from the Old Testament: Noah's sacrifice and his drunkenness; the fall of the Tower of Babel in two stages; Lot leaving Sodom and sleeping with his daughters; Joshua's military exploits (two pairs); Samson destroying the temple and his burial procession; the capture of Tirsah and the people divided between Tibni and Omri; Jehu destroying Baal-worship and adoring the golden calves; and the Chaldeans carrying away the temple pillars and removing the temple treasures. The following two prints unexpectedly show New Testament scenes—*The Nativity with the Adoration of the Shepherds* and *The Adoration of the Magi*. The series ends with a depiction of Flavius Josephus's account of the destruction of the temple in Jerusalem by the soon-to-be Emperor Titus.

At first glance Van Heemskerck's choice of paired scenes, such as *The Capture of Tirsah* and the *People of Israel Divided between Tibni and Omri*, appears puzzling, but upon closer inspection the *Clades* series proves to be internally coherent. The overall use of landscapes featuring an abundance of architectural ruins and fragmentary sculpture, as well as the smaller details, such as the crown worn by God in *Noah's Sacrifice* and then by King Nimrod in *The Tower of Babel* and *The Destruction of the Tower of Babel*, exemplify the pride and vanity of the people who are seen repeatedly to be punished. The visual narrative focuses on scenes of divine justice, and the presence of ruins alludes to sins perpetrated and punished.

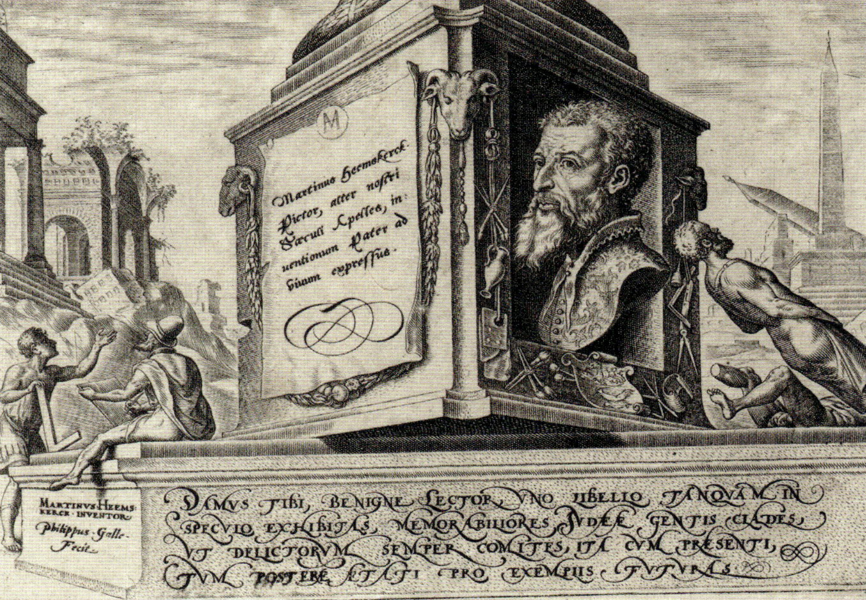

14a

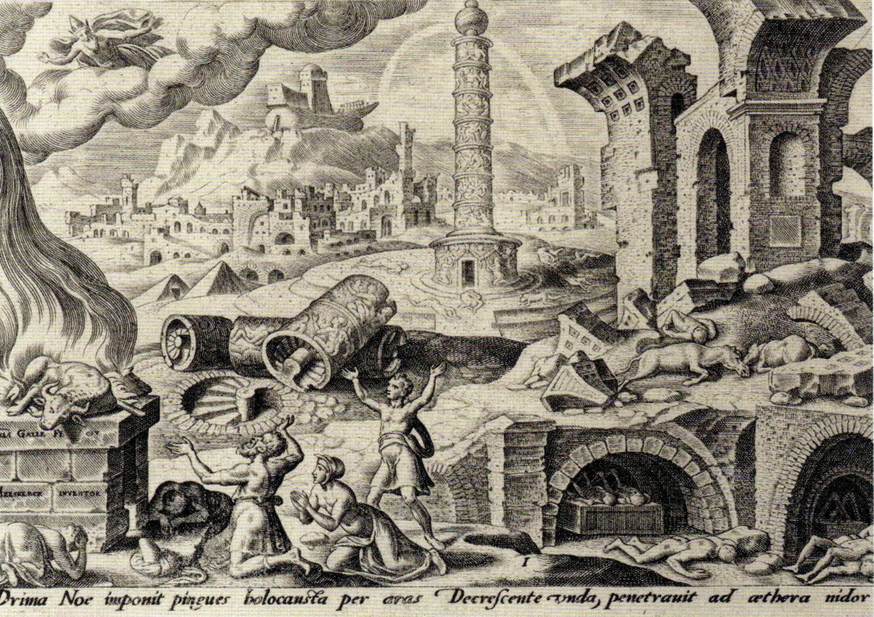

14b

The organization of the series is both chronological and strongly thematic. The predominating theme is divine justice, although this is more easily recognized in certain prints than in others. The military exploits of Joshua form a clear example, since obeisance to divine instructions results in victory over Jericho, while deviation brings defeat at the city gates of Ai and, in Achan's case, death. In the case of the *Capture of Tirsah* the connection is less obvious but present nonetheless; Omri is the instrument of God's punishment of Zimri, who had killed a reigning king and committed other sins against God. In *The People of Israel Divided between Tibni and Omri*, the latter is the chosen leader, but like Noah and Lot before him, and like Jehu after him, he could not help falling into sin himself. Also, his children did not prosper, as Jehu was anointed king of Israel in order to destroy the house of Omri's son Achab and his wife Jezebel, who had reintroduced the worship of Baal.

The architectural ruins visible in every image have different functions in the various prints. For instance, the ruins in *Noah's sacrifice* underscore the break with the past, but can also be read as a warning for the future, while in *The Tower of Babel* and *The Destruction of the Tower of Babel* the burning, collapsing building symbolizes human vanity and divine retribution. In *The Destruction of Jericho* and *The Burial of Samson* the ruins signify triumph and divine favor, while the burning temple in *The Destruction of Jerusalem by Emperor Titus* perhaps exemplifies God's abandonment of his formerly chosen people.

Van Heemskerck's choice for these grim themes may reflect contemporary events in the Low Countries. Charles V of Spain and his son Philip II after him instituted heavy taxes in their northern territories. They also supported the work of the Inquisition in its ruthless quest to quench Protestantism. This led to growing resentment among the population and nobles of the Low Countries, who tried through various means to persuade their Spanish lord to change his policies, though with little success. In 1566 a wave of iconoclasm swept over the country in protest, resulting in the destruction of many of Van Heemskerck's works, though the city of Haarlem, where he lived at the time, managed to diffuse the situation before any churches or monasteries were vandalized.

The answer from Spain was the Duke of Alva, who arrived in August 1567 and initiated the worst period of oppression. Contemporary estimates of the death-toll ranged in the tens of thousands. Dirck Coornhert, a close friend of Van Heemskerck who engraved many of his designs, put the number around 36,000. Van Heemskerck is known to have been shocked by the destruction of many of his works. In fact, he painted his last known painting a year later, thereafter devoting himself mainly to printmaking, as a supplier of drawings for print publishers and their associated engravers.

Throughout the series, Van Heemskerck produces a stage-like effect by positioning the protagonists in the lower foreground and reducing their size in relation to the background, as if the

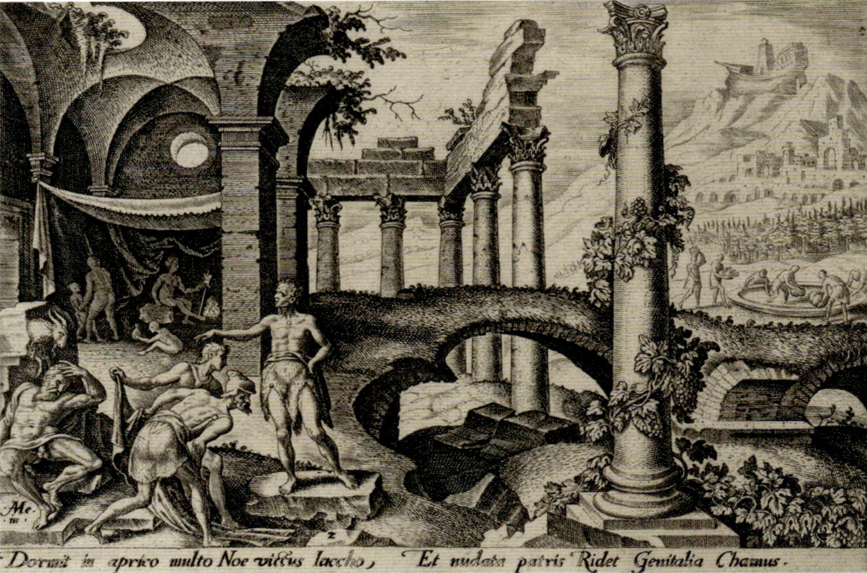

14c

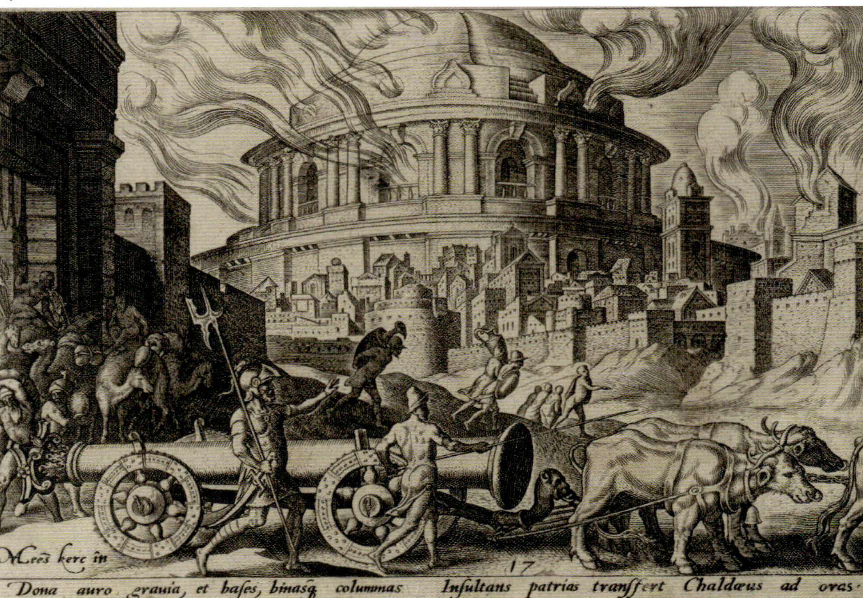

14d

historical events were being performed on a stage. This reinforces the idea that the artist intended these prints to function didactically, by showing his contemporaries the destructive consequences of sinful disobedience to God.

Frontispiece

Central to the frontispiece is a Roman socle in three-quarter view, featuring a portrait bust of the artist in a rectangular niche. Attached to the socle is a notice that reads: "Maarten van Heemskerck, painter, a second Apelles—that of our age—the father of (these) inventions, depicted from life." The socle sits on a rectangular base with an inscription introducing the twenty-one prints that follow: "The disasters visited on the Jewish people are as a mirror, an example of the punishment that one will receive for misdeeds, both now and in the future." Most striking is the attention Van Heemskerck calls to himself: he is seen sketching classical ruins, and thereby underscores his first-hand engagement with antiquity. By placing his portrait bust in the Roman socle, Van Heemskerck claims to belong to those ancient remains and to have similar status and authority. His coat of arms—a winged arm holding a pen or brush and resting on a tortoise—refers to a famous saying of Apelles, that an artist must not labor too long over a work of art. The coat of arms, which doubles as the artist's *impresa*, identifies him as a latter-day ancient and complements the argument of the text on the socle, probably composed by the humanist Hadrianus Junius.

Noah's Sacrifice

The biblical story, told in Genesis 8, relates how God, having grown dissatisfied with human disobedience, decided to wash the earth clean of people. He ordered Noah, the only righteous man, to build an ark in which he, his family, and representatives of all the animals might be kept safe. Although the *Clades* series opens with the sacrifice Noah offered after the waters had receded, the image alludes mainly to the consequences of divine justice, for the scene is filled with ruins and the cadavers of people and animals. Van Heemskerck thus admonishes his contemporaries to beware the judgment of God.

The Mocking of Noah

The story continues by showing how even Noah, the only righteous man in the world before the flood, could not avoid falling into sin: having planted vineyards, which can be seen below the ark in the background, he becomes drunk on wine, lying in his tent with his genitals uncovered. On finding him thus, his son Cham ridiculed him, whereas Cham's two brothers covered him, walking backwards to avoid seeing their father's nakedness. When Noah awoke, he cursed Cham and his offspring. Again, much of the picture is filled with ruins and debris. The text accompanying the print implicitly compares drunkenness to idolatry, placing the patriarch Noah under the sign of Bacchus: "Conquered by Bacchus, the sleeping Noah was largely exposed; and while Noah was naked, Cham laughed at his father's genitalia."

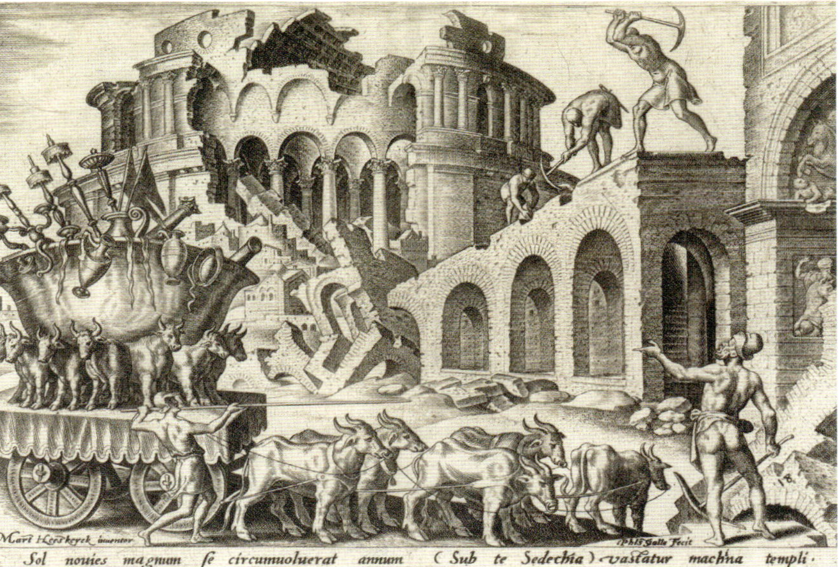

14e

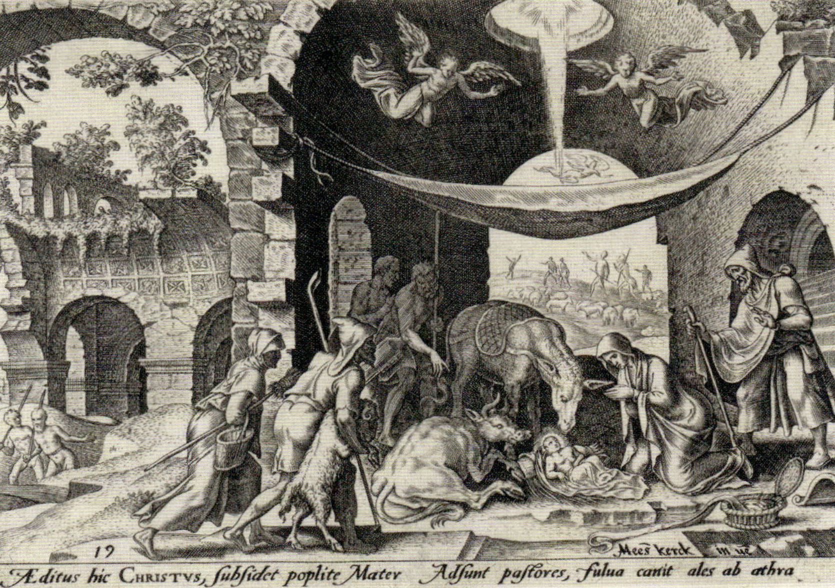

14f

*The Chaldeans Carrying Away
the Pillars of the Temple*
In 2 Kings 25:8–10 and 13–17, angered
by the disobedience of his people and in
particular of their leaders, God punished
them by allowing Nebuchadnezzar, king
of the Babylonians (or Chaldeans), to
conquer the Israelites. This resulted in the
destruction of Jerusalem and the temple.
The spoils of war included the temple
pillars and treasure, together with most
of the city's inhabitants, who were taken
captive to Babylon. Van Heemskerck has
depicted the Chaldeans marching out of
the city gate with one of the columns on an
elaborately decorated cart drawn by oxen.
The temple burns in the background, thick
smoke billowing upward. The impression
here is of divine punishment precisely
controlled, and here as elsewhere in the
series, Van Heemskerck uses fire as an
attribute of God.

*The Chaldeans Carrying Away
the Temple Treasures*
Five oxen are pulling a large cart laden
with the spoils of war away from the
city of Jerusalem that now largely lies
in ruins. Three men with pickaxes do
even more damage. In the background
the temple has crumbled like the rest of
the city, affording the viewer a glance at
the interior, which is reminiscent of the
Pantheon in Rome. Van Heemskerck's
stance on the ruins is ambiguous: as an
antiquarian he admired and studied
ancient remains; as a collector he filled
sketchbooks with drawings made
after these antiquities; as an artist he

incorporated the material he drew into
his paintings and print-designs. On
the other hand, many of the ruins of
classical buildings in his works have a
predominantly negative connotation.

*The Adoration of the Shepherds
The Adoration of the Magi*
These are the only two prints illustrating
stories from the New Testament in the
Clades series. In the far background of
the former, an angel announces to the
shepherds that Christ is born; in the
foreground, they find the Virgin Mary
and her new-born son. The Holy Family
resides in a ruined building reminiscent
of the residence of Noah and his family
in *The Mocking of Noah*; both families have
made a makeshift home for themselves in
the ruins left by the previous generations
that failed to obey God and were
punished accordingly. But while Noah
himself could not resist temptation
and became drunk, Christ shall fulfill
God's covenant with man. Marking the
momentous novelty of the coming of
Christ, the *Adoration of the Magi* takes place
in the most singular, or better, explicitly
inventive architectural construction in
the *Clades* series, adapted from Bramante's
Belvedere Staircase in the Vatican.

The Destruction of Jerusalem by Titus
The concluding print of the series is based
not on the Bible, but on Flavius Josephus'
De bello judaico (*On the Jewish War*). In 70 AD,
the future emperor Titus besieged the
rebellious city of Jerusalem, destroying it
along with the temple. In the print, Titus

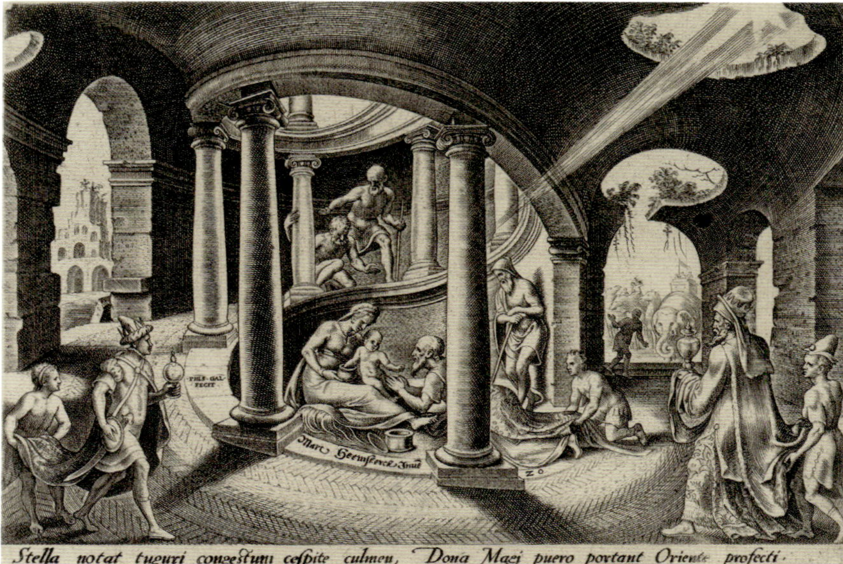

14g

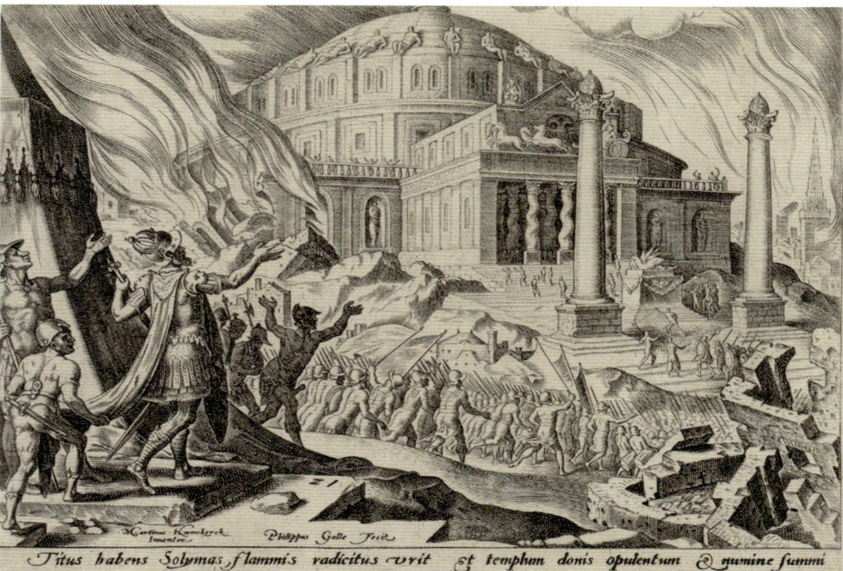

14h

surveys a scene of destruction: his
army floods into the city of Jerusalem,
in which the Pantheon-like temple is
already burning. Within the context of
the *Clades* series, this apocalyptic scene
signifies the punishment of the Jews
for their failure to acknowledge the
coming of Christ.   MG

Cornelis Cort (1533 or 1536–78)
After Federico Zuccaro (1542 or 1543–1609)
*The Annunciation Surrounded by Prophets of the
Incarnation*
1571
Engraving, 46.2 × 32.9 cm (left plate),
46.4 × 36.4 cm (right plate)
New Hollstein (Cort) 21
The British Library, London, 1917,1208.675.1-2

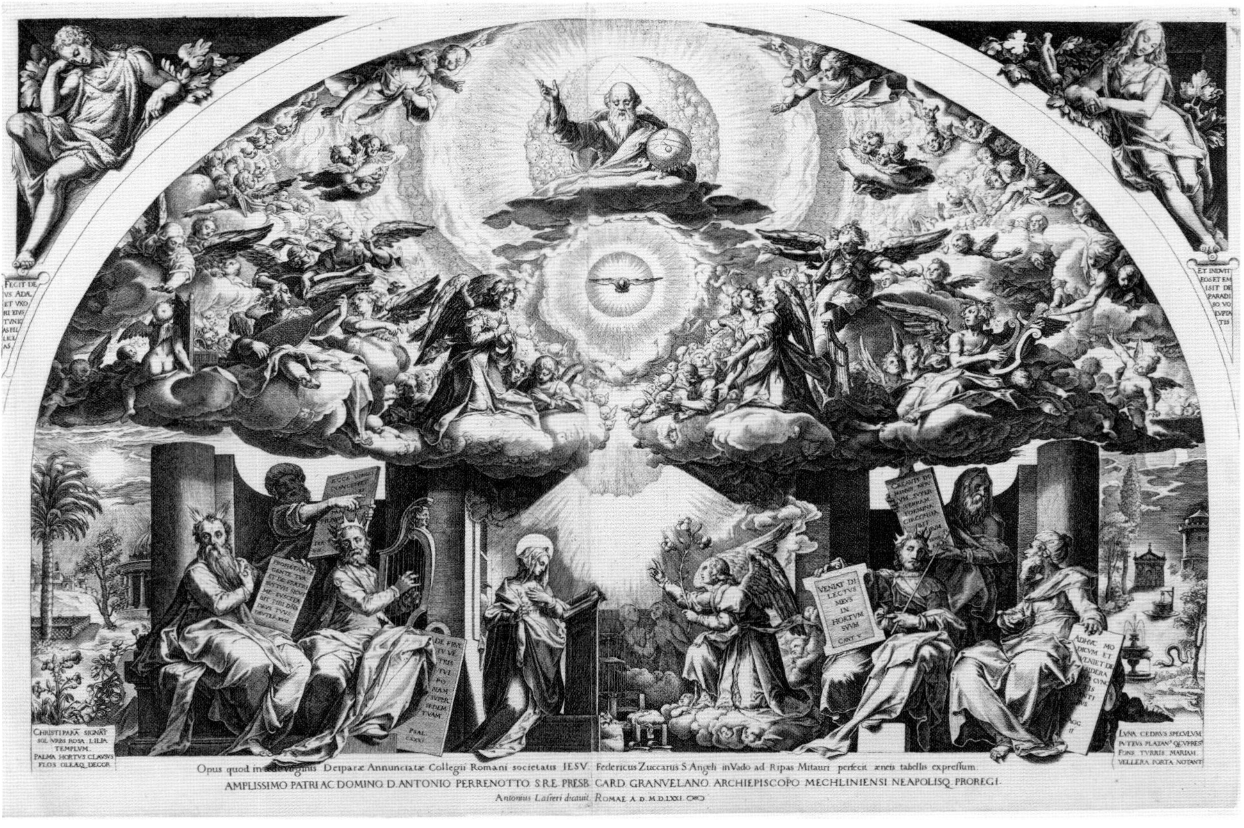

15

𝒯rained by Dirck Volckertszoon
Coornhert in Haarlem, the Dutch
master engraver Cornelis Cort produced
numerous plates for *Aux Quatre Vents*, the
Antwerp firm of Hieronymus Cock, before
moving to Italy in 1565, where he was
resident first in Venice, then in Florence
and Rome. Cort engraved *The Annunciation
Surrounded by Prophets of the Incarnation*
for the Roman print publisher Antoine
Lafreri, who dedicated it to Antoine
Perrenot, Cardinal de Granvelle; having
become Archbishop of Malines in 1559,
Granvelle was named viceroy of Naples in
1571, shortly before this print appeared.[67]
It affirms the prelate-viceroy's devotion
to the Virgin and to the Jesuit order, for
whose collegiate church, consecrated to
Mary the Virgin Annunciate and Most
Holy Mother of God, Federico Zuccaro
frescoed the Trinitarian scene on which
the print is based. The painter is identified
in the inscription below as the person
who "executed the work [here] imitated
on copper plates" by Cort (*opus quod…
Federicus Zuccarus S. Angeli in Vado ad Ripas
Mitauri perfecit aeneis tabellis expressum*).[68]
Cort relies on the linear means he had
so brilliantly codified — swelling
and tapering hatches — to articulate
sculptural forms, describe various

textures, and, most importantly, convey
the scintillant interaction of divine and
natural light. He depicts the moment
when Mary, having been illuminated by
the Holy Spirit and overshadowed by the
power of the Most High, consents to be
the mother of God, becoming the living
temple of the Lord. Cort's technique
proves adequate to portraying this
paradox of refulgent shadowing that
signifies the divine mystery at hand.

The basic structure of the image is
typological: prophets display plaques
incised with scriptural oracles of the mystery of the Incarnation, bodied forth in
their midst as the fulfilment of their inspired words. The unseen words of Mary
and the angel Gabriel, or rather, the words
visually (rather than textually) manifest
in their attitudes, gestures, and facial ex-
pressions, bring these oracles to completion, making their meaning clearly
apparent. The historical sequence begins
at left with Moses, whose plaque cites
Deuteronomy 18:15: "The Lord your God
will raise up for you a prophet [like] me

from among your people and brethren."
Moses promises that a divinely appointed
representative—namely, Jesus Christ—
shall come to mediate between God and
men, just as he himself had been chosen at
Horeb to represent the will of God to his
chosen people. Next comes David, whose
plaque quotes Psalm 131 [132]:12: "The
fruit of your womb I shall place upon your
throne." David sings of the dwelling place
he has vowed to find for the Lord, and God
responds by promising that David's progeny—that is, his lineal descendants Mary

and Jesus—shall sit upon his throne. Christ is the fruit born of the Virgin's womb, her womb the habitation of the Lord. Behind Moses and David stands Isaiah, whose plaque reads: "Behold a virgin shall conceive and bear a son (Isaiah 7:14)." This oracle proclaims God's intention of preserving his people Israel, whom he assures of eventual redemption. The sequence continues at right with Solomon, whose plaque contains an excerpt from Canticle 5: 1 [4:16], that prophesies the indissoluble unity of the Church and Christ as bride and bridegroom: "My beloved shall come to his garden." Behind David, Jeremiah displays his prophecy of the coming of Christ: "For the Lord has created a new thing on the earth: a woman encompasses a man" (Jeremiah 31:22). The woman and the man are the Virgin and Christ. Finally, Haggai cites excerpts from his oracle of the Incarnation: "But a while…and he shall come who is desired by all peoples" (Haggai 2:8).

The prophets stand against a high parapet that demarcates a chancel apse, the heart of which is filled with choirs of angels suffused by the light of the Holy Spirit. This angelic radiance signifies the presence of Christ who is seen to inhabit the Church, just as he makes a habitation of the Virgin. Above hover the dove of the Holy Spirit, and God the Father—the *Deus Artifex* (God the Artificer)—holding the orb of the created world, an allusion to the Incarnation as the supreme work of divine artifice. That Gabriel's gestures echo those of God indicates that he is the messenger of the divine will. (That Mary's gestures

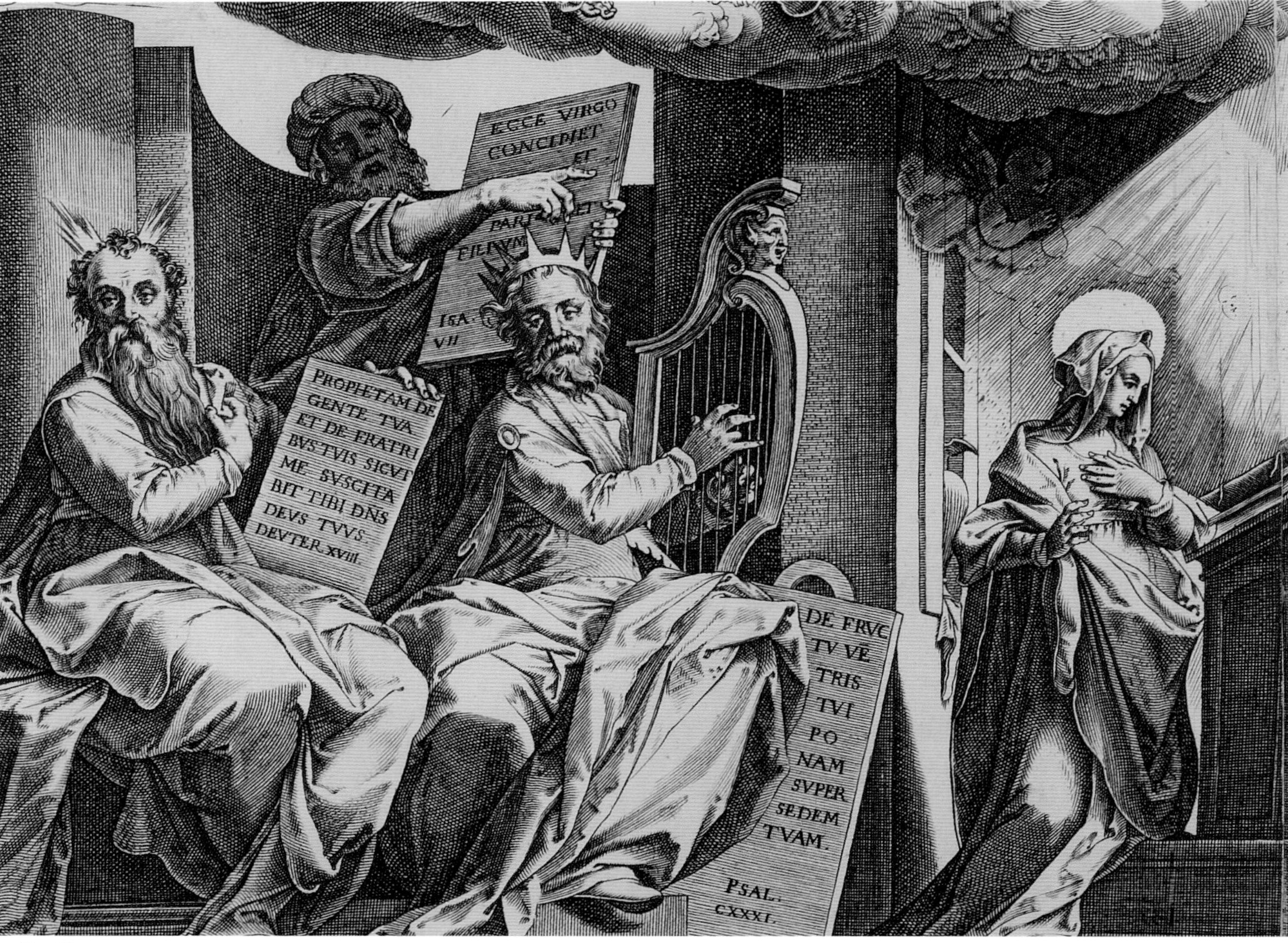

15 (detail)

resemble those of the angel directly above her reveals her angelic nature.) A symbolic Marian litany appears at the far left (daytime emblems of her motherhood) and right (night-time emblems of her virtues): sun, city, rose, lily, temple, palm, enclosed garden, flower, and beauteous olive-tree; moon, cedar, mirror, well, plane tree and cypress, fountain, tower, fleece, and gateway. The spandrels contain figures of Adam and Eve wearing the animal-skin tunics with which God clothed their shameful nakedness after they had sinned (Genesis 2:23); behind them appear the fig trees whose leaves they sewed into aprons to cover their genitals (Genesis 2:7). The texts beneath them quote Genesis 2:23, concluding with the phrase "he drove them out of the paradise of delight."

The Annunciation foreshadows the Jesuit theologian Petrus Canisius's account of the Annunciation in his great Marian treatise *De Maria Virgine incomparabili et Dei genitrice sacrosancta, libri quinque* (*Five Books on the Incomparable Virgin Mary, Most Holy Mother of God*) of 1577: Canisius visualizes the heavenly clouds opening to pour forth the Savior, who sprouts from the Virgin like the lily from the field (cf. Isaiah 45:8);[69] God descends into the most holy temple of the Virgin's body, as the bridegroom celebrating his nuptials to his bride the Church;[70] alone in her chamber she obeys the divine injunction to hear and consider what God commands, inclining her ear to the Lord (cf. Psalm 44 [45]:10).[71] WM

Philips Galle (1537–1612)
After Maarten van Heemskerck (1498–1574)
St. Peter Preaching in Jerusalem
From *Acta Apostolorum*
1575
Engraving, 21.3 × 27.4 cm
New Hollstein (Galle) 191
National Gallery of Art, Washington

16b

Philips Galle (1537–1612)
After Johannes Stradanus (1523–1605)
St. Paul Preaching in Rome
From *Acta Apostolorum*
1582
Engraving, 19.8 × 26.8 cm
New Hollstein (Galle) 219
National Gallery of Art, Washington

Designed by Maarten van Heemskerck and Johannes Stradanus and engraved by Philips Galle in 1575 and 1582 respectively, the two prints are from a series depicting the Acts of the Apostles.

St. Peter Preaching in Jerusalem, taken from Acts 2:14–40, is an event that takes place just after Christ is taken up to heaven. It is the moment foretold by Jesus, when he would return to heaven and the Holy Spirit would descend upon the apostles (Acts 1:7–8). On the day of Pentecost, when the apostles were gathered together, "a sound like the blowing of a violent wind came from heaven and filled the whole house. They saw what seemed to be tongues of fire that separated and came to rest on each of them. All of them were filled with the Holy Spirit and began to speak in other tongues" (Acts 2:2–4). Thousands of Jews from different nations, who had come to Jerusalem to celebrate the holy day, gathered before

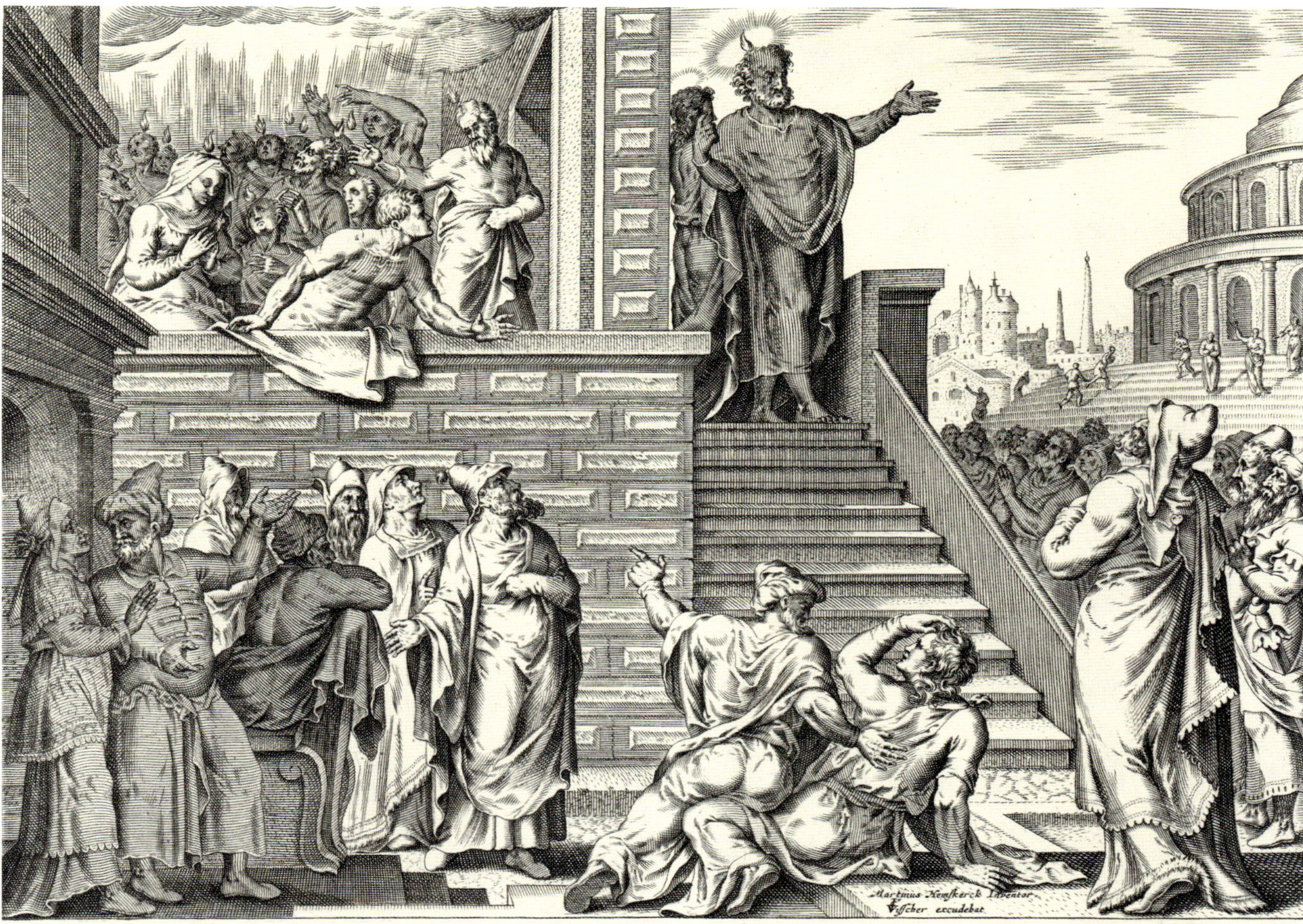

16a

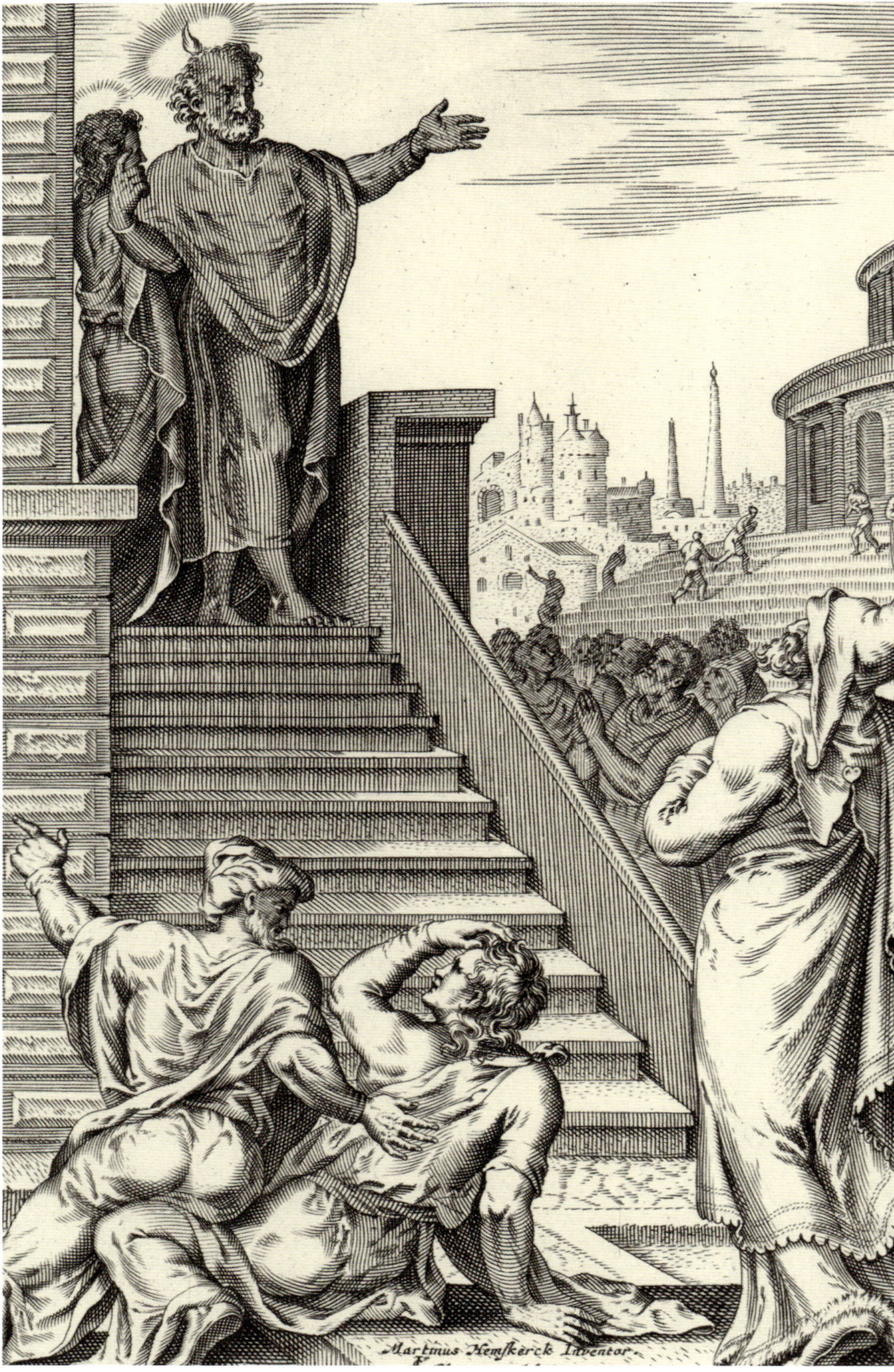

16a (detail)

them in awe because each person understood the apostles to speak in their own native language. After some in the crowd responded with suspicion, asking if the men were drunk, Peter addressed them and presented, for the first time, the complete gospel message.

Standing on top of a flight of stairs, Peter raises his left hand to the crowd, a gesture indicating speech, and points upward with his right index finger, indicating the divine source of what he is saying. A "tongue of fire" rests on his head, which emanates a halo of light. In the left background, the apostles and Mary, mother of Jesus, are gathered together and tongues of fire alight on their heads. Similar to Peter, the figure closest to the door raises his hand in a gesture of speech. Above them, a cloud represents the opening of the heavens and the Holy Spirit's descent upon them. In the left foreground, immediately below the group, scribes and Pharisees consult one another in the shadows, foreshadowing their future persecution of the apostles. In the middle foreground and right of the image, the crowd of Jews expresses various emotions, most of which reveal their humble submission to Peter's message. On the far right, a classically constructed dome represents the Temple of Jerusalem.

St. Paul Preaching in Rome, taken from Acts 28:23–29, is an event that follows his imprisonment in Caesarea. Because he was a Roman citizen, when the Jews opposed him during his trial there, Paul appealed to Caesar, and King Agrippa was forced to send him to the capital city un-der centurion guard. After his arrival, Paul arranged to meet together with the leaders of the Jews. "From morning till evening he explained and declared to them the kingdom of God and tried to convince them about Jesus from the Law of Moses and from the Prophets. Some were convinced by what he said, but others would not believe" (Acts 28:23–24).

Under the watchful eyes of the Roman guards on the left, the prisoner Paul stands in a public square, faces the crowd before him and makes a gesture of speech. Since his back faces the viewer, visual emphasis is given to the audience, which is made up of males and females, young and old, healthy and lame. The figure to the left of the man with crutches opens his arms and hands, indicating that he is receptive to Paul's Gospel message. The biblical text tells us that Paul stayed in Rome for two years, welcomed all who came to see him, and continued to preach about the life of Christ. In the right background, a second depiction of Paul, with a halo on his head, shows him standing on a pedestal and preaching to a crowd.   TR

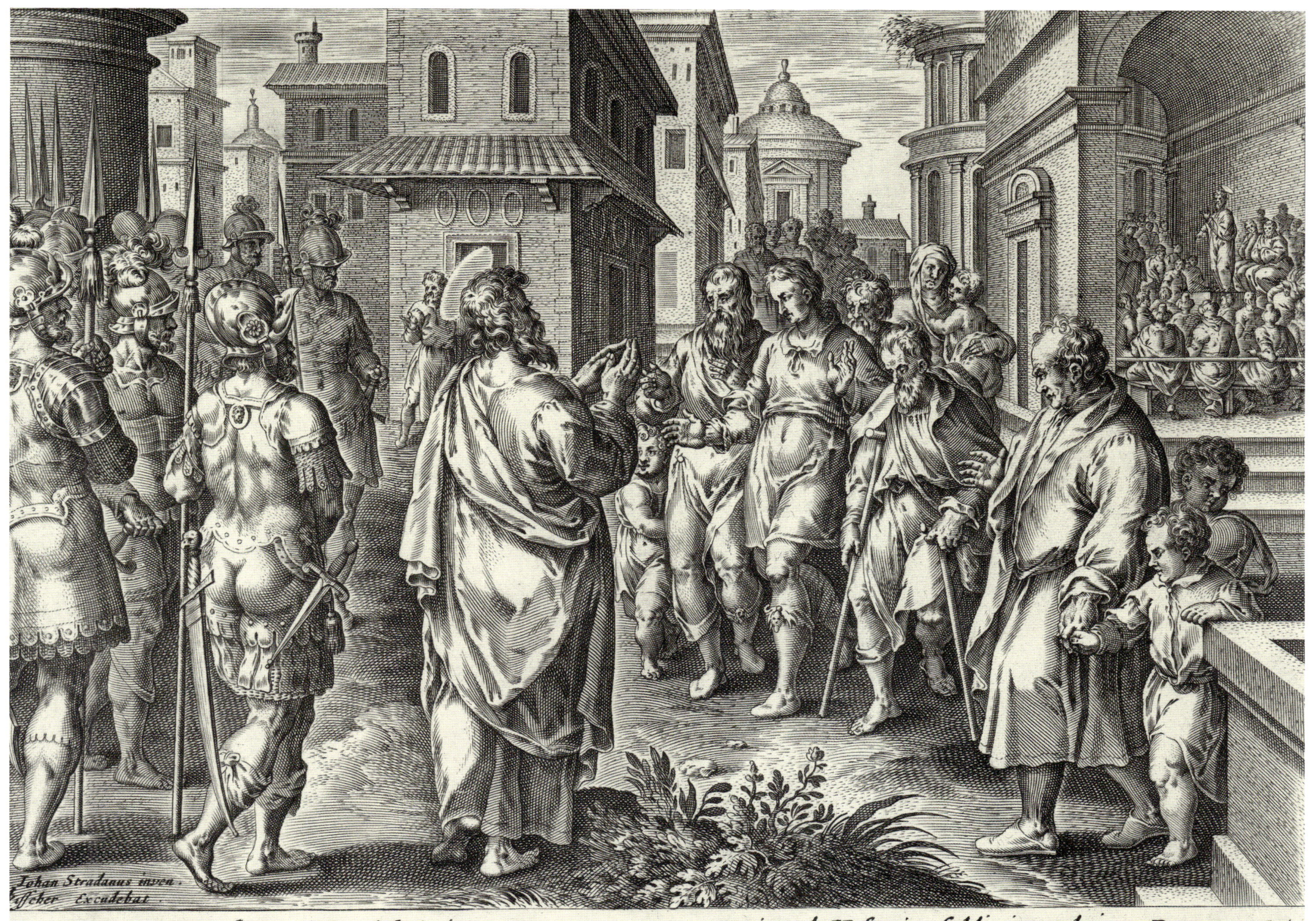

Per varios casus, per tot discrimina rerum.   Venit ad Hesperiæ sublimia culmina Romæ   35
Paulus adit Latium, et post tanta pericula tandem   Et nova Iudæis christi mysteria pandit.

Acto . 28 . 9 .

16b

17a

Adriaen Collaert (ca. 1560–1618)

After Hans Bol (1534–93)

The Good Shepherd ("…I am the door of the sheep" [Leo])

From *Emblemata Evangelica*

(Scenes from the Life of Christ)

1585

Engraving, 15.2 × 20.7 cm

New Hollstein (Collaert) 232

National Gallery of Art, Washington

17b

Adriaen Collaert (ca. 1560–1618)

After Hans Bol (1534–93)

The Parable of the Unjust Husbandmen (…The Kingdom of God shall be taken from you…" [Scorpio])

From *Emblemata Evangelica*

(Scenes from the Life of Christ)

1585

Engraving, 15.2 × 20.7 cm

New Hollstein (Collaert) 235

National Gallery of Art, Washington

*T*he inscription on the title plate to the *Gospel Emblems (Emblemata evangelica)*, a set of twelve engravings, explains that the images are adapted to the twelve celestial signs or months. It asserts that the stars in these signs had been formed by God for marking the passage of time, but had been the objects of idolatrous cults before Christ called men back to the worship of the one Creator of all things, and placed before human eyes the celestial mystical kingdom. The title plate includes depictions of the four Evangelists and still-life representations of the four seasons, and the essential meaning of the series is that the Creator is manifest in both the Gospel and nature. Each plate of the *Gospel Emblems* consists of a broad landscape, typical of Hans

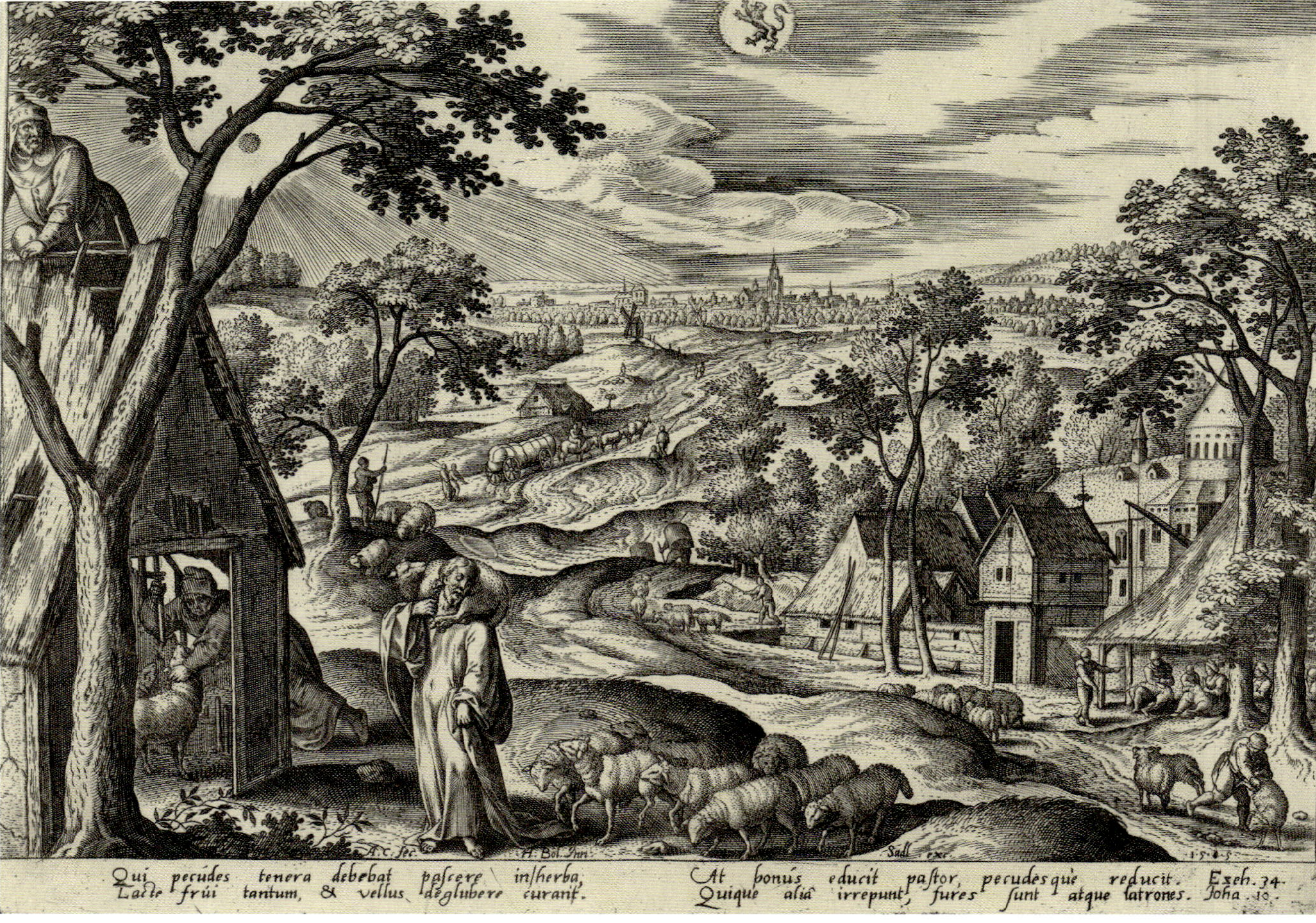

17a

Bol's work, in which events or parables from the New Testament are enacted. In a circle in the sky of each appears a sign of the zodiac (the *signa coelestia* of the title). Most of the stories are specific to times of the year, which are reflected in the landscapes and their activities: for example, the *Flight into Egypt* for Aquarius (January–February), the *Parable of the Sower* for Aries (March–April), the *Parable of the Barren Fig Tree* for Libra (September–October), and the *Virgin and Joseph at the Inn* for Capricorn (December–January). The months and seasons were commonly depicted in early modern art, as were related sets such as the planets (that is, the pagan deities representing them and the human activities associated with them), often with the signs of the zodiac.[72] Five years before the appearance of the *Gospel Emblems*, Hans Bol had also designed a set of *Four Seasons*, engraved by Johannes Sadeler, which also employed panoramic landscapes and signs of the zodiac in roundels in the sky, but featured secular allegorical figures rather than scripture illustrations.[73]

The biblical metaphor of the Good Shepherd had been depicted since early Christian times, already as here with a lamb held on the shoulders of Christ, and was common in the sixteenth century. Christ contrasted himself as the Good Shepherd with "anyone who does not enter the sheepfold by the gate but climbs in by another way," who is a "thief and a bandit" (John 10:1, cited in the print's inscription along with Ezekiel 34). At the left of the print, one of these thieves climbs on the roof of a barn, and another leans in through an opening in the wall, brandishing a knife above a sheep. At the right sheep are shorn. The bucolic landscape represents the summer sign of Leo (July–August).

The Parable of the Unjust Husbandmen, which is one of several agricultural images in the series, takes place during the harvesting of grapes and denotes Scorpio (October–November). Although Matthew 21 places Christ in the temple when he tells this parable, here, as elsewhere in the series, he is placed in the landscape of the parable itself. Women carry grapes on their backs to a wine vat in the middle ground at the center of the image, while horse-drawn carts haul barrels of wine on the road that winds through the center of the composition. At the left, Christ speaks to some of the chief priests and elders who had challenged his authority. The parable's narrative action is concentrated at the right: there is the vineyard protected by a fence and watchtower. The landowner sent several slaves to the tenants to collect his produce, but the tenants abused and even murdered the slaves. Thinking that the tenants would respect his son, the

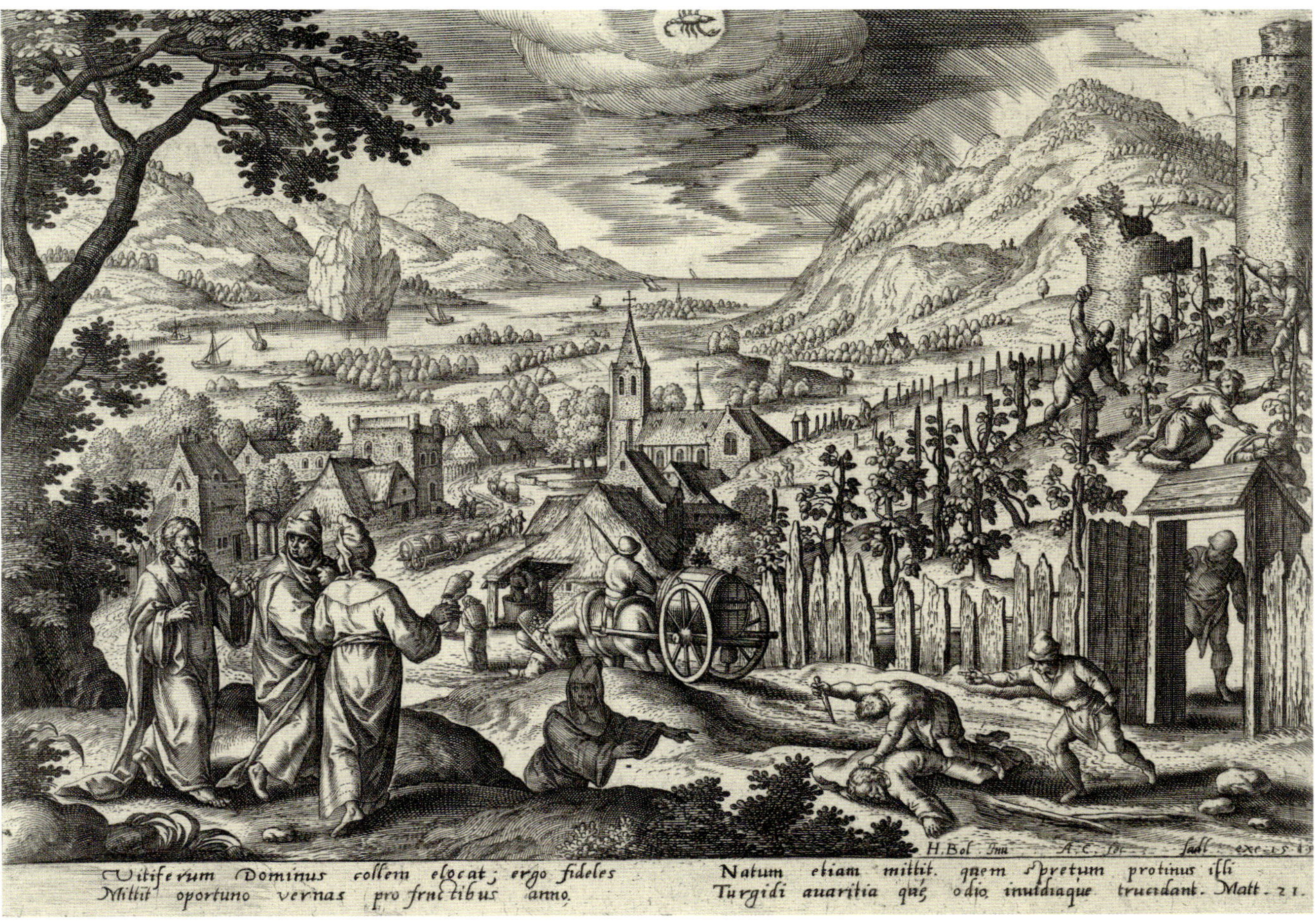

17b

landlord sent him, but "they seized him, threw him out of the vineyard, and killed him" (v. 39). Christ spoke of himself, a point confirmed in the image in which the murdered son and Christ have the same appearance (see also cat. 4).   JC

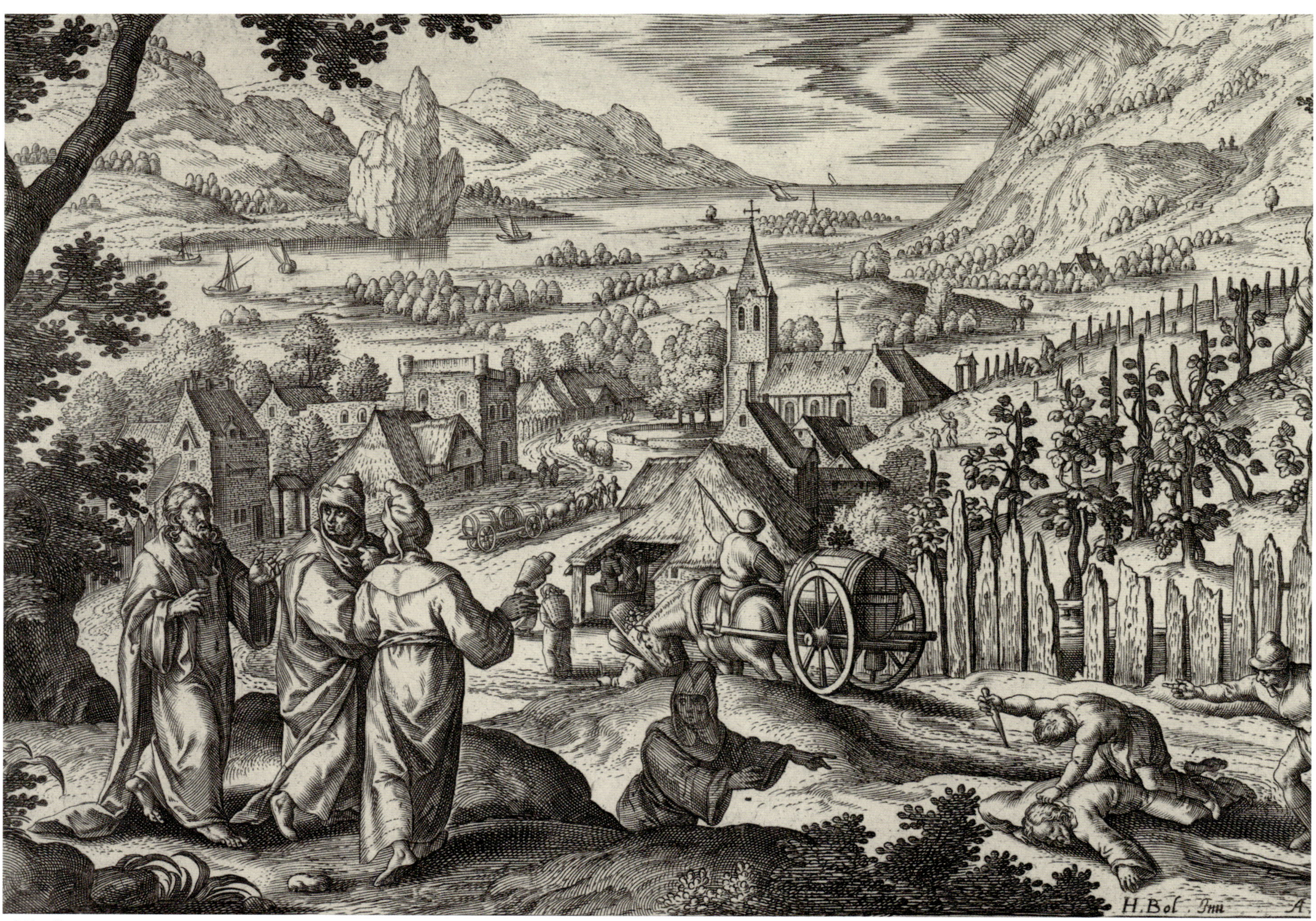

17b (detail)

Hieronymus Wierix (1553–1619)
After Crispijn van den Broeck (1524–89/91)
Allegory of the Salvation of Mankind
(Allegory of the Old Law and the New)
ca. 1586
Engraving, 26 × 20.2 cm
Hollstein (Wierix) 1802
The Metropolitan Museum of Art, New York

*H*ieronymus Wierix depicted multiple figures and symbolic objects in a landscape to compose *Allegory of the Salvation of Mankind (Allegory of the Old Law and the New)*. At left, Moses displays the Old Testament in the form of the tables of the Law, which bear Latin inscriptions from Exodus and Deuteronomy.[74] Behind Moses, John the Baptist preaches to a gathering in the center of the landscape. John, the last prophet and the first saint, acts as a liaison between the Old Testament and the New Testament, signified on the right by an open codex displaying Latin inscriptions from the gospels.[75] The Bible is supported by symbols of the four Evangelists and is crowned by the dove of the Holy Spirit, who inspired the Gospel authors Matthew, Mark, Luke and John.

Seated above the Bible is Christ. The cross he holds is balanced in the composition by a rod held by Moses. The symmetry of these instruments figures a symbolic association between them, which is grounded upon exegetical thought. Gregory of Nyssa observed that Moses's rod, by which God accomplished inexplicable wonders, was made of simple wood, like the cross, which saved mankind.[76] Ambrose asserted that, whereas God's blessing upon Moses bestowed his

rod with the power to change nature, the very words of Christ effect divine consecration.[77] The views of Gregory and Ambrose are consistent with the theological tenet that the mysteries of the Old Testament prophecies, which prefigured events of the New Testament, were fulfilled and elucidated by Christ.

Wierix elaborated this message in the foreground imagery. At left, near Moses's tablets, a skeleton embodying death delivers a fatal blow to the man lying on the ground. At right, the same man rises from his grave before the Bible. The dead and living figures illustrate Paul's declaration, "The letter killeth, but the spirit quickeneth" (2 Corinthians 3:6), which is inscribed in Latin beneath them. Exegetes identified the killing letter with the literal sense of the Old Testament and the quickening spirit with spiritual meanings revealed in the New Testament.[78] The resurrected man provides a model for worshipers, whom Wierix exhorts to progress beyond the historical foundations of the Old Testament to understand the spiritual sense of scripture elucidated through Christ.[79]   JS

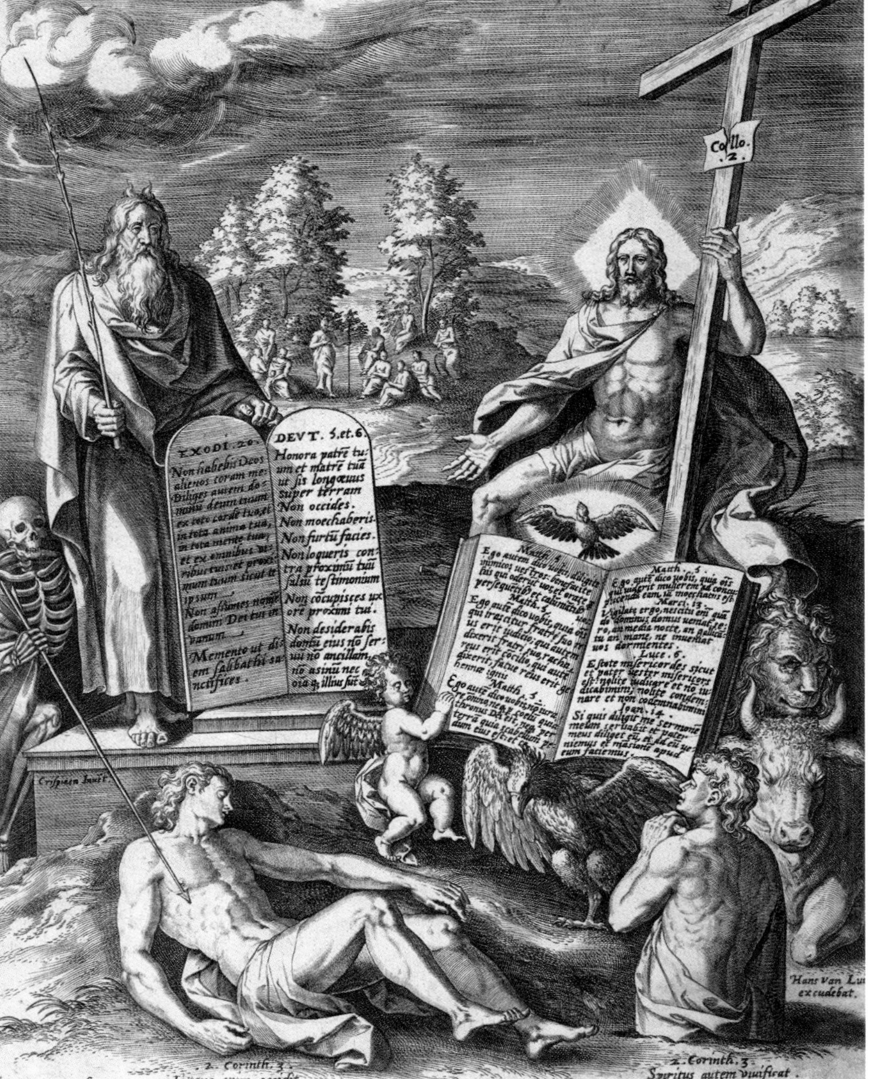

18

Worship

O Lord our God, all this abundance that we have provided for building you a house for your holy name comes from your hand and is all your own. I know, my God, that you search the heart, and take pleasure in uprightness; in the uprightness of my heart I have freely offered all these things, and now I have seen your people, who are present here, offering freely and joyously to you. O Lord, the God of Abraham, Isaac, and Israel, our ancestors, keep forever such purposes and thoughts in the hearts of your people, and direct their hearts toward you.

1 Chronicles 29:16–18

The Palace of Solomon
The Brazen Pillars in the Forecourt of the Temple
The Molten Sea on the Twelve Oxen
A Laver on a Bronze Stand
Woodcuts
In *Den Byble met groter neersticheyt gecorrigeert, ende*
op dye canten ghesedt den ouderdom der werelt, ende hoe
langhe die gheschiedenissen ende historien der Bybelen,
elc int sijne voor Christus gheboorte gheweest zijn …
(Antwerp: Jacob van Liesveldt, 1532)
American Bible Society, New York

*G*athered onto two pages of Jacob van Liesveldt's Dutch Bible of 1532 are four woodcuts illustrating 1 Kings 7. All four of the woodcuts had been used in Liesveldt's 1526 Bible (the first complete Bible in Dutch) but disposed across more pages.[80] These woodcuts, and others in the Liesveldt Bibles, are reduced, simplified, reversed, and, especially noticeable in the case of the *Molten Sea on the Twelve Oxen*, somewhat maladroit copies after woodcuts in a portion of the Old Testament in Luther's translation, *Das Ander teyl des alten testaments*, published in 1524 in Wittenberg by Christian Döring and Lucas Cranach the Elder.[81]

The first of the four illustrations in this opening depicts the palace, comprising three houses, which had been constructed in thirteen years for King Solomon (1 Kings 7:1–12). The passage on Solomon's palace constitutes a brief pause in a lengthy description of the temple that Solomon had constructed in Jerusalem to house the ark of the convenant and associated furnishings (see cat. 1).[82] The primary structure of the temple is described in chapter 6 and is illustrated in Liesveldt's Bibles. Chapter 7 describes objects crafted

for the temple and its forecourt, whose precise liturgical or ceremonial functions are largely obscure. The two large, free-standing pillars of bronze, topped with sculpted pomegranates and lilies, were named Jachin and Boaz (1 Kings 7:15–22). The king was accustomed to stand by one of the pillars on certain occasions, including in the making of a covenant, joined by the people, to follow the Lord's decrees.[83] The so-called molten sea, an enormous bronze basin that stood on statues of twelve oxen, with three facing each of the cardinal points of the compass (1 Kings 7:23–26), was set at the southeast corner of the temple.[84] Ten wheeled stands were made for smaller basins of bronze, five set on the south side and five on the north side of the temple (1 Kings 7:27–39). According to 2 Chronicles 4:6, the ten basins were for rinsing what was used for burnt offering, and the molten sea was for priests to wash in. In the dedication of the temple, Solomon offered in the forecourt "as sacrifices of well-being to the Lord" twenty-two thousand oxen and one hundred and twenty thousand sheep— "burnt offerings and the grain offerings and the fat pieces of the sacrifices of well-being."[85]

The very long tradition of representing the temple of Solomon and its furnishings, that began in antiquity, derived from a reading of the detailed descriptions in the Bible, exegetical reflections on those descriptions, and the pictorial tradition itself, which was based in part on Early Christian and Islamic buildings that were unrelated to the temple.[86] The relevant passages in Nicolas of Lyra's four-

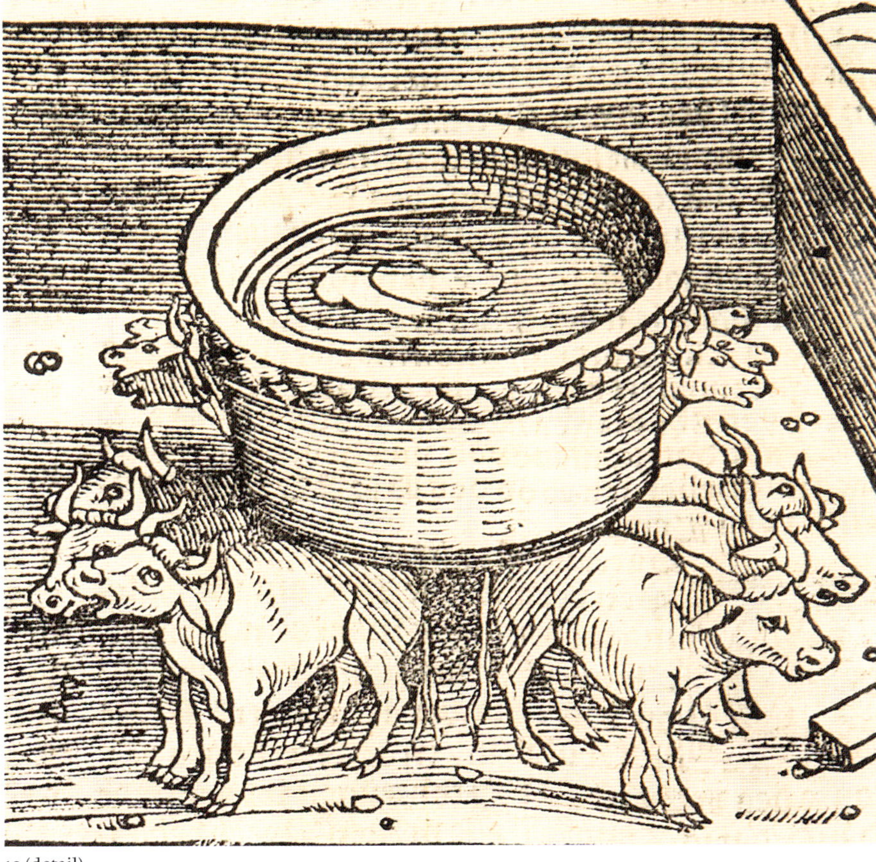

19 (detail)

teenth-century gloss on scripture, the *Postilla super totam Bibliam*, occasioned thoughtful attempts to reconstruct the appearance of the temple and its furnishings, but such reconstructions gradually became more elaborate, precise, and historically grounded (although not necessarily accurate) beginning in the mid-sixteenth century; that is, just after the publication of Liesveldt's Bibles, whose illustrations still owe their form to older models.   JC

Left page, column 1:

viercāte postē / vā olijfboomē houte / eñ twee duerē
vā duerē oft dennē houte / also dat elck duere twee
bladerē hadde / aen malcāderē hāgende / eñ maecte
daer op draepwerc vā Cherubim / palmē eñ bloem
werc / ende ouertrocse met goude / recht soot beuo-
len was.

Eñ hi timmerde oock eenen voorhof daer vnie
van drie rijen behouwender steenen / ende van een
der rijen ghescaefden Cederen.

In dat vierde iaer inder maēt Sif / so wert dat
fundamēt gelept aende huyse des HEERĒ. Eñ
inde elstē iare inder maēt Bul / dat is dye achtste
maent / wert dat huys bolmaect / so het zijn soude.

Also dat ti daer aē seuē iaer timmerde.

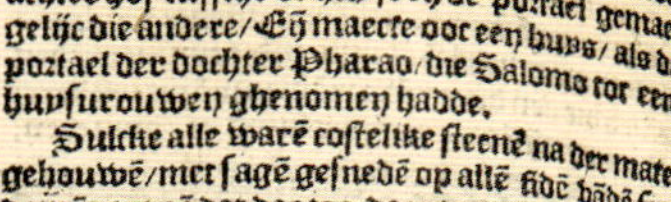

Aer aē zijn huys timerde Salomo. xiij.
iaer / dat hijt geheelijck boltimmerde / te
wetē hi timmerde eē huys bā
een huys vā wout Libanon / hondert el
voor hem / lē lāc / vijstich ellē wijt / eñ. xxx.
ellē hooch / vir viercāte / met ca-
lomnē bā ghescaefde Cederen / eñ
eñ tafelde dat deesel bouē aen
vor met Cederē / op aē die rib-
calomnē / wat elcke rije hadde
xv. calomnē / also dat alroos
die calomnē gelijc tegē malca-
derē ouer stonde / also dat elc
pāt tegē malcāderē ouer tusschē den calomnē / mette calomnen viercantich was.

Eñ hy maecte een portael
met calomnē / vijstich ellē lāc /
eñ. xxx. ellen wijt. Eñ noch een
portael voor hē met calomnē /
eñ met eē dicke pileerne. Daer
toe een portael tot eenen Coninc stoel / daer hi oordeel in

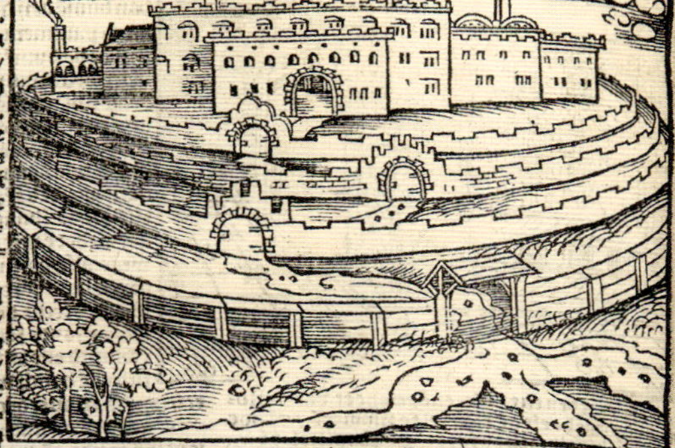

Left page, column 2:

hielt / eñ maecte se tot een vonnis portael / eñ bes-
tet met Cederē / bādē pauimēt aē / tot weder tot
bloer. Daer toe zijn huys daer hi in woonde indē
achter hof tusschē dē huyse eñ dē portael gema-
gelijc die andere. Eñ maecte oock een huys / als
portael der dochter Pharao / die Salomo tot eē
huysvrouwen ghenomen hadde.

Sulcke alle warē costelike steens na der maten
gehouwē / met sagē ghesnedē op allē sijde bādē fundamēt / tot aē dat dac toe / daer toe vor buytē tottē
groote hof toe. Die fundamētē warē oor costelike
eñ grote steene. x. eñ acht ellen groot / eñ daer op costelike gehouwē steene na der matē / eñ Cederē.
Maer den grooten hof al omme / hadde drie rijen
vā gehouwē steenē / eñ een rije vā gescaefde Cederē. Also oor den voorhof aēt huys des HEERĒ.

Eñ die Coninc Salomo sandt henē eñ liet
halē hirā vā Tyro / eend wedu we soō / vit dē
stāme Naphtali / eñ zijn vad was eē mā bā Tyro geweest / die eē meester was in metael / vol
wijshz / bsiat eñ costē / ō te arbeide alōbāde metael werc. Doe die rotte coninc Salomo quā
maecte hi alle zijn werc. Eñ maecte twee met-
talē calōnē / elc. xviij. ellen hooch / eñ een snoer
bā. xij. ellē was die mate / om beide die calōnē / eñ
hi maecte twee knoopē bā metael gegotē /
om bouē aē die calōnē te settē / eñ elcke knoop
was vijf ellē hooch / eā elcke knoopē bouē
op die calonne / warē seuē geulochtē reepkens
als ketenē / aē elcke knoop ē
rije granaet appelē ront ōme aē eē reepkē /
daer mede dē knoop bedect wert / Eñ die knop-
pē warē als die roser voor dat portael / vierel-
len groot / Eñ die granaet appelē inder rijen
rontomme warē. CC. boue eñ ondē aedē reep
die ō dē buyc dē knoops ginc / aē elcke knoo-
pe op beide calōnē / also dat alroos oen
voor dat portael des tēpel / eñ in rechte die calōnē
er hāt sette hier hi Iachin / eñ dē hi ter slinker
hāt sette hier hi Boas / Eñ het stōt also bouen
op die calōnē als roosen / Alsoe wert boleymt
dat werc der calomnen.

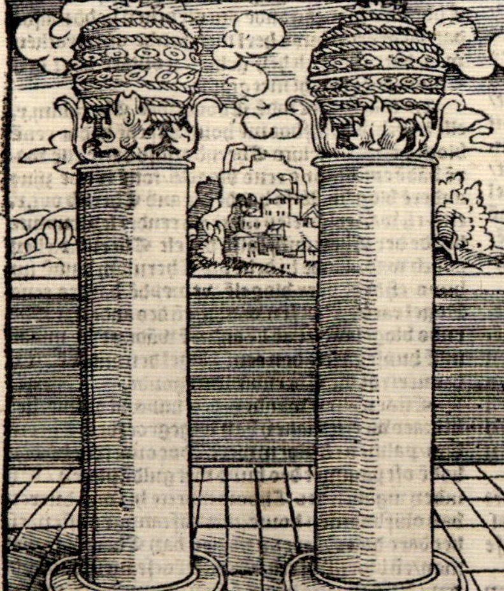

Right page, column 1:

Eñ hi maecte een gegotē zee / thic ellē wijt /
vandē eenē voorde totē anderē ront omme /
eñ vijf ellē hooch / Eñ een coorde dertich ellen
lanc was die mate ront omme. Eñ om die sel
ue zee die thien ellē wijt was / ghingē knoopē
aen haren voorde oft rant / ront omme die zee
bene / Maer die knoopē warē twee rijē ghe-
gotē / Eñ ti stont op twalef runderē / der wele
vier drie noortwaerts gekeert / drie west
waerts / drie suytwaerts / eñ drie oostwaerts
eñ die zee bouē daer op / also dat alle haer ach-
terste deelē binnenwaerts waren / Zijn dicte
was eē hāt breet / eñ sinē voort was als eens
bekers rant / als een opgegaē roose / eñ daer
ghinge twee dusent Batē in / Hy maecte oor
thien metale gestoelen / elc was vier ellē lanc
eñ vier eñ drie ellen hooch / Maer dat gestoel
te was also ghemaect / dat het siden hadde tusschē den lijste / Eñ aen den sijde tusschē den lijstē / warē leeuwē / runders / eñ Cherubim /
Eñ die sijde waren gemaect aen die lijsten / die
ouer eñ onder den leeuwē eñ runderē warē /
also dat ti onderwaert gerecht warē / Eñ eich
gestoelte hadde vier metale raders / met meta
len assen oft gestelle / Eñ optē vier hoeckē
warē scouderē gegote / die teghē die and ouer
onder aenden ketel ghelenē.

Maer dē hals middē op
gestoelte / was een elle ront eñ
hoock / ander half elle wijt / eñ
daer warē puckelkēs aedē hal
se / inde belde die viercāt warē /
eñ niet ront. Dye vier raders
stonde onder aē die side / eñ die
assche der raderē warē aēt gestoelte / Elck rat was ā half
elle hooch / eñ het warē raders
als waghē raders / eñ die assche / nauen / speekē eñ belgen /
warē al gegotē / ende die vier
scouderē op die vier hoeckē
eles gestoelte / warē oock aene
ghestoelte.

Ende aendē hals bouē op
gestoelte / een half elle hooch /
ronts om warē lijstē ende side
aēt gestoelte / Eñ hi liet op dye
placke der selfder side eñ lijstē
Cherubim / leeuwē / eñ palmboomē grauē / elc aē
den andere rontom daer aen. Op die wise maecte
hi thie gestoelte gegotē / Eenderlep mate eñ rupm
te was aey allen.

Eñ hi maecte thie metale ketelē / also dat. xl. Ga
tē in eenē ketel ghinc / eñ was vier ellen groot / eñ
op elc gestoelte was eenē ketel / Eñ hi sette vijf ghe-
stoeltē aende rechte hoecke des huys / eñ dye and
vijf aendē slincke hoeck / Maer die zee sette hp ter
rechter hant voor aen suytwaert.

Eñ hirā maecte oor potten / pannē / eñ beckē /
eñ bolepnde also alle werckē die de Coninc Salomo aenden huyse des HEEREN makten dede / Te
wetē / die twee calomnen / eñ die kenlijcke knoopē
bouen op die twee calomnen / eñ daer om twee geulochtē reepkens / om te bedeckē die twee kenlije

Right page, column 2:

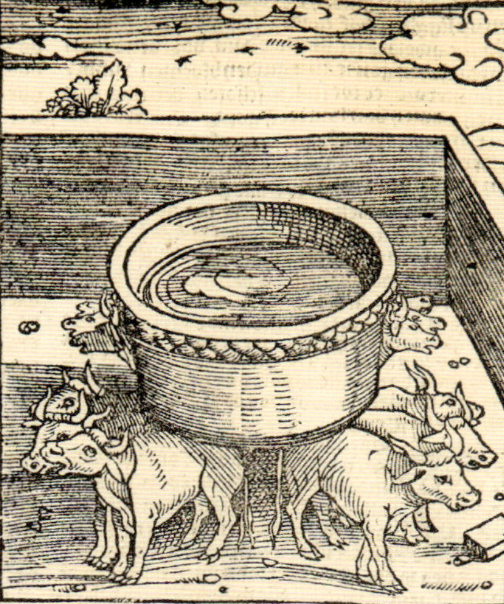

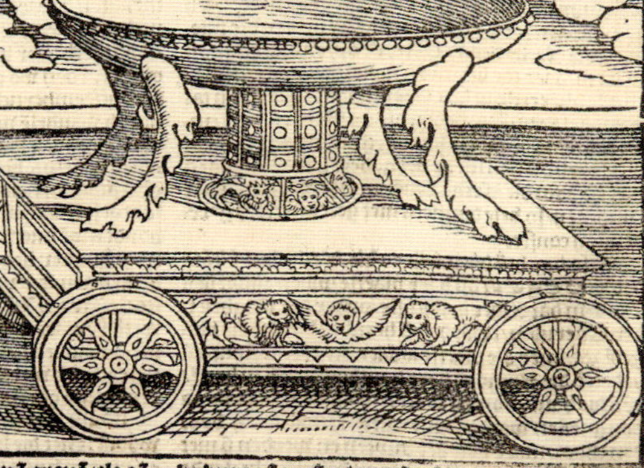

ke knoopē optē calomnē / Eñ die vier hondert gra
naet appelē aen die twee gheulochten reepkens /
te weten twee rijen granaet appelē / aen een reep-
lick te bedeckē die twee kenlicke knoopen optē
calomnen / Daer toe die thien ghestoelten / eñ thien
ketelen bouen daer op / ende dye zee / ende twalef
runderen onder die zee / Ende die pottē / ende pan
nen / ende beckens / ende alle dese batē die Hirā
den Coninck Salomo maecte / tot den huyse des
HEERĒ / waren van louterē metael / Inden
lantschap aen die Iordane liet die Coninck ghie-
ten / in dicke iremachtighe aerde / tusschen Suchoth
ende Zarthan / Ende Salomo liet alle batē ongre-
wegen / om dye seer groote menichte des metaels.

Oock maecte Salomo alle batē die tottē hu
se des HEERĒ behoordē / te wetē / eenē gul

Within the meditative tradition, Christ was said to have bled seven times (the perfect number): once at his circumcision and six times during his Passion and Crucifixion (see also cat. 29).[87] A popular theme in later medieval art and devotional literature, it was revisited in 1565 in a series of sophisticated engravings by Harmen Jansz. Muller, after designs by Maarten van Heemskerck, the final two of which are exhibited here. The episodes in this series are the circumcision, the agony in the garden, the flagellation, the crowning with thorns, Christ bearing the cross (it is his falling under this heavy burden that reopens his wounds), Christ nailed to the cross, and the

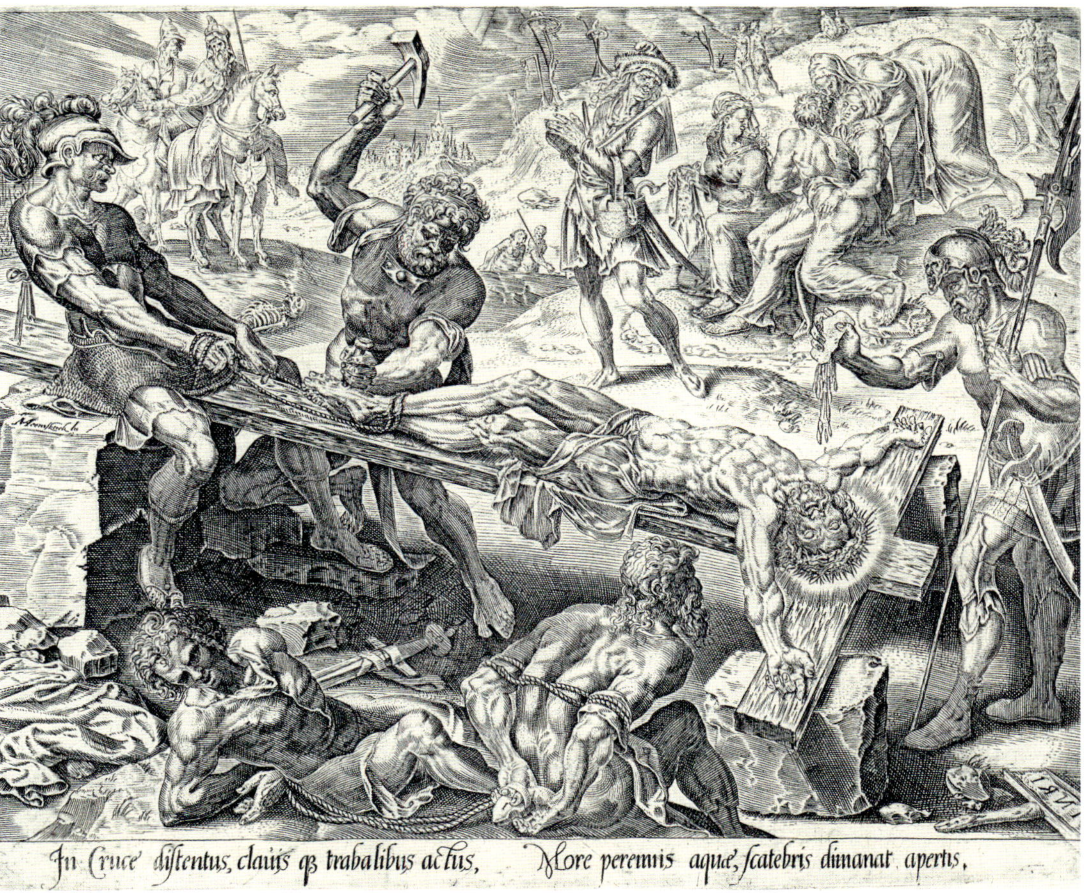

20a

centurion (commonly referred to as Longinus) piercing the side of his dead body with a lance.[88]

An explicit description of Christ nailed to the cross appears nowhere in the Bible, but was typically part of medieval Passion narratives that elaborated on Scripture, as was Mary fainting at the Crucifixion, which appears here in the background. The traditional figure of Veronica with her veil, on which Christ's features had miraculously been imprinted on his way to Golgotha, sits next to Mary—a further non-scriptural motif. Van Heemskerck also adapts an event from later in the narrative to this time early in the crucifixion: a soldier squeezes wine from a sponge for Christ rather than extending it to him on a stick moments before he died, as described in Matthew 27:48, Mark 15:36, and John 19:29. This action is rendered all the more dramatic by the very unusual inverted position of Christ's head. In the last print of the series, Van Heemskerck presents two subsequent moments, described in John 19:32–34, as simultaneous: soldiers broke the thieves' legs and then, seeing that Christ had already died, one of them pierced his side.

The inscribed text for the series is not scriptural but was written by the humanist Hadrianus Junius (Adriaen de Jonghe), who often worked with Van Heemskerck.[89] Junius recalls the affective aspects of medieval Passion literature, both in the exhortation to the reader/viewer to look (*Aspice*, he says in the *Crowning with Thorns*), and in the emphasis placed in all the distychs on Christ's blood bubbling, erupting, spewing, and flowing from his body in drops and streams. For the *Flagellation* he draws a vivid though conventional contrast between the red blood and the snow-white limbs it stains (*roseus niueos cruor inficit artus*). For all its dwelling on Christ's physical suffering, Junius's text ultimately turns to a theological interpretation of the shedding of his blood, which, as the inscription on the final print claims, washes sin away. But this blood, paradoxically, is scarcely to be found in Van Heemskerck's engravings, in which the broken and bleeding Christ of late medieval art has given way to the heroic, muscular type of both ancient and modern Italian art, that Van Heemskerck encountered during a sojourn in Rome. Even from Christ's side opened by the lance point there is no evident issue, although the blood and water that came forth were later interpreted by Thomas Aquinas and others as signs of the most important sacraments of Eucharist and Baptism.   JC

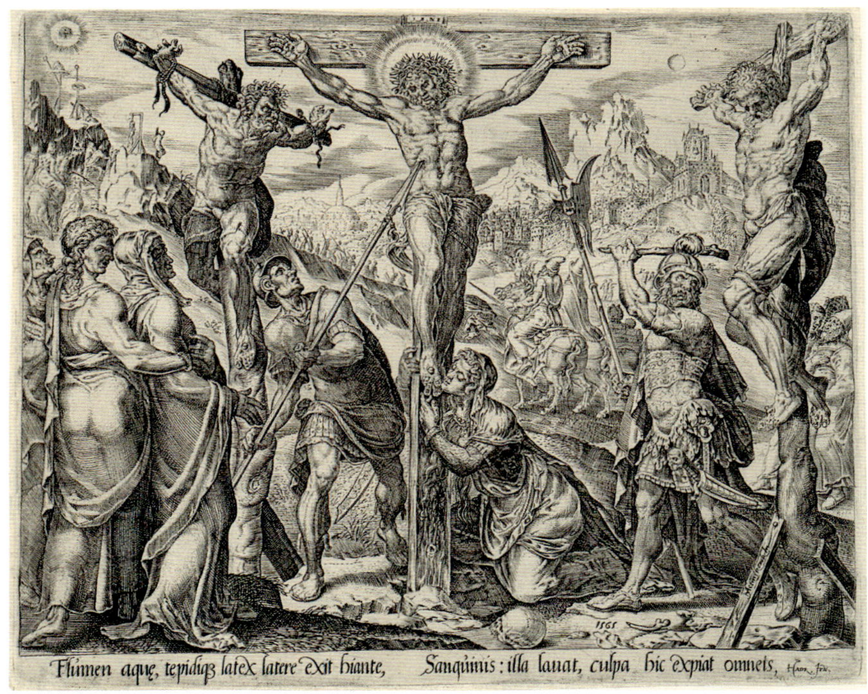

20b

21a

Jan Wierix (1553–1619) and workshop of
Philips Galle (1537–1612)
After Gerard van Groeningen (active 1561–ca. 1576)
Scientia (Self-Knowledge) Bids Sponsa (Bride) to Look into the Mirror of the Soul
ca. 1573
Engraving, 10 × 14.1 cm
Illustration 17 in *Divinarum nuptiarum conventa et acta, ad piorum admonitionem a Phillippo Gallaeo aeneis tabulis incisa, Bened. Ar. Monta. accinente* (*Covenants and Transactions of the Divine Nuptials, Engraved on Metal Plates by Philips Galle for the Instruction of the Pious, with Lyric Verses by Benito Arias Montano*) (Antwerp: Anthonis Coppens van Diest for Philips Galle, 1573–74)
New Hollstein (Van Groeningen) 295
The New York Public Library,
Astor, Lenox and Tilden Foundations

21b

Jan Wierix (1553–1619) and workshop of Philips Galle (1537–1612)
After Gerard van Groeningen (active 1561–ca. 1576)
Title-Page: Mirror of the Life of Christ
ca. 1573
Engraving, 9.7 × 14.1 cm
In *Christi Iesu vitae admirabiliumque actionum speculum a Philippo Galleo apparatum Bened. Ariae Montani singularibus distichis instructum* (*Mirror of the Life and Admirable Deeds of Jesus Christ, Prepared by Philips Galle, and Furnished with Singular Distichs by Benito Arias Montano*) (Antwerp: Anthonis Coppens van Diest for Philips Galle, 1573–74)
New Hollstein (Van Groeningen) 314
Museum Plantin-Moretus/Prentenkabinet, Antwerp–UNESCO World Heritage, Inv. No. A 1836[3]

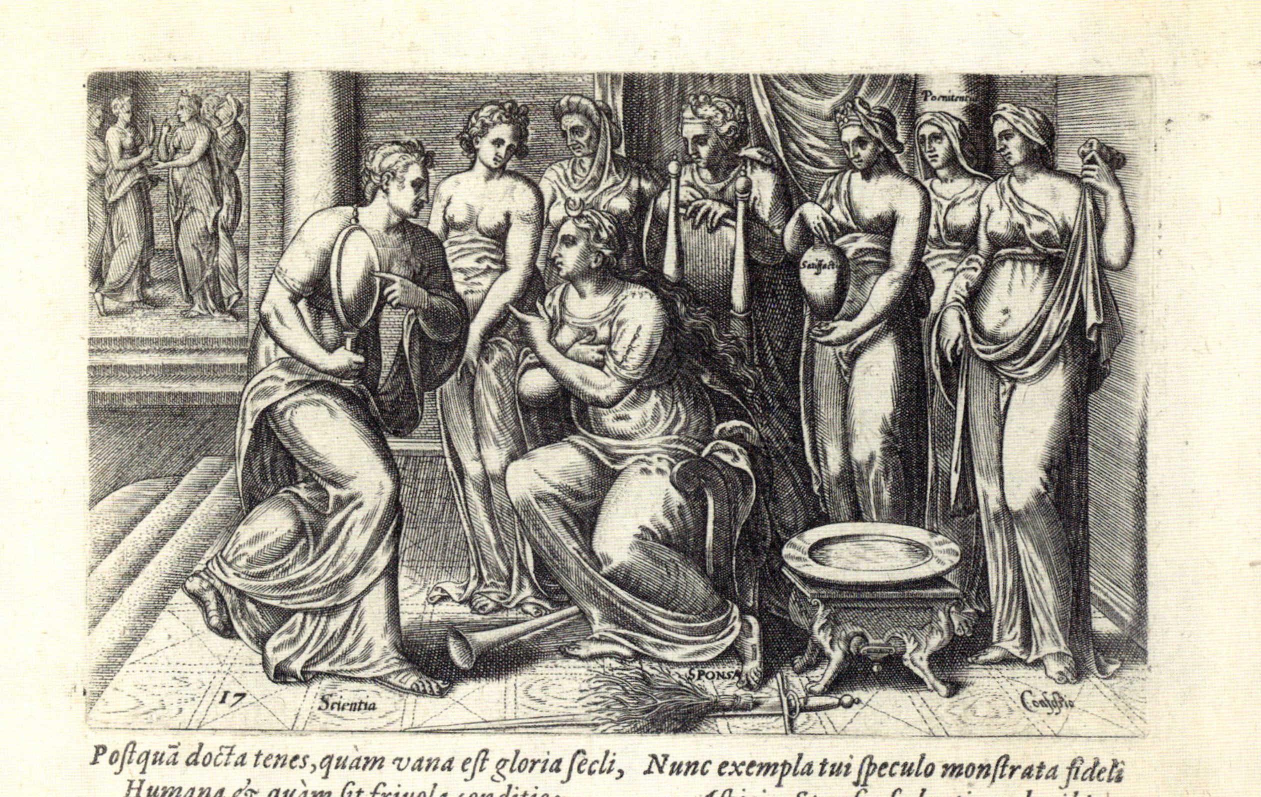

21a

$\mathcal{B}$ased on the parable of the marriage feast (Matthew 22:1–14), the *Divinarum nuptiarum conventa et acta* (*Covenants and Transactions of the Divine Nuptials*) chronicles the soul's marital journey toward her bridegroom Christ, with whom she desires to be wed spiritually. In fact, this epithalamial series also derives from Revelation 19:7–9, the call to rejoice in the marriage of the Lamb to his bride who "has made herself ready" for "the Lamb's nuptial banquet."[90] The twenty-eight allegorical scenes unfold as follows: Christ the king of kings, mindful of human salvation, sends his ministers to search the world for souls fit to be saved. They find only one willing soul (*Sponsa*), whom personifications of *Timor Dei* (Fear of the Lord), *Castigatio* (Correction), *Iustitia* (Justice), and *Poenitentia* (Penitence) then prepare for the advent of *Sponsus* (Christ the bridegroom). *Scientia* (Self-Knowledge) now appears and compels *Sponsa* to gaze into the mirror of self-knowledge, where she beholds *umbras* (shadowy images) of the sins that endanger the soul—pride, capriciousness, avarice, gluttony, luxury, ambition, and sloth. Having learned to know herself, she is instructed to look into a second mirror,

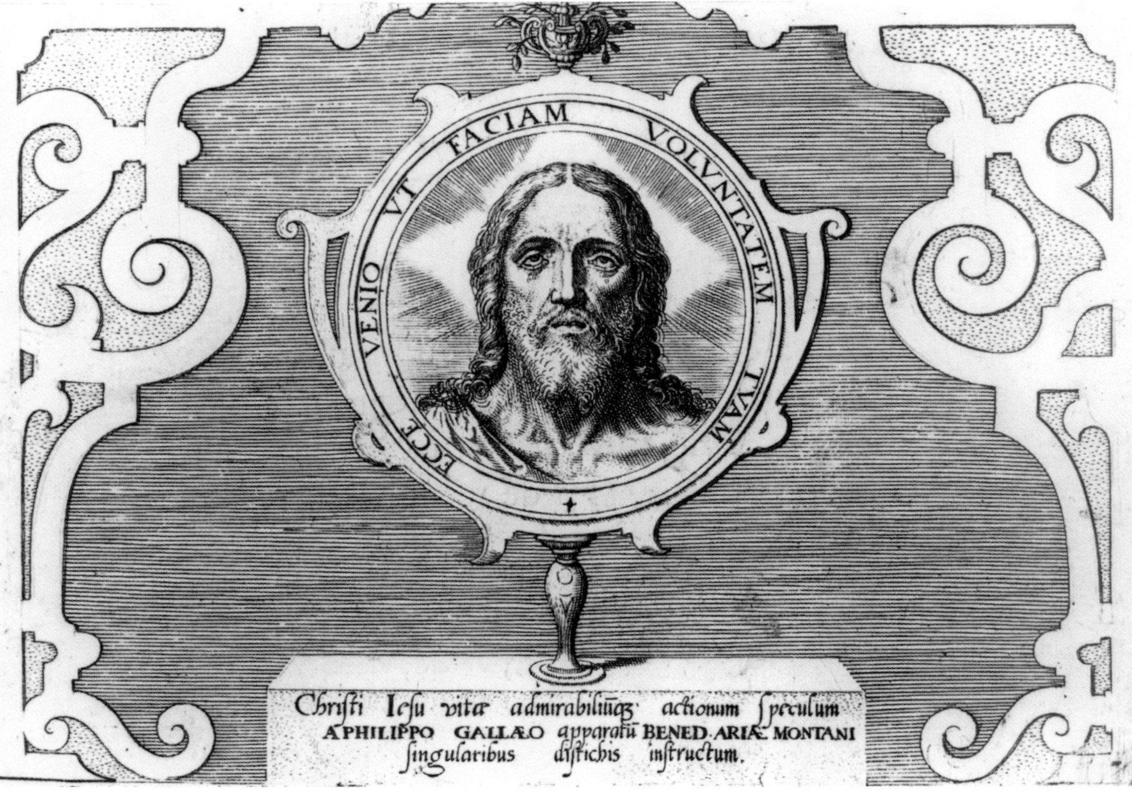

21b

where she beholds exemplary scenes from the life of Christ, after which to model herself.[91] At this point, the viewer enters the second print series, entitled *Christi Iesu vitae admirabiliumque actionum speculum* (*Mirror of the Life and Admirable Deeds of Jesus Christ*), which is embedded within the first. The fifty scenes comprised by the *Speculum* start with the *Annunciation* and end with *Pentecost* and the *Last Judgment*, incorporating key episodes from the infancy, ministry, Passion, and Resurrection of Christ. Only after viewing this Christological sequence does one re-enter the *Divine Nuptials*: transformed by her experience of Christ, *Sponsa* now encounters the theological virtues, who fill her with faith and hope in God, that engender the love of Christ (both hers in him, and his in her). At last, she meets the bridegroom, who joyfully embraces her, but since in this life spiritual union, howsoever intensely experienced, remains fleeting and contingent, bride and bridegroom are once again parted. The bride undergoes various trials before she is judged worthy to receive the crown of eternal life and to behold the Holy Trinity, into whose bosom the bridegroom finally welcomes her.

Illustration 10 in the sequence is inscribed: "In this mirror you shall contemplate the causes, effects, and limits of things, whence stolid men perish. I who am called *Scientia* show you what sort of fiction renders men miserable."[92] The fictive image, to which *Scientia* refers, consists of five scenes in which personifications of the seven deadly sins disport in tented spaces reminiscent of 2 Corinthians 5:1–10, Paul's account of this life as an earthly tent to be contrasted with the spiritual edifice of God's celestial house. These fictive and shadowy images teach *Sponsa* to engage in penitential reflection upon her own sins; confession, contrition, and satisfaction (suffering for one's sins) engender the peace of mind that allows the reformed *Sponsa* to look into the mirror held once again by *Scientia* in illustration 17.[93] The inscription declares what the mirror holds forth: "Having been taught, you ascertain how vain are the glories of this life, how trivial the human condition. Now you shall see shown in a faithful mirror, images of your bridegroom fit to be committed to memory."[94] The *Title-Page* to the *Mirror of the Life and Admirable Deeds of Jesus Christ* places us in the subject position of *Sponsa* looking into *Scientia*'s mirror. We look through her eyes at the mirror-image of ourselves refashioned into the image of the Holy Face, in other words, we see a prolepsis of our future conversion into the *imago Dei*, the likeness of Christ, that our soul aspires to portray through specular meditation on his life, death, and Resurrection. The text encircling the mirror—"I come to fashion your will"—emphasizes that Christ is the source of the meditative process we are about to undergo.[95] The motion from the *Mirror* back into the *Divine Nuptials*, confirms that by exercising ourselves in the *imitatio Christi* (imitation of Christ), we shall become fortified in faith and hope, attaining to the love of Christ, with whom our souls shall be matrimonially joined, provisionally in this life, eternally in the next. The relation between the two series is also the relation between two kinds of image: *fabulae* (poetic fictions) that represent allegorically the soul's progress toward Christ, and *specula* (veridical exempla) that represent the life of Christ as an instrument of the soul's reformatio (conversion, reformation). Whereas the former enables the votary to picture his soul's efforts to draw closer to Christ, the latter depicts Christ himself as the cause and effect of this nuptial odyssey that results in the unity of the soul's self-image with the image of Christ.   WM

Jan Sadeler (1550–1600)
After Gerard van Groeningen (active 1561–ca. 1576)
or Crispijn van den Broeck (1524–89/90)
*David Accepts the People's Offerings for the
Building of the Temple*
ca. 1575
Engraving, 10.1 × 14.2 cm
In Benito Arias Montano, *David, hoc est virtutis
exercitatissimae probatum Deo spectaculum, ex David
pastoris militis ducis exulis ac prophetae exemplis* (*David,
or the Spectacle of Well-Exercised Virtue Pleasing to God,
Comprising Examples of David the Shepherd, Soldier,
Ruler, and Prophet*) (Antwerp: Philips Galle, 1575)
Museum Plantin-Moretus/Prentenkabinet,
Antwerp–UNESCO World Heritage

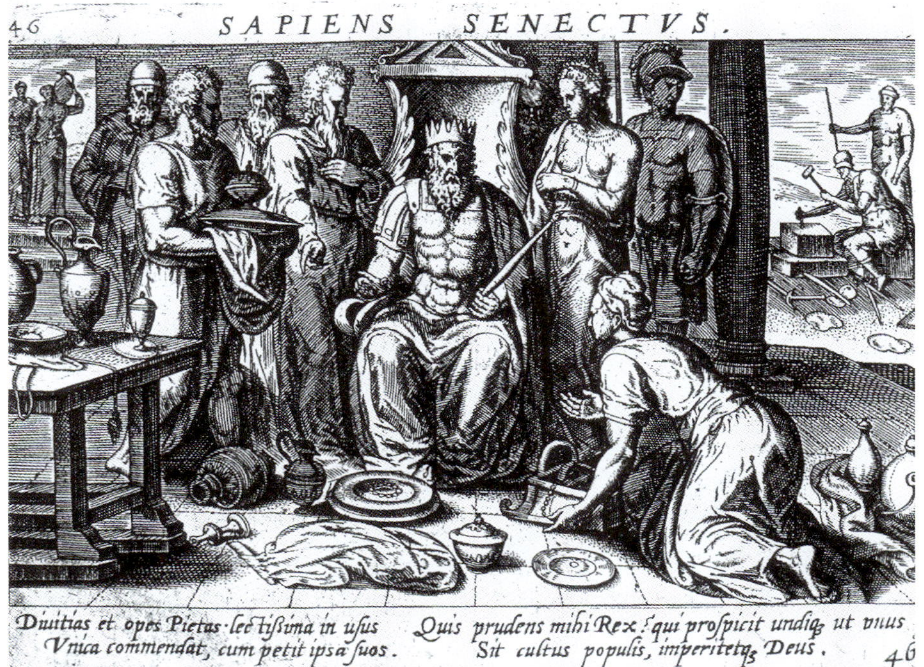

22

*P*receded by the *Humanae salutis
monumenta* (*Monuments of Human
Salvation*), the *Divinarum nuptiarum
conventa et acta* (*Covenants and Transactions of
the Divine Nuptials*), and the *Christi Iesu vitae
admirabiliumque actionum speculum* (*Mirror
of the Life and Wondrous Deeds of Jesus Christ*)
(see cat. 21), the *David* is the last of Arias
Montano's innovative scriptural emblem
books. The 48 plates illustrate exemplary
scenes from David's life, as chronicled in
1 and 2 Samuel, 1 Kings, and 1 Chronicles;
mottos above the images designate the
virtues David is seen to embody, while
tetrastichs below reflect on the meaning
these events held for him. In effect, then,
he is viewed continuously both from
without and within, just as in the Bible,
the books of Samuel and Chronicles
describe his actions, whereas the Psalms
reveal his mind, heart, and soul. As the
reader-viewer progresses through the
emblem book, he discovers how David
comes increasingly to understand the
religious significance of his pastoral,
military, royal, and prophetic deeds.
Arias Montano designed the images in
collaboration with the publisher Philips
Galle and the draughtsmen Gerard van
Groeningen and Crispijn van den Broeck.
Galle and Arias Montano dedicated the
David to King Philip II of Spain, offering
him a princely mirror in which he could
discern the lineaments of his own life
as shepherd, soldier, ruler, and prophet
to his people. Image 46, *David Accepts
the People's Offerings for the Building of
the Temple*, depicts the king gathering
the precious metals and gems he had
solicited in 1 Chronicles 29:5, as gifts
consecrated for the house of God.[96]
The scene also subtly alludes to 1 Kings
15–21, since it seems virtually (though
not actually) to portray Bathsheba
beseeching David to declare her son
Solomon his legitimate heir. Arias
Montano thereby implies that Solomon's
right of succession is expressed in and
through his prerogative of building the
temple: "He [the Lord] said to me, 'It is
Solomon your son who shall build my
house and my courts, for I have chosen
him to be my son, and I will be his father'"
(1 Chronicles 28:6). That the people are
shown offering finely worked jewels
and vessels, not simply the gold, silver,
bronze, and precious stones mentioned
in 2 Chronicles 29, underscores the theme
of divinely sanctioned artifice, which
is further emphasized by the architect
and mason dressing a temple stone in
the right background.[97] Arias Montano's
verses compress these biblical passages
into an avowal of David's singular piety:
discerning the sovereignty of the Lord, he
commends wealth and riches to these uses
(that is, the construction of the temple),
ensuring that the people venerate
God alone, whose sole privilege it is to
govern.[98] This is why, to quote the motto,
he was deemed "wise in his old age."[99]
Philip II would undoubtedly have viewed
him as an epitome of the enlightened
monarch, who directed all his resources,
artifice and wealth especially, toward
building a "house of the Lord."   WM

Anonymous copyist after Jan Wierix
(1549–ca. 1618/20)
After Pieter van der Borcht (ca. 1535–1608)
Annunciation
ca. 1575–ca. 1584
Engraving, 11.6 × 7.6 cm
In *Breviarum Romanum, ex decreto Sacrosancti Concilij Tridentini restitutum, Pii V. Pont. Max. iussu editum. Cum Kalendario Gregoriano perpetuo. Permittente Sede Apostoli*ca. (*Roman Breviary, Revised by Decree of the Tridentine Council, Issued by Order of His Holiness Pius V. With the Perpetual Gregorian Calendar. By Permission of the Apostolic See.*)
(Antwerp: Christopher Plantin, 1584)
Hollstein (Wierix Book Illustrations) 39.2
Museum Plantin-Moretus/Prentenkabinet, Antwerp–UNESCO World Heritage

*T*he *Annunciation* inaugurates the *Proprium de tempore* (*Proper of the Season*), that section of the *Roman Breviary* containing the Office of all Sundays and of the most important weekday feasts.[100] It consists of psalms, antiphons, lessons, responsories, and Gospel extracts adapted to the liturgical seasons—Advent and Christmastide, Septuagesima and Lent, Holy Week and Easter, and the Sundays after Pentecost. The image is a digest of Luke 1:26–38: whereas Gabriel's fluttering garments indicate that he has just alighted, the Holy Spirit sent by the Father already hovers over Mary; moreover, her crossed arms signal the words of consent marking the conception of Christ, "Behold, I am the handmaid of the Lord; let it be to me according to your word." Since the *Proper of the Season* opens with the Advent prayers preparatory to Christmas and Epiphany, the feasts focussing on the mystery of Incarnation, the *Annunciation* perfectly complements the chief themes of this seasonal liturgy. The print also serves to illustrate specific prayers, just as the imagery of these meditative hymns and homilies amplifies the print's meaning. For example, the *Annunciation* can be seen to portray Mary as the living *thalamus* (bridal chamber), the virginal *clausula* (small enclosure), whence in the words of the Ambrosian hymn *Conditor alme siderum* (*Kind Creator of the Stars*), Christ, the soul's bridegroom, shall emerge to save but also to judge humankind. She embodies the response of all creation to his coming: "in heaven and on earth all bend their knee before his mighty potency."[101] This hymn is sung on the first Saturday of Advent as a responsory to Romans 13:11, which, read in conjunction with the *Annunciation*, construes Mary as an epitome of our imminent salvation: "For salvation is nearer to us now than when we first believed."   WM

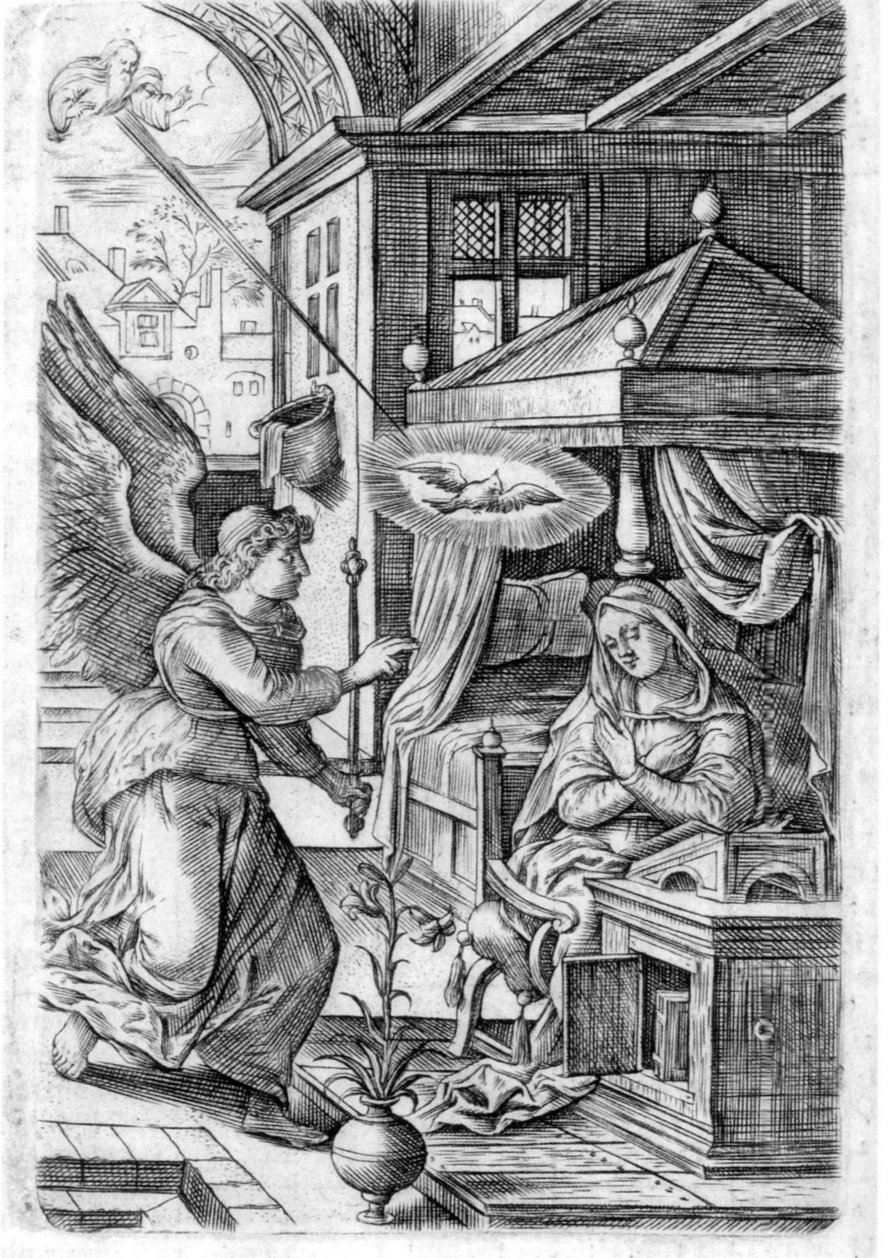

Hieronymus Wierix (1553–1619)
The Annunciation with Prayers
Before 1595
Engraving, 13.5 × 9.8 cm
Hollstein (Wierix) 1069
The British Museum, London, 1859,0709.2987

24b

Hieronymus Wierix (1553–1619)
The Circumcision with Prayers
Before 1595
Engraving, 13.5 × 9.9 cm
Hollstein (Wierix) 1070
The British Museum, London, 1859,0709.2988

Hieronymus Wierix's engraved companion pieces, *The Annunciation with Prayers* and *The Circumcision with Prayers*, demonstrate the prominence of rosary devotion in lay and monastic worship of the sixteenth century. The engravings share an identical format in which columns of Latin text frame a rectangular picture featuring a biblical event encircled by a rosary. In the first print, members of a confraternity devoted to the Virgin Mary kneel in prayer beneath the Annunciation. Two angels hover above the scene, and two hover below it, distributing rosaries to the worshipers. The work is extensively inscribed with verses of prayer. The inscriptions supplement the print's meditative function, which focused upon the image of the Incarnation. Wierix's format inverted the traditional relation between word and image in devotional books, pushing the text to the margins, around the large, central image. At the top, the Fifteen Mysteries of the Rosary are enumerated and a five-line prayer fills the bottom margin. The first part of the

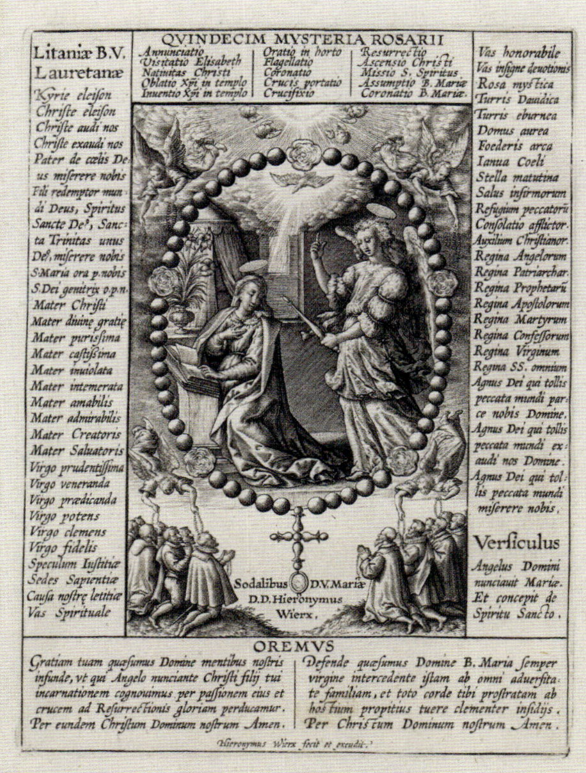

24a

litany of Our Lady of Loreto is inscribed in columns to either side.[102]

The litany concludes in the top margin and side columns of the second print, which also has a five-line prayer inscribed in the bottom margin. The Marian imagery of the preceding piece is balanced, in this engraving, with a scene from the Life of Christ: the Circumcision.[103] Wierix's imagery demonstrates that the Society of Jesus emphasized Christ in its promotion of rosary devotion.[104] Mary is present in the picture, but she occupies a marginal

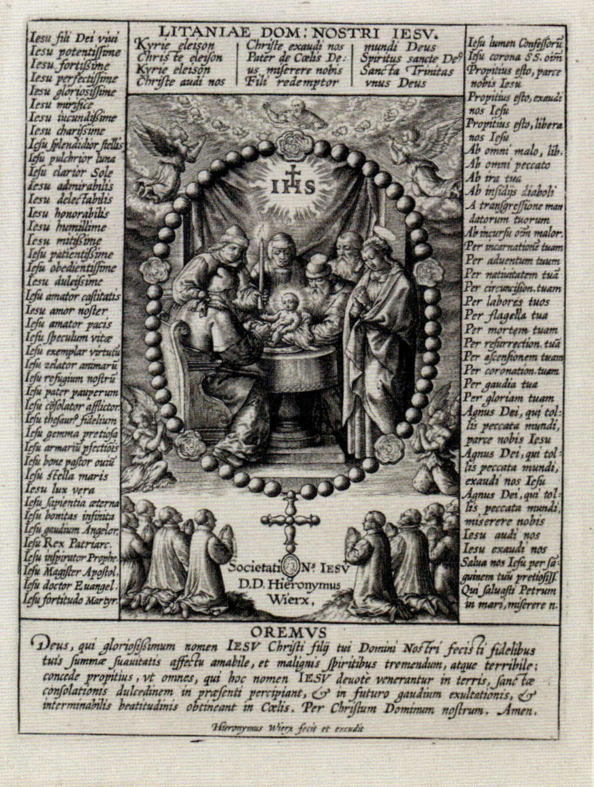

24b

position in a composition centered upon the Christ Child. Below, members of the Society of Jesus kneel in prayer. Their poses and gestures reiterate the supplications of adoring angels depicted above them. The reverential disposition of the angels and worshipers signals the importance of the Circumcision in Jesuit worship. The first shedding of Christ's blood was also the occasion upon which he received the name Jesus, after which the Jesuit order named itself.   JS

Philips Galle (1537–1612)
Baptism (Sacramentum Baptismi)
1576
From the *Seven Sacraments of the New Law*
(*Septem novae legis sacramenta*)
Engraving, 25.6 × 19 cm
New Hollstein (Galle) 266
The Metropolitan Museum of Art, New York

*I*n 1576 and 1577, the Antwerp printmaker Philips Galle produced three remarkable series of large engravings: the *Seven Sacraments of the New Law*, the *Seven Corporal Works of Mercy*, and the *Seven Spiritual Works of Mercy* (see cat. 38).[105] Each plate is densely composed of multiple images (of both biblical and contemporary scenes) and mostly biblical texts. In *Baptism*, there are nearly thirty such quotations. It is as if all the reasonably relevant texts available to the printmaker, whether seemingly redundant or not, were packed into the space with a few images. The prints' profusion of textual excerpts, gathered together under thematic headings, with little verbal commentary, recalls the overlapping traditions of florilegia and commonplace books, including those published in Antwerp by Galle's contemporaries, which gathered information, generally as simple quotations, on a wide array of topics, although most often religious, ethical, and moral.[106] Galle's prints, like those books, provided condensed material for meditation, discussion, or preaching.

The structure of each of Galle's compositions (aside from the title-pages) is nearly identical in all three series. An arched architectural frame opens onto multiple scenes set in a city- or landscape. The scenes are

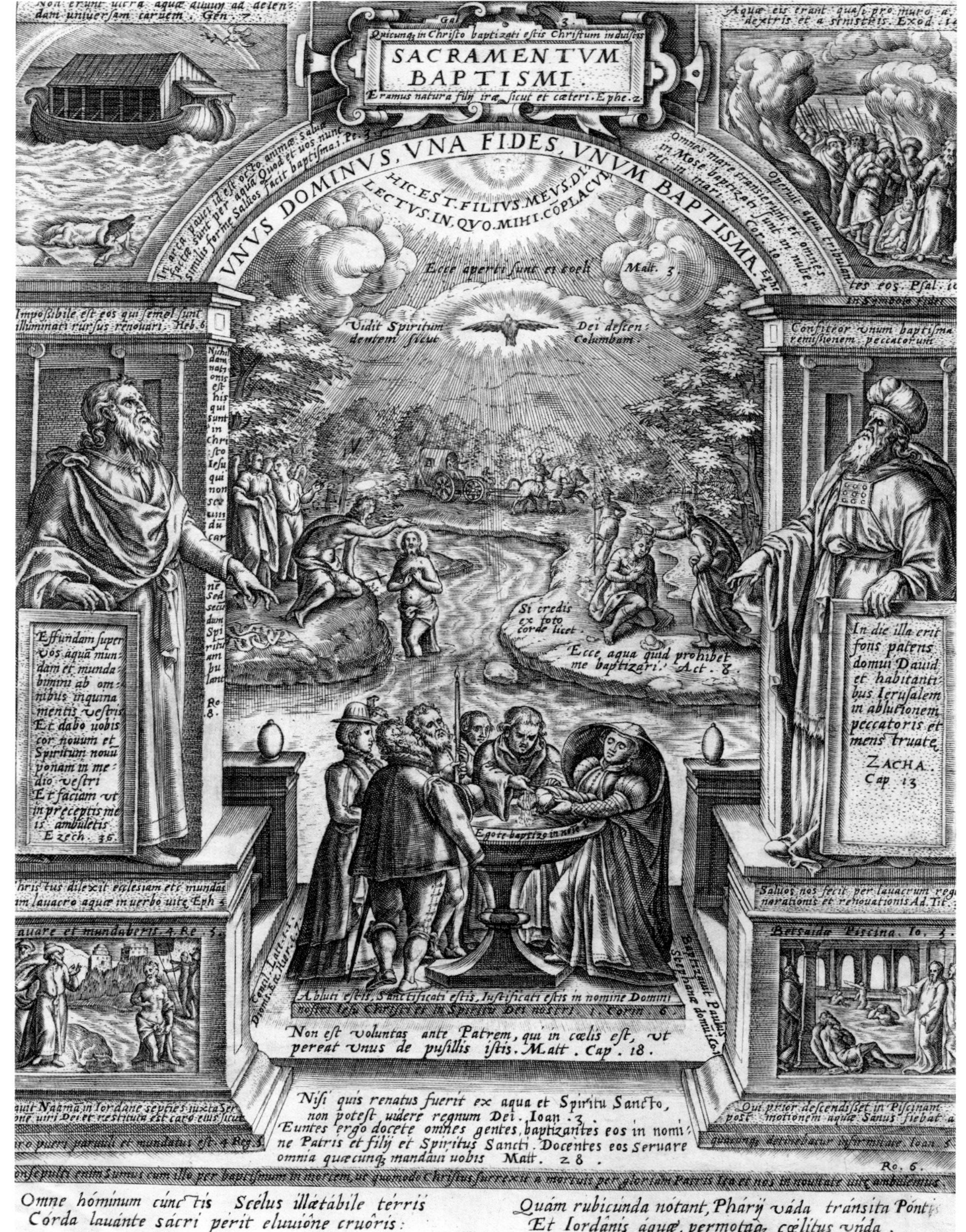

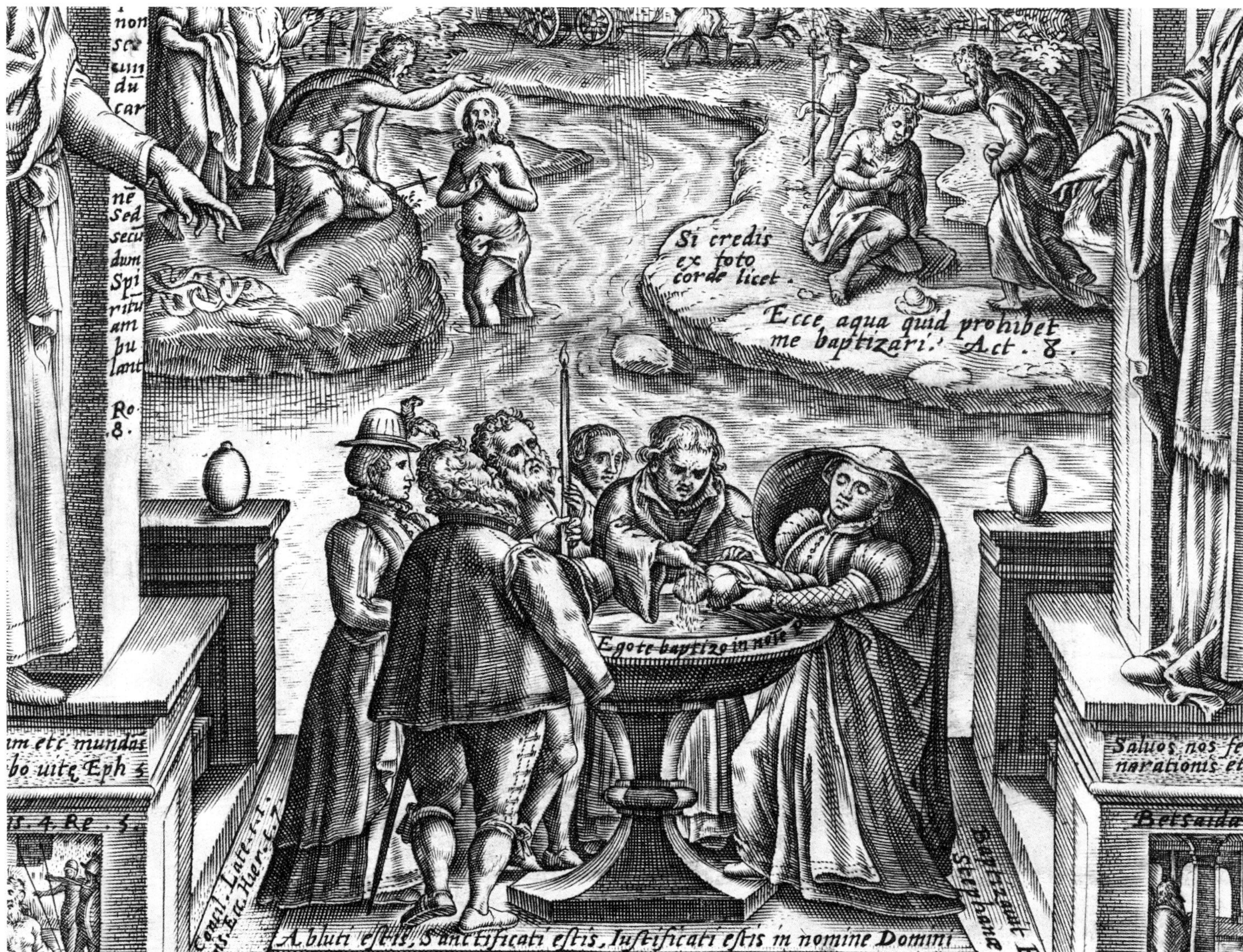

25 (detail)

tion to the pictures. For Noah's Ark and the Passage through the Red Sea, for example, not only is the relevant Old Testament passage quoted, but New Testament references tying them more closely to the theme of Baptism are also provided. For the ark, it is 1 Peter 3:20–21: "when God waited patiently in the days of Noah, during the building of the ark, in which a few … were saved through water. And baptism, which this prefigured, now saves you."

The subjects within the composition are thus linked, at least in part, typologically, so that events in the Hebrew Bible are read as prefigurations (or "types") of events in the Christian New Testament. But Galle's typology extends into his own time, juxtaposing scenes of contemporary religious life with both Old and New Testament subjects. In this sense, the Old Testament narratives are not only prefigurations of the New Testament ones, nor are they simply to be interpreted through the lens of the Gospel; rather they demonstrate a continuity of meaning that validates contemporary ritual and practice.

Galle's series of the *Seven Sacraments* is self-evidently Roman Catholic because Protestant Reformers had rejected most of these traditional sacraments. Several texts cited in the *Baptism* (Pseudo-Dionysius, the Fourth Lateran Council, the Nicene Creed) would have been more appealing to Catholics than to Protestants. Yet the emphasis on scripture in the series reflects a growing impulse in the sixteenth century to seek common ground (or persuasive argumentation) in the shared texts of all confessions. JC

linked spatially through steps, balustrades, walls, and so on, so that the space is unified visually, though not narratively. In the middle ground is usually a modern example of the subject at hand, and in the background relevant biblical narratives, usually Christological, or at least from the New Testament. In *Baptism*, in the distance is the Baptism of Christ at the left and Philip Baptizing the Eunuch at the right. On the near side of each arch, flanking it, are two prophets or other scriptural authors[107]— here Ezekiel and Zechariah—who point toward the events visible through the arch. More biblical subjects are illustrated at the four corners of each print. In the *Baptism*, it is a group of aquatic subjects with more or less relevance to the sacrament: Noah's ark (Genesis 7), Moses leading the Israelites through the Red Sea (Exodus 14), Naaman cleansed of his leprosy by washing in the Jordan (2 Kings 5), and the Pool of Bethesda (John 5). Texts relevant to the subject are also included without illustration, as, for example, Christ's injunction to the Apostles in Matthew 28 to go forth to all nations, baptizing them in the name of the Father and the Son and the Holy Spirit, which appears at the bottom of the image. Or the quotations are doubling up in rela-

Hans I Collaert (1525/30–80)

After Ambrosius Francken (?) (ca. 1544–1618)

Crucifixion with the Penitent Saint Peter

ca. 1575–80

Engraving, 20.4 × 28 cm

In *Novi Testamenti, in templo gestorum icones tredecim elegantissimi ac ornatissimi*

(Antwerp: Gerard de Jode, 1585)

New Hollstein (Collaert) 312

Spencer Collection, The New York Public Library, Astor, Lenox and Tilden Foundations

The *Thesaurus veteri testamenti* and *Novi Testamenti* of Gerard de Jode are collections of prints with biblical subjects published in Antwerp in 1585. They contain over 300 prints dating from 1575 to 1585, which were designed and engraved by different artists and arranged according to the sequence of the books of the Bible.[108]

Situated on top of the hill called Golgotha, with the city of Jerusalem and its holy temple in the background, three figures hang on crosses: Christ, in the center, and the two thieves crucified with him on either side. To emphasize his physical suffering, Collaert depicts Christ's hands and feet nailed to the cross, whereas the arms and legs of the two thieves are bound with rope to the wooden structures (both were contemporary practices). The combination of the monumental temple in the background and the figure in the left foreground, who turns his head toward Christ with his mouth open to speak, refers to Matthew 27:38: a criminal and other passers-by deride Jesus, saying "You who would destroy the temple and rebuild it in three days, save yourself! If you are the Son of God, come down from the cross."

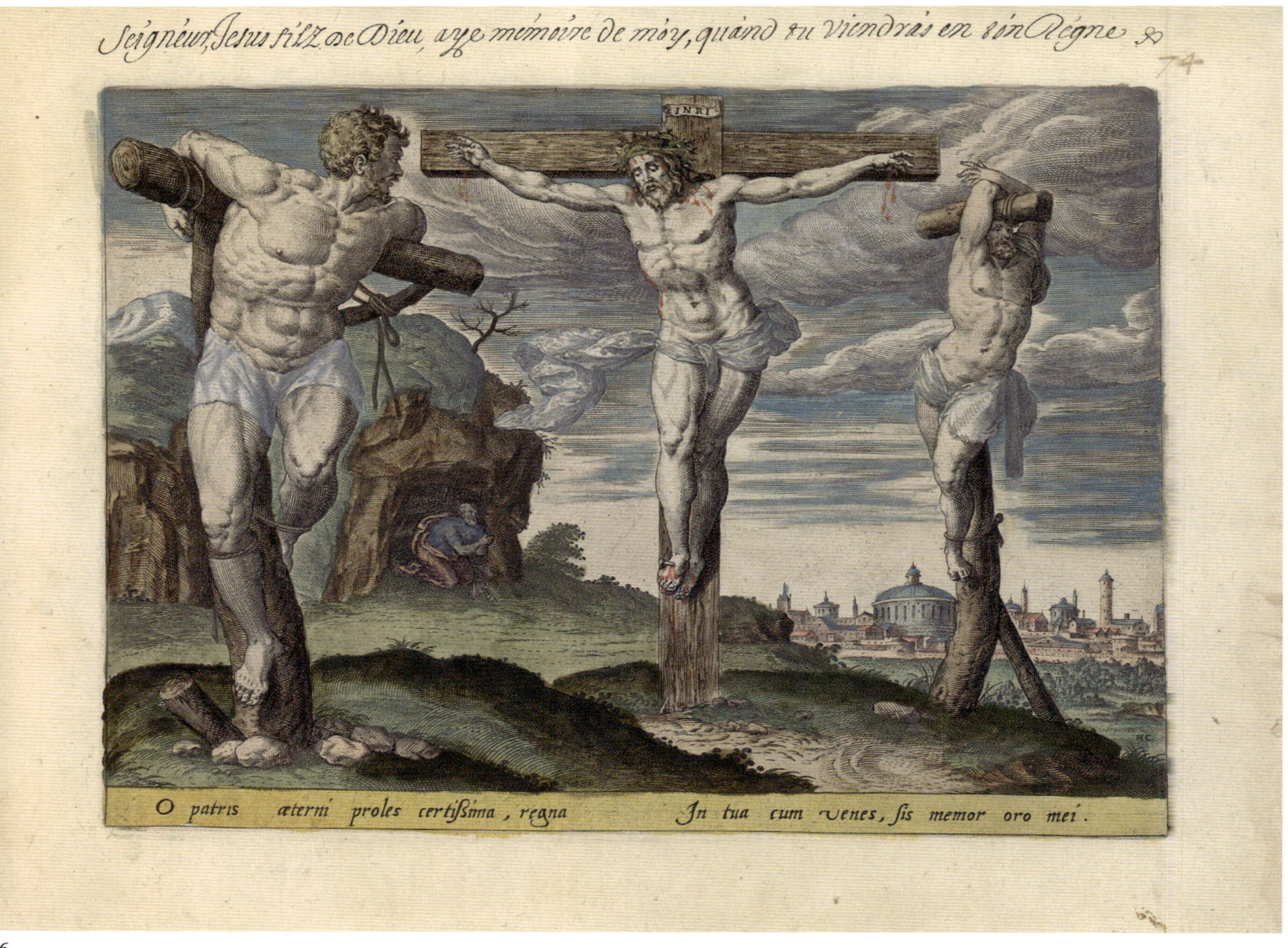

26

In contrast to the two writhing thieves, Jesus is the perfect picture of peace. Having expressed his anguish to God the night before in the Garden of Gethsemane, Christ has now fully submitted to his Father's will and to his death on the cross. His eyes are closed and his contemplative state stands in stark relief against the darkening clouds and gusty wind, whose strength is evidenced by the movment of his loincloth.

In the background, a penitent Peter kneels in the shadows of a cave, his arms raised in supplication. Before his arrest, Jesus had informed the disciples that they would all desert him. When Peter vehemently disagreed, Jesus foretold Peter's threefold denial "before the cock crows." Later that night, as predicted, Peter was accused of being a follower of Jesus and, out of fear for his life, he denied the charge three times.

In the print, Peter is situated behind the crucified Christ and begs for forgiveness. The function of this print was to assist the viewer in cultivating a personal sense of devotion. The figure of Peter provides the viewer with an example to follow, in not only developing a more intense empathy for the suffering of Christ, but also in recognizing with a penitent heart the reason why his suffering was necessary in the first place—humanity's fallen state and continual denial of God.[109]   TR

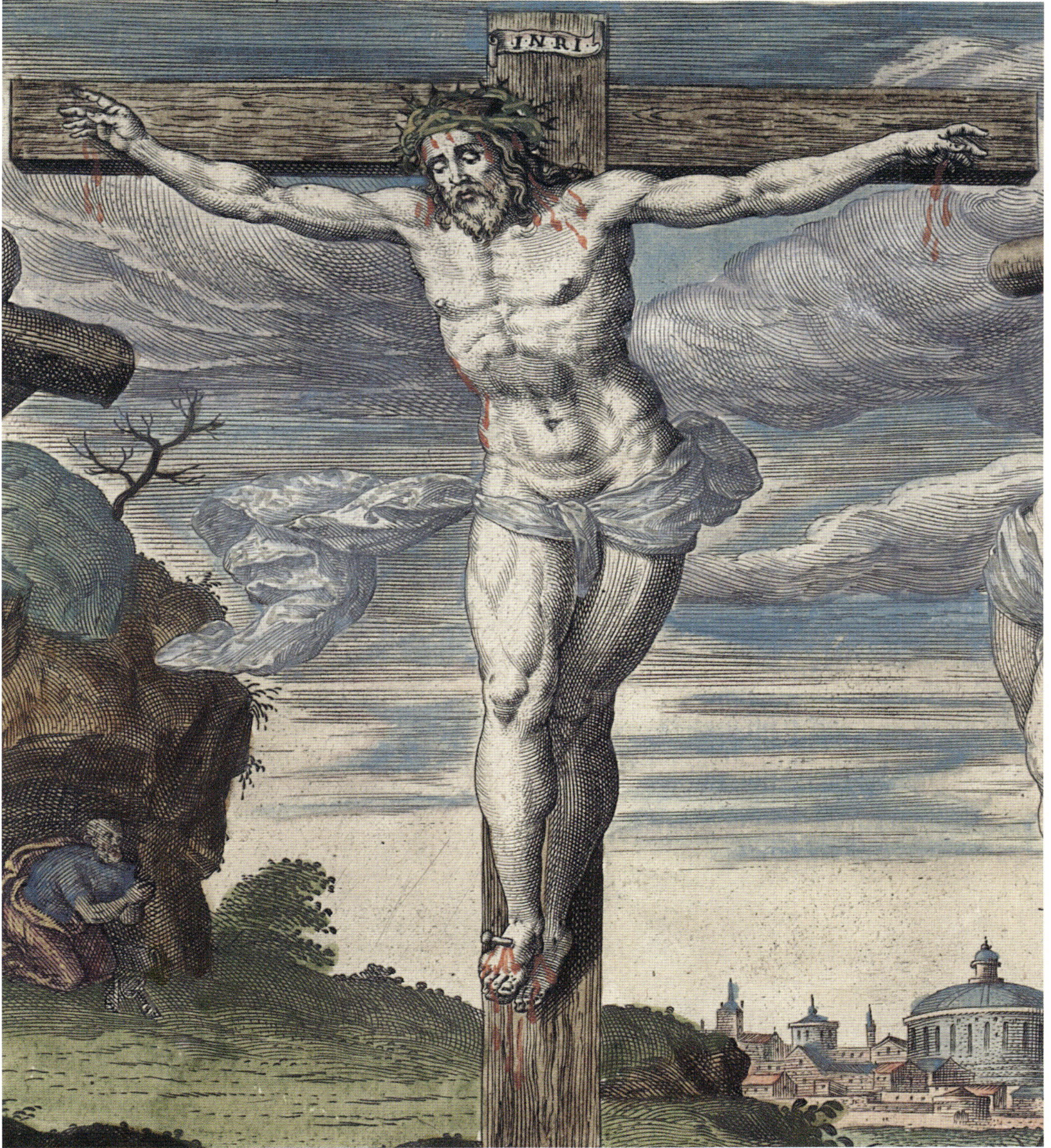

26 (detail)

27a

Hendrick Goltzius (1558–1617)
Annunciation
Plate 1 from the *Life of the Virgin*
1594
Engraving, 46.5 × 35 cm
Strauss 321
The Baltimore Museum of Art

27b

Hendrick Goltzius (1558–1617)
Adoration of the Magi in the Manner of Lucas van Leyden
Plate 5 from the *Life of the Virgin*
1594
Engraving, 46 × 35 cm
Strauss 320
The Baltimore Museum of Art

27c

Hendrick Goltzius (1558–1617)
Holy Family with the Infant Saint John in the Manner of Federigo Barocci
Plate 6 from the *Life of the Virgin*
1593
Engraving, 46 × 35 cm
Strauss 317
The Baltimore Museum of Art

*E*ngraved between 1593 and 1594 as an exercise in protean imitation, Hendrick Goltzius's *Life of the Virgin* consists of six plates depicting six versions of the Virgin's beauty: the *Visitation* in the Tuscan manner of Parmigianino, the *Nativity with Adoration of the Shepherds* in the Venetian manner of Jacopo Bassano, the *Circumcision* in the German manner of Albrecht Dürer, the *Adoration of the Magi* in the Dutch manner of Lucas van Leyden, and the *Holy Family with the Infant Saint John* in the Lombard manner of Federigo Barocci. The *Annunciation*, rather than

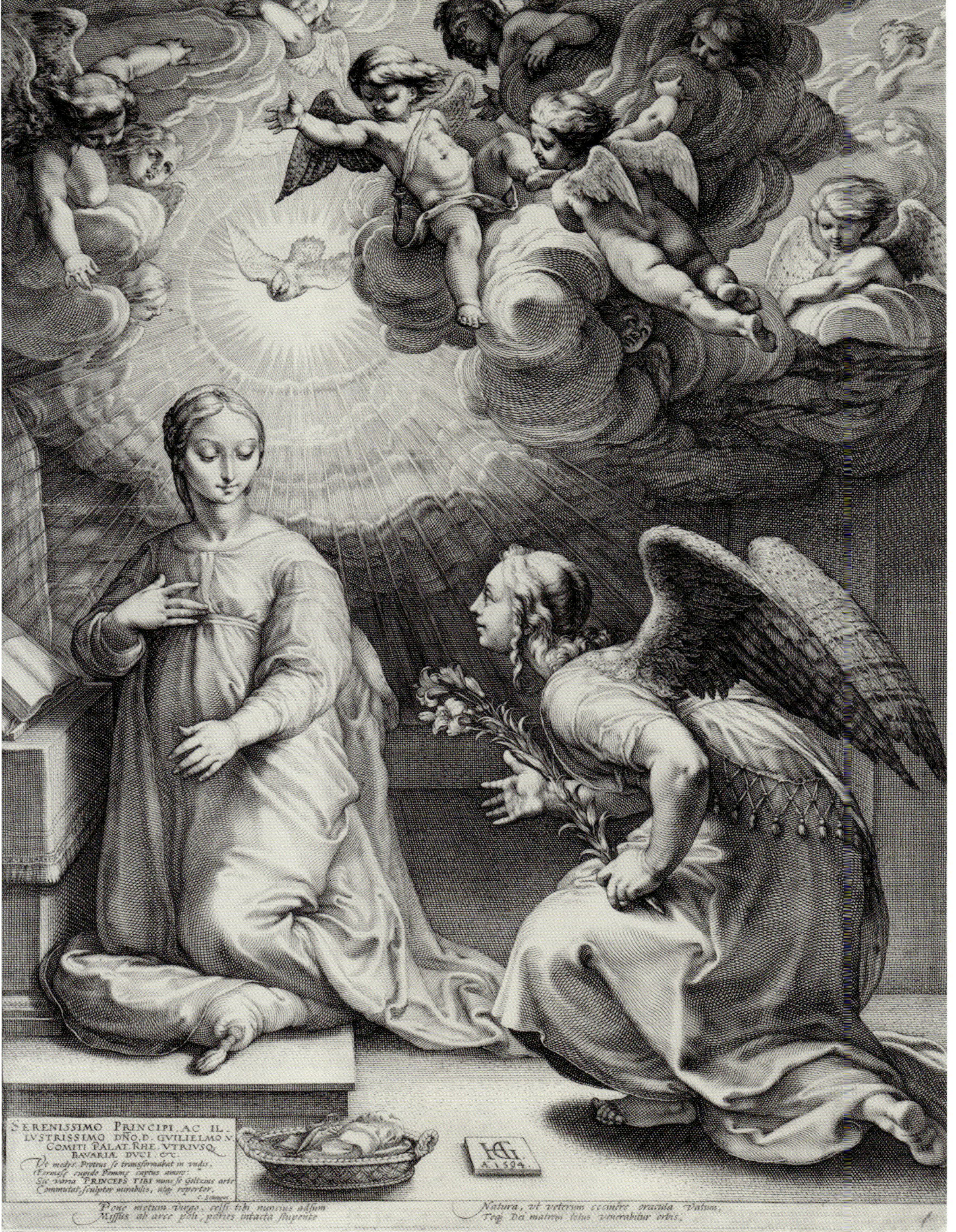

27a

imitating an identifiable master,
constitutes an amalgam of Italian *maniere*
associated with Raphael, that coalesce
into an image of the Virgin as the epitome
of lyrical beauty in all its forms: *grazia*
(grace), *leggiadria* (charm), and *venustà*
(loveliness).[110] Composed by Cornelis
Schonaeus, the dedication inscribed at
lower left in the *Annunciation*, compares
Goltzius to Proteus (and implicitly
to Vertumnus), an ancient god famed
for his powers of self-transformation:
"As Proteus, seized by eager love of
the beautiful Pomona, transformed
himself amidst the billows, so now for
you, Prince, by his mutable art Goltzius,
astonishing engraver and inventor,
wholly alters himself."[111] Goltzius is
construed as a latter-day Proteus who,
driven by love for his princely Pomona,
converts himself into the masters he
imitates, creating new works that seem
to issue not from *his* mind, heart, and
hand, but from *theirs*.[112] He folds himself
into his objects of imitation, ceding pride
of place to the Virgin, whose universal
beauty, bodily and spiritual, is seen to
encompass the beauties of every style.[113]
This conception of Mary derives from
Bernard, whose apothegm concerning
her spiritual perfection—*omnibus omnia
facta est* (she was made all things to all)—
was popularized by Ludolphus of Saxony
in his meditative treatise, the *Vita Christi*
(*Life of Christ*).   WM

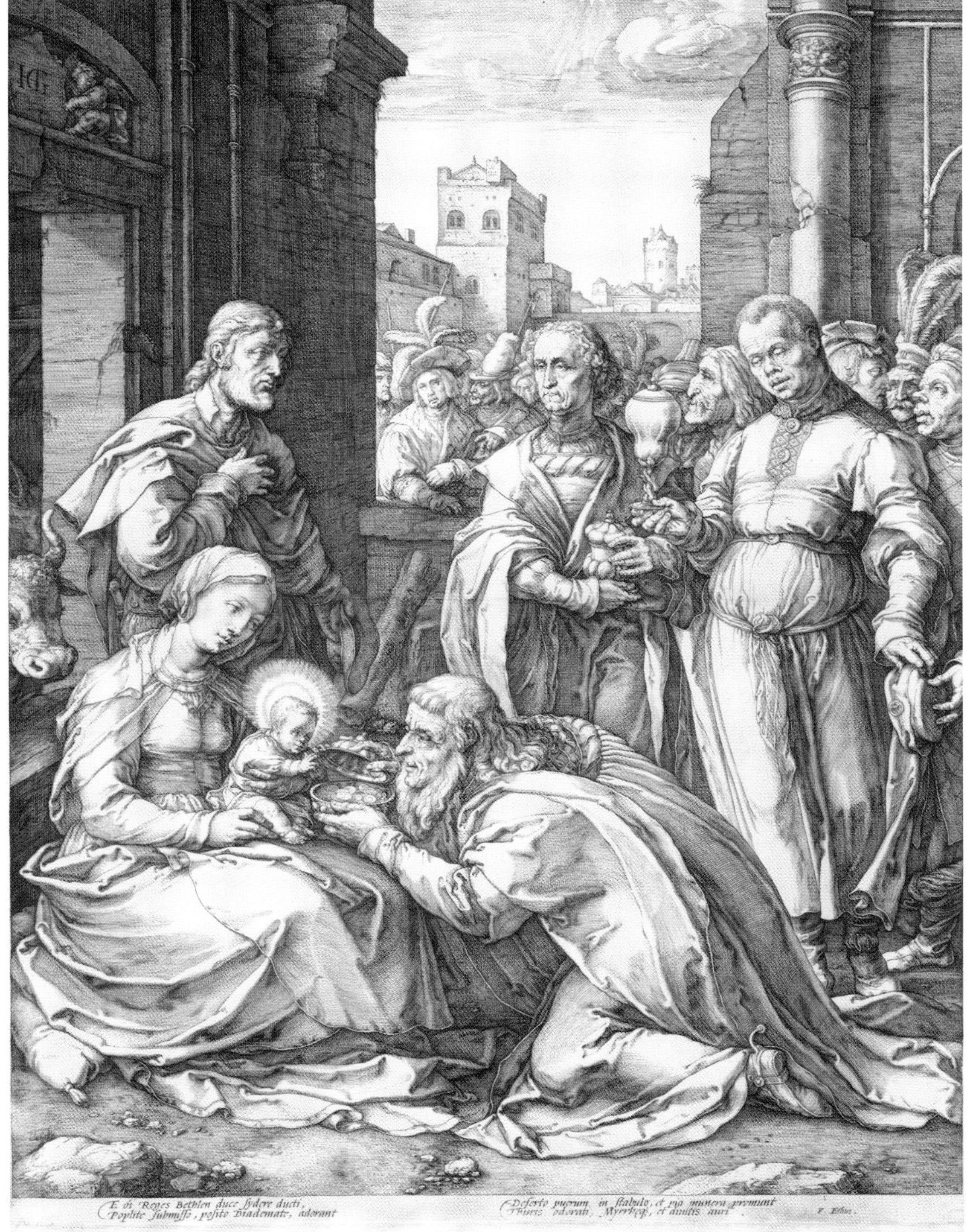

27b

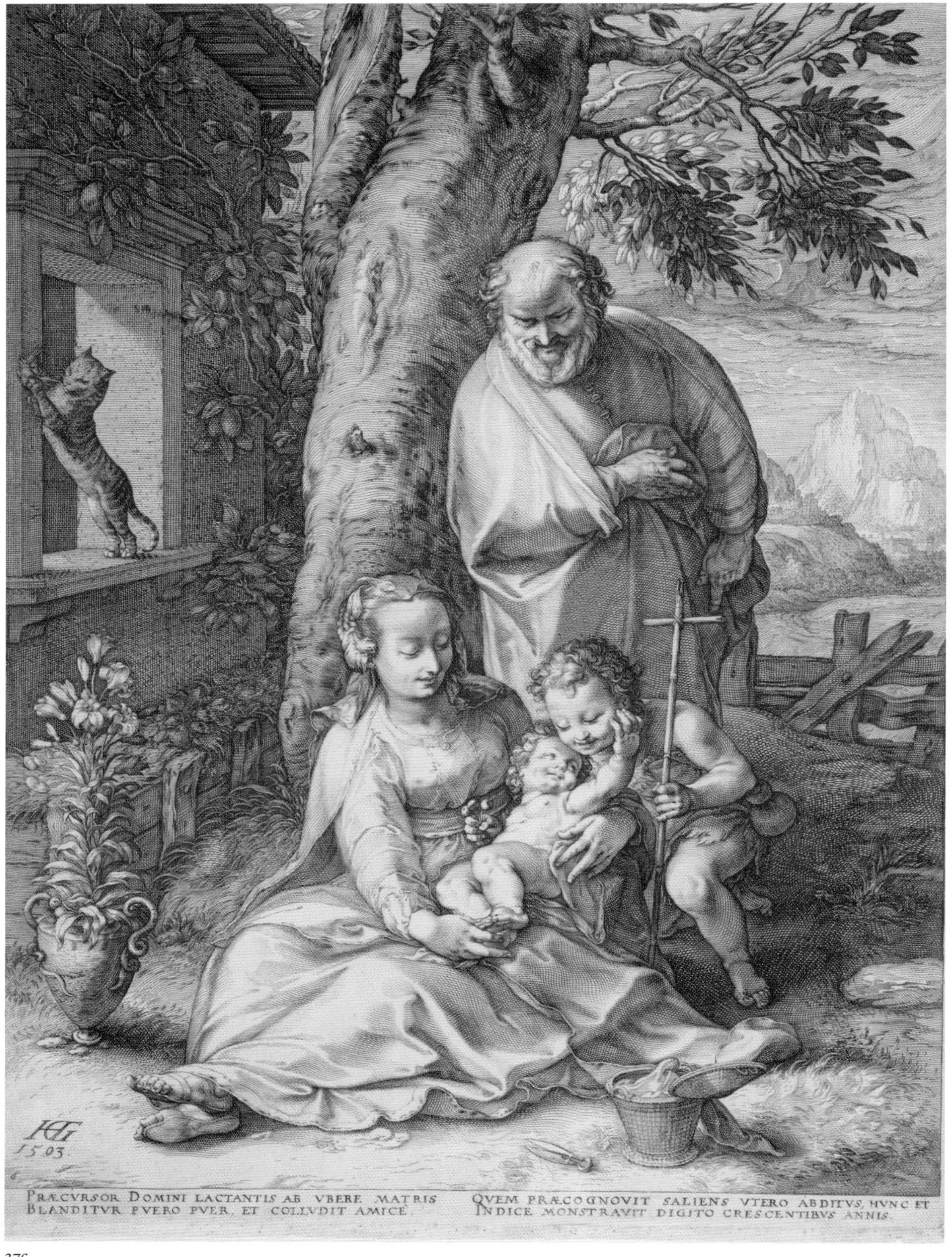

PRÆCVRSOR DOMINI LACTANTIS AB VBERE MATRIS
BLANDITVR PVERO PVER, ET COLLVDIT AMICE.
QVEM PRÆCOGNOVIT SALIENS VTERO ABDITVS, HVNC ET
INDICE MONSTRAVIT DIGITO CRESCENTIBVS ANNIS.

27c

Hieronymus Wierix (1553–1619)
After Maarten de Vos (1532–1603)
On the Night of the Lord's Birth: The Nativity of Christ
(*In nocte natalis Domini. Nativitas Christi*)
ca. 1593
Engraving, 23.3 × 14.8 cm
Imago 3 in Jerónimo Nadal, *Evangelicae historiae imagines ex ordine evangeliorum, quae toto anno in missae sacrificio recitantur, in ordinem temporis vitae Christi digestae* (*Images of Evangelical History, Following the Order of the Gospels Recited in the Sacrifice of the Mass during the Whole Year, Arranged in the Chronological Order of the Life of Christ*)
(Antwerp: Martinus Nutius, 1593)
Hollstein (De Vos) 1556;
Hollstein (Wierix Book Illustrations) 56.4
John Work Garrett Library, Johns Hopkins University

Hieronymus Wierix (1553–1619)
After Bernardino Passeri (ca. 1540–96)
At the Dawn of the Lord's Birth: On the Shepherds
(*In aurora natalis Domini. De Pastoribus*)
ca. 1593
Engraving, 23.3 × 14.6 cm
Imago 4 in Jerónimo Nadal, *Adnotationes et meditationes in Evangelia quae in sacrosancto Missae sacrificio toto anno leguntur. Cum Evangeliorum concordantia historiae integritati sufficienti. Accessit & index historiam ipsam Evangelicam in ordine temporis vitae Christi distribuens* (*Annotations and Meditations on the Gospels Read in the Most Holy Sacrifice of the Mass during the Whole Year, with an Integral Concordance of Gospel History, and in Addition, an Index Arranging Gospel History in the Chronological Order of the Life of Christ*), 2nd ed. (Antwerp: Martinus Nutius, 1595)
Hollstein (Wierix Book Illustrations) 56.5
John Work Garrett Library, Johns Hopkins University

*T*he *Nativitas Christi* (*Nativity of Christ*) forms part of the Infancy cycle in Jerónimo Nadal's *Adnotationes et meditationes in Evangelia*.[114] The two-part meditation on the Nativity begins with an image of night (*In nocte natalis Domini*—"On the Night of the Lord's Birth") and ends with an image of dawn (*In aurora natalis Domini*—"On the Dawn of the Lord's Birth").[115] These complementary images, along with their annotations and meditations, explore the shepherds' experience of Christ's birth, first in the field where they are visited by the angel, then at the stable where they contemplate the luminous child. The imagery of both scenes derives ultimately from the *Nunc Dimittis*, the prayer of thanksgiving uttered by Simeon when he first laid eyes on the infant: "for mine eyes have seen thy salvation, which thou hast prepared in the presence of all peoples, a light for revelation to the Gentiles, and for glory to thy people Israel." The radiance of Christ that brightens the night and outshines the day stands for the light of salvation that he bestows on humankind.

The captions enumerate the chief elements of *imago* 3: Bethlehem, the city of David (A); the forum where tax was paid (B); the cave where Jesus was born (C); Jesus, newly born, lying on straw before the manger (D); angels adoring the newborn child (E); the ox and the ass roused by the new light (F); the light of Christ dispelling the shadows of night (G); the Tower of Heder where the flocks were watched (H); the shepherds with their flocks at the tower (I); the angel announcing the newborn Christ to the shepherds, and with him the angelic hosts (K); the angel sent as a messenger to the souls in limbo (L); and the star and the angel sent to announce Christ to the Magi (M). Like all the images in the *Evangelicae historiae imagines*, *On the Night of the Lord's Birth* was reissued in 1595/96, as part of Nadal's meditative treatise, the *Adnotationes et meditationes in Evangelia* (*Annotations and Meditations on the Gospels*). Here lengthy texts, comprising descriptive annotations and interpretative meditations, elaborate upon the images. The annotations describe the signs made visible at Christ's birth, dwelling especially on the

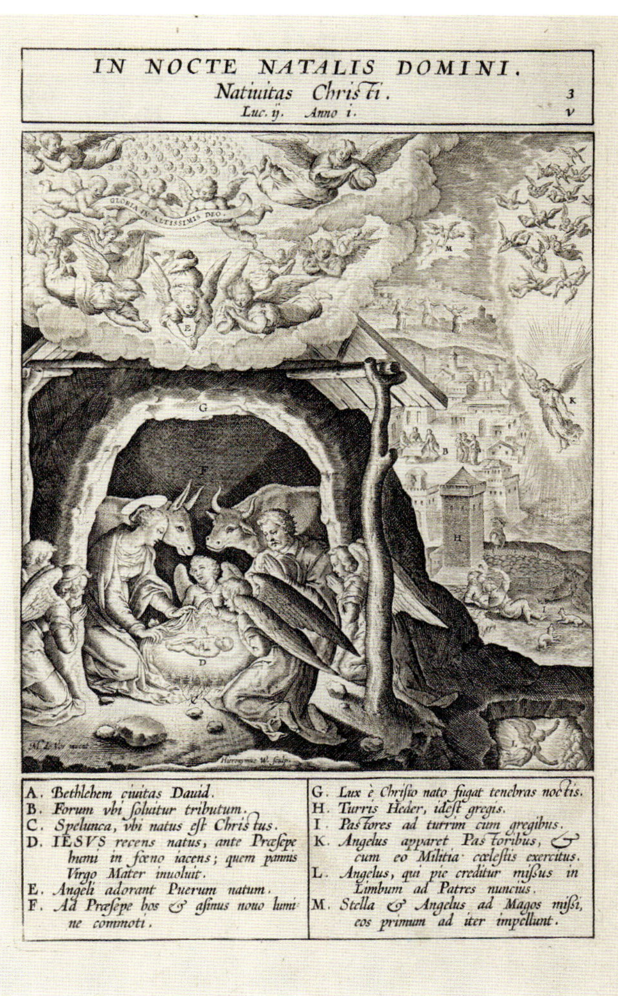

28a

appearance of light piercing the darkness (annotations G, I, K, and M). The meditation construes these chiaroscuro effects as antitheses, arguing that they signify Jesus who, being both God and man, reconciles all *paradoxa* (paradoxes). Nadal urges us to bear witness to the mystery of the Incarnation, which subsumes all antitheses, since it concerns Christ, who is human and infinite, flesh and light, in the stable and in eternity, image of the Father's boundless substance and substance of the singular Virgin's womb (*figura immensae Patris substantiae…homo ex solius virginis substantia, in eius utero*), humble in majesty, weak in power, mortal in eternity (*à maiestate tua humilitas, à virtute infirmitas, ab aeternitate tua mortalitas*).[116] These *paradoxa* resolve into a temporal antithesis, the terms of which Christ is seen to harmonize: he is both mortal and eternal, living in human time and heavenly timelessness.

De pastoribus (*On the Shepherds*) completes the two-part meditation on the Nativity that starts with an image of night and now ends with an image of dawn.[117] The captions trace the shepherds' journey to and from the Christ child: the Tower of Heder, where the shepherds conversed [about the light] (A); they discover Jesus lying in the manger (B); they understand what had been told them about the child (C); having returned to their flocks, they tell all [that they had seen and heard] (D). The lengthy annotations and brief meditation focus on their reactions to Jesus, whom they recognize as the source of the celestial

light they had first glimpsed while watching their flocks.[118] Annotation C, for example, instructs us to scrutinize their facial and bodily gestures, as indices of their growing spiritual sense of Christ, which issues from attentive contemplation of him and of Mary and Joseph.[119] The antitheses set forth in the previous chapter now resolve into a temporal paradox, that profoundly signifies the mystery of the Incarnation. The shepherds meditate on the child by tracking their past, present, and future experience of his light through the attention they confer on him in the stable: the exceptional joy they feel comes from their realization that the birth of Christ, though it occurred in historical time (*Natus est hodie ex utero matris*), partakes of eternity and is a never-ending nativity (*qui in hodie sempiterno semper nascitur…ex substantia Patris aeterni*).[120] Mediated by their present experience of Christ, their attention expands to embrace both the memory and expectation of salvation.[121] As Nadal makes clear in the meditations to *imagines* 3 and 4, the shepherds are epitomes of his ideal reader-viewers, the Jesuit scholastics who desire to meditate on Christ's birth during Christmastide (*Pastores sumus & nos*).[122]   WM

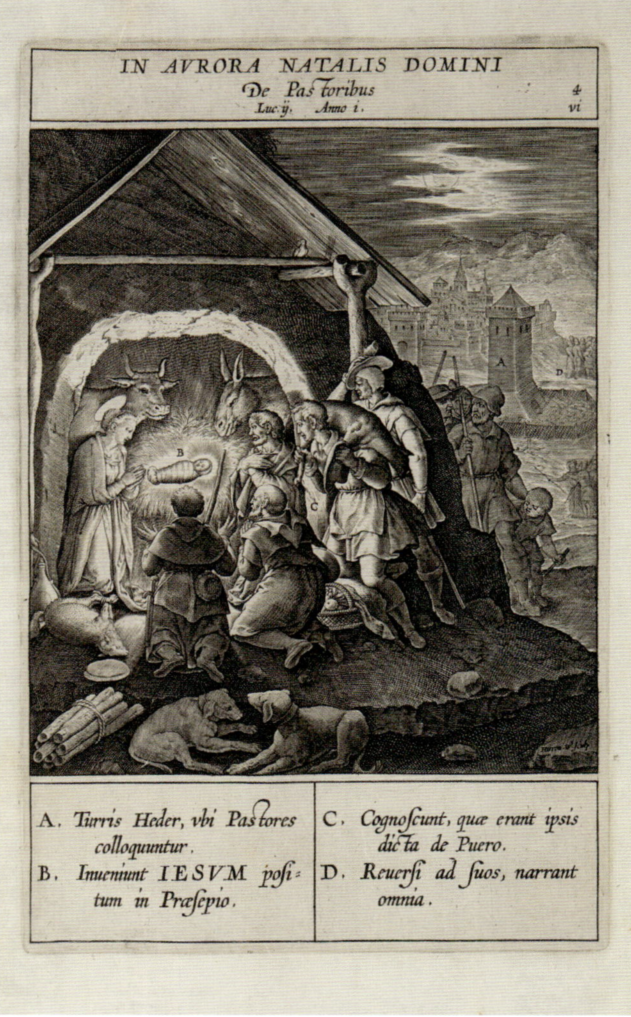

A. Turris Heder, vbi Pastores colloquuntur.
B. Inueniunt IESVM positum in Præsepio.
C. Cognoscunt, quæ erant ipsis dicta de Puero.
D. Reuersi ad suos, narrant omnia.

28b

Hieronymus Wierix (1553–1619)
After Melchior Model (active ca. 1600)
Circumcision Enframed by the Text of Psalm 6
before 1604
Engraving, 15.2 × 10.5 cm
In *Septem Psalmi Davidici. Quos vulgo poenitentiales vocitant. Septem Redemptoris nostri sanguinis effusionum formulis illustrati hactenus nusquam reperti.* (*Seven Psalms of David, Called Commonly the Penitential [Psalms], Illustrated in Patterns of the Blood Shed Seven Times by Our Savior, to be Found Nowhere Else [as Illustrated Here]*)
Hollstein (Wierix) 1062
Robert W. Woodruff Library, Emory University

*D*rawn and engraved by Hieronymus Wierix after inventions by Melchior Model, the *Septem Psalmi Davidici* (*Seven Penitential Psalms*) consists of seven diminutive images of the Passion encircled by full texts of the seven Penitential Psalms, written in continuously scrolling bands of italic letters.[123] As the title indicates, the pairing of these texts with images of the bleeding Christ was considered innovative (*hactenus nusquam reperti* —"found nowhere else"). The term *formulis* (guides, patterns, exemplars; shapes, outlines, schemes of variation; set forms of words) applies equally to the pictorial scenes and their textual frames. The flow of penitential psalms, looping round the Passion scenes, extends and ornaments the effusion of holy blood; it is as if these penitential words were the very pattern of Christ's redemptive blood, shed seven times on behalf of all sinners—at the Circumcision, Agony in the Garden, Flagellation, Crowning with Thorns, Stripping on Mount Golgotha, Nailing to the Cross, and Piercing with

the Lance (*septem Redemptoris nostri sanguinis effusionum formulis*—"patterns of the blood shed seven times by our Savior").[124] Since Psalms 6, 31, 37, 50, 101, 129, and 142 were recited to express sorrow for one's sins, they underscore the expiatory function of the blood that washes away guilt and damnation.[125] Model based his selection of scenes and psalms on Augustine's homiletic *Enarrationes in Psalmos* (*Discourses on the Psalms*): the discourse on Psalm 6, for example, associates it with the Circumcision, construing the psalmist's words as an expression of spiritual circumcision, the cutting away of one's sinful flesh and passions and reformation of oneself in the image of Christ. Augustine cites Colossians 3:10: "But from the coming of the Lord, for Whom there was a transition from the circumcision of the flesh to the circumcision of the heart, the call was made, that man should live according to the soul, that is, according to the inner man, who is also called the new man by reason of the new birth and the renewing of spiritual conversation."[126] Augustine was also the source of Model's clever conceit that associates the looping and scrolling texts with the notion of *reformatio* (reformation, in the sense of conversion, that is, the soul's turning away from sin, and conversely, its turning toward God). Augustine views penitential prayer as the soul's turning en route on a protracted and difficult journey toward God; the soul is the patient "long kept back by the [divine] physician" who deliberately impedes her turning—namely, her efforts to pray

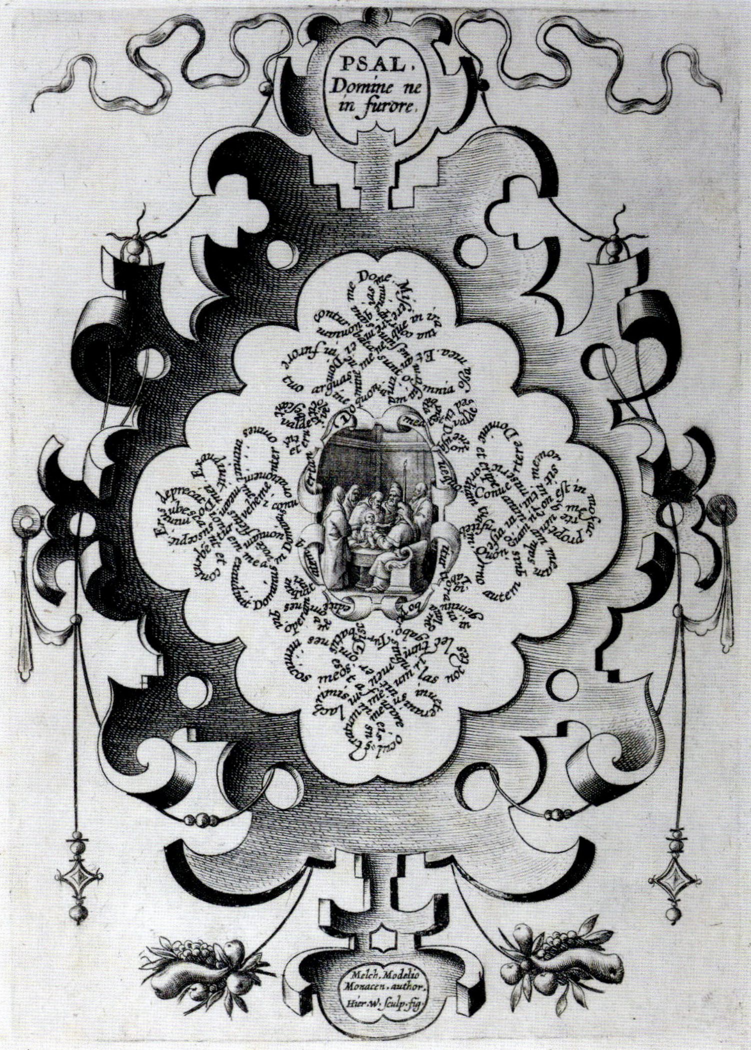

29

perfectly— until she realizes how desperate is her condition.[127] The penitent soul circumambulates (*nos convertimur*) in her efforts to secure the experience of spiritual circumcision that leads ultimately to reconciliation with God.   WM

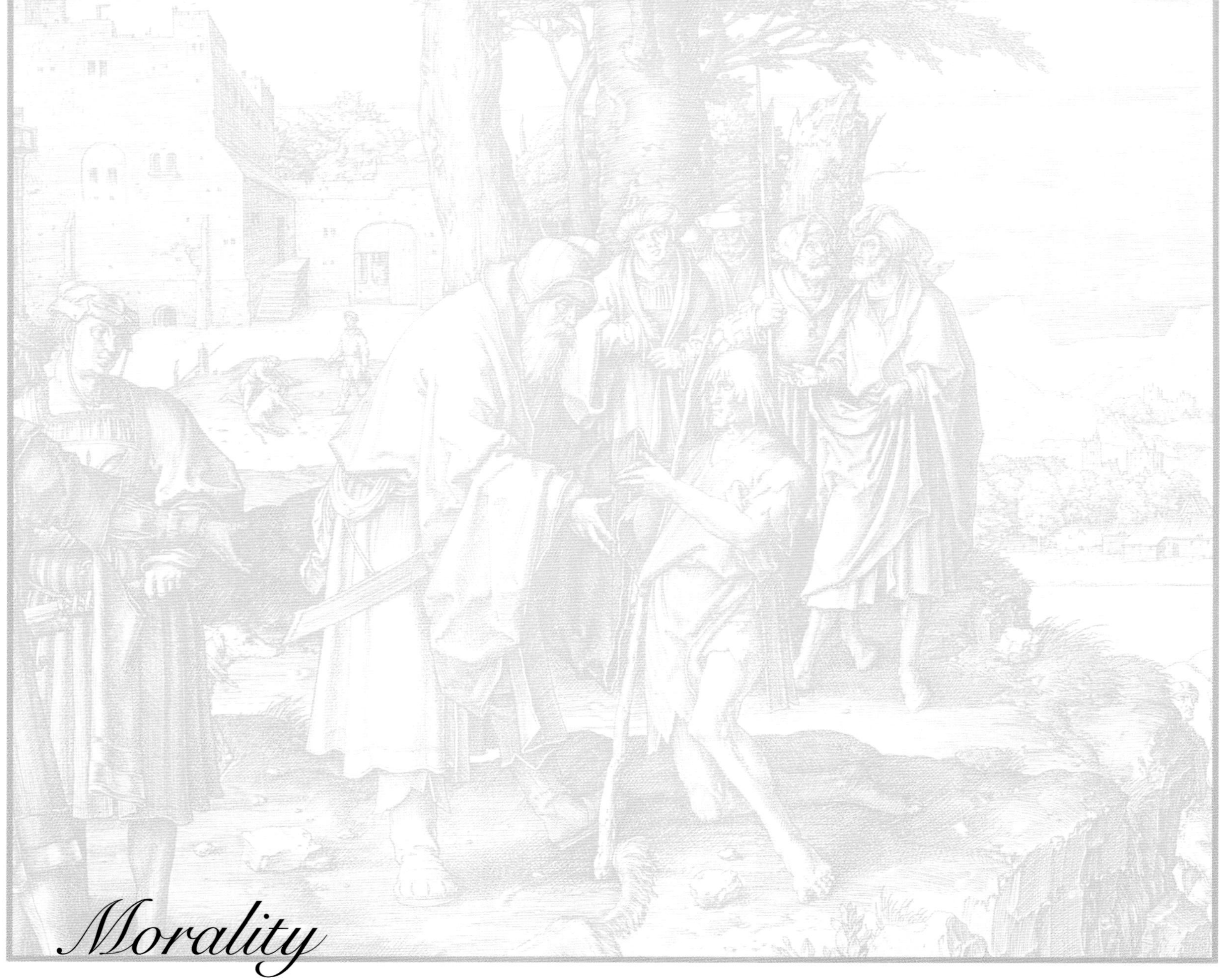

Morality

In everything do to others as you would have them do to you; for this is the law and the prophets.

Matthew 7:12

Lucas van Leyden (ca. 1494–1533)
The Return of the Prodigal Son
ca. 1510
Engraving, 18.1 × 24.5 cm
New Hollstein (Van Leyden) 78
The Baltimore Museum of Art

*L*ucas van Leyden appealed to a heterogenous audience with his elegant description of homecoming and redemption in *The Return of the Prodigal Son*. His arrangement of large figures against an unfolding landscape view is analog to diverse popular dramatizations of the Bible parable about a father's forgiveness of his youngest son, who returned home repentant after squandering his inheritance on riotous living in a foreign land. From the thirteenth through the fifteenth centuries, in France, the Netherlands and Germany, the prodigal's story was reformulated in Latin school plays, *tableaux vivants*, vernacular morality plays and rhetorical dramas.[128] Aims of entertaining, proselytizing, moralizing, and didacticism inspired plots with varied emphasis on the wasteful home-life, ruin abroad, and humbling swine-herding experienced by the prodigal prior to reconciliation with his family.

Lucas's sweeping vista integrates narrative details of the facade of his home, towns near and distant, a kneeling swineherd and celebratory calf-slaying into a spatially and temporally unified scene.[129] Imagery of farmlands and animal husbandry, which evoke medieval illustrations of the labors of the months, allude to the redemptive value of labor over the natural cycle of time. These themes amplify the meaning of renewal that attaches to the son's return home.   JS

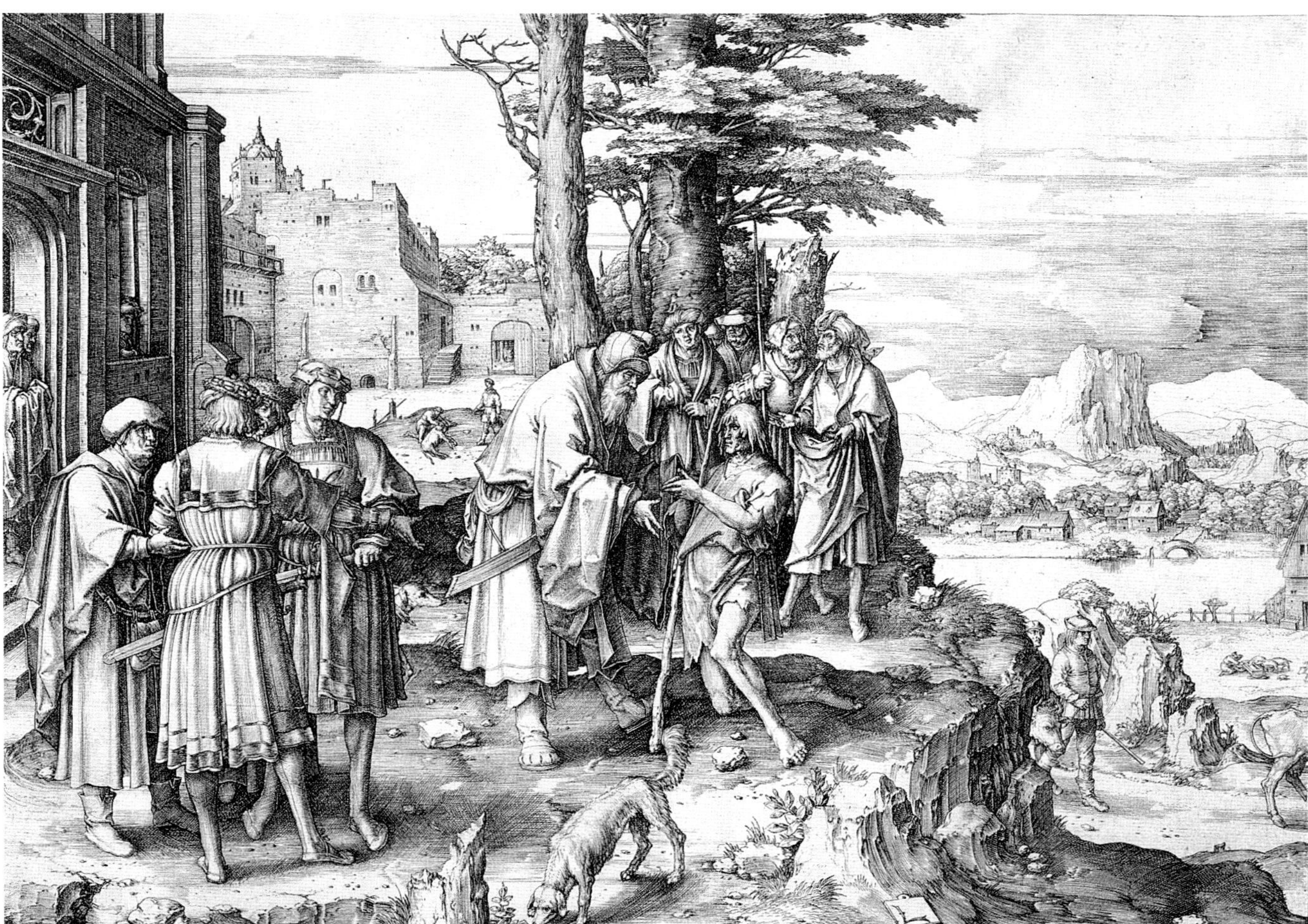

30

31a

Lucas van Leyden (ca. 1494–1533)
Adam and Eve
From *The Small Power of Women*
ca. 1517 (frame ca. 1520–30)
Woodcut, 35.2 × 23.1 cm
New Hollstein (Van Leyden) 181
The Metropolitan Museum of Art, New York

31b

Lucas van Leyden (ca. 1494–1533)
Jael Killing Sisera
From *The Small Power of Women*
ca. 1517 (frame ca. 1520–30)
Woodcut, 35.2 × 23.1 cm
New Hollstein (Van Leyden) 182
The Metropolitan Museum of Art, New York

In Lucas's second set of six woodcuts dealing with women's noxious power, the two pagan subjects drawn from the legend of Virgil have been replaced by Old Testament subjects, resulting in a series unified by its biblical subject matter as well as its misogyny.[130] This unity was enhanced in the second edition, when each woodcut was printed together with one of two decorative frames, probably designed by Lucas some years later. The alternating frames fit together to form a continuous frieze that was undoubtedly intended as wall decoration, accounting for its low rate of survival. Shown here are two prints from the only known uniform set, now divided between the Museum of Fine Arts, Boston, and the Metropolitan Museum of Art, New York, which includes Dutch texts printed in the tablets beneath the images.[131] There are also impressions with Latin inscriptions, which must have been the first to be issued, since the

Dutch translations do not fit as well into the openings and are often incomplete.[132] Whether in Latin or Dutch, the compendium of biblical inscriptions opens with the text that tells the story, while the others, often taken out of context, reinforce the general message of woman's vile and untrustworthy nature. The typeface used for the Dutch texts is like that of the Amsterdam printer Doen Pieterz, and the frame resembles those he employed in his Bible of 1530—illustrated in part with designs attributed to Lucas—suggesting that he may have been responsible for at least the second edition of the *Small Power of Women*.[133]

Although Eve was often held responsible for the Fall, Lucas's inclusion of the subject in a series on the Power of Women was highly original. He also included it in the *Large Power of Women* series and engraved the subject five times throughout his career. In keeping with the tenor of this series, Eve is represented seductively draped around a tree that echoes the shape of her body, as she offers an apple to a timorous Adam, seated awkwardly at the base of the tree. In the background we see the couple's expulsion from the Garden. The first text beneath the image (Genesis 3.6) is fairly neutral: "And when the woman saw that the tree was beautiful, good to eat, and would make one wise, she took a fruit from the living tree, ate of it and gave of it to her husband." The other biblical quotations emphasize the woman's responsibility: "The woman deceives the precious soul of man" (Proverbs 6.26);[134] "The woman made the beginning with sin and therefore

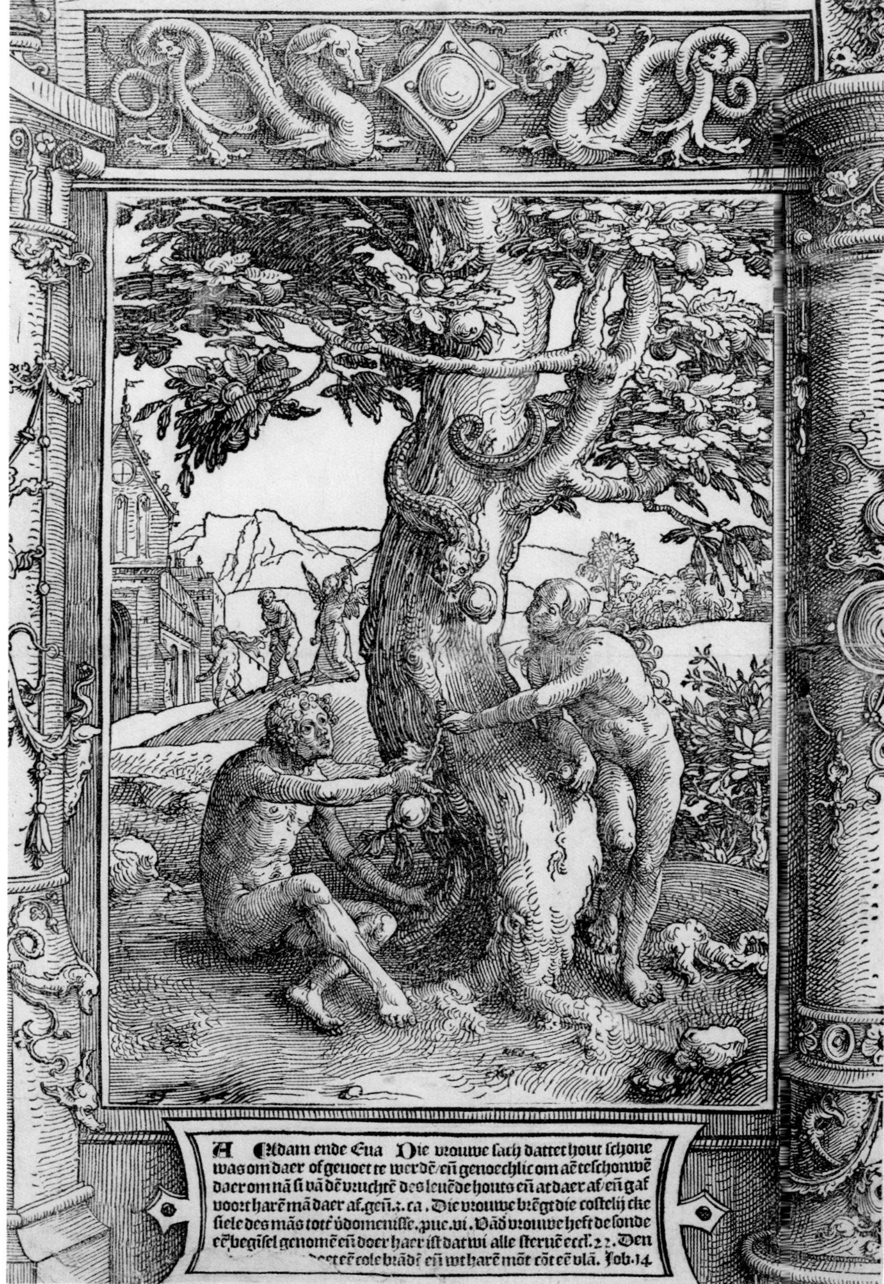

31a

we all die" (Ecclesiaticus 25.24);[135] and a quotation from Job 14 that likewise contrives to blame woman for man's mortality. This woodcut sets the tone for the images to follow.

Among these, the depiction of *Jael and Sisera* is equally unusual in a series of prints dealing with the evil power of women, for Jael, like Judith, was considered an Old Testament heroine who saved her people.

The first quotation summarizes the tale told in Judges 4:17–22: "Jael the woman went to meet Sisera and spoke to him, 'rest here by me without fear,' and after she had hidden him [from his enemies] and covered him with a cloth she drove a nail through his head with a hammer and nailed him to the ground so that Sisera's long sleep became that of death." In the foreground we see Jael driving the tent spike through Sisera's head, while in the background we witness her earlier offer of a cup of milk. In the middle ground is depicted the conclusion of the story, as Jael reveals her handiwork to Barak, leader of the Israeli forces. The killing of Sisera freed the Israelis from tyranny, yet it was not always viewed in a positive light. In fifteenth- and sixteenth-century editions of the devotional book *Zielentroost*, for example, Jael's action is cited as a violation of the commandment against murder, as is Judith's beheading of Holofernes.[136] In Lucas's woodcut the message is clearly spelled out in the second quotation: "All evil is small in comparison to the evil of a woman" (Ecclesiasticus 25.19).   WT

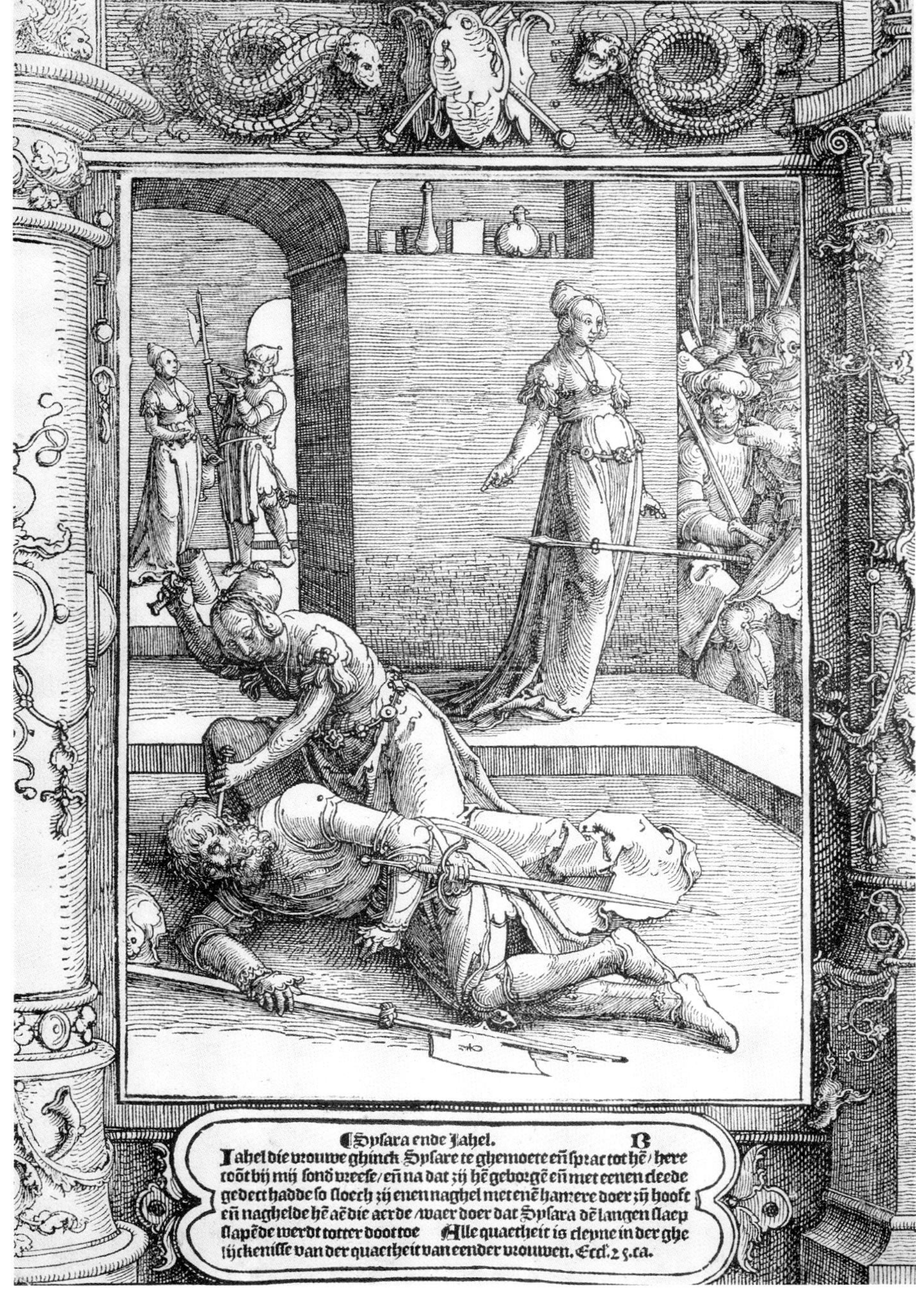

31b

Jan Swart (ca. 1500–ca. 1560)
Jesus Preaching from the Ship
ca. 1525
Woodcut, 23.8 × 26.6 cm
Hollstein (Swart) 5
The New York Public Library,
Astor, Lenox and Tilden Foundations

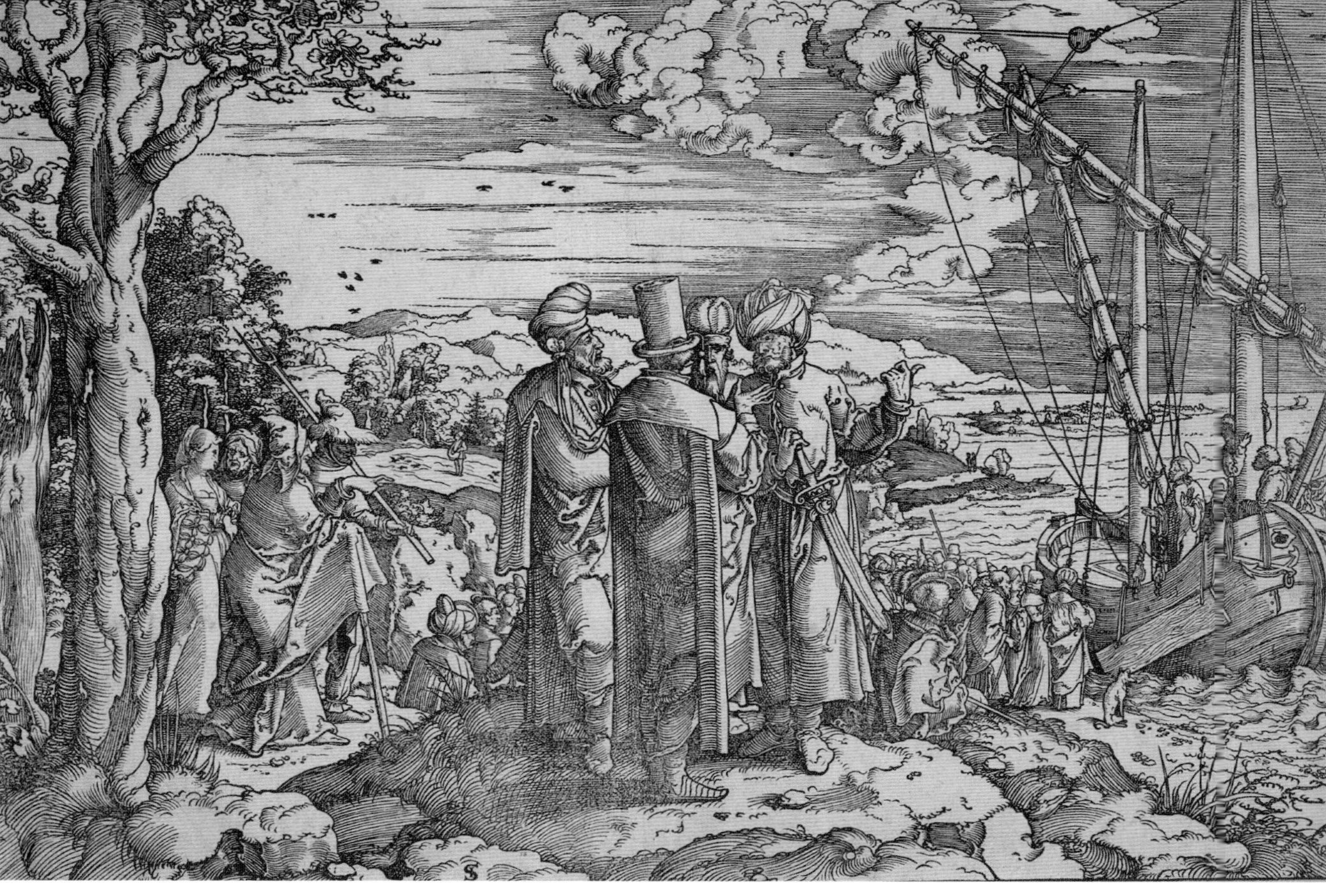

32

Jan Swart's *Jesus Preaching from the Ship* illustrates an episode described in three of the gospels, in which multitudes assemble to hear Christ preach at the lake of Genesareth.[137] Swart's vigorous, curvilinear lines imbue the scene's landscape setting with vibrant energy. Grasses sway on the shore, waves crest around the ship whereupon Christ stands, and clouds billow in the sky above him. Inland, birds circle aloft and foliage branches out in all directions. The enlivened natural forms draw our vision from place to place within the landscape.

Our gaze is further directed by a small group of pilgrims, in the left foreground, who walk toward the ship at the far right. Pointing to Christ, one of them indicates that their objective is to hear his sermon. As they join the assembled body of listeners, the pilgrims evoke the theological metaphor of members of church as an aggregate human form with Christ as its head.[138] The church's universality is suggested by the diverse dress of the seated figures, some of whom wear eastern-style turbans. Yet four men stand apart from Christ's followers, three of whom are dressed as Turks. Isolated in their own discussion, they fold their arms, frown, and gesture toward Christ, registering scepticism about his message.

Stationary in the midst of their animate surroundings, the sceptics stand parallel to a broken tree trunk at the far left of the picture. The dead tree, which is the same height as the men, figures their spiritual lifelessness. Next to the lifeless wood, a robust tree flourishes. The contrasting trees form an Edenic motif common in Netherlandish art, with the dead tree symbolizing the Tree of Knowledge and the living tree symbolizing the Tree of Life.[139] The tall trunk of the living tree parallels the ship's masts. Its spreading branches are balanced by the wooden rigging that frames Christ's figure and foreshadows his death on the cross. Visual correspondences between the tree and the ship evoke the exegetical identification of the cross with the Tree of Life. The imagery alludes to the construal of Christ as the fruit of the Tree of Life, who remits Adam's sin of tasting the fruit of the Tree of Knowledge.[140] Swart's print presents viewers with the choice of faithlessness, which ends in death, or faithful following of Christ's teachings, which promises eternal life. _s

Cornelis Anthonisz. (1505–1553)
Deathbeds of the Righteous and Unrighteous
ca. 1550
Woodcut, 42.5 × 38 cm
Hollstein (Anthonisz.) 16
The British Museum, London, 1858,0417.1017

*C*ornelis Anthonisz.'s extensive woodcut oeuvre includes around twenty moralizing prints, only a few of which are overtly scriptural. One of these, the large two-block *Deathbeds of the Righteous and Unrighteous*, draws on the medieval subject of the "Art of Dying" (*Ars moriendi*) as well as the biblical Acts of Mercy. It is a close derivation, with some elaboration, of a much larger, eight-block woodcut of around 1540—a few years earlier than Cornelis's version—attributed to the German Jörg Breu the Younger.[141]

On a single extended bed lie, foot to foot, two dying men, recalling Christ's prophecy of the end of time: "on that night there will be two in one bed; one will be taken and the other left" (Luke 17:34). Cornelis extends this image by adducing Matthew 24:40–41 for the figures in the distant landscape at right and left: of two men in the field, one will be taken; of two women grinding meal, one will be taken. The unrighteous man on the bed at the right, holding one arm over his head, twists his face in despair. His other arm is pulled by a demon in the flames of hell, described in the inscription from Job 18:21: "such is the place of those who do not know God".[142] At his bedside stand Lady World (*Werelt*),[143] who has led him astray, and Death (*Doot*), who comes to claim his body as the demon claims his soul. At the left, the righteous man clasps

his hands in prayer, surrounded by Love (*Liefde*), Faith (*Geloof*), and Hope (*Hope*). Above him, an angel labeled Grace (*Gratie*) holds a laurel wreath for him. The righteous man looks up to Christ sitting in judgment. Depicted in roundels to either side of Christ are the Six Acts (or Works) of Mercy—feeding the hungry, giving drink to the thirsty, welcoming strangers, clothing the naked, caring for the sick, and visiting the imprisoned—which, along with the angel below Christ separating sheep from goats, are drawn from Matthew 25:31–46 and are often associated with the Last Judgment.[144] Beyond the Acts of Mercy are angels holding symbols of judgment: on the left, above the righteous man, a lily denoting grace; on the right, above the unrighteous man, a sword denoting justice.

The image of a dying man lying on a bed flanked by other figures bears a striking resemblance to fifteenth-century German and Netherlandish illustrations of the *Ars moriendi*, a medieval treatise on the means to die well.[145] Most of the illustrations correspond to the part of the treatise devoted to a discussion of five temptations with which the devil confronts the dying man—Infidelity, Despair, Impatience, Vainglory, and Avarice—and how to meet them. But Cornelis's woodcut is concerned more directly with the lives led by the dying men, contrasting a pious and generous life, in which the acts of mercy were performed, with a selfish life indulging in the pleasures of the world. Although the acts of mercy were scriptural and thus not evidently either

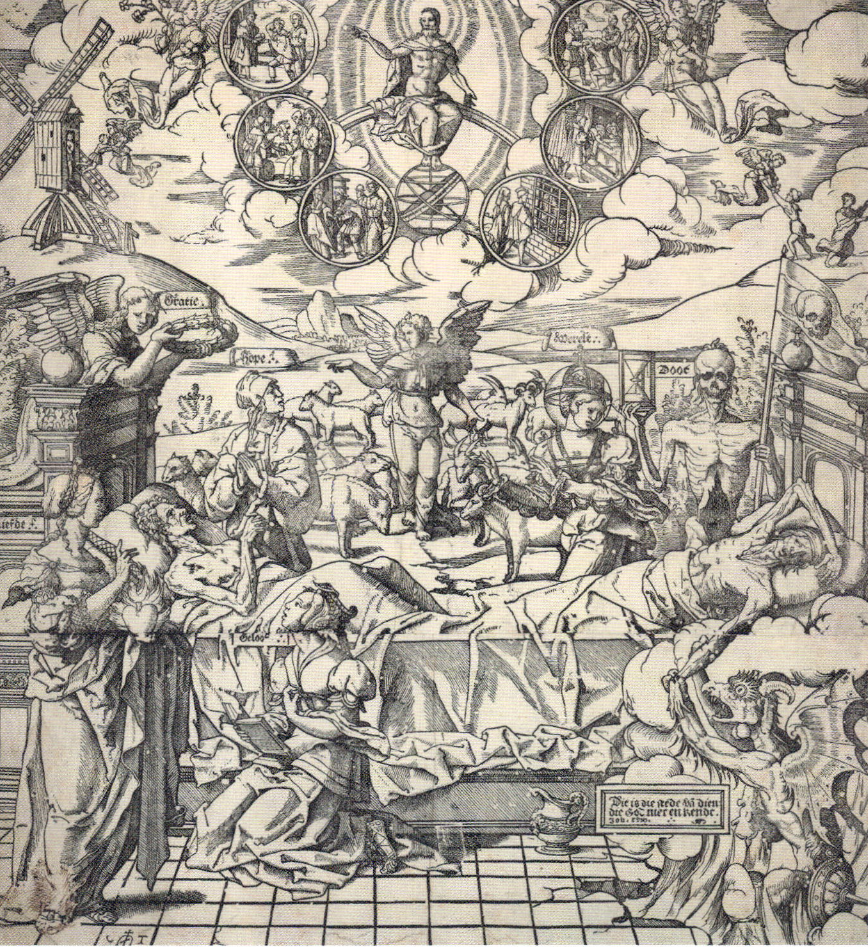

33

Catholic or Protestant, the emphasis on good works was more amenable to Catholics. Calvin, by contrast, took a position more extreme than that of Lutherans, countering the traditional import of the text by arguing that "even in these very passages where the Holy Spirit promises everlasting glory as a reward for works, by expressly terming it an 'inheritance' he is showing that it comes to us from another source. So Christ enumerates the works, which he repays with the reward of heaven, in calling the elect into possession of it; but at the same time he adds that they must possess it by right of inheritance."[146]   JC

Gratie
Hope .I.
Werelt
Doot
Liefde .L.
Geloof
Dit is die stede va dien
die Got niet en kende.
Job. rviij.

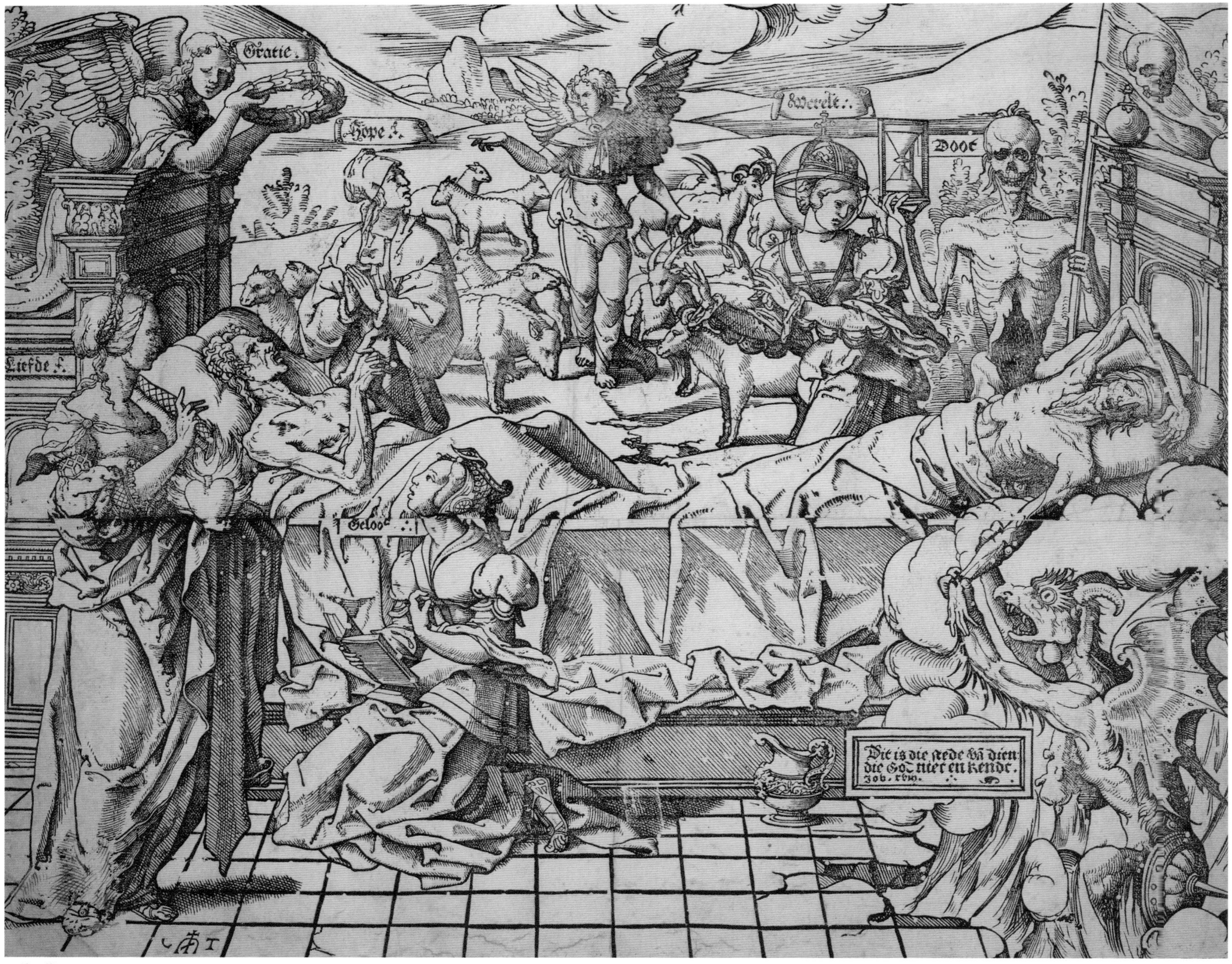

33 (detail)

Dirck Volckertsz. Coornhert (1522–90)
After Maarten van Heemskerck (1498–1574)
The Last Judgment
From *The Last Judgment and the Six Works of Mercy*
ca. 1552
Engraving, 25.8 × 19.3 cm
New Hollstein (Van Heemskerck) 330
Rijksmuseum, Amsterdam, RP-P-BI-6491X

Dirck Volckertsz. Coornhert (1522–90)
After Maarten van Heemskerck (1498–1574)
Feeding the Hungry
From *The Last Judgment and the Six Works of Mercy*
ca. 1552
Engraving, 25.5 × 19.2 cm
New Hollstein (Van Heemskerck) 331
Rijksmuseum, Amsterdam, RP-P-BI-6492X

*E*ngraved after drawings by Maarten van Heemskerck, the two prints are taken from a series of seven. The doctrine and iconographic depiction of the Last Judgment and Six Works of Mercy are drawn from the parable of The Sheep and the Goats (Matthew 25:31–46), in which judgment is entirely based on help given or refused to "the least of these."

"When the Son of Man comes in His glory all the nations will be gathered before Him, and He will separate people one from another as a shepherd separates the sheep from the goats, and He will put the sheep at his right hand and the goats at the left. Then the king will say to those at His right hand, 'Come, you that are blessed by my Father, inherit the kingdom prepared for you… For I was hungry and you gave me food, I was thirsty and you gave me something to drink… Truly I tell you, just as you did it to one of the least of these who are members of my family, you did it to me.' Then He will say to those at His left hand, 'You that are accursed, depart from me into the eternal fire prepared for the devil and his angels; for I was hungry and you gave me no food, I was thirsty and you gave me nothing to drink… Truly I tell you, just as you did not do it to one of the least of these, you did not do it to me.'"

The six works of mercy, therefore, are good deeds that the faithful must perform for others during their lifetime in order to gain a place in heaven. The six works are: providing for the hungry, providing for the thirsty, clothing the naked, taking in the stranger, ministering to the sick, and comforting those in prison (see also cat. 33).

In *The Last Judgment*, Christ Pantocrator sits on his heavenly throne surrounded by angels and dispenses judgment upon the saved and the damned. In the foreground, three classical figures are thrown to the ground and hide their faces, referring to Revelation 20:11: "And I saw a great white throne, and him that sat on it, from whose face the earth and the heaven fled away." On the left, the devil leads those who are rejected into hell, and on the right angels lead the blessed to their heavenly kingdom. In the middle, between the two men in the foreground, a figure is shown rising up out of the earth. This

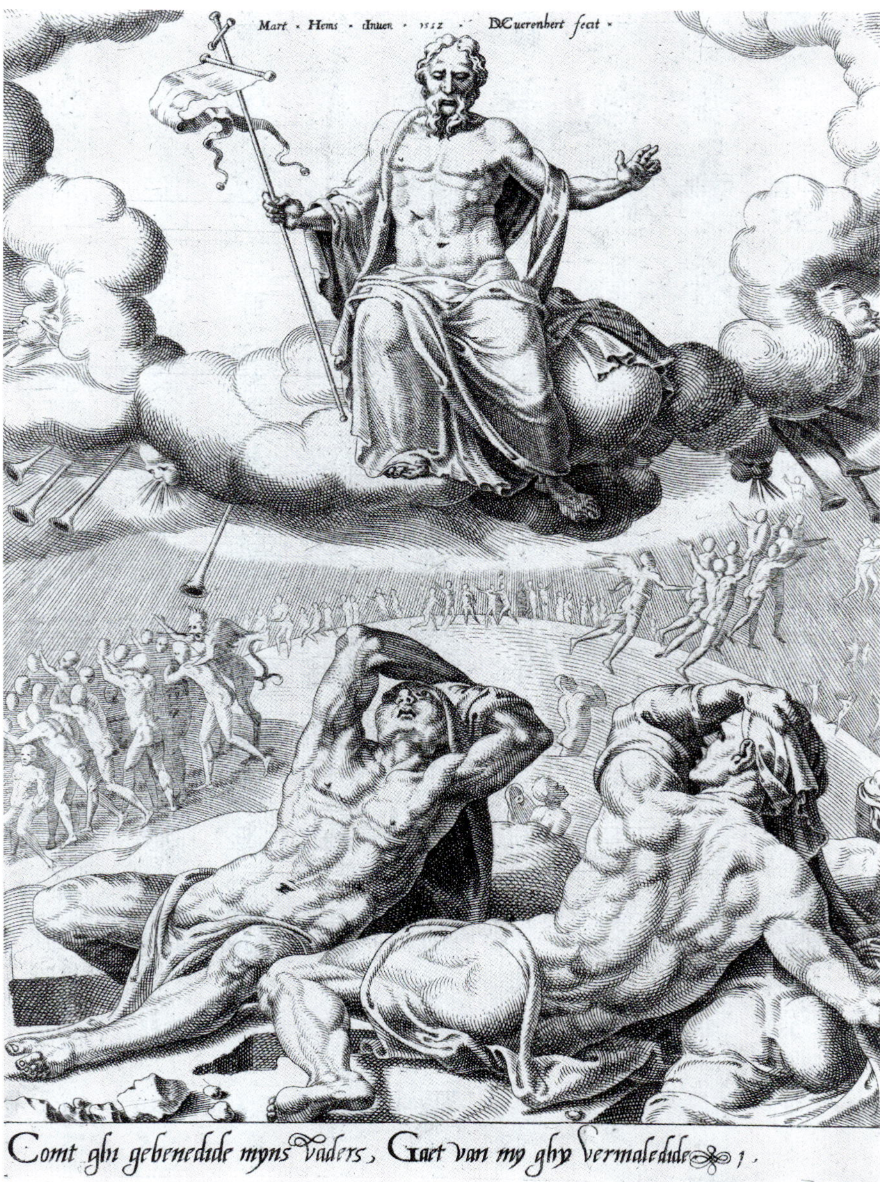

34a

illustrates the Christian belief that there will be a general resurrection of the dead at "the end of time," as prophesied by the apostle Paul when he said, "…he hath appointed a day, in which he will judge the world…" (Acts 17:31) and "…there shall be a resurrection of the dead, both of the just and unjust" (Acts 24:15). In *Feeding the Hungry*, Christ, who stands behind the crowd on the right with a halo of light around his head, looks on as a group of people provide food to the hungry. The young man in the center turns his head to the right and visually emphasizes the separated group of people in the background, who refuse to aid "the least of these." TR

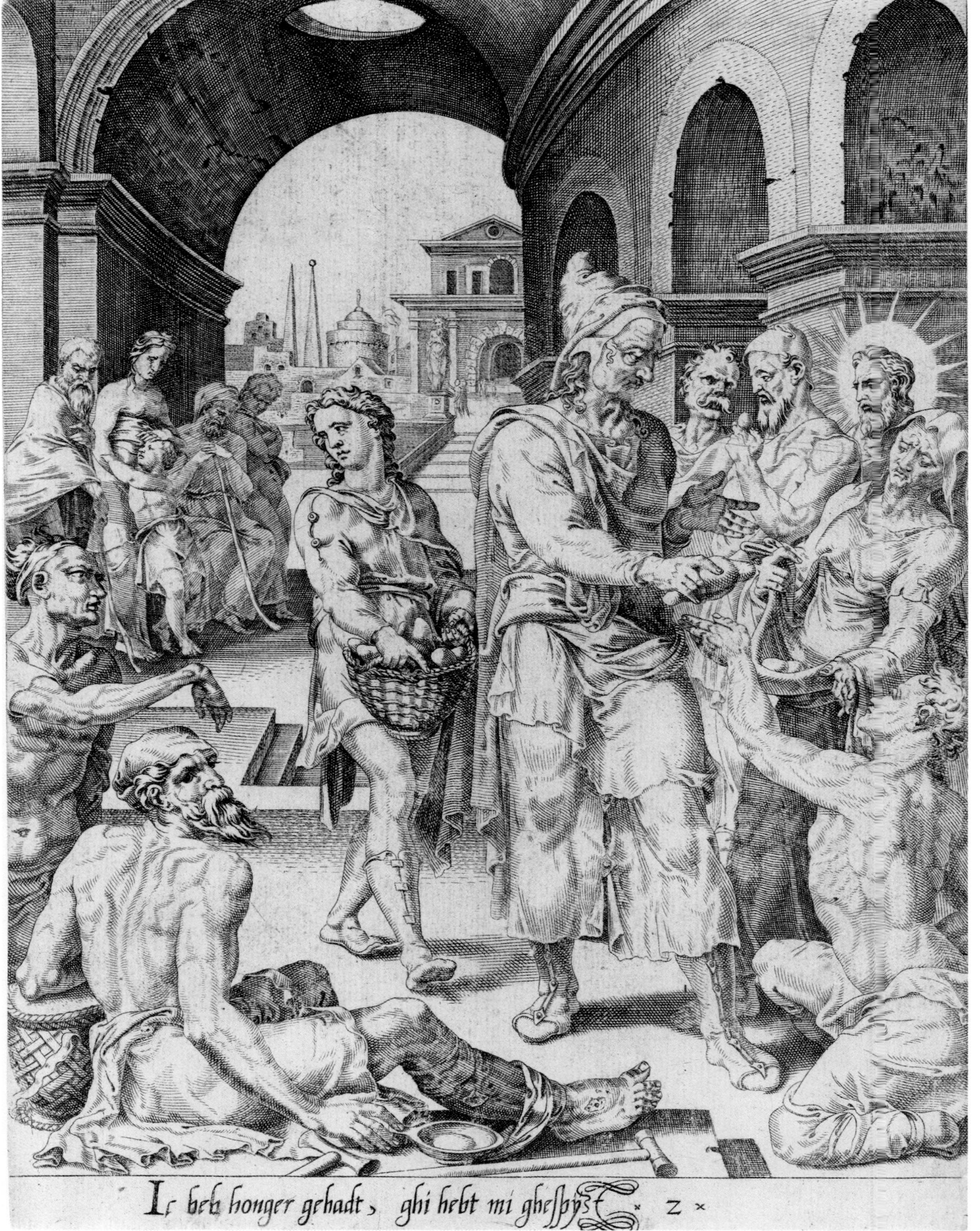

34b

35

Pieter van der Borcht (ca. 1535–1608)
Christ in the House of Martha and Mary
ca. 1590
Etching and engraving, 22.2 × 28.5 cm
New Hollstein (Van der Borcht) 78
Rijksmuseum, Amsterdam, RP-P-1891-A-16313

*S*et within a sixteenth-century domestic interior, the print depicts the story of Christ visiting the home of Martha and Mary. As Luke 10:38–42 tells it, as soon as Christ entered, Mary immediately sat at his feet listening to his teaching. Martha, on the other hand, was distracted by all the preparations that needed to be made. Annoyed by her sister's refusal to help, Martha turned to Jesus and said, "Lord, don't you care that my sister has left me to do the work by myself? Tell her to help me!" Jesus' response, which is written in Latin in the lower margin of the print, was rather to reprimand Martha: "Martha, Martha, you are worried and upset about many things, but only one thing is needed. Mary has chosen what is better, and it will not be taken away from her." Where one focuses his or her attention, therefore, conveys one's priorities and Jesus makes it clear that Mary, not Martha, is the one whose attention is focused in the right direction.

Similar to paintings of the subject by Pieter Aertsen and Joachim Beuckelaer, the design of the print poses a similar question to the viewer. In the foreground, three women are busy preparing a meal in the kitchen. One tends to a pot over a blazing fire, while two others prepare the fish to be cooked. The room itself and the activity in it, especially the raucous scene of the boy chasing the dog chasing the cat

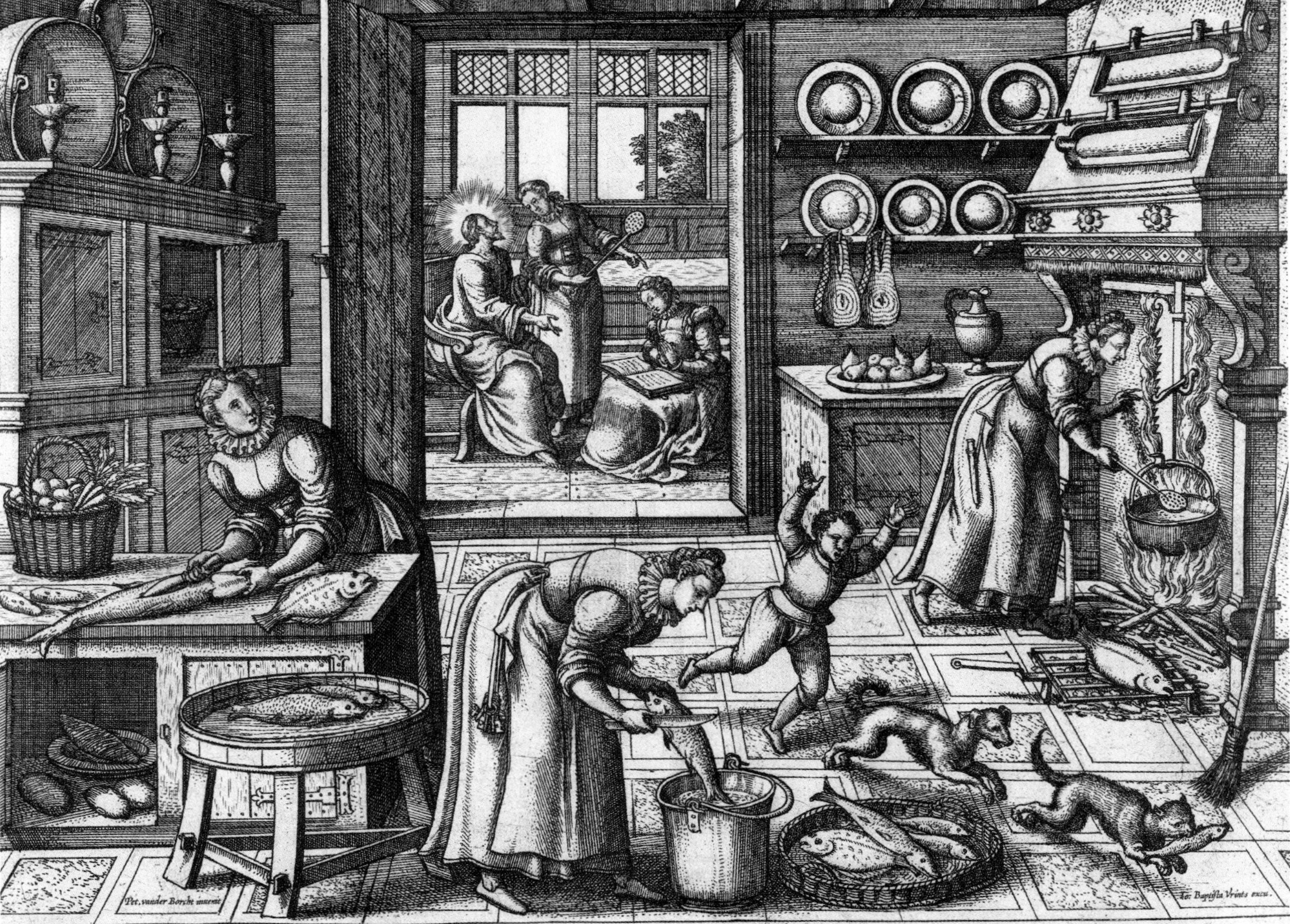

35

with a fish in its mouth, encourage the viewer to pan the space and fix on the activity unfolding. After a closer look, however, the viewer discovers the background vignette that depicts the moment when Christ explains to the distracted Martha that it is Mary, with her hands folded and a book in her lap, who is more devout. To see through to the religious scene in the background, then, the viewer, like Mary, must forego the distracting activity in the foreground and focus his or her attention on "the one thing that is needed."[147]   TR

Philips Galle (1537–1612)

After Pieter Bruegel the Elder (ca. 1525/30–1569)

The Parable of the Wise and Foolish Virgins

ca. 1560–63

Engraving, 22.2 × 22.8 cm

New Hollstein (Galle) 147

The Metropolitan Museum of Art, New York

Designed by Pieter Bruegel the Elder and engraved by Philips Galle, the print portrays one of three parables told by Jesus, including the Parable of the Talents and The Sheep and the Goats, to illustrate the unknown hour of his Second Coming, or Last Judgment, and the diligence that should be paid in keeping a watchful eye. In the parable, ten virgins are given the honor of attending a wedding. When they go outside to wait for the bridegroom, five wise virgins are prepared for his delayed arrival because they bring with them jars of oil for their lamps. The other, foolish virgins are not prepared because they did not bring the necessary extra oil and their lamps burn out. When the bridegroom arrives, they are away buying more oil and, thus, are excluded from the ceremony. The groom is clearly a metaphor for Jesus and the wedding banquet is heaven. Similar to the two other parables told in the same chapter, the story has a clear apocalyptic theme: be prepared for the day of reckoning.

The image depicts the moment of the bridegroom's arrival and is divided into four quadrants. The lower half is demarcated by clouds and three angels. The center angel bears a scroll with a Latin text that reads: "Look! Here is the bridegroom! Come out to meet him! (Matthew 25:6)"[148] The two angels on either side blow the trumpets of doom. In the lower left, five

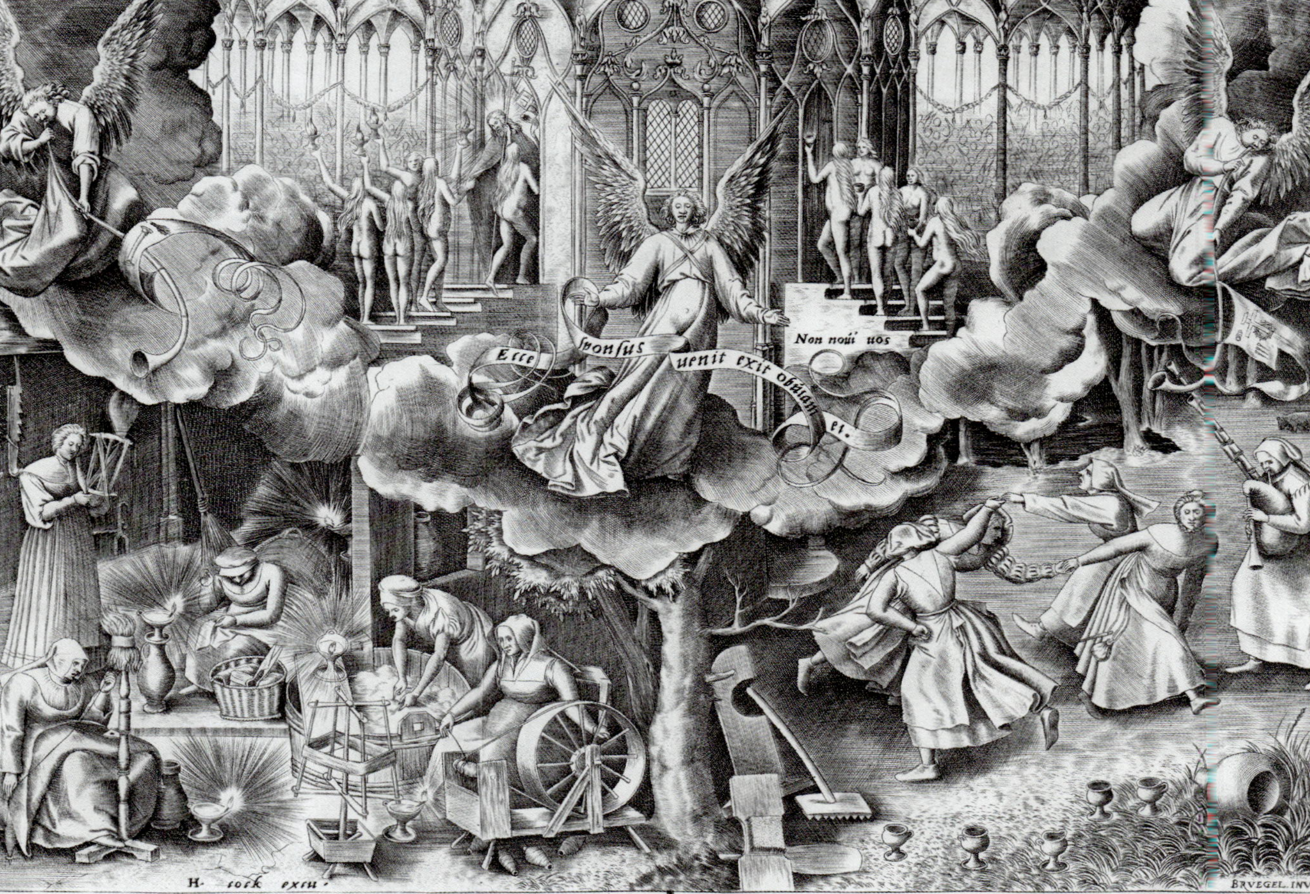

36

"wise" virgins are busy at work preparing themselves for the bridegroom; their lamps are filled with oil and their flames shine bright. In the lower right, five "foolish" virgins dance to the tune of a bagpipe, often a symbol of folly in sixteenth-century Netherlandish art. They are carefree and unconcerned with preparing themselves for the impending wedding, as is indicated by the neglected lamps lying empty in the grass in the foreground. The two scenes are separated by a tree whose branches on the left, the side of the wise virgins, blossom with leaves, while those on the right, the side of the foolish virgins, are barren.

The upper portion portrays the culmination of the story, when the bridegroom arrives for the banquet. On the central angel's right, traditionally the blessed side, the five wise virgins hold their illuminated lamps high and Christ meets them at the door to invite them into the ceremony, a heavenly realm represented by Gothic church-like architecture. On the angel's left, traditionally the side of the damned, the five foolish virgins climb the stairs holding their empty lamps; they are met only by a closed door and are denied access to the festivities inside. Engraved on the steps below them, a Latin text reads: "I know you not" (Matthew 25:12).

Bruegel departs from the biblical story, in which we are told that the virgins had all fallen asleep when the bridegroom arrived, by depicting the blessed as diligent laborers and the foolish as squandering their time. This type of representation became popular in sixteenth-century Netherlandish prints, when humanist literature and moral guidebooks increasingly contrasted the virtue of Labor and the vice of Sloth.[149]   TR

Philips Galle (1537–1612)

The Idler Refuses to Work during Harvest Time

From *The Idler's Punishment*

ca. 1565

Engraving, 20.8 × 24.9 cm

New Hollstein (Galle) 67

Museum Plantin-Moretus/Prentenkabinet,
Antwerp–UNESCO World Heritage,
Inv. No. OP 13544, Cat. No. III/598

Philips Galle (1537–1612)

The Idler Chased Away from the Table of Those Who Have Worked

From *The Idler's Punishment*

ca. 1565

Engraving, 20.9 × 25 cm

New Hollstein (Galle) 68

Museum Plantin-Moretus/Prentenkabinet,
Antwerp–UNESCO World Heritage,
Inv. No. OP 13546, Cat. No. III/599

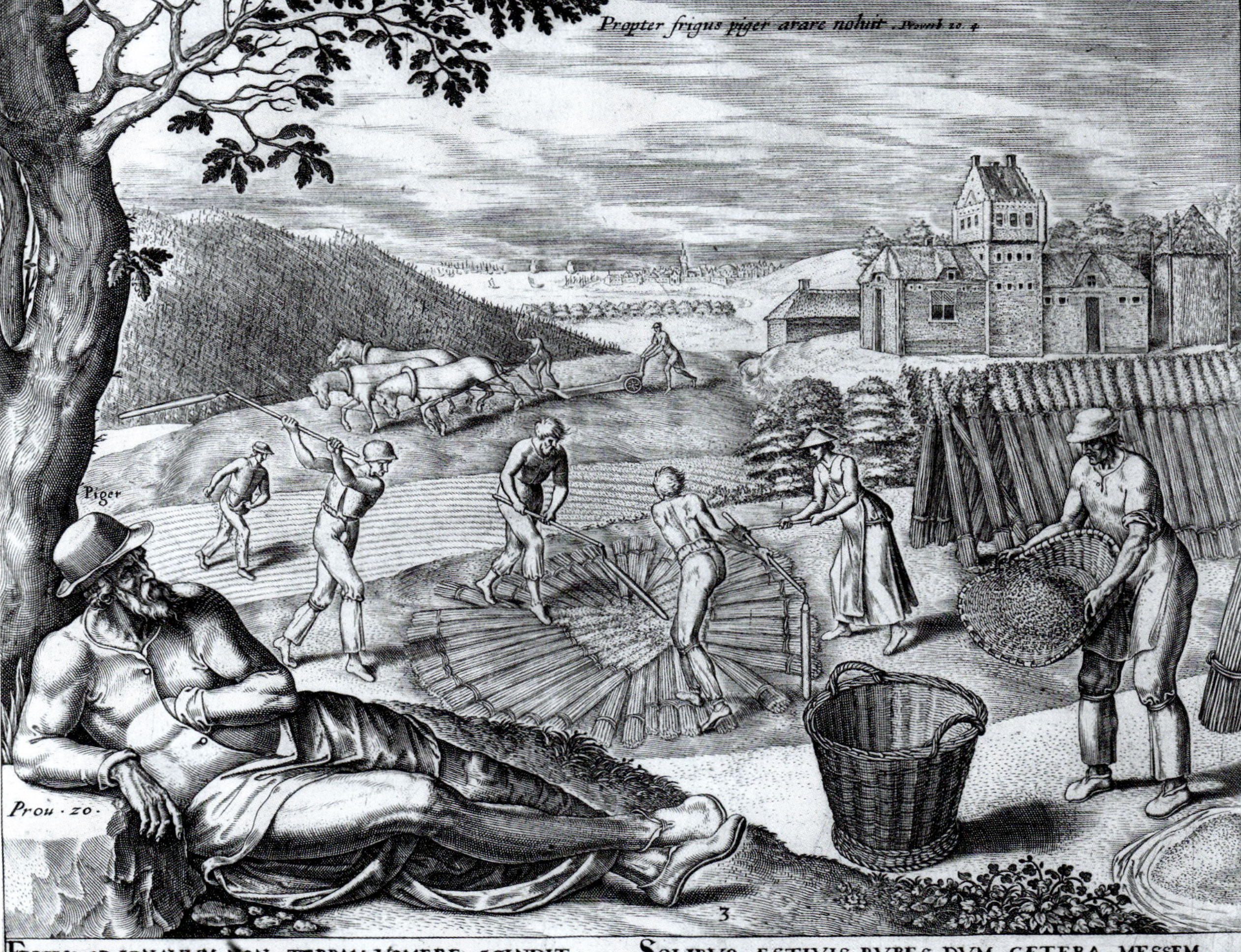

37a

*D*esigned by Philips Galle around 1565, *The Idler's Punishment* is a series of four numbered plates, all of which contain Latin verses in the lower margins written by Hadrianus Junius, a friend of Galle's.[150] The subject of the second print in the series, *The Idler Struck Down by Poverty and Want*, is taken from Proverbs 6:10–11: "A little sleep, a little slumber, a little folding of the hands to rest and poverty will come on you like a bandit and scarcity like an armed man." Because the sluggard has neglected his labors in the field, while others reap the harvest (illustrated in the first print), he is struck down by the personifications of Poverty (*Inopia*) and Want (*Egestas*).

In the third image, *The Idler Refuses to Work during Harvest Time*, the man continues his idleness in the field, illustrating Proverbs 20:4: "A sluggard does not plow in season; so at harvest time he looks but finds nothing." While he lounges in the shade of a tree on the left, the figure on the right shows the inside of a basket that is empty. The moral of the story is made explicit in the final print, *The Idler Chased Away from the Table of Those Who Have Worked*: the sluggard, obliged to beg, is chased away from the table of his neighbors who, unlike him, have worked for their daily bread. It is a poignant illustration of 2 Thessalonians 3:10: "If any should not work, neither should he eat."

In the mid-sixteenth-century Netherlands, the proponents of both the emerging capitalist economic system and the strong work ethic embedded in Calvinism held high regard for those who were diligent laborers. In contrast, those who were able, yet chose not to work, were treated with disdain. Whereas almsgiving and good works for the poor had been religious obligations during the Middle Ages, Galle's print series shows clearly that during this period people did not feel the need to offer charity to those who were able to work, but did not. The belief that idlers were potential criminals who should be set to work is expressed in Dirk Volckertsz. Coornhert's treatise *Boeventucht ofte middelen tot mindering der schadelyke ledighghangers* (The Correction of Knaves, or Ways of Reducing the Numbers of Harmful Loiterers), written in 1567. Coornhert links poverty and crime, and calls for the establishment of workhouses, something that would emerge in Amsterdam toward the end of the century: "for if able-bodied beggars receive sustenance rather than punishment, the country will soon be full of scoundrels who will plague the righteous with theft, pillage and murder."[151] TR

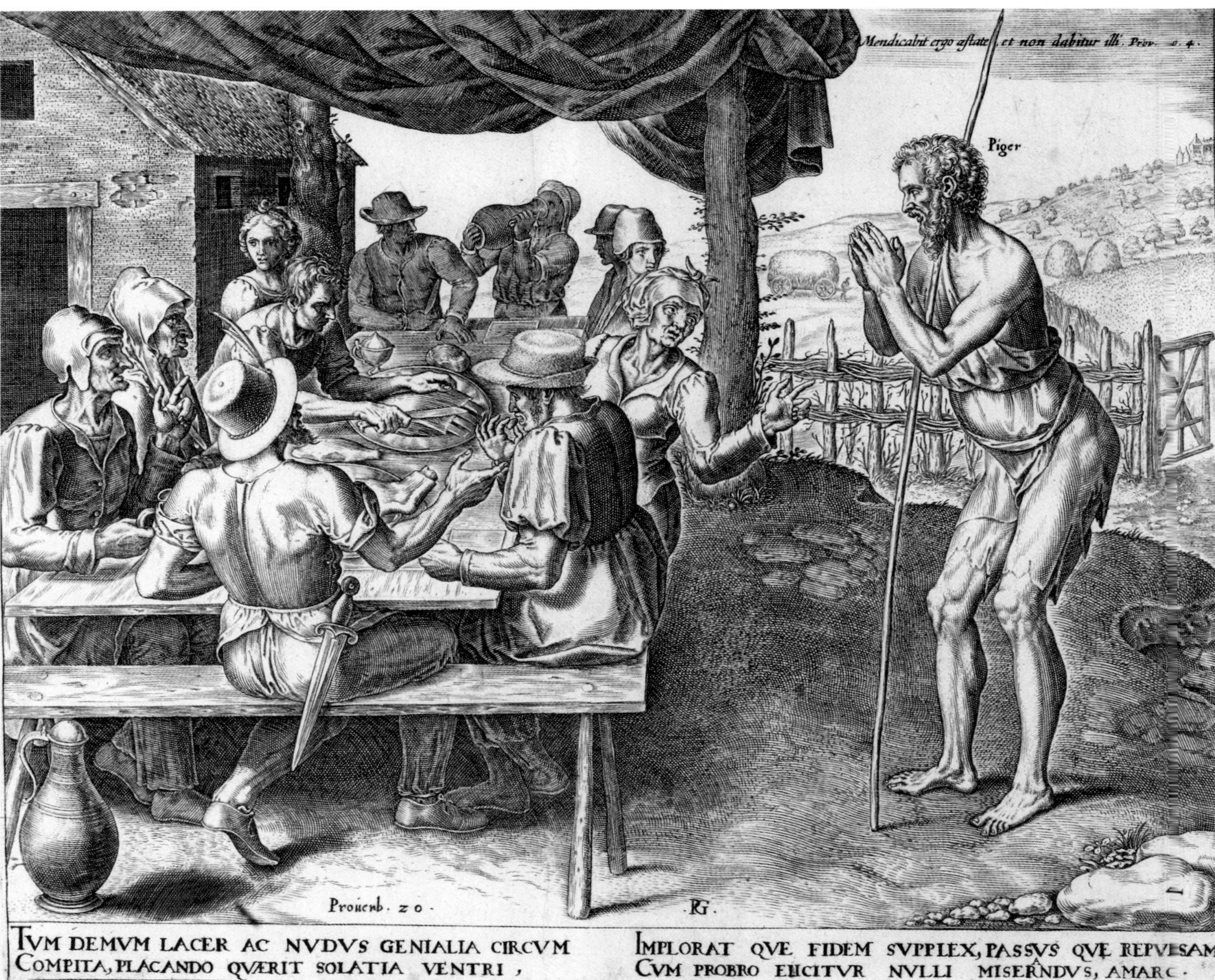

37b

38

Philips Galle (1537–1612)

Correcting Sinners (Peccantes Corrigere)

1577

From *The Seven Spiritual Works of Mercy*
(Septem opera misericordiae spiritalia)

Engraving, 26.0 × 19.0 cm

New Hollstein (Galle) 250

Museum Plantin-Moretus/Prentenkabinet,
Antwerp–UNESCO World Heritage,
Inv. No. OP 12223, Cat. No. III/G.576

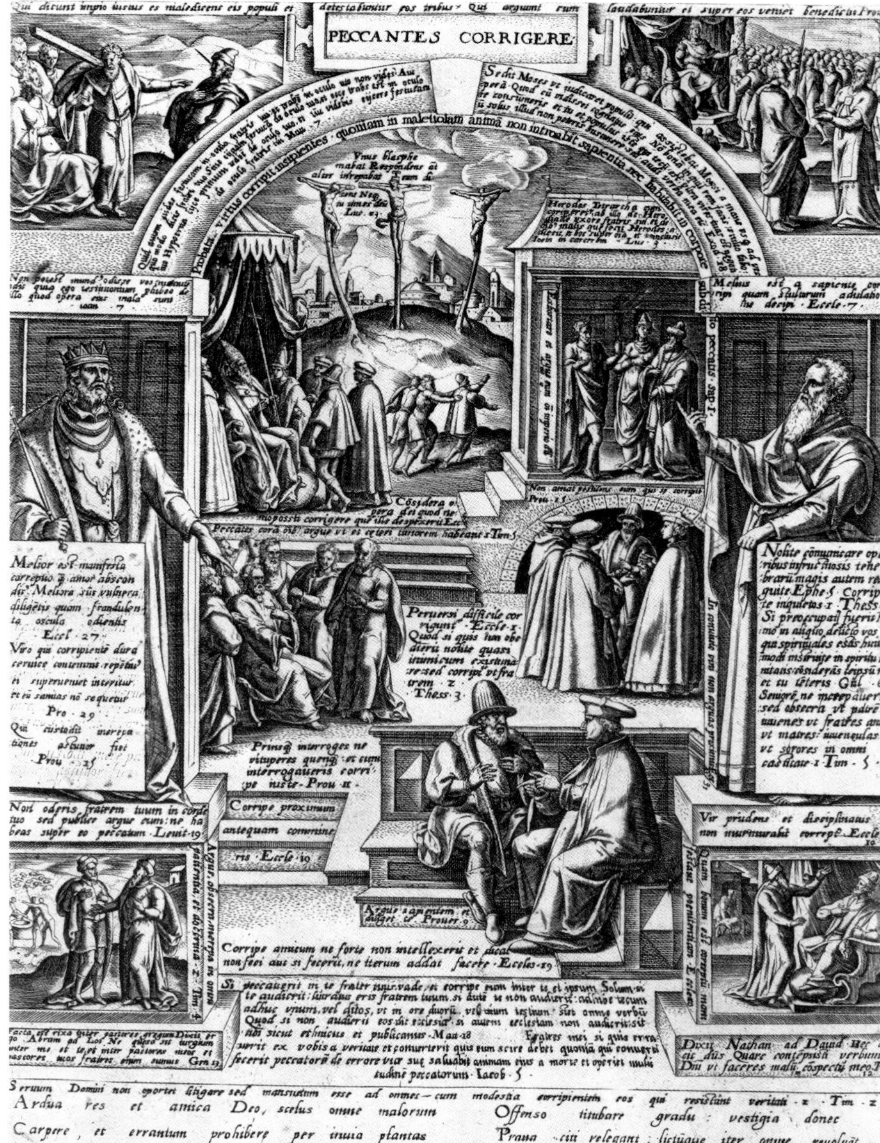

Like Philips Galle's *Baptism* (cat. 25), *Correcting Sinners* is part of his three series from 1576–77 that comprise compositions dense with narrative vignettes and mostly biblical texts, not all of which are illustrated. The subject of one of Galle's series, the *Seven Corporal Works of Mercy*, was frequently depicted (see, for example, cat 33, 34), but the parallel series, *The Seven Spiritual Works of Mercy*, from which *Correcting Sinners* is drawn, is rarely met. The Seven Spiritual Works of Mercy are to instruct the ignorant, to counsel the doubtful, to correct sinners, to bear wrongs patiently, to forgive offences willingly, to comfort the afflicted, and to pray for the living and the dead. Unlike the Corporal Works, the Spiritual Works, which were codified in the thirteenth century, derived from diverse passages in the Bible, not all of them spoken by Christ.[152]

Like the other works in Galle's series of 1576–77, *Correcting Sinners* is structured with two biblical authorities—in this instance Solomon and Paul—flanking and pointing toward several biblical and contemporary scenes visible through the arched opening on which they stand. Further scenes appear on the corners of the arch. The print is filled with rebukes, among them: in the background, one thief on the cross chastises the other for deriding Christ and not fearing God (Luke 23:39–41); at the lower right, Nathan, filled with righteous anger that David killed the husband of Bathsheba in order to take her for himself, asks, "Why therefore has thou despised the word of the Lord, to do evil in my sight?" (2 Kings 12:9). More general statements accompany figures in contemporary dress, such as the two figures at the lower center, one of whom admonishes the other according to Ecclesiasticus 19:13: "Reprove a friend, lest he may not have understood, and say: I did it not: or if he did it, that he may do it no more."

The non-biblical inscription below the image proclaims that it is a lofty (or difficult) thing, favorable to God, to decry every impious act, to prevent the errant from straying into the wilderness. But the print also problematizes over-zealous or misguided attempts at correction. As Ecclesiastes 7:14, quoted in the center of the image, darkly instructs: "Consider the works of God, that no man can correct whom he hath despised."[153] The vignette at the upper left of the image illustrates Christ's warning against hypocritical judgment: "first take the log out of your own eye, and then you will see clearly to take the speck out of your neighbor's eye" (Matthew 7:5).

In spite of the seemingly severe subject of the print, it carries suggestions of the tolerance and peacemaking that sometimes mark the works of Galle and others in the late sixteenth-century Netherlands. One of the inscriptions in the center of the print, for example, comes from Paul's third letter to the Thessalonians, wherein he urged his readers to avoid anyone who did not heed his word, "Yet do not esteem him as an enemy, but admonish him as a brother" (v. 15). In the lower left of the print, because the land could not support the herds and flocks of both Abraham and his brother Lot, and strife had arisen between their followers, Abraham tells Lot, "Let there be no quarrel, I beseech thee, between me and thee, and between my herdsmen and thy herdsmen: for we are brethren" (Genesis 13:8).   JC

Philips Galle (1537–1612)
After Anthonie van Blocklandt (1533/4–83)
Christ and the Samaritan Woman at the Well
From *Christ and Women from the Gospels*
ca. 1577–79
Engraving, 21 × 25.9 cm
New Hollstein (Galle) 159
The British Museum, London, 1868,0612.437

Christ and Women from the Gospels is a series of prints that Philips Galle engraved after designs by Anthonie van Blocklandt. The first of these prints is *Christ and the Samaritan Woman at the Well*. Galle's inscription relates that Christ asked a Samaritan woman to give him a drink of water from a well.[154] In the gospel account, the stranger asked why a Jew should ask a Samaritan for a drink. He responded, "Whosoever drinketh of this water, shall thirst again; but he that shall drink of the water I will give him, shall not thirst for ever" (John 4:13). When she asked Christ for this water, he told her to bring her husband to the well. She replied that she had no husband. Christ then said that previously she had had five husbands, to which she remarked that he must be a prophet. Christ identified himself as the Messiah, whereupon the woman, believing in him, spread the news to her countrymen.

In Galle's picture, this biblical narrative is enacted by elegant mannerist figures placed in frieze-like arrangements against a landscape setting. Onlookers focus attention to the center of the composition, where Christ and the woman interact. Responsive poses and dynamic gestures invest their exchanges with visual tension. The pictorial synergy of the image signals the mystical union between

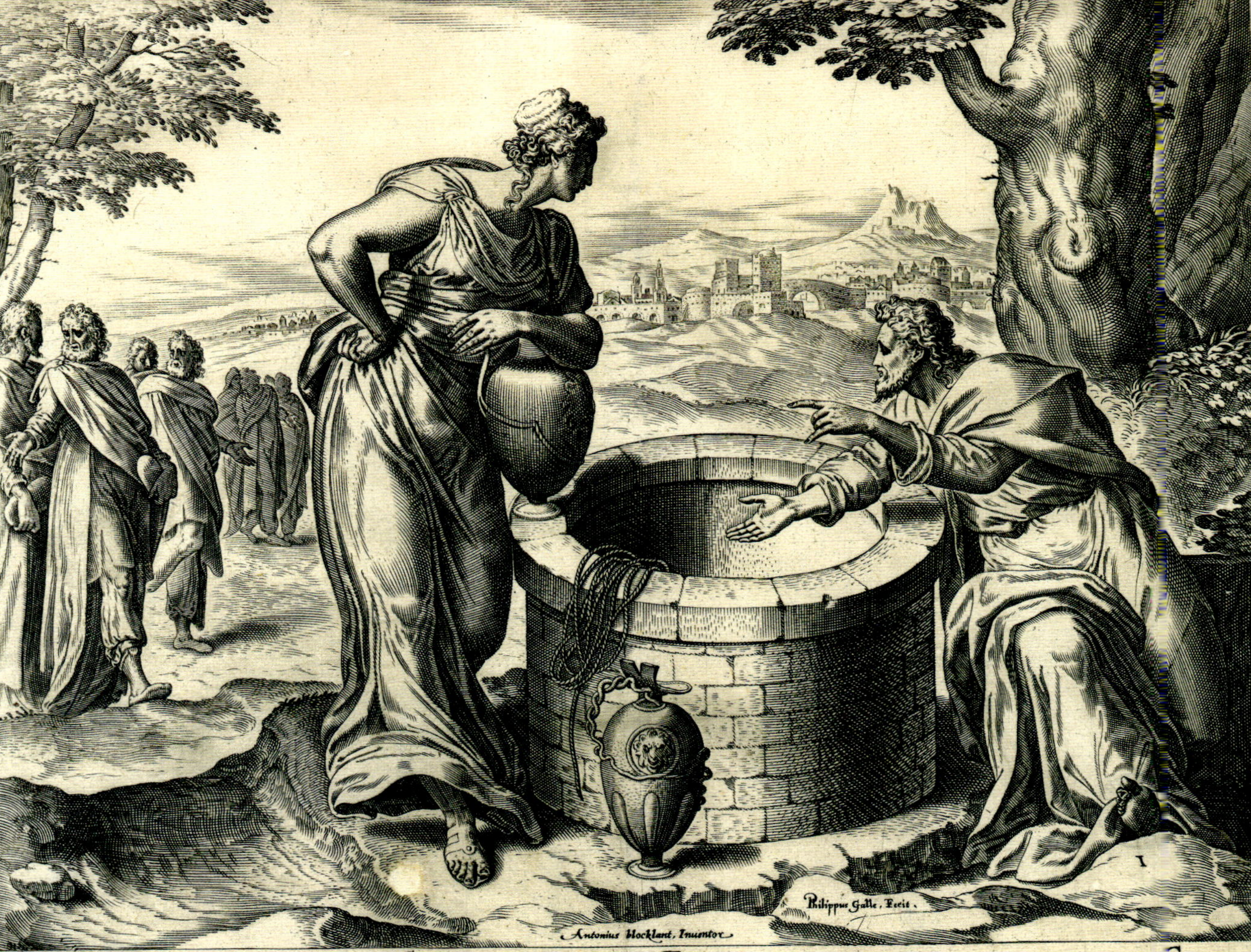

39

Christ and the woman, whom Augustine designated as a type for the Church. Augustine asserted that the Samaritan woman, a foreigner to the Jews, prefigured the Church, which would be born of the Gentiles.[155] He elaborated that, when Christ bid her to call her husband, he referred to himself, revealing that he was already the soul's bridegroom. Augustine identified the water offered by Christ as the sacramental fountain of everlasting life and he compared the Samaritan woman's agency in spreading the faith to the clergy's preaching of the Gospels. Galle's prints present the women of the gospels as models for the faithful to emulate, in striving toward union with Christ through the ministry of the Church.   JS

Hendrick Goltzius (1558–1617)
The Eight Beatitudes
ca. 1578
Engraving, 23.2 × 18.2 cm
Strauss 29
The Metropolitan Museum of Art, New York

Hendrick Goltzius's *Eight Beatitudes* (*Octo Beatitudines*) is composed in the same format used by the young artist for other prints executed for, or under the aegis of, the printmaker/publisher Philips Galle in Haarlem around 1578, consisting of a central image framed by vignettes illustrating Bible passages, as in Goltzius's *Dissent in the Church* (cat. 51). Here the main scene is of Christ preaching to a crowd gathered around him; the subsidiary scenes illustrate the Beatitudes articulated at the beginning of his Sermon on the Mount (Matthew 5:3–10), supplemented by images of the four Evangelists at the corners. The eight Beatitudes begin at the upper left and proceed counter-clockwise. The inscriptions reproduce the text of the Beatitudes, but the images exemplifying them are drawn from elsewhere in the Bible. They are not identified, and the viewer would be presumed to recognize them. For "Blessed are the meek, for they will inherit the earth" at the lower left, for example, Goltzius shows the woman described as a sinner in Luke 7:36–50 (traditionally identified as Mary Magdalen) bathing Christ's feet with her tears and drying them with her hair. Across from this scene, illustrating "Blessed are the pure in heart, for they will see God," is the Annunciation, with the dove of the Holy Spirit hovering over

Mary, who kneels as she is approached by the angel telling her that she will bear a son, Jesus, who will be called the Son of God (Luke 1:26–39). Above that, the peacemaker of the seventh Beatitude is Abigail, wife of Nabal, who appeases David and defuses the threat of violence with the offer of a feast (1 Samuel 25). At the upper right, the stoning of the proto-Apostle, Stephen (Acts 7:58–60), exemplifies the final Beatitude: "Blessed are those who are persecuted for righteousness's sake, for theirs is the kingdom of heaven."

The theme of persecution is continued in the following verse, when Christ shifts to a second-person address. It informs Goltzius's entire print, appearing as the larger inscription at the bottom: "Blessed are you when people revile you and persecute you and utter all kinds of evil against you falsely on my account. Rejoice and be glad, for your reward is great in heaven" (Matthew 5:11). The theme of religious persecution resonated during the confessional conflicts in the Netherlands in the later sixteenth century, and, like the *Dissent in the Church*, Goltzius's *Eight Beatitudes* may have been occasioned by events such as the violence against Catholics in St. Bavo's Church in Haarlem on 29 May 1578.[156]   JC

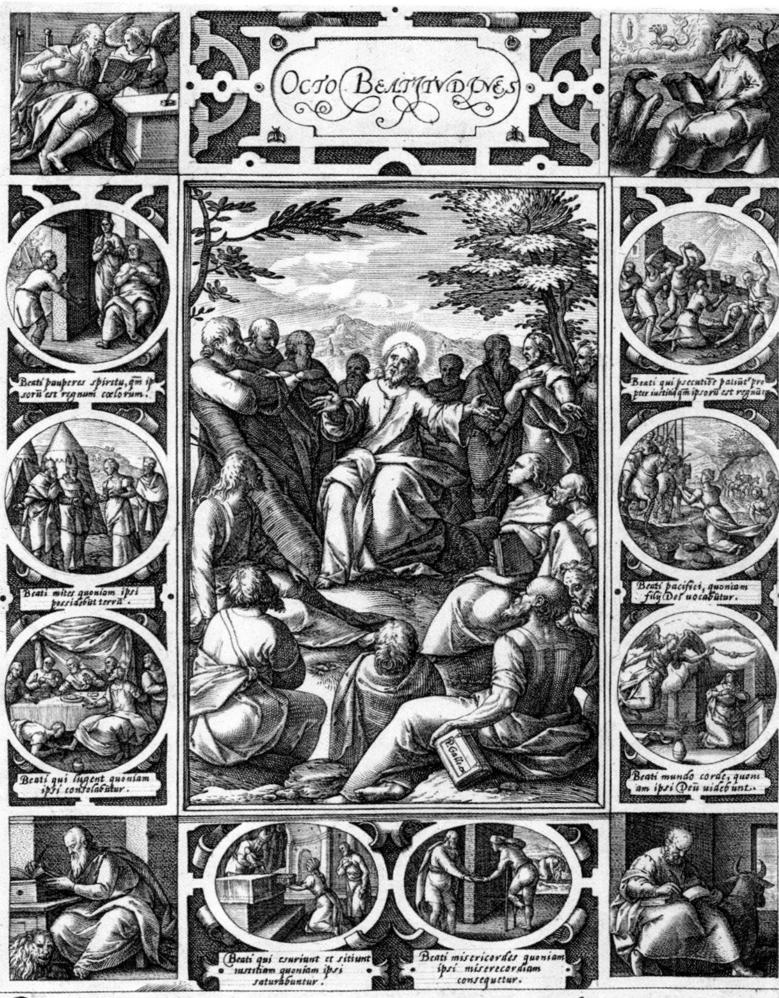

40

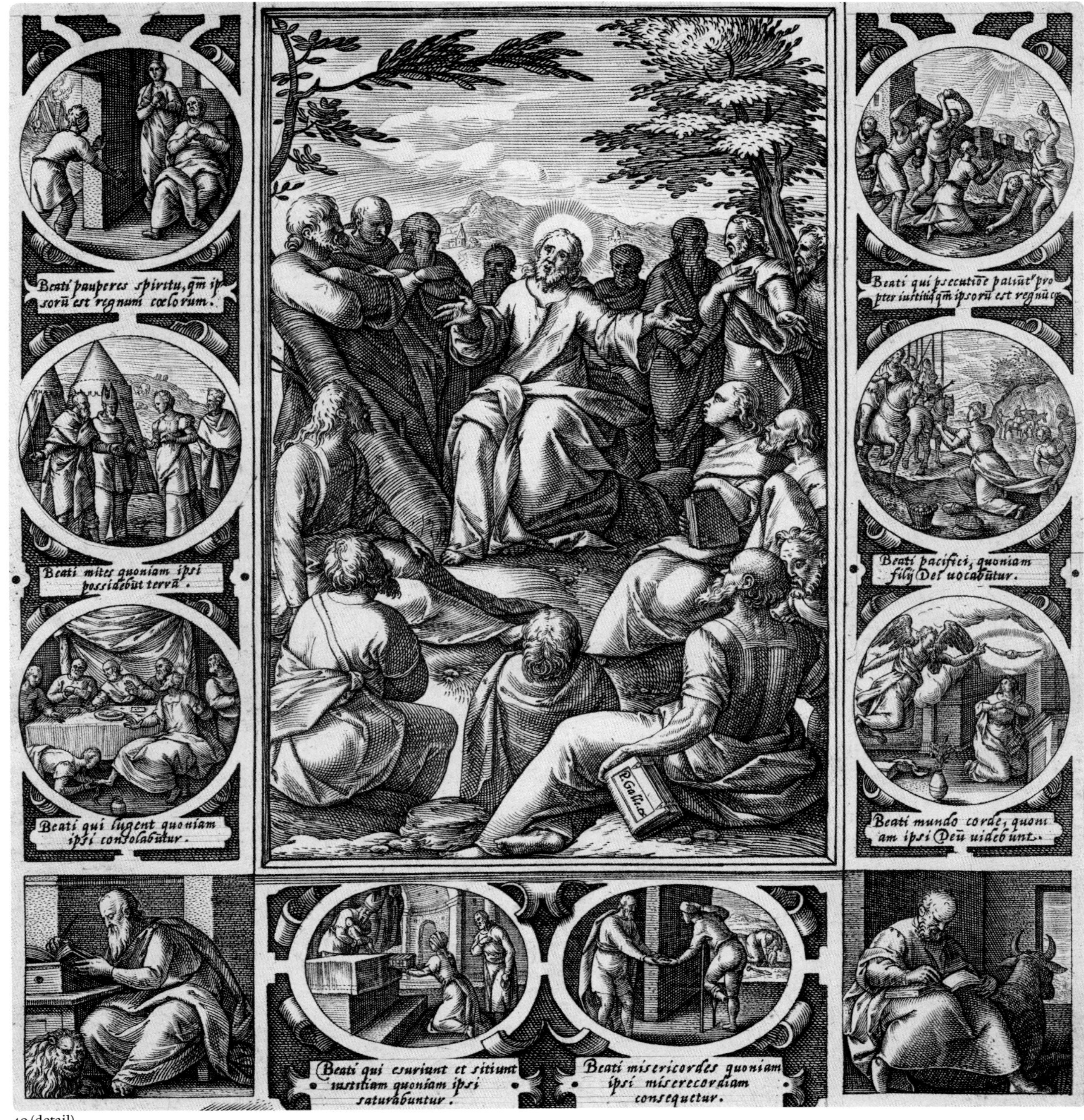
Beati pauperes spiritu, qm ipsoru est regnum coelorum.
Beati mites quoniam ipsi possidebut terra.
Beati qui lugent quoniam ipsi consolabuntur.
Beati qui psecutide paciut propter iustitia qm ipsoru est regnu cœ
Beati pacifici, quoniam filij Dei uocabutur.
Beati mundo corde, quoniam ipsi Deu uidebunt.
Beati qui esuriunt et sitiunt iustitiam quoniam ipsi saturabuntur.
Beati misericordes quoniam ipsi misericordiam consequetur.

40 (detail)

*A*ntoon Wierix's series of the Eight Beatitudes represents each Beatitude with an allegorical image rather than a biblical narrative, as in Hendrick Goltzius's roughly contemporaneous print (cat. 40). These small, delicate engravings are sacred emblems, a term that has been used broadly since the sixteenth century, but now refers most often to symbolic religious images combined with text.[157] Such emblems, often published by the score and even hundreds in books, were extremely popular from the second half of the sixteenth century to well past the end of the seventeenth century. In addition to *The Eight Beatitudes*, Antoon Wierix created numerous emblems on religious and moral subjects.[158]

Each of Wierix's emblems in this series consists of the biblical text of the Beatitude inscribed at the bottom of the image, an animal or heart occupying the central area, and a banderole with a related text toward the top, which explicates, reinforces, or paraphrases the scriptural passage. Each of these texts is taken from Augustine's homily on Christ's Sermon on the Mount, which was well known throughout the Middle Ages and early modern period, quoted by Thomas Aquinas and other theologians, and even excerpted in the Roman breviary.

Some of the emblems use more common imagery than others. The fifth plate, for example, *Blessed Are the Merciful, for They Will Receive Mercy* (Matthew 5:7), shows a pelican (albeit one born of the artist's fantasy rather than observation) that has plucked her own breast so that her children might feed from her blood. The pelican's supposed self-sacrifice was used already in the Early Christian *Physiologus*, and commonly throughout the medieval and early modern periods (by Dante, Shakespeare, and many others) as a metaphor for Christ's bloody sacrifice on the cross.[159] To each side of the pelican are lilies, which are here related to the mercy that Christ shows to the saved at the Last Judgment, in which scene his is sometimes shown flanked by a lily and a sword (see cat. 33, 34). The inscription on the banderole proclaims: "The merciful succor so that the wretched may be freed."

The lily appears again in the following emblem, *Blessed are the Pure in Heart, for They Will See God* (Matthew 5:8), but this time superposed on a heart as a symbol of purity, as it was often used in association with the Virgin Mary. Above is Augustine's comment, "This is a pure heart because it is a simple heart."

The heart—depicted in the shape of a valentine in this period—was often used as a symbol of the soul or its dwelling place in Christian emblematics, as in Antoon Wierix's very popular series, *Cor Iesu amanti sacrum*, of ca. 1600.[160] In Wierix's *Blessed Are Those Who Mourn, for They Will Be Comforted*, the heart is anthropomorphized with two crying eyes. The Augustinian inscription reads: "They mourn like those knowing what they have lost and to what depths they have sunk."   JC

Gillis van Breen (active 1597–1602)
After Karel van Mander (1548–1606)
The Commandment to Love One Another
ca. 1599
Engraving, 29.5 × 19.8 cm
New Hollstein (Van Mander) 91
The Metropolitan Museum of Art, New York

Seven New Testament texts in Dutch are marshalled in Gillis van Breen's engraving after a design by Karel van Mander, to exhort the viewer to love others. A half-length female figure with exposed breast, holding an infant, personifies Charity. The commandment to love one another, as Christ has loved us and as we love ourselves, is given three times: from John 13:34 at the upper left, Matthew 22:36 in the center, and Romans 13:9 at the bottom. Charity or Love (*Liefde*) is futher praised in passages from 1 Corinthians 13:2, 1 Peter 4:8, and 1 Timothy 1:5. Inscribed in a book at the lower center of the engraving is the phrase "all of the law and the prophets," suggesting the Old Testament complement to the New Testament texts, made explicit in the text across the top of the engraving: "In everything do to others as you would have them do to you; for this is the law and the prophets" (Matthew 7:12). The Law, in the form of several of the Ten Commandments, is folded into the lowermost inscription, Romans 13:8–10, which, adding love, summarizes: "Love does no wrong to a neighbor; therefore, love is the fulfilling of the law" (v. 10).

Van Mander, whose historical legacy rests at least as much on his extensive writings on art and artists, particularly *Het Schilder-boek* of 1604, as on his paintings and designs for prints, wrote several times of the iconoclasm that erupted in 1566 from the Protestant Reformation, and destroyed much of the Catholic art in the Netherlands, not concealing his anger and disgust, calling it "mindless fanaticism," the work of the "evil hands" of the "senseless mob," and so on.[161] More broadly, he referred on more than one occasion to "art-hating Mars", and decried the bellicose conditions even as he wrote[162]—conditions that followed from the time when "Luther began to stir up the peaceful world with his teachings."[163] Van Mander was personally affected by political upheaval; the anonymous *vita* of Van Mander attached to the second edition of the *Schilder-boek* provides extensive description of the attacks that he and his family endured from the Catholic malcontents, how they were forced to move from one place to another.[164] But he declined to write in any detail of the troubles in his time, both because he felt ill-suited to the task and, somewhat cryptically, "on account of the anxiety and danger threatened by raging, treacherous discord."[165] It is not to be wondered, then, that Van Mander would design an engraving that explicitly calls for mutual love among neighbors.

The use of shared sacred scripture offered an ecumenical means toward mutual love in the religious conflict in the Netherlands, evident in numerous prints of the period. The priority of text over images in Van Mander's composition is accentuated by the finely rendered script and the strapwork cartouches on which it is engraved. Such calligraphy and orna-

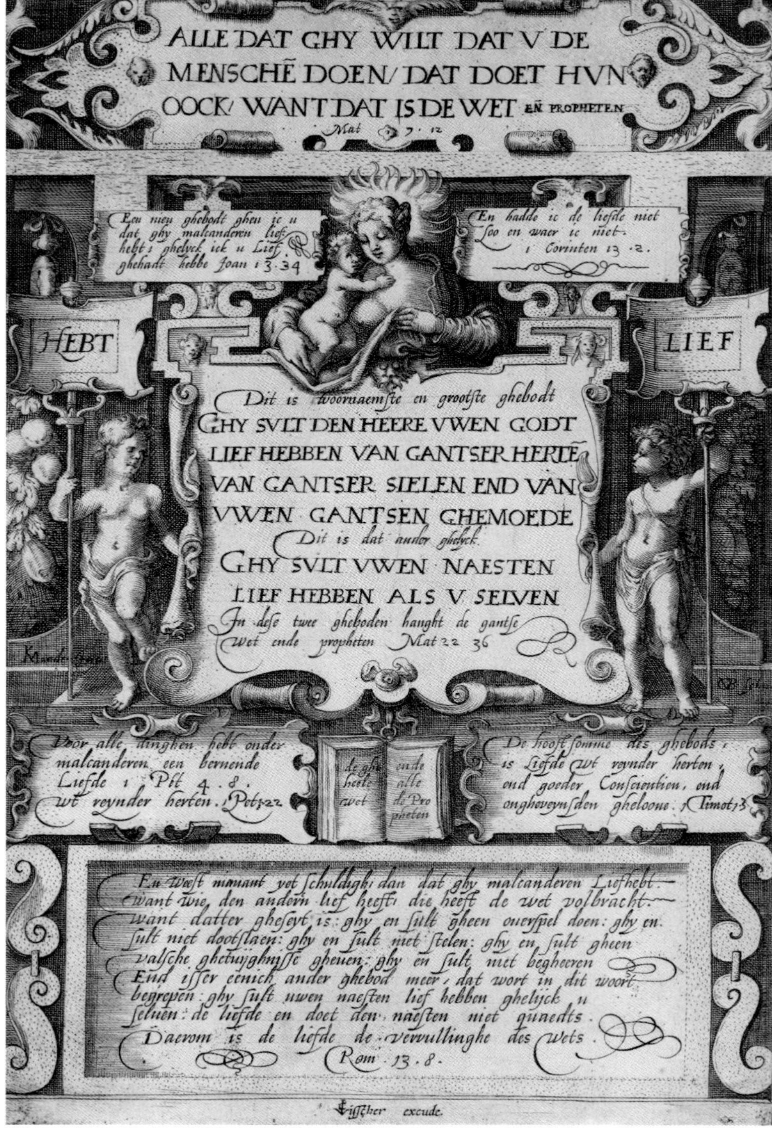

mental elements had been popular in more limited form on prints for decades, and had been featured in copybooks such as Hans Vredeman de Vries's *Exercitatio Alphabetica* of 1569 and the *Theatrum Artis Scribendi* of 1594.[166] Van Mander's composition may also have participated in an increasing tendency, not only to aestheticize text but also to monumentalize it, to use it as a substitute for, rather than complement to, figural forms. The visual presentation of text was especially useful for scripture in confessions with aniconic proclivities. This tendency achieved its apogee in large paintings of text, mostly biblical, in Dutch homes and Reformed churches of the seventeenth century.[167]   JC

Hieronymus Wierix (1553–1619)
After Maarten de Vos (1532–1603)
The Christian Knight
ca. 1590
Engraving, 30.1 × 39.6 cm
Hollstein (Wierix) 1795
The British Museum, London, 1870,1008.2868

The Christian knight (or soldier)—the *eques* (or *miles*) *christianus*—was a leitmotif in European culture throughout the Middle Ages and into the seventeenth century, exemplified by Christian heroes of history and legend, foremost among them the dragon-slayer, Saint George. The idea of the Christian soldier was easily allegorized, based most directly on a passage in Paul's letter to the Ephesians, 6:10–17:

> "Put on the whole armor of God, so that you may be able to stand against the wiles of the devil.… [T]ake up the whole armor of God, so that you may be able to withstand on that evil day, and having done everything, to stand firm. Stand therefore, and fasten the belt of truth around your waist, and put on the breastplate of righteousness. As shoes for your feet put on whatever will make you ready to proclaim the gospel of peace. With all of these, take the shield of faith, with which you will be able to quench all the flaming arows of the evil one. Take the helmet of salvation, and the sword of the Spirit, which is the word of God."

Paul's metaphor of spiritual armor gained great impetus in the sixteenth century through the publication, first in 1504 and subsequently in many editions

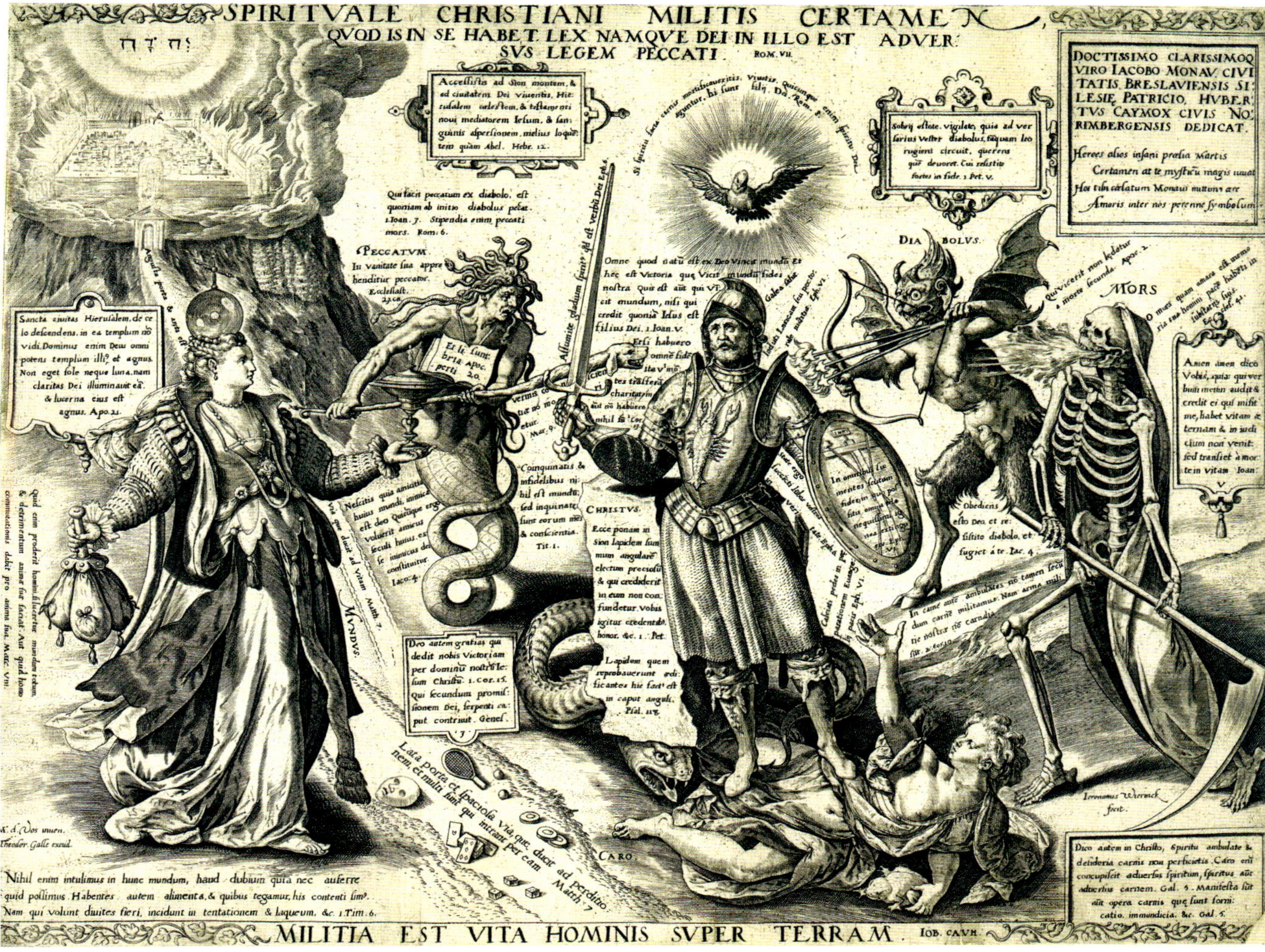

43

and languages, of Erasmus's extremely popular *Enchiridion Militis Christiani* (*Handbook of the Militant Christian*).

Around the turn of the seventeenth century, Hieronymus Wierix engraved several prints in Antwerp featuring the Christian Knight.[168] Phrases from Ephesians 6 are inscribed next to the armor protecting the knight in the most elaborate of these engravings, designed by Maarten de Vos and published by Gerard de Jode.[169] The knight, over whom the dove of the Holy Spirit hovers, engages in spiri-

tual battle with personifications of the World (*Mundus*),[170] Sin (*Peccatum*), the Devil (*Diabolus*), Death (*Mors*), and the Flesh (*Caro*). As the majuscule inscription at the bottom of the engraving, quoting Job 7:1 (a passage cited by Erasmus at the beginning of the *Enchiridion*), proclaims, "The life of man upon earth is a warfare," and the composition is densely packed with biblical texts that elaborate this struggle. The path is straight and the gate narrow to the knight's ultimate goal, the Heavenly Jerusalem at the upper left of the image, as

the inscribed passage from Matthew 7 tells us, in contrast to the spacious path that leads to perdition, here strewn with the instruments of frivolity—a tennis racket and balls, cards, dice, backgammon markers, and a theater mask—at the feet of the figure of the World. But the battle is waged internally, according to the inscription at the top of the print, which cites Romans 7, a battle between the law of God that dwells in the spiritual soldier's mind and the law of sin that dwells in the members of his body. JC

Politics and Polemics

Indeed an hour is coming when those who kill you will think that by doing so they are offering worship to God.

John 16:2

44

Lucas van Leyden (ca. 1494–1533)
Cain Killing Abel
1524
Engraving, 11.8 × 7.7 cm
New Hollstein (Van Leyden) 13
The British Museum, London, 1848,0078.127

*I*n *Cain Killing Abel*, Lucas van Leyden defined historical contexts for his subject and his art. This picture illustrates the Old Testament account of Adam and Eve's son, Cain, murdering his brother Abel, after God showed favor to Abel's sacrifice of a lamb from his flock over Cain's sacrifice of grain from his harvest (Genesis 4:3–8). In a landscape with trees, Cain grabs Abel's hair, swinging a deadly blow with an ass's jaw-bone. These details recall Petrus Christus's grisaille painting of an archivolt carving of Abel's murder in the *Nativity*, ca. 1465.[171] Lucas's robust, muscular portrayal of Cain contrasts with the stiff, non-muscular stone figures painted by Christus and his predecessors.[172]

In Lucas's engraving, Cain's fleshiness evokes the allegory of Abel's slaying as a struggle between flesh and spirit.[173] Abel, who prefigures Christ, embodies spirituality and Cain, who prefigures Christ's persecutors, embodies fleshly sins.[174] Lucas situated the first murder in pre-Roman antiquity by inventively depicting the brothers in animal skins.[175] While signaling temporal disjunction between viewers and the Old Testament event, the pelts and jawbone also signify cultural dissociation, as they allude to the pictorial "wild-man" motif, and construe Cain's act as barbaric.[176]   JS

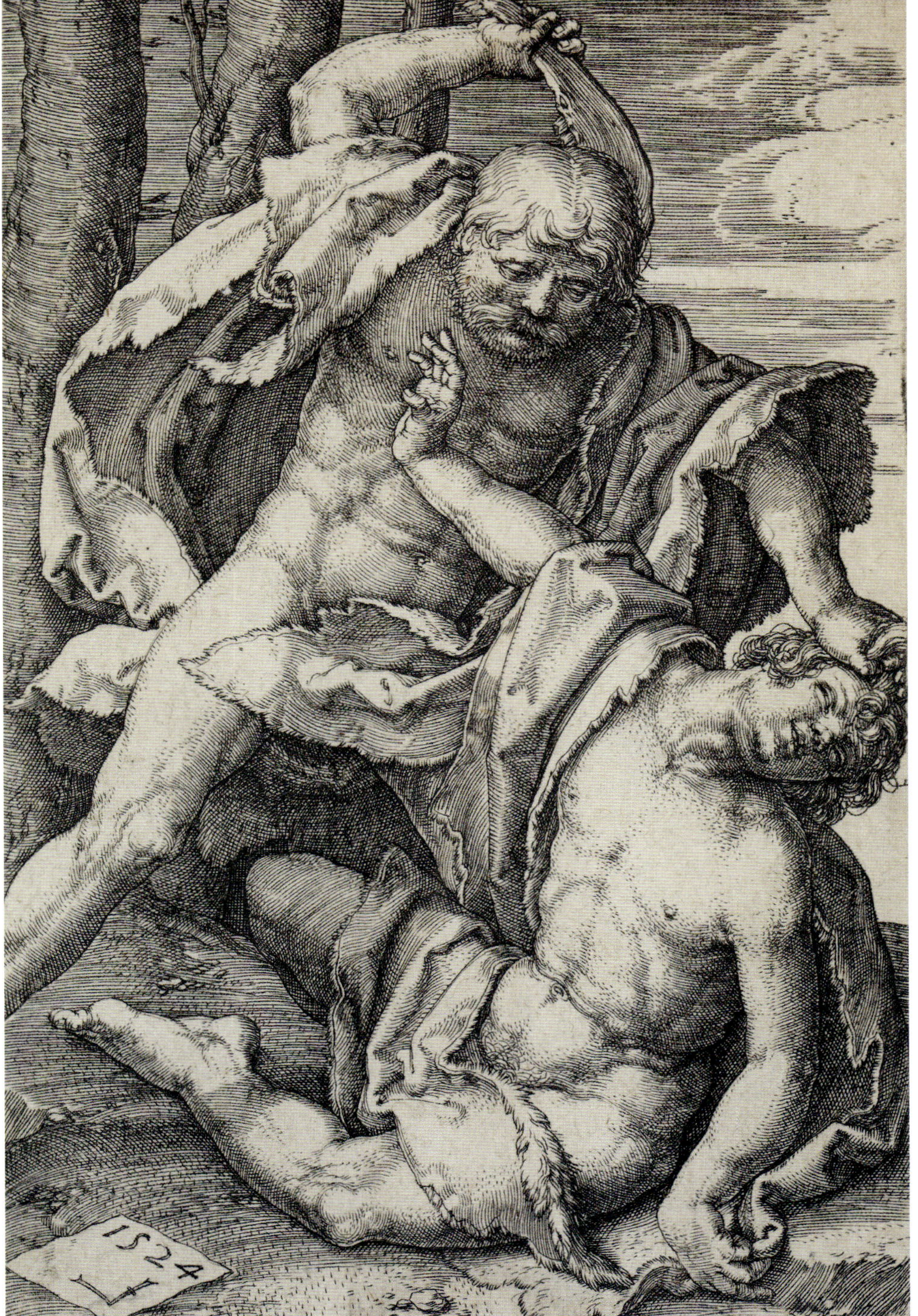

44

Philips Galle (1537–1612)

After Maarten van Heemskerck (1498–1574)

Isaiah's Prophesy over Jerusalem

1564

Engraving, 17.9 × 29 cm

New Hollstein (Galle) 69; New Hollstein

(Van Heemskerck) 169

The Royal Library of Belgium, Brussels

*P*hilips Galle engraved *Isaiah's Prophesy over Jerusalem* after a drawing by Maarten van Heemskerck, whose symbolic imagery portends heavenly intervention in the worldly habits of the Israelites. Seated in the foreground, the prophet looks out over Jerusalem and expressively raises his hands to the sky. The inscription in the print's lower margin, authored by Latin scholar and humanist Hadrianus Junius, explains Isaiah's gesture: "The troubled prophet held up his hands. Isaiah strongly admonished the wicked people to atone."[177] The Latin verses, which evoke the account of Isaiah's vision (Isaiah 1:1–31), situate the scene in biblical history.

The dwelling place of the wicked multitude unfolds as an extensive city view, set within a mountainous landscape. Egyptian obelisks signify the pagan rituals and idolatry practised by the wicked inhabitants of the land.[178] These architectural monuments embody the cause of God's wrath, whereas natural elements allude to redemption through Christ. The brilliant sun, shining in the upper left corner, recalls Isaiah's invitation for sinners to "walk in the light of the Lord" (Isaiah 2:5), and the flourishing branches in the lower right corner recall the proclamation that the "branch of the Lord shall be beautiful and glorious" (Isaiah 4:2).

The imagery agrees with contemporary devotional theorizing on the spiritual meaning of landscape and the interpretation of astronomical events as divine portents.[179]

Cosmic symbolism that amplifies the apocalyptic tenor of Isaiah's vision may also allude to millennialist ideology, espoused by Protestant reformers in the Netherlands who sought to establish the "New Jerusalem."[180] Through his work, Van Heemskerck, a Catholic humanist, engaged in the polemical discourse on idolatry, which was then turning some Protestants against religious imagery.[181] While explicating Isaiah's condemnation of idolatrous worship, his picture also advocates religious art. The natural element of water surrounding the man-made pagan monuments reflects images of them. The depicted reflections display the skill of the artist who rendered them, but also demonstrate that the action of light and the reflective processes in nature are agents of image-making.[182] Asserting that created images are manifestations of divine power, the artist set forth an argument for the sanction of religious picturing.   JS

46a–e

Philips Galle (1537–1612)

After Maarten van Heemskerck (1498–1574)

The Story of Daniel, Bel and the Dragon

1565

A series of ten engravings, each ca. 20.5 × 24.6 cm, from which:

a. *Daniel Refusing to Worship Bel*

b. *Cyrus Showing Bel and His Food to Daniel*

c. *The Destruction of the Statue of Bel*

d. *Habakuk Bringing Daniel Food in the Lion's Den*

e. *Daniel's Accusers Cast into the Lion's Den*

New Hollstein (Galle) 93, 94, 98, 100, 102; New Hollstein (Van Heemskerck) 226, 227, 231, 233, 235

The British Museum, London, D,5.85 (a); D,5.86 (b); D,5.94 (c); D,5.96 (d); D,5.98 (e)

*D*esigned by Maarten van Heemskerck in 1565 and engraved by Philips Galle,[183] the five engravings are from a series of ten depicting the events of the extended, or apocryphal, book of Daniel, chapter 14. The prophet Daniel was the most highly esteemed friend of King Cyrus. The Babylonians worshipped Bel, whose statue was given large quantities of food and drink daily. The nightly disappearance of the feast convinced Cyrus that Bel was a living god. However, to prove the illegitimacy of the god, when Daniel was alone with the king, he spread ashes on the temple floor and sealed the doors. When the two returned the next morning, although the food was gone, Daniel pointed to the numerous footprints in the ashes. The footprints led to a hidden door under the altar, and proved that the temple priests came in each night to eat the offerings in secret. Angry at the hoax, Cyrus ordered the priests killed and gave the altar over to Daniel to destroy.

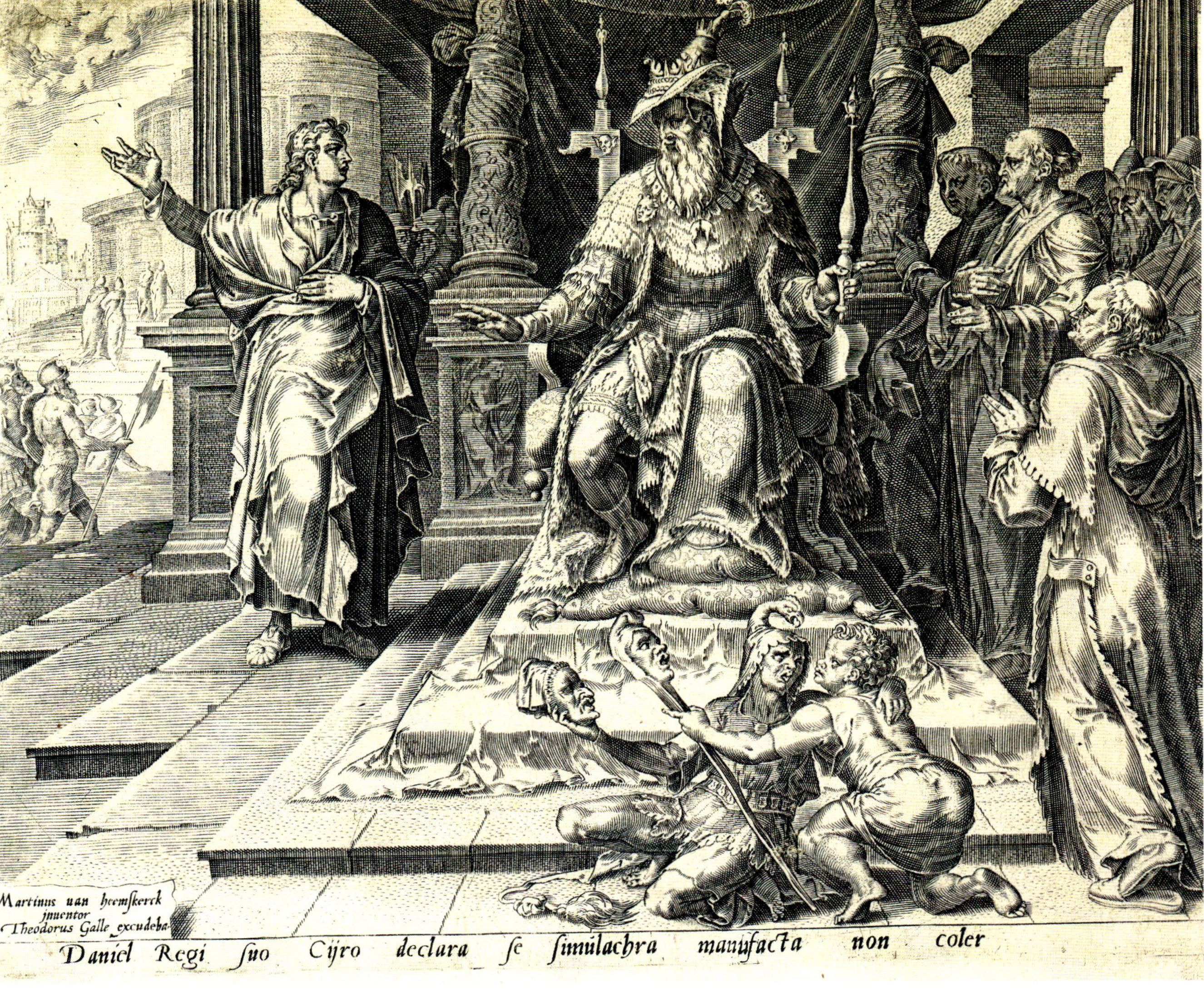

46a

In the first print, *Daniel Refusing to Worship Bel*, Cyrus is shown sitting on his throne; he holds a scepter in one hand and offers a gesture of caution to Daniel with the other. The prophet Daniel stands on the left and gestures with his right hand toward the temple in the background. In the lower margin, a Latin text reads, "Daniel Regi suo Cijro declara se sim lach-ra manufacta non coler" (Daniel declares to his king Cyrus that he would not wor-ship the manufactured likeness). On the right, a cluster of temple priests listen in on the dialogue. The second image, *Cyrus Showing Bel and His Food to Daniel*, illus-trates the action taking place in the tem-ple at the moment Cyrus conveys his faith in Bel. Bel's statue is situated on a pedestal surrounded by burning incense. Servants bring his nightly meal to set on the table before him. On the right, the priests exit the temple at the king's command. In the Latin text: "Rex Danielem ad Bel m d cit ostendens quam multa comedat bibatq[ue]" (The King says to Daniel: see how much food and drink Bel consumes).

The third print reproduced here, the sixth of the series, follows prints that depict Daniel spreading the ashes and exposing the fraudulent priests. The im-age illustrates the moment when King Cyrus gives the altar over to Daniel to destroy. On the left, the two men look on as Bel's statue is toppled and beheaded. In the right foreground, a child urinates in the god's mouth. In the center of the image, the altar has been removed and the stairs used by the priests to sneak into the temple each night are revealed. In the

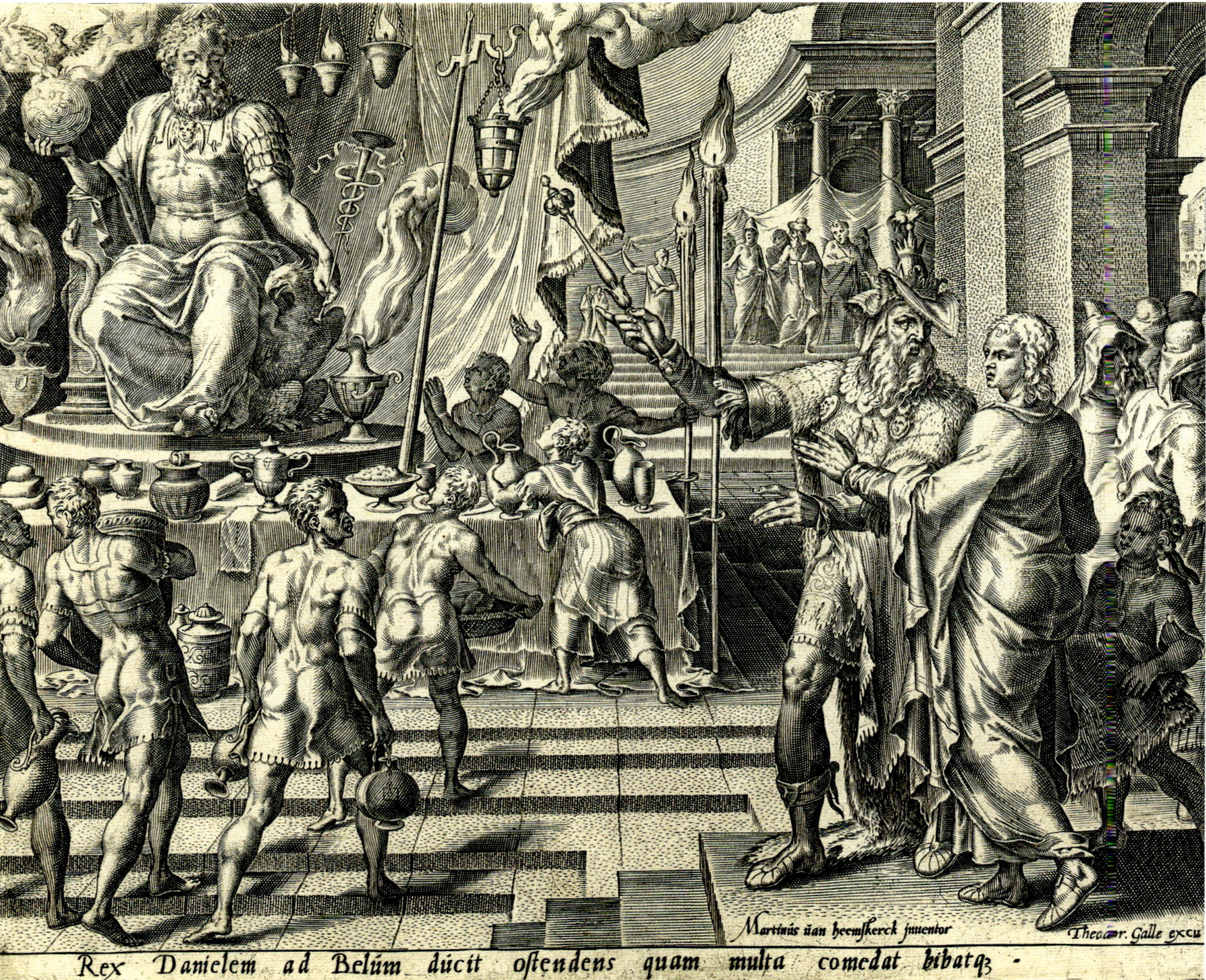

46b

lower margin, the Latin text reads, "Rex iratus sacerdotes interficere iubet, Danielq[ue] Belum cum templo subuertit" (The king, angered, ordered the execution of the priests, and Daniel overthrew Bel with his temple).

As a result of the king's conversion, the Babylonians became indignant and worried that he had become a Jew. In response, they demanded that Daniel be handed over to them and that he be thrown into the lion's den, where he remained for six days.

To provide for Daniel, an angel of God appeared to the prophet Habakkuk and told him, "Take the lunch you have to Daniel in the lions' den at Babylon" (Daniel 14:34). The fourth print, eighth in the series, illustrates the moment when Habakkuk responds to the angel with hesitation and "the angel of the Lord seized him by the crown of his head and carried him by the hair; with the speed of the wind, he set him down in Babylon above the den" (Daniel 14:36). Daniel is shown praying, unharmed in the den with seven lions, and receiving food from the miraculous transportation of Habakkuk.

"On the seventh day the king came to mourn for Daniel. When he came to the den he looked in, and there sat Daniel! The king shouted with a loud voice, 'You are great, O Lord, the God of Daniel, and there is no other besides you!'" (Daniel 14:40). The final print of the series shows Daniel on the far left, having been pulled out of the den, standing next to the king. The two men look on as soldiers throw "into the den those who had attempted

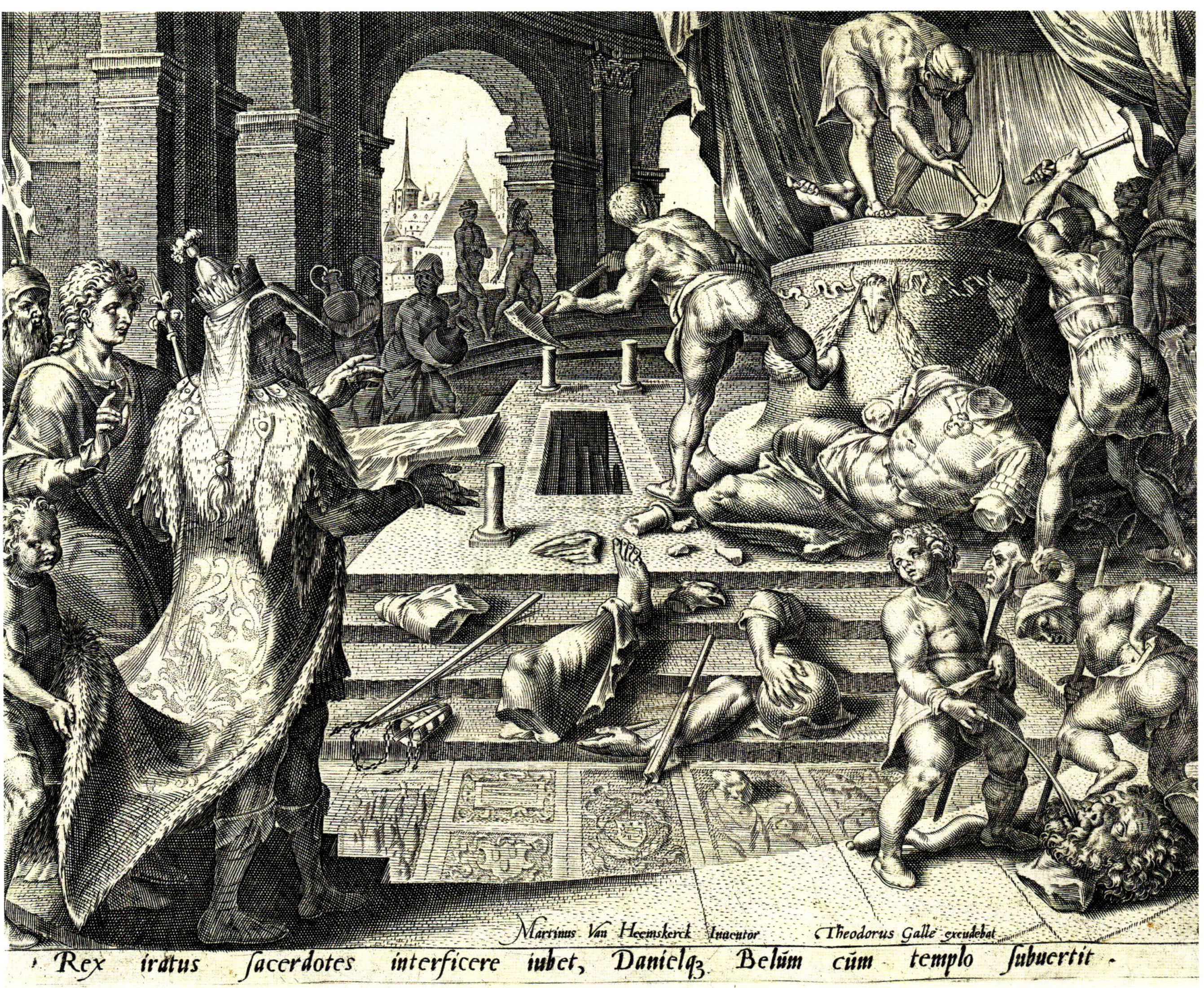

46c

[Daniel's] destruction, and they were instantly eaten" (Daniel 14:42).[184]

Although the tale of Daniel, Bel and the dragon is rarely depicted in art, it was referenced many times during the Reformation and it has been argued that this series in particular shows Protestant sympathies. For example, in *Daniel Refusing to Worship Bel*, the fraudulent priests on the right wear monks' clothing and are tonsured.[185] As Eleanor Saunders explains, the story was the subject of controversy as early as 1533. In that year, an Amsterdam chamber of rhetoricians was punished for having presented a play about Daniel and Bel without receiving the proper approval. The reason behind the reprimand, she argues, was that the subject of the play mocked the clergy.[186] In addition, by the mid-1560s, a number of Netherlandish songs referred to the idol of Bel when criticizing Catholic images.[187] TR

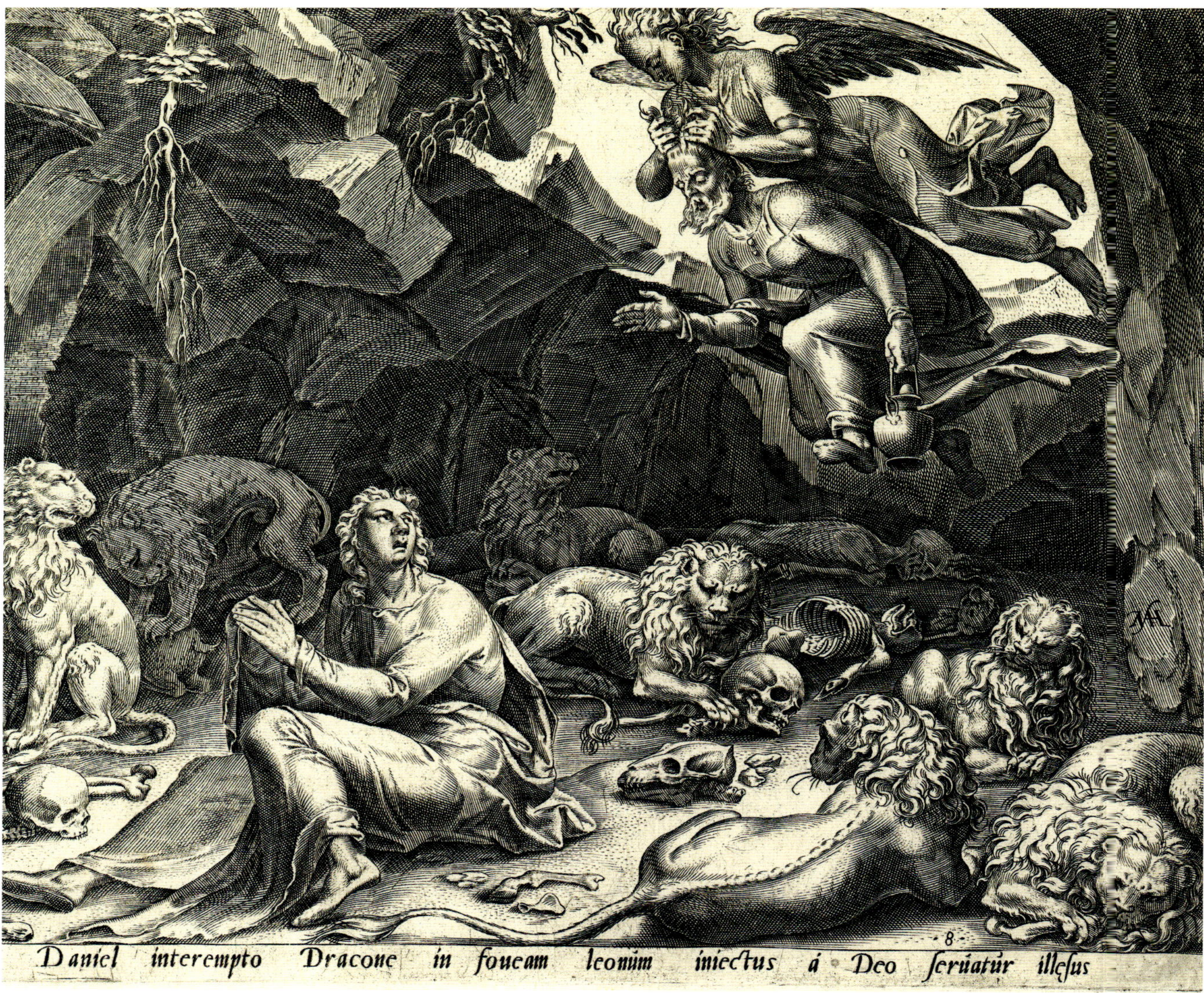

46d

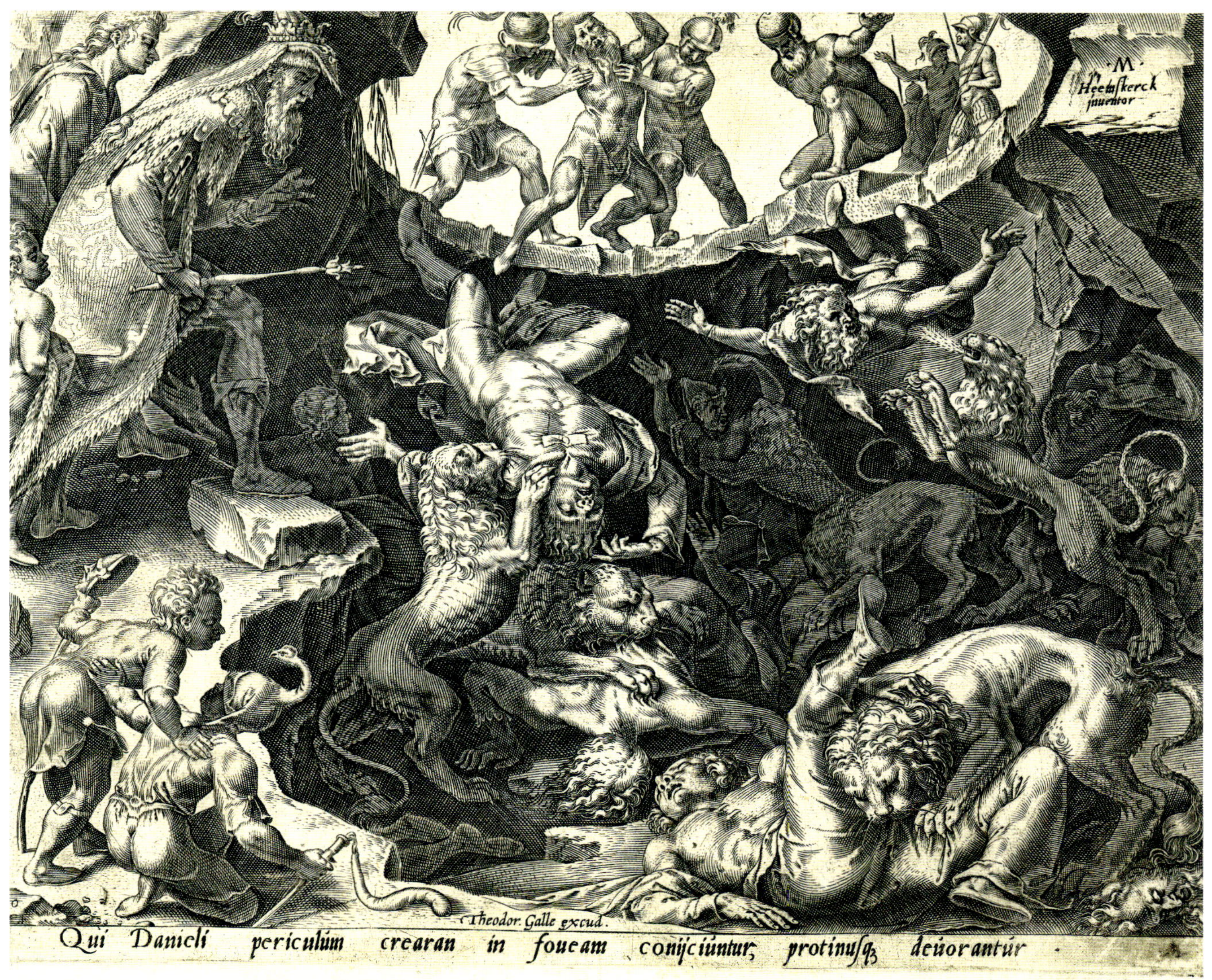

M
Heemskerck
inuentor
Theodor. Galle excud.
Qui Danieli periculum crearan in foueam conijciuntur, protinusq devorantur

46e

Harmen Jansz. Muller (1540–1617)
After Maarten van Heemskerck (1498–1574)
Thou Shalt Have No Other Gods Before Me
From *The Ten Commandments*
ca. 1566
Engraving, 21.2 × 24.9 cm
New Hollstein (Van Heemskerck) 65;
New Hollstein (Muller) 9
Museum Plantin-Moretus/Prentenkabinet,
Antwerp–UNESCO World Heritage,
Inv. No. 3 11825, Cat No. III/M.224

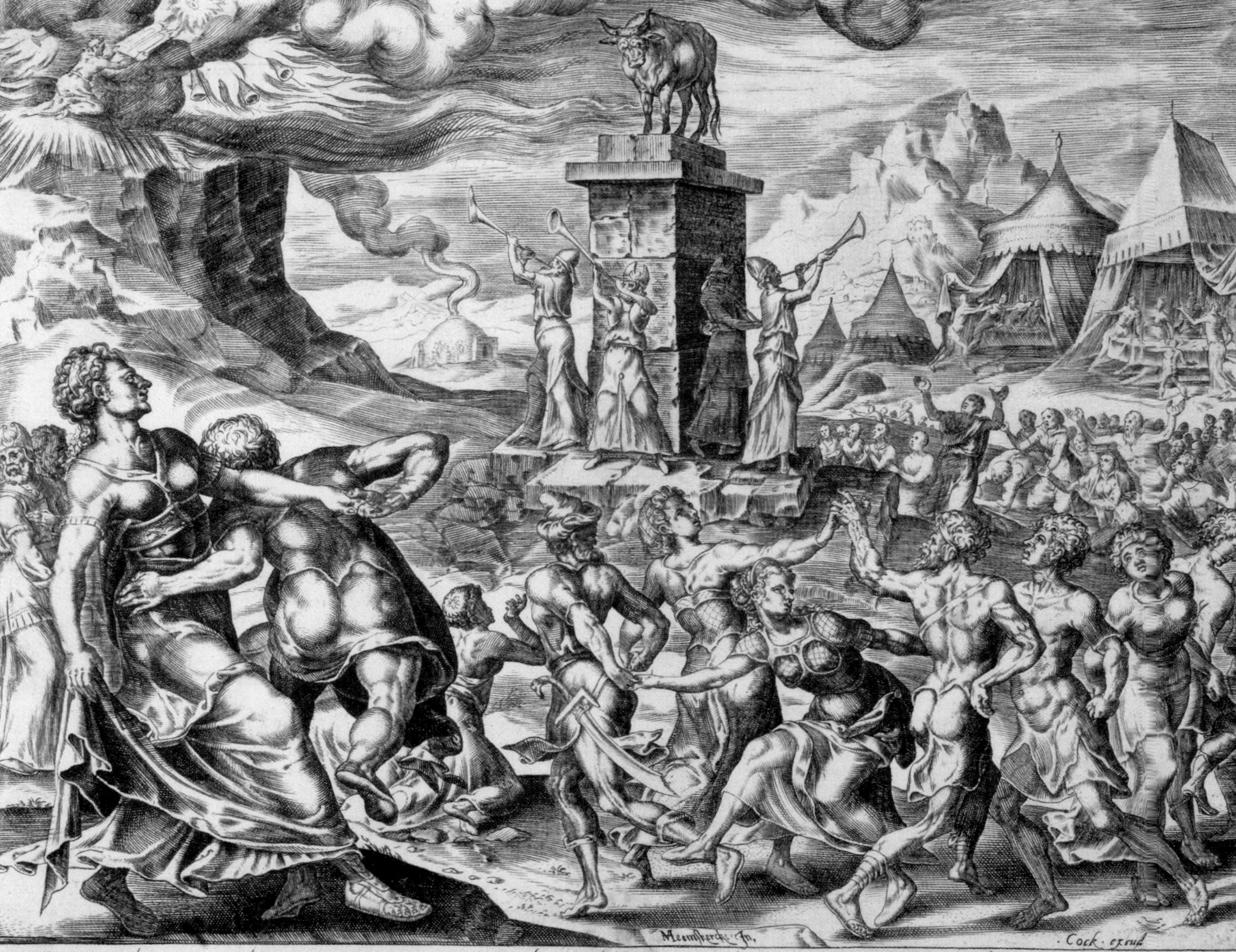

47

*D*esigned by Maarten van Heemskerck around 1566, the print comes from a series depicting illustrations of the Ten Commandments, which was engraved by Herman Jansz Muller and published by Hieronymus Cock. The Haarlem painter Van Heemskerck was the first Northern artist to devote a considerable part of his energy to the production of print designs, which were mainly published by Cock and etched or engraved by a circle of colleagues. Van Heemskerck made around one hundred paintings, but the prints after his designs total some six hundred, a number unrivalled in his time.[188]

The iconography of the series is loosely based on Lucas Cranach's woodcuts.[189] To illustrate the First Commandment, the artist has depicted a moment when the law was broken: the Israelites dancing around a golden calf, significantly, just as Moses was receiving the Decalogue from God on Mount Sinai. God the Father, in the form of clouds, thunder and lightning, descends on the mountain peak in the far left distance. Moses and Aaron kneel in awe while holding the stone tablets. Exodus 32 explains that, because Moses was away so long on the moun-

tain, forty days and forty nights, the Israelites lost faith and demanded that Aaron make for them an idol that they could see and worship.

After Aaron fashioned the golden calf, seen here placed on a pedestal in the center, "the people sacrificed burnt offerings sat down to eat and drink and got up to indulge in revelry" (Exodus 32:5–6). To represent the festive occasion, Van

Heemskerck has portrayed the multiple intertwined, dancing figures in the foreground, in a manner reminiscent of Italianate bacchanalia. Having visited Italy himself many years earlier, Van Heemskerck was well acquainted with the bacchic visual tradition taken from antique sarcophagi, and employed it in many of his paintings for Northern humanist patrons. TR

Harmen Jansz. Muller (1540–1617)
After Maarten van Heemskerck (1498–1574)
Athaliah Destroying the Royal Progeny
From *The Story of Joash and Queen Athaliah*
ca. 1567
Engraving, 19.2 × 24.8 cm
New Hollstein (Van Heemskerck) 139;
New Hollstein (Muller) 29
Rijksmuseum, Amsterdam, RP-P-1890-A-15408

48b (not illustrated)
Harmen Jansz. Muller (1540–1617)
After Maarten van Heemskerck (1498–1574)
The Destruction of the House of Baal
From *The Story of Joash and Queen Athaliah*
ca. 1567
Engraving, 18.8 × 24.8 cm
New Hollstein (Van Heemskerck) 142;
New Hollstein (Muller) 32
Rijksmuseum, Amsterdam, RP-P-1904-3359

Designed by Maarten van Heemskerck and engraved by Herman Jansz. Muller, the two prints are taken from a series of four numbered plates that illustrate the events of 2 Kings 11. All four images contain Latin verses in the lower margin written by Hadrianus Junius.[190]

The story begins when Ahaziah, the King of Judah, is killed. After his death, there is confusion over his successor, and his mother, Athaliah, decides that she should rule Judah as Queen. Taking advantage of the confusion, Athaliah proceeds mercilessly to exterminate the entire royal lineage in her own family. However, one of her grandchildren, Joash, is rescued by his aunt Jehosheba. She and her husband, the high priest Jehoiada, hide the boy in the temple in Jerusalem for six years. In the seventh year of Athaliah's reign, Jehoiada leads a revolt in favor of Joash and, conspiring with five army commanders and most of the religious and political leaders in Judah, succeeds in establishing the seven-year-old boy as king. Athaliah, hearing the crowd's celebration of the sudden coronation, goes to the temple to investigate the commotion. She is immediately captured, led to the city gate, and executed. 2 Chronicles 24:7 explains that during her reign, Queen Athaliah had directed that sacred objects from the temple of the Lord be put into the temple of Baal in Jerusalem. In response to her death, the people went to the temple of Baal and tore it down.

In a scene similar to the Slaughter of the Innocents in the book of Matthew, *Athaliah Destroying the Royal Progeny* shows the moment the aspiring queen orders the execution of all contenders for the throne. Guards draw their swords against children and young men, while in the foreground Jehosheba shields her nephew Joash, indicated by the crown on his head. On the far left, Jehosheba escapes the massacre with Joash and takes the child to the Jewish temple in the background.

In *The Destruction of the House of Baal*, the final print of the series, Joash, now king, holds the hand of his uncle Jehoiada and is accompanied by his army as they proceed to tear down the idols of the temple. The floor is littered with broken statues, in the center a guard kills the temple priest, and in the background multiple figures attempt to topple a statue of the pagan god.

The destruction of religious icons was a hot topic in 1567; just one year earlier, Dutch Protestants had openly revolted against the Roman Catholic Church, invaded churches, and destroyed altarpieces, statues, and relics. It has been argued that in this image, along with other scenes depicting the destruction of idols, Van Heemskerck offers his own commentary on iconoclasm.[191]   TR

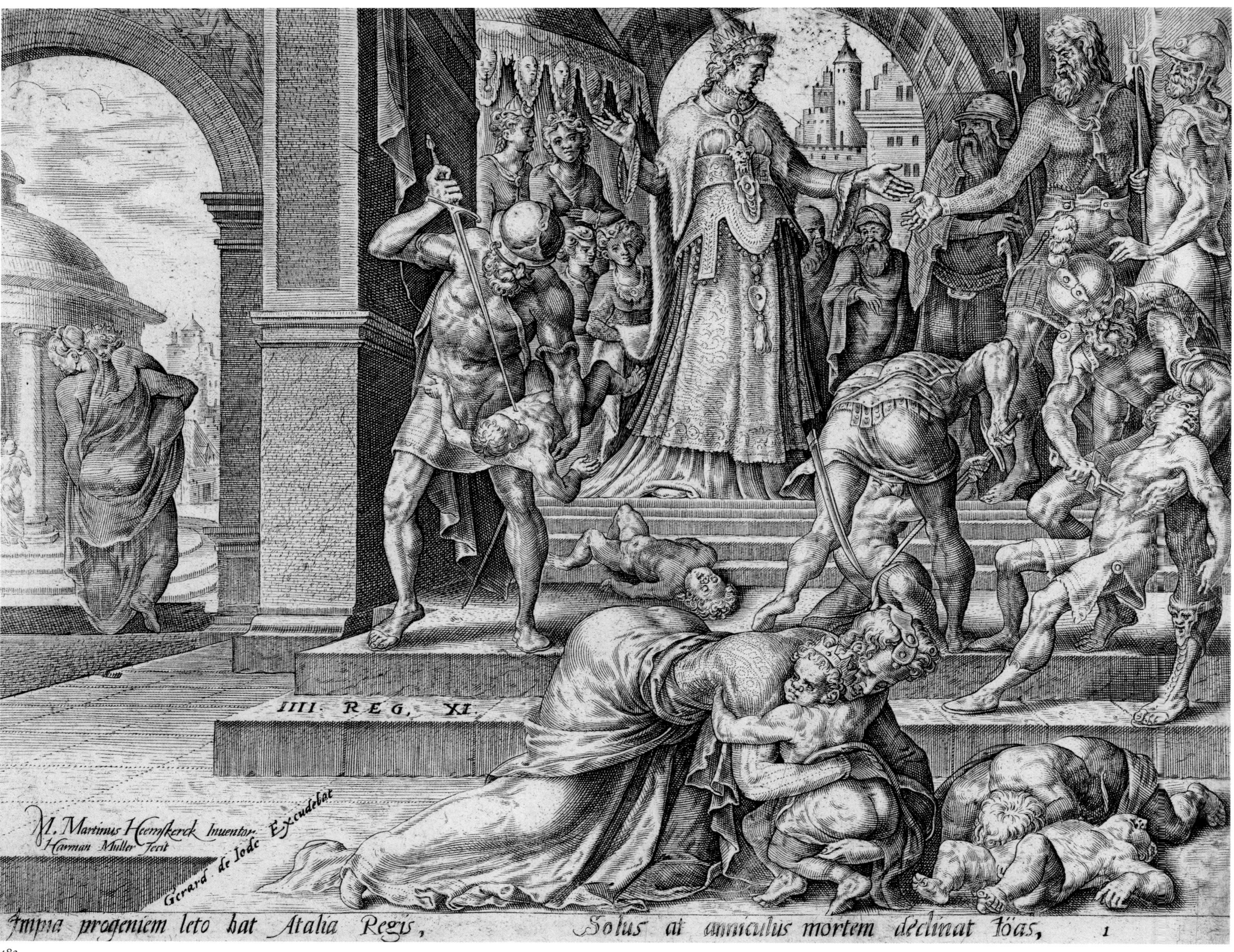

48a

IIII REG. XI.
M. Martinus Heemskerck Inuentor.
Harman Muller fecit
Gerard de Iode Excudebat
Impia progeniem leto bat Atalia Regis,   Solus at anniculus mortem declinat Ioas,   1

Pieter Nagel (active ca. 1567–84)

After Gerard van Groeningen (active 1561–ca. 1576)

Allegory of Law and Grace

ca. 1567

Engraving, 22 × 32.5 cm

New Hollstein (Van Groeningen) 158

Museum Plantin-Moretus/Prentenkabinet,

Antwerp–UNESCO World Heritage,

Inv. No. OP 15118, Cat. No. III/N.2

Pieter Nagel's print is a biblical allegory that derives from a composition that emerged from the workshop of the German artist Lucas Cranach in the late 1520s, and appeared in the Netherlands already in 1530 as part of a Bible title-page published in Antwerp.[192] By the time Nagel produced his print around 1567, the iconography had appeared throughout northern Europe in a wide variety of media. The allegory embodies important Lutheran precepts on Law and Grace.

A nude man at the center of the composition faces a choice, rather like Hercules at the Crossroads, between Law on the viewer's left and Grace on the right. The dichotomy, which informs the individual motifs of the image, is articulated in the inscription below: "The Law was given by Moses, Grace and Truth by Jesus Christ our Lord." The tree that is barren on the side of Law, and foliate on the side of Grace, divides the composition into two antithetical halves. An Old Testament prophet on the left and John the Baptist on the right compete for the man's attention. The composition illustrates the Lutheran idea that the Law brings humans to an awareness of their sin and wretchedness; hence the quotation from Romans 3:20 on the banderole at the up-

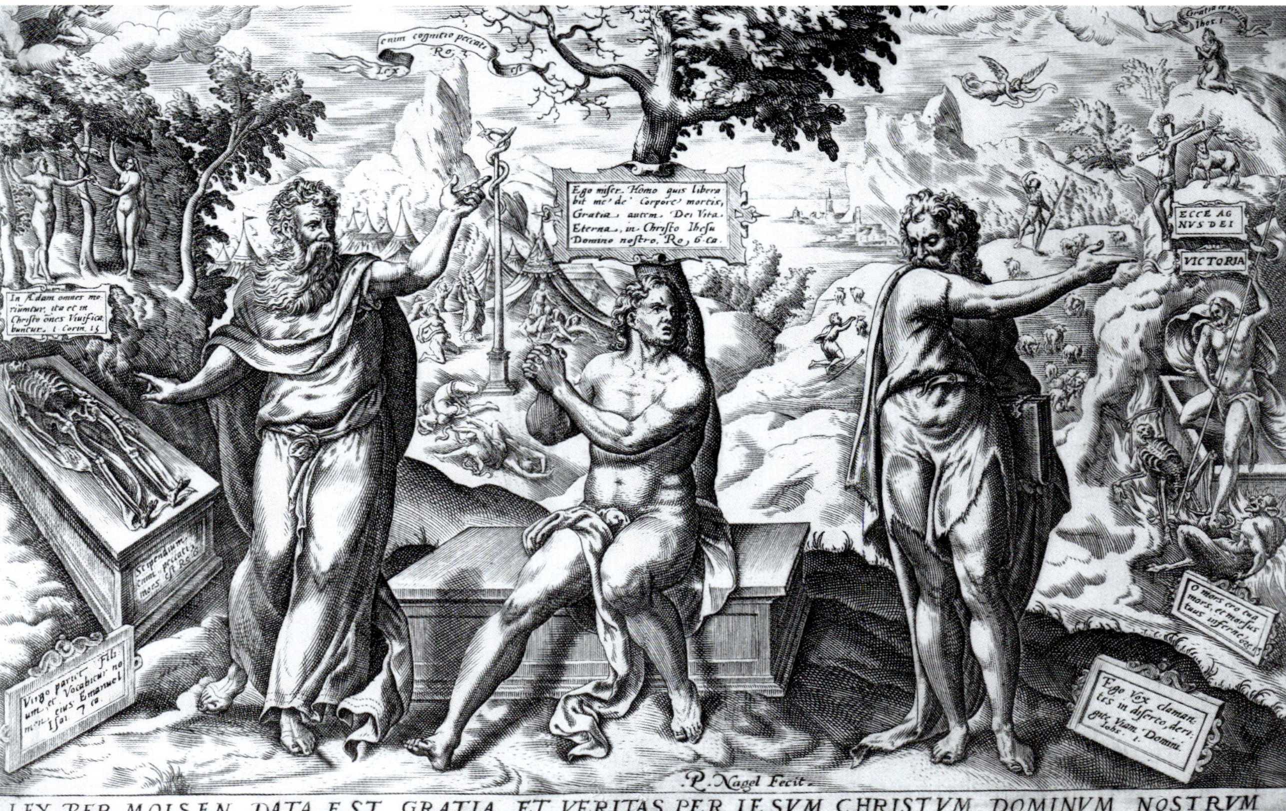

49

per left: "for through the law comes the knowledge of sin." But such knowledge cannot save them, because humans are incapable of following the Law without Christ. On the skeleton-topped tomb at left is the dire conclusion: "the wages of sin is death" (Romans 6:23).

Also on the Law side of the composition, Adam and Eve take the forbidden fruit, Moses receives the tablets of the Law from divine hands reaching from a cloud, and the brazen serpent rises before the tents of the Israelites in the desert. The brazen serpent was commonly understood as a prefiguration of the crucifixion of Christ, but it appears here as a sign, not so much of the historical event of the crucifixion, but of justification through the crucifixion.[193] At the top of the hill on the Grace side is the Annunciation, with the infant Christ, carrying a cross, flying to Mary as the Word Incarnate. Below them are the Lamb of God, the crucified Christ, and the Resurrected Lord victorious over sin and death, this latter a motif that became quite common in the sixteenth and early seventeenth centuries.

The man who wrings his hands in despair angles his body toward the side of Law, but his head turns toward John the Baptist and the side of Grace, his choice announced in the inscription above his head, derived from Romans 7:24: "Wretched man that I am! Who will liberate me from this body of death? But thanks be to God for eternal life in Jesus Christ our Lord." It is a *summa* of Luther's theology of justification by faith alone.   JC

Hendrick Goltzius (1558–1617)
The Judgment of Solomon
ca. 1578/1604
Engraving, 23.6 × 18.3 cm
Strauss 66
The New York Public Library,
Astor, Lenox and Tilden Foundations

$\mathcal{T}$he story of the Judgment of Solomon, told in 1 Kings 3:16–28, is well known and often represented. Two women appeared before King Solomon with two infants, one dead, one living. Each claimed the living child for her own. Solomon ordered the living child cut in half and divided between the two mothers. The false mother accepted the arrangement, but the true mother urged the king to spare the child—her son—and Solomon, in his wisdom, restored the child to his mother. But in Goltzius's engraving the story has become an allegory of rulers and the Church. Most remarkably, the wise Old Testament king has been turned into a "cruel prince," blindfolded (as Justice often is, but here with negative connotations), accompanied by an owl, which, ambiguously, could represent either wisdom or malevolence in the early modern period. The two women are labeled as the "False Church" and the "True Church." The dead infant is Barrabas, who was released instead of Christ at the behest of the crowd before Pilate, and the living infant, dangled upside-down by a soldier whose sword is already slicing into his back, is Christ. The inscription next to the infant Christ adds to his name "in his members," drawing on Paul's description (in 1 Corinthians 12) of the baptized as members of Christ's body (and thus of the Church), and referring to those in the background of the image who are martyred by burning at the stake, hanging, beheading, and drowning.

Surrounding the cruel prince are advisers, each named for one of the means of execution (Doctor Fire, Doctor Noose, Doctor Sword, and Doctor Water), who illustrate one of the passages quoted in the inscription at the lower right: "If a ruler listens to falsehood, all his officials will be wicked" (Proverbs 29:12). The quotation of Proverbs 14:28—"The glory of a king is a multitude of people; without people a prince is ruined"—suggests the symbiotic relationship of ruler and subjects, but two passages quoted from Exodus, in which the Egyptian Pharaoh is speaking, advocate the suppression and even extermination of the people: "Come, let us deal shrewdly with them, or they will increase" (Exodus 1:10): "When you act as midwives to the Hebrew women, and see them on the birthstool, if it is a boy, kill him; but if it is a girl, she shall live" (Exodus 1:16). The passage from John 16:2, like the visual motif of the attack on Christ and his members, confirms the negative judgment on such acts, evoking the persecution of heretics or of those at odds with the authorities: "Indeed, an hour is coming when those who kill you will think that by doing so they are offering worship to God."

Both sides of the religio-political conflict in the sixteenth-century Netherlands had opportunity to oppress

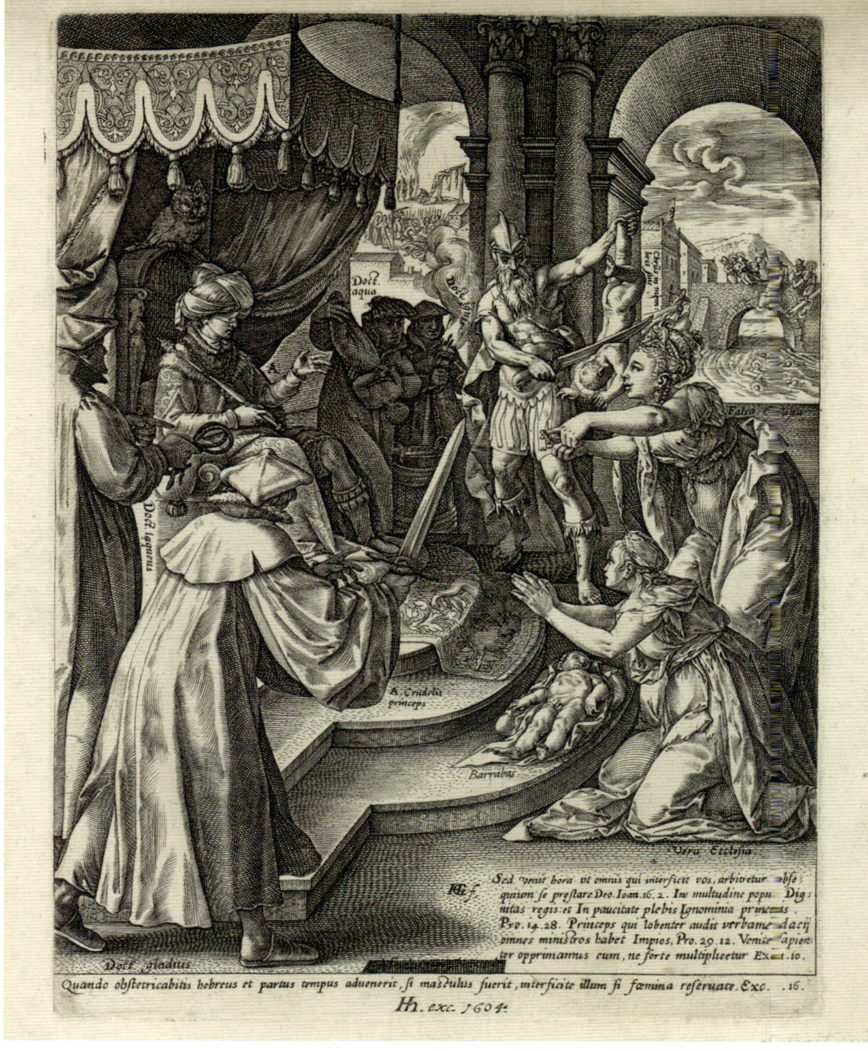

50

the other, and both were accused of it. The print is not explicit about who comprises the "True Church" and the "False Church." Hendrick Goltzius remained a Catholic throughout his life, but tended toward tolerance, also addressed in his engraving of *Dissent in the Church* (cat. 51). The print was probably engraved around 1578, when Goltzius was in the circle of Philips Galle and Dirck Volckertsz. Coornhert, who were both also Catholic with ecumenical inclinations. Hendrick Hondius, who published the print in 1604, was Protestant and even anti-Catholic, but, like many printmakers, was also ready to produce prints of an ambiguous or even contrary theological or ecclesiological position.[194]   JC

51

Hendrick Goltzius (1558–1617)
Dissent in the Church (*Dissidium in Ecclesia*)
ca. 1578
Engraving, 24 × 18.5 cm
Strauss 63
The Metropolitan Museum of Art, New York

*I*n or around 1578, the young Hendrick Goltzius engraved about twenty large religious images, mostly allegories, each featuring a central image surrounded by a frame containing subsidiary images, decorative elements, and texts, which consist almost exclusively of scriptural quotations.[195] Although produced in Haarlem, some, or probably all, were published in Antwerp by Philips Galle, whose address appears on seven of them and who may have been partially responsible for the format.[196] Goltzius's prints, lacking any title-page(s), were probably not intended to form a single coherent group.

In *Dissent in the Church*, what would seem to be a mêlée is the conglomeration of different biblical episodes of violence done to those blessed by God, each keyed by a number to a text in the margin. Dominating the foreground is Cain murdering Abel (see also cat. 44). At the left, Joseph is lowered into the pit by his brothers. At the right, Ishmael strikes Isaac, who drops his ball from a game of bowling. Just behind them, Saul aims his spear at a fleeing David, endeavoring to nail him to the wall. Further back, the prophet Jeremiah is struck, and the prophets Jehu and Zacharias are slain. In the apse of the church, the unfaithful steward in the parable of Luke 12, trusting that his lord's return is far off, begins to strike the menservants and maidservants.

Violence in the church recalls the disturbing events in Haarlem on 29 May 1578, the feast of Corpus Christi, when anti-Spanish soldiers, so-called Beggars (*Geuzen*), robbed Catholic churchgoers and stabbed a priest to death in St. Bavo's church. The church was subsequently closed and, in November of that year, given over to the Reformed congregation, seemingly validating the use of violence in sectarian conflicts. The *Dissent in the Church* may have a topical significance specific to St. Bavo's,[197] but it treats more broadly an issue of significant concern in the Netherlands in the sixteenth century, that of theological disagreement (often with political ramifications) that led to the persecution of some Christians by other Christians. Goltzius's inscription below the image quotes the ominous warning of John 16:2: "Indeed, an hour is coming when those who kill you will think that by doing so they are offering worship to God."[198]

Goltzius's voice is one of many of the period decrying intolerance in the church, regardless of confession. Since the early 1570s, the issue had concerned in particular Dirck Volckertsz. Coornhert, Goltzius's mentor, who accused the ministers of the Reformed Church of sinking to the level of the Roman Catholic Church in persecuting and killing their enemies—so-called heretics—now that they had gained power. Coornhert held the most liberal view conceivable, that even atheists should be tolerated, and argued that the path to strengthening the Christian faith

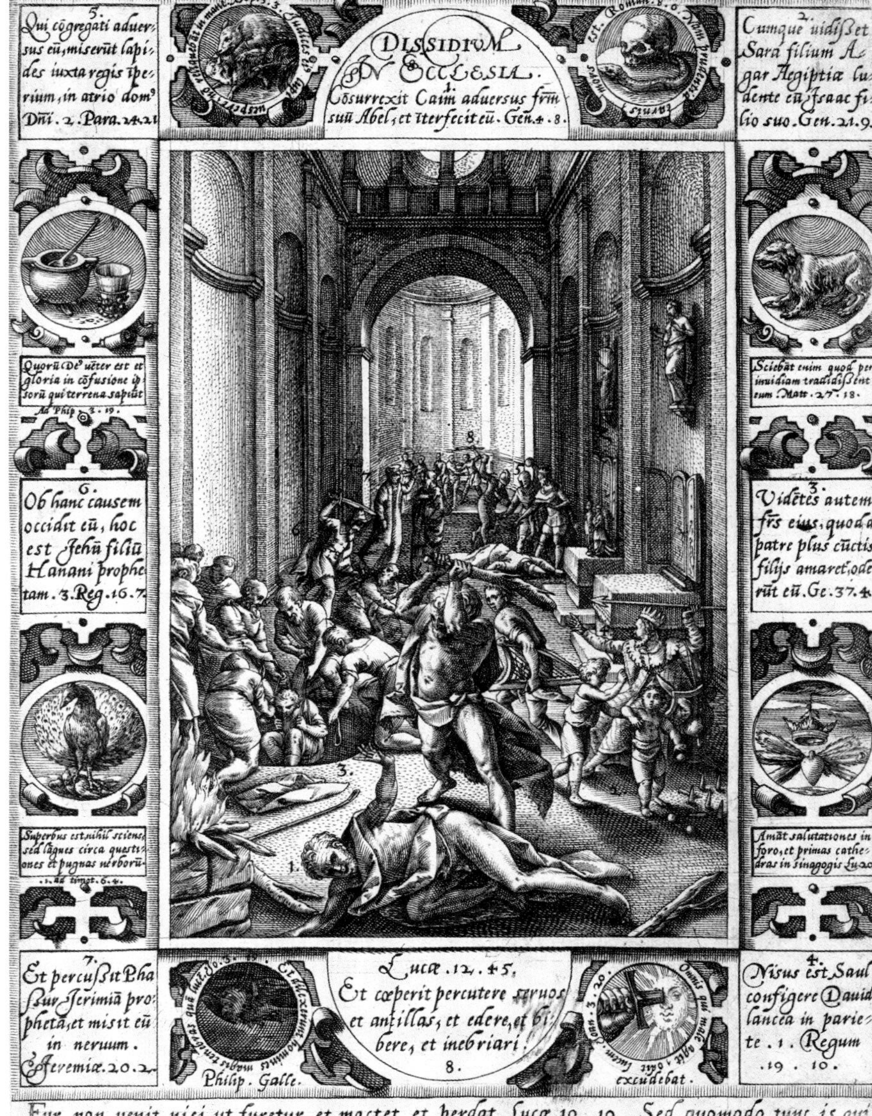

and suppressing heresy lay not in persecuting heretics, real or imagined, but in achieving doctrinal concord based on the mutually acceptable sources of the faith: the canonical scriptures and the Apostles' Creed.[199] But the voices of tolerance were ultimately overwhelmed by the whirl- wind of Reformed dominance in Holland. By 1578, William of Orange's repeated efforts to maintain a religious peace, including the guarantee, in 1577, of freedom of worship, were failing. In April 1581, public Catholic worship in Haarlem was forbidden. JC

Jan Wierix (1549–ca. 1618)

Christ Gives the Symbols of Power to Philip II and Pope Gregory XIII

ca. 1572–80

Engraving, 23 × 29.4 cm

Hollstein (Wierix) 1920

The British Museum, London, 1862,0208.66

The divine right of absolutist rulers was a mainstay of political theory of the early modern period, and was applied by Jan Wierix in his portrayal of King Philip II of Spain and Pope Gregory XIII, kneeling before Christ.[200] Christ, his right hand raised in blessing, hands to Philip and Gregory the globe of the world, surmounted by a cross and a crown that encompasses a sword and olive branch, symbols of war and peace. On the ground behind Philip is a pyramid inscribed "The Undefeated Catholic Faith" (*Fides Invicta Catholica*).

Religion and politics were bound particularly closely in the Eighty Years' War, in which the Dutch sought independence from Spain. Although the relationship was highly complex and shifting, anti-Spanish and anti-Catholic sentiments were most often allied, and political independence generally meant the exclusion of Catholic worship, as at Haarlem (see cat. 51); and (re-)subjugation by the Spanish generally meant the imposition of Catholic worship, as at Antwerp in 1585. Both sides of the conflict enlisted scriptural authority for their positions. In the "glory" at the top of the print, where one might expect to see the dove of the Holy Spirit or a tetragrammaton representing God, appears the text of Wisdom 14:7, "For blessed is the wood, by which justice

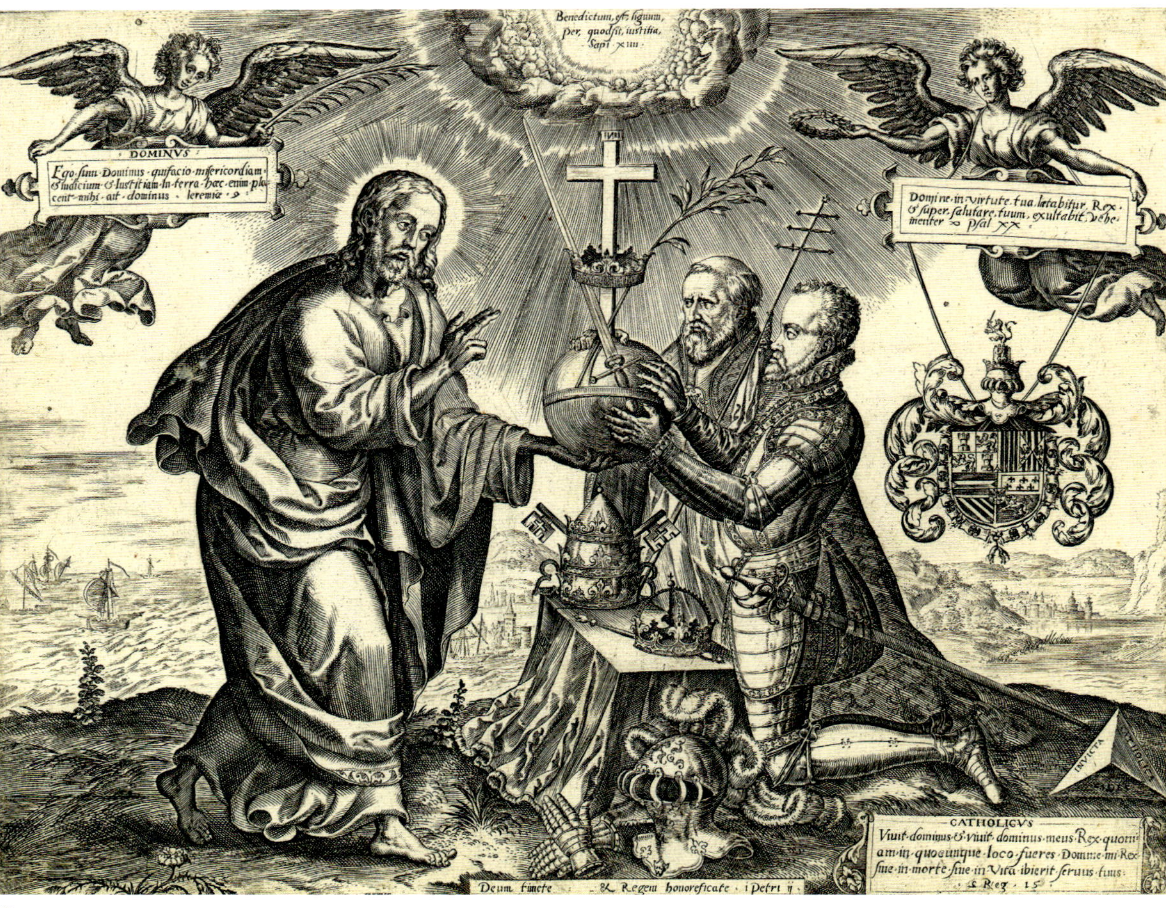

52

cometh," positing Christ's cross as the basis of Catholic rule. The term "Lord" appears several times in the print. The angel at the left holds an inscription from Jeremiah 9:24: "I am the Lord that exercise mercy, and judgment, and justice in the earth: for these things please me, saith the Lord." The angel at right proffers Psalm 20:2: "In thy strength, O Lord, the king shall joy; and in thy salvation he shall rejoice exceedingly." The inscription at the lower center of the print, from 1 Peter 2:17, draws Christ and Philip closer together: "Fear God. Honor the king." The inscription at the lower right, drawn from 2 Kings 15:21 and labeled "Catholic," is a pledge of loyalty, of Philip to Christ and of the Catholic viewer to Philip: "As the Lord liveth, and as my lord the king liveth: in what place soever thou shalt be, my lord, O king, either in death, or in life, there will thy servant be."

Such imagery was readily fungible in the confessional conflicts of the later sixteenth century. The figures of Philip and Gregory were soon copied in a complex composition by Theodor de Bry, that showed them kneeling at some distance from Christ, separated from him by the devil and the sinful world, while the leader of the Protestant opposition, William of Orange, kneels directly before Christ.[201] JC

Catalog notes

1

1 See Rosier 1997, 1:69–70.

2 On Vorsterman's 1528 Bible and Jan Swart's illustrations for it, see Beets 1915; Den Hollander 1997, 87–94, 350–54; and Rosier 1997, 1:4, 5, 16–19, 164–70.

3 Schramm 1923, 6–7 and figs. 47–48, 59–62; Rosier 1997, 1:14, 16. Vorsterman's woodcuts to Exodus 37–38 are similar to, but differ from, the illustrations in Jacob van Liesveldt's complete Bible of 1526, whose illustrations Vorsterman had elsewhere used (Rosier 1997, 1:16).

4 See, for example, the illustration from the third quarter of the fifteenth century of the *Postilla* (Koninklijke Bibliotheek, The Hague, 128 C 8).

2

5 On the genesis of the Biblia Sacra, see Hänsel 1991, 24–28; and Rosier 1997, 1:80–81, 322–25.

6 On Arias Montano's participation as draughtsman, see Hänsel 1991, 27–28.

7 On this allegorical frontispiece, see ibid., 31–33; and Rosier 1:323.

8 "And the king stood by the pillar and made a covenant before the Lord, to walk after the Lord and to keep his commandments and…to perform the words of this covenant that were written in this book."

9 For a full discussion of this frontispiece, see the Introduction, 30–31, 33, 35–36 . See also New Hollstein (Van der Borcht Book Illustrations) 423 (2:3), with full bibliography.

3

10 For a full discussion of this frontispiece, see the Introduction, 31–36. See also Hollstein (Wierix Book Illustrations) 1.1 (1:4), with full bibliography.

11 Alternatively, this may represent the waters "flowing down toward the sea of the Arabah, the Salt Sea, [that] were wholly cut off" (Joshua 4:16).

4

12 For a full discussion of this frontispiece, see the Introduction, 31–33, 36. See also Hollstein (Wierix Book Illustrations) 1.2 (1:4), with full bibliography.

5

13 For a fuller discussion of this frontispiece, see the Introduction, 33–34, 36–37. See also Hollstein (Wierix Book Illustrations) 1.3 (1:5), with full bibliography.

14 John 1:29

15 Joshua 4:14.

6

16 Shalev 2003, 56–80, esp. 63–71.

17 Matamoro also taught Arias Montano to draw; on the latter's praise of his former teacher in the preface to Nehemiah, see ibid., 61–63, and on the form and function of the map of ancient Jerusalem, adapted from Pieter Laickstein's earlier map, see Delano-Smith and Ingram 1991, 121; Hänsel 1991, 38–39; Rubin 1999, 135–39; and Shalev 2003, 61–63. As Shalev notes, Arias Montano altered Laickstein's map in one significant respect, changing the plan of Solomon's temple to match his own, as elucidated in the tractate *Exemplar, sive, de sacris fabricis liber* (*Exemplar, or Book on Sacred Edifices*), in volume 8 of the *Biblia Sacra*; see ibid., 63. For all citations from the preface, see Benito Arias Montano, "Benedicti Ariae Montani in Ierosolymorum descriptionem praefatio," in Arias Montano 1568–73, vol. 1, unpaginated.

18 Ibid.: "Demonstrabat saepè ille mihi puero, & ex ore narrantis pendenti omnia ferè illius regionis loca, quo singula modo essent, ut quondam habuisse viderentur, ut nunc haberent: ita ut ego ipse iam adolescens simulachra illa locorum ab eodem demonstrata ac depicta referre expeditissimè aliis possem, à quo etiam magnum & elegantissimum totius Ierosolymae urbis, & suburbij exemplum suis coloribus in tela depictum accepi. Quantum autem illa per hunc virum menti meae impressa, sacrorum locorum imago mihi utriusque Testamenti libros postea legenti ad multa, quae in illis libris continentur, cognoscenda contulerit, non est quòd referam."

7

19 On the *Humanae salutis monumenta*, see the Introduction, 66–75, esp. note 209, with full bibliography.

20 The emblem is an image-text construction generally formed of three parts: a picture, motto, and commentary; the latter comments on the relation between the epigrammatic motto and the pictorial image, which are found to be complementary, antithetical, or some shade between. The parts together constitute a poetic conceit enshrining a truth to be discerned through the hermeneutics of viewing and reading. On the early history of the emblem, see Miedema 1968; for an excellent summary of the current state of emblem studies, see the essays in Dimler 2007.

21 Christopher Plantin, "Christophorus Plantinus lectori s.," in Arias Montano 1571, unfoliated.

22 See Introduction, 71–72.

23 Deuteronomy 2:7.

24 Arias Montano 1571, unfoliated [*imago* 17]: "Constantiae fructus." "Fideli Deo s."

25 Ibid.: "Felix qui monitisque Dei verbisque benigni/ Audiit, ille sacrae compos erit patriae."

26 "In tabulam Israëlitarum Iordanem transeuntium. Ode sapphica XVII.," in ibid., unfoliated [*ode* 17]: "Sed fides constans animíque magni,/ Quae semel certo radiata verbo,/ Tramitem ostensum subit, atque caeli/ Prospicit alti// Templa, lux unde & favor, ac potentis/ Vis tenax verbi, penetrare praesens/ Turbidi fluctus maris, ac secundo/ Grati a ductu."

27 Ibid.: "Tunc probat sortis memor et prioris,/ Digna quam multis fuerint periclis,/ Quamque contento repetenda cursu/ Munera dia./ Sic et Aegypti miseris redempta/ Vinculis felix manus, advocanti et/ Obsequens verbo, tenuit quietis/ Regna beatae./ Hinc inaccessos trepidare mentes,/ Hinc opes visa est solito priores,/ Largius turbae venienti in usum/ Fundere tellus."

28 On this *monumentum*, see New Hollstein (Van der Borcht Book Illustrations) 912 (3:55). On Van der Borcht and his association with the publisher Plantin, see Bowen and Imhof 2008, 322–26; on Abraham de Bruyn and Plantin, 9–31.

29 Arias Montano 1571, unfoliated [*imago* 19]: "Quis tam multa brevi dicat potuisse comari/ Tempore, vir nisi qui credidit et studuit?"

30 "In tabulam terrae distributae. Ode tricolos tetrastrophos. XIX.," in Arias Montano 1571, unfoliated [*ode* 19]: "Haec ipse nullis indigus arbiter/ Novo colono dividit, et bonos/ Commendat exercere in usus,/ Non propriae referenda laudi./ Valde stupenti tam cito plurium/ Cessisse regnorum imperium sibi?/ Et ante quam possent obiri/ Cuncta oculis, potuisse vinci."

31 Christopher Plantin, "Tabul. XIX. Argum.," in Arias Montano 1571, 10–11.

8

32 The Latin text in the lower margin reads: "Egressvs Zacharias non poterat loqvi. et cognovervnt qvod visionem vidisset in templo." ("When Zacharias came out, he was unable to speak. And they understood that he had a vision in the temple.") Translation by Christopher Lakey.

33 Serlio 1611. This English version was translated directly from the Dutch 1553 version.

34 In the lower margin, a Latin verse reads, "Amen amen dico vobis anteqvam Abraham fieret ego svm." ("I say to you: Amen, Amen. Before Abraham was, I am.") Translation by Christopher Lakey.

35 Below the lamb, in the lower margin, a Latin verse reads, "Domvs mea domvs orationis vocabitvr, vos avtem fecistis eam spelvncam latronvm." ("My house shall be called a house of prayer, but you have made it a den of thieves.") Translation by Christopher Lakey.

9

36 Nadal wrote his texts in response to unidentified images that formed the basis for the several sets of drawings upon which the *modelli* by Passeri and De Vos were ultimately based. Birgit Ulrike Münch has recently argued that Willem van Branteghem's *Iesu Christi vita* may have been Nadal's primary source ("Sola Scriptura? Mapping the Passion Cycle during the Era of Confessional Clashes," Historians of Netherlandish Art Conference, Baltimore/Washington, DC, 2006). On the genesis of the images for the *Adnotationes et meditationes in Evangelia*, see Wadell 1985. The 153 images were published separately in 1593 under the title *Evangelicae historiae imagines* (*Images of Gospel History*). On the *Adnotationes et meditationes*, see Melion 2003, with full bibliography (89, nn. 1, 7). On *imago* 90, see Hollstein (Wierix Book Illustrations) 56.76 (2:41).

37 The Roman numerals identify the chapters to which the images correspond.

38 On *definitio per descriptionem*, see Fumaroli 1980b.

39 The right corner figure calls attention to the publican and the pharisee, expounding them to his companion and encouraging us to consider their significance. For a fuller discussion of this print, see the Introduction, 80–82.

10

40 Van Ruusbroec 1989, 112, 113, 152, and 153, lines 58–62; 68–74; 444–46, and 511–514; Ruusbroec 1985, 41, 119.

41 Dutch Book of Hours, Flanders early 15th c., Brugge, Grootseminarie ter Brugge, MS. 72–175, fol. 64 recto.

42 Jerome 1892, 98 (Letter 53, to Paulinus, 5).

43 Deschamps 1960–61 (Gerard Zerbolt van Zutphen, *De libris teutonicalibus*, Chapter 7, 93–95).

44 Claesz's graphic style and, to a greater degree, the painting tradition it emulated, may have informed Karel van Mander's critical categories of "understanding" and "variety," which required skillful description of "foreign things" (Van Mander 1604, fol. 35r, line 12). See also Smith 2007, 2:347–65.

11

45 Jacobowitz and Stepanek 1983, 214–17; Filedt Kok 1988.

46 Below the engraved scenes, inscriptions were printed in Dutch or French from Exodus 34:9; Psalm 87: 4 and Esther 7:3.

47 Previous groupings included Moses, the Pentecost, and Elijah preaching. Hesdin of Amiens, *Biblia Pauperum* (c. 1450–1455), Museum Meermano Westreenianum, The Hague, MS. 10 A 15 fol. 37r; *Biblia Pauperum*, Netherlands or Germany (1465), Library of Congress Rare Books, Washington, DC, 35.

48 Earlier books grouped Roman soldiers falling to the ground as Christ made himself known (John 18: 6) with Samson slaying the Philistines (Judges 15:15) (*Speculum Humanae Salvationis*, Keulen [ca.1450], Museum Meermano Westreeniam, The Hague, MS. 10B 34 fol. 17v; *Speculum Humanae Salvationis*, Germany? [1400–1500], Museum Meermano Westreenianum, The Hague, MS. 10 C 23 fol. 20v) or, with the Foolish Virgins and the Apocalypse, Museum Meermano Westreenianum, The Hague, MS. 10 A 15 fol. 29v, and Library of Congress Rare Books, Washington, DC, *Biblia Pauperum*, 20.

49 Netherlandish writers associated Esther with Christ's Passion. Dirc van Delf 1938 (De spieghel der menscheliker behoudenesse, XXXIX).

50 Museum Meermano Westreenianum, The Hague, MS. 10 C 23 fol. 43r; Museum Meermano Westreenianum, The Hague, MS. 10 B 34 fol. 40r.

51 Library of Congress, Washington, DC, *Biblia Pauperum*, 36; Museum Meermano Westreenianum, The Hague, MS. 10 A 15 fol. 37v.

52 Jerome 1892, 99 (Letter 53, to Paulinus, 8). Dirc van Delf 1938, *Tafel*, 575–76 (zomerstuk, XLVI).

12

53 On the subject of Christ in the Winepress, see Thomas 1936; Gessler 1942; Vloberg 1946, 172 83; Weckwerth 1960; Schiller 1971 72, 2:128 29, 228 29; Mâle 1986, 110 16. Marrow 1979, 83 94, discusses its relationship with narrative scenes, especially the Bearing of the Cross.

54 Quoted by Schiller 1971–72, 2:228.

55 Thomas 1936, 115ff.; Weckwerth 1960, 97–98; Marrow 1979, 85.

56 See especially Marrow 1979, 83–94.

57 Weckwerth 1960, 97.

58 Marrow 1979, 86. The subject was used in the later sixteenth century as a

frontispiece to an engraved Passion series by Jacques de Gheyn II and Zacharias Dolends after Karel van Mander (New Hollstein [Van Mander] 36–49).

59 See Mâle 1986, 112 16.

60 See Schiller 1971–72, 2:228; Weckwerth 1960, 106–107.

61 Wierix's engraving cannot be dated with precision. It was granted a privilege for publication by Joachim de Buschere, a secretary to the Council of Brabant, who performed that service for many Wierix prints, but only a few of those are dated—in 1602 (Hollstein [Wierix] 76, 77, 78), 1603 (Hollstein [Wierix] 80, 81), 1607 (Hollstein [Wierix] 1662), and 1613 (Hollstein [Wierix] 1813). Buschere's documented privileges for books date from 1577 (Voet 1969–72, 2:269) and 1589–1600 (Van den Branden 1990, 73–80, whose publication covers only the years to 1600).

62 On catching Christ's blood in chalices, see Vloberg 1946, 149–58. It has been suggested that the introduction of chalices into representations of the subject was a response to attacks on the doctrine of the Real Presence in the eucharist by John Wycliffe and John Huss and their followers in the decades around 1400 (Weckwerth 1960, 99–100).

13

63 For the distinction between iconic and narrative, see Ringbom 1984.

64 On the *arma Christi*, see Berliner 1955; Schiller 1971–72, 2:184ff.; Suckale 1977. See also cat. 43.

65 It is from this passage that the term Man of Sorrows (or Suffering) (*vir dolorum*) comes. It is usually applied to a post-crucifixion image of the suffering Christ but may also be used for a pre-crucifixion Christ, as here.

14

66 Scenes more commonly depicted were: Noah's Sacrifice, the Mocking of Noah, the Tower of Babel, the Destruction of the Tower of Babel, Lot and his Family Leaving Sodom, Lot Making Love to his Daughters, Samson Destroying the Temple of the Philistines, the Burial of Samson, the Nativity with the Adoration of the Shepherds, and the Adoration of the Magi. Less common were: the Destruction of Jericho, the Destruction of Ai and the Stoning of Achan, the King of Ai Hanged, the Corpse of the King of Ai Brought to the City Gates, the Capture of Tirsah, the People of Israel Divided between Tibni and Omri, Jehu Destroying the Temple of Baal, Jehu Adoring the Golden Calves, the Chaldeans Carrying away the Temple Pillars, the Chaldeans Carrying away the Temple Treasures, and the Destruction of the Temple by Titus.

15

67 Cort engraved the print at the start of his third sojourn in Rome (1572–78), on which see Sellink 2000, esp. xxx. There are three virtually identical autograph versions of *The Annunciation Surrounded by Prophets of the Incarnation*, all dated 1571, on which see New Hollstein (Cort) 20–22 (53–55), with full bibliography.

68 The inscription also names his place of birth—Sant'Angelo in Vado, located in Le Marche.

69 Canisius 1577, 304. The lily held by the angel Gabriel derives from and alludes to this famous passage from Isaiah 45.

70 Ibid., 236.

71 Ibid., 238.

17

72 On the signs of the zodiac in early modern art, see Stedelijk Museum Sint-Niklaas 1994; for the Gospel Emblems specifically, pp. 44–46, 114–27.

73 See Stedelijk Museum Sint-Niklaas 1994, 132, 134.

18

74 Exodus 20:3–8; Deuteronomy 5:16–21.

75 Matthew 5: 22, 28, 34, 35 and 44; Mark 13:35–36; Luke 6:36–37; John 14:23.

76 Gregory of Nyssa 1979, 58–59.

77 Ambrose 2007, 324 ("On the Mysteries," 9, 51–52).

78 Thomas Aquinas 2007, 4:538–45 (q. 106, a. 2).

79 Wierix's formulation endorses his allegorical idiom insofar as it agrees with Gregory the Great's dictum that allegory reveals spiritual meaning by elaborating upon the typical sense derived from historical exposition (Gregory 1844, 1.1, The Epistle, III).

19

80 Rosier 1997, 1:14–15, 159, 196–200. On Liesveldt's 1532 Bible, see Den Hollander 1997, 393–96.

81 For the illustrations in *Das Ander teyl des alten testaments*, see Strachan 1957, 45 and figs. 78–79; Naredi-Rainer 1994, 158–59.

82 Solomon's Temple and its furnishings are also described in 2 Chronicles 3–4, a much later text.

83 2 Kings 23:3; see also 1 (3) Kings 11:14.

84 1 Kings 7:39.

85 1 Kings 8:62–64.

86 On representations of Solomon's temple and its furnishings, see Mirimonde 1975; Gutmann 1976; Rosenau 1979; Naredi-Rainer 1994; Tuzi 2002.

20

87 The number of bleedings was sometimes given as five, as by Jacobus de Voragine, in his *Golden Legend* (Voragine 1993, 1:74).

88 The choice of subjects varies, in both literary and visual treatments; see Clifton 2001, 68–69.

89 The distychs were published posthumously by Junius's grandson as "In septem, quas vocant, Christi haemorrhagias" in a book entitled *Poëmatum* (Junius 1598, 188–89). This book includes numerous poems by Junius that appear on prints of varied subjects after Heemskerck, five series of which were engraved by Muller. On the relationship between Heemskerck and Junius, with especial regard to the *Poëmatum*, see Veldman 1974.

21

90 On Arias Montano's scriptural sources, see Hänsel 1991, 107, 108. On the *Divinarum nuptiarum conventa et acta*, see ibid., 100–15; New Hollstein (Van Groeningen) 286–313 (2:69–87); Melion 2005a, 98–107, 200–01; Hollstein (Wierix

Book Illustrations) 6, 7, 13, and 32 (1:51–59, 86–87, and 185–86); and Melion 2009, 37–104. On the *Christi Iesu vitae admirabiliumque actionum speculum*, see Hänsel 1991, 101, 111, 115–18; New Hollstein (Van Groeningen) 313–64 (2:88–120); Hollstein (Wierix Book Illustrations) 7 (1:54–59); and Melion 2005a, 98–107.

91 These scenes are veridical *specula* (mirror-images), rather than *umbrae* (shadowy images) or *fabulae* (fictive images), according to the usage of Arias Montano.

92 Illustration 10: "Hoc speculo rerum causas, finesque, modosque/ Inspicies, homines ut pereant stolidi./ Ipsa tibi quae sum dictata Scientia, monstro,/ Mortaleis qualis fabula habet miseros."

93 The personifications of *Confessio*, *Poenitentia*, and *Satisfactio* watch from behind *Sponsa*'s chair at right.

94 Illustration 17: "Postquam docta tenes, quam vana est gloria secli,/ Humana & quam sit frivola conditio;/ Nunc exempla tui speculo monstrata fideli/ Aspicies Sponsi, sed retinenda tibi."

95 "Ecce venio ut faciam voluntatem tuam."

22

96 On the *David*, see New Hollstein (Van Groeningen) 265–85 (2:54–57); and Melion 2005a.

97 These workmen are a reference to 1 Chronicles 22:6–16: "Then he called for Solomon his son, and charged him to build a house for the Lord, the God of Israel. David said to Solomon, 'My son, I had it in my heart to build a house to the name of the Lord my God. But the word of the Lord came to me, saying, "You have shed much blood and have waged great wars; you shall not build a house to my name… Behold a son shall be born to you; he shall be a man of peace. I will give him peace from all his enemies round about; for his name shall be Solomon, and I will give peace and quiet to Israel in his days. He shall build a house for my name, He shall be my son, and I will be his father, and I will establish his royal throne in Israel for ever." Now, my son, the Lord be with you, so that you may succeed in building the house of the Lord your God, as he has spoken concerning you….You have an abundance of workmen: stonecutters, masons, carpenters, and all kinds of craftsmen without number, skilled in working gold, silver, bronze, and iron. Arise and be doing! The Lord be with you!'"

98 "Divitias et opes Pietas lectissima in usus/ Unica commendat, cum petit ipsa suos.// Quis prudens mihi Rex? qui prospicit undique ut unus/ Sit cultus populis, imperitetque Deus."

99 "Sapiens senectus."

23

100 On the *Annunciation*, see Hollstein (Wierix Book Illustrations) 39.2 (1:219). As Bowen and Imhof 2008, 141–55, have shown, the publisher Plantin commissioned multiple plates of prints such as the *Annunciation* to be used in the various editions of the reformed *Breviarum Romanum*, *Missale Romanum*, and *Officium B. Mariae Virginis* that he produced between 1568 and 1589. He received the right to publish the new breviary in 1568, the new missal in 1570, and the book of hours in 1572, on which see Bowen 1997, 63–66.

101 Plantin 1584, 113: "Conditor alme siderum,/ Aeterna lux credentium,/ Christe redemptor omnium,/ Exaudi preces supplicum/…/ Vergente mundi vespere,/ Uti sponsus de thalamo,/ Egressus honestissima/ Virginis matris clausula./ Cuius forti potentiae/ Genu curvantur omnia,/ Caelestia, terrestria,/ Nutu fatentur subdita/ Te deprecamur agie,/ Venture iudex saeculi."

24

102 In Dillingen, in 1558, the Jesuit writer Peter Canisius (b. Netherlands 1521, d. Germany 1597) administered the first printing of the litany of Our Lady of Loreto, containing 49 invocations of the Virgin Mary. In 1571 the Jesuit leader Otto Truchseß gained papal approval for wider use of the litany; see Heal 2007, 150–51.

103 On the spiritual significance of the Circumcision in Netherlandish devotional art, see Melion 2001. On symbolic correspondences between the rosary and Christ's circumcision in Netherlandish art, see Steinberg 1983, 47–50.

104 The Circumcision and events in Christ's life were stressed in Jesuit rosary devotion. This practice is consistent with Ignatius of Loyola's *Spiritual Exercises*, which incorporated meditative prayer oriented toward the imitation of Christ; see Mullett 1999, 93.

25

105 New Hollstein (Galle) 249–72 (2:178–208); Clifton 2008b. On Galle's *Seven Corporal Works of Mercy*, see also Van Bühren 1998, 130–36, 293–97.

106 On florilegia and commonplace books, see Lechner 1962; Rouse and Rouse 1979; Goyet 1996; Moss 1996; and Havens 2001.

107 Or, in one case, Church Fathers.

26

108 See Mielke 1975.

109 The Latin text in the lower margin reads: "O patris aeterni proles certissima, regna In tua cum venes, sis memor oro mei." (Oh most resolved Son of our heavenly Father, while you come into your kingdom, I beg that you remember me.) Translation by Christopher Lakey.

27

110 On the *Annunciation*, see Leeflang 2003, 210–15, no. 75; Jürgen Müller in Müller, Roettig, and Stolzenburg 2002, 40–41, no. 44; Melion 2007b, 395–98; and Melion 2009, 369–94.

111 The dedication is addressed to Wilhelm V, Duke of Bavaria: "Ut mediis Proteus se transformabat in uncis,/ Formosae cupido Pomonae captus amore:/ Sic varia Princeps Tibi nunc se Goltzius arte/ Commutat, sculptor mirabilis, atque repertor."

112 Goltzius and Schonaeus mix two fables concerning transformation, pairing Proteus with Pomona, the beloved of Vertumnus; on Goltzius's interest in the Ovidian tale of Vertumnus and Pomona,

see Sluijter 2000, 70–85.

113 One might frame this imitative procedure in terms of decorum: rather than emulating these masters, that is, striving to surpass them, he impersonates their signature styles, foregrounding their art, not his own, as the privileged means through which he decorously pays homage to the Virgin.

28

114 On the *Adnotationes et meditationes in Evangelia*, see cat. 9, especially note 1.
115 On *imago* 3, see Hollstein (Wierix Book Illustrations) 56.4 (2:12); and Melion 2007b, 406–26.
116 Nadal 1595, 18.
117 On *imago* 4, see Hollstein (Wierix Book Illustrations) 56.5 (2:12); and Melion 2007b, 406–26.
118 Like several other chapters forming the continuation of a sequence, that on the dawn of the Lord's birth consists of extensive annotations followed by a short meditation. In chapters such as these, the *adnotationes* usurp much of the *meditatio*'s form and function, while the *meditatio* proper serves as a coda.
119 Nadal 1595, 24.
120 Ibid.
121 Ibid., 23.
122 Ibid., 24.

29

123 On the *Septem Psalmi Davidici*, see Hollstein (Wierix) 1061–68 (5:159–62); and Melion 2009, 261–92. Antoon Wierix engraved the final print in the series, *Soldier Piercing the Side of Christ on the Cross, Enframed by the Text of Psalm 142*.
124 In the meditative tradition, Christ's wounds are seen to reopen when his mantle is stripped off and his congealed scabs loosened. The Circumcision was often connected to the Passion, as the first willing sacrifice made by Christ on behalf of sinful humankind. On the Seven Bleedings of Christ, see also cat. 20.
125 Numbered as such in the Septuagint and the Vulgate, these psalms appear as numbers 6, 32, 38, 51, 102, 130, and 143 in the Hebrew Bible.
126 Augustine 1847–57, 1:35. Following Augustine, the Circumcision was often interpreted as the promulgation of the new doctrine of spiritual circumcision that abrogates the rite prescribed under the Old Law.
127 Augustine 1847–57, 1:37.

30

128 The play *Verloren Zoon* was performed by *rederijkers* at a church in Dendermonde in 1420, at Oudenaarden in 1547 and in Lier in 1548; see Te Winkel 1922, 403. The play *Courtois d'Arras* was popular in late-medieval France; see Symes 2002. Latin school plays on the prodigal son were performed through the 16th century; see Kelly 1974.
129 At right, the kneeling swineherd and cow recall Albrecht Dürer's print of the prodigal son; see Beets 1913, 41. Lucas's depiction has been identified with faith and repentance; see Jacobowitz and Stepanek 1983, 94. The son's bony figure and staff recall the impoverished vagabond in Hieronymus Bosch's *Wayfarer* (Rotterdam, Museum Boymans-van Beuningen) and *Haywain* shutters (Madrid, Museo Nacional del Prado).

31

130 Scholars concur in dating the series to the middle of the second decade. Filedt Kok 1996, 19, found that some impressions are printed on paper with the same watermark as Lucas's *Abraham and Issac*, which he dates to 1517. On Lucas's first series on the subject, see Jacobowitz and Stepanek 1983, 102–20.
131 Filedt Kok 1996, 19.
132 Jacobowitz and Stepanek 1983, 166–67.
133 Ibid., 166. Filedt Kok 1978, 50, has suggested that humanist friends of the publisher may have supplied the inscriptions. See also Matile 2000, 16–20.
134 Translation of this passage was assisted by the modern Dutch translation cited by Filedt Kok 1978, 50.
135 This is an apocryphal book, also known as the Book of Sirach.
136 Veldman 2006, 124.

32

137 The evangelists reported that wondrous events occurred at that time, including an extraordinary catch of fishes (Luke 5:2); the miraculous replication of loaves and fishes (Mark 6:32–44); Jesus walking on water, and Peter's recognition of him as the Son of God (Matthew 14:22–33).
138 Ruusbroec 1985, 143.
139 Falkenburg 2001, 274.
140 See Bonaventure 1882–1902, 8:86a-b. Also see Van Maerlant 1918, 90–109, 126–27.

33

141 New Hollstein (Breu) 17. The priority of Cornelis's version, assumed by Gibson 1981, 435, is rejected by Armstrong 1990, 162 n. 18, who also dismisses the connection he attempts to draw between Cornelis's woodcut and contemporaneous *rederijker* theater. The most significant differences between the two woodcuts occur in the upper half of the compositions: Cornelis has changed the positions of Christ's arms to the more traditional up on the side of the saved and down on the side of the damned; he has shifted the positions of the angels and replaced their trumpets with the lily and sword that appear hovering by Christ in the earlier version; and he has added the two scenes at the right and left of the background landscape. Cornelis's woodcut, of which there is only this one extant impression, has not been dated more precisely than the later 1540s or early 1550s. On Cornelis's print, see Armstrong 1990, 84–86.
142 Above the demon is a blank space in a billow of smoke; in the comparable space of the German woodcut is inscribed 1 Peter 5:8: "Discipline yourselves, keep alert. Like a roaring lion your adversary the devil prowls around, looking for someone to devour."
143 For another representation of Lady World, see cat. 43.
144 On the Acts of Mercy, see Van Bühren 1998; for the association of the Acts of Mercy with the Last Judgment and deathbeds, see esp. pp. 64–68. See also cat. 34 and Clifton 2008b. Since the Middle Ages, the number of Acts of Mercy was

often put at seven, with an additional work, burying the dead, drawn from the Book of Tobit.

145 On the *Ars moriendi*, see O'Connor 1942; Shestack 1967, nos. 4–15.
146 Calvin 1960, 822 (3.18.2). For an anti-Catholic series of prints on good works of ca. 1560, see Horst 1990.

35

147 See also Craig 1983; Meadow 1995; Falkenburg 1996; Sullivan 1999.

36

148 Orenstein 2001, 208.
149 Ibid.

37

150 See Junius 1598, 185.
151 Veldman 2000, 128–29.

38

152 Van Bühren 1998, 20 21.
153 Also quoted in the print is Ecclesiastes 1:15: "The perverse are hard to be corrected."

39

154 "Cvm petit e liqvido mvlier samararitidos orae fonte vndam implorat pvtealea mvnera Christvs."
155 Augustine 2004, 101–107 (Tractate 15, on John 4:1–42).

40

156 Suggested by Strauss 1977, 1:78.

41

157 See Dekoninck, Guiderdoni-Bruslé, and Van Vaeck 2006, 9–14, 93–94. That the term emblems was used for narrative as well as hieroglyphic images in the sixteenth century is evident in Adriaen Collaert's *Gospel Emblems* of 1585 after Hans Bol (cat. 17). See also cat 7. The Beatitudes were the subject of an emblem book variously attributed to Edward Manning and Edward Mico, which was published in London in 1665: *Ashrea: Or, The Grove of Beatitudes, Represented in Emblemes: And, by the Art of Memory, To be read on our Blessed Savior Crucifi'd: With Considerations and meditations suitable to every Beatitude, and to the holy time of Lent.*
158 See, for example, Hollstein (Wierix) 421–22, 425, 445–62, 1673–76, 1742, 1774, 1850–59, many of which are quite similar in format and motifs to the Beatitudes.
159 Antoon Wierix represented the self-sacrificing pelican in other emblems as well (Hollstein [Wierix] 422, 1676).
160 Hollstein (Wierix) 445–62, where the title is translated as *The Human Heart Vanquished by the Infant*. The emblems were copied many times in the seventeenth century.

42

161 Van Mander 1994–99, 1:74, 202, 222, 274, and passim (see also 2:23).
162 "While art-destroying, unscrupulous Mars startles and horrifies our lands with thunderous gunfire and causes Time's grey hairs to stand on end, it is to be wondered that there are still so many practitioners of our peace and prosperity loving art of painting to be found among our countrymen, the Netherlanders" (Van Mander 1994–99, 1:457; see also 1:301, 305).
163 Van Mander 1994–99, 1:198. In commenting on Van Mander's text, Hessel Miedema draws on the passage in discussing the conflicting evidence for Van Mander's religious proclivities (2:23).
164 Van Mander 1994–99, 1:21-22, 25 (see also 2:58).
165 Van Mander 1994–99, 1:50.
166 See De Jong and De Groot 1988, 117–19; Worthen 1991–92.
167 See Mochizuki 2008.

43

168 Hollstein (Wierix) 1791, 1793. In the simplest of the compositions, the knight, holding sword and shield (on which are emblazoned the Instruments of the Passion, also known as the *arma Christi*), stands on seven swords, each representing one of the Seven Capital Sins. Each of these two versions is after a composition by Girolamo Olgiato and is paired with an image of a sinner in danger of dropping into the "pit of Hell." On the *miles christianus* in the art and literature of the sixteenth and seventeenth centuries, see Knipping 1974, 1:92–94; Wang 1975.
169 Wierix also produced a reduced version of this composition (Hollstein [Wierix] 1796). The present engraving was produced for a German client, Hubert Caymox of Nuremberg (1554–1601), who dedicated it to the Silesian intellectual, Jacob Monavius of Wroclaw (Breslau) (1546–1603), who, as part of an international circle of intellectuals, was in contact with, among others, the Antwerp geographer Abraham Ortelius, the Flemish philosopher Justus Lipsius, and the Franco-Netherlandish botanist Carolus Clusius. Caymox was part of a publishing family with ties to De Jode from the mid-1560s. See Meurer 1993, esp. 24–28. Crispijn de Passe "dedicated and consecrated" a series of emblematic engravings to Caymox, "exceptional devotee of the art of printmaking," in 1594 (Hollstein [De Passe] 629–36); see Veldman 2001a, 76–77, 111. Caymox's death in 1601 provides a terminus ante quem for the print.
170 On the figure of "Lady World" in this print, see De Jongh 2000, 64–65. For another representation of Lady World, see cat. 33.

44

171 Washington, DC, National Gallery of Art.
172 Dirk Bouts's *Annunciation*, ca. 1445 (Madrid, Museo Nacional del Prado) and Hubert and Jan van Eyck's Ghent Altarpiece, 1432 (Ghent, St. Bavo's cathedral). See Hand and Wolff 1989, 44–45. On the impact of Italian art see Jacobowitz and Stepanek 1983, 221, cat. no. 87. In a woodcut of ca. 1525, modeled after Jan Gossaert's design, Cain is muscular and unclothed (Hollstein [Gossaert] 4).
173 Augustine 1887, XV, 18, 299. See also Silver and Smith 1978.
174 Van Maerlant 1983, 1:23–24, 903–36.
175 On history as theme, see Bangs 1980.
176 A jaw-bone also appears in "Cain Killing Abel," Spieghel Historiael, West Flanders, ca.1325–35, Den Haag, Koninklijke Bibliotheek MS. KA 20, fol. 5ra. See Schapiro 1942. Biblical references to wild-men include Judges 13–16, Genesis 16:12, and Daniel 4:29–30.

45

177 "Exagitat vates tensis ad sidera palmis isacidum dvrae scelerata piacvla gentis."
178 The structures were inspired by Heemskerck's observation of archeological specimens in Rome. See Veldman 1974.
179 See Silver 1999.
180 An example is the Anabaptist movement in Antwerp during the 1530s; see Waite 1987.
181 Saunders 1978–79.
182 On the critical category of *reflexy-const* see: Melion 1991, 70–77.

46

183 The second edition was published by Philips Galle's son Theodoor.
184 The Latin text reads: "Qui Danieli pericul m crearan in foueam conijci ntur, protinusq[ue] de orantur." (Those who attempted danger to Daniel were thrown into the lion's den and devoured straightaway.) All Latin translations by Christopher Lakey.
185 Bangs 1977, 9.
186 See Saunders 1978–79, 76.
187 Ibid.

47

188 Veldman 2000, 132.
189 Ibid., 137.

48

190 See Junius 1598, 180.
191 Saunders 1978–79.

49

192 The literature on the subject is extensive; for a discussion in English, see Koerner 1993, 363–410. The most extensive treatment is now Reinitzer 2006 (1:241 for Nagel's print). On the allegory's appearance on the title-page of *La saincte Bible …*, published in French translation by Martin Lempereur (or De Keyser), see Clifton 2008a.
193 See Ehresmann 1966–67.

50

194 On Hondius's religious inclinations, see Orenstein 1996, 33–35, 98–101. For an interpretation of the print as firmly opposed to Spanish Catholic rule in the Netherlands, see Tanis and Horst 1993, 74–75.

51

195 Strauss 1977, 1: 66–81, 124–147.
196 Goltzius's prints were produced just after Galle's series of the Seven Sacraments, Seven Works of Corporal Mercy, and Seven Works of Spiritual Mercy, and bear some affinities with them (see cat. 25, 38). Some of these prints by Goltzius were republished by Hendrick Hondius (Orenstein 1996, 98–100).
197 On the events in St. Bavo's, see Overmeer 1912, 101–104; Voogt 2000, 40, 92. See also the catalog entry for Goltzius's *Eight Beatitudes* (cat. 40).
198 Also quoted in his Judgment of Solomon (cat. 50).
199 On the tolerance issue, see Bonger 1954, Güldner 1968, Voogt 2000.

52

200 The print, previously attributed to Hieronymus Wierix and now given to Jan (Johannes) Wierix in the recent Hollstein catalog, may be dated between Gregory's elevation to the papacy in 1572 and Philip's conquest of Portugal in 1580, which does not yet appear here in the king's coat of arms. On the attribution of prints bearing the monogram IH.W to Jan Wierix, see Van Zuyven-Zeman 2004, xv. On the print, see Rijksmuseum Het Catharijneconvent 1986, 110; Tanis and Horst 1993, 94–95.
201 Rijksmuseum Het Catharijneconvent 1986, 111; Tanis and Horst 1993, 90–91.

References

Hollstein (Anthonisz.)
De Hoop Scheffer, D., ed., *Hollstein's Dutch & Flemish Etchings, Engravings and Woodcuts ca. 1450–1700: Volume XXX: Cornelis Anthonisz T(h)eunissen to Johannes den Uyl,* compiled Ger Luijten. Amsterdam: Van Gendt, 1986.

Hollstein (Claesz)
Hollstein, F. W. H., ed., *Dutch & Flemish Etchings, Engravings and Woodcuts ca. 1450–1700: Volume IV: Brun–Coques.* Amsterdam: Menno Hertzberger, n.d.

Hollstein (Gossaert)
Hollstein, F. W. H., ed., *Dutch & Flemish Etchings, Engravings and Woodcuts ca. 1450–1700: Volume VIII: Goltzius–Heemskerck.* Amsterdam: Menno Hertzberger, n.d.

Hollstein (De Passe)
Boon, K. G. and J. Verbeek, *Dutch & Flemish Etchings, Engravings and Woodcuts ca. 1450–1700: Volume XV: Van Ostade–De Passe.* Amsterdam: Menno Hertzberger, n.d.

Hollstein (Swart)
Boon, K. G., ed., *Hollstein's Dutch & Flemish Etchings, Engravings and Woodcuts ca. 1450–1700: Volume XXIX: Samuel de Swaef to Jan Thesing,* compiled Dieuwke de Hoop Scheffer, George S. Keyes, and Ger Luyten. Blaricum: A. L. van Gendt, 1984.

Hollstein (De Vos)
De Hoop Scheffer, D., ed., *Hollstein's Dutch & Flemish Etchings, Engravings and Woodcuts 1450–1700: Maarten de Vos,* compiled Christiaan Schuckman, 3 vols, Rotterdam: Sound & Vision Interactive, 1995–96.

Hollstein (Wierix)
Van der Stock, Jan, and Marjolein Leesberg, eds, *Hollstein's Dutch & Flemish Etchings, Engravings and Woodcuts 1450–1700: The Wierix Family,* compiled Zsuzsanna van Ruyven-Zeman in collaboration with Marjolein Leesberg, 10 vols, Rotterdam: Sound & Vision, 2003–04.

Hollstein (Wierix Book Illustrations)
Van der Stock, Jan, ed., *Hollstein's Dutch & Flemish Etching, Engravings and Woodcuts 1450–1700: The Wierix Family, Book Illustrations,* compiled Harriet Stroomberg, 2 vols, Ouderkerk aan den Ijssel: Sound & Vision, 2006–07.

New Hollstein
(Van der Borcht Book Illustrations)
Luyten, Ger, ed., *The New Hollstein Dutch & Flemish Etchings, Engravings and Woodcuts 1450–1700: Peeter van der Borcht, Book Illustrations,* compiled Hans Mielke and Ursula Mielke, 6 vols, Ouderkerk aan den Ijssel: Sound & Vision, 2005–07.

New Hollstein (Breu)
Kaulbach, Hans-Martin, ed., *The New Hollstein German Engravings, Etchings and Woodcuts 1400–1700: Jörg Breu the Elder and the Younger,* compiled Guido Messling, 2 vols, Ouderkerk aan den Ijssel: Sound & Vision, 2008.

New Hollstein (Collaert)
Leesberg, Marjolein, and Karen L. Bowen, eds, *The New Hollstein Dutch & Flemish Etchings, Engravings and Woodcuts 1450–1700: The Collaert Dynasty,* compiled Ann Diels and Marjolein Leesberg, 8 vols, Ouderkerk aan den Ijssel: Sound & Vision, 2005–06.

New Hollstein (Cort)
Leeflang, Huigen, ed., *The New Hollstein Dutch & Flemish Etchings, Engravings and Woodcuts 1450–1700: Cornelis Cort,* compiled Manfred Sellink, 3 vols, Rotterdam: Sound & Vision, 2000.

New Hollstein (Van Doetecum)
Luijten, Ger, and Christiaan Schuckman, eds, *The New Hollstein Dutch & Flemish Etchings, Engravings and Woodcuts 1450–1700: The Van Doetecum Family,* compiled Henk Nalis, 4 vols, Rotterdam: Sound & Vision Interactive, 1998.

New Hollstein (Galle)
Sellink, Manfred, ed., *The New Hollstein Dutch & Flemish Etchings, Engravings and Woodcuts 1450–1700: Philips Galle,* compiled Manfred Sellink and Marjolein Leesberg, 4 vols, Rotterdam: Sound & Vision, 2001.

New Hollstein (Van Groeningen)
Luijten, Ger, ed., *The New Hollstein Dutch & Flemish Etchings, Engravings and Woodcuts 1450–1700: Gerard van Groeningen,* compiled Christiaan Schuckman, 2 vols, Rotterdam: Sound & Vision Interactive, 1997.

New Hollstein (Van Heemskerck)
Luyten, Ger, ed., *The New Hollstein Dutch & Flemish Etchings, Engravings and Woodcuts 1450–1700: Maarten van Heemskerck,* compiled Ilja M. Veldman, 2 vols, Roosendaal: Koninklijke van Poll, 1993–94.

New Hollstein (Van Leyden)
Luyten, Ger, ed., *The New Hollstein Dutch & Flemish Etchings, Engravings and Woodcuts 1450–1700: Lucas van Leyden,* compiled Jan Piet Filedt Kok, with the assistance of Bart Cornelis and Anneloes Smits. Rotterdam: Sound & Vision Interactive, 1996.

New Hollstein (Van Mander)
Leeflang, Huigen, and Christiaan Schuckman, eds, *The New Hollstein Dutch & Flemish Etchings, Engravings and Woodcuts 1450–1700: Karel van Mander,* compiled Marjolein Leesberg. Rotterdam: Sound & Vision, 1999.

New Hollstein (Muller)
Luijten, Ger, and Christiaan Schuckman, eds, *The New Hollstein Dutch & Flemish Etchings, Engravings and Woodcuts 1450–1700: The Muller Dynasty,* compiled Jan Piet Filedt Kok and Harriet Stroomberg, 3 vols, Rotterdam: Sound & Vision, 1999.

Strauss
Strauss, Walter L., ed., *Hendrik Goltzius 1558–1617: The Complete Engravings and Woodcuts.* 2 vols, New York: Abaris Books, 1977.

Bibliography

Alcina Rovira 1997
Alcina Rovira, J. F. "La fama de las odas de Arias Montano entre poetas y humanistas luteranos." In *Humanismo y pervivencia del mundo clásico. II. Homenaje al Profesor Luis Gil*, 3 vols, ed. José Ma. Maestre Maestre, Joaquin Pascual Barea, L. Charlo Brea, 3: 1447–55. Cádiz: Universidad de Cádiz, 1997.

Alcina Rovira 1998
Alcina Rovira, J. F. "Los *Humanae salutis monumenta* de Benito Arias Montano." In *Anatomía del humanismo: Benito Arias Montano, 1598–1998. Homenaje al profesor Melquiades Andrés Martín: actas del simposio internacional celebrado en la Universidad de Huelva del 4 al 6 de noviembre de 1998*, ed. Luis Gómez Canseco, 111–47. Huelva: Servicio de Publicaciones, Universidad de Huelva, 1998.

Ambrose 2007
Ambrose. "On the Mysteries." In *Nicene and Post-Nicene Fathers: Second Series, Volume X: Ambrose: Select Works and Letters*, ed. Philip Schaff and Henry Wallace. New York: Cosimo, 2007.

Amstelredamus 1523
Amstelredamus, Alardus. *Passio Domini nostri Iesu Christi, sive Scopus meditationis Christianae, ex optimis quibusque Poetis Cristianis, ijsque vetustissimis concinnatus*. Amsterdam, 1523.

Arblaster 2004
Arblaster, Paul. "'*Totius Mundi Emporium*': Antwerp as a Centre for Vernacular Bible Translations, 1523–1545." In *The Low Countries as a Crossroads of Religious Beliefs*, ed. Arie-Jan Gelderblom, Jan L. de Jong, and Marc van Vaeck, 9–31. Intersections: Yearbook for Early Modern Studies 3 (2003). Leiden and Boston: Brill, 2004.

Arias Montano 1568–73
Arias Montano, Benito, ed. *Biblia Sacra Hebraice, Chaldaice, Graece, & Latine, Philippi II. Reg. Cathol. pietate, et studio ad sacrosanctae Ecclesiae usum*, 8 vols. Antwerp: Christopher Plantin, 1568–73.

Arias Montano 1571
Arias Montano, Benito. *Humanae salutis monumenta B. Ariae Montani studio constructa et decantata*. Antwerp: Christopher Plantin, 1571.

Arias Montano 1593
Arias Montano, Benito. *Antiquitatum Iudaicarum libri IX., in quis, praeter Iudeae, Hierosolymorum, & Templi Salomonis accuratam delineationem, praecipui sacri ac profani gentis ritus describuntur...adiectis formis aeneis*. Leiden: Franciscus Raphelengius, 1593.

Armstrong 1990
Armstrong, Christine Megan. *The Moralizing Prints of Cornelis Anthonisz*. Princeton: Princeton University Press, 1990.

Atkinson 1964
Atkinson, D. *Acolastus: A Latin Play of the Sixteenth Century by Gulielmus Gnapheus*. London, Ontario, 1964.

Auerbach 1953
Auerbach, Erich. *Typologische Motive in der mittelalterlichen Literatur*. Schriften und Vorträge des Petrarca-Instituts Köln 2. Krefeld: Scherpe, 1953.

Augustine 1847–57
Augustine. *Expositions on the Book of Psalms*, 6 vols, trans. and ed. J. Tweed, T. Scratton, H. M. Wilkins et al. Oxford and London: J. H. Parker, 1847–57.

Augustine 1887
Augustine. *The City of God*, trans. Marcus Dods. A Select Library of the Nicene and Post-Nicene Fathers of the Christian Church 2. Buffalo, N.Y.: Christian Literature, 1887.

Augustine 2004
Augustine. "Tractate 15 on John 4:1–42." In *Homilies on the Gospel of John, Homilies on the First Epistle of John and Soliloquies*. Nicene and Post-Nicene Fathers of the Christian Church. Whitefish, Montana: Kessinger, 2004.

Bailey 2003
Bailey, Gauvin Alexander. *Between Renaissance and Baroque: Jesuit Art in Rome, 1565–1610*. Toronto, Buffalo, and London: University of Toronto Press, 2003.

Bangs 1977
Bangs, Jeremy D. "Maerten van Heemskerck's Bel and the Dragon and Iconoclasm." *Renaissance Quarterly* 30 (1977): 8–12.

Bangs 1980
Bangs, Jeremy D. Review of *Lucas van Leyden*, by R. Vos; *Lucas van Leyde– grafiek*, by J. P. Filedt Kok; and *Lucas van Leyden Studies*, ed. J. P. Filedt Kok, W. Th. Kloek, and I. M. Veldman. *Sixteenth-Century Journal* 11 (1980): 91–97.

Van Barrefelt 1592
Van Barrefelt, Hendrik Jansen. *Imagines et figurae bibliorum*. Leiden: Franciscus Raphelengius, n.d. [ca. 1592].

Beets 1913
Beets, Nicolaas. *Lucas de Leyde*. Brussels and Paris: G. van Oest, 1913.

Beets 1915
Beets, Nicolaas. *De Houtsneden in Vorsterman's Bijbel van 1528. Afbeeldingen der Prenten van Jan Swart, Lucas van Leyden, e.a.* Amsterdam: Uitgegeven van Wege het Koninklijk Oudheidkundig Genootschap, 1915.

Berliner 1955
Berliner, Rudolf. "Arma Christi." *Münchner Jahrbuch der bildenden Kunst* 6 (1955): 35–152.

Bertini 1998
Bertini, Giuseppe. "Otto van Veen,

Cosimo Masi, and the Art Market in Antwerp at the End of the Sixteenth Century." *The Burlington Magazine* 140 (1998): 119–20.

Bevers 1994
Bevers, Holm. "Willem van Haecht composuit – Zu einem Aspekt der Antwerpener Stichproduktion um 1570." In *Die Malerei Antwerpens— Gattungen, Meister, Wirkungen. Studien zur flämischen Kunst des 16. und 17. Jahrhunderts. Internationales Kolloquium Wien 1993*, ed. Ekkehard Mai, Karl Schütz, and Hans Vlieghe, 179–85. Cologne: Verlag Locher, 1994.

Biemans 1984
Biemans, J. A. A. M. *Middelnederlandse bijbelhandschriften*. Corpus Sacrae Scripturae Neerlandicae Medii Aevi. Catalogus. Leiden: Brill, 1984.

Bleyerveld 2000–01
Bleyerveld, Yvonne. "Chaste, Obedient, and Devout: Biblical Women as Patterns of Female Virtue in Netherlandish and German Graphic Art, ca. 1500–1750." *Simiolus: Netherlands Quarterly for the History of Art*, 28 (2000–01): 219–50.

Bleyerfeld 2001
Bleyerveld, Yvonne. "Van de tiran verlost: Het boekje *Tyrannorum praemia. Den loon der tyrannen* van Willem van Haecht (1578)." In *Prentwerk / Print Work 1500–1700*, ed. Jan de Jong, Mark Meadow, Bart Ramakers, and Frits Scholten, 127–53. Nederlands Kunsthistorisch Jaarboek 52 (2001). Zwolle: Waanders Uitgevers, 2002.

Bonaventure 1882–1902
Bonaventure. *Opera Omnia*, 10 vols. Quaracchi: College of Saint Bonaventure, 1882–1902.

Bonger 1954
Bonger, Hendrik. *De Motivering van de Godsdienstvrijheid bij Dirck Volckertszoon Coornhert*. Arnhem: Van Loghum Slaterus, 1954.

Boon 1982
Boon, K. G. "Patientia dans les gravures de la Reforme aux Pays-Bas." *Revue de l'Art* 56 (1982): 7–25.

Boorsch and Lewis 1985
Boorsch, Suzanne, Michal Lewis, and R. E. Lewis. *The Engravings of Giorgio Ghisi*. Exh. cat. Saint Louis: The Saint-Louis Art Museum; New York: The Metropolitan Museum of Art, New York; Los Angeles: Grunwald Center for the Graphic Arts, University of California, 1985.

Bowen 1997
Bowen, Karen Lee. *Christopher Plantin's Books of Hours: Illustration and Production*. Nieuwkoop: De Graaf Publishers, 1997.

Bowen 2003
Bowen, Karen Lee. "Illustrating Books with Engravings: Plantin's Working Practices Revealed." *Print Quarterly* 20 (2003): 3–34.

Bowen and Imhof 2008
Bowen, Karen Lee, and Dirk Imhof. *Christopher Plantin and Engraved Book Illustrations in Sixteenth-Century Europe*. Cambridge: Cambridge University Press, 2008.

Van den Branden 1990
Van den Branden, L. "Drukoctrooien toegekend door de raad van Brabant tot 1600." *De Gulden Passer* 68 (1990): 5–88.

Van Branteghem 1537
Van Branteghem, Willem. *Dat leven ons Heeren Christi Jesu figuerlijck uuten text der vier Evangelisten, met al die Evangelien ende Epistelen vanden gheheelen iare, ende Prophetien van Christo, met somighe ghebeden*. Antwerp: Mattheus Cromme, 1537.

Van den Broecke 1996
Van den Broecke, Marcel P. R. *Ortelius Atlas Maps: An Illustrated Guide*. Westrenen, 't Goy: HES Publishers, 1996.

De Bruin 1970
De Bruin, C. C., ed. *Het Luikse Diatessaron*. Corpus Sacrae Scripturae Neerlandicae Medii Aevi. Series minor 1: Harmoniae evangeliorum1. Leiden: Brill, 1970.

De Bruin 1993
De Bruin, C. C. *De statenbijbel en zijn voorgangers: Nederlandse bijbelvertalingen vanaf de Reformatie tot 1637*, ed. F. G. M. Broeyer. Haarlem and Brussels: Nederlands Bijbelgenootschap, 1993.

Bruyn 1987
Bruyn, Josua. "Toward a Scriptural Reading of Seventeenth-Century Dutch Landscape Paintings." In *Masters of 17th-Century Dutch Landscape Painting*, ed. Peter C. Sutton, 84–103. Exh. cat. Amsterdam: Rijksmuseum; Boston: Museum of Fine Arts; Philadelphia: Philadelphia Museum of Art, 1987.

Van Bühren 1998
Bühren, Ralf van. *Die Werke der Barmherzigkeit in der Kunst des 12.–18. Jahrhunderts: Zum Wandel eines Bildmotivs vor dem Hintergrund neuzeitlicher Rhetorikrezeption*. Hildesheim: Georg Olms Verlag, 1998.

Burger, Den Hollander, and Schmid 2004
Burger, C., A. den Hollander, and U. Schmid, eds. *Evangelien-harmonien des Mittelalters*. Studies in Theology and Religion 9. Assen: Brill, 2004.

Buser 1976
Buser, Thomas. "Jerome Nadal and Early Jesuit Art in Rome." *The Art Bulletin* 58 (1976): 424–33.

Calvin 1960
Calvin, John. *Institutes of the Christian Religion*, ed. John T. McNeill, trans. Ford Lewis Battles. The Library of Christian Classics 20. Philadelphia: The Westminster Press, 1960.

Canisius 1577
Canisius, Peter. *De Maria Virgine incomparabili, et Dei genitrice sacrosancta, libri quinque*. Ingolstadt, 1577.

Clifton 2001
Clifton, James. "A Fountain Filled with Blood: Representations of Christ's Blood from the Middle Ages to the Eighteenth Century." In *Blood: Art, Power, Politics and Pathology*, ed. James M. Bradburne, 65–87, 249–50. Exh. cat. Frankfurt: Schirn Kunsthalle and Museum für Angewandte Kunst, 2001.

Clifton 2008a
Clifton, James. "A Lutheran Image on the Title-Page of the Last Bible without a Confessional Label." *Ephemerides Theologicae Lovanienses* (ETL) 84 (2008): 69–86.

Clifton 2008b
Clifton, James. "'Appositis exemplis, ac sententiis illustrata': Philips Galle's Series of the Sacraments and the Works of Mercy." In *Infant Milk or Hardy Nourishment? The Bible for Lay People and Theologians in the Modern Period*, ed. Wim François, 297-335. Bibliotheca Ephemeridum Theologicarum Lovaniensium (BETL). Leuven: Peeters, 2008.

Van der Coelen 1999
Van der Coelen, Peter. "Emblemata Sacra? Biblical Picture Books and Emblem Literature." In *The Emblem Tradition and the Low Countries: Selected Papers of the Leuven International Emblem Conference, 18–23 August, 1996*, ed. John Manning, Karel Porteman, and Marc van Vaeck, 261–78. Imago Figurata Studies 1b. Turnhout: Brepols, 1999.

Craig 1983
Craig, Kenneth M. "Pars ergo Marthae transit: Pieter Aertsen's 'Inverted' Paintings of Christ in the House of Martha and Mary." *Oud Holland* 97 (1983): 25–39.

Cromme 1538
Cromme, Mattheus, publ. *Dat nieuwe Testament ons Heeren Jesu Christi*. Antwerp, 1538.

Dackerman 2002
Dackerman, Susan. *Painted Prints: The Revelation of Color in Northern Renaissance & Baroque Engravings, Etchings & Woodcuts*. Exh. cat. Baltimore: The Baltimore Museum of Art, 2002.

Daly and Dimler 2005
Daly, Peter M., and G. Richard Dimler, S. J., eds. *The Jesuit Series, Part Four (L–P)*. Corpus librorum emblematum. Toronto, Buffalo, and London: University of Toronto Press, 2005.

Danielou 1960
Danielou, Jean, S. J. *From Shadows to Reality: Studies in Biblical Typology of the Fathers*. London: Burns & Oates, 1960.

Dekoninck 1999
Dekoninck, Ralph. "Entre Réforme et Contre-Réforme: Les *Imagines et figurae bibliorum* d'Hendrik Jansen van Barrefelt et Pieter van der Borcht." *Quaerendo* 29 (1999): 96–131.

Dekoninck 2004
Dekoninck, Ralph. "*Imagines peregrinantes*: The International Genesis and Fate of Two Biblical Picture Books (Barrefelt and Nadal) Conceived in Antwerp at the End of the Sixteenth Century." In *The Low Countries as a Crossroads of Religious Beliefs*, ed. Arie-Jan Gelderblom, Jan L. de Jong, and Marc van Vaeck, 49–64. Intersections: Yearbook for Early Modern Studies 3. Leiden and Boston: Brill, 2004.

Dekoninck 2005
Dekoninck, Ralph. *Ad imaginem. Status, fonctions et usages de l'image dans la littérature spirituelle jésuite du XVIIᵉ siècle*. Travaux du Grand Siècle 26. Geneva: Librairie Droz, 2005.

Dekoninck, Guiderdoni-Bruslé, and Van Vaeck 2006
Dekoninck, Ralph, Agnès Guiderdoni-Bruslé, and Marc van Vaeck. *Emblemata Sacra: Emblem Books from the Maurits Sabbe Library, Katholieke Universiteit Leuven*. Exh. cat. Philadelphia: Francis A. Drexel Library, Saint Joseph's University, 2006.

Delano-Smith and Ingram 1991
Delano-Smith, Catherine, and Elizabeth Morely Ingram. *Maps in Bibles, 1500–1600: An Illustrated Catalogue*. Travaux d'Humanisme et Renaissance 256. Geneva: Librairie Droz, 1991.

Deschamps 1960–61
Deschamps, J. "Middelnederlandse vertalingen van Super modo vivendi (7de hoofdstuk) en De libris teutonicalibus van Gerard Zerbolt van Zutphen." *Handelingen van de Koninklijke Zuidnederlandse Maatschappij voor Taal- en Letterkunde en Geschiedenis* 14 (1960): 67–108; 15 (1961): 175–220.

Dimler 2007
Dimler, G. Richard, S. J. *Studies in the Jesuit Emblem*. AMS Studies in the Emblem 18. New York: AMS Press, 2007.

Dirc van Delf 1938
Dirc van Delf. *Tafel van den kersten Ghelove. Naar de handschriften uitgegeven, ingeleid en van aateekeningen voorzien*, ed. L. M. Daniëls. Antwerp: Tekstuitgaven van Ons geestelijk erf, 1938.

Ehresmann 1966–67
Ehresmann, Donald L. "The Brazen Serpent, a Reformation Motif in the

Works of Lucas Cranach the Elder and His Workshop." *Marsyas* 13 (1966–67): 32–47.

Engammare 1994
Engammare, Max. "Les Figures de la Bible: Le destin oublié d'un genre littéraire en image (XVIe–XVIIe siècles)." *Mélanges de l'École française de Rome* 106 (1994): 549–91.

Fabre 1992
Fabre, Pierre-Antoine. *Ignace de Loyola: Le lieu de l'image*. Paris: Editions de l'Ecole des Hautes Etudes en Sciences Sociales, 1992.

Falkenburg 1994
Falkenburg, Reindert L. *The Fruit of Devotion: Mysticism and the Imagery of Love in Flemish Paintings of the Virgin and Child, 1450–1550*, trans. Sammy Herman. Oculi: Studies in the Arts of the Low Countries 5. Amsterdam and Philadelphia: John Benjamins Publishing Company, 1994.

Falkenburg 1996
Falkenburg, Reindert. "Matters of Taste: Pieter Aertsen's Market Scenes, Eating Habits, and Pictorial Rhetoric in the Sixteenth Century." In *The Object as Subject: Studies in the Interpretation of Still Life*, ed. Anne W. Lowenthal, 13–27. Princeton: Princeton University Press, 1996.

Falkenburg 2001
Falkenburg, Reindert. "Pieter

Bruegel's Series of the Seasons: On the Perception of Divine Order." In *Liber Amicorum Raphaël de Smedt. 2. Artium Historia: Action and Revelation*, ed. Joost vander Auwera, 253–76. Leuven: Peeters, 2001.

Filedt Kok 1978
Filedt Kok, Jan Piet. *Lucas van Leyden–grafiek*. Amsterdam: Rijksmuseum, 1978.

Filedt Kok 1988
Filedt Kok, Jan Piet. "Een biblia pauperum met houtsneden van Jacob Cornelisz. en Lucas van Leyden gereconstrueerd." *Bulletin van het Rijksmuseum* 36 (1988): 83–116.

Filedt Kok 1990
Filedt Kok, Jan Piet. "Jacques de Gheyn II: Engraver, Designer, and Publisher, I–II." *Print Quarterly* 7 (1990): 248–81, 371–96.

Filedt Kok 1991–92
Filedt Kok, Jan Piet. "Hendrick Goltzius–Engraver, Designer and Publisher 1582–1600." In *Goltzius-Studies: Hendrick Goltzius (1558–1617)*, ed. Reindert Falkenburg, Jan Piet Filedt Kok, and Huigen Leeflang, 159–218. Nederlands Kunsthistorisch Jaarboek 42–43 (1991–92). Zwolle: Waanders Uitgevers, 1993.

Filedt Kok 1996
Filedt Kok, Jan Piet. "On the Authorship, Printing Quality and

Production of the Prints of Lucas van Leyden." In *The New Hollstein Dutch & Flemish Etchings, Engravings and Woodcuts 1450–1700: Lucas van Leyden*, ed. Ger Luyten, compiled Jan Piet Filedt Kok, with the assistance of Bart Cornelis and Anneloes Smits, 8–28. Rotterdam: Sound & Vision Interactive, 1996.

Filedt Kok, Hinterding, and van der Waals 1994–95
Filedt Kok, Jan Piet, Erik Hinterding, and Jan van der Walls. "Jan Harmensz. Muller as Printmaker, I–III." *Print Quarterly* 11 (1994): 223–64, 351–78; 12 (1995): 3–29.

Foucart 1985
Foucart, Jacques. "Quelques inédits d'Otto Vaenius." In *Rubens and His World. Bijdragen opgedragen aan Prof. Dr. Ir. R.-A. D'Hulst*, 97–108. Antwerp: Het Gulden Cabinet, 1985.

Foucart 1998
Foucart, Jacques. "*L'accueil de la Vierge dans les cieux* à l'église de Poligny: une revanche pour Otto Venius." In *Curiosité: Études d'histoire de l'art en l'honneur d'Antoine Schnapper*, ed. Olivier Bonfait, Véronique Gérard Powell, and Philippe Sénéchal, 27–34. Paris: Flammarion, 1998.

François 2004
François, Wim. "Die 'Ketzerplakate' Kaiser Karls in den Niederlanden und ihre Bedeutung für

Bibelübersetzungen in der Volkssprache. Der 'Proto-Index' von 1529 als vorläufiger Endpunkt." *Dutch Review of Church History* 84 (2004): 198–247.

François 2006
François, Wim. "Vernacular Bible Reading and Censorship in Early Sixteenth Century: The Position of the Louvain Theologians." In *Lay Bibles in Europe 1450–1800*, ed. M. Lamberigts and A. A. den Hollander. 69–96. Bibliotheca Ephemeridum Theologicarum Lovaniensium 198. Louvain, Paris, and Dudley, MA: Peeters, 2006.

Freedberg 1978
Freedberg, David. "A Source for Rubens's Modello of the *Assumption* and *Coronation of the Virgin*: A Case Study in the Response to Images." *The Burlington Magazine* 120 (1978): 432–42.

Freedberg 1989
Freedberg, David. *The Power of Images: Studies in the History and Theory of Response*. Chicago and London: University of Chicago Press, 1989.

Fumaroli 1980a
Fumaroli, Marca. *L'age de l'éloquence: Rhétorique et "res literaria" de la Renaissance au seuil de l'époque classique*. Hautes études médiévales et modernes 43. Geneva: Librairie Droz, 1980.

Fumaroli 1980b
Fumaroli, Marca. "Définition et description: scolastique et rhétorique chez les Jésuites des XVIe et XVIIe siècles." *Travaux de linguistique et de littérature* 18 (1980): 37–28.

Gessler 1942
Gessler, J. *Over en om de Mystieke Wijnpers te Aarschot en Elders.* Leuven: Boon-Hecking, 1942.

Gibson 1981
Gibson, Walter S. "Artists and *Rederijkers* in the Age of Bruegel." *The Art Bulletin* 63 (1981): 426–46.

Göttler 2005
Göttler, Christine. "Saintly Patronage: Peter Paul Rubens and Bishop Maximilian Villain de Gand on the Cathedral of Tournai." In *Sponsors of the Past: Flemish Art and Patronage 1550–1700*, ed. Hans Vlieghe and Katlijne van der Stighelen, 135–56. Turnhout: Brepols, 2005.

Goyet 1996
Goyet, Francis. *Le sublime du "lieu commun": L'invention rhétorique dans l'Antiquité et à la Renaissance.* Paris: Honoré Champion, 1996.

De Graaf 1958
Graaf, B. de. *Alardus Amstelredamus (1491–1544): His Life and Works, with a Bibliography.* Amsterdam: M. Hertzberger, 1958.

Gregory 1844
Gregory the Great. *Morals on the Book of Job by St. Gregory the Great*, trans. J. H. Parker. London: J. G. F. and J. Rivington, 1844.

Gregory of Nyssa 1979
Gregory of Nyssa. "A Sermon for the Day of the Lights or On the Baptism of Christ." In *The Faith of the Early Fathers: A Source-book of Theological and Historical Passages* 2, trans. and ed. W. A. Jurgens. Collegeville, Minnesota: Liturgical Press, 1979.

Grieten 1995
Grieten, Stefan. "Reconstructie van het altaarstuk van het Antwerpse Meerseniersambacht. Nieuwe gegevens over Otto van Veen, Erasmus II Quellinus en Balthazar Beschey." *Jaarboek van het Koninklijk Museum voor Schone Kunsten Antwerpen* (1995): 135–58.

Güldner 1968
Güldner, Gerhard. *Das Toleranz-Problem in den Niederlanden im Ausgang des 16. Jahrhunderts.* Lübeck: Matthiesen, 1968.

Gutmann 1976
Gutmann, Joseph, ed. *The Temple of Solomon: Archaeological Fact and Medieval Tradition in Christian, Islamic and Jewish Art.* Missoula, Montana: Scholars Press, 1976.

Haberditzl 1908
Haberditzl, F. M. "Die Lehrer des Rubens." *Jahrbuch der kunsthistorischen Sammlungen des allerhöchsten Kaiserhauses* 27 (1908): 191–235.

Haeger 1986
Haeger, Barbara. "Cornelis Anthonisz's Representation of the Parable of the Prodigal Son: A Protestant Interpretation of the Biblical Text." In *Renaissance en Reformatie en de Kunst in de Noordelijke Nederlanden*, 133–50. Nederlands Kunsthistorisch Jaarboek 37. Bussum: Fibula-Van Dishoeck, 1986.

Hamilton 1981
Hamilton, Alistair. "From Familism to Pietism: The Fortunes of Pieter van der Borcht's Biblical Illustrations and Hiël's Commentaries from 1584 to 1717." *Quaerendo* 11 (1981): 271–301.

Hand and Wolff 1989
Hand, John Oliver, and Martha Wolff. *Early Netherlandish Painting. The Collections of the National Gallery of Art Systematic Catalogue.* Washington, DC: National Gallery of Art and Cambridge University Press, 1989.

Hänsel 1991
Hänsel, Sylvaine. *Der Spanische Humanist Benito Arias Montano (1527–1598) und die Kunst.* Spanische Forschungen der Görresgesellschaft, 2nd ser., 25. Münster: Aschendorffsche Verlagsbuchhandlung, 1991.

Hänsel 1993
Hänsel, Sylvaine. "Las 'Humanae salutis monumenta' de Benito Arias Montano y el problema de una iconografía contrareformista de la historia sagrada." *Cuadernos de arte e iconografía* 6 (1993): 497–506.

Harris 2004
Harris, Jason. "The Religious Position of Abraham Ortelius." In *The Low Countries as a Crossroads of Religious Beliefs*, ed. Arie-Jan Gelderblom, Jan L. de Jong, and Marc van Vaeck. 89–139. Intersections: Yearbook for Early Modern Studies 3 (2003). Leiden and Boston: Brill, 2004.

Havens 2001
Havens, Earle. *Commonplace Books: A History of Manuscripts and Printed Books from Antiquity to the Twentieth Century.* New Haven: Beinecke Rare Books and Manuscript Library, 2001.

Heal 2007
Heal, Bridget. *The Cult of the Virgin Mary in Early Modern Germany: Protestant and Catholic Piety, 1500–1648.* Cambridge and New York: Cambridge University Press, 2007.

Henry 1983
Henry, Avril "The Living Likeness: The Forty-Page Blockbook *Biblia Pauperum* and the Imitation of Images in Utrecht and other Manuscripts." *Journal of the British Archaeological Association* 136 (1983): 124–36.

Henry 1984
Henry, Avril "*Biblia Pauperum*: The Forty-Page Blockbook and The Hague, Rijksmuseum Meermanno-Westreenianum, MS. 10. A. 15." *Scriptorium* 38 (1984): 31–41.

Henry 1987
Henry, Avril. *Biblia pauperum: A Facsimile and Edition*. Ithaca: Cornell University Press.

Den Hollander 1997
Den Hollander, August A. *De Nederlandse Bijbelvertalingen 1522–1545 / Dutch Translations of the Bible 1522–1545*. Bibliotheca Bibliographica Neerlandica 33. Nieuwkoop: De Graaf Publishers, 1997.

Den Hollander 2003
Den Hollander, August A. *Verboden bijbels: Bijbelcensuur in de Nederlanden in de eerste helft van de zestiende eeuw*. Oratiereeks. Amsterdam: Amsterdam University Press, 2003.

Horace 1929
Horace. *Satires, Epistles and Ars poetica*, trans. H. Rushton Fairclough. Rev. ed. Cambridge: Harvard University Press, 1929.

Horst 1990
Horst, Daniel R. "Een zestiende-eeuwse reformatorische prentenreeks van Frans Huys over de Heilsweg van de Mens." *Bulletin van het Rijksmuseum* 38 (1990): 3–24.

Hughes 1980
Hughes, Anthony. "Naming the Unnameable: An Iconographical Problem in Rubens's 'Peace and War.'" *The Burlington Magazine* 122 (1980): 157–65.

Jacobowitz and Stepanek 1983
Jacobowitz, Ellen S., and Stephanie Loeb Stepanek. *The Prints of Lucas van Leyden & His Contemporaries*. Exh. cat. Washington: National Gallery of Art, 1983.

Jacobszoon and Bouwenszoon 1589
Jacobszoon, Jan Paedts, and Jan Bouwenszoon, publs. *Biblia. Dat is, de gantsche Heylighe Schrift, grondelick ende trouwelick verduytschet. Met verclaringhe duysterer woorden, redenen ende spreucken, ende verscheyden lectien, die in ander loflicke Oversettinghen ghevonden, ende hier aen de cant toe-ghesettet zijn. Met noch rijcke aenwijsinghen, der ghelijck ofte ongelijck stemmenden plaetsen, op het alderghewiste, met Scheyt-letteren ende Versen, ghetale (daer een yeghelick Capittel nae Hebreischer wijse, mede onderdeylt is) verteeckent*. Leiden, 1589.

Jerome 1892
Jereome. "Leter 53 (to Paulinus)." In *Jerome: Letters and Select Works*, trans. W. H. Freemantle and ed. Philip Schaff. Nicene and Post-Nicene Fathers of the Christian Church, 2nd ser., 6. Edinburgh: T&T Clark, and Grand Rapids: Wm. B. Eerdmans, 1892.

De Jong and De Groot 1988
De Jong, M., and Irene de Groot. *Ornamentprenten in het Rijksprentenkabinet, I, 15de & 16de eeuw*. Amsterdam: Rijksprentenkabinet, Rijksmuseum; and The Hague: Staatsuitgeverij, 1988.

De Jongh 2000
De Jongh, Eddy. "The Changing Face of Lady World." In *Questions of Meaning: Theme and Motif in Dutch Seventeenth-Century Painting*, 59–82, trans. and ed. Michael Hoyle. Leiden: Primavera Pers, 2000.

Junius 1598
Junius, Hadrianus. *Poëmatum liber primus continens pia et moralia carmina …* Leiden: Ex officina Ludovici Elzevirij, 1598.

Kat 1952
Kat, Johannes F. M. *De verloren zoon als letterkundig motief*. Amsterdam: J. Babeliowsky, 1952.

Kelly 1974
Kelly, Genevieve. "The Drama of Student Life in the German Renaissance." *Educational Theatre Journal* 26 (1974): 291–307.

De Keyser 1530
De Keyser, Marten, publ. *La saincte Bible en Francoys*. Antwerp, 1530.

Klemm 1979
Klemm, Christian. "Weltdeutung–Allegorien und Symbole in Stilleben." In *Stilleben in Europa*, 140–218. Exh. cat. Münster: Westfälisches Landesmuseum für Kunst und Kulturgeschichte; and Baden-Baden: Staatliche Kunsthalle, 1979.

Knipping 1974
Knipping, John B. *Iconography of the Counter-Reformation in the Netherlands: Heaven on Earth*. 2 vols, Nieuwkoop: De Graff, 1974.

Koerner 1993
Koerner, Joseph Leo. *The Moment of Self-Portraiture in German Renaissance Art*. Chicago and London: The University of Chicago Press, 1993.

Kölker 1963
Kölker, A. J. *Alardus Aemstelredamus en Cornelius Crocus: Twee Amsterdamse Priester-Humanisten. Hun leven, werken en theologische opvattingen. Bijdrage tot de kennis van het Humanisme in Noord-Nederland in de eerste helft van de zestiende eeuw*. Nijmegen: Dekker & Van de Vegt, 1963.

Krahn 1968
Krahn, Cornelis. *Dutch Anabaptism: Origin, Spread, Life and Thought 1450–1600*. The Hague: Martinus Nijhoff, 1968.

Lazure 2000
Lazure, Guy. "Perceptions of the Temple, Projections of the Divine: Royal Patronage, Biblical Scholarship,

and Jesuit Imagery in Spain, 1580–1620." *Calamus Renascens: Revista de humanismo y tradición clásica* 1 (2000): 155–88.

Lazure 2007
Lazure, Guy. "Nadal au Nouveau Monde. Une traduction poétique des *Evangelicae historiae imagines*, Pérou, ca. 1614." In *Emblemata Sacra: Rhétorique et herméneutique du discours sacré dans la littérature en images*, ed. Ralph Dekoninck and Agnès Guiderdoni-Bruslé, 321–31. Imago Figurata 7. Turnhout: Brepols, 2007.

Lechner 1962
Lechner, Joan Marie. *Renaissance Concepts of the Commonplaces*. New York: Pageant Press, 1962

Leeflang 2003
Leeflang, Huigen. "A Proteus or Vertumnus in Art: The Virtuoso Engravings, 1592–1600." In *Hendrick Goltzius (1558–1617): Drawings, Prints and Paintings*, ed. Huigen Leeflang and Ger Luijten, 203–33. Exh. cat. Amsterdam: Rijksmuseum, New York: The Metropolitan Museum of Art, and Toledo, Ohio: The Toledo Museum of Art, 2003.

Van Liesveldt 1526
Van Liesveldt, Jacob, publ. *Dat oude ende dat nieuwe testament*. Antwerp, 1526.

Van Liesveldt 1538
Van Liesveldt, Hansken, publ. *Den Bybel met groter neersticheyt gecorrigeert, ende op dye canten ghesedt den ouderdom der werelt, ende hoe lange die gheschiedenissen ende historien der Bybelen, elc int sijne voor Christus gheboorte gheweest zijn, ende daer bi vergadert wt Fasciculus temporum, ende uut dye Cronike van alder werelt, die principael historien der machtiger Heydenscher Conincrijcken, daer die heylige scrift oock dicwils af vermaent.* Antwerp, 1538.

Van Maerlant 1918
Van Maerlant, Jacob. *Jacob van Maerlant's Strophische Gedichten*, ed. J. Verdam en P. Leendertz Jr. Leiden: Bibliotheek van Middelnederlandsche Letterkunde, 1918.

Van Maerlant 1983
Van Maerlant, Jacob. *Rijmbijbel*, ed. M. Gysseling. Corpus van Middelnederlandse teksten (tot en met het jaar 1300), series 2: Literaire handschriften, 3. 2 vols, The Hague: Nijhoff, 1983.

De Maeyer 1955a
Maeyer, Marcel de. *Albrecht en Isabella en de schilderkunst: Bijdrage tot de geschiedenis van de XVIIe-eeuwse schilderkunst in de Zuidelijke Nederlanden.* Verhandelingen van de Koninklijke Vlaamse Academie voor Wetenschappen, Letteren en Schone Kunsten van België 9. Brussels: Paleis der Academiën, 1955.

De Maeyer 1955b
Maeyer, Marcel de. "Otto Venius en de tapijtreeks 'De Veldslagen van Aartshertog Albrecht.'" *Artes Textiles* 4 (1955): 105–111.

Mâle 1986
Mâle, Émile. *Religious Art in France: The Late Middle Ages: A Study of Medieval Iconography and Its Sources*, trans. Marthiel Mathews. Princeton: Princeton University Press, 1986.

Van Mander 1604
Van Mander, Karel. *Het schilder-boeck, waerin voor eerst de leerlustighe Ieught den grondt der edel vry schilderconst in verscheyden deelen wort voorghedraegen.* Haarlem, 1604, repr. Utrecht: Davaco Publishers, 1969.

Van Mander 1994–99
Van Mander, Karel. *The Lives of the Illustrious Netherlandish and German Painters, from the First Edition of the Schilder-boeck (1603–1604) . . . .* ed. Hessel Miedema. 6 vols, Doornspijk: Davaco, 1994–99.

Marrow 1979
Marrow, James H. *Passion Iconography in Northern European Art of the Late Middle Ages and Early Renaissance: A Study of the Transformation of Sacred Metaphor into Descriptive Narrative.* Kortrijk: Van Ghemmert, 1979.

Matile 2000
Matile, Michael. *Die Druckgraphik Lucas van Leyden und seiner Zeitgnossen: Bestandeskatalog der Graphischen Sammlung der ETH Zürich*. Basel: Schwabe, 2000.

Mauquoy-Hendrickx 1976
Mauquoy-Hendrickx, Marie. "Les Wierix illustrateurs de la Bible dite de Natalis." *Quaerendo* 6 (1976): 28–63.

Mauquoy-Hendrickx 1978–83
Mauquoy-Hendrickx, Marie. *Les estampes des Wierix conservées au Cabinet des Estampes de la Bibliothèque Royale Albert Ier*, 3 vols. Brussels: La Bibliothèque, 1978–83.

McGrath 1984
McGrath, Elizabeth. "Rubens's *Susanna and the Elders* and Moralizing Inscriptions on Prints." In *Wort und bild in der niederländischen Kunst und Literatur des 16. und 17. Jahrhunderts*, ed. Herman Vekeman and Justus Müller Hofstede, 73–90. Erftstadt: Lukassen Verlag, 1984.

Meadow 1995
Meadow, Mark. "Aertsen's *Christ in the House of Martha and Mary*, Serlio's Architecture and the Meaning of Location." In *Rhetoric–Rhétoriqueurs–Rederijkers*, ed. Jelle Koopmans, et al., 175–96. Amsterdam: Koninklijke Nederlandse Akademie van Wetenschappen, 1995.

Melion 1991
Melion, Walter S. *Shaping the

Netherlandish Canon, Karel van Mander's Schilder Boeck. Chicago and London: University of Chicago Press, 1991.

Melion 1992
Melion, Walter S. "Piety and Pictorial Manner in Hendrick Goltzius's Early Life of the Virgin." In *Hendrick Goltzius and the Classical Tradition*, 44–51. Exh. cat. Los Angeles: Fisher Gallery, University of Southern California, 1992.

Melion 1995
Melion, Walter S. "Self-Imaging and the Engraver's *virtù*: Hendrick Goltzius's *Pietà* of 1598." In *Image and Self-Image in Netherlandish Art, 1550–1750*, ed. Reindert Falkenburg, Jan de Jong, Herman Roodenburg, and Frits Scholten, 104–43. Nederlands Kunsthistorisch Jaarboek 46 (1995). Zwolle: Waanders, 1995.

Melion 1998
Melion, Walter S. "Artifice, Memory, and *Reformatio* in Hieronymus Natalis's *Adnotationes et meditationes in Evangelia* of 1595," *Renaissance and Reformation* 22 (1998): 5–34.

Melion 1999
Melion, Walter S. "*Ad ductum itineris et dispositionem mansionum ostendendam*: Meditation, Vocation, and Sacred History in Abraham Ortelius's *Parergon*." *The Journal of The Walters Art Gallery* 57 (1999): 49–72.

Melion 2001
Melion, Walter S. "*Cordis circumcisio in spiritu*: Imitation and the Wounded Christ in Hendrick Goltzius's *Circumcision* of 1594." In *Prentwerk / Print Work 1500–1700*, ed. Jan de Jong, Mark Meadow, Bart Ramakers, and Frits Scholten, 31–77. Nederlands Kunsthistorisch Jaarboek 52 (2001). Zwolle: Waanders Uitgevers, 2002.

Melion 2003
Melion, Walter S. "The Art of Vision in Jerome Nadal's *Adnotationes et meditationes in Evangelia*." In Jerome Nadal, *Annotations and Meditations on the Gospels, Volume I: The Infancy Narratives*, trans. and ed. Frederick A. Homann, S.J., 1–96. Philadelphia: Saint Joseph's University Press, 2003.

Melion 2005a
Melion, Walter S. "Benedictus Arias Montanus & the Virtual Studio as a Meditative Place." In *Inventions of the Studio: Renaissance to Romanticism*, ed. Michael Cole and Mary Pardo, 73–107, 196–201. Chapel Hill and London: The University of North Carolina Press, 2005.

Melion 2005b
Melion, Walter S. "*Mortis illius imagines ut vitae*: The Image of the Glorified Christ in Jerome Nadal's *Adnotationes et meditationes in Evangelia*." In Jerome Nadal, *Annotations and Meditations on the Gospels. Volume III: The Resurrection Narratives*, trans. and ed. Frederick A.

Homann, S.J., 1–32. Philadelphia: Saint Joseph's University Press, 2005.

Melion 2007a
Melion, Walter S. "*Haec per imagines huius mysterij ecclesia sancta [clamat]*: The Image of the Suffering Christ in Jerome Nadal's *Adnotationes et meditationes in Evangelia*." In Jerome Nadal, *Annotations and Meditations on the Gospels. Volume II: The Passion Narratives*, trans. and ed. Frederick A. Homann, S.J., 1–73. Philadelphia: Saint Joseph's University Press, 2007.

Melion 2007b
Melion, Walter S. "The Meditative Function of Hendrick Goltzius's *Life of the Virgin* of 1593–94." In *Image and Imagination of the Religious Self in Late Medieval and Early Modern Europe*, ed. Reindert Falkenburg, Walter S. Melion, and Todd M. Richardson, 379–426. Proteus: Studies in Early Modern Identity Formation 1. Turnhout: Brepols, 2007.

Melion 2009
Melion, Walter S. *The Meditative Art: Studies in the Northern Devotional Print, 1550–1625*. Early Modern Catholicism and the Visual Arts. Philadelphia: Saint Joseph's University Press, 2009.

Meurer 1993
Meurer, Peter H. "Der Nürnberger Verlag Caymox und die Kartographie." *Quaerendo* 23 (1993): 24–43.

Miedema 1968
Miedema, Hessel. "The Term *Emblema* in Alciati." *Journal of the Warburg and Courtauld Institutes* 31 (1968): 234–50.

Mielke 1975
Mielke, Hans. "Antwerpener Graphik in der 2. Hälfte des 16. Jahrhunderts. Der Thesaurus veteris et novi Testamenti des Gerard de Jode (1585) und seine künstler." *Zeitschrift für Kunstgeschichte* 38 (1975): 29–83.

Mielke 2005
Mielke, Ursula. "Introduction." In *The New Hollstein Dutch & Flemish Etchings, Engravings and Woodcuts 1450–1700: Peeter van der Borcht, Book Illustrations*, ed. Ger Luyten, compiled by Hans Mielke and Ursula Mielke, 1:vii–xi. Ouderkerk aan den Ijssel: Sound & Vision, 2005.

Mirimonde 1975
Mirimonde, A. P. de. "A propos d'une gravure publiée par Christophe Plantin et d'un tableau flamand du Musée de Gray: Le Temple de Jérusalem (architecture, culte, musique). *Jaarboek van het Koninklijk Museum voor Schone Kunsten Antwerpen* (1975): 213–43.

Mochizuki 2008
Mochizuki, Mia M. *The Netherlandish Image after Iconoclasm, 1566–1672: Material Religion in the Dutch Golden Age*. Aldershot, England, and Burlington, Vermont: Ashgate, 2008.

Moffitt 1990
Moffitt, John F. "Francisco Pacheco and Jerome Nadal: New Light on the Flemish Sources of the Spanish 'Picture-within-the-Picture.'" *The Art Bulletin* 72 (1990): 631–38.

Moss 1996
Moss, Ann. *Printed Commonplace-Books and the Structuring of Renaissance Thought*. Oxford and New York: Clarendon Press, 1996.

Von zur Mühlen 1997
Von zur Mühlen, Ilse. "*Imaginibus honos*–Ehre sei dem Bild: Die Jesuiten und die Bilderfrage." in *Rom in Bayern: Kunst und Spiritualität der ersten Jesuiten*, ed. Reinhold Baumstark, 161–70. Exh. cat. Munich: Bayerisches Nationalmuseum, 1997.

Müller, Roettig, and Stolzenburg 2002
Müller, Jürgen, Petra Roettig, and Andreas Stolzenburg. *Die Masken der Schönheit: Hendrick Goltzius und das Kunstideal um 1600*. Exh. cat. Hamburg: Hamburger Kunsthalle, 2002.

Müller-Hofstede 1957
Müller-Hofstede, Justus. "Zum Werke des Otto van Veen, 1590–1600." *Bulletin–Musées Royaux des Beaux-Arts de Belgique* 6 (1957): 127–74.

Müller-Hofstede 1959
Müller-Hofstede, Justus. "Otto van Veen, der Lehrer des P. P. Rubens." PhD diss., Albert-Ludwigs-Universität, 1959.

Mullett 1999
Mullett, Michael A. *The Catholic Reformation*. New York: Routledge, 1999.

Nadal 1595
Nadal, Jerome. *Adnotationes et meditationes in Evangelia quae in sacrosancto Missae sacrificio toto anno leguntur*. Antwerp: Martinus Nutius, 1595.

Nadal 1607
Nadal, Jerónimo. *Adnotationes et meditationes in Evangelia quae in sacrosancto Missae Sacrificio toto anno leguntur: Cum Evangeliorum concordantia historiae integritati sufficienti. Accessit & index historiam ipsam Evangelicam in ordinem temporis vitae Christi distribuens. Editio ultima: In qua Sacer Textus ad emendationem Bibliorum Sixti V. et Clementis VIII. restitutus.* Antwerp: I. Moretus, 1607.

Nadal 2003
Nadal, Jerome. *Annotations and Meditations on the Gospels, Volume I: The Infancy Narratives*, trans. and ed. Frederick A. Homann, S.J. Philadelphia: Saint Joseph's University Press, 2003.

Naredi-Rainer 1994
Naredi-Rainer, Paul von. *Salomos Tempel und das Abendland: Monumentale Folgen historischer Irrtümer*. Cologne: Dumont Buchverlag, 1994.

Navarro López 1990–91
Navarro López, Joaquín Luis. "La influencia horaciana en Benito Arias Montano: A propósito de la oda VI de los 'Humanae salutis monumenta.'" *Anales de la Universidad de Cádiz* 7-8 (1990–91): 439–53.

Navarro López 1991
Navarro López, Joaquín Luis. "Dos versiones diferentes de la oda XI de los 'Humanae salutis monumenta.'" *Excerpta philologica* 1, part 2 (1991): 545–63.

Navarro López 1996
Navarro López, Joaquín Luis. "El poema I de los 'Humanae salutis monumenta' de Benito Arias Montano." *Revista de estudios Extremeños* 72 (1996): 1027–39.

Nicolau 1949
Nicolau, Miguel, S.J. *Jerónimo Nadal, S.I. (1507–1580) sus obras y doctrinas espirituales*. Madrid: Consejo Superior de Investigaciones Cientificas, Patronato Raimundo Lulio, Instituto Francisco Suárez, 1949.

Norris 1940
Norris, Christopher. "Rubens before Italy." *The Burlington Magazine* 76 (1940): 184-94.

O'Connor 1942
O'Connor, Mary Catharine. *The Art of Dying Well: The Development of the Ars moriendi*. New York: Columbia University Press, 1942.

Orenstein 1996
Orenstein, Nadine M. *Hendrick Hondius and the Business of Prints in Seventeenth-Century Holland*. Studies in Prints and Printmaking 1. Rotterdam: Sound & Vision Interactive, 1996.

Orenstein 2001
Orenstein, Nadine, ed. *Pieter Bruegel the Elder: Prints and Drawings*. Exh. cat. New York: Metropolitan Museum of Art, 2001.

Overmeer 1912
Overmeer, W. P. J. *De Hervorming te Haarlem*. Haarlem: J. W. Boissevain & Co., 1912.

Parshall 1978
Parshall, Peter. "Lucas van Leyden's Narrative Style." *Nederlands Kunsthistorisch Jaarboek* 29 (1978): 185–238.

Parshall 1984
Parshall, Peter. "Review of *The Prints of Lucas van Leyden and his Contemporaries* by Ellen S. Jacobowitz; Stephanie Loeb Stepanek." *Simiolus: Netherlands Quarterly for the History of Art* 14 (1984), pp. 41–45.

Parshall 1997
Parshall, Peter. Review of *The New Hollstein: Dutch & Flemish Etchings, Engravings and Woodcuts 1450–1700: Lucas van Leyden*, by Jan Piet Filedt Kok. *Simiolus: Netherlands Quarterly for the History of Art* 25 (1997): 236–38.

Patigny 2003
Patigny, G. "La chapelle Sainte-Ursule à l'église Du Sablon de Bruxelles: l'union de l'art et de la destinée humaine." *Annales d'histoire de l'art et de l'archéologie* 25 (2003): 33–49.

Plantin 1568
Plantin, Christopher. "Tabularum in Regiis Bibliis depictarum brevis explicatio." In *Biblia Sacra Hebraice, Chaldaice, Graece, & Latine, Philippi II. Reg. Cathol. pietate, et studio ad sacrosanctae Ecclesiae usum*, ed. Benito Arias Montano, vol. 1, unfoliated. Antwerp: Christopher Plantin, 1568.

Plantin 1584
Plantin, Christopher, publ. *Breviarum Romanum, ex decreto Sacrosancti Concilij Tridentini restitutum, Pii V. Pont. Max. iussu editum. Cum Kalendario Gregoriano perpetuo. Permittente Sede Apostolica. Antwerp, 1584.*

Post 1954
Post, R. R. *Kerkelijke verhouding in Nederland vóór de Reformatie van 1500 tot 1580.* Utrecht: Spectrum, 1954.

Van de Put 1920
Van de Put, A. "Otto Vaenius and Archduke Ernest," *The Burlington Magazine* 37 (1920): 184–90.

Reinitzer 2006
Reinitzer, Heimo. *Gesetz und Evangelium: Über ein reformatorisches Bildthema, seine Tradition, Funktion und Wirkungsgeschichte.* 2 vols, Hamburg: Christians Verlag, 2006.

Rheinbay 1995
Rheinbay, Paul. *Biblische Bilder für den inneren Weg: Das Betrachtungsbuch des Ignatius-Gefährten Hieronymus Nadal (1507–1580).* Egelsbach: Hänsel-Hohenhausen, 1995.

Riggs 1977
Riggs, Timothy A. *Hieronymus Cock, Printmaker and Publisher.* New York and London: Garland, 1977.

Rijksmuseum 1986
Kunst voor de beeldenstorm: Noordnederlandse kunst 1525–1580. Exh. cat. Amsterdam: Rijksmuseum.

Rijksmuseum Het Catharijneconvent 1986
Ketters en papen onder Filips II. Exh. cat. Utrecht: Rijksmuseum Het Catharijneconvent, 1986.

Ringbom 1984
Ringbom, Sixten. *Icon to Narrative: The Rise of the Dramatic Close-up in Fifteenth-Century Devotional Painting.* 2nd ed. Doornspijk: Davaco, 1984.

Ríos 1928
Ríos, Román. "Los *Monumenta Humanae Salutis* de Benito Arias Montano." *Revista Española de Estudios Bíblicos* 3 (1928): 56–67.

Rodríguez de Ceballos 1974
Rodríguez de Ceballos, A. "Las 'Imágenes de la historia Evangélica' del P. Jerónimo Nadal en el marco del jesuitismo y la contrareforma." *Traza y baza* 5 (1974): 77–95.

Van Roey 1968
Van Roey, J. "Het Antwerpse geslacht van Haecht (Verhaecht). Tafereelmakers, schilders, kunsthandelaars." In *Miscellanea Jozef Duverger: Bijdragen tot de kunstgeschiedenis der Nederlanden*, 1:216–29, 2 vols. Ghent: Vereniging voor de Geschiedenis der Textielkunsten, 1968.

Rooses 1888
Rooses, Max. "De plaatsnijders der *Evangelicae historiae imagines.*" *Oud Holland* 6 (1888): 277–88.

Rosenau 1979
Rosenau, Helen. *Vision of the Temple: The Image of the Temple of Jerusalem in Judaism and Christianity.* London: Oresko Books, 1979.

Rosier 1997
Rosier, Bart A. *The Bible in Print: Netherlandish Bible Illustration in the Sixteenth Century*, trans. Chris F. Weterings, 2 vols. Leiden: Foleor, 1997.

Rouse and Rouse 1979
Rouse, Richard H., and Mary A. Rouse. *Preachers, Florilegia and Sermons: Studies on the Manipulus florum of Thomas of Ireland.* Studies and Texts 47. Toronto: Pontifical Institute of Mediaeval Studies, 1979.

Rubin 1999
Rubin, Rehav. *Image and Reality: Jerusalem in Maps and Views.* Jerusalem: Hebrew University Magnes Press, 1999.

Russell 1990
Russell, H. Diane, with Bernardine Barnes. *Eva/Ave: Woman in Renaissance and Baroque Prints.* Exh. cat. Washington: National Gallery of Art, 1990.

Ruusbroec 1985
Ruusbroec, John. *The Spiritual Espousals and Other Works.* Ed. J. A. Wiseman. New York, Mahwah, and Toronto: Paulist Press, 1985.

Van Ruusbroec 1989
Van Ruusbroec, Jan. *Boecsken der Verclaringhe*, ed. G. de Baere, trans. Ph. Crowley and H. Rolfson. Corpus Christianorum 101. Tielt: Lannoo, 1989.

Sánchez Salor 1998
Sánchez Salor, Eustaquio. "Obras de Arias Montano." In *Arias Montano y su tiempo*, ed. A. Albar Ezquerra, J. Gil, E. Sanchez Salor, et al., 149–72. Exh. cat. Mérida : Iglesia de la Preciosa Sangre, Centro de Exposiciones de San Jorge, 1998.

Saunders 1978
Saunders, Eleanor A. "Old Testament Subjects in the Prints of Maarten van Heemskerck: 'Als een claere spiegele der tegenwoordige tijden.'" PhD diss. Yale University, 1978.

Saunders 1978-79
Saunders, Eleanor A. "A Commentary on Iconoclasm in Several Print Series by Maarten van Heemskerck." *Simiolus: Netherlands Quarterly for the History of Art* 10 (1978–79): 59–83.

Schapiro 1942
Schapiro, Meyer. "Cain's Jaw-Bone that Did the First Murder." *The Art Bulletin* 24 (1942): 205-212.

Schiller 1971-72
Schiller, Gertrud. *Iconography of Christian Art*, trans. Janet Seligman. 2 vols, Greenwich, Connecticut: New York Graphic Society, 1971–72.

Schramm 1923
Schramm, Albert. *Luther und die Bibel, Volume 1: Die Illustration der Lutherbibel*. Leipzig: Verlag von Karl W. Hiersemann, 1923.

Seitz 1989
Seitz, Christopher R. *Figured Out: Typology and Providence in Christian Scripture*. Louisville: Westminster John Knox Press, 1989.

Sellink 2000
Sellink. Manfred. "Introduction." In *The New Hollstein Dutch & Flemish Etchings, Engravings and Woodcuts 1450–1700: Cornelis Cort*, ed. Huigen Leeflang and compiled by Manfred Sellink, 1:xxiii–xxxiv. Ouderkerk aan den Ijssel: Sound & Vision, 2000.

Serlio 1611
Serlio, Sebastiano. *The Book of Architecture*. London, 1611, repr. New York: Arno Press, 1980.

Sesé Sanz 1998
Sesé Sanz, Juan Carlos. "Análisis y pedagogía de una traducción dieciochesca de los 'Monumenta' de Arias Montano." In *Actas. Congreso Internacional sobre Humanismo y Renacimiento*, 2:639–47. 2 vols. León: Universidad de León, Secretariado de Publicaciones, 1998.

Shalev 2003
Shalev, Zur. "Sacred Geography, Antiquarianism, and Visual Erudition: Benito Arias Montano and the Maps in the Antwerp Polyglot Bible." *Imago Mundi* 55 (2003): 56–80.

Shestack 1967
Shestack, Alan. *Master E.S.: Five Hundredth Anniversary Exhibition*. Exh. cat. Philadelphia: Philadelphia Museum of Art, 1967.

Silver 1993
Silver, Larry. "Graven Images: Reproductive Engravings as Visual Models." In *Graven Images: The Rise of Professional Printmakers in Antwerp and Haarlem, 1540–1640*, ed. Timothy Riggs and Larry Silver, 1–45. Exh. cat. Chicago: Mary and Leigh Block Gallery, Northwestern University, 1993.

Silver 1999
Larry Silver. "Nature and Nature's God: Landscape and Cosmos of Albrecht Altdorfer." *The Art Bulletin* 81 (1999): 194–214.

Silver and Smith 1978
Silver, Larry, and Susan Smith. "Carnal Knowledge: The Late Engravings of Lucas van Leyden." *Nederlands Kunsthistorisch Jaarboek* 29 (1978): 239–98.

Sluijter 2000
Sluijter, Eric Jan. *Seductress of Sight: Studies in Dutch Art of the Golden Age*. Studies in Netherlandish Art and Cultural History 2. Zwolle: Waanders Publishers, 2000.

Smith 2007
Smith, Jamie L. "So moeti den schilt draghen; Dien God veruwede met roder greine: Jan van Eyck's Critical Principles of Oil Painting and Their Middle Dutch Antecedents." PhD diss. Johns Hopkins University, 2007.

Smith 2002
Smith, Jeffrey Chipps. *Sensuous Worship: Jesuits and the Art of the Early Catholic Reformation in Germany*. Princeton and Oxford: Princeton University Press, 2002.

Spengler 1996
Spengler, Dietmar. "Die *Ars Jesuitica* der Gebrüder Wierix," *Wallraf-Richartz-Jahrbuch* 57 (1996): 161–94.

Stedelijk Museum Sint-Niklaas 1994
Stedelijk Museum Sint-Niklaas. *Sterren in Beelden: Astrologie in de Eeuw van Mercator*. Exh. cat. Sint-Niklaas: Stedelijk Museum Sint-Niklaas, 1994.

Steenbergen 1968
Steenbergen, G. J. "De Apostelspelen van Willem van Haecht." In *Liber alumnorum Prof. Dr. E. Rombauts*, 161–77. Leuven: Universiteitsbibliotheek, 1968.

Steinberg 1983
Steinberg, Leo. *The Sexuality of Christ in Renaissance Art and in Modern Oblivion*. New York: October Books, 1983.

Van der Stock 1998
Van der Stock, Jan. *Printing Images in Antwerp: The Introduction of Printmaking in a City, Fifteenth Century to 1585*, trans. Beverley Jackson. Studies in Prints and Printmaking 2. Rotterdam: Sound & Vision Interactive, 1998.

Strachan 1957
Strachan, James. *Early Bible Illustrations: A Short Study Based on Some Fifteenth and Early Sixteenth Century Printed Texts*. Cambridge: Cambridge University Press, 1957.

Strauss 1977
Strauss, Walter L. *Hendrik Goltzius, 1558–1617: The Complete Engravings and Woodcuts*, 2 vols. New York: Abaris Books, 1977.

Stroomberg 2007

Stroomberg, Harriet. "Introduction." In *Hollstein's Dutch & Flemish Etching, Engravings and Woodcuts 1450–1700: The Wierix Family, Book Illustrations*, ed. Jan van der Stock, compiled Harriet Stroomberg, 2:3–7. Ouderkerk aan den Ijssel: Sound & Vision, 2007.

Suckale 1977

Suckale, Robert. "*Arma Christi*: Überlegungen zur Zeichenhaftigkeit mittelalterlicher Andachtsbilder." *Städel-Jahrbuch* 6 (1977), 177–208.

Sullivan 1999

Sullivan, Margaret. "Aertsen's Kitchen and Market Scenes: Audience and Innovation in the Art of Pieter Aertsen." *The Art Bulletin* 81 (1999): 236–66.

Symes 2002

Symes, Carol. "The Appearance of Early Vernacular Plays: Forms, Functions and the Future of Medieval Theater." *Speculum* 77 (2002): 778–831.

Tanis and Horst 1993

Tanis, James, and Daniel Horst. *Images of Discord: A Graphic Interpretation of the Opening Decades of the Eighty Years' War*. Exh. cat. Bryn Mawr, Pa.: Bryn Mawr College Library, 1993.

Thomas 1936

Thomas, Alois. *Die Darstellung Christi in der Kelter. Eine theologische und kulturhistorische Studie*. Düsseldorf: Schwann, 1936.

Thomas Aquinas 2007

Thomas Aquinas. *Summa Theologica*, trans. Dominican Province. 10 vols. First published 1947. Charleston, S.C.: Forgotten Books, 2007

Tuzi 2002

Tuzi, Stefania. *Le Colonne e il Tempio di Salomone: La storia, la leggenda, la fortuna*. Rome: Gangemi Editore, 2002.

Veldman 1974

Veldman, Ilja M. "Maarten van Heemskerck and Hadrianus Junius: The Relationship between a Painter and a Humanist." *Simiolus: Netherlands Quarterly for the History of Art* 7 (1974): 35–54.

Veldman 1977

Veldman, Ilja M. *Maarten van Heemskerck and Dutch Humanism in the Sixteenth Century*, trans. Michael Hoyle. Maarssen: Gary Schwartz, 1977.

Veldman 1986a

Veldman, Ilja M. "De boekillustratie als inspiratiebron voor de Nederlandse prentkunst van de zestiende eeuw." In *Eer is het Lof des Deuchts: Opstellen over renaissance en classicisme aangeboden aan Dr. Fokke Veenstra*, ed. H. Duits, A.-J. Gelderblom, and M. B. Smits-Veldt, 261–77. Amsterdam: Batafsche Leeuw, 1986.

Veldman 1986b

Veldman, Ilja M. *Leerrijke reeksen van Maarten van Heemskerck*. Exh. cat. Haarlem: Frans Halsmuseum, 1986.

Veldman 1986c

Veldman, Ilja M. "Lessons for Ladies: A Selection of Sixteenth and Seventeenth-Century Dutch Prints." *Simiolus: Netherlands Quarterly for the History of Art* 16 (1986): 113–27.

Veldman 1990

Veldman, Ilja M. *De Wereld tussen Goed en Kwaad: Late prenten van Coornhert*. The Hague: SDU uitgeverij, 1990.

Veldman 1992

Veldman, Ilja M. "Images of Labor and Diligence in Sixteenth-Century Netherlandish Prints: The Work Ethic Rooted in Civic Morality or Protestantism?" *Simiolus: Netherlands Quarterly for the History of Art* 21 (1992): 227–64.

Veldman 2000

Veldman, Ilja M. "Representations of Labor and Diligence in Late Sixteenth-Century Netherlandish Art: The Secularization of the Work Ethic." In *The Public and Private in Dutch Culture of the Golden Age*, ed. Arthur K. Wheelock Jr, and Adele Seeff, 123–40. Newark: University of Delaware Press, 2000.

Veldman 2001a

Veldman, Ilja M. *Crispijn de Passe and His Progeny (1564–1670): A Century of Print Production*. Studies in Prints and Printmaking 3. Rotterdam: Sound & Vision Publishers, 2001.

Veldman 2001b

Veldman, Ilja M. *Profit and Pleasure: Print Books by Crispijn de Passe*. Studies in Prints and Printmaking 4. Rotterdam: Sound & Vision Publishers, 2001.

Veldman 2006

Veldman, Ilja M. *Images for the Eye and Soul: Function and Meaning in Netherlandish Prints (1450–1650)*. Leiden: Primavera Pers, 2006.

Veldman and Van Schaik 1989

Veldman, Ilja, and Karin van Schaik. *Verbeelde boodschap: De Illustraties van Lieven de Witte bij 'Dat leven ons Heeren' (1537)*. Haarlem: Nederlandse Bijbelgenootschap, and Brussels: Belgisch Bijbelgenootschap, 1989.

Visser 1969

Visser, C. Ch. G. *Luthers Geschriften in de Nederlanden tot 1546*. Assen: Van Gorcum, 1969.

Visser 1988

Visser, Piet. "Jan Philipsz Schabaelje and Pieter van der Borcht's Etchings in the First and Final State. A Contribution to the Reconstruction of the Printing History of H. J. Barrefelt's *Imagines et figurae Bibliorum*." *Quaerendo* 18 (1988): 35–76.

Vlieghe 1981

Vlieghe, Hans. "Rubens and Van Veen in Contest. A Marginal Note." In *Ars auro prior. Studia Ioanni Bialostocki sexagenario dicata*, ed. J. A. Chróscicki, N. Cieslinska, et al., 477–82. Warsaw: Panstowowe Wydawn. Nauk., 1981.

Vlieghe 1998
Vlieghe, Hans. *Flemish Art and Architecture, 1585–1700*. New Haven and London: Yale University Press, 1998.

Vloberg 1946
Vloberg, Maurice. *L'Eucharistie dans l'art*. Paris: Arthaud, 1946.

Voet 1969–72
Voet, Leon. *The Gold Compasses: A History and Evaluation of the Printing and Publishing Activities of the Officina Plantiniana at Antwerp*. 2 vols, Amsterdam: Vangendt & Co., London: Routledge & Kegan Paul, and New York: Abner Schram, 1969–72.

Vogl 1987
Vogl, Alphons. *Der Bilderzyklus "Der Triumph der Kirche" von Otto van Veen*. Munich: Tuduv, 1987.

Voogt 2000
Voogt, Gerrit. *Constraint on Trial: Dirck Volckertsz Coornhert and Religious Freedom*. Sixteenth Century Essays & Studies 52. Kirksville, Missouri: Truman State University Press, 2000.

De Vooys 1928
De Vooys, C. G. N. "Een Allegorie van Willem van Haecht in woord en beeld." *Oud Holland* 45 (1928): 147–8.

Voragine 1993
Voragine, Jacobus de. *The Golden Legend: Readings on the Saints*, trans. William Granger Ryan. 2 vols, Princeton: Princeton University Press, 1993.

Vorsterman 1528
Vorsterman, Willem, publ. *De Bibel. Tgeheele Oude ende Nieuwe Testament met grooter naersticheyt naden Latijnschen text gecorrigeert, ende opten cant des boecks die alteratie die hebreeusche veranderinge, naerder hebreeuscer waerheyt der boecken die int hebreus zijn, ende die griecsce der boecken die int griecs zijn, ende dinhout voor die capittelen gestelt. Met schoonen figueren ghedruct, ende naerstelijc weder oversien*. Antwerp, 1528.

Vorsterman 1532
Vorsterman, Willem, publ. *Den Bibel. Tgeheele Oude ende Nieuwe Testament*. Antwerp, 1532.

Wadell 1969
Wadell, Maj-Brit. *Fons Pietatis: Eine ikonographische Studie*. Göteborg: Elanders Boktrykeri aktiebolag, 1969.

Wadell 1985
Wadell, Maj-Brit. *Evangelicae Historiae Imagines: Entstehungsgeschichte und Vorlagen*. Gothenburg Studies in Art and Architecture 3. Göteborg: Acta Universitatis Gothoburgensis, 1985.

Waite 1987
Waite, Gary K. "The Anabaptist Movement in Amsterdam and the Netherlands, 1531–1535: An Initial Investigation into its Genesis and Social Dynamics." *Sixteenth Century Journal* 18 (1987): 249–65.

Walch 1985
Walch, Nicole. "Deux eaux-fortes anonymes en relation avec le tableau d'Otto van Veen, *Le Christ mort soutenu par un ange*." *De gulden passer* 61–63 (1985): 629–43.

Wang 1975
Wang, Andreas. *Der "Miles Christianus" im 16. und 17. Jahrhundert und seine mittelalterliche Tradition. Ein Beitrag zum Verhältnis von sprachlicher und graphischer Bildlichkeit*. Mikrokosmos: Beiträge zur Literaturwissenschaft und Bedeutungsforschung 1. Bern: Herbert Lang, and Frankfurt am Main: Peter Lang, 1975.

Weckwerth 1960
Weckwerth, Alfred. "Christus in der Kelter: Ursprung und Wandlungen eines Bildmotives." In *Beiträge zur Kunstgeschichte: Eine Festgabe für Heinz Rudolf Rosemann zum 9. Oktober 1960*, 95–108. Munich: Deutscher Kunstverlag, 1960.

Te Winkel 1922
Te Winkel, Jan. *De ontwikkelingsgang der Nederlandsche Letterkunde II. Geschiedenis der Nederlandsche letterkunde van Middeleeuwen en Rederijkerstijd (2)*. 2nd printing. Haarlem: De erven F. Bohn, 1922.

Worthen 1991–92
Worthen, Amy Namowitz. "Calligraphic Inscriptions on Dutch Mannerist Prints." In *Goltzius-Studies: Hendrick Goltzius (1558–1617)*, ed. Reindert Falkenburg, Jan Piet Filedt Kok, and Huigen Leeflang, 261–306. Nederlands Kunsthistorisch Jaarboek 42–43 (1991–92). Zwolle: Waanders Uitgevers, 1993.

Wuhrmann 1998
Wuhrmann, Sylvie. "Une étude en gris. Le *Triptyque du déluge* de Jérôme Bosch." *Artibus et historiae* 19 (1998): 61–136.

Ziadé 2007
Ziadé, Raphaëlle. *Les martyrs Maceabéas, de l'histoire juive au culte chrétien: les hómelies de Grégoire de Nazianzé et de Jean Chrysostome*. Leiden: Brill, 2007.

Van Ruyven-Zeman 2004
Van Ruyven-Zeman, Zsuzsanna. "The Wierix Family: Introduction." In *Hollstein's Dutch & Flemish Etchings, Engravings and Woodcuts 1450–1700: Volume LXIX: The Wierix Family: Introduction and Guide to the Catalogue*, ed. Jan der Stock and Marjolein Leesberg, compiled Zsuzsanna van Ruyven-Zeman in collaboration with Marjolein Leesberg, xiii–xlv. Rotterdam: Sound & Vision, 2004.

Photographic Acknowledgements

American Bible Society, New York:
Courtesy of The American Bible Society.
Photography: Bill Orcutt: 1, 19

The Baltimore Museum of Art:
The Baltimore Museum of Art:
Garrett Collection.
Photography By: Mitro Hood:
27a (BMA 1946.112.12045);
27b (BMA 1946.112.12049);
27c (BMA 1946.112.12050)

The Baltimore Museum of Art:
Gift of Alfred R. and Henry G. Riggs, in
Memory of General Lawrason Riggs:
30 (BMA 1943.32.305)

The British Library, London:
By permission of the Trustees of the
British Library: 15

The British Museum, London:
Image © Trustees of the British Museum:
8a, 8b, 8c, 10, 24a, 24b, 33, 39, 43, 44, 46a,
46b, 46c, 46d, 46e, 52

**Georgia Museum of Art, The
University of Georgia:**
Georgia Museum of Art,
The University of Georgia;
Gift of Alfred H. Holbrook: 20a

Georgia Museum of Art,
The University of Georgia;
Gift of Alfred H. Holbrook and the
Museum Patrons: 20b

**John Work Garrett Library, The Johns
Hopkins University:**

Special Collections,
The Sheridan Libraries of The Johns
Hopkins University: 7a, 9, 28a, 28b

**The Metropolitan Museum of Art,
New York:**
The Metropolitan Museum of Art,
Harris Brisbane Dick Fund, 1953
Image © The Metropolitan Museum of
Art: 12 [53.601.19(132)]; 25 [53.601.14(67)];
40 [53.601.14(61)]; 51 [53.601.14(63)]

The Metropolitan Museum of Art,
The Elisha Whittelsey Collection,
The Elisha Whittelsey Fund, 1949
Image The Metropolitan Museum
of Art: 13 (49.95.1038); 42 (49.95.1779)

The Metropolitan Museum of Art,
The Elisha Whittelsey Collection,
The Elisha Whittelsey Fund, 1951
Image The Metropolitan Museum of Art:
18 (51.501.6702)

The Metropolitan Museum of Art,
Rogers Fund, 1922 (22.10.4)
Image The Metropolitan Museum of Art:
31a (22.10.4); 31b (22.10.6)

The Metropolitan Museum of Art,
Harris Brisbane Dick Fund, 1928
Image The Metropolitan Museum of Art:
36 [28.4(27)]

**Museum Plantin-Moretus/
Prentenkabinet,
Antwerp–UNESCO World Heritage:**
14a, 14b, 14c, 14d, 14e, 14f, 14g, 14h, 21b, 37a,
37b, 38, 47, 49

National Gallery of Art, Washington:
Rosenwald Collection, Image courtesy of
the Board of Trustees, National Gallery of
Art, Washington: 17a (1964.8.366); 17b
(1964.8.369)

Alisa Mellon Bruce Fund, Image courtesy
of the Board of Trustees, National Gallery
of Art, Washington: 16a (1974.33.11); 16b
(1974.33.42)

New York Public Library:
Print Collection,
Miriam and Ira D. Wallach Division of Art,
Prints and Photographs,
The New York Public Library,
Astor, Lenox and Tilden Foundations:
Cover, 21a, 32, 50

Spencer Collection,
The New York Public Library,
Astor, Lenox and Tilden Foundations: 26

**Pitts Theology Library,
Emory University:**
Courtesy of the Pitts Theology Library,
Candler School of Theology,
Emory University: 2a, 2b, 3, 4, 5, 6

Rijksmuseum, Amsterdam
Courtesy of Rijksmuseum,
Amsterdam:
11, 34a, 34b, 35, 48a, 48b

**Robert W. Woodruff Library,
Emory University:**
Manuscript, Archives, and Rare Book
Library,
Emory University: 7b, 29

Index

"